PERCY BYSSHE SHELLEY

Shelley and the Baths of Caracalla, 1845, by Joseph Severn, courtesy of the Keats–Shelley Memorial Association, Rome.

PERCY BYSSHE SHELLEY
A Biography

Exile of Unfulfilled Renown, 1816-1822

James Bieri

Newark: University of Delaware Press

Associated University Presses
2010 Eastpark Boulevard
Cranbury, NJ 08512

The paper used in this publication meets the requirements of the American National Standard for Permanence of Paper for Printed Library Materials Z39.48-1984.

Library of Congress Cataloging-in-Publication Data
Bieri, James.
    Percy Bysshe Shelley: a biography: exile of unfulfilled renown,
  1816-1822 / James Bieri
       p.   cm.
    Includes bibliographical references and index.
    ISBN 0-87413-893-0 (alk. paper)
    1. Shelley, Percy Bysshe, 1792–1822—Last years.   2. Shelley, Percy Bysshe, 1792–1822—Homes and haunts—Italy.   3. Poets, English—Homes and haunts—Italy.   4. Poets, English—19th century—Biography. 5. British—Italy—History—19th century.   6. Italy—Intellectual life—1789–1900.   I. Title.

PR5432.B538 2005
821'.7—dc22   2004012679

SECOND PRINTING 2006
PRINTED IN THE UNITED STATES OF AMERICA

Contents

List of Illustrations   7

1. The Dark Autumn of Suicides   11
2. Albion House: The Last English Year   32
3. "Paradise of exiles, Italy"   55
4. Euganean Isles of Misery: Venice   75
5. Paradise of Devils: Naples   98
6. Roman Tragedy and Creativity   116
7. Leghorn's "sad reality"   133
8. "a voice from over the Sea"   149
9. Florentine Voices: Unacknowledged Legislator
   and Sophia Stacey   160
10. Poetic Mothers: Pisa and Leghorn   182
11. Baths of San Giuliano   202
12. "Emily . . . my heart's sister"   219
13. "A Love in desolation masked"   236
14. The Last Pisan Winter   264
15. Drawn to the Sea   283
16. A "watery eclipse"   305
17. Life Terminable and Interminable   329

Notes   355
Selected Bibliography   399
Index   423

Illustrations

Frontispiece Shelley and the Baths of Caracalla,
    1845, by Joseph Severn   2

Fig. 1. Leigh Hunt by Benjamin Robert Haydon, c. 1811   92

Fig. 2. John Keats, miniature by Joseph Severn, 1819   93

Fig. 3. Albion House, Marlow   94

Fig. 4. Horace Smith, from a portrait by J. J. Masquerier   94

Fig. 5. William Shelley by Amelia Curran, 1819   95

Fig. 6. Parish church of San Giuseppe a Chiaia, Naples   95

Fig. 7. Sophia Stacey by Bouton, c. 1818   96

Fig. 8. Villa Valsovano, Leghorn   97

Fig. 9. Convent of Santa Anna, Pisa   97

Fig. 10. Percy Bysshe Shelley, watercolor by
    Edward Williams, 1821 or 1822   257

Fig. 11. Mary Wollstonecraft Shelley by Richard
    Rothwell, 1841   258

Fig. 12. Jane Williams by George Clint, ?1820s–1830s   259

Fig. 13. Edward Ellerker Williams, pastel self-portrait   260

Fig. 14. Lady Mount Cashell (Mrs. Mason), miniature   260

Fig. 15. Villa Magni with the *Don Juan*, 1822, watercolor
    by Captain Daniel Roberts, R.N.   261

Fig. 16. Edward John Trelawny, lithograph by
    Seymour Kirkup   262

Fig. 17. Shelley's grave, Protestant Cemetery, Rome   262

Fig. 18. Sir Percy Florence Shelley, color drawing/painting   263

Fig. 19. Lady Jane Shelley, photograph   263

PERCY BYSSHE SHELLEY

1

The Dark Autumn of Suicides

THE SHELLEY FAMILY'S SWISS SUMMER ENDED WITH A TWO-DAY WAIT in Le Havre for favorable winds that became so strong they all suffered seasickness during the stormy twenty-six-hour Channel crossing. Stepping ashore at Portsmouth on September 8, 1816, Shelley, despite a violent headache, immediately wrote to Byron of the safe arrival of his "Childe."[1] Shelley went on to London and the others left the next day for Bath to await Claire's baby. When Shelley reached his Marchmont Street lodgings in London the next day, Fanny promptly called. However, Shelley's lawyer, Longdill, was out of town, so his financial settlement with his father was delayed.

Shelley delivered Byron's third canto to Murray, whose initial cordiality would soon turn to antipathy. After Shelley and Douglas Kinnaird engaged Murray in some hard bargaining on the sale price for the third canto, Shelley wrote Murray for the proofs of *Childe Harold* in order to correct them as Byron requested. Upon learning that Byron had—without telling Shelley—arranged with Murray for the conservative William Gifford to do the proofreading, Shelley complained of Murray's "ill will" and gently chastised Byron.[2]

Mary located rather fashionable lodgings in Bath near the Roman Baths at 5 Abbey Churchyard, the home of the publisher and editor of the *Bath Herald.* She immediately resumed work on *Frankenstein.* Claire—"Mrs. Clairmont"—found modest quarters several blocks away at Mrs. Gilbert's rooming house, 12 New Bond Street. She rented a piano and soon sent Byron the first of four long letters. Solicitous of Byron's health, she attributed Shelley's "violent spasms in the head" to the "vile & nauseous animal Polidori."[3] Ignoring Claire, Byron would only write to Shelley.

After contacting Longdill about drawing up his will and arranging his finances with his father,[4] Shelley went to Marlow where

Mary joined him in the search for a rural house. On September 24, Shelley signed the will he drafted in Switzerland, its provisions unaltered. Claire's two bequests totaling £12,000 were in stark contrast to the absence of any mention of Fanny. Her financial dependence upon Godwin received a blow from Shelley's other action on the twenty-fourth, his settlement with his father. This agreement left Shelley short of the £300 he had promised Godwin. Rather than receiving £2000 outright, Shelley had to await the sale of bank stocks. However, Whitton apparently advanced Shelley £1700 on Timothy's "indispensable condition that Shelley should pay all his debts."[5] Because Longdill controlled the disbursement of these new funds, Shelley effectively was limited to his £250 quarterly allowance.[6]

Shelley, in Bath, told Claire the latest London news which she passed on to Byron. A reviewer of *Alastor* had censured "its indecency" but Claire thought it an "innocent poem" and that "its most chaste author" had written a work that "puts one more in the mind of a sober Nun's habit than a lady's ball dress."[7]

Sometime before September 24, Shelley saw Fanny Godwin for the second time since returning from Switzerland. She wrote Mary she was "angry" with Shelley and expressed "great uneasiness" about his health. Hinting at wanting a haven with Shelley and Mary, her situation had become more desperate because her two aunts left London without deciding if Fanny could teach in their Dublin school.[8]

Fanny's anger toward Shelley was more evident after Godwin received Shelley's £200, not the £300 he expected. Fanny attacked Shelley for not seeing her before signing the financial arrangement and accused him of knowing about the shortfall without telling her. She also attacked Shelley for inflicting "unnecessary pain and anxiety" upon Godwin and for making her "the author of a glaring falsehood" by distorting her story about Mrs. Godwin. When she concluded by calling Mary and Shelley "vulgar souls," Mary dismissively commented that Fanny's letter was "stupid."[9] Neither she nor Shelley sensed the hopelessness behind Fanny's anger.

Godwin's outrage soon followed. Finding his name on Shelley's check, he returned it demanding another be made out to "Joseph Hume," Godwin's tactic to conceal Shelley's support.[10] Fanny's fate now seemed to hang on the thread of this returned check. Shelley promptly made out a new check to "Hume," which Godwin probably received October 8.

Fanny, not waiting for the check's arrival, left Skinner Street forever on either October 7 or October 8. She took the mail coach to Bath, arriving there on the eighth for a brief stopover before continuing on to Bristol. That day, Mary recorded "Letter from Fanny," a now-lost letter she probably wrote before leaving home. If Fanny indicated in this letter that she would be in Bath on her way to visit Wollstonecraft relatives in Wales, did she meet Shelley or Mary there for the last time?[11] Was she upset by what transpired at the meeting, or upset that the meeting did not occur? Mary did not record a meeting in her journal but lines Shelley would write about his last meeting with Fanny could suggest it was in Bath on October 8.[12] Claire reportedly said many years later, "Fanny G. inters [?] w S. at Bath."[13] Fanny possibly asked Shelley if she could join their Bath household and was rejected because of the need to preserve the secrecy of Claire's pregnancy. Such a rejection obviously would have contributed to what transpired next.

Whether or not Fanny saw Shelley or Mary in Bath, stopping there reflected her wish to be saved from the fatal plan she was prepared to carry out. She continued by coach to Bristol where that same day, the eighth, she wrote both Mary and Godwin to alert them of her intent. On October 9, Mary noted in her journal, "In the evening a very alarming letter comes from Fanny." Fanny wrote to Godwin, "I depart immediately to the spot from which I hope never to remove."[14] Claire would recall that in her letter to Godwin Fanny said she was "disgusted with life" and that in her letter to Shelley she told him "to come to see her buried." Claire said that Shelley, upon reading Fanny's letter, "jumped up thrust his hand in [his] hair—I must be off."[15] Shelley "crushed" the letter into "his pocket and rushed off, and would not let any one see it."[16] Fanny told neither Godwin nor Mary and Shelley that she was taking a coach to Swansea, eighty-six miles from Bristol. Shelley inexplicably had gone to Bristol on September 30 and, after reading Fanny's letter, he immediately went there again. He returned at two in the morning of October 10 with "no particular news." Unaware that Fanny had died earlier that same night, October 9, Shelley returned to Bristol the morning of the tenth. He returned to Bath at eleven that night after finding "more certain trace."[17] Godwin, responding to Fanny's letter, set off on the afternoon of the tenth for Bristol where he searched for her unsuccessfully on the eleventh. His path and Shelley's never crossed. Godwin then went to Bath, finding lodgings near the residence of Shelley and Mary whom he made no effort to see. Maintaining his cold rejection of them in this time of family crisis, Godwin walked about Bath before returning to London where Shelley's letter soon informed him of his adopted daughter's fate.

Shelley had left for Swansea on the eleventh, returning the next day to Bath with what Mary called "the worst account." Whether or not he saw Fanny's body, he probably saw the notice printed that day in the Swansea *Cambrian* with its anonymous details. "A most respectable looking female" had arrived at the Mackworth Arms Inn the evening of the ninth. After taking tea in her room she dismissed the maid. Alarmed when she failed to appear the next day, the staff broke into her room to find her dead, clad in her blue skirt and white blouse, a silk-lined fur-trimmed coat and hat nearby. She had died of an overdose of laudanum. A note was found on the table next to the laudanum bottle:

> I have long determined the best thing I could do was to put an end to the existence of a being whose birth was unfortunate, and whose life has only been a series of pain to those persons who have hurt their health in endeavouring to promote her welfare. Perhaps to hear of my death will give you pain, but you will soon have the blessing of forgetting that such a creature ever existed as[18]

The signature apparently had been torn off and burned, possibly to preserve Fanny's anonymity, although the paper reported her clothing included her mother's stays marked "M.W." and her stockings initialled "G." Among her possessions was the gold watch Shelley and Mary had bought for her in Geneva. She had told a fellow coach passenger that she was going to Ireland, but the mere eight shillings sixpence in her purse indicated Swansea was her planned destination.[19]

Fanny's death was never publicly recognized as a suicide; the coroner's jury reported her as "found dead." Although this avoided the ignominy of a suicide's burial as prescribed by law, she apparently had been buried before Shelley arrived in Swansea.[20] Godwin, responding to the tragic news in Shelley's letter, said, "I did indeed expect it." Godwin imposed a blanket of censorship over the matter, promulgating the family story that Fanny died of illness in Ireland. He asked Shelley not go to Swansea and only told his wife the truth.[21] A year later, Charles Clairmont still believed Fanny was alive.[22]

Mary, in mourning clothes, worked with stoical discipline on *Frankenstein* with its subplots of family tragedy. Writing to Byron, Claire said Fanny's "so horrible" death had "melancholy and distressing circumstances . . . Poor Shelley's health is broken up."[23]

His depression and guilt over Fanny's death apparently contributed to one of Shelley's most compulsive food rituals, keeping an account in ounces of how much food he ate for breakfast, lunch, dinner, and tea.[24] This ritual soon was interrupted as bailiffs were after him because of his £516 carriage debt to Charters. Although not in prison, Shelley technically was under arrest and in the custody of the marshal for what Charters claimed was a £1000 debt.[25]

Peacock observed that Fanny's death was a "deeply tragic event" for Shelley, and Claire said "after Fanny's suicide he was a changed man & acted more cautiously toward women."[26] Shortly after her suicide, Shelley drew an idealized burial site with stairs bordered by three large urns containing plants with drooping blossoms. Above the urns, he wrote, "These cannot be forgotten— years" and by a graveside tree, "Breaking thine indissoluble sleep" with the single word, "miserable." Lower on the page Shelley wrote, "It is not my fault—it is not to be attributed to me." Later, he apparently added the words, "When said I so?" Guilt, denial, and continuing guilt were his legacy, as from the potted anenome-like flower at the bottom he drew a line to the words, "drew this flower plot in October 1816 and now it is 1817."[27]

Shelley wrote two verse fragments to Fanny on the reverse side of the drawing.[28] The first, written shortly after Fanny's suicide, has two initial lines Mary omitted when she published the others without comment in 1839: "Friend had I known thy secret grief / Should we have parted so." These lines, and the next, reflect Shelley's guilt over failing to read Fanny's "secret grief" at his last meeting with her. They could indicate this meeting occurred in Bath just before her death:

> Her voice did quiver as we parted,
>   Yet knew I not that heart was broken
> From which it came, and I departed
>   Heeding not the words then spoken.

The other fragment, written some months later, movingly evokes Fanny as the infant of Mary Wollstonecraft. Shelley, recalling phrases from Wollstonecraft's Norway letters, began his lines,

"Thy little footsteps on the sands" and ended them joining Fanny with her mother: "Thine eyes are dark—thy hands are still cold / And she is dead—& thou art dead."[29]

Godwin reportedly said years later "that the three girls were all equally in love with [Shelley] and that the eldest put an end to her existence owing to the preference given to her younger sister."[30] Although Fanny wished to live with Mary and Shelley, Godwin did not believe she and Shelley were having a love affair. The family rebuffs Fanny experienced were compounded, as her suicide note implied, by the shame of her illegitimate birth.[31] During melancholic moods, Fanny must have dwelt on her mother's two suicide attempts and—as her suicide note indicated—on being a financial burden upon Godwin. Mary later wished that Fanny had lived a few months longer when Shelley and Mary married; "she would have been saved for my house would then have been a proper assylum for her."[32]

Shelley occupied himself after Fanny's death reading Lucian's satirical dialogues, *Don Quixote,* and Montaigne's *Essays.*[33] In November, he received Byron's letter from Milan which he regretted reading to Claire as it made her "wretched." Shelley replied to Byron that as "Poor Clare's time approaches ... She has lost much of the animation & lightness which perhaps you do not ever remember in her." Warning Byron of England's "tumultuous state," he hoped "a calm & steady" populace could promote "reform ... without revolution" and avoid "illiterate demagogues for masters."[34]

After twenty years of war, England in 1816 was experiencing economic depression, high unemployment, food shortages, constant threats of rioting, and talk of revolution. Cobbett's rousing call to the laboring class, "Address to Journeymen and Labourers," sold 40,000 copies during November 1816.[35] Shelley's concern that the populace might be provoked to violence received some support two weeks after writing Byron when the second Reform demonstration in London provoked the Spa Fields riot.[36]

Before Fanny's death, Shelley had reestablished contact with Leigh Hunt, sending *Hymn to Intellectual Beauty* for publication in Hunt's *Examiner* under his nickname, "Elfin Knight." Hunt's response in the October 6 *Examiner,* "The Elfin Knight, the first opportunity" unfortunately was not immediately followed up as Hunt promptly mislaid the *Hymn.* By November, Shelley's continuing money concerns led him to contact his solicitor Hayward for help in getting an advance on a new *post obit* loan.[37] Godwin joined in, soliciting a deal with his friend George Dawe, successful artist and moneylender. Shelley rejected Godwin's "exorbitant" proposal involving Dawe, a "mean spirited wretch,[38] but the efforts of Hayward and Godwin apparently bore fruit when Shelley received £100 from Mrs. Godwin.

December brought startling developments for Shelley and his family. On the first, a letter from Leigh Hunt evidently requested money—possibly for public charity—as Shelley promptly sent him a check for £50.[39] Several days later, while Shelley was house-hunting in Marlow, Mary wrote her "Sweet Elf" wondering why Hunt did not acknowledge Shelley's check. She had her own news, which she was afraid Shelley would "look grave on." She asked, "Tell me shall you be happy to have another little squaller?" Only nineteen, Mary believed she was pregnant for the third time in less than two and one-half years. She would be happy if he soon found a house with a garden and if they could live "absentia Clariae."[40] Only the former request was fulfilled.

Returning soon from Marlow, Shelley found another letter from Hunt enclosing £5, interest on the £50 Shelley had sent. Shelley returned the £5 to Hunt, who had made clear he needed several hundred pounds. What most exhilarated Shelley was Hunt's news that his December 1 *Examiner* contained the first favorable public recognition of Shelley as a poet. Under the title "Young Poets," Hunt cited Shelley, John Keats (one of whose sonnets Hunt had already published), and John Hamilton Reynolds. Hunt apologized for mislaying Shelley's *Hymn,* but added, "we shall have no hesitation in announcing him for a very striking and original thinker. His name is PERCY BYSSHE SHELLEY, and he is the author of a poetical work entitled *Alastor, or the Spirit of Solitude.*" Unable to locate this copy of the *Examiner,* Shelley wrote Hunt, "let me lay aside preliminaries & their reserve; let me talk with you as with an old friend."[41]

Shelley accepted Hunt's invitation to visit him, saying he would try "to spend one evening with you." Having found and leased a house in Marlow, Shelley asked Peacock to oversee its renovation and left for Hampstead to visit Hunt at his cottage in the Vale of Health. Shelley, clearly "pleased with Hunt,"[42] stayed several days. At Hunt's home he met John Keats, who at twenty-one was three years younger than Shelley. Perhaps another guest that December weekend was Horace Smith, a prosperous stockbroker and writer, soon one of Shelley's close friends. Smith was immediately impressed with Shelley, a "fair, freckled, blue-eyed, light-haired, delicate looking person, whose countenance was serious and thoughtful." Smith had long felt that Shelley was "a grievously over-punished man" and had "recently read his poems with a profound admiration of his genius." Although Shelley was "naturally more disposed to seriousness than to levity," Smith thought his smiles indicated he enjoyed Hunt's notorious bantering. Strolling on Hampstead Heath, Smith found the talkative Shelley "a psychological curiosity, infinitely more curious than Coleridge's Kubla Khan, to which strange vision he made reference." However, Shelley talked mostly of Plato.[43]

Hunt provided an intimate, lively, artistic, and intellectual family scene that Shelley had not experienced since the Newtons. Marianne Hunt and her husband already had four of their ten children. The oldest, six-year-old Thornton, quickly developed a special relationship with Shelley. Later a successful journalist, Thornton remembered Shelley entering "unreservedly into the sports and even the thoughts of children." Shelley invited Thornton to take long walks on the heath and "into regions which I then thought far distant." Shelley talked with Thornton as they walked briskly until the young boy, fatigued by the long ramble, was carried home "in his arms, or on his shoulder, or pickback."[44]

Shelley's friendship with Hunt was timely and fortunate as his next trauma quickly unfolded. The day after returning to Bath, December 15, Shelley received a letter from Thomas Hookham with the shattering news of the discovery of Harriet's body on December 10. At Shelley's request, Hookham was trying to locate Harriet and the two children when word reached Hookham that "she had destroyed herself." Hookham questioned the report but confirmation came from a friend of Mr. Westbrook's "that she was taken from the Serpentine river on Tuesday last, apparently in an advanced state of pregnancy." Noting she was called "Harriet Smith," Hookham said the inquest jury gave the verdict "*found drowned.*" He believed the children were in London and well.[45]

Shocked by this news, Shelley and Mary took a walk and discussed future plans, including marriage and expanding their family. They naïvely assumed that Shelley would fetch three-and-a-half-year-old Ianthe and two-year-old Charles to join ten-month-old William. Mary did not confirm to Shelley that she was pregnant and, after dinner, Shelley left for London. Accompanied by Hunt, Shelley spent December 16 trying to learn what he could of Harriet's last months and began his fruitless attempt to regain his two children. Writing Mary that night, Shelley, "somewhat faint & agitated," was experiencing "agonising sensations." After he had told Longdill he "was under contract of marriage to you," the solicitor believed he would certainly get his children. Shelley added, "Hunt said very delicately that this would be soothing intelligence for you."

If this was Shelley's offhand marriage proposal, he hinted that Leigh Hunt, with "his kind speeches about you," encouraged their marriage. Trying to square his "contract" with his disavowal of marriage, he told Mary marriage would be "inferior in value to that greatest of benefits—yourself." Still wavering about marriage, he told her if the Westbrooks contested his getting the children he would end their challenge by entering into a "nominal union" with Mary, "a mere form . . . [not] barren of good."

Shelley then gave a garbled version of Harriet's last days:

It seems this poor woman—the most innocent of her abhorred & unnatural family—was driven from her father's house, & descended the steps of prostitution until she lived with a groom of the name of Smith, who deserting her, she killed herself—There can be no question that the beastly viper her sister, unable to gain profit from her connexion with me—has secured to herself the fortune of the old man—who is now dying—by the murder of this poor creature. Everything tends to prove, however, that beyond the mere shock of so hideous a catastrophe having fallen on a human being once so nearly connected with me, there would, in any case have been little to regret. Hookham, Longdill—every one does me full justice;—bears testimony to the up[rightness &] liberality of my conduct to her:—T[here] is but one voice in condemnation of the dete[s]table Westbrooks. If they should dare to bring [it] before Chancery—a scene of such fearful horror would be unfolded as would cover them with scorn & shame.[46]

Shelley's sources for this story are uncertain. Trying to deal with his guilt over Harriet's death and preserve his sense of rectitude, he impulsively blamed Eliza for her sister's death. The unfounded accusation he had heard from some source about Harriet's "prostitution" he never repeated again.

Shelley last saw Harriet on April 22, 1815, in connection with infant Charles's appearance in court. After granting Harriet £200 annually the next June, he bequeathed her £6000 and each of their children £5000. In June 1816, Harriet, to no avail, wrote Peacock to request from Sir Timothy an increase in her allowance.[47] She had recently written John Frank Newton from her father's house offering to come help take care of his sick wife and family: "To the unhappy there is nothing so delightful as being of use to others."[48] If the Boinville family lore is correct, Harriet visited Bracknell in September and Mrs. Boinville supposedly took her on long walks to ease her depression. Sometime later, Harriet wrote Mrs. Boinville from London that if she did not come by a certain date she would commit suicide. Because of a delay in the mail, Mrs. Boinville arrived too late.[49]

Shelley apparently was seeking Harriet's whereabouts by mid-November. Hookham's difficulty in locating her was understandable given the information that emerged at her inquest, the day after her body was found. On the inquest day, December 11, her death notice appeared in the London *Sun*, the first of several that had escaped Shelley's eye during his stay with Hunt: "Yesterday [December 10] a respectable female far advanced in pregnancy was taken out of the Serpentine River and brought home to her residence in Queen Street, Brompton, having been missed for nearly six weeks. She had a valuable ring on her finger. A want of honour in her own conduct is supposed to have led to this fatal catastrophe, her husband being abroad."[50]

This last sentence formed part of the several stories that have been handed down concerning Harriet's life before she died. The hearsay story Shelley related of Harriet descending into prostitution and committing suicide after being deserted by a "groom" named "Smith," was repeated several times many years later with the added notion that the groom came from a "very humble grade of life."[51]

A second story had Harriet unfaithful to Shelley before he left her. In May 1817, Godwin wrote to William Baxter he knew "from unquestionable authority, wholly unconnected with Shelley," that Harriet had become "a woman of great levity" and had been "unfaithful" to Shelley before they separated: "Afterwards she was guilty of repeated acts of levity, & had latterly lived in open connection with a colonel Maxwel."[52]

Hearing this from Godwin the following month, Shelley wrote Mary what has been called "one of the most controversial letters of Romantic biography."[53] Shelley said: "I learn just now from Godwin that he has evidence that Harriet was unfaithful to me *four months* before I left England with you. If we can succeed in establishing this our connexion will receive an additional sanction, & plea be overcome."[54] Shelley's emphasis on *"four months"* suggests his surprise that the presumed unfaithfulness occurred earlier than when he told Mary before their elopement that Harriet was in love "with Major Ryan."[55] Four months before their elopement would have been late March or early April, when Shelley and Harriet were remarried and Harriet became pregnant with Charles. Godwin was a stickler for facts and his information about Harriet cannot be discounted unequivocally. However, self-interest and sense of propriety possibly led him to promulgate the idea Harriet was to blame for his daughter's elopement with Shelley. It seems improbable that Harriet was unfaithful to Shelley in 1814, but a brief affair with Ryan was possible early that year when, accompanied by Eliza, she was apart from Shelley.[56] Shelley continued for years to believe in Harriet's 1814 unfaithfulness.[57]

A year before her death, Charles Clairmont absolved Harriet of infidelity with Ryan, "an Irish adventurer whom she commissioned to take all possible legal advantage of Shelley."[58] Claire, who had heard of Major Ryan but never met him, also was convinced that Harriet had not been unfaithful to Shelley. Years later she wrote it was not Harriet's "fault" that Shelley left her, but that "he fell desperately in love with Mary."[59] The Mr. Ryan whom Shelley and Harriet met in 1812 in Dublin and entertained in London in 1813, and who contacted Shelley and Mary in early 1815 to obtain money for Harriet, was in all likelihood also the Major Ryan and the Irish adventurer.[60]

Ryan's role reappears in Godwin's story—in his letter to Baxter—that Harriet lived with an army officer named Maxwell at the time of her death. That the Army Lists record both Major Matthew Ryan and Lieutenant Colonel Christopher Maxwell in the same regiment suggests Harriet met the thirty-six-year-old Maxwell through Ryan.[61] Claire's account, probably the most accurate available, was that Harriet's lover "was a Captain in the Indian or Wellington Army" who was "ordered abroad." With Eliza Westbrook's "concurrence," Harriet lived near Chapel Street with a "decent couple" who believed that Harriet, under another name, "was a lady's maid, was married and that her husband was abroad as a Courier." Eliza, wanting Harriet's affair concealed from Shelley, apparently told her parents Harriet was visiting "friends in the country." Harriet, "very low" after not hearing from Maxwell, told her sister that "he did not really love her and meant to abandon her—for she remarked I don't think I am made to inspire love, and you know my husband abandoned me."[62] In a similar account, derived in part from Claire's information, the army captain promised to write Harriet. She then had to move to cheaper lodgings but "her former landlady refused to forward her letters to her new address."[63]

These versions match salient details given by witnesses at Harriet's inquest, held at the Fox and Bull Tavern in Knightsbridge.[64] The witness who found her body on December 10 said it "must have lain in the Water some days." Another witness, who accompanied Harriet when she took the rooms at 7 Elizabeth Street near Hans Place, testified that Harriet was married but not living with her husband. That this witness—who observed her "lowness of Spirits" for several months—identified Harriet's body could suggest she had not been in the water more than a few days (her last letter was written December 7). However, she possibly was identified by her clothing or ring. Her landlady on Elizabeth Street testified that she had been staying there for nine weeks, paying from month to month, before she left on November 9. She stated that Harriet "appeared in a family way" and was "very desponding and gloomy." The maid testified that Harriet "said very little" and spent most of her time in bed. Harriet's behavior "was proper" except for her "continual lowness of Spirits."

The official inquest report did not mention Harriet was pregnant when she drowned, but she undoubtedly was and Maxwell most likely was the father of her unborn child.[65] Harriet's inquest was conducted with delicacy and some secrecy to avoid involving the Westbrooks. She was referred to as Harriet Smith and the verdict "found dead" avoided mentioning suicide. Murder was ruled out by stating there were "no marks of violence" on her body, and no determination of a date of death was made. The secrecy about Harriet's death continued when she was buried December 13 and her inquest name, "Harriett Smith," appeared on the burial register with the double *t* she and her family were accustomed to using. Strangely, the same record lists the burial of "Benjamin Smith" two days earlier on December 11. Both he and Harriet were listed as living on Mount Street.[66]

Harriet left her lodgings on Elizabeth Street November 9 after dinner at four o'clock. With Eliza's help, she probably moved without her parent's awareness to live with Benjamin Smith and his wife, the "decent couple," near Chapel Street.[67] According to inquest testimony, her parents, alarmed after she was missing from her Elizabeth Street lodgings for a week and knowing of her depression, had the Serpentine dragged for her body.[68] Either she had talked of drowning herself or the Serpentine's proximity to Chapel Street made it a likely suicide spot. The death of Smith, thirty-three years older than Harriet, must have been the final blow that precipitated a severely depressed Harriet to her death. Not having received the letters held by her former landlady from her lover—the father of her unborn child—she felt once more abandoned and unworthy of a man's love. Her final letter to Eliza, containing messages for Shelley and her parents, was written on Saturday evening, December 7. She probably drowned herself that same night.

Shelley read Harriet's letter sometime after Eliza had seen it. The most tragic letter Shelley ever read, it added more anguish to his already shattered feelings. After her greeting to "My dearest & much belo^d Sister," a slip in her first sentence suggests her ambivalence about taking her own life: "When you read this letr. I shall be more [sic] an inhabitant of this miserable world. do not regret the loss of one who could be never be anything but a source of vexation & misery to you all belonging to me. Too wretched to exert myself lowered in the opinion of everyone why should I drag on a miserable existence embittered by past recollections & not one ray of hope to rest on for the future."

She asked forgiveness from Eliza, a "dear amiable woman" and wished "that I had never left you oh! that I had always taken your advice. I might have lived long & happy but weak & unsteady have rushed on my own destruction." Addressing her last message to Shelley, she wanted him to have Charles and Eliza to have Ianthe:

My dear Bysshe let me conjure you by the remembrance of our days of happiness to grant my last wish—do not take your innocent child from Eliza who has been more than I have, who has watched over her with such unceasing care.—Do not refuse my last request I never could refuse you & if you had never left me I might have lived but as it is, I freely forgive you & may you enjoy that happiness which you have deprived me of. There is your beautiful boy. oh! be careful of him & his love may prove one day a rich reward ... Now comes the sad task of saying farewell—oh I must be quick. God bless & watch over you all..You dear Bysshe. & you dear Eliza. May all happiness attend ye both is the last wish of her who loved ye more than all others. My children I dare not trust myself there. They are too young to regret me & ye will be kind to them for their own sakes more than for mine My parents do not regret me. I was unworthy of your love & care. Be happy all of you. so shall my spirit find rest & forgiveness. God bless you all is the last prayer of the unfortunate Harriet S—[69]

Harriet was still receiving her adequate annual income, £200 from Shelley and £200 from her father. Shelley had heard her wealthy father was seriously ill and "confined to his room" at the time Harriet died.[70] However, there is no indication her father was not planning to continue to support Harriet whose two children were apparently with Eliza in the Westbrook home during at least the final months of Harriet's life. Coping with the difficulties she faced was beyond Harriet's strengths. Shelley bore responsibility for leaving Harriet, but it became evident in the almost two and a half years since his elopement with Mary that Harriet lacked the emotional resources to rebuild her life. It seems a correct judgment that many women in even more difficult situations did not commit suicide.[71]

Shelley's understanding of Harriet's vulnerabilities grew in the months after her death, compounding and deepening his pain over her death. Hunt commented: "It was a heavy blow to him; and he never forgot it. For a time, it tore his being to pieces . . . he was not without remorse for having no better exercised his judgment with regard to the degree of intellect he had allied himself with, and for having given rise to a premature independence of conduct in one unequal to the task."[72]

After the initial shock of Harriet's death, Shelley suppressed his grief, guilt, and depression under a blanket of denial and feverish activity connected with trying to retrieve Ianthe and Charles. His initial surface calmness, according to Peacock, "grew into a deep and abiding sorrow." Peacock acutely noted that during a visit Shelley angrily attacked a gardener for ruining a "beautiful tree."[73]

When Shelley wrote Byron about Harriet's death, he alluded to Fanny's death, saying it affected him more deeply than Harriet's.[74] However, some months later, after failing to regain his children, Shelley's intense feelings over Harriet's death apparently surfaced. He wrote the Hunts of a "constant pain in my side" and of "such a depression of strength & spirits" that he could hardly hold his pen while writing. Mary thought Shelley was "worse than I have known him for some time."[75] Walking one evening with Peacock, Shelley fell "into a gloomy reverie" and remarked he would "take a great glass of ale every night" to "help deaden my feelings." He then confessed that "thinking of Harriet" led to thoughts and feelings "I would not tell any one else."[76]

Shelley initially dealt with his guilt by accusing Eliza of being her sister's murderer in letters to Mary and to Byron. Eliza, he claimed, had murdered Harriet to get her father's money. He mentioned his "persecution" by Eliza, "a libidinous & vindictive woman" and a "viper."[77]

Masking these feelings, in his effort to regain his children he wrote Eliza in a conciliatory tone and twice tried unsuccessfully to see her. Again writing her, he wanted "exclusive and entire charge" of Ianthe who, he proposed, along with her brother, should live temporarily with Leigh Hunt. Shelley denied believing Eliza or her father behaved ill "towards the unhappy victim" but she could have "acted more judiciously." Bearing Eliza "no malice," he apologized for contacting his lawyer. However, he handed Eliza ammunition by saying Mary was "the lady whose union with me you may excusably regard as the cause of your sister's ruin."[78] These words must have jolted Mary if she read them quoted by Eliza in her later sworn affidavit against Shelley.[79] Years later, in 1839, Mary expressed the lingering effects from this charge of her responsibility in Harriet's death: "Poor Harriet to whose sad fate I attribute so many of my own heavy sorrows as the atonement by fate for her death."[80]

Shelley's contact with his children by Harriet had been minimal. His solicitor twice stated that his client had never seen Charles; any contact Shelley had with his son was fleeting.[81] Ianthe, only a year old when her father eloped with Mary, had seen little of him the previous six months. Shelley perhaps last saw Ianthe in April 1815, when she was twenty-two months old. Mr. Westbrook actively backed Eliza in keeping Shelley from the two children who, at the time of their mother's death, were in Warwick under the care of a minister.[82] Ignoring requests from Shelley and Leigh Hunt for the children's deliverance, the Westbrooks soon took decisive legal action to deprive Shelley of his offspring.

After Harriet's death, Mary had numerous reasons for wishing to be married. Pregnant, she was aware that her mother turned to marriage under similar circumstances. Marriage would restore Mary's relationship with her father, and she must have hoped it would deepen the wedge between Shelley and Claire. Immediately answering Shelley's mention of marriage in his December 16 let-

ter, she was non-committal about when it took place but they "must
be [married] in London."[83] Peacock advised Shelley to marry as
soon as possible but Shelley was conflicted.[84] He believed marriage would provide leverage in a Chancery contest for his children
but his disastrous marriage to Harriet did not lessen his principles
against matrimony.

Godwin, agitating for an early marriage, apparently had pursued
the possibility of Shelley getting a divorce just before Harriet's
death.[85] His daughter's marriage to the future baronet would remove the social stigma he felt about Mary's unmarried motherhood, replacing it with the title-in-waiting of Lady Shelley. The
marriage also promised relief to his financial woes. Upon hearing
of Harriet's death, Godwin invited Shelley to Skinner Street, his
first admittance into Godwin's home since eloping with Mary. In
his best withholding style, Godwin orchestrated a gradual return.
Shelley showed up on December 18, but Godwin had absented himself and after talking two hours to the detested Mrs. Godwin he returned to Bath. Finally, Godwin received his future son-in-law at
Skinner Street on December 27. The next day Godwin accompanied Shelley to obtain a licence for the marriage to be solemnized
two days later at the Parish Church of St. Mildred on Bread Street.
Mary, a minor, needed her father's signature on the licence. Shelley, repeating his Edinburgh tactic, made oath on the licence of
having resided in St. Mildred Parish for four weeks.[86] Shelley, a
marriage disparager, and Godwin, no longer a marriage disparager, went through the legal niceties that would equalize each at
two marriages.

Mary, who came to London with Shelley, now had her first meeting with her father in two and a half years. Godwin, upon leaving
the licence office, called on her at the Hunts. It is unclear what dra-
matics, if any, transpired before the marriage. In one dubious report by Mrs. Godwin, twice transmitted years later by Claire, Mary
threatened to kill herself and their son if Shelley did not agree to
marry her.[87] An 1818 rumor was that Mrs. Godwin pressured the
recalcitrant couple by writing them that Godwin was in such despair that if they did not marry he would commit suicide.[88]

The Godwins attended the marriage of Mary and Shelley on December 30 in St. Mildred's. Godwin's long-term coldly hostile rejection of Mary quickly changed to flattery and effusive warmth.
Shelley took care to write the heavily pregnant Claire in Bath the
day of the marriage. He wryly observed that the "magical" effects

the ceremony had on Godwin's behavior—"polished & cautious attentions to me & Mary"—did not deceive him. Shelley felt "antipathy" for Mrs. Godwin but "Her sweet daughter is very dear to me." His mentioning sending only £20 to Charles Clairmont signaled Claire not to expect Harriet's death to release more money. He reassured Claire that the Godwins were ignorant about her pregnancy and that her letter that day "relieved me from a weight of great anxiety." Downplaying the marriage's importance, he attributed it to the pressures of the Godwins who "will now be satisfied & quiet."

Claire knew Mary wanted this marriage to strengthen her position in their competition for Shelley's affection. Claire also knew that Shelley wanted the marriage to gain custody of his children, to placate Mary, and perhaps to appease his parents, who soon heard of the wedding through Whitton. In his letter to Claire, the most moving moment was his allusion to the dead Fanny: ". . . how dreadfully melancholy Skinner St. appears with all its associations. . . . But I am resolved to overcome such sensations—if I do not destroy them I may be myself destroyed. . . . Kiss Willy & yourself for me."[89]

Shelley observed that the marriage brought out the worst of Godwin's hypocritical behavior. Godwin disguised the marriage in his diary as a social call, secreting a more complete account in the 1814 pages of his journal, as if to erase that year's elopement. Mrs. Godwin wrote of the "flattering prospects" she and her husband were enjoying from Mary's marriage to the eldest son of a "Baronet," adding that for health reasons the Shelleys might spend the summer in Italy.[90] Godwin, denying future monetary recompense, protested, "I care but little, comparatively, about wealth."[91] Godwin's hollow rapprochement with Shelley would not last.

After returning with Shelley to little William and the imminently expecting Claire on New Year's Day, Mary noted laconically in her journal, "a marriage takes place," misdating it the "29th."[92] Resuming the half-finished *Frankenstein,* she wrote of little William Frankenstein's murder by the monster.[93] Back in London several days later, Shelley discovered that John Westbrook, moving aggressively to block his claim on Ianthe and Charles, had placed his two grandchildren under the protection of the Court of Chancery by settling upon them a £2000 trust.[94] Westbrook then filed a bill in Chancery Court, petitioning the Lord Chancellor that the children not be given over to their father, emphasizing Shelley's marital behavior and only secondarily his religious beliefs. The petition stated Shelley had "deserted" his wife and "unlawfully cohabited" with "Mary Godwin." Further, the petition stated that Shelley "vows himself to be an Atheist" and his *Queen Mab* "and other Works . . . blasphemously derided the Truth of the Christian revelation and denied the Existence of a God."[95]

Eliza Westbrook, in affidavits, testified she knew Shelley's handwriting well and produced nine of his letters to Harriet. Eliza also quoted the passage from Shelley's recent letter to her that Mary might be regarded as causing Harriet's ruin.[96] After conferring all day with his solicitor, Longdill, Shelley wrote Mary summarizing the Westbrooks' "insidiously malignant" petition. Shelley's defense would focus on their charges against his beliefs, charges the Chancellor could use to take his children from him. Shelley vowed that the Westbrooks would not have his children. He thought the Chancellor would give his children to his father "if they must be denied to me."[97]

With only five days to prepare an answer for the hearing, Shelley hoped to verify Godwin's rumor of Harriet's unfaithfulness four months before he eloped with Mary. Omitting this unverifiable charge, his defense statement of January 18 began with a denial that he had deserted Harriet. Rather, they "agreed" because of "certain differences" to live "apart from each other."[98] Whitton, unable to persuade Shelley not to oppose John Westbrook's bill, was certain the Lord Chancellor would not allow Shelley custody of his children. Further, Shelley would open himself up to further criminal charges of blasphemy and sedition by the evidence introduced of *Queen Mab* and *A Letter to Lord Ellenborough*. Whitton agreed with Shelley that the Lord Chancellor would turn to Sir Timothy.[99]

Shelley favored a strategy emphasizing an aggressive defense of his principles concerning marriage, religion, and politics. His attorneys wanted to downplay the importance of these beliefs and emphasize the inadequacy of the Westbrooks as guardians. The brief Longdill prepared for Shelley's courtroom attorneys outlined this defense of denigrating the Westbrooks, but it contained personal language about Shelley that must have boomeranged on his prospects. Longdill derogated the "boyish and silly" *Queen Mab*, saying that despite its "violent Phillipics" against marriage, Shelley had "married twice before he was 25!" He compared Shelley's family's wealth to John Westbrook's having "formerly kept a Coffee House." As for "illiterate and vulgar" Eliza Westbrook, Longdill presented Shelley's old grievance that her "advice" and "*man-agement*" made her responsible for his marriage.[100]

This inauspicious defense, taking the low ground, probably frustrated Shelley. Before the hearing, he wrote Byron that Eliza's persecutory Chancery petition would "deprive" him of his children and "throw me into prison . . . [for] being a <u>Revolutionist</u> & an <u>Atheist</u>." He had been led to believe he could "purchase victory" if he recanted, but he had "too much pride" for that.[101]

Unfortunately, none of Shelley's three attorneys was of the same caliber as the Westbrooks' attorney, the eminent Sir Samuel Romilly. In addition to his legal experience and impressive speaking ability, his Whig background communicated to the conservative Lord Chancellor that liberal political beliefs did not square with Shelley's behavior. Romilly, like Shelley, supported Sir Francis Burdett's reform efforts and Catholic emancipation. Having been an MP from Horsham, Romilly knew the Shelley family.

Lord Chancellor Eldon, the able arch-conservative who would decide the case, formed with Sidmouth and Castlereagh the reactionary triumvirate that ran Lord Liverpool's Tory government. Eldon did not get Timothy Shelley's vote for chancellor of Oxford in his unsuccessful 1809 bid. Shelley first mentioned Eldon in his 1812 *An Address, to the Irish People,* citing his repression of freedom of the press. Eldon's attacks on a free press and civil rights continued. Opposed to easing capital punishment for minor theft, he condemned a man to hanging for stealing seven shillings. Eldon heard Shelley's case during the 1816–1819 interval in which "The liberties of British citizens were more drastically curtailed than in any other peacetime period of modern history."[102] A consummate authoritarian bureaucrat, Eldon shared one thing with Shelley, forfeiting his fellowship at Oxford's University College for running away to Scotland to get married.

Eldon heard the case in open court on January 24. Romilly argued Shelley's irreligious beliefs in *Queen Mab* made him unfit to raise his children. Shelley's attorney, Basil Montagu, countered by stating *Queen Mab* was never published and Shelley wrote it for his own amusement. Montagu requested dismissal of the petition with costs.[103] Eldon, in an action unfavorable for Shelley, delayed his decision, announcing that any future hearing would be held in his private chamber. The day of the hearing was little William's birthday and Mary hoped his second year would "be more peaceful." Hearing the "bad news" about the delayed decision, Mary went to London the next day.[104]

Eldon was determined to keep the proceedings private and outside the purview of the press. A notice printed in the *Examiner* about the Chancery case threatened to lead to legal action against Hunt.[105] Shelley wrote to Claire that "the malice of these monsters" would lead to "some such punishment as imprisonment & fine."[106]

While Eldon deliberated, Shelley prepared a further declaration of his case which Godwin forcefully edited. Shelley's declaration contained a temperate statement refusing to retract his beliefs about marriage and religion: "If I have attacked religion, it is agreed that I am punishable, but not by the loss of my children." As for marriage, it is "in its present state . . . a mischievous and tyrannical institution." Further, "delicacy forbids" he say more "than that [he and Harriet] were disunited by incurable dissensions, and rendered incapable, by that marriage contracted at eighteen [sic] years of age."[107] Again, there was no suggestion that he had left Harriet against her wishes.

Accompanied by Leigh Hunt, Shelley listened as Eldon handed down his judgment on March 27, effectively depriving him of his children. Eldon said "the father's principles cannot be misunderstood," Shelley's "conduct" and principles were "highly immoral" and he could not deliver "over these children for their education exclusively to what is called the care to which Mr. Shelley wishes it to be entrusted."[108]

Shelley presumably could appeal to the House of Lords but Peacock wryly noted "Liberal law lords were then unknown."[109] Depriving the parent of the guardianship of his children was a precedent-setting decision that continues to be cited in legal circles. Refusing to place the children under the guardianship of the Westbrooks, Eldon asked a Master of Chancery to recommend guardians from those proposed by Shelley and the Westbrooks.

A prolonged guardianship battle, unresolved for eighteen months, left the hapless children in emotional limbo. Shelley proposed for guardian his solicitor, Longdill. When the Master initially recommended the Westbrooks' proposed guardian, the Reverend Kendall, an outraged Longdill appealed to Eldon who requested a new set of guardians be proposed.[110] This time, Longdill's proposed guardians, Thomas Hume, M.D., and his wife, were selected. Thomas Moore, visiting the home while Shelley's children lived there, described Mrs. Hume as "clever, warm-hearted." However, the Humes' plan was that Ianthe would shun fashionable clothes— they violated "all feelings of feminine Delicacy and Decency"—and would avoid reading most novels. The final guardianship plan called for annual support of £120 from Shelley and £80 from West- brook. Shelley could visit his children once a month or twelve times a year but one of the Humes had to be present.[111] As it turned out, the children's fates took divergent courses.

2

Albion House: The Last English Year

Cㅣᴀɪʀᴇ's ᴅᴀᴜɢʜᴛᴇʀ ᴡᴀs ʙᴏʀɴ ᴊᴀɴᴜᴀʀʏ 12 ᴡʜɪʟᴇ sʜᴇʟʟᴇʏ ᴡᴀs visiting the Hunts. After writing Shelley the news, Mary wrote Byron, saying offhand she was now "Mary W. Shelley." When Shelley returned to Bath, he also wrote Byron about the "beautiful" baby.[1] Like her mother, the infant was illegitimate and of uncertain name. Claire and the Shelleys called her Alba ("Dawn"), Italian for the early morning hour of its birth and a feminine form of her father's nickname, Albé. Later, Byron chose the name Allegra and Claire had her christened as Clara Allegra Byron.

Shelley, impulsively pretending he had a sedentary nature, in December had leased for some twenty-odd years a large house in Great Marlow, called Albion House, at £63 a year. Robert Madocks, a local cabinetmaker, apparently was the agent for the property's owner, Mr. Tylecote.[2] Shelley lived there almost a year, longer than any other residence of his adult life. An ungainly rambling structure, it resembled the rural hotel it quickly became after Shelley and Mary occupied it in March. Albion House faced toward the distant Thames, where Shelley soon had a boat. For privacy, Shelley leased some adjoining acreage and Peacock reported that to avoid scandalous rumors, he "held no intercourse with his immediate neighbours," saying, "I am not wretch enough to tolerate an acquaintance."[3] According to another acquaintance, Shelley ordered "his upholsterer to notify the inhabitants that the coming family would associate with no one in the village, would never go to church, and would do as they chose in defiance of public opinion ... a room was hung with black for the reception of Lord Byron."[4]

The Shelleys engaged the fashionable Bath firm of English, English, and Beck to furnish and decorate Albion House.[5] In his most ostentatious domestic display, Shelley again deferred paying his bills to commercial establishments, leaving England without paying the firm's £1,192 bill, which he supposed was £800.[6]

Albion House had "a good dining room, library 36 feet by 18, drawing room 30 feet by 18, study, 5 best bedrooms, 2 large nurseries, each 30 feet by 20, water closet, 6 or 7 attics, convenient offices, good garden and pleasure-ground . . . 4 acres of land may be had."[7] Shelley's library, "large enough for a ball-room," was decorated—like Hunt's—with life-sized statues of "the Vatican Apollo and the celestial Venus."[8]

Awaiting renovation of Albion House, Mary joined Shelley in London for a few weeks at the Hunts'. When not discussing literature and politics, Hunt indulged his passion for time-limited sonnet-writing competitions. Thornton Hunt, whom Mary called her husband's "protégé," recalled Shelley's "pleasure" in frightening him by screwing up his "long and curling hair into a horn" and making "frightful gestures as some imaginative monster." The frightened boy retaliated one day when Shelley was waiting anxiously to hear from Chancery about his children's fate. After again being teased by Shelley, Thornton said he hoped Shelley "would be beaten in the trial and have his children taken from him." Shelley fell "listlessly back in his chair" from the shock but soon "folded his arms around me and kissed me."[9]

Leigh Hunt's "crowning anecdote" involved Shelley's going to Hunt's home on a bitter cold winter's night and finding a woman "in fits" lying upon the snow-covered ground. Unable to get nearby residents to take in the woman while he went for a doctor, Shelley implored a man stepping from a carriage to assist him but was rebuffed. Assisted by the woman's son, Shelley took her some distance to Hunt's house and called a doctor, who said she would have perished had she lain longer in the snow. After sending them safely home the next day, Shelley received her "thanks full of gratitude."[10]

A close friendship developed among Leigh Hunt, Shelley, and Horace Smith. Shelley thought it "odd" that Smith, "the only truly generous person I ever knew, who had money to be generous with, should be a stockbroker! And he writes poetry too."[11] Shelley again met Keats at Hunt's. Hunt admired Keats, but professed his closest friend was Shelley. Keats, after first meeting Hunt in October 1816, was encouraged by Hunt to publish his first volume of poetry. However, Shelley—echoing Godwin's advice that he vehemently had rejected—early in his acquaintance with Keats advised the younger poet while they walked on Hampstead Heath not to publish his "first blights."[12] Keats's rejection of the advice did not stop

Shelley from calling at the printer's shop to facilitate publication of Keats's volume.[13]

As Hunt observed, "Keats did not take to Shelley as kindly as Shelley did to him."[14] Hunt believed Keats was sensitive about his modest social-class origins and felt uncomfortable with Shelley's privileged background. Trying to establish his own poetic voice, Keats wanted to avoid the influences of Shelley's poetic style and of Hunt's editorializing. When Shelley later invited him to Marlow, Keats declined, remarking that he wanted his "own unfettered scope."[15] Except for Charles Cowden Clarke, Keats's friends disliked Shelley, finding his radical religious and political views scarcely less palatable than his argumentative and attacking behavior. Keats usually became quiet and uninvolved during Shelley's heated exchanges with his friends.

One friend of Keats who disliked Shelley was the artist Benjamin Robert Haydon, a Tory and rabid Christian. At Horace Smith's dinner party early in 1817, Haydon "resolved to gore [Shelley] without mercy" after Shelley commented about "that detestable religion, the Christian," saying the Ten Commandments were not the basis of "all codes of law." Keats and Smith remained silent. Haydon also took offense when Shelley said "he could not bear the inhumanity of Wordsworth in talking of the beauty of the shining trout as they lay after being caught."[16]

Keats's friend, the artist Joseph Severn, was "shocked and disturbed" when Shelley, after attacking Severn's "Christian creed," outlined a poem comparing "the Blessed Saviour with a mountebank, whose tricks he identified with miracles." When Shelley proclaimed Shakespeare's disbelief in Christianity, Severn countered with a string of quotations. After Hunt and Keats said that Severn had the best of the argument, "Shelley declared he would study the subject and write an essay upon it." Shelley's essay, *On Christianity,* probably written shortly after, possibly was stimulated by this encounter.[17]

William Hazlitt, the brilliant critic friend of Hunt and Godwin, also developed antipathetic feelings toward Shelley. However, one night at Hunt's, Hazlitt and Shelley apparently agreed on "monarchy & republicanism." On another occasion, Hazlitt, a staunch Bonapartist, reportedly was offended by Shelley's "cutting him up."[18] Shelley regretted that another of Hunt's friends whom he admired, Charles Lamb, shunned him because of the "calumny of an enemy," possibly Godwin.[19]

Mary had cautioned Shelley not to contact Hogg on his return to London after Harriet's death, but Hogg dined at the Hunts' with Shelley, Godwin, Hazlitt, and a new acquaintance, Walter Coulson.[20] In mid-February, Shelley signed a new will, keeping Peacock and Byron as executors. The will's provisions for Mary, Claire, Hogg, Peacock, and Byron were unchanged. Harriet's bequest was deleted and Shelley raised the provision for each of his children by her to £6000. William, now his legitimate son, was provided the same amount.[21]

To keep the Godwins ignorant of her motherhood and the baby's parentage, Claire and her baby made separate appearances in London. Alba stayed with Marianne Hunt while Claire reverted to being Miss Clairmont and her child passed for that of a London friend.[22] It is unclear when Godwin came to know of Claire's child and its parentage; neither he nor his wife ever mentioned Alba.

London was the center of much popular agitation and Lord Liverpool's government was about to implement a program of political repression. In late January, several days after Eldon heard the Chancery suit, the Prince Regent was mobbed upon leaving Parliament and his carriage window broken. At the end of January, the radical reform delegates of the Hampden Clubs convened in London at the Crown and Anchor Tavern with petitions for Annual Parliaments, Universal Suffrage, and the secret ballot.[23] In February, Shelley wrote *A Proposal for Putting Reform to the Vote throughout the Kingdom*, the first of two pamphlets with the pseudonym, "The Hermit of Marlow." By February 22 he was arranging revisions of his pamphlet with the publisher, Charles Ollier and his brother James, a new firm that Hunt also had recommended to Keats. Shelley told Ollier to print five hundred copies and advertise in all the morning papers.[24]

Shortly after his reform pamphlet appeared, Shelley was in London on March 7, the day his father gave his only reported speech in the House of Commons. A Horsham reform petition was being discussed and Sir Timothy briefly testified to the orderly nature of the Horsham reform meeting. Increasingly conservative, his last known vote in Parliament, on June 23, 1817, was in favor of the Tory government's suspension of habeas corpus.[25]

In his *Proposal,* which he hoped would be sold by William Hone, the radical bookseller, Shelley ostensibly positioned himself with the moderate reformers represented in the press by such journals as Leigh Hunt's *Examiner.*[26] However, Shelley's implicit message in the *Proposal* was more radical than that espoused in the *Examiner*. His republican aims were in accord with the democratic beliefs of the radical reformers but he feared a violent revolution of the "untutored multitude" unless gradual means were used.[27] To bridge this gap between goals and means, Shelley used an adroit rhetoric in his *Proposal* similar to that in his essay, *On Christianity*.[28] He believed that Christ, like himself, was a humanitarian radical reformer who, living under conditions much like those in England of 1817, had to couch his message in moderate terms for it to be accepted.

The working-class misery of 1817—mass unemployment, food shortages, and outbreaks of rioting—had deepened the animosity between the radical and moderate reform groups. Shelley, in his *Proposal*, reached out to radicals, citing Major Cartwright and William Cobbett and sending both copies. To achieve radical reform "gradually and with caution," Shelley advocated immediate annual Parliaments but believed universal male suffrage should be delayed. The vote for women was not even considered. Shelley's clever writing showed how far he had matured as a political writer since his 1812 Irish *Address* and *Proposals*. However, he ended his 1817 *Proposal* in the language of his aristocratic liberalism with its disdain of the ignorant masses' readiness to have the vote; universal suffrage was "fraught with peril" in the "present unprepared state of public knowledge and feeling." The right to vote should, "at present," only go to those who paid "a certain small sum in *direct taxes*." To extend the franchise to all adult males "would be to place power in the hands of men who have been rendered brutal and torpid and ferocious by ages of slavery."

Attacking the "bullying and swindling" involved in choosing the House of Commons—a "hospital for lunatics"—Shelley proposed a countrywide reform referendum. However, the referendum would be a fait accompli with revolutionary implications. If it went unheeded by the government, "Parliament would have rebelled against the People then."[29]

Shelley, characteristically pledging £100 to finance the plan, sent Ollier a list of forty-one individuals, editors, and organizations to receive his *Proposal*. The list's broad geographical scope attests to Shelley's comprehensive knowledge about major actors in the reform movement, mostly moderates.[30]

Aside from Hunt's plaudits in the *Examiner*, Shelley's pamphlet received little response, partly because government repressions were falling in place in March, including The Habeas Corpus Suspension Act and The Seditious Meetings Act. Southey, scorning reform, soon listed Shelley's *Proposal* among publications he attacked in the conservative *Quarterly Review*.[31]

Once ensconced at Albion House, the Shelleys' houseguests would include the Hunt family, Godwin, Horace Smith, Hogg, Walter Coulson, and William Baxter. Peacock visited frequently, much to Mary's annoyance. Godwin arrived first, staying four days in early April. Claire, rejoining the Shelley household, left Alba with the Hunts.[32] Each adult was writing a deeply personal work: Godwin's *Mandeville*, Mary's *Frankenstein*, and Shelley's *Laon and Cythna*. Claire was completing a now lost "book"; later in the year Shelley and Mary co-authored *History of a Six Weeks' Tour*. Another visitor, Hunt, was preparing *Foliage* and Peacock was composing his long poem, *Rhododaphne*. As if commemorating this literary outburst, Shelley would write reviews of *Frankenstein*, *Mandeville*, and *Rhododaphne*.

Shelley's other outpouring was money. His expenses included Claire and her child, Godwin, Peacock on his £100–120 annuity, and Hunt, who received £1400 from Shelley sometime in 1817.[33] Charles Clairmont, abroad, received occasional support. Shelley's household staff included Elise, a cook, and Harry, both manservant and gardener. By early summer a young woman from around Marlow, Amelia (Milly) Shields, became Alba's nursemaid.

In early April, Mary finished her draft of *Frankenstein* in time for the arrival of the Hunts, their four children, Alba, and Marianne Hunt's sister, Bessy Kent. Shelley, seeking solitude while composing *Laon and Cythna*, escaped regularly to his boat on the Thames and the seclusion of Bisham Wood. Mary, four months pregnant, wrote a fair copy of *Frankenstein* while Marianne Hunt, newly pregnant, scraped Shelley's plaster casts of Apollo and Venus.[34]

Despite Shelley's wish to avoid neighbors, several townsfolk got to know him. One recalled his laughter upon finding that someone had lengthened his boat's name from "Vaga" to "Vagabond."[35] Shelley's reading included a history of the French Revolution—*Laon and Cythna*'s historical underpinning—and Spenser, whose stanza form he adopted in his poem. Hunt recalled Shelley's "great, though peculiar, and often admiring interest" in reading the Bible at this time. His favorites were the book of Job, the Epistle of James, and the Sermon on the Mount.[36]

Shelley, taking the verses from James to heart, during his Marlow stay engaged in his most sustained works of charity toward the poor. Marlow was a poverty-stricken lace-making center whose "miserably remunerated" women lost their health eking out an existence for their families. Peacock recalled Shelley's continual visits "amongst this unfortunate population," his financial help relieving "the most pressing cases of distress." Hunt said that Shelley "inquired personally into the circumstances of his petitioners; visited the sick in their beds . . . and kept a regular list of industrious poor, whom he assisted with small sums to make up their accounts."[37] Mrs. Madocks remembered that on his "sacred" visits he carried little money, giving his charges a sum on a "little billet . . . sometimes on the leaf of a book" to be cashed for "as much as half a crown." He came home once without shoes because, having no paper, he "gave the poor man his shoes." Shelley dispensed money to his pensioners on Saturday evenings. When absent from town, he left a bag of coins for this purpose with Mrs. Madocks. In the cold winter of 1817–1818 Shelley provided sheets and army blankets for the poor, stamping the blankets with "Shelley" in large letters to avoid confiscation by the pawnbrokers.[38]

Countering rumors that Shelley was a "keeper of a seraglio" at Albion House, Hunt said Shelley "was extremely difficult to please in such matters" and lived "like a hermit" at Marlow. Shelley arose early, "walked and read," ate a spare breakfast, and then composed *Laon and Cythna* all morning. Finishing a "dinner of vegetables," he visited "the sick and the fatherless" or conversed with friends. After reading to Mary, he was in bed by ten o'clock.[39]

Shelley wrote out the last thirteen pages of fair copy for *Frankenstein* in mid-May and then wrote the novel's preface.[40] Clarifying the controversial issue of Shelley's contribution to *Frankenstein*, Robinson notes that Shelley—collaborating actively in all phases of the novel's production, including its final printing—was the "able midwife" to Mary's "creative genius," writing "more than 4000 words" of the text.[41] When he wrote the publisher of having changed "such few instances of baldness of style," Shelley was slighting his extensive editorial contribution.[42] However, the substantive conception, plot, and structure of *Frankenstein* unquestionably were Mary's. Shelley kept a hovering eye on her work, accepting her "carte blanche to make what alterations you please."[43]

Frankenstein has achieved a cultural influence beyond any work of Blake, Wordsworth, Coleridge, Byron, Keats, or Shelley. Beginning the novel at age eighteen, Mary determinedly wrote *Frankenstein* during ten stressful, busy months. Completed when she was nineteen, published anonymously when she was twenty, Mary's work was the kind of human drama she criticized her husband for not writing in his poetry.

Neither Godwin nor Shelley escaped Mary's anger in *Franken-stein*. The Shelley-like Victor Frankenstein, "pale student of un-hallowed arts," echoed the name Shelley chose for himself in *Victor and Cazire*. Henry, another of Shelley's poetic names, became one of the monster's murder victims. His next victim, Victor's aptly named bride and sisterly cousin, Elizabeth, is murdered on her bridal bed before the marriage is consummated.

The rejected monster's sadistic carnage begins with the murder of Victor's young brother William. Considering the numerous Williams in Mary's life—her son, her half brother, and her father—the name of the monster's first victim was an overdetermined, strange choice.

Six months pregnant, Mary twice in May drew in her journal black crescent moons and an "A" above them with the words, "a let-ter." This code, if not about mounting financial debts, perhaps in-volved keeping Alba's parentage secret.[44] Another annoyance for Mary was the seventy-five-guinea bill for Claire's piano, just ar-rived from London. Hunt, an opera critic who sang and played the piano, had written to his well-known musical friend Vincent No-vello to fulfill Shelley's expansive desires for a piano that was "*grand*." Three years later, it was another bill Shelley was trying to pay.[45]

Later in May, Shelley took Mary to London by boat to deliver the manuscript of *Frankenstein* to Murray for possible publication. Her stepmother being in Paris, Mary pleased Godwin by staying with him even if "my bedchambers are by no means fit to receive a future ornament of the English baronetage."[46] Shelley and Mary saw Mozart's *Don Giovanni,* the beginning of Shelley's more for-mal musical education. The ballet following the opera featured the *danseuse* Mlle Milanie, who "enchanted" Shelley.[47]

Escaping Godwin's financial badgering, Shelley soon returned to Marlow, leaving Mary with her father. Three days later she com-plained of not hearing from him "since you left me." Back in Marlow, Mary heard Marianne discuss an anxiety dream that elicited Shelley's twenty-three-stanza poem, "Marianne's Dream," featuring a huge black anchor floating Magritte-like in the sky.

Mary, wishing to publish *Frankenstein* anonymously, correctly believed people would assume Shelley was the author. After Murray's rejection, Shelley submitted *Frankenstein* to his old bookseller Lackington, who accepted it. Shelley made adroit profit arrangements for its author, "a friend . . . not . . . at present in England." He also finessed a major correction Lackington wanted and arranged to oversee the revisions and proofreading.[48]

After staying at Albion House two and a-half months, Leigh, Marianne, and Thornton Hunt, accompanied by Shelley, left for London. Shelley saw Longdill about the Chancery machinations and continued seeking financial help for the improvident Hunt. Visiting the poet-banker Samuel Rogers for a loan, Shelley only got information about Byron's latest whereabouts. Upon returning to Albion House, Shelley probably talked to Mary about the Chancery proceedings, their money problems, his health, and the awkward rumors that Alba was Claire's child by Shelley. Composing the poem "To William Shelley," he told his son of their anticipated "contented exile" in "serene and golden Italy."[49]

Shelley, "very unwell" after returning from London, wrote Byron complaining of the "relapse of my constitutional disease." He had a cough and was concerned about his lungs. In the unusually cold, wet summer, damp Albion House had mildewed books and paint peeling from the walls. Shelley told Byron he was considering going to Italy, not only for his physical "disorder" but to escape England's "tyranny civil and religious," fearing the Chancery would take William from them in addition to his first two children. His anger at Byron's continued silence was barely disguised. Having completed about half of *Laon and Cythna*, he had just read Byron's *Manfred* "with the greatest admiration" but it made him "dreadfully melancholy." Testily asking Byron about his plans "with regard to little Alba," Shelley mentioned how difficult it was to "temporize" with servants and visitors about Alba's "feigned" name and parentage.[50] It was two more months before they heard from Byron.

Shelley worked rapidly on *Laon and Cythna*, completing his "380th stanza" in early August. Having allotted himself from April through August to complete the poem,[51] he displayed remarkable self-discipline considering his health, visitors, family anxieties, and deepening money problems. According to Medwin, Shelley told him that he and Keats had "mutually agreed" to write a long poem—the longest each would write—in what may have been a "friendly rivalry." There was no mention of a contest.[52] Keats's poem, *Endymion,* was also on a timetable. Somehow, Shelley found time in July and August to translate Aeschylus's *Prometheus Bound* and read more Aeschylus, Homer, Plutarch, Spenser, and a history of Afghanistan, Persia, Tartary, and India.[53]

With all the Hunts gone by mid-July, Mary resumed editing the journal and letters she and Shelley had kept during their 1814 elopement trip. Published without their names in November, *History of A Six Weeks' Tour* included the first printing of *Mont Blanc.*

Mary's annoyance with the visits of Hogg and Peacock led Shelley to suggest the men meet at Peacock's.[54] Using nicknames for one another, Shelley became the Conchoid, Hunt was La Caccia, and John Newton possibly was Demogorgon. Despite Mary, Peacock frequented Albion House and once, finding her at home, waited to enter until she asked him in. She complained to Shelley that uninvited Peacock, consuming their food and drink, "morally disgusts m[e]."[55] Nevertheless, she later spent a week copying Peacock's completed long poem, *Rhododaphne.*

In nearby Egham, Shelley sought out Dr. Furnivall from Bishopsgate days. Furnivall, also attending Mary, became more scathing about her domination of Shelley. According to Furnivall's daughter, he "was very indignant" at Mary's "dictatorial ways with Shelley, ordering him about as if he had been a dog." Calling Mary "a toad," Furnivall "tried to make Shelley rebel against her dictation." Shelley, uncertain "what he should do" when Furnivall said he should be "master" in his house, was told, "Divide the house . . . give her the outside and keep the inside for yourself. Shelley laughed, but did nothing." Furnivall "hated Shelley's principles [but] always spoke kindly" of him even though Shelley paid only one of seven guineas he owed Furnivall.[56]

Finding Shelley, Peacock, and Hunt discussing and justifying suicide, Furnivall placed some dissecting knives on the table asking if one of them would "like to make the experiment."[57] Despite his lung complaint, Shelley took long walks to Hampden and Virginia Water with Peacock and Hogg. Peacock "never saw Shelley tired . . . Delicate and fragile as he appeared, he had great muscular strength."[58] Thornton Hunt also remarked upon Shelley's physical "grit." Despite a "sense of weakness in the chest, which attacked him on any sudden effort," Shelley towed his boat on the

Thames, pulled oars even though he preferred to steer, and once was the most active male helping the women up a steep incline. Thornton believed Mary's later reputation as a "Wilful Woman" was evident in her "temper being easily crossed, and her resentments taking a somewhat querulous and peevish tone."[59] Mary's willful need to have her resistant husband satisfy Godwin's incessant financial demands surfaced in late September. Arriving in London, Shelley received Mary's letter saying she was "very anxious . . . whether you can do any thing for my father."[60]

Shelley's greater concern was appealing the Chancery Master's decision giving Ianthe and Charles to the Westbrooks' choice of guardian. Mary's anger continued to surface. On his twenty-fifth birthday, Shelley received no present from Mary, something she blamed on Marianne Hunt. Scolding Marianne for not finding her a nurse, Mary advised pregnant Marianne to stop wearing stays. Angry that Shelley supported Claire, Mary wondered why Shelley should spend £70 a year to support Alba and only £100 to support Ianthe and Charles.[61]

Amid this tension, Shelley secluded himself composing *Laon and Cythna.* Like his previous long poems, *Queen Mab* and *Alastor,* it was written during his wife's pregnancy. Mary gave birth on September 2 to a daughter, Clara Everina. Neither parent notified Hogg, Mary's solace and companion when her first daughter was born and died. Shelley's health, as it had after Mary's two previous childbirths, immediately declined.

Soon completing his draft of *Laon and Cythna,* Shelley began his dedication stanzas to Mary, "So now my summer task is ended, Mary, / And I return to thee, mine own heart's home." It was a brief return. The day he finished his draft, September 23, Shelley went to London with Claire and the *Frankenstein* manuscript to which he had added, "I feel pleasure in dwelling on the recollections of childhood."[62] This theme also appeared in his *Laon and Cythna* notebook:

> If it were possible that a person should give a faithful history of his being from the earliest epochs of his recollection, a picture would be presented such as the world has never contemplated before. A mirror would be held up to all men in which they might behold their own recollections, & in dim perspective their shadowy hopes & fears,—all that they dare not, or that daring and desiring, they could not expose to the open light of day.

Only "with difficulty" can one "visit the intricate & winding chambers" of thought which "is like a river whose rapid & perpetual stream flows outwards;—like one in dread who speeds thro the recesses of some haunted pile & dares not look behind."[63] Shelley obsessively reworked his early emotional history in drafting the dedication stanzas of Laon and Cythna.[64]

Shelley also drafted in this notebook an ad for a villa near Naples and possibly placed it in a London paper while there much of the time until the end of November.[65] In late September, he again sought out his physician, William Lawrence, last consulted in 1815 when Shelley had similar symptoms of pulmonary distress. Writing Byron after his latest consultation with Lawrence, Shelley painted a dire picture of his health which, without "care," could "speedily" terminate "in death." Italy was recommended "as a certain remedy for my disease."[66] Lawrence perhaps prescribed Pisa with its famous medical school and the renowned Dr. Andrea Vaccà Berlinghieri.[67] Shelley assured Byron that if he did winter in Pisa, he would bring Alba with him.

Lawrence also prescribed that Shelley stop writing poetry, imaginative effort being considered bad for recuperation. Hearing this "edict," Mary was concerned Shelley would not finish "my pretty eclogue."[68] During the summer, Shelley began Rosalind and Helen: A Modern Eclogue, reflecting Mary's relationship with Isabel Booth and her efforts to have Shelley write more human-interest poetry. Shelley viewed Rosalind and Helen as "not an attempt in the highest style of poetry."

A temporary adoptee in the family at this time was a local girl, Polly Rose. She later recalled often meeting Shelley "going or coming from his island retreat near Mendenhall Abbey . . . his eyes like a deer's, bright but rather wild; his white throat unfettered." Sometimes he returned "fantastically arrayed" with a wreath of wild flowers on his head. With his customary frightening playfulness, Shelley would slide Polly on the table or vividly tell a ghost story. He startled neighbors by wandering in Bisham Wood at night, explaining he was a necromancer trying to raise the devil. Polly remembered Shelley, after buying crayfish from a street vendor, directed his servant Harry to release them into the Thames. The day he departed Marlow, Shelley gave Polly his favorite plate filled with his usual diet of raisins and almonds.[69]

During Shelley's extended time in London in the early fall, Mary, in frequent letters, discussed their marital relationship. Recovering slowly from her delivery, left in charge of a large household, lonely for her husband, feeling ignored by guests, and angry at Peacock's presence, she implored Shelley to return to Marlow. Criticizing his indecisiveness about their future plans, she rejected his early October suggestion that she pack up Albion House and join him in London preparatory to going to Italy.[70] Italy was his preference; the south coast of Kent was hers. Having long since decided to leave dank Albion House, Mary told Shelley to never again take a lease. Further, she disliked his vague optimism about their financial affairs.

Claire, returned from London, hinted to Mary that Shelley, still in London, was working on another *post obit* bond. Resenting Shelley's confidences to Claire, Mary warned him repeatedly that if he pursued a slow *post obit* negotiation "Alba must go before it is finished."[71] After she told Shelley to take care of her father financially before they left for Italy, he wrote Godwin a check for £20.[72]

By early October, Mary, sensing Shelley was avoiding her, "most earnestly" entreated him to come home. Not understanding "what you are doing," she threatened to wean Clara and join him in London.[73] She asked Shelley to write Dr. Furnivall for advice because she was not producing enough milk for Clara, ill from the supplemental cow's milk. Little William was misbehaving, competing with his new sister and Alba, whom Mary found "lively and uncommonly interesting."[74]

Shelley was adept at eliciting criticisms from Mary, who accused him of "<u>capitulations</u>" to "capricious" Byron.[75] Regretting coming to Marlow, ambivalent about going to Italy, she felt most deeply her father's disapproval: "the idea of his silent disapprobation makes me weep as it did in the days of my childhood."[76]

Shelley avoided Godwin. He wrote to Mary from the Hunts' of his "violent bowel complaint" and "pain in the side." Soon he advised her to come to London, having "suffered for the last two days . . . very great [anxiety]."[77] When a Marlow attorney called twice at Albion House concerning Shelley's debts, Mary urged him to stay in London.[78] Days earlier, he had been arrested in London for two days at the instigation of Captain Pilfold, who unsuccessfully tried to get Sir Timothy to cover his son's unpaid obligation. Whitton estimated Shelley's debts were at least £1500 and Horace Smith later stated Shelley had given nearly £5000 to his literary dependents, including Godwin.[79]

Shelley's friendship with his uncle foundered on the shoals of his unpaid debts but Horace Smith knew how to preserve his warm friendship for Shelley. When he did accede to Shelley's requests, he charged the highest legal rate of interest and insisted on prompt repayment. In early October Shelley, after repaying Smith £60—money Shelley probably gave to Hunt—borrowed £250 more from Smith, telling Mary Smith surely would loan him more to go to Italy.[80]

Returning briefly to Marlow in late October with his new friend and financial advisor, Walter Coulson, Shelley began dictating to Mary a translation of Spinoza's *Tractatus Theologico-Politicus*. He had first recognized his enduring interest in Spinoza by quoting him in his *Queen Mab* note, "There is no God." Returning to London, Shelley rented lodgings at 19 Mabledon Place. Mary, with Elise, left a weaned Clara with Claire and Milly Shields for a ten-day stay in London. The scarlet evening gown with a deep décolletage Mary ordered revealed her sloping shoulders.[81] On November 18 Hunt and Keats called. After *Laon and Cythna* was published some weeks later, Keats wrote: "Shelley's poem is out & there are words about its being objected too as much as Queen Mab was. Poor Shelley I think he has his Quota of good qualities, in sooth la!!"[82]

While Mary was with him in London, Shelley wrote his most eloquent statement of his objections to the English political scene, *Address to the People on the Death of the Princess Charlotte*. Two consecutive events prompted its composition, the November 6 death of Princess Charlotte in childbirth and the next day's brutal execution by hanging and beheading of the three leaders of the working-class Derbyshire uprising. This rebellion, involving government *agents provocateurs,* was "one of the first attempts in history to mount a wholly proletarian insurrection."[83] Hunt's *Examiner* protested the hypocritical spectacle of bloody executions on the day of national mourning for the princess as the Tory press effectively used the princess's death to keep news of the executions from the public. Eager to get his message quickly before the public, Shelley began his pamphlet on November 11, finishing it the next day.[84] Signing it "The Hermit of Marlow," Shelley preceded the title with "We Pity the Plumage, but Forget the Dying Bird," an altered quote from Paine's *Rights of Man.* Shelley said "thousands of the poorest poor" women die in childbirth and "none weep for them—none mourn for them." Naming the executed leaders, Shelley spoke of their being "shut up in a horrible dungeon for many months . . . They too had domestic affections and were remarkable for the exercise of private virtues." He attacked capital punishment and cited the economic slavery of the laboring class by the moneyed "double aristocracy." Echoing Paine's imagery, Shelley concluded in his finest republican style: "Let us follow the corpse of British Liberty slowly and reverentially to its tomb: and if some glorious Phantom should appear and make its throne of broken swords and sceptres and royal crowns trampled in the dust, let us say that the Spirit of Liberty has arisen from its grave and left all that was gross and mortal there, and kneel down and worship it as our Queen."

During November, Shelley was twice visited in London by Isabel Baxter Booth's husband, David Booth, and her father, William Baxter. Booth had no use for Shelley but Isabel's father, twice a guest at Albion House, had extolled Shelley.[85] Baxter praised his "rare genius . . . truly republican frugality and plainness of manners . . . [his] delicacy of moral tact that might put to shame (if shame they had) many of his detractors . . . [he is] so amiable that you have only to be half an hour in his company to convince you that there is not an atom of malevolence in his whole composition."[86] Now Baxter backed off Shelley, influenced by Booth who would not let his wife Isabel accept Shelley's invitation to accompany them to Italy. During the second visit, Shelley apparently attacked the "prejudices" of Booth and Baxter. Booth was convinced that "little Auburn" (Alba) was Claire's child and that Shelley slept alternately with Mary and Claire. After this meeting, Baxter did not answer Shelley's repeated invitations to visit Marlow, but did procure blankets for Shelley's Marlow poor.[87]

Shelley's conflicts with Booth and Baxter probably contributed to the unfinished *Rosalind and Helen* being "thrown aside."[88] The poem contrasts Rosalind's unhappy traditional marriage (Isabel and Booth) with the unmarried love of Helen and Lionel (Mary and Shelley.) Sharing themes with *Laon and Cythna* of brother–sister incest, madness, exile, and enchainment, *Rosalind and Helen* might have been titled *Lionel,* over half the poem focusing on this veiled portrait of Shelley as a "visionary youth," "of great wealth and lineage high," who knew "love" as early as he knew life. His "wild and queer" verses evoking the hatred of priests, Lionel "left his native land" only to return unrecognizable four years later with "some disease of mind" which passed as he lived with Helen "near the sea."

Shelley transforms Helen/Mary into a Claire-like figure whose erotic singing and harp playing elicit a *liebestod* scene of sexual embrace. His ostensible poem of Mary's reconciliation with Isabel Booth seems more Shelley's fantasy of his desire for Claire. At this time, Shelley's feelings for Claire again became more overtly sexual and her musicality elicited erotic verses about her. The two poems entitled "To Constantia" and some verse fragments, composed in the latter half of 1817, are among his most sensuous love lyrics. The longest "To Constantia" poem, "Thy voice, slow rising like a Spirit, lingers," appeared January 1818 in Munday's *Oxford University and City Herald* under the pseudonym "Pleyel."[89] Claire transcribed the poem, which was kept secret from Mary.[90] Shelley's pseudonym for Claire came from the musically talented Constantia Dudley in Charles Brockden Brown's *Ormond.* Peacock believed Brown's heroine held "the very highest place" in Shelley's pantheon of ideal females. Pleyel, a famous piano maker, was also Clara Wieland's lover in Brown's *Wieland.* When Henry Pleyel's wife died in childbirth, he married Clara. The longer "To Constantia" begins:

> Thy voice, slow rising like a Spirit, lingers
> O'ershadowing me with soft and lulling wings;
> The blood and life within thy snowy fingers
> Teach witchcraft to the instrumental strings.

Shelley's line, "I am dissolved in these consuming extacies," leads to his declaration, "I have no life, Constantia, but in thee." In the final stanza, Claire has a "power" in her dark eyes as he, "lingering" over her "lips . . . breath . . . and hair," ends tearfully:

> And from thy touch like fire doth leap:
> Even while I write my burning cheeks are wet
> Alas, that the torn heart can bleed but not forget.[91]

If his "torn heart" alludes to his feelings when Claire turned from him to Byron, Claire's inconstancy belies calling her "Constantia," as in the closing lines of his shorter "To Constantia" lyric where he addressed Claire, "But thy false care did idly wear / Its withered leaves in a faithless bosom!" Shelley, his heart also "withered," possibly had become sexually intimate with Claire only to experience her turning to Byron.[92] Reacting to Mary's moon-like erotic coldness, Shelley's heart was like a "rose" grown "pale and blue"

In the gaze of the nightly moon;
For the planet of frost, so cold and bright,
Makes it wan with her borrowed light.

(4–6)

With Mary a frosty moon, Shelley, on the manuscript page of the longer "To Constantia," seemingly expressed his sexual frustration with her: "To thirst and find no fill." If Claire did resist Shelley's sexual advances in 1817, she nevertheless later adopted the name Constantia.

Peacock was also under Claire's spell. She rejected his marriage proposal, probably in early 1818, saying years later he was too old for her. Despite her rejection, Peacock kept her company until she left for Italy.[93]

Shelley's problems publishing *Laon and Cythna* were anticipated when he wrote Byron that, unlike *Queen Mab,* it was "interwoven with a story of human passion." The passion was incest, treated covertly in Byron's recent *Manfred* and overtly in his *Parisina.* Shelley suggested another problem, his attack on religion in *Laon and Cythna:* "I am not of your opinion as to religion [because] I am careless of the consequences as they regard myself." Feeling "persecution bitterly," he could "but die [or] be torn to pieces, or devoted to infamy most undeserved."[94]

The bitter consequences soon began. Shelley sent four sheets of his poem by mid-October to several potential publishers before the Olliers accepted it.[95] Unaware of the poem's explosive religious and sexual content from the sheets they saw, the Olliers in late October advertised for early January publication, "*Laon and Cythna; or, the Revolution of the Golden City, a Poem in twelve cantos.* By Percy Shelley." Shelley also engaged a second publisher for the poem, the older, politically liberal firm of Sherwood, Neely, and Jones. The first resistance to the poem came from the printer, Buchanan McMillan, whose government connections sensitized him to the potential for blasphemous libel. By November 21, when 750 copies had been printed, McMillan changed references to God in Shelley's preface. Shelley called him "an obstinate old dog . . . as immaculate as the Lamb of God."[96] In late November, Shelley requested twelve copies from Ollier and urged him to advertise the poem, which had been excerpted in Hunt's *Examiner.*

As December began, Shelley first alerted Godwin that because of his health he was considering going to Italy "in favour of life."[97]

Responding to Godwin's alarm about losing his provider, Shelley said his health was "materially worse" due to periodic feelings "of a deadly & torpid kind" that affected his vision such that he could see "blades of grass & the boughs of distant trees . . . with microscopical distinctness." His "lethargy & inanimation" led to sleeping "hours on the sofa"; when awake he was "prey to the most painful irritability of thought." Although his earlier "pulmonary attack" was in abeyance, this added "symptom sufficiently shows the true nature of my disease to be consumptive." Italy's warmth would help him avoid death and its "train of evil consequences" for those dependent upon him. He had changed his eating habits, but "I cannot persevere in the meat diet." Having just read *Mandeville,* he warmly praised Godwin's novel.[98] Without notifying him, Godwin sent Shelley's enthusiastic critique of *Mandeville* to the *Morning Chronicle* where it appeared before his longer review in Hunt's *Examiner,* signed "E.K." for Elfin Knight.

Godwin refused to return Shelley's praise, expressing dislike for *Laon and Cythna.* Shelley countered, saying he was reassured because his works that Godwin liked "hold a very low place in my own esteem." *Laon and Cythna* would "leave some record of myself . . . the communications of a dying man. . . . in many respects a genuine picture of my own mind." He believed his power as a poet "consists: in sympathy & that part of imagination which relates to sentiment & contemplation." Not "formed . . . in common with the herd of mankind," he was aware that much of his writing lacked "tranquillity which is the attribute & the accompaniment of power."[99]

He had little tranquility when a critical onslaught arrived from Ollier, who had just read the poem and wanted to withdraw as publisher. A fledgling publisher, Ollier feared *Laon and Cythna* would drive away his trade and lead to his arrest and prosecution for blasphemous libel because of the poem's anti-religious passages. Incest was not a civil crime punishable by law in England until 1908, but the incest theme of *Laon and Cythna* was another thorn for Ollier. Recently, Hunt's *Story of Rimini* was attacked in *Blackwood's Magazine,* its author trying "to render Rimini a story not of incest, but of love."[100] The *Edinburgh Review* judged *Manfred's* "incest . . . is not a thing to be at all brought before the imagination." Ollier was aware of these attacks and rumors about Hunt's sexual relationship with his sister-in-law, Byron's supposed incestuous relationship with his half sister, and Shelley's reputed "seraglio at Marlow." Shelley had been attacked for his treatment of Harriet, for being a seducer of Mary, considered by some a prostitute, and had lost his children because of his radical views on sex and marriage.

Ollier's concern about the anti-religious views in *Laon and Cythna* had a basis as there was frequent persecution of the press in the aftermath of the 1817 government suppressive measures. Several trials for blasphemous libel were attracting attention and James Williams's prosecution was announced in the issue of the *Examiner* containing excerpts from *Laon and Cythna*. William Hone's trial, after six months' imprisonment, was heard by Lord Chief Justice Ellenborough in December.[101]

Shelley, reacting to these trials, urged Ollier not to show fear or knuckle under to the government: "if they see us tremble . . . they will feel their strength. . . . You lay yourself prostrate, & they trample on you."[102] Shelley was correct. Williams's attorney, admitting his client's guilt and asking for clemency, received fines and imprisonment. However, Hone successfully defended himself and was acquitted of the blasphemous libel charges in late December.

Ollier proposed altering the poem and Shelley accepted immediately: "No one is to be blamed, however heavy and unexpected is my disappointment."[103] Ollier arrived mid-December and for two days Shelley, initially "inflexible," oversaw changing passages dealing with anti-religious and incestuous ideas. The title change underscored Ollier's desire to eradicate the poem's incest theme. *Laon and Cythna* became *The Revolt of Islam*.

Shelley realized he had to revise his poem for it to be published. Peacock recalled that Shelley's "friends finally prevailed upon him" to make the alterations, presided over by a "literary committee." Shelley "contested . . . step by step . . . sometimes adopting, more frequently modifying, never originating, and always insisting that his poem was spoiled."[104]

In addition to Shelley and Ollier, the advisory committee probably included Mary, Peacock, and possibly Claire. Of the forty-three passages changed in the poem's 4,818 lines, more dealt with religion than with incest. "God" became "Power" and "Christian" became "Iberian." Shelley subtly substituted for "Christ" the early Hebrew version of Jesus, "Joshua." Cythna, originally Laon's "little sister," became an "orphan." The final paragraph of Shelley's Preface, dealing with the incest theme, was deleted. Shelley had written, "the personal conduct of my Hero and Heroine . . . was intended to startle the reader from the trance of ordinary life." His aim was "to break through the crust of those outworn opinions on which established institutions depend" by appealing "to the most universal of all feelings," love, including sexual passion.[105]

Receiving praise from Thomas Moore about *Laon and Cythna,* Shelley told him the poem was "suppressed" and would appear with its new title "in about a fortnight." He underplayed the changes, saying they amounted to substituting *"friend* or *lover* for . . . *brother* & *sister."* Moore's connections with government officials led Shelley to avoid mentioning that there were more revisions intended to forestall blasphemous libel.[106]

Eager to circulate his revised poem, Shelley urged Ollier repeatedly to recall *Laon and Cythna* and get *The Revolt of Islam* out "to all the principal Reviews." Paying for his own advertising, he told Ollier to advertise more "vigorously" and *"make* the Booksellers subscribe."

The influential Tory *Quarterly Review* received both versions, calling them "the same poem." The *Quarterly*'s scathing reviewer a year later was not Southey, as Shelley believed, but John Taylor Coleridge, nephew of the poet. He accused Shelley of reproducing "the same poison" in the revision as in the original but acknowledged "beautiful stanzas." He struck at Shelley's "magic cauldron" of cures of social ills, "among which Mr. Shelley specifies with great *sang froid* the commission of incest!" Hunt, attacked as Shelley's "leader," later mounted a spirited defense of Shelley in the *Examiner.*

Surprisingly, the most appreciative and insightful review of *The Revolt of Islam* appeared in the Tory *Blackwood's Magazine.* The review, reflecting Thomas De Quincey's critical admiration, rejected Shelley's political views but extolled his powerful and sensitive depictions of love: "Mr. Shelley has proved himself to be a great poet. Around his lovers, moreover, in the midst of all their fervours, he has shed an air of calm gracefulness, a certain majestic monumental stillness . . . and realizes in them our ideas of Greeks struggling for freedom." Shelley was praised for "very rare strength and abundance of poetic imagery and feeling." The reviewer, J. G. Lockhart, calling Shelley "a scholar, a gentleman, and a poet," hoped he would "select better companions" than "Johnny Keats" in order to "securely promise himself abundance of better praise."[107]

In addition to the *Quarterly*'s "malignant" review,[108] Shelley was vilified privately by John Murray. Sending his copy of *Laon and*

Cythna to John Wilson Croker, who later savaged Keats's *Endymion,* Murray asked him to keep "under Lock & Key" this "avowed defense of Incest—the author is the vilest wretch in existence."[109] Shelley, allied with Hunt's "sect," could not buffer the establishment's attack. Because the incest theme was central to his political aim in *Laon and Cythna,* its suppression in *The Revolt of Islam* had to be a blow to Shelley.

"I have written fearlessly," Shelley proclaimed in his Preface, which ended, "Love is celebrated everywhere as the sole law which should govern the moral world."[110] Shelley's invoking of incest as the basis of a sexually based political revolution undoubtedly reflected his personal issues, but he knew incest's prominence in Greek myth and drama, and in the novels of his time. The incest theme in *Laon and Cythna* served Shelley's radical intent to present love as the basis for future revolutions rather than the violence and revenge of the French Revolution. Implicitly, Shelley was challenging his elder, Wordsworth, and his conservative, power-based political views.[111]

Shelley considered *Laon and Cythna* "illustrative of such a Revolution as might be supposed to take place in a European nation," a "*beau ideal* as it were of the French Revolution. . . . The authors of it are supposed to be my hero & heroine whose names appear in the title."[112] Thus, Shelley's political theme involved the theme of women's equality. The bloodless revolution fomented by the sibling lovers—advocates of nonviolence—fails not because of their behavior but from being crushed by violent, rapacious tyrants and priests.

In his dedication stanzas to Mary, Shelley praised her courage in defying social convention to live with him. Mary merges with other strong women—including Mary Wollstonecraft—from whom Shelley formed the ideal Cythna, Laon's proto-feminist co-revolutionary sister. Her independence, strength, wisdom, and initiative match her brother's attributes. Astride her "giant" horse, she will rescue her prostrate "faint" brother.

The poem's most indelible images of combat occur in the first canto as a struggle between "An Eagle and a Serpent wreathed in fight." This fierce fight between good and evil, with its sexual overtones, ends in a draw of exhaustion as the "Hung high" serpent "Fell to the sea," "lifeless, stark, and rent" and the eagle departs "on the exhausted blast."[113] The ambiguous sex of each antagonist resembles the bisexual characters in Ovid's *Metamorphoses,* which Shelley had recently read.[114]

Embedded within *Laon and Cythna*'s political message are scenes and events reflecting Shelley's life and personality. Laon, recounting (Canto II) his childhood, recreates Shelley's early life at Field Place,[115] "our bright home" with "fair daughters," none of whom "wandered forth / To see or feel," a family on which "a darkness had descended" until "this home of happy spirits" was "as a dungeon to my blasted kind." Just as the *Alastor* Poet was "early" exiled from "cold fireside and alienated home," Laon is driven into exile like one of "Ocean's wrecks" whose "Guilt and Woe / Framed a dark dwelling for their homeless thought."

Rebuffed by "Heartless and false" friends, Laon sought affection from his "little sister" Cythna, "A second self, far dearer and more fair" and "all I had / To love in human life." Cythna's intuitive "female mind" is imbued with his revolutionary fervor "for free and equal man and woman." She declares she too will lead a revolution with her manifesto (II.42), "Can man be free if woman be slave?"

As part of their equality, both Laon and Cythna suffer sexual degradation and abuse after being abducted and separated. Laon's ordeal, a "sexual form of torture,"[116] is to be stripped naked and raised to a platform upon a "column's dizzy height" where, bound in chains for days, he hallucinates devouring his beloved Cythna's corpse.

> A woman's shape, now lank and cold and blue,
> The dwelling of the many-coloured worm
> Hung there, the white and hollow cheek I drew
> To my dry lips—what radiance did inform
> Those horny eyes? whose was that withered form?
> Alas, alas! it seemed that Cythna's ghost
> Laughed in those looks, and that the flesh was warm
> Within my teeth!
>
> (III.26)

Laon, unbound and nurtured by a Lind-like old "Hermit," suffers another "milder madness . . . of clinging sadness." Treated by the old man's skillful "soothing words," Laon's "madness" lifted "from my brain."

Cythna's parallel cannibalistic fantasy—of being given Laon's flesh to eat—occurs while enslaved in a cave (VII.15) after having been raped and impregnated by her captor sultan, Othman. Cythna, curing her delusional madness by her own self-understanding and wisdom, successfully converted her male captors. Her final trauma was to bear the female child from her rape only to have it taken from her.

Laon rejoins Cythna, who has brought the revolution to its near conclusion before it fails. They convince the citizens not to take revenge on Othman but this forgiveness is short-lived. After Cythna rescues Laon from the sultan's slaughter, they find an old "ruin" where the siblings have protracted sexual intercourse as Laon "felt the blood that burned / Within her frame mingle with mine" in the "mute and liquid ecstacies" of their "sweet and sacred" incestuous union.

Weaving his political message of non-violent revolution through love, sexual equality, and forgiveness, Shelley's epic ends as Cythna and Laon are betrayed by the tyrant Othman at the urging of the "Christian Priest." After dying in a fiery immolation, their spirits are transported in the "divine canoe" of a child "with silver-shining wings," the spirit of the deceased daughter that Cythna bore by Othman. The hero and heroine embody Shelley's "affirmation of hope and perseverance"[117] as essential to the never-ending political struggle for freedom. Soon, Claire and her daughter would voyage with the Shelleys in their hopeful quest for a more peaceful place.

3

"Paradise of exiles, Italy"

Plans for Italy were still unsettled on December 16 when an ad to let Albion House appeared in two London papers. Shelley wrote Byron subtly prodding him about Alba, saying his "uncertain" affairs kept him in England.[1] Claire, considering christening her baby Clara, awaited Byron's suggestion. Byron, exploring sending the child to Italy or "placing" her in England, intended to give her the name "Biron (to distinguish her from little Legitimacy)" and planned "to christen her Allegra . . . a Venetian name."[2]

Horace Smith visited Shelley in late December and recalled their last woodland walk. Shelley, excitedly "swinging his arms to and fro," quoted Plutarch and Bacon on the advantages of atheism and reason over "superstition" and "perverted religion." Although Smith was "many years older . . . I could almost fancy that I had been listening to a spirit from some higher sphere."[3] Later, when Shelley was in England, Smith agreed to act as his financial agent, receiving and forwarding his income to Italy and saving Shelley brokerage fees.

Apparently during Smith's visit, he and Shelley each composed a sonnet about Ozymandias (Rameses II). The two possibly were reading the Greek historian Diodorus. If Shelley saw the 1817 accounts of Giovanni Belzoni's 1816 retrieval of the monumental head of Rameses II, he certainly did not see the head, which did not arrive in England until March 1818. Shelley's "Ozymandias," his finest sonnet, was announced in Hunt's *Examiner* January 4 and published there a week later, signed with Shelley's coined Latin word for dormouse, "Glirastes."[4] About this time, the first copies of *Frankenstein* arrived and Shelley sent a copy to Sir Walter Scott, assuring him he was not the unidentified author.[5]

One Marlow resident recalled Shelley often spent "whole nights in his boat" and occasionally made his "abode at a small inn down the river."[6] Shelley's wish for escape probably was heightened by Godwin's eight letters early in January. Receiving the first, Shelley developed a "severe" ophthalmia, which Mary attributed to his visiting the poor.[7] When Hogg arrived for a two-week visit, Mary also became "unwell."[8] Godwin, planning to visit an unresponsive Shelley, worried he might contract his ophthalmia.[9] Reading *Paradise Lost*, Shelley, like blind Milton, soon had Mary reading to him and writing his letters because of his ophthalmia.

On Claire's daughter's first birthday, she wrote Byron in anguish over breaking her bond with her baby, fearing that if Allegra lived with Byron she might become "sickly & wasted" under his "improper management." Perceptively, she told Byron he was caring when "sole master & lord" but when "more on a par" with another, he became suspicious and "very often cruel." After writing her letter that Byron never acknowledged, Claire copied part of the verses "To Constantia."[10] His eyes improving, Shelley finished reading the "Hymns" of Homer and began translating them the day Godwin arrived.

A series of events now resolved Shelley's indecision about when to go to Italy. His eye problem recurred January 22, perhaps causing Godwin's departure that day. Three days later, Claire excitedly noted, "the House Sold. Great Rejoicing."[11] Needing to settle money matters before leaving England, Shelley took Claire and Peacock to London to consummate with William Willats the *post obit* loan Godwin long had been negotiating.[12] Shelley signed documents promising not to leave England without giving Willats sufficient notice and received £2000 for an "Indenture covenant." It required him to pay Willats £4500 within three months of Sir Timothy's death, a debt Mary paid in 1845. Godwin, furious at Shelley for leaving him only part of the £2000, icily wrote him they needed to talk, if Shelley had the "courage." No "witness" should hear what he had to tell Shelley,[13] who avoided Godwin for the next five weeks despite receiving ten letters from him in that period. Godwin received between £750 and £900, the balance of the £2000 probably was part of the £1400 Shelley gave to Hunt before leaving for Italy.[14]

Keats was with Shelley at Hunt's home in early February and wrote his brothers that the three engaged in a sonnet competition, "On the Nile," apparently won by Hunt.[15] Claire enjoyed the company of Peacock and Hogg for a week before returning with Shelley on the fifth to Marlow where Mary was taking charge of moving the household. Some volumes from the sizeable library went with them, but most, to be shipped abroad later, stayed with Peacock, along with the piano.

Shelley left Marlow for the last time February 7, followed shortly by Claire, Allegra, and the nursemaid Milly Shields. After a brief sojourn at the New Hummums Family Hotel, Shelley rented quarters at 119 Great Russell Street, near the residence of Charles and Mary Lamb. Arriving later, Mary, displeased with Shelley's choice of lodgings, looked unsuccessfully elsewhere.

Claire and Peacock became a pair, and they all attended again Mozart's *Don Giovanni.* The next evening Keats joined the Shelleys, Claire, Peacock, and Hogg for an evening of music at the Hunts'. Despite Horace Smith's efforts, it was the last time Shelley saw Keats, who would leave London a week before Shelley.[16]

Shelley's final month in England was a round of cultural activities. Hunt spied Mary at the opera "with her great tablet of a forehead, & her white shoulders unconscious of a crimson gown."[17] Among the plays they attended was a musical version of Byron's *The Bride of Abydos* starring Edmund Kean. At the British Museum they saw the Elgin Marbles and the casts of Phidias. The immense "Panorama of Rome" was exhibited on the Strand and Peacock showed them the Library at India House, his future place of employment.[18] There were no visits with Godwin. Mary copied the incomplete *Rosalind and Helen,* part of which was printed before they left England.[19] In early March, Shelley called on Mr. Baxter and Mary possibly saw Isabel.[20] At the Hunts', the Shelleys met Vincent Novello and the critic Henry Robertson.[21]

Shelley, after writing to John Murray offering to take books to Byron, forgot them. He remembered Hunt's *Foliage,* containing two sonnets about Shelley, his "high-hearted friend." Similar praise came from Horace Smith whose "Sonnet: To the Author of *The Revolt of Islam*" was published in Hunt's *Examiner* early February.[22] Despite these accolades from friends, including Hunt's laudatory review of *The Revolt of Islam* in the *Examiner,* Shelley left England correctly anticipating hostile reviews of *The Revolt* in the *Quarterly Review.*

For legal reasons, on March 9, two days before leaving London, the three children were christened at St. Giles-in-the-Fields. William, two, and Clara Everina, six months, were recorded as the "children of Percy Bysshe Shelley Esq., and Mary Wollstonecraft his wife." Clara Allegra, fifteen months, was registered as "reputed daughter of Rt. Hon. George Gordon, Lord Byron, Peer, of no fixed residence, traveling on the Continent, by Clara Mary Jane Clairmont."[23] Godwin and his wife did not attend. Effecting a reconciliation, Mary wrote her father on the fourth and the next day he called. The Godwins likely continued to suspect, with David Booth, that Allegra was Shelley's child. When Godwin called on Mary on the sixth, Shelley arrived, reinstating their awkward relationship. Their final night in London, March 10, Godwin came by, said farewell and gave Mary letters of introduction to his two friends in Italy, Lady Mount Cashell and Maria Gisborne.[24]

Before leaving London, Shelley wrote a lukewarm review of Peacock's "Greek and Pagan poem," *Rhododaphne*.[25] Peacock joined the Shelley party their last evening to attend the first Rossini performance in England, *Il Barbiere di Siviglia*.[26] After the Hunts joined them for a farewell supper, Shelley fell asleep on the sofa. Hunt and Marianne did not disturb him to say goodbye. Peacock dreaded returning to an empty Marlow where he filled his shelves with Shelley's books and placed Claire's piano "in the parlour . . . Oh! how that touch enchanted!"[27] Peacock kept her piano tuned and in his possession for several years. His £100 a year subsidy from Shelley continued until his India House appointment, in May 1819.

At five in the morning of March 11, Shelley, Mary, Claire, Elise, Milly, William, Clara, and Allegra departed for Dover. Shelley, owing Charters over £500, had another coachmaker prepare his carriage.[28] Shelley wrote his banker from Dover to honor what he owed Peacock, Godwin, Ollier, and the agent for Albion House, a total of £327.[29]

Despite stormy seas, they decided to embark on a ship ominously named the *Lady Castlereagh*. Leaving England forever on March 12, Shelley made his third Channel crossing with Mary and Claire feeling alienated from his Field Place family and from the society that, branding him a blasphemous adulterer, had taken away his older children and censored his creative efforts.

In Calais, Shelley bought a calèche to supplement his carriage for their trip to Milan by way of Lyon. Before setting off, he wrote Hunt that "motion" gave them "excellent spirits . . . even when the mind knows there are causes for dejection."[30]

Skirting Paris, they headed for Lyon on March 13. A horned moon guided them to the locked gate of the small fortified town of St. Omer where a woman shrieked across the moat demanding to know these invaders' identity. Accompanied by a dozen soldiers, three huge gates clanked shut behind them before they reached their "magnificent" hotel.[31] Through "dismal" country with a "very disagreeable" postilion, Shelley read aloud each day their guidebook, Schlegel's *Lectures on Dramatic Art and Literature*.[32] After Reims and St. Dizier, they wound through the more inviting scenery of the Marne valley, retracing their 1814 elopement route from Chaumont to Langres and Dijon.[33] Arriving in Lyon on March 21 after eight tiring days on the road, they rested for four days. To take them to Milan across the border of the Kingdom of Sardinia-Piedmont and into Austrian-occupied Lombardy, they hired a *voiturier*. Shelley wrote to Byron, alerting him to their pending arrival in Milan. Scolding Marianne Hunt for having "defrauded" him of a farewell kiss, Shelley had improved "spirits & health" in Lyon's warm weather.[34]

Leaving Lyon on March 25, they were stopped two days later at le Pont-de-Beauvoisin, the border of France and Savoy. French soldiers were at one end of the bridge, Piedmontese at the other. The entourage grew anxious after learning a traveler was turned back to Lyon the day before because his passport was refused. They were allowed to pass only after an hour-long discussion in the middle of the bridge. However, Shelley's trunk of books was confiscated and sent ahead to Chambéry for perusal by the priest-censor who, they were told, burned works by Rousseau and Voltaire. Fortunately, Shelley met a canon who, according to Claire, "knew his father at the Duke of Norfolk's." The Norfolk connection apparently saved Shelley's books, which followed him to Italy.[35]

In Les Eschelles, they ascended the narrow Roman road into the valley of the Grottes des Eschelles whose looming rocky cliffs and caves helped inspire Shelley's *Prometheus Unbound*. Impressive rocks not "less than 1000 feet in perpendicular height sometimes overhang the road on each side & almost shut out the sky." He was reminded of a scene "described in the Prometheus of Aeschylus—Vast rifts & caverns in the granite precipices—wintry mountains with ice & snow above." Anticipating Demogorgon in his cave, he observed how "One old man lame & blind crawled out of a hole in the rock."[36]

In Chambéry, there was a prearranged meeting with Elise's "Mother, father-in-law and little girl," identified by Claire as "Monsieur et madame Romieux et la petite Aimée." The child, if not Elise's stepsister, may have been her illegitimate daughter. A year earlier Mary, at Elise's urging, bought clothes in London for Aimée. Claire soon referred to Elise as "a mother."[37]

Before sunrise they left Chambéry and passed through some of the trip's most beautiful scenery in the Isère River Valley, including the snow-covered Alps lit by the rosy dawn. Leaving St. Jean-de-Maurienne, they approached Mont Cenis in snow as high as the carriage. Mary found it "dreadful" going, the narrow road skirting the edge of precipices and crossing narrow bridges spanning Alpine chasms. After a night in Lanslebourg, they ascended Mont Cenis on a better road, Shelley singing exuberantly "all the way."[38]

On crossing into Italy, they were struck by the scenic transformation of their adopted country. Under a cloudless blue sky, primroses shone and fruit trees blossomed as they arrived on March 30 in "delightfully clean" Susa. Shelley was delighted with "the first things we met in Italy," including the triumphal arch of Augustus with "magnificent proportions in the Greek taste" and the pretty "*blonde* woman of light & graceful manners" who picked them a nosegay of violets.[39]

In Turin, they attended the opera but could hardly hear the two lead singers over the audience's "perpetual talking."[40] They arrived on April 4 in Milan where the Locande Reale became their headquarters for the next four troubled weeks. Milan's cathedral, its gleaming white exterior recently completed, impressed Shelley as an "astonishing work of art," whether seen under "the solid blue . . . serene depth of this Italian Heaven, or by moonlight when the stars seem gathered among those sculptured shapes is beyond any thing I had imagined architecture capable of producing." He told Peacock his retreat for reading *The Divine Comedy* was a "solitary spot . . . behind the altar where the light of day is dim & yellow under the storied window."[41] The first evening they found cheap seats in La Scala's pit, the first of four performances there. The audience's talking again drowned out the singing but they found the ballet much more accomplished than that in England.

Shelley's detailed letters to Peacock were intended to be a major record of their Italian experience. He expected his letters would be "longer if not more entertaining" when "I am a little recovered from my journey." With Claire gone, he inquired if Peacock intended pursuing his relationship with Marianne de St. Croix. Mary, writing to the Hunts, asked if Peacock was "in despair" after Claire's refusal of his marriage proposal. Shelley, his health having improved more than his spirits, had a "thirst to be settled" so he could, from among his "many literary schemes," begin "one in particular."[42]

Tasso fascinated Shelley. He was reading Tasso's life and planned to devote "this summer & indeed the next year" composing "a tragedy" about "Tasso's madness." He told Peacock: "But, you will say I have no dramatic talent. Very true in a certain sense; but I have taken the resolution to see what kind of a tragedy a person without dramatic talent could write."[43] Shelley's interest in Tasso, a possible influence on *Alastor*, went back at least to 1815 and was stimulated further upon reading Byron's *Lament of Tasso* in 1817.[44] Shelley identified with the youthful, idealistic Tasso, persecuted by adults for his solitary wandering, and whose "soul was drunk with Love" from birth. Shelley had written Byron in 1817 that his "wonderfully impressive . . . lines in which you describe the youthful feelings of Tasso . . . make my head wild with tears." Shelley's dissatisfaction with Byron's poem probably included Byron's fatalistic view that Tasso submitted to his incarceration.[45] Shelley's Italian rivalry with Byron had begun.

Shelley and Mary, thinking of summering at nearby Lake Como, set off on April 9 on a three-day search for a paradisiacal lakeside home. The trip gave Mary a rare chance to be alone with Shelley without Claire. Shelley was ecstatic about Lake Como, telling Peacock it "exceeds anything I ever beheld in beauty, with the exception of the arbutus islands of Killarney." On their boat trip from Como up the lake to Tremezzo, Shelley's keen botanical eye identified chestnut, laurel, bay, myrtle, fig, and olive trees that "overhang the caverns & shadow the deep glens which are filled with the flashing light of the waterfalls."

The house with the most beautiful setting, the sixteenth-century Villa Pliniana, enraptured Shelley. Built around an intermittent spring described by Pliny the Younger, it was "once a magnificent palace . . . now half in ruins."[46] Its "immensely large, but ill furnished" apartments could accommodate Milord's expansive needs if he visited them. Pliniana, built on the water's edge, exemplified the marine homes that attracted Shelley. Soon to complete *Rosalind and Helen,* he set the poem's beginning at Lake Como, incorporating his description of Villa Pliniana into that of "Helen's home."

The signal event at Como was Shelley's encounter with the local police. Only Claire recorded this "Curious adventure." Shelley decided that his pistol, loaded since leaving England, should be discharged to assure its proper functioning. Walking alone "pretty far" to an isolated spot, he was followed by two police who, despite his protests, took him into custody for illegally carrying arms. The courteous local prefect, learning Shelley was an Englishman, kept his gun until he "heard from Madame Shelley that her husband had no intention of shooting himself through the head." Mary's certification released the pistol.[47]

This incident, ending the dream of a summer on Lake Como, may have stemmed from a possible contact—personal or by mail— with the mysterious lady. In any event, it was time to confront the emotionally wrenching issue of Allegra's departure. If Byron received Shelley's letter from Lyon, he did not respond. The day after returning from Como, Shelley wrote Byron inviting him to "spend a few weeks with us this summer" at Villa Pliniana, "which I imagine we have chosen."[48] Shelley's uncertainty was justified; the house negotiations failed later in April. Byron replied, saying he refused to visit if Claire were there. Sending a messenger to collect Allegra, he implied that Claire was not to see her again. Byron's letter, arriving April 21, created agitation and conflict in the household. Claire snapped back at Byron, "If you will not regard me as her mother, she shall never be divided from me . . . you have all the power in your hands . . . spare me." She ended with characteristic self-abnegation, "Whatever my fate may your's still be great and glorious as it has been."[49]

Byron's current fate included a busy sex life yielding "a Clap." Among his growing "Whore-hold," the "Gonorrhea *gratis*" he contracted was the "first of such maladies—which I believe not to have been purchased." About this time he estimated his two-year expenses "laid out on Sex" involving "at least two hundred of one sort or another" as over £2500.[50] Shelley had heard the rampant rumors circulating in Milan of Byron's sexual profligacy. Claire noted on April 24 that Shelley had a "curious" encounter in the Milan post office with a Venetian, having heard some Byronic scandal. Claire's reaction was, "hear no agreeable news of Albè." Mary, without mentioning the strange encounter, noted, "Albe Albe everywhere."[51] In Shelley's jaundiced view, Italian women were a "mixture of the coquette & prude . . . the worst characteristics of English women." However, the women were "better than the men . . . a tribe of stupid & shrivelled slaves [without] a gleam of intelligence." He also disliked the "very great" number of Englishmen in Milan who—perhaps projecting his own guilt—"ought to be in their own country at the present crisis."[52]

After receiving Byron's provoking letter, Shelley, "unwell," angrily wrote his most candid letter to Byron. He doubted Byron's truthfulness about not receiving his Lyon letter, unable to "conceive" it did not arrive. As the "third person in this painful controversy" between Claire and Byron, he had "the invidious office of mediation" but "would willingly" present arguments on Claire's behalf. After accusing Byron of implying Claire would have no future contact with Allegra, he lectured him on a mother's "more acute" feelings for her child than those of the father: "Besides she might say, 'What assurance have I of the tenderness of the father for his child, if he treats the feelings of the mother with so little consideration?'" Attacking Byron's power and status needs, Shelley continued, "surely rank & reputation & prudence are nothing in comparison to a mother's claims." After denying having influenced Claire, Shelley was at his most blunt: "Your conduct must at present wear the aspect of great cruelty however you justify it to yourself." Pressing further, Shelley brought up Byron's sexual behavior. Professing not to believe the "Stories . . . improbable & monstrous . . . propagated of you at Venice" and "which the multitude believe of you," he noted, "they cannot say more at Como than they do at Venice." He would send Milly with Allegra and Byron's messenger after Claire and Byron "come to an understanding." He insisted that Byron not "place me in a degrading situation" of reimbursing him for Allegra's incurred expenses. Mary would have disagreed that the expenses were "extremely trifling."[53]

Byron then wrote to Hobhouse that Shelley, in Milan "with the bastard & its mother," would not send Allegra "unless I will go & see the mother." He had dispatched a messenger for the child and "between Attorneys . . . Whores . . . wives [and] children . . . my life is made a burthen."[54] Stubborn and vain, Byron used a sty in his eye as an excuse not to go to Milan. Part of his aversion to Claire was to avoid encouraging her continued attraction to him. Unsure of his sexual control with her, some months later he wrote to his half sister that he avoided "seeing" Claire "for fear the consequence might be an addition to the family."[55]

Byron's messenger had to wait in Milan several days until Shelley received more conciliatory word from Byron. In his return letter, Shelley apologized for the "misunderstandings" but blamed

Byron for not writing to Claire, adding, "I cannot well refuse to let her see your letters."[56]

Allegra went to Byron accompanied by Elise, rather than her nursemaid Milly Shields. Shelley's words to Byron—that Mary parted with Elise "solely that Clare & yourself may be assured that Allegra will be attended almost with a Mother's care"—again suggest Elise had been a mother. Elise, twenty-three, was more mature than the younger, homesick Milly, who spoke only English and whose probable illiteracy precluded her writing about Allegra. Harsh feelings must have been expressed between Claire and Shelley, who probably warned her she might lose Allegra forever. Years later, he admonished Claire for her decision.[57]

The separation devastated Claire, whose journal ceased abruptly for a month. She had just turned twenty before Allegra left April 28. Claire later asserted that she sent Allegra believing she had an earlier understanding from Byron that he would not remove her from his home until she was seven years old.[58]

The reduced family, unable to negotiate a house, departed for Pisa May 1 carrying Godwin's letters of introduction to Lady Mount Cashell in Pisa and Maria Gisborne in Leghorn (Livorno). Writing to Hogg for the first time since leaving England, Shelley apologized for not saying goodbye, recommending he read his letters to Peacock and the Hunts for details of his travels. Shelley now counted his closest friends in England to be Hunt, Peacock, and Horace Smith, who remarried shortly after Shelley left for Italy.

They headed southeast on the old Roman road across the fertile plain of the Emilia Romagna. After overnight stops in Piacenza, Parma, and Modena, they dined in Bologna. Pushing on, they climbed the Apennines into Tuscany amid violent winds that made Claire fearful the carriage would blow over. On May 4, Shelley wrote his first poetry in Italy, the lines, "Listen, listen, Mary mine, / To the whisper of the Apennine." From the resort village of Barberino, their guide skirted west of Florence, originally on Shelley's itinerary. Descending into the Arno River valley, they arrived in Pisa on May 7.

From their lodgings on the Lungarno at Le Tre Donzelle, the sight of the emaciated, yellow-faced, and red-dressed prisoners in ankle chains cleaning the streets made them question their plans to settle into Pisa. Relieved to hear from Elise of Allegra's safe arrival in Venice, they climbed the Leaning Tower, admired the Duomo, and left Pisa. They apparently did not contact Lady Mount

Cashell—now going by the name of Mrs. Mason—perhaps because of Godwin's peculiar letter of introduction.[59] A year passed before they met her.

In nearby Leghorn, which Mary thought a "stupid town,"[60] they took rooms at L'Aquila Nera before finding larger quarters at La Croce di Malta. Mary immediately sent her father's letter of introduction to Maria Gisborne. Godwin reminded Maria that she had taken newborn Mary into her home for a week shortly after the death of Maria's friend, Mary Wollstonecraft.[61] She was then Maria James Reveley, married to the architect Willey Reveley and the mother of Henry Reveley, who was born early in 1789. Shortly after Maria was widowed at age twenty-nine in 1799, she rejected the widower Godwin's earnest marriage proposal and secretly married an unsuccessful businessman, John Gisborne. The Gisbornes and young Henry went to Rome in 1801, moved later to Pisa, and settled in Leghorn by 1815. Henry, more fluent in Italian than English, studied civil engineering at Rome and Pisa.[62]

The Gisbornes immediately called and Mary found Maria Gisborne "reserved yet with easy manners." The Shelleys returned the call the next day at the Gisbornes' home, Casa Ricci. Mary, reinstating her bond with Maria of twenty-one years earlier, talked long with her about her parents. She found Mrs. Gisborne "a lady of great accomplishments, and charming from her frank and affectionate nature"[63] and must have wished her father had succeeded in marrying her rather than Mrs. Clairmont. The Shelleys and the Gisbornes saw each other almost daily for the next several weeks, enjoying evening walks in and around the city.

Shelley, as well as Mary and Claire, read Wieland's *Aristippus*, criticizing its "impudent" French translator for omitting too much of the original German to accommodate "fastidious" readers.[64] Shelley soon began translating it, including passages likely to offend proper readers. Mary read extensively in French, Italian, and Latin, while Shelley read Euripides and another life of Tasso. Shelley, having read *Hamlet* before leaving Milan, further satisfied his taste for tragedy with the manuscript John Gisborne loaned him of the Cenci family story, with its theme of incest and parricide. Mary spent several days in late May copying the manuscript.[65] The tragic intrafamilial themes of *Hamlet* and the Cencis resonated with Shelley, whose interest in Tasso waned.

Shelley's dismissive attitude toward John Gisborne was evident when, a year later, he considered him "an excessive bore" with "little thin lips receding forehead & a prodigious nose." Shelley's mini-dissertation on noses, including his own, reflected his fascination with human physiognomy. Gisborne's nose was "quite Slawken-burgenian . . . once seen never to be forgotten and which requires the utmost stretch of Christian charity to forgive. I, you know, have a little turn up nose; Hogg has a large hook one but add both them together, square them, cube them, you would have but a faint idea of the nose to which I refer."[66]

Dissatisfied with Leghorn, a "noisy mercantile" town, Mary notified the Hunts that they intended "to pass the summer at Florence" and that Elise, from Venice, sent word that Allegra, dressed in lace-trimmed trousers, was treated "like a little princess."[67] Godwin wrote that Shelley's letters gave him "great pain" as the topic of money "converted" Shelley "into a kind of being at which my nature revolts."[68]

Claire, reacting to Byron's few lines in Elise's letter, expressed the hope that Allegra had given her father some "knocks" to repay "all your unkindess to me in innocent coin." However, she asked Byron, "My dearest & best friend," to send a lock of his hair.[69] She did not find the rather shy bachelor Henry Reveley communicative like Peacock, but he did show the newcomers the steam engine he was constructing. Henry occasionally joined the Gisbornes and Shelleys on evening walks along the harbor *molo* (quay) or into the hills to Montenero.

Eager to leave Leghorn, they decided to spend a month in the mountain spa resort of Bagni di Lucca, sixty miles north, before moving on to Florence. Shelley spent two days finding a house in Bagni di Lucca, whose medicinal baths perhaps were suggested by "the physician" they had met, Mr. Bilby.[70] Shelley described to Peacock the "very fine" scenery of Bagni di Lucca, "a kind of watering place . . . where the most fashionable people resort." They had stayed in Leghorn a month only because of the "very aimiable & accomplished Lady Mrs. Gisborne, who is the sole attraction in this most unattractive of cities."[71]

Leaving Leghorn June 11, they traveled through the walled city of Lucca and up the Serchio River to Bagni di Lucca, nestled along the river Lima. The ascent from the town square to their house, Casa Bertini, took them past the villa of Napoleon's sister, Princess Pauline, married to Prince Borghese. Mary would find her "handsome" but disapproved of her associations "with the high ministerial English."[72] She probably would not have approved of Pauline's semi-nude sculpture by Canova.

Casa Bertini, perched on a hill with a view of the higher peaks of the Apennines, is adjacent to a house where Montaigne had stayed. The Shelleys' casa, built by Domenico Bertini in 1471, is a short distance down the street from the baths of Terme Bagno alla Villa. Just above Casa Bertini is Casa del Chiappa, whose owner, Signore G. B. del Chiappa, visited the Shelleys the first evening.[73]

Mary was pleased with Casa Bertini. It was small but "commodious and exceedingly clean," with fresh paint and new furniture. There was a small garden that ended with "an arbour of laurel trees so thick the sun does not penetrate it."[74] Mary invited the Gisbornes to come enjoy the mountains and "delightful" walks in the woods. Although Chiappa was "a stupid fellow," upon his recommendation they hired Paolo Foggi at "3 pauls a day" as cook and household manager. A woman received less "to do the dirty work." Mary believed Paolo was almost "a servant worth a treasure" were it not for his tendency "to cheat us," a harbinger of future serious trouble from him. Mary found Bagni di Lucca "very quiet" and pleasant, as she and Shelley daily read a canto of Ariosto's *Orlando Furioso* and took walks together. However, she felt isolated. They avoided their Italian neighbors and kept away from the English, who soon invaded Bagni di Lucca for the summer season. Only away from Maria Gisborne five days, Mary wrote she felt an "exile ... from your presence so long—that I quite long to see you again."[75]

Mary's loneliness was part of a broader pattern of emotional uneasiness in the household. She told Maria Gisborne in this mid-June letter that "Mr Shelley is tolerably well," a cautiously vague characterization she would repeat. The last day of June Mary and Shelley rode horseback up a long winding mountain trail through chestnut woods full of singing birds to Il Prato Fiorito, a lovely "flowery meadow at the top of one of the neighboring Apenines [sic]."[76] Shelley recalled the odor from the field of jonquils almost made him faint, an impression recorded in *Rosalind and Helen* and *Epipsychidion*.[77] This scenic spot, still unspoiled, affords panoramic views of the surrounding mountains that inspired Shelley to ask Mary to join him on an overnight trip to the shrine atop Monte San Pellegrino, twenty-two miles distant. Mary cautiously inquired of Maria Gisborne if this might not be an unsafe trip requiring them to "sleep in one of the houses on the mountain." They did not go. Two years later, Shelley would make the pilgrimage alone.

This failed excursion seemingly signaled continuing emotional strain among Shelley, Mary, and Claire. Two days before the Il Prato Fiorito excursion, Shelley, perhaps unknown to Mary, wrote the first of two brief, cryptic letters to his publisher and unofficial banker, Ollier. These letters, among other puzzling mysteries that punctuated Shelley's life, underscore how veiled he kept much of his life. In this first letter, Shelley wrote "In great haste" across the top and instructed Ollier to pay £10 to a person bringing an undated note signed "A. B." Further, "*on no account*" was Shelley's name to be mentioned. Payment of the note was of "great consequence."[78] About August 16, a similar letter instructed Ollier to honor a draft for £20, signed "A. B.", that someone would present to him. Shelley wrote in a footnote, "I had just sealed my other letter when I discovered the necessity of writing again."[79] In this other letter, Shelley enclosed "6 pieces of writing" representing his completion of *Rosalind and Helen* and a letter addressed to someone in London which he asked Ollier to post. Perhaps Shelley's footnote about having sealed his letter before discovering he needed to write again was a ruse intended to mislead Ollier from associating "A. B." with the enclosed London letter, which may have informed a third party to send "A. B." for the £20. Presumably, Ollier would not have known this third party to whom the London letter was addressed. This eliminated Peacock, Hunt, and Hogg. Horace Smith possibly was the third party arranging for an as yet unknown anonymous publication of Shelley's.[80] However, in late July Shelley wrote his banker to reimburse Smith for the £150 he had borrowed from him. Shelley could have reimbursed Smith in a similar fashion without the secrecy of a third party. More likely, Shelley was supporting some unknown person.[81]

During July, Shelley and Mary took more frequent evening horseback rides. Claire initially joined them until, on August 8, she was "unlucky." Falling from her horse, she "hurt her knee so as to knock her up for some time."[82] This was Claire's second such mishap. In mid-July, she and Shelley had set off for Lucca when she fell off her horse, delaying the excursion until the next day.[83]

In early July, Shelley, Mary, and Claire began attending the Sunday evening dances at the Casino. Shelley wrote Godwin that the two women refrained from dancing either "from philosophy or protestantism." Only Italians frequented the Casino dances and

Shelley teased Peacock that the "exquisitely beautiful" waltzes might make it "a little dangerous" to their "newly unfrozen senses and imaginations," however the Italian women were "far removed from . . . beauty or grace." He wryly observed, "except in the dark— there could be no peril."[84]

Shelley probably used the local baths but his favorite indulgence was his solitary nude bathing each midday "in a pool or fountain, formed in the middle of the forests by a torrent . . . surrounded on all sides by precipitous rocks" and a waterfall. He would "undress and sit on the rocks, reading Herodotus, until the perspiration has subsided, and then to leap from the edge of the rock into the fountain—a practice in the hot weather exceedingly refreshing."[85]

Shelley's fascination with Bagni di Lucca's atmospheric phenomena anticipated his poem, "The Cloud." He took "great delight in watching the changes of atmosphere . . . the growth of the thunder showers . . . which break & fade away towards evening into flocks of delicate clouds." At night, watching what he thought was Jupiter (actually Saturn), he recalled last summer's Venus whose "divine and female nature" had a "soft yet piercing splendour." He had "forgotten to ask the ladies if Jupiter produces on them the same effect."[86]

The timely arrival of the books confiscated in Chambéry was a boon to Shelley and his future readers. In addition to reading and annotating his seven volumes of Herodotus's *Histories*,[87] he read Aeschylus's *The Persians*, Xenophon's *Memorabilia Socratis*, Aristophanes' *The Clouds*, and Barthélemy's *Anacharsis*. During the first month in Bagni di Lucca, Shelley probably began and abandoned his opening scene of his drama *Tasso*.[88] Being "totally incapable of original composition,"[89] he turned to translation on July 7.

Shelley began applying his gift for translation to the banquet scene of Plato's *Symposium*, motivated in part by his disdain of the Christian biases of writers' presentations of the Greeks' sexual life: "There is no book which shows the Greeks precisely as they were; they seem all written for children, with the caution that no practice or sentiment highly inconsistent with our present manners should be mentioned."[90] Shelley's rapid, nonstop translation of the *Symposium* attests to his fascination with its theme of love. He worked eleven consecutive mornings translating, and spent several more days correcting his writing. It took Mary over two weeks to transcribe his work.[91]

Shelley wrote Godwin that translating the *Symposium* had "excited" him "to attempt an Essay upon the cause of some differences in sentiment between the antients & moderns with respect to the subject of the dialogue."[92] The "subject" of the dialogue—between Alcibiades and Socrates—was the homosexuality and pederasty of classical Greece that informed the speeches on love in the all-male banquet scene of the *Symposium.* Shelley's essay, *A Discourse on the Manners of the Antient Greeks Relative to the Subject of Love,* was one of two spawned by his translation.

Shelley's translation, of which he was rightfully proud, has been judged to reflect more of Plato's poetic beauty than more literal translations.[93] Unfortunately, substantial portions of Alcibiades' account of his sexual relationship with Socrates were part of Mary's excisions when she published Shelley's translation.

Translating the *Symposium* was somewhat daring. Plato's ideas were considered too corrupting for Oxford and Cambridge students, who were not even required to read the bowdlerized eighteenth-century translations. Following the censorship of *Laon and Cythna,* the desexualization of Shelley's work continued when cut and altered versions of his *A Discourse* and his *Symposium* translation were published by Mary in 1840. The uncensored *Discourse* was first printed in 1931 in a limited private edition. Not until 1949 were the *Symposium* and *A Discourse* generally available as Shelley wrote them.

Shelley's brief essay, *On Love,* and his longer *A Discourse,* are his most important prose statements on the nature of love and sex.[94] Complaining in *On Love* that he "found my language misunderstood," he described love as "that powerful attraction towards all that we conceive, or fear, or hope beyond ourselves." He placed the basis of love in the feeling of loss and emptiness—"the chasm of an insufficient void"—filled by seeking a sympathetic bond with another, and supposed this process originates in early infancy.

The subject of homosexuality in *A Discourse* was more sensitive than incestuous love in *Laon and Cythna* and *Rosalind and Helen.* Unlike incest, homosexuality was not treated openly in literature. In homophobic England, denial was so great that language was lacking to discuss homosexuality, a word not yet coined and referred to in Blackstone's legal *Commentaries* as "The horrible sin not to be named among Christians."[95] Male homosexuality in England had been a capital offense from 1533. By the early nineteenth century, in contrast to more enlightened laws in other European countries and America, there were renewed efforts in England for executing these miscreants, as they were called. Shelley, aware of such homophobia, wrote to Peacock in mid-August that *A Discourse* was a "subject to be handled with delicate caution which either I cannot or I will not practise in other matters, but which I acknowledge to be necessary."[96]

About the time Shelley wrote *A Discourse*, Jeremy Bentham—who began writing on "Paederasty" in 1774—was working on an extensive indictment of English attitudes toward homosexuality and proposing sodomy law reform.[97] Shelley and Bentham were aware of the lack of technical language for discussing homosexuality. In *A Discourse*, Shelley complained, "The laws of modern composition scarcely permit a modest writer to investigate the subject with philosophical accuracy."[98] *A Discourse* was a "pioneering . . . sophisticated historical–psychological perspective" on Greek homosexuality, a topic that awaited renewed discussion by an English scholar for a century and a half.[99]

The physical aspect of homosexuality gave Shelley the most difficulty in *A Discourse*. His tendency to spiritualize love existed alongside his daringness to discuss taboo sexual themes. Grappling with Greek pederasty in *A Discourse*, Shelley was aware of its pervasiveness in Plato's *Symposium* and *Phaedrus*, and in the plays of the Greek dramatists. Reading these dramas in the original Greek, Shelley recognized the hypocritical, prudish censorship by contemporary translators of the four-letter words they contained and of frequent allusions to cross-dressing.

Shelley's repeated expressions of revulsion in *A Discourse* for the unnamed anal intercourse included "ridiculous," "disgusting," "detestable violation," "gross," "unrefined," and an "operose and diabolical . . . machination." Rejecting "that a lover" would "associate his own remembrance" of love "with images of pain and horror," Shelley proposed that Greek male lovers achieved sexual gratification by using fantasies to trigger emissions.

Shelley's fascination with androgynous male physique infused *A Discourse*. Greek males' beauteous forms were "firm yet flowing . . . their gestures animated at once with the delicacy and . . . boldness." He believed in ancient Greece males more often were called "beautiful" and females were denoted as "handsome."[100]

In *A Discourse*, Shelley appealed for toleration of sexual orientation, linking sexual bigotry to the "invidious" derogation of women's "intellectual nature." Probably harking back to his own early sexual experience, he said "the usual intercourse endured by almost every youth of England with a diseased and insensible prostitute" made "ludicrous" society's castigation of the sexual practices of earlier societies. Believing the "earlier dramatic English writers" were often more "frightfully obscene" than the Romans, Shelley praised Shakespeare's "sentimental attachment towards persons of the same sex" in his sonnets as "wholly divested of any unworthy alloy."[101]

With Mary's urging, in early August Shelley "took advantage of ten days of dubious inspiration to finish" *Rosalind and Helen.* This comment went with the manuscript to Ollier. Shelley, disparaging his "light and unstudied" poem as one that will not interest "that prig the public," asked Ollier to send *Endymion,* which Shelley had not read. He thought Keats "has a fine imagination and ought to become something excellent; but he is at present entangled in the cold vanity of systems."[102]

In late July, Shelley wrote Godwin of experiencing "busy thoughts and dispiriting cares which I should shake off."[103] On his birthday, he again inscribed "thoughts" in Mary's journal. Clearly restless by mid-August, he was finding Bagni di Lucca confining emotionally and creatively. Having completed *Rosalind and Helen* with Lionel (Shelley) dead and Helen (Mary) living with Rosalind, it was as if he desired to see someone else. Fearing the August heat in Florence, they decided to stay put and renewed their lease on Casa Bertini into September.[104]

However, Shelley became bored and on August 16 he wrote of getting away alone on "a short excursion of a week or so, to some of the neighboring cities."[105] He abandoned this idea that same day when Elise's second letter in two days brought news that Allegra was no longer with Byron but was under the care of Isabella Hoppner and her husband, Richard Belgrave Hoppner, the British consul in Venice.[106] Concerned by this change, Shelley and an agitated Claire departed for Venice the next day, August 17. Before leaving, Shelley sent his second payment through Ollier to the mysterious "A. B." in London.

The Hoppners later said they initiated Allegra's removal to their home because of their concern about her living with Byron.[107] He had moved into the Palazzo Mocenigo on the Grand Canal and presided over a household of fourteen servants and a menagerie of monkeys, a wolf, a fox, two mastiffs, and caged birds. What Byron called his "miscellaneous harlotry" included "nine whores" at this time by his count. He was again out of condoms and a "violent quarrel" in late July between two of his jealous lovers may have contributed to the Hoppners' concern about Allegra. Byron at this time viewed Allegra as "very pretty" and "remarkably intelligent," but with "a devil of a Spirit" that was "Papa's."[108]

Shelley's decision to accompany Claire to Venice probably provoked Mary's anger and feeling of abandonment. Once again he was running off with Claire, leaving her alone with the children. Soon after leaving Bagni di Lucca he wrote Mary of his "most delightful respite"; the pain in his side disappeared "since I left you."[109] Paolo Foggi accompanied Shelley and Claire as far as Florence.

After their departure, Mary wrote "work" in her journal, writing out Shelley's additions to *Rosalind and Helen* and considering a writing project her father suggested, and Shelley seconded, a history of the era of Charles I and Cromwell. Mary, asking Maria Gisborne to "come and cheer my solitude," mentioned their plan to go to Naples sometime after the fall equinox. They were "in high debate" about the safest way to travel with little William and Clara, by land or sea.[110] This was the first mention of a plan to go to Naples, a destination perhaps related to some contact Shelley had with the mysterious lady and/or to his two notes to Ollier about secret payments to "A. B." Naples, Shelley's first Italian destination when at Marlow, probably had other attractions beside the winter warmth.

The three days it took Mary to write out Shelley's emendations to *Rosalind and Helen* meant he wrote more than a "conclusion," as he told Ollier. *Rosalind and Helen* was his first literary testament to his depressed feelings in Italy, his isolation from Mary, and his turning again erotically to Claire. Lionel seemingly expresses Shelley's feelings:

> I wake to weep,
> And sit through the long day gnawing the core
> Of my bitter heart, and, like a miser, keep,
> Since none in what I feel take pain or pleasure,
> To my own soul its self-consuming treasure.
>
> (775–79)

Shelley wrote Peacock that "the concluding lines are natural," expressing what he was experiencing in his life.[111] The poem begins with an unexpected meeting on the deeply wooded shore of

Lake Como between the estranged friends, Helen and Rosalind, "That sweet strange lady-friend."(l.91) The Italian form of the name Helen would loom large in Naples and the Como visit possibly involved the mysterious lady. The poem concludes with Lionel's death and the reconciliation of Rosalind and Helen, whose children marry. Whatever Shelley's experiences had been near Villa Pliniana, as he walked with his loaded pistol, it now became the place where Rosalind died "ere her time."

Four days after Shelley left, Mary noted that Clara, not quite a year old, was "not well." Two days later, Clara apparently "Very unwell," Shelley's letter from Florence arrived saying he had engaged a *vetturino* to take them by carriage to Padua. He and Claire "shall only sleep three nights on the road." Paolo had returned to Bagni di Lucca. Shelley reported that Claire had changed her plans, she now wanted to stay in Padua while Shelley called on Byron. Knowing Claire's changeableness, Shelley added skeptically, "But we shall see." After saying Florence was "the most beautiful city I ever saw," he got to the vexed issue of Mary's hurt feelings, asking if she was "very lonely" and did she "ever cry? If you love me you will keep up your spirits." He wanted her to tell the "truth" as he would be "flattered" not "by your sorrow" but "by your cheerfulness."[112] Knowing she was unhappy about his leaving, he did not want to hear of her unhappiness. He closed saying he would be happy if she were productive, as when he was away from her in Geneva and she began *Frankenstein*. Unfortunately, the family tragedies in her novel began to unfold in life.

4

Euganean Isles of Misery: Venice

Aᴏᴛᴇʀ ꜱʜᴇʟʟᴇʏ ᴀɴᴅ ᴄʟᴀɪʀᴇ ʟᴇꜰᴛ ꜰʟᴏʀᴇɴᴄᴇ, ᴛʜᴇʏ ꜱᴘᴇɴᴛ ᴛʜᴇ next two nights in bedbug-ridden beds in Bologna and Padua. Shelley wrote to a jealous Mary soon after arriving in Venice and avoided details of his trip with Claire, saying their travels "contained nothing which may not be related another time." Claire did change her mind and accompanied him to Venice from Padua by gondola down the River Brenta and its canal. Their gondolier volunteered that Byron, living "very luxuriously," spent "great sums of money." As they crossed the lagoon from Fusina to Venice after dark in a "violent storm," Claire was "a little frightened in our cabin" but Shelley appreciated the black gondola's "extraordinarily soft" couches and blinds to keep out the light.[1] Writing to Peacock, he drew a gondola, likening it to "moths of which a coffin might have been the chrysalis."[2]

At their Venice inn, the waiter immediately began talking of Byron. The next morning, Shelley and Claire went to the Hoppners and, uncertain of their reception, Shelley waited in the gondola while Claire went in. He was soon fetched by Richard Hoppner, and his wife Isabella, a rather prim Swiss mother of an infant, quickly summoned Elise and Allegra. Shelley observed to Mary that Allegra was taller, less lively, but "as beautiful as ever." The Hoppners confirmed the rumors about Byron's lifestyle and discussed how Shelley should approach Byron. They decided Claire's presence should be concealed because Hoppner said Byron "often expresses his extreme horror" of her arrival, threatening to leave Venice instantly if she comes. Shelley called at the Palazzo Mocenigo at three that afternoon.

Byron, delighted to see Shelley, quickly learned the purpose of his visit was Claire's desire to see Allegra. Shelley apparently led Byron to believe that Mary, Claire, and the children were in Padua. Trying to relax Byron's hold on Allegra, Shelley mentioned their plans to live in Florence and suggested Allegra might visit her mother there. These ploys apparently had some effect as Shelley told Mary that Byron said: "after all I have no right over the child. If Clare likes to take it—let her take it." If Claire were "imprudent" enough to try to keep her, Byron would not "refuse to provide for it, or abandon it." Byron was noncommittal about any permanent arrangements but, to Shelley's surprise, he was willing to have Allegra visit her mother in Padua for a week. Byron vetoed sending Allegra to Florence for fear the Venetians would think he had tired of her, adding to his "reputation for caprice."[3] Byron later maintained he always agreed to let Allegra visit her mother should Claire be living nearby.

Shelley was pleased by Byron's "willingness & good humour," telling Peacock that Byron had "changed into the liveliest, & happiest looking man I ever met."[4] Another visitor commented that at thirty, Byron looked forty, his face "pale, bloated, and sallow" and "grown very fat."[5]

Besides sex and swimming, Byron's other enthusiasm was horseback riding on the Lido and he insisted Shelley join him for a ride. Shelley reluctantly agreed, leaving Claire "anxiously" awaiting him at the Hoppners'. After crossing the lagoon to the Lido in Byron's gondola in the late afternoon, they had the most famous horseback ride made by poets.

Writing to Mary before dawn the next morning, Shelley told of riding "along the sands of the sea" conversing about their "feelings . . . [and] affairs," Byron expressing "great professions of friendship & regard for me." They "talked of literary matters," and Byron, saying his fourth canto was "very good . . . repeated some stanzas of great energy to me."[6]

This ride, probably embellished with other Lido rides, became the opening of one of Shelley's most intriguingly autobiographical poems, *Julian and Maddalo; A Conversation:*

> I rode one evening with Count Maddalo
> Upon the bank of land which breaks the flow
> Of Adria towards Venice: a bare strand
> Of hillocks, heaped with ever-shifting sand,
> Matted with thistles and amphibious weeds
> Such as from earth's embrace the salt ooze breeds
>
> This ride was my delight. I love all waste
> And solitary places; where we taste

> The pleasure of believing what we see
> Is boundless, as we wish our souls to be:
>
> (1–6,14–17)

Balancing his inner sense of isolation, Shelley delighted in his renewed social and intellectual communion with Byron, even as he pointed out his friend's narcissism:

> So, as we rode, we talked; and the swift thought,
> Winging itself with laughter, lingered not,
> But flew from brain to brain,—such glee was ours,
>
> We descanted, and I (for ever still
> Is it not wise to make the best of ill?)
> Argued against despondency; but pride
> Made my companion take the darker side.
> The sense that he was greater than his kind
> Had struck, methinks, his eagle spirit blind
> By gazing on its own exceeding light.
> Meanwhile the sun paused ere it should alight
> Over the horizon of the mountains—Oh!
> How beautiful is sunset, when the glow
> Of heaven descends upon a land like thee,
> Thou paradise of exiles, Italy!
>
> (28–30, 46–57)

At Bagni di Lucca, the Gisbornes arrived August 25 to alleviate Mary's loneliness. Three days later, Shelley's long letter from Venice arrived and Mary had an immediate "consultation" with the Gisbornes.[7]

A crucial section of Shelley's letter was later torn away, deleting what occurred after he and Byron returned to Palazzo Mocenigo from their ride. The two poets likely talked into the small hours of the morning before Shelley returned to his inn and continued his letter to Mary. Byron apparently had made a generous offer. Perhaps still believing Mary and Claire were with the children in Padua, Byron gave them the use of a villa he had leased from Hoppner as a summer residence but had never used. It was Casa I Capuccini in Este, south of Padua, nestled among the Euganean Hills near Petrarch's home and tomb.

Eager to get Mary and the children to Este as quickly as possible, Shelley instructed her to "pack up directly," get up at four the next morning, and take the post to Lucca where Paolo could hire a *vetturino* for the daylong trip to Florence. Shelley would send £50 to Florence to get them to Este.

Mary's consultation with the Gisbornes involved the advisability of making such a long, hot, and hard journey with Clara, probably not recovered from being ill a week earlier. Feeling guilty, Shelley ended his letter trying to soften Mary's anger. She "must soon come & scold me if I have done wrong & kiss me if I have done right—for I am sure I do not know which—& it is only the event that can shew." What the event would show was the tragic loss of Mary's daughter as a result of Shelley's efforts for Claire and Allegra.

Shelley apparently told Byron of Mary's true whereabouts before leaving Venice for Este.[8] Although unaware of Clara's recent illness, Shelley was placing a tremendous burden on Mary to transfer the household and make a difficult journey with two young children, even with the aid of Paolo and Milly. Heeding Shelley's call, Mary had to "bustle" and was "packing" on her twenty-first birthday, August 30.[9] It was to be a sad repeat of three years earlier when she noted the "bustle of moving" as she and her week-old premature baby daughter, soon dead, went alone to new lodgings.

On the last day of August, Maria Gisborne accompanied Mary, William, Clara, Milly, and Paolo as far as Lucca. Arriving in Florence after a hot, all-day trip on rough roads, they waited the next day for a passport signature. The arduous route to Padua via Bolgona took four days. Waiting at I Capuccini for Mary, Shelley composed his lines "O Mary dear, that you were here; The Castle echo whispers 'Here!'" It was Shelley's trick of bouncing his voice off the adjacent castle walls. Shelley and Claire probably had been at I Capuccini a week or ten days when Mary arrived September 5 to be greeted by her "very anxious" husband who expected them several days earlier.

Mary's journal entry recorded the toll of the arduous, hot six-day trip: "poor Clara is dangerously ill." Fatigued from the journey, Clara developed dysentery on arrival. It was aggravated by teething and a week later, Mary wrote Maria Gisborne that Clara was somewhat better but "still in a frightful state of weakness and fever . . . so thin . . . you would hardly know her again."[10]

The small agricultural village of Este was a bad location for a seriously ill baby. Mary, deciding the local doctor was a "stupid fellow," called in one "who appears clever" from Padua, twenty miles distant.[11] Meanwhile, Shelley, although ill "from taking poison in Italian cakes," began writing "his drama of Prometheus."[12] Shelley had completed twenty-six manuscript pages of the first act of *Prometheus Unbound* by September 22,[13] composing in the villa's summerhouse at the end of a vine-trellised pergola.[14]

Byron was eager for a visit from Shelley who, on September 13, wrote he was "an anxious prisoner" as Clara "had been dangerously ill" but was "now better."[15] Three days later, Shelley, still "very ill" from the poison, went with Claire to Padua to see the "Medico," about whom Shelley had doubts.[16] Shelley returned a week later to the Padua physician with Claire, who had an appointment with the doctor for an unstated problem, probably gynecological and possibly involving being pregnant.

If Claire was pregnant, it was not by Byron. He wrote his half sister that, fearing another pregnancy, he had not seen her in Venice. Byron said Claire was to return Allegra after a month "and then return herself to Lucca—or Naples where she was with her relatives."[17] Shelley probably told Byron about possibly going to Naples. Mary commented on Byron's fear of Claire years later, saying that he "feared" Claire and "did not spare her."[18]

Shelley and Claire arrived in Padua on September 22 too late for her appointment and rescheduled it for the early morning, two days later. Shelley decided to go alone to Venice to find a more capable doctor for little Clara and to visit Byron. Before leaving Padua, he wrote Mary that he would meet her and Clara in Padua on September 24 to take them back to Venice. In order for Mary to accompany Claire for her early morning doctor's appointment in Padua, Shelley told Mary she and the baby would have to get up at three thirty in the morning. Although "somewhat uneasy" about "My poor little Clara," he felt "secure there is no danger." Encouraging Mary to continue her work on "Charles the 1st," he asked her to bring the translation she was writing of Alfieri's *Myrrha*, a tragedy of father–daughter incest.[19]

Shelley and Mary, with perilously ill Clara, departed Padua for Venice the morning of September 24 to see Dr. Francesco Aglietti, whom Byron recommended. Clara became increasingly weak and began having facial convulsions. At Fusina, having forgotten their passports, the Austrian soldiers tried to prevent them from proceeding but relented under Shelley's vehement protests. Crossing the lagoon, Clara was worse when they reached their inn in Venice that afternoon. Shelley wrote Claire the next day that Dr. Aglietti was not home and upon returning, he found Mary in "dreadful distress." Clara was worse and when another physician arrived he told Shelley "there was no hope." Clara died within an hour, "silently, without pain . . . she is now buried." Mary was "reduced . . . to a kind of despair." They accepted the Hoppners' invitation to stay at their house. After stating that all this misery "must be borne," Shelley's next sentence to Claire was later obliterated (probably by Claire). It apparently read, "Meanwhile forget me & relive [or revive] not the other thing." Shelley ended, "And above all—my dear girl take care of yourself."[20]

What Shelley asked Claire not to relive or revive perhaps involved their close relationship during their three weeks together after leaving Mary at Bagni di Lucca. Asking Claire to "forget me" perhaps was Shelley's attempt to dampen their relationship and possible sexual intimacy. Claire's trips to the Padua physician could have been to obtain an abortion, as suggested by Shelley's admonition, "take care of yourself" and not "relive . . . the other thing." Shelley disapproved of abortion, but under the circumstances he could have condoned it. If Claire conceived shortly after leaving Bagni di Lucca, she would have been four weeks pregnant when she and Shelley first went to Padua on September 16.[21]

Clara Everina Shelley, one year and three weeks old when she died, was buried in the Lido cemetery for foreigners.[22] For Mary, the loss of her second daughter was devastating and marked the beginning of her depressive withdrawal from Shelley. She wrote, "This is the Journal of misfortunes . . . my poor Clara . . . dies the moment we get [to Venice]." Not until early November did Mary write to Maria Gisborne of Clara's death. Godwin, learning the tragic news from Mary in late October, lectured her sternly not to be a "very ordinary" person by indulging "long in depression and mourning."[23]

Mary reacted to Clara's death by turning inward, increasingly closing out her feelings, including her sexual feelings, for Shelley. She resented Claire for having persuaded Shelley to leave her in Bagni di Lucca and was angry at Shelley for going with Claire. She resented both Claire and Shelley for their relationship and, perhaps more unconsciously, she resented that her daughter had died and Claire's survived.

Shelley and Mary stayed five days with the Hoppners before returning to Este. Without Shelley, she had several meetings with Byron, the first time on the Lido while she visited Clara's grave. This meeting perhaps resulted in Byron allowing Allegra to stay longer at Este.[24] The following day Mary visited Byron at the Palazzo Mocenigo, meeting his mistress, La Fornarina. Byron ad-

mired *Frankenstein* and probably showed Mary his recently begun *Memoirs,* which she encouraged him to publish. She took his
manuscripts of "Mazeppa" and "Ode on Venice" to Este to copy
and later offered to copy the first canto of *Don Juan.*[25]

Upon returning to Este, the Shelleys found Claire was again in
Padua. Her doctor visits to Padua were not unnoticed by Elise and
Paolo, who soon would begin a romance. While Mary transcribed
Byron's poetry, Shelley launched his *annus mirabilis* of greatest
productivity by finishing in early October the first act of *Prometheus
Unbound.*

Within four months of Clara's death the Shelleys conceived another child. Shelley's strong views on contraception surfaced in
1819 while writing *A Philosophical View of Reform.* Under a heading, "Malthus principle," he alluded to the vaginal sponge:

> The sexual intercourse by no means presents, as has been supposed,
> the [?] horrendous alternative of a being . . . for whom there is no sub-
> sistence, or the revolting expedients of infanticide and abortion. Any
> student of anatomy must be aware of an innocent, small and almost im-
> perceptible precaution by which all consequence of this kind are pre-
> vented, and the ends of an union of two persons of opposite sexes in
> every other respect fulfilled. . . . It is curious to remark how few med-
> ical men of any considerable science have more children than they can
> comfortably maintain.[26]

Shelley's wry comment on physicians' use of contraception
probably reflected his own practice. He shared Godwin's disdain
for Malthus's callous attitudes toward the lower classes but told
Peacock he was not sanguine about population control anytime
soon. Mentioning his family's "bad spirits," Shelley said they would
soon leave for "Florence Rome & Naples at which last city we shall
spend the winter, & return northwards in the spring." His scenic
descriptions of the nearby Euganean Hills, including Petrarch's
home and tomb, suggest he had begun *Lines written among the
Euganean Hills.*[27]

In early October, a despondent Shelley made a day's excursion
to the top of Monte Rua, the tallest of the modest peaks near Petrarch's home in Arqua Petrarca, and began composing *Lines
written among the Euganean Hills.* Like *Rosalind and Helen,* it
took Mary's urging for Shelley to complete *Euganean Hills* in December. He wrote that she tried without success "to extinguish . . .
[his] . . . delineating sadness."[28] The finely wrought initial three

verse-paragraphs of *Euganean Hills* express both Shelley's sadness and his characteristic defense of hopefulness. In the pre-dawn, atop his mountain-island overlooking the sea-like plain of Lombardy, his "deep wide sea of misery" hopefully holds "Many a green isle." Like a storm-tossed mariner, he is enclosed in "the solid darkness black" whose "ship has almost drank / Death."

Mary's cold withdrawal of love and verbal harshness are suggested next in lines she probably did not see until shortly before Shelley sent them to Ollier:

> Senseless is the breast, and cold,
> Which relenting love would fold;
> Bloodless are the veins and chill
> Which the pulse of pain did fill;
> Every little living nerve
> That from bitter words did swerve
> Round the tortured lips and brow,
> Are like sapless leaflets now
> Frozen upon December's bough.
>
> (16–44)

From his mountaintop, amid these "waters of wide Agony," he sees Venice, "Ocean's nursling," its sun-illumined towers— "obelisks of fire"—are "Sepulchres" that will sink into a "watery bier." "Chained" Venice, having succumbed to political slavery, may "awake" to freedom. Byron appears as "a tempest-cleaving Swan" who, "Driven from his ancestral streams," might bring "joy" but the city's "sins and slaveries foul / Overcloud" his "sunlike soul!"

As "Noon descends," Shelley tried to erase the "Pain" of "remembered agonies" with a wishful fantasy of "The frail bark of this lone being":

> Other flowering isles must be
> In the sea of life and agony:
> Other spirits float and flee
> O'er that gulph: even now, perhaps,
> On some rock the wild wave wraps,
> With folded wings they waiting sit
> For my bark, to pilot it
> To some calm and blooming cove,
> Where for me, and those I love,
> May a windless bower be built,
> Far from passion, pain, and guilt
>
> (335–45)

The poem ends with a wish for "the love which heals all strife" and that "the earth grow young again."

One strife, little William's persisting symptoms, caused his frightened parents to take him to Venice in mid-October for better medical care.[29] Staying in a hotel, they saw the Hoppners frequently. Mary was repulsed by Venice's dirtiness and the sight of "zucce" (pumpkins) in the "dirty" streets made her "sick." The "horrid smell" of canals that were "never cleaned . . . makes my head ache."[30]

Seemingly oblivious to such realities, the two poets, when not riding on the Lido, were talking until two or three in the morning at Palazzo Mocenigo. Shelley soon wrote Byron he was "so dreadfully sleepy" he could not visit that night.[31] Shelley praised Byron's stanzas in *Childe Harold* 4 about the nymph Egeria, echoed in *Prometheus Unbound.*[32] Peacock's dislike of Byron's poem led Shelley to write Peacock that "The spirit in which it is written is, if insane, the most wicked & mischievous insanity that ever was given forth." Branding Byron's "obstinate & self-willed folly," Shelley believed the "real root" of "these expressions of contempt & desperation" was Byron's sex life. Shelley still found Italian women "contemptible . . . ignorant . . . disgusting . . . bigotted . . . filthy. . . . Countesses smell so of garlick that an ordinary Englishman cannot approach them." Byron "is familiar with the lowest sort of these women" and "allows fathers & mothers to bargain with him for their daughters . . . and associates with wretches who seem almost to have lost the gait & physiognomy of man, & who do not scruple to avow practices which are not only not named but I believe seldom ever conceived in England." Shelley added, "But that he is a great poet, I think the address to Ocean proves" and "he has a certain degree of candour while you talk to him, but unfortunately it does not outlast your departure."[33]

Shelley's comment on "wretches" probably alluded to Byron's homosexual predilections.[34] Writing Hogg, Shelley repeated his disgust at Byron's "practising aphrodisiacs at a great rate." Shelley, able to minister to the English impoverished poor but unable to relate to humble Italians as easily as Byron, told Hogg, "the [Italian] men are . . . below criticism."[35]

Mary remained in Venice while Shelley went to Este October 24 to return Allegra to Byron. While he spent three or four days with Claire at I Capuccini, Mary paid a last visit to Clara's grave with Isabella Hoppner. Returning with Allegra, Shelley joined Mary in saying goodbye to the helpful Hoppners before departing for Este. Shelley, angry about Byron's obstinacy and pettiness in prohibiting Claire greater access to Allegra, wrote to Peacock that his arguments with Byron were "in vain" and "for his sake I ought to hope that his present career must end up soon by some violent circumstance" which would "reduce our situation with respect to Alba into its antient tie."[36] Shelley's bitter aftertaste from his latest personal contact with Byron lingered. More than a year and a half passed before he communicated again with Byron.

Julian and Maddalo filled that void, presenting the two poets' differing philosophies and Shelley's response to the tragic losses that beset him and Mary soon after they arrived in Italy. Planning to publish *Julian and Maddalo* anonymously and evasive about when it was written, Shelley probably worked on it from late 1818 or early 1819 to about August 1819.[37] The Byron figure, Count Maddalo, was portrayed in the preface as caustically brilliant, witty, and cynical, "a person of consummate genius, and capable, if he would direct his energies to such an end, of becoming the redeemer of his degraded country . . . it is his weakness to be proud: he derives, from a comparison of his own extraordinary mind with the dwarfish intellects that surround him, an intense apprehension of the nothingness of life. . . . His passions and his powers are incomparably greater than those of other men" but he is unable to use "the latter in curbing the former." Maddalo's "ambition preys upon itself . . . it is on his own hopes and affections only that he seems to trample."

Julian the Apostate, a Roman emperor (CE 331–63) with anti-Christian views, probably provided Shelley's poetic name.[38] Julian was "an Englishman of good family, passionately attached to those philosophical notions which assert the power of man . . . [for] immense improvements . . . by the extinction of certain moral superstitions. . . . Without concealing the evil in the world, he is for ever speculating how good may be made superior. He is a complete infidel, a scoffer at all things reputed holy."

The third key figure in *Julian and Maddalo*, the maniac, is clearly Shelley.[39] In his preface, Shelley guardedly says: "Of the Maniac I can give no information. He seems disappointed in love. He was evidently a very cultivated and amiable person when in his right senses." The maniac is absent from the poem's title but occupies two-thirds of the poem and half of those lines are devoted to the maniac's monologue, his profound argument with himself.

Julian and Maddalo is a veiled introspective, autobiographical analysis of a period of marital discord and personal despair from the late summer of 1818 to the summer of 1819.

The two poet-exiles' ride along the Lido epitomized the creative spark Shelley got from his reunion with Byron after being separated for two years. The opening invocation to Tasso in the completed fourth canto of *Childe Harold* renewed Shelley's interest in that poet's madness; the maniac in *Julian and Maddalo* perhaps stemmed from their talk of Tasso. About this time Byron read to an impressed Shelley what he was writing, the first canto of *Don Juan*. Shelley told Peacock that *Don Juan*'s stinging Dedication stanzas to Southey were "more like a mixture of wormwood & verdigrease than satire. The poor wretch will writhe under the lash."[40] Byron's longtime aversion to the poet laureate was fueled by the rumors Southey had spread, which Shelley might have told Byron, about the Genevan "League of Incest." Byron gained revenge with the theme of sexual impotence, attacking "quite adry, Bob" Southey and the "intellectual eunuch Castlereagh."[41]

Don Juan became the great epic commentary on Regency England, not the revolutionary epic Shelley had urged Byron to write. In his preface to his revolutionary epic, *Laon and Cythna*, Shelley had indirectly admitted his competition with Byron.[42] Shelley, now ready to start a more powerful revolutionary epic, was spurred by Byron's increased poetic skill. Within a matter of days after their initial ride, Shelley had begun his greatest dramatic poem, *Prometheus Unbound*.

Shelley harbored, but could not fully accept, Maddalo–Byron's dark views on life. A lyric Shelley probably composed before starting *Julian and Maddalo*, "The Two Spirits—An Allegory," is a dialogue contrasting the two poets' different life-views.[43] The Maddalo-like spirit cautions:

> Oh thou, who plumed with strong desire
> Would float above the Earth, beware!
> A Shadow tracks thy flight of fire—
> Night is coming!

(1–4)

The Julian-like spirit replies:

> The deathless stars are bright above;
> If I should cross the shade of night

Within my heart is the lamp of love,
And that is day!

(9–12)

In *Julian and Maddalo,* such optimism elicits Maddalo's dismissive, "You talk Utopia." But Julian, undaunted, replies with the credo of *Prometheus Unbound:*

and those who try, may find
How strong the chains are which our spirit bind:
Brittle perchance as straw. We are assured
Much may be conquered, much may be endured,
Of what degrades and crushes us. We know
That we have power over ourselves to do
And suffer—*what,* we know not till we try;
But something nobler than to live and die

(179–87)

Maddalo, proposing they visit the madman, assures Julian, "his wild talk will shew / How vain are such aspiring theories." Julian has the final words of the debate, hoping "to prove" that what will cure the maniac is to "be beloved with gentleness":

And being scorned, what wonder is they die
Some living death? This is not destiny,
But man's own wilful ill."

(209–11)

Julian's confrontation with the maniac at the island madhouse, the poem's emotional center, is best discussed later as part of the deepening schism in Shelley's relationship with Mary.

The Shelley household, departing I Capuccini in early November for Naples, traversed terrible roads for two days to reach Ferrara. Mary's dour realism contrasted with Shelley's optimism in their accounts of the trip. When the bad roads necessitated getting oxen, Mary vowed they would not make the same travel arrangements again. Shelley, noting the "deep & clayey" roads, was sure they would improve "the rest of the way."[44]

Reliving his boyhood farm experiences, Shelley enthused over the "oxen of immense size & exquisit beauty" they stopped to see. Comparing English and Italian farmyards, he observed "vast heaps of many coloured zucki or pumkins [provided] winter food for the hogs." Among the turkeys and fowls wandering about were "two or three dogs who bark with a sharp hylacticism."

In Ferrara, the literary haunts of the Renaissance poets Ariosto, Tasso, and Guarini fascinated Shelley. What most beguiled him in the 160,000-volume library containing Ariosto's grave was his inkstand and a medal depicting the dead poet with "an upraised serpent." He delighted in analyzing the poets' handwriting, telling Peacock, "You know I always seek in what I see the manifestation of something beyond the present & tangible object." Ariosto had "small firm & pointed" handwriting, expressing "a strong & keen but circumscribed energy of mind." By contrast, Tasso's larger handwriting turned "smaller," revealing "an intense & earnest mind exceeding at times its own depth."[45] Shelley's graphological analysis of Tasso's personality closely parallels that in his unfinished "Scene for Tasso" and he gave Tasso's physical features in this fragment to the maniac when he later resumed writing *Julian and Maddalo*.[46]

Shelley sent Peacock a splinter from the door of Tasso's reputed prison cell, a more "decent dungeon" than those in Venice's Doges' Palace. Observing "a Penitent . . . completely enveloped in a ghost like drapery of white flannel," Shelley thought it "a striking instance of the power of the Catholic superstition over the human mind."

Sightseeing in Bologna for two days was the basis of the next of Shelley's letters to Peacock, who enthusiastically read each to anyone who called. Mary, with an eye to its future publication, recopied and edited the Bologna letter before sending it. Two visits to the *pinacoteca* provided Shelley's most detailed descriptions of paintings. He particularly enthused over the paintings of female figures, having become "tired indeed" of the "monotonous & agonized" theme of "J[esus] C[hrist] Crucified." One saint, an "animated mummy," evoked Shelley's query, "Why write books against religion, when one can hang up such pictures." Mary tried to soften this criticism and deleted Shelley's passage describing Guido and his mistress, who was poisoned "by another lover, a rejected one of course."

The maiden in Guido's *Rape of Proserpine* had "languid & half unwilling eyes" and his nursing Madonna was animated by "the spirit of a love almost insupportable from its intensity." Raphael's *St. Cecilia* had "deep dark eloquent eyes," her countenance "calmed by the depth of its passion & rapture."[47] He later expressed a preference for Raphael's "loveliness" over "a certain rude, external, mechanical quality" in Michelangelo.[48] The next day, after revisiting the *pinacoteca*, they rode up Monte Albano to the Basilica of the Madonna[49] and Shelley took a "strikingly picturesque" moonlight walk through the city's colonnaded streets.

Beginning a ten-day trip to Rome, they avoided the strenuous mountainous route to Florence, traveling southeast to Faenza and Cesena before crossing the Rubicon. They reached the Adriatic at Rimini and, after spending the night at Cattólica, headed inland into the Apennines at Fano on the Via Flamina. The inn at Fossombrone was so "miserable" they neither slept nor got undressed. Relying on his guidebook,[50] Shelley wrote Peacock they followed the banks of the Metaurus River whose steep cliffs and pinnacles, Mary thought, made a beautiful "Promethean" scene, almost as fine as Les Eschelles. Shelley was impressed by the Roman Legion's enduring chisel marks visible in the rocks and by ephemeral low windblown clouds "like curtains of the finest gauze removed one by one."[51] Dropping south, after "miserable" nights at Scheggia and Foligno, they came upon Spoleto, which Shelley found "the most romantic city I ever saw" with its castle "of tremendous magnitude" above the aqueduct and torrent below.

The journey's most spectacular sight came the next day at Terni, where they spent an afternoon and early evening viewing the Cascades of Mármora. Shelley's description of the falls, perhaps his longest of any natural phenomenon, Godwin later incorporated in his novel *Cloudesley*. After the glaciers of Montanvert and the source of the Arveiron, Shelley believed the cascade's three-hundred-foot drop "the grandest spectacle" he ever saw, the cascading water "comes in thick tawny folds flaking off like solid snow gliding down a mountain . . . like the folding of linen thrown carelessly down." The water was shaped "wholly unlike anything any thing I ever saw before . . . white as snow, but thick & impenetrable to the eye." Moving on because of their bad inn, Shelley considered "spending some time next year near this waterfall."

After spending the night within the medieval walls of Nepi, they crossed the Campagna di Roma November 20 and entered the city, their resting place for a week before going to Naples. After some difficulty, they found a comfortable hotel where the mysterious lady possibly also was a guest. Mary's postscript to Shelley's letter to Peacock said they would remain in Naples until "the end of February" and then return to Rome.[52] This definite and accurate date for concluding their stay in Naples suggests something other than the weather determined the length of their stay there.

They were disappointed by St. Peter's on their first day of sight-seeing but a visit to the Forum and the Colosseum cemented Shelley's fascination with Rome. Returning to the Colosseum the next three days, he conveyed his detailed observations to Peacock with the injunction, "Come to Rome." He found the Colosseum was now "an amphitheatre of rocky hills overgrown by the wild-olive the myrtle & the fig tree." A visit to the pyramid of Cestius and the adjacent Protestant Cemetery evoked Shelley's touching tribute to the spot so tragically important to his future: "The English bur[y]ing place is a green slope near the walls, under the pyramidal tomb of Cestius, & is I think the most beautiful & solemn cemetery I ever beheld."[53]

After going to the Vatican and revisiting the Colosseum, Shelley began his unusual, unfinished story, *The Coliseum.* Possibly written to counter Byron's nihilism,[54] it is a tale of a young, self-isolated male stranger who meets in the Colosseum an old blind oracular man and his young daughter Helen. Events soon to unfold in Naples make it perhaps significant that Helen is the only person named in the story. The Shelley-like young man "avoided, in an extraordinary degree, all communication with the Italians" but occasionally would "converse with some accomplished foreigner." The young man will tell his two new acquaintances: "it is painful for me to live without communication with intelligent and affectionate beings. You are such, I feel."

According to Mary, Shelley intended the young stranger to be Greek, "nurtured from infancy exclusively in the literature of his progenitors." Shelley described the youth's "never to be forgotten" face as having "the eager and impassioned tenderness of the statues of Antinous . . . [with] an expression of profound and piercing thought . . . his eyes deep, like two wells of crystalline water which reflect the all-beholding heavens." His was "a timid expression of womanish tenderness and hesitation, which contrasted, yet intermingled strangely, with the abstracted and fearless character that predominated in his form and gesture."

Medwin said of this description, "There never was drawn a more perfect portrait of Shelley himself."[55] Shelley had seen the androgynous statues of Antinous the previous day in the Vatican. Mary believed the youth's feminine quality was due to his greater "resemblance" to a fourth figure omitted in the story: "Shelley conceived the idea of a woman . . . named Diotima . . . his instructress and guide."[56] In Shelley's *Symposium* translation, Diotima was "the stranger Prophetess" who imparted her ideas of love to Socrates.

The old man, envisioning his daughter Helen's death before his own, utters, "It has happened . . . that men have buried their children." The daughter tries to soothe the youth's guilt, but his final words reflect Shelley's own feelings of loss, rejection, and emotional isolation at this time: "I live a solitary life, and it is rare that I encounter any stranger with whom it is pleasant to talk; besides, their meditations . . . do not always agree with mine; and though I can pardon this difference, they cannot."

One person Shelley apparently encountered again in Italy was the mysterious lady whose romantic approaches he had politely refused before leaving England, probably in 1814. According to Medwin, she first followed him to Geneva and, "her constancy . . . untired," she then followed him in Italy: "During his journey to Rome and Naples, she once lodged with him at the same hotel, en route, and finally arrived at the latter city the same day as himself. He must have been more or less than man, to have been unmoved by the devotedness of this unfortunate and infatuated lady. At Naples, he told me that they met and when he learnt from her all those particulars of her wanderings, of which he had been previously ignorant; and at Naples she died. Mrs. Shelley . . . was unacquainted with all those circumstances."[57]

Diotima's absence in Shelley's story is paralleled by the absent mysterious lady who seemingly reappeared in Naples. This lady apparently played a role in Shelley's despondency in Naples and perhaps in his adoption of an infant there to whom he gave the name Elena (Helen). Medwin publicly alluded to these events as early as 1833:

> Fortune did not seem tired of persecuting him, for he became the innocent actor in a tragedy here [Naples], more extraordinary than any to be found in the pages of a romance. The story as he related it to myself and Byron, would furnish perfect materials for a novel in three volumes, and cannot be condensed into a few sentences. . . . Certain it is, that Shelley, as may be judged from his 'Lines written in Despondency,' must have been most miserable at Naples. . . . His departure from Naples was, he said, precipitated by this event.[58]

It is not known if Shelley knew this lady was in Rome during the week he was there with his family. Leaving Rome alone for Naples on November 27, a day before his family's departure, he wrote Peacock that his prior departure "was necessary to procure lodgings here [Naples] without alighting at an Inn."[59] This desire for his family's privacy by avoiding inns in Naples was one possible reason for his prior departure. However, a more secret agenda was behind going to Naples, filled with rumor-spreading visiting English. According to Mary, when they learned there was no danger of being attacked by robbers en route to Naples, "Shelley went on first to secure us lodgings and we followed a day or two later."[60]

If Shelley had more personal reasons involving the mysterious lady for leaving Rome early, his quicker travel with a *vetturino* gave him two full days in Naples before his family arrived. Shelley, spending only two nights on the road, had among his traveling companions a "Calabrian priest" who had "the most frantic terror of robbers on the road & he cried at the sight of my pistol." Upon approaching Naples, Shelley felt horror when seeing a man murder a youth with a knife made the fearful priest laugh. Angry at the priest, Shelley "never felt such an inclination to beat any one."[61]

Mary's group left Rome November 28 and would spend three nights before arriving in Naples. After stopping in Velletri, they crossed the Pompine marshes to Terracina on the coast. The road was guarded and they were warned to wait for daylight before proceeding to Gaeta. Their tiring journey ended the evening of December 1 when, with Vesuvius's flames for a backdrop, Mary and her family arrived in Naples, where Shelley had found lodgings beside the sea.

Fig. 1. Leigh Hunt by Benjamin Robert Haydon, c. 1811, courtesy of the National Portrait Gallery, London.

Fig. 2. John Keats, miniature by Joseph Severn, 1819, courtesy of the National Portrait Gallery, London.

Fig. 3. Albion House, Marlow, Shelley's last home in England. Photograph by author.

Fig. 4. Horace Smith, engraved by Finden from a portrait by John James Masquerier.

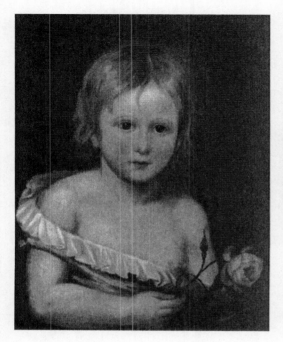

Fig. 5. William Shelley
by Amelia Curran, 1819,
courtesy of The Carl F.
Pforzheimer Collection of
Shelley and His Circle, The
New York Public Library,
Astor, Lenox and Tilden
Foundations.

Fig. 6. Parish church
of San Giuseppe a
Chiaia, Naples, where
Elena Adelaide Shelley
was baptized.
Photograph by author.

Fig. 7. Sophia Stacey by Bouton, c. 1818, from photograph, copyright Rodney
M. Bennett 1994, courtesy of Rodney M. Bennett.

Fig. 8. Villa Valsovano, Leghorn, from late nineteenth-century photograph by W. Hall Griffin, showing Shelley's rooftop tower where he composed *The Cenci*.

Fig. 9. Convent of Santa Anna, Pisa, abode of Emilia Viviani. Photograph by author.

5

Paradise of Devils: Naples

THEIR ROOMS AT 250 RIVIERA DI CHIAIA OVERLOOKED THE ADJACENT royal gardens and the bay, which was "encompassed by the mountainous island" of Capri, "the lofty peaks which overhang Salerno," the woody promontories of Posillipo, and "the lofty isle" of Ischia. From the garden, Vesuvius was "a smoke by day & fire by night is seen upon its summit, & the glassy sea often reflects its light or shadow."[1]

A year later, Mary wrote, "I never found my spirits so good since I entered upon *care* as at Naples, looking out on its delightful Bay." However, the scenic beauty could not eclipse all her underlying "care." She went on to say that because of the city's inhabitants, "It is a paradise inhabited by devils."[2]

Shelley's Neapolitan devils, internal and external, created some of the most mysterious episodes of his life. Outwardly, the three months in Naples were marked largely by social isolation punctuated by occasional vigorous sightseeing. For Shelley, it was a time of depression, physical symptoms, secretive actions, domestic strain, and a group of poems not shown to Mary.

The record Shelley and Mary left of their stay in Naples is fragmentary, evasive, and censored. Claire's journal, missing for this period, began again after they left Naples. Mary's journal entries, more clipped than usual, were omitted for thirty-one days in January and February. Shelley's Naples letters are devoid of personal concerns except for brief references to his depression and ill health. Mary mentioned Claire only once in her Naples journal; references to Shelley concerned his reading and letter writing. Most of their sightseeing occurred before December 22 and after February 10. Between these two dates, upsetting events occurred in Naples.

Shelley's secretive Neapolitan experience seems to mirror that of the secretive heroine of Madame de Staël's novel *Corinne, or*

Italy, which he and Mary read soon after arriving in Naples.[3] Medwin thought *The Coliseum* "promised to rival, if not surpass 'Corinne'" and that Shelley, like de Staël's heroine, "meant to have idealized himself in the principal character."[4] *Corinne* described places the Shelleys' would visit in and around Naples but it had more personal meaning. Mary first read the novel in 1815 when her infant daughter died and Shelley was involved with Claire. After Hogg left the household, Mary recorded "a fuss," her word for a quarrel with Shelley. She would use the word again about events on leaving Naples.

Intriguing parallels exist between *Corinne*'s three major figures and Shelley, Mary, Claire, and the mysterious lady. The novel involves the titled Oswald's love for two half sisters, Corinne and Lucile.[5] A depressed Oswald, advised by his physician to go to Italy to avoid consumption, in Rome first meets wealthy, young, and beautiful Corinne, surrounded in mystery. Only Corinne's maid knows her real name and place of birth. Corinne falls in love with Oswald and the two travel to Naples where they climb Vesuvius. Corinne makes the ascent on a litter, as would Claire. Revealing her life story, Corinne tells Oswald that her half sister was chosen to marry him. He returns to England, followed by Corinne, who secretly observes him in London while he falls in love with her half sister. Corinne returns to Italy, relinquishing Oswald to her half sister in an unhappy marriage. Oswald becomes ill and, with his wife and daughter, returns to Italy where he visits the ill Corinne just as she dies.

Several days after visiting Herculaneum in early December, Shelley, Mary, and perhaps the unmentioned Claire, set out on an all-day boat excursion.[6] The underwater plant life seen through the translucent water Shelley later incorporated into *Ode to the West Wind*. Crossing the Bay of Pozzuoli to Cape Miseno, they came ashore to see the Elysian Fields. The landscape disappointed Shelley whenever they disembarked, "while from the boat the effect of the scenery was inexpressibly beautiful." In the Bay of Baiae, the sight of submerged ruins of "antique grandeur . . . in the transparent sea" also appeared in his *Ode*. Going ashore at Lake Avernus, legendary entrance to Hades, the volcanic topography became more interesting. Passing through "the cavern of Sybil," they approached one of several volcanic lakes, future imagery for *Prometheus Unbound*. Lake Avernus, "once a chasm of deadly & pestilential vapours," was now a "windless mirror" reflecting Roman ruins, a scene "far more beautiful than the Elysian fields." Crossing to Pozzuoli, the volcanic landscape and mud jets of Solfatara were less appealing to Shelley than their descriptions in classical poetry. They sailed back to Naples by moonlight under a radiant evening star.[7]

Attending a Rossini opera in the newly rebuilt Teatro San Carlo, Shelley thought the interior was "beautiful" but "the boxes are so dear & the pit so intolerable that I fear we shall visit it seldom."[8] Just after reading *Corinne*, the Shelleys, on December 16, made the ascent to the summit of Vesuvius.

Shelley, describing this strange outing several days later to Peacock, made clear that Claire accompanied them.[9] At Resina, he and Mary mounted mules for the ascent but four men carried Claire in a chair on their shoulders, "much like a member of parliament after he had gained his election & looking with less reason quite as frightened." Whether Claire's physical condition necessitated her being carried, or she was identifying with Corinne, Shelley did not say. Perhaps she avoided riding after her falls in Bagni di Lucca. As in *Corinne*, they wound upward through the lava beds to the hermitage of San Salvador to receive food from "an old hermit." Vesuvius was for Shelley, "after the glaciers the most impressive expression of the energies of nature I ever saw." Ascending across "a vast stream of hardened lava . . . the waves of the sea changed into hard black stone by enchantment . . . once a sea of liquid fire." Standing in "a black shower of ashes" on the volcano's summit, Shelley observed, "The lava like the glacier creeps on perpetually with a crackling sound as of suppressed fire."

As they descended by torchlight after the sun had set between Capri and Ischia, Shelley was seized by "a state of intense bodily suffering" and his guides "conducted me I know not how to the hermitage." Pandemonium broke out as the guides, with "horrible cries," became "complete Savages." As Shelley moved ahead of the party, the guides threatened to leave Claire seated in her litter "in the middle of the road" until "my Italian servant promised them a beating, after which they became very quiet." They arrived home at ten o'clock, Mary noting all were "very much fatigued" and Shelley "very ill."[10]

Shelley ended his letter to Peacock: "I have depression enough of spirits & not good health, though I believe the warm air of Naples does me good. We see absolutely no one here." This last sentence, perhaps hiding some contact with the mysterious lady, was intended for Mary's eyes. In a postscript, she told Peacock to address his next letters "to Livorno."

Shelley soon wrote Hunt of having "neither good health or spirits" and a visit from him would "be a relief."[11] Shelley mentioned Byron's offer to loan Hunt the "4 or £500" needed to get him—but not "all your family"—to Italy. Lonely and missing his male friends, Shelley suggested Hunt bring Peacock for an Italian spring reunion. Shelley correctly guessed that Hunt would be "uncomfortable" accepting Byron's loan. Writing Hogg, he again commented, probably misleadingly, "in Naples I have no acquaintance." He told Hogg he liked Rome best and mentioned reading *Corinne:* "my thoughts point again to the majestic and eloquent desolation of what Corinna calls the 'City of the Dead.'"[12]

On December 22, three days after seeing the statues at the Royal Museum, Shelley, Mary, and Claire went to Pompeii. Delighted and "astonished" with Pompeii, Shelley underscored its Greek origins: "I can now understand why the Greeks were such great Poets. . . . They lived in a perpetual commerce with external nature and nourished themselves upon the spirit of its forms." He observed, "Their temples were mostly upaithric [open to the sky]," a word he had introduced into the English language in *Laon and Cythna.*[13] Finding the tombs at Pompeii "the most impressive things of all," he anticipated *Ode to the West Wind* by observing, "The wild woods surround them . . . you hear the late leaves of autumn shiver & rustle in the stream of inconstant wind as it were like the step of ghosts."[14]

Almost two months elapsed before the Shelleys ventured forth on another excursion. Writing his Pompeii letter to Peacock a month after their visit, Shelley was still concerned about his condition: "O if I had health & strength & equal spirits . . . At present I write little else but poetry, & little of that." Having completed his "1st Act of Prometheus," he discussed other literary aspirations: "I consider Poetry very subordinate to moral & political science, & if I were well, certainly I should aspire to the latter; for I can conceive a great work, embodying the discoveries of all ages, & harmonizing the contending creeds by which mankind have been ruled. Far from me is such an attempt & I shall be content by exercising my fancy to amuse myself & perhaps some others, & cast what weight I can into the right scale of that balance which the Giant (of Arthegall) holds." Shelley, alluding to Spencer's *Faerie Queene,* whose giant was drowned for arguing for justice, considered himself "of the Giant's faction."[15] What he was writing were sad verses that he did not show Mary, who was copying *Euganean Hills* and revising *Frankenstein*.[16]

After December 22, the Shelleys' accounts of their lives in Naples become even more opaque. Mary repeated daily that Shelley read Livy silently but Winckelmann—their art history guide— "aloud to me." Her only journal mention of Claire, on December 27, was, "Clare is not well." Mary recorded "Visit Virgil's tomb" the next day, and they spent the evening of January 1 at Madame Falconet's, the wife of Shelley's banker. Early in the New Year, after again seeing the statues at the Royal Museum, Shelley and Mary rode the horses he kept for exercise. Riding, he told Peacock, was "absolutely essential for my health," physicians believing it was beneficial for chronic gonorrhea, hepatitis, kidney disease, and consumption.[17] However, Mary became "stiff" from the "very hard galloping." By mid-January, Shelley was under the care of an "English surgeon" for "a disease [of] the liver which he will cure." Shelley reported "using mercury & Cheltenham salts with much caution & some success for this last ten days."[18] Late in February, one of the "pretty schemes" of his doctor, John Roskilly, was to put caustic on his side: "You may guess how much quiet I have had since it was laid on."[19] This painful procedure, a remnant of "humoral" medicine, possibly opened a suppuration in Shelley's side to which peas or gentian root were applied in the belief it would draw out the poison. Roskilly possibly thought Shelley had chronic hepatitis.[20] Still confident about his physician, Shelley told Peacock, Roskilly "has done me important benefit."

When Mary later printed this letter to Peacock, she omitted Shelley's reference to taking mercury, which was also used for venereal disease.[21] The debilitating effects of his various medical "cures," and of his depression, perhaps affected Shelley's physical appearance. Charles MacFarlane, a nineteen-year-old Englishman who became acquainted with Shelley in Naples, recalled many years later—with probable coloration—that he "read on his countenance and in the whole of his delicate excited frame the words, 'Death, early death!'"[22]

Toward mid-January, Mary's skipped journal entries reflected domestic troubles. She wrote Maria Gisborne of not being "in very good spirits today" because they were "dreadfully teized." Specifically, "We have got rid of our Italian Paolo" who had lately "cheated us through thick and thin" of £100. Shelley wrote Peacock,

"Elise has just married our Italian servant & has quitted us; the man was a great rascal & cheated enormously; this match was very much against our advice."[23] Mary later added more details:

[Elise] formed an attachment with Paolo when we proceeded [from Este] to Rome, & at Naples their marriage was talked of—We all tried to dissuade her; we knew Paolo to be a rascal and we thought so well of her that we believed him to be unworthy of her. An accident led me to the knowledge that without marrying they had formed a connexion; she was ill we sent for a doctor who said there was danger of a miscarriage—I wd not turn the girl on the world without in some degree binding her to this man—we had them married at Sir. W. A'Courts [the British consul]—she left us; turned catholic at Rome, married him & then went to Florence.[24]

This 1821 letter to Mrs. Hoppner concerns what became known in Shelley biography as the "Hoppner scandal," including the mystery of Shelley's "Neapolitan" child and Paolo Foggi's attempts from at least 1820 to blackmail Shelley. The "Hoppner scandal" (chapter 13) stemmed from Elise's accusations that in Naples Claire had a child by Shelley which was placed in a foundling home. Mary denied this in her 1821 letter to Mrs. Hoppner.

Claire's being "not well" December 27 possibly was due to being pregnant. It is unlikely she would have undertaken the Vesuvius trip ten days before, even in a litter, had she been close to delivery. However, if she had become pregnant sometime from mid-August to early September she would have been three to four months pregnant at the time of the Vesuvius ascent. Being carried by a litter rather than riding a mule could reflect her pregnant condition.

Claire, possibly pregnant by Shelley, could have miscarried on December 27, despite Mary's implication to Isabella Hoppner that Claire's December 27 illness was a menstrual problem.[25] Her visits to the doctor in Padua with Shelley perhaps concerned difficulties in her pregnancy, including efforts to obtain an abortion. Shelley's subsequent deleted admonition to Claire, "forget me & relive [or "revive"] not the other thing," possibly concerned an abortion. Naples was full of English travelers who could spread the gossip about Claire being pregnant. Their prior determination to leave Naples by the end of February might have reflected a desire to leave the city before her pregnancy was advanced. Shelley repeatedly emphasized their social isolation in his letters from Naples. After the January 1 visit to his banker's home, the only other recorded social contact was when Dr. Roskilly dined with them February 14.

The significant and probably not accidental loss of Claire's journal from June 1818 to early March 1819, and Mary's skipped journal entries the second half of January and most of February, suggest the Shelley family was concealing much that occurred in Naples. Just before leaving Naples, Shelley registered a female infant as born on December 27, listing himself as the father and Mary as the mother. It is unlikely that this baby was Claire's. Paolo Foggi, having "cheated" the Shelleys, was dismissed sometime before January 22 and a year later was attempting to blackmail Shelley.

In 1936, three important documents were located in the Naples archives: the birth registration, the baptismal certificate, and the death certificate of an infant girl Shelley represented as his and Mary's child.[26] On February 27, 1819, the day before he and his family left Naples, Shelley appeared before the registrar for the District of Chiaia and obtained a birth registration stating that on that date "at 7 p.m. Before me . . . has appeared PERCY SHELLEY of England—age twenty-six—Proprietor—domiciled at Riviera di Chiaia—Number 250—who has declared that on the twenty-seventh day of the month of December One Thousand Eight Hundred and Eighteen, was born to him and to Mary [?]Padurin, his legitimate wife—of England—aged twenty-seven—a girl whom he has presented us and to whom the name of Elena Adelaide was given."[27] In addition to Shelley, two men witnessed and signed the birth registration, a young hairdresser neighbor at 223 Riviera di Chiaia and an older cheesemonger. Shelley's signature, but not Mary's, is on the birth registration. Her incorrect age is closer to that of Elise.

The baptismal record states the child was baptized February 27, 1819, at the parish church of San Giuseppe a Chiaia, several blocks up the Riviera di Chiaia from the Shelleys' residence. The parish priest, Francesco Boccaccio, baptized her as "Elena Adelaide daughter of Percy Shelley and of Mary Godwin lawfully begotten." Gaetana Musto was listed as "Midwife." If the midwife was present at the baptism, it could indicate the child was born more recently than the date on her birth certificate. It is unlikely Mary attended either the baptism or the birth registration; the single word "Pack" appeared in her journal that day.

The third document is an extract from the 1820 death records of the Montecalvario district of Naples, the poorer neighborhood of

narrow and hilly streets just north of the Shelleys' residence.
It stated that two men appeared before the official registrar on
June 10, a cheesemonger, Antonio Liguori, age twenty-five, living
at Vico Canale 48, and a young potteryman from a nearby street.
The faulty spelling of the certificate stated they declared that
"at three a.m." on June 9 "has died at her home ELENA SCHELLY
of Naples, aged fifteen months and twelve days . . . domiciled
at Vico Canale No 45, daughter of Bercy Schelly—Proprietor
[Landowner]—and of Maria Gebuin—domiciled at Leghorn."[28] It
further stated that the certifying official, accompanied by the two
witnesses, had "visited . . . the deceased person" to verify the "actual death." No resident of the house in which Elena died at Vico
Canale 45 appeared either in person or by name in relation to the
death certificate.

The old working-class neighborhood of Montecalvario appears
little changed since the time of the child's death.[29] The building at
Vico Canale 45 was never a foundling hospital; the records of the
only one at that time in Naples, Ospedale Annunziata, reveal Shelley did not deposit or collect a child there.[30] If Elena Adelaide was
born December 27, 1818, she would have been almost eighteen
months old at her death; the younger age on the death certificate
coincides with the date of the birth registration, the end of February 1819. Shelley presented her in person when she was registered
so it is unlikely, but not impossible, he would have been able to present a newborn infant as two months old. A birth date as late as mid-
January, when Mary's journal entries cease for a week, is possible.

Shelley possibly selected December 27 as the child's birth date
in order to conceal association with its actual mother. This date,
and its six-month counterpart, June 27, had a personal significance
and fascination for Shelley from perhaps as early as 1810, certainly
by 1814.[31] In addition to Elena Adelaide's birth date, twenty-seven
appears on the birth registration as Mary's age. Holmes pointed
out that Shelley, writing The Cenci during the summer of 1819,
used December 27 as the date on which Count Cenci's two sons
were murdered.[32] This date does not appear in the source Shelley
used for his tragedy.

Naples apparently was Shelley's original Italian destination
when at Albion House in 1817. Later, from Bagni di Lucca, both
Shelley and Mary wrote of going to Naples.[33] Byron, after talking
to Shelley in Venice, wrote his half sister in September that Claire
and the Shelleys would return either to Lucca or Naples. The

Naples plans were set by October 8 when Shelley wrote Peacock they would winter in Naples, returning "northwards in the spring." He was beset with disturbing "events," but only mentioned Clara's death. They left Este in early November for Naples with the intention of leaving that city the end of February.

Establishing Elena Adelaide's parentage is one of the great bafflements Shelley left for his biographers. The Gisbornes, tight-lipped, apparently were the only friends in whom the Shelleys confided about the child. The lawyer Shelley would hire in Leghorn, Federico del Rosso, and possibly the physician Roskilly in Naples, probably knew most of the details. It is possible but not likely that the name Elena Adelaide indicates one parent was English, the other Italian. That Shelley adopted a female foundling child as an act of restitution for Mary's loss of Clara seems improbable. Mary's becoming pregnant in Naples about two weeks before Shelley registered Elena Adelaide adds to the certainty that she was not the mother. If Shelley chose the name Elena (Helen), he might have been associating it with Helen in one of the two works he was composing at this time, the motherless daughter in *The Coliseum* and the Mary-like woman in *Rosalind and Helen*.

Mary probably knew something but not all about the infant and its parentage before leaving Naples. It seems unlikely, but possible, that she did not know Shelley was hurriedly carrying out the baptism and registration late on February 27, the eve of their departure for Rome. By waiting until the last minute Shelley may have been trying to avoid being caught by the legal authorities in Naples. That the Shelleys had planned since November to leave Naples the end of February might suggest they knew when the child was to be born. Medwin wrote that Shelley told him "his departure from Naples was precipitated by that event," the death of the mysterious lady. Assuming she was the mother, either her death or her relinquishing the child could have led to its adoption. Medwin's assertion, "that on quitting Naples he was afraid of being arrested,"[34] if accurate, could reflect Shelley's anxiety about the fraudulent birth registration. A number of locals had to be involved in the illegal adoption, possibly including the hostile Paolo. The adoption aside, Shelley may have been under political surveillance. Local authorities were clamping down on the secret revolutionary society of the Carbonari, who instigated a failed uprising in Naples the next year. Claire, late in life, wondered if Shelley were involved with the Carbonari; Byron certainly was. Rome, within The Papal States, afforded Shelley some protection from the Kingdom of the Two Sicilies.[35]

Paolo, probably dismissed by mid-January, was in a prime position to blackmail Shelley. He possibly knew something about the child Shelley adopted and understood that the story of its being the child of Shelley and Claire would appeal to the hypocritical, wealthy English who condemned Shelley's radical ideas on free love and atheism. Shelley later mentioned Paolo was in league with some English in Leghorn in his blackmail efforts.[36]

Elise Foggi, if she were the child's mother, probably would not have spread the story about Elena Adelaide. Elise wrote Mary from Florence in July 1821 that she was nursing a baby daughter born in early March.[37] Because Elise did not mention any other child, her pregnancy by Paolo in Naples possibly ended in a miscarriage. Since Elise and Paolo did not meet until early September, she probably was no more than three months pregnant in late December. Paolo was not Elena Adelaide's father and Elise was not her mother unless she conceived Elena earlier in Milan or Venice, an unlikely possibility.

If not Mary, Claire, or Elise, the mother of Elena Adelaide could be associated with the mysterious lady, the "Incognita" whom Medwin asserted arrived in Naples the same day as Shelley. Although Medwin's accounts of the lady have been dismissed by some biographers as either myth or Shelley's delusion, Dowden's 1883 "romantic guess," seconded by Richard Garnett, was that the "English lady who died in Naples . . . might have left a child in Shelley's guardianship."[38] In his Shelley biography, Dowden would not dismiss as entirely "fanciful . . . the strange story related by Medwin of the unfortunate and infatuated lady—young, married, and of noble connections—who had declared her love to Shelley." Dowden's belief that the story's very strangeness "deserves implicit credence" seems sound. He noted that Claire Clairmont told William Michael Rossetti that she knew the woman's identity and had seen her, something she later related in part to Edward Silsbee.[39] Cameron aptly stated, "Although the story sounds more like romance than reality, there was perhaps some truth to it."[40] The Corinne-like identity of the woman hangs over Shelley's life as had other figures from novels that Shelley enacted in his life. Several months after leaving Naples, Claire too read *Corinne*.[41]

In his (at least) four explicit accounts of Shelley's relationship with the mysterious lady, Medwin never revealed her name, saying her "disappearance from the world of fashion, in which she moved, may furnish to those curious in such inquiries a clue to her identity."[42] Medwin also alluded to Shelley's relationship with the mysterious lady in two of his novels, *The Angler in Wales* (1834) and *Lady Singleton* (1843). In *The Angler,* Medwin implied a love affair between the Shelley figure and the lady. In *Lady Singleton,* Lady Augusta's attempted seduction of the Shelley-like Herbert Vivian meets with his rebuff. Nora Crook has noted that Medwin used some of this same wording from *Lady Singleton* when writing about the mysterious lady in his 1847 Shelley biography.[43] After Shelley's death, Medwin discussed the story with Byron who was "equally acquainted with the story, as told to us mutually, and which he [Shelley] more than once made a subject of conversation with me during my visit at Pisa." Medwin reported that Byron said "There was a Mrs.—— once fell in love with Shelley for his verses."

Medwin's accounts, including the lady's death in Naples, are believable despite the reconstructed conversations. With its exotic, Corinne-like quality, it is perhaps the most Shelleyan of all stories told about him, reflecting his attraction to the secret and hidden. Who was the mysterious lady and what was her relationship to Elena Adelaide? Cameron conjectured from Medwin's information that "Mrs.——" was from a famous titled family, apparently married to a commoner.[44] It is possible that Shelley was asked to assume responsibility for the infant he called his "Neapolitan charge."

An intriguing but inconclusive link to the mysterious lady and Elena Adelaide, first suggested by Roe and discussed by Cameron and Stocking,[45] involves Lady Charlotte Susan Maria Campbell Bury (1775–1861) and her daughters. Lady Charlotte, youngest daughter of the Duke of Argyll and the Duchess of Hamilton, was remarkable for her beauty and her passion for belle lettres. She was an early patroness of Sir Walter Scott who, with Monk Lewis, frequented her Edinburgh parties in the early 1800s. Later the anonymous author of a diary critical of the royal court, Lady Charlotte wrote romantic novels. The first, *Self-Indulgence* (1812), was followed by others with such titles as *Flirtation* and *The Divorced.* In her long travel poem, *The Three Great Sanctuaries of Tuscany* (1833), considered Shelleyan in tone and imagery, she omits mentioning Shelley but cites Milton, Scott, and Byron.[46] Through her friend, Oxford's Charles Kirkpatrick Sharpe, whom Shelley may have seen in Edinburgh, Lady Charlotte was familiar with Shelley's writing at the time of his expulsion from Oxford. Widowed with six daughters and two sons in 1809, Lady Charlotte Campbell became Lady-In-Waiting (1809–1814) to the Princess of Wales, later Queen Caroline. Lady Charlotte's travels on the Continent coincide with the three European trips Shelley made in 1814, 1816, and 1818–1822.[47]

In 1814, the year Medwin said that Shelley was first approached by the lady, thirty-nine-year-old Lady Charlotte Campbell left Princess Caroline's service, taking her children to Geneva, Genoa, Milan, and Lausanne.[48] She was back in London in late 1815, where her eldest daughter Eliza had married (September 1815) Sir William Gordon Cumming, baronet. Returning to Italy with her children in 1817, Lady Charlotte married her son's tutor, Reverend Edward John Bury, in Florence on March 17, 1818. Now Lady Charlotte Bury, she was at least several months pregnant when she married. Bury, about Shelley's age, must have known him at University College where Bury received his Oxford B.A. in 1811 and his M.A. in 1817. After her first child by Bury, a daughter, died in infancy, Lady Charlotte conceived their second child in October 1818. That November she was in Rome when Shelley was there a week before going to Naples. Lady Charlotte gave birth in Rome on July 9, 1819, to a daughter, Bianca Augusta Romana, the day before the Shelleys departed Rome for Leghorn.

Lady Bury's two oldest daughters, Eliza (b. 1797) and Eleanora (b. 1799), were in Naples while Shelley was there. A younger sister, Harriet (b. 1803), wrote that in February 1818 her sister Eliza, having "bad" health, went to Naples accompanied by her unattractive baronet husband, William Gordon Cumming. Eliza, whose marital and social status matched that Medwin attributed to the mysterious lady, could have had an out-of-wedlock child in Naples, mimicking her mother's maternal behavior at that time. Lady Bury reportedly told one of her daughters in an unhappy marriage to commit adultery and get a divorce.[49] Eliza was joined in Naples in April 1818 by her romantically adventurous sister Eleanora, engaged to distant Henry Paget, Earl of Uxbridge (later 2nd Marquis of Anglesey), living in England. Eleanor had ardent suitors in Italy, including the married Duc de Berry.[50] If not Eliza, who would bear thirteen children, Eleanora was the most likely of Lady Charlotte's daughters to have been Elena Adelaide's mother. One acquaintance considered Eleanora "critically beautiful, and nothing more."[51] Her younger sister Harriet, with her mother in Florence, wrote in May 1818 of a family crisis involving her mother, Eleanora, and possibly Eliza, the latter two in Naples.[52] Eleanora left Naples sometime in 1819, returning to England to marry Henry Paget that August. She died nine years later after having three children. One of Lady Charlotte's younger daughters, Adelaide Constance, probably was no older than twelve in 1818.[53] Adelaide, the only one of the three younger sisters mentioned in Harriet Campbell's journal, undoubtedly was too young to be Elena Adelaide's mother. However, Lady Charlotte possibly influenced the child's name. She recently gave her new daughter an Italian first name (Bianca) and had named another daughter Adelaide. Lady Charlotte would dedicate her 1833 poetry volume, *Three Sanctuaries*, to Queen Adelaide, who made Lady Charlotte's daughter Emma one of her Ladies of the Bedchamber. In Florence on February 27, 1821, Harriet married Lord Tullamore, who came to Italy in 1820 with his half brother, Shelley's Eton friend James Tisdale. She became the second Countess Charleville and had five children before dying in Naples in 1848.

The Campbell–Shelley connection surfaced in Pisa late November 1820 when Claire noted that she and Mary saw the "Campbells." Medwin, also in Pisa at that time, reported "Lady Charlotte Bury's daughters visited" Emilia Viviani.[54] In Florence, May 1821, Claire met at Casa Boutourlin the first Countess Charleville and her daughter by her first marriage, Louisa Tisdale.[55] The following year, Claire would meet Elise Foggi at Casa Boutourlin.

Although it is possible one of the Campbell daughters was the mother of Elena Adelaide Shelley, no Campbells died in Naples while Shelley was in Italy. Shelley may have told Medwin the mysterious lady had died, but many years later Claire reported she knew her identity but respected the dead Shelley's wish that it be kept secret. Claire said the lady was still alive and had been pregnant by Shelley. Mary's silence on the point and Claire's vow of secrecy to Shelley are suggestive of his paternity of Elena. He made clear in his 1821 letter to Mary that what most outraged him was Elise's accusation that he would abandon his own child. He did not deny having fathered a child nor did he deny Elise's accusation of having an affair with Claire. It was to Edward Silsbee that Claire clearly implied late in her life that Shelley had fathered Elena Adelaide with the mysterious lady. Silsbee recorded, in his crimped style, the three times Claire spoke of the mysterious lady and Shelley:

Lady at Naples married a [blank space] true story was married—
Shelley "had a Scrape" with her or got into to use C's words—She was
a person I have heard of or might C. says—Mrs. S. knew it—Lines in
Dejection inspired by this event more or less. C—has the secret—says
she would tell if the person is dead thinks she must be—is under promise of secrecy—remarked Shelley had a great infatuation or weakness
for women C. has told me the lady at Naples was a person well known.
She was knowing of it—Shelley told her. She is under promise to Shelley never to divulge it. I am the first one who has ever asked her about
it Claire said today April 7th the lady spoken of at Naples is alive. She
told me before she was a person known in the world either for fame or
rank & that the Story was to her knowledge true Shelley told her of it
at the time. She never will tell the particulars & has grown shy as to saying anything abt. It—more so every time I speak to her about it & says
as she always did She is under a promise of secresy[56]

Claire, as Stocking noted, used the word "scrape" to refer to an
out-of-wedlock pregnancy.[57] The mysterious lady would have conceived sometime from mid-March to early April if Elena Adelaide
were born December 27 or slightly earlier; if she were born sometime up to late February 1819, the conception may have been as
late as early June.[58] If Shelley fathered the child in Italy, the most
likely time was between April 4 and May 1, the dates he was in Milan and around Lake Como. However, he could have been in contact with the mother in London before leaving England on March
11. If so, this would rule out the Campbell sisters as candidates for
Elena's mother. Shelley's letters to Peacock make clear he was depressed while in Milan, the time he was developing his interest in
Tasso and his madness. Some lines in two Milan letters to Peacock
were heavily crossed out. Mary ignored, but Claire reported in ex-
tenso, Shelley's "Curious adventure" with suicidal overtones during his long solitary walk at Como with his pistol. Mary made no
daily journal entries for the next week. Claire also noted Shelley's
"curious *rencontre* at the post office with a Venetian" on April 24,
an incident Mary again omitted mentioning directly.[59] As if anticipating the revised opening of *Rosalind and Helen* with Helen's "remorse" and "suffocating sorrow," Shelley, musing on Marlow,
wrote Peacock after his trip to Lake Como: "The curse of life is that
whatever is once known can never be unknown. You inhabit a spot
. . . you think you leave it, you leave it not,—it clings to you."[60]
Shelley's paternity of Elena Adelaide is consistent with his assuming legal and financial responsibility for her. In the three ref-

erences to Elena Adelaide in his letters to the Gisbornes, he refers to her as "My," never as "Our Charge." Clearly, Mary's involvement with the child was minimal. Shelley's paternity is also suggested by the act of placing himself in jeopardy with the law by registering her as his and Mary's child. He felt a deep responsibility for the child despite the increased conflict it brought to his relationship with Mary. Keeping in close touch with Elena Adelaide's situation after leaving Naples, Shelley's financial support of her (and Paolo's blackmail) had to create a repetition of Mary's resentment about his support of Allegra. Mary must have known of the child when they left Naples, as Shelley's letter to the Gisbornes in early April 1819 makes clear.[61] The false birth certificate insured Shelley's claim to Elena Adelaide and meant that upon returning to England with her she would have the legal status of a biological child. Shelley, concerned that Chancery might remove his children by Mary from him, perhaps knew that in England in 1818 legal adoption was not possible.[62] Years after Shelley's death, Medwin, angry at Mary, hinted at Shelley's paternity when he said he had materials that could incriminate Shelley concerning something that happened in Naples.[63]

When and how much did Mary know of Shelley's involvement with the mysterious lady? The gaps in Mary's journal in January and February strongly suggest she was preoccupied after Paolo and Elise departed sometime before January 22. Writing that day to Maria Gisborne, a depressed Mary commented that the "annoyances" and "care" that continued to trouble her "came from outward circumstances in a great part, and not from my self." This seems an indirect accusation of Shelley as the cause of their "care." It is likely these "outward circumstances" included some knowledge of Shelley's contacts with the mysterious lady, as well as the problems with Paolo and Elise. Mary ended this late January letter to Maria Gisborne, "the devil is getting more and more power in the world every day."[64]

Shelley probably told Mary as little as possible about the mysterious lady, just as later he kept from her details of his relationship with Emilia Viviani. Medwin wrote that had Mary "been able to disentangle the threads of the mystery" she would not have attributed his depression in Naples to "physical causes."[65] Whatever her partial ignorance, she must have been attempting to conceal what went on in Naples when, in 1839, she wrote her notes to Shelley's 1818 poems to which Medwin is referring. Mary stated that "Shelley suffered greatly in health" in Naples, including the "severe bodily pain" of his doctor's ineffective cures. She was aware of his deep depression, which he attempted to hide with the outward "appearance of cheerfulness," by having "escaped to solitude," and by writing "verses, which he hid from me from fear of wounding me." She had "unspeakable regret and gnawing remorse" for not being "more alive to the nature of his feelings, and more attentive to soothe them," thinking his "melancholy" was due to "the constant pain to which he was a martyr."[66] The severity of Shelley's depression, expressed in his verses, lends credence to Trelawny's later report that Shelley told him he attempted suicide in Naples.[67]

Beginning in Naples and extending into 1820, Shelley composed a series of melancholy verses, including the excruciating "maniac" additions to *Julian and Maddalo*. Sending these shorter verses to Ollier in late 1820, Shelley wrote, "The Julian & Maddalo & the accompan[y]ing poems are all my saddest verses raked into one heap."[68] Shelley's unrealized intention was to publish *Julian and Maddalo* with these "saddest verses," which probably included the 1818–1819 "Stanzas written in Dejection—December 1818, Near Naples," "Misery.—A Fragment" ("Invocation to Misery"), "The Past," "On a Faded Violet," "Sonnet: Lift Not the Painted Veil," and possibly the 1820 "The Question" and "Death."[69] With *Julian and Maddalo* as the centerpiece, a unifying theme was Shelley's depressive estrangement from Mary. Part of that estrangement included hiding a number of these poems from Mary. When she first published some but not all of the "saddest verses" with *Julian and Maddalo* in 1824, Mary dispersed the poems so as to keep them well "dissociated."[70] Medwin believed "Stanzas written in Dejection," "Misery.—A Fragment" ("Invocation to Misery"), and "To a Faded Violet" were written in Naples after the death of the mysterious lady.[71] However, the latter two also reflect subsequent losses during 1819.

"Stanzas written in Dejection—December 1818, Near Naples," composed as "I sit upon the sands alone" (l.15), expresses Shelley's emotional isolation and despair in repeated cadences that echo the sea's recurring "tone" that "Arises from its measured motion, / How sweet! did any heart now share my emotion." The lament, "Alas, I have nor hope nor health / Nor peace within nor calm around," leads to yearnings for death that sadly anticipate his actual fate:

Yet now despair itself is mild,
Even as the winds and waters are;
I could lie down like a tired child
And weep away the life of care
Which I have borne and yet must bear
Till Death like Sleep might steal on me
And I might feel in the warm air
My cheeks grow cold, and hear the Sea
Breathe o'er my dying brain its last monotony.

(28–36)

Shelley's closing words, " . . . for I am one / Whom men love not, and yet regret," evoked Baudelaire's admiration.[72]

In February, after a day trip to Caserta, they visited Lago d'Agnano's extinct volcanic crater where Shelley stopped the guides from demonstrating that dogs could suffocate from carbon dioxide rising from the grotto. Continuing on, they encountered King Ferdinand.[73] Despite the rain, on February 23 the Shelleys set off for the Greek temples at Paestum. Five miles from Paestum, a swollen river forced them to abandon their carriage and walk. Spending only two hours among the ruins, Shelley later explained to Peacock the architectural differences among each of the three temples. Closing their three-day journey, they revisited Pompeii before returning to Naples.

Shelley possibly visited Pompeii again with Charles MacFarlane a day or two later. During the Shelleys' final visit to the Royal Museum on February 26, MacFarlane, also there, heard "an unmistakable and most interested-looking English gentleman" speaking of a statue's "gracefulness" in a "tone of voice . . . peculiarly soft and touching." Shelley, "thin" and "pale," looked "in delicate health . . . his eye was rather sunken or hollow, but at the same time uncommonly quick, brilliant, and glancing." Despite looking sad, Shelley's "melancholy frequently irradiated with liveliness and even joyfulness." Dressed "negligently" but "neatly," Shelley, despite "personal peculiarities," was obviously "a true thoroughbred English gentleman." He and MacFarlane conversed "as if we had been old acquaintances."

MacFarlane learned Shelley's name the next day when the two were formally introduced on the Via Toledo by Dr. Roskilly. MacFarlane recalled riding with an "exhilarated" Shelley to Pompeii in a *calesso* they hired, drawn by two black horses. After touring Pompeii, Shelley's mood darkened as they sat talking on a lava rock near the water watching the sun set over the sea. MacFarlane later thought Shelley's somber mood matched that in "Stanzas written in Dejection." However, returning to Naples, Shelley joked with the Italian driver and, stopping in Torre Annunciata, he became intrigued with a machine making pasta. Approached by a group of beggars, Shelley gave them all his coins. When MacFarlane commented "poor creatures," Shelley replied, "they are happier than I" and probably "happier than you." Shortly after Shelley left Naples Roskilly told MacFarlane that he "was in a very poor way when he started on the journey."[74]

Mary, writing to Maria Gisborne the day before Shelley adopted Elena Adelaide, had no plans to return to Naples. She said that after three months in Rome, they would "be at Florence in the summer" and hoped the Gisbornes would join them.[75] Shelley was more ambiguous about their future address after Rome. Writing the day of Elena Adelaide's birth registration and baptism, he told Ollier that after three months he would use his permanent Italian mailing address, "Mr. Gisborne, Livorno."[76] Before long, their plan was to return to Naples.

Shelley's feverish Elena Adelaide activity February 27 delayed their departure from Naples the next day until two o'clock. Paolo's replacement, Vincenzo Gavita, drove their carriage pulled by the horses Shelley now owned. Stopping that night at Capua, Mary wrote in her journal, "a most tremendous fuss."[77] That Mary had never characterized a quarrel with Shelley "tremendous" indicates strong feelings were vented. Seventeen years later, revisiting this quarrel, she wrote in her novel *Lodore* that the Shelley-like Saville, after leaving Naples for Rome with his Neapolitan wife, is attacked by her in an inn in a "jealous freak" involving a "concealed . . . sad truth."[78] Perhaps Shelley, in another fait accompli, waited until they reached Capua to tell Mary of his illegal action the night before in claiming the child as theirs. Subsequent events revealed that Shelley had made financial arrangements for Elena Adelaide's care before leaving Naples and intended to return by June to include her within his family.

6

Roman Tragedy and Creativity

AFTER CAPUA, THE SHELLEY ENTOURAGE STAYED AT THE INN IN Gaeta an extra day, strolling the seashore and woods. In Terracina, Shelley was impressed by the "precipitous conical crags of immense height" but Mary, several weeks pregnant, found the next day's trip to Velletri "most fatiguing."[1] Passing through Albano, they arrived in Rome the evening of March 5 and found temporary lodgings at La Villa di Parigi. Claire resumed her journal on March 7, the day they moved into rooms in the Palazzo Verospi at 300 Corso, a hub of the city's social and intellectual scene.[2]

Sightseeing began the day they moved into the Corso. In quick succession they revisited the Colosseum, St. Peter's, and the Vatican Museum. They made the first of many drives to the Villa Borghese and its Gardens, and walked to the Capitol, the Forum, the Trevi Fountain, and the Pantheon. Revisiting the Pantheon at night, they were impressed by seeing the moon through the dome's aperture, its yellow rays illuminating the floor. Shelley considered the Pantheon's coffered dome "the visible image of the universe . . . the perfection of its proportions [is like] the unmeasured dome of Heaven."[3] His fondness for sculpture brought them frequently to the statue gallery in the Capitol Museum.

Soon the three paid the first of many evening calls on their neighbor at 310 Corso, sixtyish Signora Marianna Candida Dionigi. A talented artist, writer, and honored member of ten academies, she soon had them listening with rapt appreciation to the "Singing Boys" at Mass in St. Peter's. Shelley, delighted after hearing the *Miserere* sung at a private concert, later was disappointed they could not get tickets for its public performance during Holy Week in the Sistine Chapel.[4] Mary found Signora "very old—very miserly & very mean,"[5] but Shelley and Claire enjoyed her frequent evening *conversazioni* or salons accompanied by her Spartan refreshment, cold water.

116

Their social life included two calls by Lord Guildford, whom Byron called an "aged nondescript."[6] Claire's journal reveals their visits to the Palazzo Doria's picture galleries and the Baths of Caracalla. Passing Nero's villa on the Palatine, they met Pius VII, "on the brink of the Grave," whom previously they had seen in St. Peter's.[7] Amid all this sightseeing, Mary, "dreadfully tired," wrote Marianne Hunt hinting about her pregnancy and noting that three-year-old William now spoke more Italian than English.[8]

Amid this March sightseeing, all three continued their reading and separate artistic pursuits. Claire resumed music lessons, Mary took drawing lessons, and Shelley, immersed again in Lucretius, Plutarch, and the plays of Euripides, began three months of intense creativity.

One monument that especially intrigued Shelley was the Triumphal Arch of Titus, commemorating the Roman victory over Jerusalem. He described it twice in his long letter to Peacock and a third time in his notebook. Its scenes "of Hebrew desolation" depicted the Roman "barbarous and enraged soldiery" with "captives in every attitude of humiliation & slavery." Shelley wryly commented that monuments are designed to express "that mixture of energy & error which is called a Triumph . . . Rome is no more than Jerusalem."

The Baths of Caracalla provided a secluded retreat when Shelley soon resumed *Prometheus Unbound.* His letter to Peacock made clear that Caracalla's physical beauty stimulated his creativity. With its "towers & labyrinthine recesses hidden & woven over by wild growth of weeds & ivy . . . Never was any desolation more sublime & lovely." Severn's famous retrospective idealized portrait of Shelley, pencil in hand and perched high among the ruins, reflected what Shelley wrote in the Preface to *Prometheus Unbound:* "This Poem was chiefly written upon the mountainous ruins of the Baths of Caracalla, among the flowery glades, and thickets of odiferous blossoming trees, which are extended in ever widening labyrinths upon its immense platforms and dizzy arches suspended in the air. The bright blue sky of Rome, and the effect of the vigorous awakening spring in that divinest climate, and the new life with which it drenches the spirits even to intoxication, were the inspiration to this drama."

Shelley had begun parts of acts II and III in the final months of 1818, but most of these two acts were composed in less than thirty days in Rome during March and April 1819. After this prodigious pace of composition, he wrote Peacock in early April that *Prometheus Unbound* "is just finished" and he would send it "in a month of two." However, later in 1819 he would compose a fourth act and add "lyrical insertions" to earlier acts.[9] Continuing his *annus mirabilis*, he completed *Julian and Maddalo* and *The Cenci* during the summer. Before the end of October he had composed the ninety-one stanzas of *The Mask of Anarchy*, the long *Peter Bell the Third*, and *Ode to the West Wind*, and later wrote act IV of *Prometheus Unbound*.

That this sustained period of creativity occurred during the warm season from March through October 1819 is characteristic of Shelley's poetic productivity. Eighteen of his twenty longest poetic works were begun (or resumed) during warm months; only *Epipsychidion* was started in winter, during a mild, pleasant period in Pisa. Mary commented, "The extreme heat always put Shelley in spirits."

Shelley's productivity in Rome perhaps was fostered by Mary's being pregnant, as at Marlow when he composed *Laon and Cythna*. He also was working under something of a time deadline. Less than a month after arriving in Rome they decided to return to Naples by May. After writing Peacock March 23 that he had "no more than a few months" to be inspired by the artistic beauty of Rome, he wrote two weeks later that they would return to Naples "in a month or six weeks" and probably stay until early 1820. Writing to the Gisbornes of these new plans, Shelley invited them to come to Naples, knowing they undoubtedly would not. He wrote that a "combination of circumstances which Mary will explain to you, leads us back to Naples in June, or rather the end of May, where we shall remain until the ensuing Winter. We shall take a house at Portici or Castel a Mare until late in the Autumn."[10] These two small coastal towns south of Naples could provide seclusion from prying English and Neapolitans, forestalling rumors when Elena Adelaide joined the family. Mary wrote to Leigh Hunt, "In a couple of months we shall return to Naples where circumstances will keep us a long time."[11]

Mary, not fully forthcoming, wrote Maria Gisborne about what Shelley had called the "combination of circumstances" taking them back to Naples. Mentioning neither Shelley's health nor Elena Adelaide, she said, "one reason for going" was her pregnancy. An "eminent English surgeon" was to be in Naples and she desired his presence for her pregnancy and childbirth. They would stay "all the summer and perhaps the autumn somewhere along the shores of the Bay." Mary then mentioned a more ominous circumstance taking them from Rome: "We are delighted with Rome, and nothing but the Malaria would drive us from it for many months."[12] By late April, Mary wrote the Gisbornes that they had moved up the date of their departure for Naples to May 7, explaining it was for health reasons as "The physicians prognosticate good effects to Shelley from a Neapolitan summer—he has been very unwell lately & is very far from well now." Their intention to live near Pompeii in Castellammare probably involved the medicinal springs Shelley sought. Mary vainly urged the Gisbornes to join them there as "we shall most likely live a solitary life & not see a single creature."[13] The physician Mary wanted was the renowned Scottish surgeon then practicing in Rome, Dr. John Bell. He planned to be in Naples because his celebrated patient, Princess Pauline Borghese, Napoleon's sister, would be there.

Shelley had arrived in Rome suffering and questioning Dr. Roskilly's painful treatment. Seeking an exceptional physician with progressive ideas, Shelley called on Bell two weeks after arriving in Rome.[14] Both men had sought exile in Italy after being ostracized for advanced views and Bell's wife's description of her husband could be that of Shelley: "he would readily give his last guinea, his time and his care, to any who required them."[15] Returning Shelley's call, Bell became the family's physician and possibly countermanded Roskilly's painful treatment. Experienced in cutting for kidney stone, Bell may have suspected Shelley's pain was a nephritic disorder for which he prescribed a diuretic. Among Bell's extensive prescriptions written in Mary's journal was an opiate in the form of "a strong cordial."[16] Claire wrote to Byron that Bell ordered Shelley "to pass the summer at Naples" and if "any consumptive symptoms" were present "by the approach of next winter he must pass the cold season at Tunis."[17] Consumption, a somewhat vague diagnosis, included emaciation as well as pulmonary problems. Subsequent evidence suggests Shelley's longstanding lung complaints may have involved a tubercular disease that later was in remission.[18]

Shelley told Peacock his "spirits [are] not the most brilliant in the world, but that we attribute to our solitary situation." He could not contemplate returning to England even though he missed his friends, whom he tallied as "you Hogg & Hunt." All the rest "who know or hear of me" regard him "as a rare prodigy of crime & pollution whose look might even infect." Mary occasionally called on Mrs. Bell and a Mr. Davies accompanied them to the Vatican Easter festivities. Claire received some attention from men, including Signora Dionigi's son.[19]

Mary's melancholy lifted somewhat in mid-March when she wrote to Marianne Hunt, "now I begin to live." However, by early April she confided to Leigh Hunt that she suffered "ten times" more "from ill spirits" in Italy than before. Not acknowledging anger toward Shelley, she vented her displeasure about Hogg. She felt Bell was helping Shelley but the "myriad of medecines" were less beneficial than the "bright sun of the blue sky" as cold "casts him back."[20] Still anxious about the lawsuit against her father, Mary wrote Maria Gisborne of being "so devoured by ill spirits, that I hardly know what or where I am." Her great consolation was precocious William, no longer "Willmouse," but "Will-man" or "little Will."[21]

Mary was in a writing lull as Shelley continued with *Prometheus Unbound.* Her successful Promethean myth, *Frankenstein,* was still presumed to be Shelley's. In William Hone's 1819 verse parody about "the Vampyre crew" that "hatched" *Frankenstein,* the "wretch abhorred" monster was attributed to what "shuddering Sh——y saw in a horrid dream." Byron, informing his publisher Murray that *Frankenstein* was by Mary, not Shelley, thought it "a wonderful work for a Girl of nineteen—*not* nineteen indeed—at that time."[22]

Completing the draft of act III of *Prometheus Unbound* in early April, Shelley quickly turned to *Julian and Maddalo* and *The Cenci.* Realizing that the idealized, classical, and abstract style of *Prometheus Unbound* would limit its audience, these new works, with more "natural" language, would have people caught in such excruciating human crises as insanity, incest, and parricide. Shelley probably wrote most of *Julian and Maddalo* in Rome beginning in March 1819, leaving blank pages for much of the maniac's soliloquy which he returned to and finished in August.[23]

Shelley's fascination in Leghorn with the incestuous and parricidal story of Beatrice Cenci was reactivated in April in Rome, the home of the Cenci family. The story was much in the air as a source for tragic drama. Stendhal, in Italy while Shelley was there, later wrote *Les Cencis.* Accompanied by Mary and Claire, Shelley saw at the Palazzo Colonna the reputed portrait of Beatrice Cenci, supposedly by Guido Reni. One of two "Beatrice" portraits they saw in Rome, it was neither of Beatrice nor by Reni. Mary noted that

"Shelley's imagination became strongly excited" and he urged her to write a tragedy about Beatrice. Feeling her "incompetence," she "entreated him to write it instead."[24] However, Mary soon began her own story of father–daughter incest, *Mathilda*.

Visiting the Cenci Palace in the Jewish ghetto of Rome, Shelley found it a "vast and gloomy pile of feudal architecture." His particular interest was "a passage, dark and lofty and opening into gloomy subterranean chambers." A few days later, Mary noted, Shelley "writes his tragedy."[25]

Claire, re-reading the Cenci story, could not resist comparing Byron to Count Cenci, who had raped his daughter, Beatrice. She wrote Byron, "I am sorely afraid to say that in the elder Cenci you may behold [yourse]lf some twenty years hence but if I live Allegra shall never be a Beatrice."[26] Claire answered a letter from Mrs. Hoppner, who wrote that a wealthy English widow had offered to adopt Allegra if Byron renounced his claim to her, which he refused to do.[27] Claire, writing to Byron of her guarded support of the widow's proposal and chiding him about his wild mistress, the Fornarina,[28] was unaware that Byron a month earlier wrote to Hobhouse, "I am in love—and tired of promiscuous concubinage—& have now an opportunity of settling for life." He had fallen in love with Countess Teresa Gamba Ghiselli Guiccioli of Ravenna, only nineteen and the third wife of Count Guiccioli, almost forty years her senior.[29]

In mid-April, signs of ill health appeared in the Shelley household. Dr. Bell called and Mary noted Shelley was very "unwell." Quickly well enough to walk to the Capitol with Mary, Shelley soon received a most welcome visit from Sir William Drummond, the skeptical philosopher he esteemed and whose treatise, *Academical Questions*, he cited in *Queen Mab*.[30] After Dr. Bell called repeatedly, Mary wrote to Maria Gisborne in late April, "We already begin to feel or think we begin to feel the effects of the Roman air—producing colds—depression & even fever to the feeblest of our party."[31] Their plan to soon go to Naples was still in force but Claire much later reported that when Dr. Bell told them to leave Rome by May 1, Shelley refused.[32]

This decision not to return to Naples was a fateful change they would deeply regret. What led Shelley to veto the move is unknown. There is no record of his having any contact with Lady Charlotte Bury, living in Rome and about to give birth. On April 23, Mary and Claire, during one of their frequent drives in the Borghese Gardens, spotted their old acquaintance Amelia Curran, last seen in the Godwin home in early 1818. Having first gone to Italy in 1814 to study painting, she now resided in Rome, probably supplementing her modest inheritance by painting portraits of English visitors.[33] The next day, the Shelleys called at her home, 64 Via Sistina, at the top of the Spanish Steps. She was out but returned their call on the twenty-seventh, Claire's unnoticed twenty-first birthday. Mary and Claire began spending time each day with Amelia. Claire, reading *Corinne*, sat for her portrait by Amelia Curran on May 5 and 6 but detested the likeness, destined to hang in Newstead Abbey, Byron's ancestral home. Their lease at 300 Corso expired May 7 and instead of leaving for Naples the Shelleys moved next door to Amelia at 65 Via Sistina, the last house on the Trinita dei Monti.[34]

Shelley sat for Amelia Curran on May 7 and 8, but the portrait, which neither the artist nor Mary liked, was unfinished until after his death. It has become the misleading image by which so many have misperceived Shelley. Amelia then successfully painted William, his pink cheeks, delicate mouth, and large eyes a melding of each parent's best features. Mary's portrait, begun in late May, displeased her as making her "a great dowdy."[35] If Shelley stayed in Rome to provide some support for their artist friend by having the family portraits painted, it was his most tragic example of charity.[36]

Explaining to Maria Gisborne why they planned to "stay another month in Rome," Mary said "an old friend . . . has induced us to stay longer." Shelley found "the air of the Corso" did not agree with him and "the Trinita dei Monti . . . is the best air in Rome." Mary was anxious to retrieve any letters Maria might have forwarded on to Naples.[37] In this brief period of misplaced optimism, Mary enjoyed Amelia's company. Shelley, probably adding to *Julian and Maddalo*, perhaps was loathe to leave Rome just at that time. On May 23, he went alone to Albano, perhaps searching for a healthier place in the hills. At the end of May, Mary wrote to Maria Gisborne that Bell had advised them to "pass the summer in as cool a place as possible" because of William, "who is so very delicate—and we must take the greatest possible care of him this summer."[38] In a story she wrote later, Mary identified Albano as a place to recover from "the mal'aria fever" contracted in Rome.[39]

They now gave up on Naples. Dr. Bell's plans had changed when Princess Borghese cancelled going to Naples for Bagni di Lucca. Mary, determined to have Bell rather than an Italian doctor attend her for the baby she expected in October, told Maria Gisborne that they would go to Bagni di Lucca, Lucca, or the Baths of Pisa. Assuming William was well enough, they planned to leave for Lucca on June 7. She thought they likely would winter in Pisa, recommended by Bell for Shelley's health.[40]

The day before moving to Via Sistina, Shelley apparently was involved in another strange episode, perhaps a panic reaction. Both Mary and Claire wrote in their journals that Shelley had an "adventure at the Post Office" on May 6, *not* the similar adventure Medwin recounted in his biography that took place a year later in the Pisa post office. Both this post office incident and the one in Pisa, but probably not the earlier encounter in the Milan post office, were minor versions of the Keswick and Tanyrallt panic reactions. Mary and Claire called this Rome incident an "adventure," not an attack, suggesting Shelley had not been physically threatened.[41] It is perhaps significant that three Italian episodes—each about a year apart—occurred at post offices, where Shelley probably received upsetting news not relayed to either Mary or Claire. The nature of this Rome post office "adventure"—real or fantasized—is unknown but it led Shelley to move the family the next day to Via Sistina.[42] Under the guise of better air, he perhaps felt more secure next to Amelia Curran's residence. The day they moved, after his first sitting for Amelia, he took an evening walk with the family and Dr. Bell.

A more ominous event occurred two days after Shelley's trip to Albano when, on May 25, Mary noted, "William is not well." On May 30, she wrote Maria Gisborne of his "dangerous attack of worms" but the past two days he was "convalescent."[43] Dr. Bell called every day from May 27 to June 1 leaving prescriptions; Mary recorded in her journal that little William received strong purgatives to treat his worms.[44] On June 2, Mary noted, "William becomes very ill in the evening" and Claire recorded Bell called three times and "I sit up with Willy." Never robust, he probably was weakened by his attack of worms and by the treatment he endured. William apparently had contracted malaria, part of the epidemic that intermittently swept Rome in 1819, 1820, and 1821.[45] Thought literally to be caused by "bad air," malaria was the disease Mary had feared might drive them from Rome; unfortunately it had only lifted them from the Corso to the higher air atop the Spanish Steps. On June 3 a desperately hopeful Mary noted that William was "very ill but gets better in the evening" and that Amelia Curran called. It was Mary's last journal entry for two months. On this day, because of her "dreadful anxiety," Mary had Claire write to Maria Gisborne about William's condition, which Claire described as "a complaint of the Stomach." Two days later, Mary added to the letter that "William is in the greatest danger . . . Yesterday he was in the convulsions of death and he was saved from them. . . . The misery of these hours is beyond calculation—The hopes of my life are bound up in him." She said Shelley was more exhausted than she from watching over their son.[46] William died June 7 "at noon-day," as Claire noted in her journal. Shelley had watched over William for sixty hours without sleep until death came.[47]

Mary's moving account of the ordeal of William's death in her 1826 novel, *The Last Man*, described their unceasing vigil for a fortnight until "without convulsion or sigh, the frail tenement was left vacant of its spiritual inhabitant." She closed her story, "I was a fool to remain in Rome all this time: Rome noted for Mal'aria, the famous caterer of death."

William's death devastated Mary. Only twenty-one, she had lost her third child, the son who was her most cherished offspring. Her depression, having lessened somewhat, now intensified. Shelley, too, deeply felt William's death, writing Peacock that his "greatly improving" health had suffered "a relapse."[48] Chancery had deprived him of his two children by Harriet and now little William was his third child by Mary to die. His tender feelings toward William were expressed in response to Hogg's letter of condolence: "He had lost all shade of ill-temper, and had become affectionate and sensible to an extraordinary degree, his spirits had a very unusual vivacity—it was impossible to find a creature more gentle and intelligent.—His health and strength appeared to be perfect; and his beauty, the silken fineness of his hair, the transparence of his complexion, the animation and deep blue colour of his eyes were the astonishment of everyone. The Italian women used to bring each other to look at him when he was asleep."[49]

William was buried the day after his death in the Protestant Cemetery near the pyramid of Cestius. Shelley drew in his manuscript notebook a pair of eyes overlooking a pyramid and asked Amelia Curran to design a grave monument, "a mere pyramid."[50] Some weeks later, Amelia had a touch of malaria and William's grave marker was never completed. Shelley immediately wrote Peacock of William's death, asking him to tell "all my friends" as it was "a great exertion" to write. He added, "it seems to me as if,

hunted by calamity as I have been, that I should neve[r] recover
any cheerfulness again." He told Peacock they would depart for
Leghorn the next day, having written the Gisbornes to lease them
a house for a month.[51] Leaving Rome for the last time on June 10,
they began a sad week's journey north to Leghorn. Only Claire's
brief account of the journey survives. They returned to the lovely
waterfall at Terni and went on to Lake Trasimeno, arriving in
Leghorn June 17.[52]

Shelley carried to Leghorn the manuscripts and continuing
ideas for the unfinished *Prometheus Unbound, The Cenci,* and *Julian and Maddalo,* the creative legacy of three months in Rome before disaster struck. The diversity of Shelley's poetic genius leaps
out in the differences among these three works. *Prometheus Unbound,* subtitled *A Lyrical Drama,* has prompted musical analo-
gies, its operatic scenes and aria-like passages deepening Shelley's radical message of social and political change from the
earlier *Queen Mab* and *Laon and Cythna. The Cenci,* written in a
contrasting mode, is a tragic, historically based drama whose psychological subtlety is carried by what Shelley called "matter-of-
fact" calamitous human actions.[53] Written to appeal to the public,
Shelley wanted it staged with a particular lead actress in mind. *Julian and Maddalo,* building upon the introspection of *Alastor,* is an
intensely private poem of the most personal anguish. Shelley
wrote to Ollier that *Julian and Maddalo* was not to be printed with
Prometheus Unbound. It was in a "different style, in which I am
not yet sure of myself, a *sermo pedestris,* an ordinary conversation
but still a sermon with a message, a way of treating human nature
quite opposed to the idealism of that drama."[54]

Shelley's writing pace did not slacken after William's death. In
August, turning from *Prometheus Unbound* to darker themes, he
completed *The Cenci* and probably the additions to the maniac's
soliloquy in *Julian and Maddalo.* In early September he wrote Ollier that *Prometheus Unbound* was "long finished." Act IV, if not
yet begun, awaited composition in November and December,
about the time their new child was expected.[55]

Shelley recognized the originality of *Prometheus Unbound* in his
early April letter to Peacock: "It is a drama with characters &
mechanism of a kind yet unattempted; & I think the execution is
better than any of my former attempts."[56] The "mechanism" was
to have the drama's characters represent different aspects of the
human psyche, making *Prometheus Unbound* "wholly a psycho-

drama."[57] *Prometheus Unbound* is Shelley's most ambitious effort to create through poetry a metapsychology, a depiction of the structure and function of the human mind.[58]

Shelley's special fondness for *Prometheus Unbound* was expressed in letters to his frustrating, uncommunicative publisher, Charles Ollier: "It is in my judgment, of a higher character than any thing I have yet attempted; and is perhaps less an imitation of any thing that has gone on before it. . . . a poem in my best style . . . the most perfect of my productions . . . the best thing I ever wrote . . . my favourite poem." He urged Ollier "to pet him and feed him with fine ink and good paper."[59] Shelley reportedly later said: "If that is not durable poetry, tried by the severest test, I do not know what is. It is a lofty subject, not inadequately treated, and should not perish with me. . . . It is original; and cost me severe mental labour. Authors, like mothers, prefer the children who have given them the most trouble."[60] Recognizing it would lack popular appeal, he told Hunt it was "written only for the elect," to Ollier that it would sell "twenty copies," and to John Gisborne that "it was never intended for more than 5 or 6 persons." He soon heard the criticism that *Prometheus Unbound* was too obscure. Hunt, in 1821, apologized to Shelley for not reviewing the difficult *Prometheus Unbound*, saying it was too abstract to be recommended to general readers.[61] Godwin did not finish it and Peacock considered Shelley's poetry too full of "day-dreams and nightmares."

However, Shelley wanted his *Prometheus Unbound* to have a sharper political edge than that of Aeschylus. Rejecting Aeschylus's compromising reconciliation between Prometheus and Zeus, Shelley's Prometheus would be victorious over the tyrant Jupiter. In his Preface, Shelley also rejected Milton's Satan from *Paradise Lost* in favor of the "more poetical" Prometheus because Satan had "taints of ambition, envy, revenge, and a desire for personal aggrandisement." Moreover, those with "religious feeling" render Satan into "something worse." Writing the last half of his Preface in October after reading the savage review of *Laon and Cythna* in the April 1819 *Quarterly Review,* an incensed Shelley saw himself attacked as one of the "miserable crew of atheists" who, borrowing from Wordsworth's "religious mind," had "degraded and perverted" the older poet's "pure and holy" poetry.[62] Alluding to Wordsworth and Byron, Shelley asserted that the writings of "a great contemporary" can no more be excluded than "all that is lovely in the visible universe." Having translated *Prometheus Bound* for Byron in Geneva, Shelley knew Byron's shorter, more pessimistic "Prometheus" ode that Mary transcribed.[63]

In his Preface, Shelley acknowledged having, "what a Scotch philosopher characteristically terms, 'passion for reforming the world:' ... For my part I had rather be damned with Plato and Lord Bacon, than go to Heaven with Paley and Malthus." Asserting "Didactic poetry is my abhorrence," his aim in poetry had been "to familiarise the highly refined imagination of the more select classes of poetical readers with beautiful idealisms of moral excellence." Perhaps criticizing Godwin's overly rational *Political Justice,* he added, "until the mind can love, and admire, and trust, and hope, and endure, reasoned principles of moral conduct are seeds cast upon the highway of life which the unconscious passenger tramples into dust."

Shelley's identification with Prometheus and his punishments was akin to his identification with Ahasuerus, the Wandering Jew. Prometheus, a god-like human fated to live forever, was persecuted and exiled for defying the father-god's authority by bringing fire to humankind and for refusing to reveal to his father—Jupiter in Shelley's drama—the prophecy about his downfall.

Prometheus Unbound, a tale of human regeneration, has the central point "that when love fails all is lost unless love can be revived."[64] Prometheus and his love, Asia, separated in act I, celebrate their reunion in act IV with joyful erotic abandon that masterfully creates the unbound feeling of the fullness of love and sexuality.[65] The fourth act, not an unnecessary afterthought, is vital to the whole drama, "a masterpiece of symmetrical structure."[66] Shelley's radical social vision was that unbinding sexual repression was essential for political freedom.

The drama opens with Prometheus enduring three thousand years being "bound to the Precipice," suffering "pain, pain ever, for ever," from "spears" of glacial ice piercing his skin, from "burning cold" chains eating "into my bones," and from the eagle's beak—infected with Jupiter's diseased saliva—tearing his heart. To resolve his oedipal dilemma, Prometheus acknowledges that, when "eyeless in hate" toward his tyrant-father Jupiter, he had placed a curse on the tyrant. Wishing to renounce the curse he has repressed, Prometheus cannot recall it even though "I hate no more." In a dialogue between Prometheus and "Thy mother," The Earth, the Phantasm of Jupiter recalls Prometheus's hateful curse:

> I curse thee! let a sufferer's curse
> Clasp thee, his torturer, like remorse;
> 'Till thine Infinity shall be
> A robe of envenomed agony;
> And thine Omnipotence a crown of pain,
> To cling like burning gold round thy dissolving brain.
>
> (I.286–91)

Upon hearing his curse, Prometheus is set upon by Jupiter's emissary Mercury and his band of obscene "fiends," the Furies, intending to inflict more pain to make Prometheus reveal his secret. Viewing the "execrable shapes" of the Furies, "ministers of pain, and fear, / . . . mistrust, and hate," Prometheus observes with Shelleyan subtlety, "Methinks I grow like what I contemplate." Still awaiting release from his sadomasochistic state, Prometheus expresses Shelley's Actaeon persona, of being "some struck and sobbing fawn" pursued and devoured by "lean dogs."

Unaware of the nature of masochism, Prometheus asks how can anything "exult in its deformity?" The Fury's reply expresses Shelley's awareness of what perverse and non-perverse love can have in common:

> The beauty of delight makes lovers glad,
> Gazing on one another: so are we.
>
> So from our victim's destined agony
> The shade which is our form invests us round
>
> (I.465–66, 470–71)

Shelley's observation—that the gratification lovers receive from perceiving the partner's pleasure is akin to the sadist's gratification from observing the humiliation, powerlessness, and pain inflicted upon the satisfied masochistic partner—has led a contemporary critic to comment, "Perhaps no other passage of Romantic poetry expresses such a profound realization of the nature of sexual perversion."[67]

The Furies' next torment is the bitter lesson of the Prometheus-like crucified Christ. In his most extended poetic commentary on Jesus, Shelley's admiration for the man is equaled by the harsh knowledge of his message's subversion by institutionalized Christianity. Commenting on this failed enlightenment of Christ—and of the French Revolution—a Fury delivers perhaps the drama's most biting lines:

> Behold an emblem: those who do endure
> Deep wrongs for man, and scorn, and chains, but heap
> Thousandfold torment on themselves and him.
>
> (I.594–96)

Prometheus remains hopeful despite hearing a Fury's words expressing Shelley's skepticism, lines Yeats echoed with deeper despair in "The Second Coming," questioning mankind's moral advancement. Shelley wrote:

> The good want power, but to weep barren tears.
> The powerful goodness want: worse need for them.
> The wise want love; and those that love want wisdom;
> And all best things are thus confused to ill.
>
> (I.625–28)

However, from the "dim caves of human thought" come Spirits, harbingers of "the soul of Love," expressing Shelley's hope for enduring poetic influence. Not from "mortal blisses" but from ". . . the aerial kisses / Of shapes that haunt thought's wildernesses" will he create "Forms more real than living man, / Nurslings of immortality!"

Buoyed by the Spirits' prophecy of the return of "Wisdom, Justice, Love, and Peace," Prometheus anticipates replacing his sexual onanism by loving intercourse with

> Asia! Who, when my being overflowed,
> Wert like a golden chalice to bright wine
> Which else had sunk into the thirsty dust.
>
> (I.809–11)

Act II mirrors act I. Asia, like Prometheus, is isolated in the wintry Indian Caucasus, awaiting her sister Panthea. Repeating Prometheus's repression in act I, Panthea can only remember the first of two dreams that will restore Asia to her lost love. Asia's transformation expresses Shelley's understanding of interrelated forms of erotic passion. With homoerotic sisterly passion, Panthea sleeps "linkèd" with Ione while dreaming of a sexual encounter with Prometheus. Panthea's dream climaxes as Prometheus's love "Steamed forth like vaporous fire," and she felt "His presence flow and mingle thro' my blood / . . . And thus I was absorb'd." Panthea's sexual dream has become the feminine counterpart of that of the *Alastor* Poet. Panthea's homoerotic experience with Ione has reawakened her sexual passion for Prometheus, which can now be transmitted to Asia. Shelley achieves this transfer through his fascination with the hypnotic power of eyes.[68] Asia asks to look into Panthea's eyes that she might "read his written soul":

> Thine eyes are like the deep, blue, boundless heaven
> Contracted to two circles underneath
> Their long, fine lashes, dark, far, measureless,
> Orb within orb, and line thro' line inwoven.

> (II.i.114–17)

Gazing into her sister's eyes, Asia receives Panthea's first dream, Prometheus's smiling face. Asia then receives a fleeting glimpse of a "shape," as Panthea recalls her unremembered second dream, the written message "O Follow, Follow!" transformed into sound as The Echoes lead Asia and Panthea to the realm of Demogorgon, Shelley's most inventive poetic creature. The lifting of repression by Prometheus and by Panthea are necessary steps in the transformation from perverse love to the mutual passion of Prometheus and Asia.

Asia and Panthea descend into Demogorgon's cave, "Like a volcano's meteor-breathing chasm." Veiled Demogorgon sits on an "ebon throne" with a "snake-like Doom coiled underneath." Demogorgon, the unknowable center of Shelley's mythic psyche, can only be described by Panthea as "a mighty darkness / Filling the seat of power" that, "shapeless," has neither "form, nor outline; yet we feel it is / A living spirit." Asia's queries to the inscrutable Demogorgon only elicit responses using her concepts. Provoked, Asia demands of Demogorgon, "Utter his name . . . Who reigns? . . . Whom calledst thou God?" Demogorgon informs her, "the deep truth is imageless," and "Fate, Time, Occasion, Chance, and Change? To these / All things are subject but eternal Love."

Undergoing her final transformation, Asia goes to meet Prometheus, who is startled by the radiant beauty of her change. Enveloped in erotic desire for Prometheus, Asia celebrates her rediscovered libidinal rapture:

My soul is an enchanted boat,
Which, like a sleeping swan, doth float
Upon the silver waves of thy sweet singing;
And thine doth like an angel sit
Beside the helm conducting it,
Whilst all the winds with melody are ringing.

(II.v.72–77)

Asia's transformation is a psychic journey backwards from the rationalistic quizzer of Demogorgon to desire-driven thought, a re-creative regression combining love and reason:

We have pass'd Age's icy caves,
And Manhood's dark and tossing waves,
And Youth's smooth ocean, smiling to betray;
Beyond the glassy gulphs we flee
Of shadow-peopled Infancy,
Through Death and Birth, to a diviner day;

(II.v.98–103)

Before Asia can reunite with Prometheus, she awaits his final transformation by Demogorgon in relation to his internalized, punishing father, Jupiter. This final coming to terms with the father is accomplished in act III when Jupiter is subdued by Demogorgon, allowing Prometheus finally to be unbound from his emotional chains. Now it is revealed that the rape of Thetis by Jupiter's "quick flames," "penetrating presence," and venomous "Numidean" snake, had produced double-gendered Demogorgon, who announces to her/his father the secret that she/he is "Mightier than thee: and we must dwell together / Henceforth in darkness." Jupiter and his "Detested prodigy" twist together like "a vulture and a snake," sinking down into the "dark void" of Demogorgon's cave of the unconscious. Demogorgon's purging of Jupiter, the psychological climax of the drama, is followed anticlimactically by Hercules's perfunctory unbinding of Prometheus, now reunited with Asia.

After the Earth gives her cave to Prometheus and Asia for their eventual lovemaking, the Spirit of the Hour receives Asia's nuptial conch shell, its "mighty music" sounding the fall of Jupiter. The view of humanity's change concluding act III is one of Shelley's finest expressions of the potential for human freedom. In each human, "sparks of love and hope" would end "common, false, cold, hollow talk / Which makes the heart deny the *yes* it breathes." Proclaiming women's freedom from this "unmeant hypocrisy . . . of self-mistrust," Shelley anticipates women "Speaking the wisdom once they could not think, / Looking emotions they once feared to feel." Gone would be "Thrones, altars, judgement-seats, and prisons" with their "Sceptres, tiaras, swords, and chains, and tomes / Of reasoned wrong, glozed on by ignorance." Beyond a time when humans no longer would be "Flattering the thing they feared, which fear was hate," Shelley builds toward his radical ultimate vision of humanity's possibilities, largely defined cautiously in negatives:[69]

> The loathsome mask has fallen, the man remains
> Sceptreless, free, uncircumscribed, but man
> Equal, unclassed, tribeless, and nationless,
> Exempt from awe, worship, degree, the king
> Over himself; just, gentle, wise: but man
> Passionless; no, yet free from guilt or pain,
> Which were, for his will made, or suffered them,
> Nor yet exempt, tho' ruling them like slaves,
> From chance, and death, and mutability,
> The clogs of that which else might oversoar
> The loftiest star of unascended heaven,
> Pinnacled dim in the intense inane.
>
> (III.iv.193–204)

Humanity's "unascended" goals are unrealized both in terms of not being fully imagined and in terms of not yet being attained.

Adding act IV in late 1819, Shelley returned to this final message to give it the firm voice of Demogorgon, the most powerful "intense inane" of his imagining. Act IV is Shelley's own testament of determined perseverance and resilience in the face of dashed hopes during the time he composed *Prometheus Unbound,* one of the most stressful periods of his life. The deaths of Clara and William, the depressive and secret events of Naples, the growing estrangement from Mary, and his painful physical symptoms were the "sad realities" against which he applied his creative powers. Begun when he was twenty-six, completed at age twenty-seven, *Prometheus Unbound,* Shelley's masterpiece, is a remarkable expression of the dire need today for envisoning a more just, humane, and loving world.

7

Leghorn's "sad reality"

DURING THEIR "MELANCHOLY JOURNEY" FROM ROME TO LEGHORN, Shelley admitted to Peacock he had "neither the health nor the spirits to take notes," twice exclaiming, "O that I could return to England!" Leghorn, initially, was to be a brief stopping place until they caught up with Dr. Bell in Florence to attend Mary's late fall delivery. Shelley had received Peacock's parcels of books containing *Nightmare Abbey* and thought the character based on himself—tower-loving Scythrop—was "admirably conceived & executed."[1]

Renewing daily social contacts with the Gisbornes and Henry Reveley, the despondent travelers decided to stay longer in Leghorn, leasing for three months the Villa Valsovano, "a little country house, in a pretty verdant scene near Livorno."[2] Amid farmland just outside the old city wall on the road to Montenero, the three-story house still has a small glass-enclosed room on the tiled terrace rooftop that Shelley called "Scythrop's tower," his study for reading and writing. Affording a panorama from the islanded Mediterranean across the plains to the Apennines, in this hot perch Shelley listened to the renditions of Rossini by "vine-dressers singing all day" and resumed writing *The Cenci*.[3] The "dazzling sunlight and heat" in Shelley's tower retreat, unbearable to others, revived his "health and spirits."[4]

Mary's depression and emotional distancing from Shelley seemingly influenced the icy imagery of "Misery.—A Fragment," possibly written in Leghorn. This was the only one of the "saddest verses" Mary delayed publishing until 1839; she may have never published it had not Medwin done so seven years earlier.[5] One of Shelley's most confessional poems, Mary as "misery" is a "Lady, whose imperial brow / Is endiademed with woe." Shelley entreats her:

> Come, be happy!—sit near me,
> Shadow-vested Misery:

Coy, unwilling, silent bride,
Mourning in thy robe of pride,
Desolation—deified!

(1–5)

Fated "Like a sister and a brother / Living in the same lone home,"
theirs was "an evil lot, and yet / Let us make the best of it." Recognizing she has "a love thou darest not utter," he catalogued her
emotional and sexual coldness in a chilling series of phrases unmatched in his poetry—"thy frozen pulses," "thine icy bosom,"
"thy lips are cold," "thine arms . . . chill and dead"—concluding
with "And thy tears upon my head / Burn like points of frozen lead."
He urged her to "Hasten to the bridal bed— / Underneath the
grave 'tis spread" as only in a "sleep that lasts alway" will their
"hearts be grown / Like two shadows into one." Another of Shelley's "saddest" verses, the sonnet, "Lift not the painted veil,"
echoed his despair of finding love.

Shelley's despondency at Leghorn over Mary's withdrawal was
starkly documented in *Julian and Maddalo* and *Athanase: A Fragment*. Her anguish over her children's deaths apparently evoked
Shelley's "A Vision of the Sea," probably written the next spring.
Inspired by storm-driven waterspouts they observed from Shelley's Leghorn tower,[6] the poem—seemingly allegorizing little
William's death[7]—depicts an anguished shipwrecked mother and
her infant in "the terror of the tempest." Aboard the battered, sinking ship, "Twin tigers" grip the "vibrating" deck and "At the helm
sits a woman more fair / Than Heaven" who "clasps a bright child
on her upgathered knee." As the ship sinks, one tiger is crushed
fighting a "sea-snake" while "A blue shark is hanging within the
blue ocean, / The fin-winged tomb of the victor." The other tiger is
dispatched when a boat appears with twelve oarsmen whose "Hot
bullets burn" in his breast. The immersed mother "grasps . . . im-
petuously" with one hand the final fragment of the ship while, with
her other hand, "she sustains her fair infant." Their precarious
fate is left unresolved.

Shelley wrote of another woman's fate in *The Cenci*. His only major work he shared with Mary during its composition, it had the realism about "character and incident" she vainly encouraged Shelley to pursue. Mary considered act V of *The Cenci* "the finest thing
he ever wrote"[8] and Godwin "was glad to see Shelley at last descending to what really passes among human creatures." Gaining

"a new idea of Shelley's powers" amid "passages of great strength," Godwin thought "the character of Beatrice is certainly excellent."[9] Shelley knew *The Cenci* was a powerful dramatic work; among his friends who prized it above all his other works was Horace Smith.

Daily visits with the Gisbornes led Maria to become "very much attracted to Shelley," according to Mary, who criticized Maria's controlling Henry Reveley as if he were still a boy.[10] Part of the problem was Claire, whom Maria Gisborne viewed as a sexual temptation for her son. Shelley, writing to Peacock, compared Maria Gisborne favorably with Mrs. Boinville except for less "elegance and delicate sensibility of . . . mind." Although reserved, she was a "democrat and atheist" whom he visited late each afternoon to read Spanish together. Under Maria's tutelage, Shelley soon was reading the plays of Calderón, whose "dramatic power" he thought approached Shakespeare's.[11]

Hearing no word from Venice in months, Claire was unaware that Byron was spending June and July in Ravenna with Teresa Guiccioli. In August, Allegra joined Byron in following the Guicciolis to Bologna, where Teresa's accommodating husband provided her lover an apartment in the family palace. Byron toyed with going to South America and wrote to his half sister that Allegra "speaks nothing but Venetian" and has "a particular liking of Music." Her mother was resuming music lessons from the best teacher in Leghorn.[12]

Shelley, nearing completion of *The Cenci* and eager to get his play on the stage before any competition, asked Peacock to negotiate its presentation at Covent Garden Theatre.[13] He told Peacock it was an "eminently dramatic" tragedy well known in Italy and "generally known among the English." He emphasized having treated the subject, father–daughter incest, with "peculiar delicacy," and included a translation of the manuscript on the Cenci family Mary had transcribed in Leghorn a year earlier. He wanted the translation affixed to the play, along with a print of Beatrice.[14] Knowing the play's success was nil if he were known to be its author, Shelley asked Peacock "to preserve complete incognito" and "Of course you will not shew the Mss. to any one." He wanted Eliza O'Neill to play Beatrice, as the part "precisely fitted her," but expressed little hope Edmund Kean would be available to play Count Cenci. Peacock, recalling how enthralled Shelley was with Miss O'Neill when they saw her act, believed he drew the character of Beatrice with her in mind.[15]

Mary wrote Amelia Curran in mid-September that Shelley's tragedy was *"a deep secret,"* only Peacock knew about it in England and "with S.'s public & private enemies it would certainly fall if known to be his." Eliza Westbrook "alone would hire enough people to damn it—it is written with great care & we have hopes that its story is sufficiently polished not to shock the audience."[16] When Shelley wrote Ollier in mid-October stating he was sending him a box with copies of the printed drama, he asked him not to open the box. Neither Ollier nor "others" were to see its contents.[17] Shelley previously had written to Hunt about *The Cenci*, telling him "I mean to dedicate it to you." After completing the drama, Shelley drafted his warm Dedication to Hunt, predating it "Rome, May 29. 1819."[18]

Seeking a wider audience, Shelley said in his Dedication that *The Cenci* was a deliberate break from his earlier published work, which had "been little else than visions which impersonate my own apprehensions of the beautiful and the just." These works had "literary defects incidental to youth and impatience; they are dreams of what ought to be, or may be. The drama which I now present to you is a sad reality." Further, he would "lay aside the presumptuous attitude of an instructor." He wrote in his long Preface of having taken "great care" to avoid "mere poetry," there being "scarcely . . . a detached simile." He had "written more carelessly; that is, without an over-fastidiousness and learned choice of words." However, Shelley—always exacting about having his works printed accurately—oversaw the printing of two hundred fifty copies in Leghorn about the time he sent *The Cenci* to Peacock in September. If he sent Peacock this printed version, Shelley removed the title page with his name and the Dedication to Hunt, wanting to preserve his anonymity while the play was under consideration by the theater.[19]

Peacock, a bachelor devoted to his mother, avoided mentioning sex in his satirical works. Now employed at the East India Company and no longer Shelley's financial dependent,[20] he neither cared for *The Cenci* nor expected it to be accepted for the stage. He had advised Shelley how to handle the incest theme, a theatrical taboo, and appreciated that Shelley was feared as a genius with a dangerous pen.[21] Peacock was not surprised when the manager of Covent Garden, rejecting *The Cenci*, expressed "great admiration . . . of the author's powers, and great hopes of his success with a less repulsive subject." Drury Lane apparently also rejected

Shelley's play. Incest themes appeared on the French stage but the English government kept tighter censorship over the theater than over the press.[22] Shelley, hearing in mid-October of Peacock's distaste for the play, wrote Maria Gisborne that Peacock "is a nursling of the exact & superficial school of poetry." Shelley was still waiting in mid-December to hear if *The Cenci* had been accepted for the stage.[23] After hearing of its rejection, Shelley was "persuaded that they must have guessed at the author" but the theater manager asserted that the morally unacceptable incest theme, not the author, caused the rejection.[24]

The Tory establishment kept the feared radical's *The Cenci* off the stage, but Shelley was right when he wrote Ollier, it "will succeed as a publication."[25] The first edition, printed in Italy, sold off quickly. The London second edition (1821) made *The Cenci* Shelley's only major work to have two authorized editions in his lifetime. Evoking long critical reviews in 1820–1821, *The Cenci* garnered more response than his earlier works. Conservative critics, reviled by its "disgusting" topics, lambasted it as "a dish of carrion." Most, however, also grudgingly recognized the power of Shelley's writing and occasionally, as in *Blackwood's,* his genius. Hunt published two glowing reviews and the reviewer in the liberal *Theatrical Inquisitor* included copious quotes with his praise for the "unparalleled . . . beauty" of this "first dramatic effort."[26] Byron considered *The Cenci* "a work of power, and poetry" but found its subject "essentially undramatic" and wished Shelley had not used Jacobean dramatic form.[27] Keats, after reading *The Cenci* and marking it with many notes, wrote Shelley advising that he "might curb your magnanimity." Reportedly, an older Wordsworth thought it "the greatest tragedy of the age," altering his earlier comment, "Won't do."[28]

In 1886, years after Robert Browning was unsuccessful in having *The Cenci* performed in London, the drama was first produced by The Shelley Society in England. Government censorship still prohibited a public performance and with some difficulty a theater was found in outlying Islington. George Bernard Shaw, a Shelley Society member, commented after seeing the play, "Shelley and Shakespeare are the only dramatists who have dealt in despair of this quality."[29] *The Cenci* was produced in Paris (1891), Moscow (1919–1920), Prague (1922), and London (1922, 1926). Antonin Artaud's 1935 adaptation (with sets by Balthus) launched the Theatre of Cruelty.[30] Performances of *The Cenci* continued in the last half of the twentieth century.

Shelley's drama relates Count Francesco Cenci's forcible rape of his daughter Beatrice and her subsequent conspiracy to have him murdered. Cenci, patriarch of a rich Catholic family, exercised his sadistic, paternal phallocentric power as part of a larger corrupt collusion with Pope Clement VIII. The play opens as Cardinal Camillo tells his friend Count Cenci, "The matter of the murder is hushed up" if Cenci will give a third of his property to the Pope. In this manner, Cenci's habitual crimes enrich the Vatican coffers.

Cenci, alluding to his pending rape of his daughter, tells Camillo his aim is to enjoy his victim's soul-murder:

> The dry fixed eyeball: the pale quivering lip,
> Which tell me that the spirit weeps within
> Tears bitterer than the bloody sweat of Christ.
>
> (I.i.111–13)

Shelley felt about Count Cenci the way he did about an incest perpetrator in a Calderón play, "a prejudiced savage . . . abhorring that which is the unwilling party to his crime." Writing Maria Gisborne about reading Calderón's "perfectly tremendous" incest scene after completing *The Cenci*, he told her, "Incest is like many other *incorrect* things a very poetical circumstance."[31] For Shelley, the Cenci story was "perhaps [the most] fearful domestic tragedy which was ever acted on the scene of real life."[32]

Beatrice's rape by her father—not in Shelley's sources—was but one major change he made from the material he had read. The readily available Italian manuscripts of the "Relation of the Death of the Family of Cenci" were legends combining family fact and fiction.[33] Shelley perhaps had more than one version of the "Relation" when writing *The Cenci*. The lost "Relation" version he sent to Peacock probably was similar to the one Mary Shelley printed with *The Cenci* (not the lost Gisborne version) in 1839.[34]

To develop Cenci's evil nature, Shelley kept him alive in the first four of the play's five acts. In Pieracci's 1816 drama, *Beatrice Cenci*, the count had died when the play began.[35] Although Count Cenci is clearly the most evil person in Shelley's works, Shelley could not condone Beatrice's identification with her father's sadism and power.

Inevitably, readers identify more with Beatrice than with Prometheus; his symbolic rape by a vulture's polluted beak is eclipsed by Beatrice's real polluting punishment inflicted by her father's infected phallus. The severity of her trauma complicates the play's central moral dilemma: Was Beatrice justified in taking revenge upon her father, a revenge Prometheus renounced? A negative answer seems supported by Shelley's comments in the play's Preface and by the notion that two wrongs do not make a right. By offering no resolution of the play's moral dilemma,[36] Shelley underscores that his basic moral–artistic stance is to point out the inadequacies of conventional moral precepts. The difficult emotional demand of *The Cenci* is that we both condemn and love Beatrice, requiring us to move "beyond a conventional standard of ethical judgment."[37] The optimistic message concluding act III of *Prometheus Unbound,* tyranny's "loathsome mask has fallen," contrasts with *The Cenci*'s tragic ending; Beatrice's head will fall to the executioner's ax.

Beatrice—"with a look"—first communicated her parricidal intentions to the lying, treacherous priest Orsino, perhaps the play's most interesting character (III.i.360–61). Her powerful gaze may account for two full faces—drawn with the most detailed eyes Shelley ever sketched—in his draft notebook.[38] Wily, deceiving Orsino, goaded by his sexual fantasies of Beatrice and scheming to seduce her and promote the conspiracy to kill her father so as to get her money, remarks:

> Yet I fear
> Her subtle mind, her awe-inspiring gaze,
> Whose beams anatomize me nerve by nerve
> And lay me bare, and make me blush to see
> My hidden thoughts.
>
> (I.ii.83–87)

Orsino also commented on the power of Beatrice's self-analysis—before it was blinded by her rape—in words suggestive of Shelley's mixed feelings about his own introspective bent:

> That 'tis a trick of this same family
> To analyse their own and other minds.
> Such self-anatomy shall teach the will
> > Dangerous secrets
>
> (II.ii.108–11)

In the play's ironic dramatic crux, the Pope's Legate arrives with a warrant for Cenci's arrest and execution just after his murder by Beatrice's hired assassins. Her father's unnecessary pre-emptive murder does not faze Beatrice.[39]

In his Preface, Shelley's implicit affirmation that Prometheus was a greater figure than Beatrice underscores the tragic theme of honor which *The Cenci* shares with Calderón's plays.[40] Shelley wrote:

> Undoubtedly, no person can be truly dishonoured by the act of another; and the fit return to make to the most enormous injuries is kindness and forebearance, and a resolution to convert the injurer from his darkest passions by peace and love. Revenge, retaliation, atonement, are pernicious mistakes. If Beatrice had thought in this manner she would have been wiser and better; but she would never have been a tragic character

Shelley vindicated Beatrice somewhat; her trauma produced a flawed reality testing in which she could not judge the moral soundness of her actions.

Beatrice's brother, twenty-eight-year-old Giacomo, like twenty-seven-year-old Shelley, was the eldest son in a wealthy family whose wife, in "bitter words" complains that her husband does not adequately support her or their children. Shelley was fascinated by Giacomo, a minor figure in the "Relation," whose lines fill one-sixth of the play.[41] The scene (I.iii) portraying Cenci's perverse delight in front of guests upon receiving word of the deaths of the two exiled "disobedient and rebellious" sons he had disowned—perhaps "the most dramatic in the play"[42]—touches Shelley's own tortuous history.

Shelley reportedly said he wrote *The Cenci* "to see how I could succeed in describing passions I have never felt . . . I don't think much of it. It gave me less trouble than anything I have written of the same length."[43] Such passions include Beatrice's emotional pain and psychic disorientation following her severe sexual trauma. Beatrice "speaks wildly" to her stepmother, Lucretia: "My brain is hurt / My eyes are full of blood; just wipe them for me." Lucretia, uncomprehending, believes Beatrice has "no wound," mistaking Cenci's infected blood and semen as "only a cold dew / That starts from your dear brow . . ." (III.i.1–5). Beatrice's explicit tactual description of her father's contaminating semen must be Romantic poetry's most disturbing sexual image.[44] In poignant last words, Beatrice asks Lucretia—as they both await decapitation—to tie "My girdle for me, and bind up this hair / In any simple knot."

This was one of Shelley's two favorite scenes in the play. The other (IV.i.141–57), was the diseased curse Cenci lays upon his violated daughter. Shelley explained, "as it often happens respecting the worst part of an author's work, it is a particular favourite with me."[45] Cenci's curse is that Beatrice be infected with his venereal disease and become "encrusted round / With leprous stains" and "speckled like a toad; parch up / Those love-enkindled lips." Further, her limbs should have "loathed lameness" and her eyes become blind. The curse ends with Cenci's wish that his daughter bear his venereally disfigured infant—"A hideous likeness of herself"—who would turn hatefully against its mother and "hunt her . . . to a dishonoured grave." Either Shelley or Mary made an ink drawing in their joint notebook of the murdered Count on his bed, nail wounds in his head, eye, and throat.[46]

Alone in his tower, Shelley wrote most of *The Cenci* the first seven weeks in Leghorn. He told Peacock he was "much better" and "materially changed" since finishing it. Medwin reported that Shelley told him "it was with the greatest possible effort, and struggle with himself, that he could be brought to write *The Cenci*."[47]

Mary's dead son preoccupied her. She wrote Amelia Curran and Maria Gisborne that, having lost interest in "Everything on earth," she dwelt on little William amid the "wretchedness & despair that possesses me."[48] On August 4, Shelley's twenty-seventh birthday, Mary resumed her journal with an entry implicating her alienation from Shelley as part of her deepening depression: "We have now lived n̶o̶w̶ five years together & if all the events of the five years were blotted out I might be happy—but to have won & then cruelly lost the associations of four years is not an accident t̶h̶a̶t̶ to which the human mind can bend to without much suffering."[49]

Godwin was incensed to hear from his daughter that his letters only increased her depression. He again lectured her as "a father and a philosopher" about her unseemly "depression" which lowered her "character" and put her "among the commonality and mob of your sex." These were bitter words from the husband of suicidal Mary Wollstonecraft to her daughter. Godwin asked, "What is it you want that you have not?" As for Shelley, "You have the husband of your choice, to whom you seem unalterably attached, a man of high intellectual endowments, whatever I & some other persons may think of his morality. . . . You have all the goods of fortune." Most brutally, her only excuse for being depressed is "because a child of three years old is dead!" Unless she changed from her "selfishness and ill-humour," her "nearest connections . . . will finally cease to love you, and scarcely learn to endure you."[50]

Mary was now writing *The Fields of Fancy*, later called *Mathilda*.[51] Godwin—having praised *The Cenci*—after reading this novel of a father's incestuous feelings for his daughter, found Mary's story's subject "disgusting and deplorable" and hid the manuscript.[52]

Shelley wrote Amelia Curran in August of his "ill spirits & ill health" and of Mary's being "wretchedly depressed." Repeating this to Hunt, he said he could not expose Mary in her "state" to her "hard-hearted" father and had written Godwin for the first time in a year "to entreat him to soothe her in his next letter." The result, Shelley said, was Godwin's letter to Mary calling her husband "a disgraceful and flagrant person" who was obliged "to give him *more* money (after having given him £4,700)." Shelley had not shown Godwin's letter to Mary but had "bought bitter knowledge with £4,700" and wished "it were all yours now!"[53] Hunt, whose appreciative review of *Rosalind and Helen* had appeared in the *Examiner* in May, was the Shelleys' most supportive and active correspondent in the trying weeks after William's death.

The portrait Hunt sent to Shelley—hoping he would carry it "about with you, like the pot of Basil in Boccaccio"[54]—took almost a year to arrive in Leghorn. Shelley, a strong partisan of Boccaccio, wrote Hunt in September a lengthy appreciation of "this most divine writer" whose "more serious theories of love agree especially with mine." He added, Boccaccio's maxim, "A kissed mouth doesn't miss a chance, on the contrary, it recurs as does the moon," would benefit "the common narrow-minded conceptions of love."[55]

In mid-August, a week after finishing *The Cenci*, Shelley sent Hunt *Julian and Maddalo* for publication. Among its mysteries are the deceptive composition dates given by Shelley and Mary. She knew the complete poem by 1820 but Shelley probably concealed from her when he actually wrote the sections of the maniac's soliloquy reflecting his painful marital estrangement.[56] Shelley told Hunt he did not "particularly wish this Poem to be known as mine, but at all events I would not put my name to it—I leave you to judge whether it is best to throw it in the fire, or to publish it—So much for *self self* that burr that will stick to one." He said Hunt would recognize "two of the characters" in the poem and the maniac "is also in some degree a painting from nature, but, with respect to time and place, ideal."[57] Hunt saw through this transparent veil, despite Shelley's effort to obscure the poem by saying it was composed the previous year in Este. Shelley also tipped his hand to Ollier about the autobiographical nature of *Julian and Maddalo,* saying it was "drawn from dreadful realities."[58]

Shelley also was devious to Claire about the poem. Aware that Allegra was in the poem, Claire received Shelley's assurance that *Julian and Maddalo* "never was intended for publication."[59] Shelley asked Hunt to give the "little Poem" to Ollier "for publication but without my Name." After saying Peacock would correct the proofs, Shelley changed his mind and asked Hunt, apparently wanting to deny Peacock any further private Shelleyan marital material.

The earlier debate as to whether the maniac in *Julian and Maddalo* represented Shelley, Byron, Tasso, or a composite of them, attests to Shelley's success in veiling his agonized marital situation in the madman's soliloquy. The bitter one hundred fifty lines for which no draft manuscript exists were probably added before Shelley sent the poem to Hunt in August 1819. Not only does the madman experience actual situations in Shelley's life, the identification of Shelley as the maniac—described much like Shelley—is suggested several times by Maddalo.[60]

The maniac's soliloquy indicated he had experienced "some deadly change in love" from a woman who "had abandoned him." To hide his pain, the maniac had to "wear this mask of falshood even to those / Who are most dear," trying to avoid "more changed and cold embraces." The maniac continues, as if addressing Mary, as to why he hides his grief from her:

> "O Thou, my spirit's mate!
> Who, for thou art compassionate and wise,
> Wouldst pity me from thy most gentle eyes
> If this sad writing thou shouldst ever see,
> My secret groans must be unheard by thee;
> Thou wouldst weep tears, bitter as blood, to know
> Thy lost friend's incommunicable woe.
>
> (337–43)

To reveal the secret of his grief, the maniac, in psychotic-like discourse, converses with his hallucinated lost love in a devastating passage that exceeds the depressive icy imagery of Mary's withdrawal. She, "Death's dedicated bride," has deserted him emotionally for a "ghastly paramour," making "the tomb / Thy bridal bed." Mary at this time was writing in *Mathilda* of her depressed heroine telling her poet friend that, being "in love with death," she contemplates her "shroud" as her "marriage dress."[61]

The maniac, angry and accusatory, equates his partner with a poisonous "serpent" who turns on him and asks: "Didst thou not seek me for thine own content? / Did not thy love awaken mine?" Denying her accusation "that I am proud," the maniac argues, "Never one / Humbled himself before, as I have done!" and likens himself to an "instinctive worm" who, trampled upon, dies writhing. In the poem's most damning passage, Shelley seemingly accuses Mary of wishing he had castrated himself:

> "That you had never seen me! never heard
> My voice! And, more than all, had ne'er endured
> The deep pollution of my loathed embrace!
> That your eyes ne'er had lied love in my face!
> That, like some maniac monk, I had torn out
> The nerves of manhood by their bleeding root
> With mine own quivering fingers! so that ne'er
> Our hearts had for a moment mingled there
> To disunite in horror!
>
>   (420–28)

Continuing his complaint of her verbal abuse, he "can forget not . . . / . . . those curses." The self-pitying maniac lapses into one of Shelley's iconic self-concepts, the oversensitive, caring soul suffering undeserved abused from his mate:

> *Me*, who am as a nerve o'er which do creep
> The else-unfelt oppressions of this earth,
> And was to thee the flame upon thy hearth,
> When all beside was cold: that thou on me
> Shouldst rain these plagues of blistering agony—
> Such curses are from thy lips once eloquent
> With love's too partial praise!
>
>   (449–55)

After complaining, "I live to show / How much men bear and die not!", the maniac—in a passage for which Shelley left no draft for Mary's eyes—expressed the woman's revulsion to his physical attractiveness in their lovemaking:

"Thou wilt tell,
With the grimace of hate, how horrible
It was to meet my love when thine grew less;
Thou wilt admire how I could e'er address
Such features to love's work. . . .this taunt, though
   true,
(For indeed nature nor in form nor hue
Bestowed on me her choicest workmanship)
Shall not be thy defence: for since thy lip
Met mine first, years long past, since thine eye
   kindled
With soft fire under mine, I have not dwindled
Nor changed in mind or body, or in aught
But as love changes what it loveth not
After long years and many trials.

                                        (460–72)

Mary's verbal attacks, revealed by Shelley in *Julian and Maddalo,* were fostered by her jealous resentment over his relationship with Claire.[62] In *Mathilda,* Mary wrote of the poet, Woodville: "I called him my friend but I viewed all he did with jealous eyes. If he did not visit me at the appointed hour I was angry, very angry, and told him . . . 'You are cruel, very cruel, to treat me who bleed at every pore in this rough manner.'" Woodville responded: "beware how you injure it [my friendship] with suspicion. Love is a delicate sprite and easily hurt by rough jealousy."[63]

The poem ends as Julian, revisiting Venice, meets Maddalo's now-grown daughter who tells him that the woman who deserted the madman had returned to him two years[64] after Julian left Venice, her "imperious mien" now "meek" as if "remorse brought her low." However, she left him again, evoking Julian's characterization of her as a "tough" woman. In the final lines, Julian refuses to share with the reader the daughter's account of "how / All happen'd." His final, "but the cold world shall not know" is only partially true. The maniac's agonized feelings and thoughts are those of Shelley.

The portrait of Shelley provided by the maniac fits that in perhaps his most confessional poem, *Athanase,* probably begun before leaving England and continued in Italy through the summer of 1819. That December he sent *Athanase: A Fragment* to Ollier— the 124 lines of fair copy in his own hand—wanting it published with *Julian and Maddalo* "because it is som[ewhat the same] character as that poem."[65] Mary, initially unaware of both these poems that Shelley wanted published anonymously, later dated *Athanase* differently each time she published it as *Prince Athanase, Part I*.[66] Athanase, not a Prince in the fragment Shelley wanted published, is perhaps his most accurate, if sentimentalized, self-description as a much-traveled weak youth, prematurely gray, and deeply depressed. Having a "gentle yet aspiring mind," he was "Fearless . . . scorning all disguise." Echoing Shelley's introductory letter to Godwin, Athanase was "a child of Fortune & of Power / Of an ancoestral name the orphan chief":

> His soul had wedded Wisdom, & her dower
> Is love & justice, clothed in which, he sate
> Apart from men, as in a lonely tower.
>
> (31–33)

Athanase is not one of Shelley's more accomplished poems, due in part to his struggle with Dante's *terza rima*, later mastered in *The Triumph of Life*. Shelley's personal crisis of 1819 infuses his portrayal of Athanase who, like the maniac, suffers "grief" from a "secret pain" and "Some said that he was mad." Like the maniac, Athanase's friends "idly" "debate" his state, "Babbling vain words and fond philosophy" like Julian and Maddalo. The poem's intense isolation, despair, and disillusionment led Reiman to suggest *Athanase* expressed Shelley's precocious midlife crisis.[67] Athanase is disappointed that "he never found relief" from his altruistic, humanitarian efforts on behalf of others, including his financial generosity with "his many friends." Athanase's malaise reflects Shelley's disillusionment by mid-1819 that those toward whom he had extended himself—Mary, Godwin, Peacock, and Hunt—had treated him with hostility, insensitivity, or insufficient appreciation of his efforts.[68]

Candor is lacking in *Athanase*, with its idealized personality and contradictory passages about Athanase's knowledge of what is causing his grief. Unwilling to confide, Athanase has no "secret crime" because "his heart" understood no "ill." This moral infallibility, linked with the denial that Athanase indulged "evil joys which fire the vulgar breast," suggests the sexual basis of his grief, a sexual "withering up his prime" that leaves his "vernal spirit sere." Although protesting "He knew not" what caused his grief, Shelley speaks of Athanase's stratagems for not responding when others asked the "cause of his disquietude." If *Athanase* seemed designed to tease the reader about Shelley's undisclosed secret grief, *Julian and Maddalo* suggested the answer.

The phrase, "eyeless nightmare grief," captures Shelley's message in *Athanase*. Shelley's recurrent ophthalmia probably contributed to his fascination with blindness as symbolic castration. Blindness permeates his long translation of Euripides' *The Cyclops* he was drafting in the same notebook with *Athanase*.[69] Enticing the reader to decode his message, Shelley added a note to his completed fair copy of *Athanase:* "The Author was pursuing a fuller developement of the ideal character of Athanase, when it struck him that in an attempt at extreme refinement and analysis, his conceptions might be betrayed into the assuming a morbid character. The reader will judge whether he is a loser or a gainer by this diffidence."

The other fragments Shelley excised from *Athanase* included the Lind-like figure of Zonoras and lines about a "blight" on the "green / Leaves" of his "manhood." The draft of *Athanase* indicates the abandoned longer version was to have told of the hero's disappointment in his loved one. Like the maniac, Athanase suffers her desertion and return.[70]

Shelley's despair over Mary's withdrawal was openly expressed in lines faintly penciled in a notebook, dated "Livorno, August 1819" in which "My dearest M.," who has "left me in this dreary world alone," now "sittest on the heart of pale despair." Shelley, who "cannot follow thee," entreats her to "return." On the opposite page is a capsule verse of their sad present state:

> The babe is at peace in the womb
> The corpse is at rest within the tomb
> We begin in what we end—.[71]

Mary's *Mathilda*, begun in earnest on Shelley's birthday, has been called "a crucial biographical document, and one of the first case histories of an acute depression, the more rare for being written by the patient."[72] The poet Woodville's lovely bride Elinor died six months before he and Mathilda met, a death perhaps compounded of Harriet's death and the loss of the mysterious lady of Naples, perhaps Eliza or Eleanora Campbell. Mathilda, in her despair, becomes jealous of Woodville. Mathilda, as if she were Mary suspecting her role in *Julian and Maddalo*, unburdens her feelings of being a pawn in Woodville's career aspirations: "perhaps he is already planning a poem in which I am to figure."[73]

Shelley, seemingly not content with being drained financially by Godwin, found in Leghorn another opportunity both to dissipate hundreds more of his sorely needed pounds and to sour another relationship. He was attracted to a new water-engineering project, Henry Reveley's steamship, intended to zip from Leghorn to Genoa to Marseille. Shelley as shipping magnate was an entre-preneurial fantasy combining his enthusiasms for science, tech-nology, and water travel. By the end of September, after consulta-tion with Mary, Shelley had committed his overextended resources to the Gisbornes to finance further work on the steam engine.

Early in September, Charles Clairmont, on his way to teach in Vi-enna, arrived from Spain for a two-month visit. Shelley quickly sought to benefit from Charles's proficient Spanish, and Mary too became a Spanish scholar. They were no sooner all reading Calderón's plays when news from England turned Shelley from in-trospective to political poetry.

8

"a voice from over the Sea"

ENGLAND'S MAJOR 1819 POLITICAL EXPLOSION WAS THE AUGUST 16 Manchester Massacre in St. Peter's Field, quickly called "Peterloo," mocking the Tory government victory at Waterloo. Reading about the horrible event in early September, Shelley immediately wrote Ollier: "the torrent of my indignation has not yet done boiling in my veins." He waited "anxiously [to] hear how the Country will express its sense of this bloody murderous oppression of its destroyers." Equating the event with Beatrice's violation, he quoted to Ollier and to Peacock her contemplation of action against her father: "Something must be done . . . What yet I know not." Shelley thought "the terrible & important news of Manchester" was "the distant thunders of the terrible storm that is approaching," but doubted an armed revolt unless the country's "financial affairs" deteriorated further.[1]

Shelley soon began drafting the ninety-one ballad-like stanzas of his most powerful political poem, *The Mask of Anarchy: Written on the Occasion of the Massacre at Manchester.* Shelley told Peacock that the reformists' spokesman, Henry "Orator" Hunt, had behaved "with great spirit & coolness in the whole affair," a view Byron did not share.[2] Shelley did not mention writing the anti-government *The Mask of Anarchy,* realizing that Peacock, at the East India Company, was an adjunct of the Tory government attacked in the poem. He had written to Peacock just before hearing of Peterloo about England's "very disturbed state." Either "change should commence among the higher orders, or anarchy will only be the last flash before despotism."[3] Shelley still feared a working-class revolt would lead to greater despotism.

Peterloo "really was a *massacre* . . . without question a formative experience in British political and social history."[4] *The Mask of Anarchy* became the event's poetic capstone. The issues put forth by the reformists gathering in St. Peter's Field included those

149

Shelley enunciated in his 1812 *Declaration of Rights*: freedom of the press, the right of assembly, the right to organize politically, extension of the vote, and elimination of rotten boroughs. Manchester, like other large industrial cities, had no representation in Parliament. What Shelley correctly wrote Peacock in January 1819 from Naples employed the imagery of *The Mask of Anarchy*: "you [write] from the habitations of men yet unburied; tho the Sexton Castlereagh after having dug their graves stands with his spade in his hand evidently doubting whether he will not be forced to occupy it himself."[5] These graves were dug at Manchester. The repressive English *ancien régime* under the Prince Regent and his Tory ministers—Castlereagh, Sidmouth, and Eldon—was losing its authoritarian control in the face of widespread popular dissent. Class conflict pitted a fragmenting ruling class against a reformist working class. In between was a wavering middle class that Peterloo helped galvanize for the 1832 Reform Act. The reform revolution in 1819 was led by radical constitutionalists who, opposing the ultra-radical conspiratorial insurrectionists, promoted their cause openly in the widely circulated, inexpensive radical press.

The successful July gathering of fifty thousand in Birmingham set the stage for Manchester's August gathering, organized by "Orator" Hunt. The gentry had been surprised and threatened by the peaceable nature and discipline at the gatherings of those they considered rabble. The threatened Government's response to this rising popular movement could only be repression or concession. By 1819, only the former alternative was possible.[6]

Secret assassination plots, including the ill-fated Cato Street Conspiracy being hatched in late 1819, could be infiltrated easily and squelched, but not the openly conducted mass meetings. The Government in London allowed the rally only to quickly support the violence of the troops at St. Peter's Field. Predictably, the victims became the villains as Government repression soon began "the most sustained campaign of prosecutions in the courts in British history."[7] Indicted and jailed were not only "Orator" Hunt and the other organizers of the Manchester meeting, but leading writers and publishers who supported reform. Within months, Parliament passed the Six Acts allowing searches without warrants, limiting the size of meetings, increasing stamp duties on periodicals, and granting greater power to prosecute seditious libel. Two of these laws are still in force.

The mounted, saber-wielding local Yeomanry at Manchester, not the Army's Hussars, inflicted the most grievous butchery on the unarmed eighty thousand assembled citizens listening to the beginning of "Orator" Hunt's speech. One of the eleven killed was a child. Among more than four hundred wounded were one hundred women and girls. Female Reform Societies had appeared and women voted with the men at radical meetings.

The writer Samuel Bamford recounted the carnage at St. Peter's Field as the cavalry "began cutting the people . . . their sabres were plied to hew a way through naked held-up hands and defenceless heads; and then chopped limbs and wound-gaping skulls were seen. . . . Women, white-vested maids, and tender youth, were indiscriminately sabred or trampled." In ten minutes the open field, almost "deserted," was strewn with "caps, bonnets, hats, shawls, and shoes, and other parts of male and female dress, trampled torn, and bloody." The dismounted Yeomanry "were wiping their sabres" among the "mounds" of the "crushed" and "smothered."[8] Shelley, reading of the Yeomanry's role, perhaps remembered that Harriet Grove's father headed the local Yeomanry in Wiltshire.

Shelley had read in the August 22 *Examiner* Leigh Hunt's rousing editorial excoriating the Tory government as "these Men in Brazen Masks of Power" who led "thousands of human beings to slaughter and be slaughtered for the greater security of a corrupt Government." Hunt concluded by quoting the infamous line by "a pathetic court poet," Wordsworth, supporting Tory warmongering: "Carnage is God's daughter," a line Shelley parodied in his notebook:

> A Poet of the finest water
> Says that Carnage is Gods daughter
> This poet lieth as I take
> Under an immense mistake
> As many a man before has done
> Who thinks his spouse's child his own.[9]

Among the late August *Examiner* articles that influenced *The Mask of Anarchy* was Sir Francis Burdett's open letter which won him several months in jail.[10] Many others who protested in print were imprisoned or slated for prosecution, including Richard Carlile. Outraged over the massacre, Carlile soon published

152   PERCY BYSSHE SHELLEY

anonymously Shelley's *Declaration of Rights* in his radical *Republican*. Thanks to Carlile, the 1812 *Declaration* was Shelley's only work to be printed at the time in response to Peterloo. In October 1819, Carlile was convicted and imprisoned for reprinting Paine's *The Age of Reason*, the same Paine who influenced Shelley's *Declaration*. Carlile's trial would evoke Shelley's spirited November letter to Hunt.

Shelley called *The Mask of Anarchy* and his other political poems written at this time his "exoteric species" of works.[11] Called "the greatest poem of political protest ever written in English,"[12] *The Mask*'s subtlety transcends its immediate time and place.

Composing quickly as he had *The Cenci*, Shelley probably wrote most of *The Mask of Anarchy* in the week before September 23, the day he mailed it to Hunt for printing in the *Examiner*. Hunt had printed vitriolic attacks on the government immediately after Peterloo. By the time he received Shelley's poem, the prosecution of the writers had begun to freeze the radical press. Hunt grew cautious. His imprisonment with his brother John in 1812 for attacking the Prince Regent made him familiar with Government revenge. Never as politically radical as Shelley, Hunt's republican sympathies were not his strong suit. Hunt suppressed *The Mask of Anarchy*, not publishing it until 1832, the safe year of the Reform Act. Rationalizing his delay, Hunt weakly deflected his fears about himself onto fears about Shelley: "I thought that the public at large had not become sufficiently discerning to do justice to the sincerity and kind-heartedness of the spirit that walked in this flaming robe of verse."[13]

Hunt's caution deprived Shelley of the greater public recognition he sought, but only Shelley, in Italy, was safe from prosecution. His absence from England deprived his works from receiving whatever impetus for publication he could have provided. Hunt, burdened by an increasing family and decreasing income, was withdrawing from political concerns. About the time Shelley sent him *The Mask of Anarchy*, Hunt had started a new periodical, *The Indicator*, that contained "nothing . . . political or critical."[14] Shelley scolded Hunt, "But you will never write politics" and urged him to present in the *Examiner* what was really happening in England. He enclosed his famous political sonnet, "England in 1819." Shelley made other ineffective publishing appeals to Hunt during this productive period of political writing in the last half of 1819 and the first half of 1820.[15] Five of Shelley's major 1819 works—*Julian and*

Maddalo, The Mask of Anarchy, Peter Bell the Third, the Carlile letter to the *Examiner,* and *A Philosophical View of Reform*—rested in oblivion until after his death, the last until 1920.

The Mask of Anarchy begins with a not uncharacteristic line of self criticism:

> As I lay asleep in Italy
> There came a voice from over the Sea,
> And with great power it forth led me
> To walk in the vision of Poesy.
>
> (1–4)

Aroused from exile's sleep, Shelley aimed to strip away the masks and masquerade of the government's enslaving anarchy to reveal a more humane vision. Shelley began *The Mask* by parading the government's leaders in a *danse macabre masque,* a literary form in his recent reading, Petrarch's *Trionfo della Morte,* which he used again in *Charles the First* and *The Triumph of Life.*[16] His four masked riders—imagery from the biblical Four Horsemen of the Apocalypse[17]—were the Government's top power mongers whose grotesque and profane acts cannot be hidden behind the masks they wear. Shelley's intent was that the masses remove the masks of power they have given their ruling icons and break away from their anarchic, self-destructive identification with murderous power. The tentacles of this self-imposed tyranny extended into all reaches of society, including "Bishops, lawyers, peers, and spies."

Leading the masque of death is Castlereagh, the minister most detested by Shelley and object of his satiric wrath since 1811. Bloody suppressor of the Irish rebellion, then War Secretary, and Foreign Secretary since 1812, Castlereagh wrote Metternich after Peterloo, "Although we have made an immense progress against radicalism, the monster still lives . . . but we do not despair of crushing him."[18] Shelley responded in *The Mask:*

> I met Murder on the way—
> He had a mask like Castlereagh—
> Very smooth he look'd, yet grim;
> Seven bloodhounds followed him:
>
> All were fat; and well they might
> Be in admirable plight,

> For one by one, and two by two,
> He tossed them human hearts to chew,
> Which from his wide cloak he drew.
>
> (5–13)

Shelley is condemning Castlereagh's economically lucrative, "fat" agreement with the seven other countries in the Holy Alliance to postpone abolition of the slave trade.

Following Castlereagh, "Next came Fraud," Lord Chancellor Eldon. After depriving Shelley of his children by Harriet, Eldon was a "Masked Resurrection" in Shelley's bitter 1817 poem, "To the Lord Chancellor." In *The Mask,* Eldon wore

> . . . an ermined gown;
> His big tears, for he wept well,
> Turned to mill-stones as they fell;
> And the little children, who
> Round his feet played to and fro,
> Thinking every tear a gem,
> Had their brains knocked out by them.
>
> (15–21)

Next was Lord Sidmouth, Home Secretary, whose spies and informers sent him Shelley's Irish pamphlets in 1812. Sidmouth, "Hypocrisy," riding "On a crocodile," is "Clothed with the * * [Bible] as with light."

The fourth figure, Anarchy as a skeleton of death, mocks the corpulent Prince Regent he represents:

> Last came Anarchy: he rode
> On a white horse, splashed with blood;
> He was pale even to the lips,
> Like Death in the Apocalypse.
>
> And he wore a kingly crown;
> And in his grasp a sceptre shone;
> On his brow this mark I saw—
> "I am God, and King, and Law!"
>
> (30–37)

The military, "hired murderers," were joined by bowing "Lawyers and priests, a motley crowd," to proclaim:

"Thou art King, and God and Lord;
Anarchy, to Thee we bow,
Be thy name made holy now!"

And Anarchy, the skeleton,
Bowed and grinned to every one,
As well as if his education
Had cost ten millions to the nation.

(71–77)

Anarchy's procession of all-male idolaters, intent on completing his ruin of the national economy ("the Bank"), fill his prisons ("Tower"), and fully corrupt "his pensioned parliament," has its movements blocked by the first of two female figures, a "maniac maid" whose "name was Hope . . . / But she looked more like Despair." Hope, lying prostrate "in the street, / Right before the horses' feet" and "Expecting" to be trampled by "Murder, Fraud, and Anarchy," is saved by the "image" of Shelley's next activist female inspiratrix, Liberty, who urges "Men of England, Heirs of Glory" to:

"Rise, like lions after slumber,
In unvanquishable number,
Shake your chains to earth like dew,
Which in sleep had fall'n on you.
Ye are many—they are few.

(368–72)

The evanescent image of Liberty, "a mist, a light" that grows to a "Shape" only to disappear from sight as "empty air," is Shelley's ambitious aim in *The Mask* to replace rigid visual icons with nonvisual words that, flowing and moving like the wind, are mutable and emerging. Ironically, the poem's most lasting memory traces are from the icon of Anarchic monarchy, the grinning skeleton of death.

Some consider *The Mask* Shelley's "most ambivalent" political poem, its "meaning . . . not obvious,"[19] but Liberty clearly calls for two reactions from reformers, "a great Assembly" from all over England "to Declare . . . that ye / Are . . . free," and nonviolent resistance in the face of another onslaught.

"And if then the tyrants dare
Let them ride among you there;

Slash, and stab, and maim, and hew;
What they like, that let them do.

"With folded arms and steady eyes,
And little fear, and less surprise,
Look upon them as they slay
Till their rage has died away.

(340–47)

Shelley's call for massive nonviolent resistance appealed to Gandhi when he read the poem.[20] This pacifist call is not undone or confused by the provocative ending of *The Mask*, "Ye are many—they are few," or by the more provocative opening of another poem fueled by Peterloo, "Ode to the Assertors of Liberty": "Arise, arise, arise! / There is blood on the earth that denies ye bread." The reformers' "holy combat" is not civil war but the war over one's own sense of enslavement: "The slave and the tyrant are twin-born foes." As in *Prometheus Unbound*, the concept of freedom will be victorious over that of oppression.[21]

After Peterloo, other reformers advocated Shelley's two recommendations in *The Mask*, mass meetings and nonviolent resistance. However, a December general strike never materialized and the reformers went into disarray.[22] With unabated zeal, Shelley was chiding Hunt the next May, "you never speak politics." He asked him to suggest "any bookseller who would like to publish a little volume of *popular songs* wholly political & destined to awaken & direct the imagination of the reformers. I see you smile but answer my question."[23] Hunt again failed to respond. Shelley's volume of songs—another stillborn political publication—would have been a popular companion to the 1820 *Prometheus Unbound* volume, appealing to a different audience. Shelley by this time had written at least nine poems for his proposed *"popular songs,"* but only one was published during his lifetime, "Ode to the Assertors of Liberty," retitled, "An Ode written October, 1819, before the Spaniards had recovered their Liberty."[24] The *"popular songs"* included the acid "To S.[idmouth] and C.[astlereagh]," its title neutered first by Medwin's 1832 "Similes," and then by Mary's 1839 "For Two Political Characters of 1819." When she published Shelley's political song, "What Men Gain Fairly," her omission of the most telling line, "With those whom force or falsehood has made strong," led one scholar to wonder what additional political censorship she wielded over other songs.[25]

One of Shelley's most powerful political songs, partially printed first in 1926 as "A Ballad: Young Parson Richards," was retitled "Ballad of the Starving Mother" when printed in full in 1970.[26] While a parson feeds his dog, a famished woman with a dying babe at her "flaccid" breast begs him for food. After relating being seduced, impregnated, and deserted by a "ruiner," in desperation, considering prostituting herself to the parson, she lectures him about God, including a jibe pitting the biblical word against Malthus's stern ideas on overpopulation:

> "O God! this poor dear child did I
>   At thy command bear and cherish—
> Thou bad'st us increase and multiply—
>   And our tyrants bid us perish.[27]

The mother collapses, her dead child "stiff as frozen straw" upon her "white cold breast." The "surly," unbending parson recognizes the child is his.

Hypocritical church–state sexual politics and Peterloo still preoccupied Shelley as he drafted his sonnet, "England in 1819," with its renowned lines on the debauched royal family whose members spawned illegitimate children, engaged in brother–sister incest, and sold commands to army officers who bribed a royal mistress:

> An old, mad, blind, despised, and dying King;
> Princes, the dregs of their dull race, who flow
> Through public scorn,— mud from a muddy spring;
> Rulers who neither see nor feel nor know,
> But leechlike to their fainting country cling
> Till they drop, blind in blood, without a blow.
>
> (1–6)

Shelley, well aware his explosive sonnet would not be published by the cautious Hunt, told him, "I do not expect you to publish it, but you may show it to whom you please."[28]

With the completion of *The Mask of Anarchy*, it was time to leave Leghorn where, Mary later recalled, she felt "horror" from what she "suffered."[29] John Gisborne had departed September 12 for England to obtain "a situation" for Henry Reveley and was carrying Shelley's fair copy of the first three acts of *Prometheus Unbound*.[30] Mary was uncertain in mid-September, telling Amelia Curran that Shelley had not yet "recovered from his fatigue at

Rome and continually frightens me by the approaches of dysentery."[31] Still expecting Dr. Bell to be in Florence to attend Mary's expected late-October delivery, Shelley and Charles Clairmont left on September 23 to find lodgings. Shelley, returning from Florence "very unwell" two days later, had rented an apartment for six months in a pensione in the Palazzo Marini near Piazza Santa Maria Novella. The landlady, Madame Marveilleux du Plantis, had recently met the Shelleys in Leghorn through the Gisbornes.[32]

Shelley, following Leigh Hunt's suggestion that they write each other on Monday mornings, wrote in late September that he had some hope the birth of Mary's child might "relieve ... some part of her present melancholy depression."[33] However, the word "part" indicated his realization of her tendency to be chronically depressed. Mary commented years later of having "been pursued all my life by a mixed lowness of spirits which superinduces a certain irritability which often spoils me as a companion." She made the "sad Confession" that "To be as I ought to be towards others ... I need to be a little tipsy ... I wish I were made otherwise. ... I hate & despise myself for it—without being able to bring a remedy."[34]

Shelley told Hunt that "one of our motives in going to Florence" was Dr. Bell. Perhaps another reason was Henry Reveley's interest in Claire. Either before leaving Leghorn, or sometime the next year, Claire rejected a marriage proposal from timid Henry. The Gisbornes did not want Henry to marry and certainly not to penniless Claire, never Maria's favorite. Henry's marriage five years later at age thirty-five made his mother and stepfather incensed at his independence.[35] Before leaving Leghorn, Shelley committed himself financially to backing Henry's steamboat and agreed to edit Henry's letters to him to improve his written English.

Mary, upset about separating from Maria Gisborne, on departing September 30 left in Maria's hand a note with Byron's lines indicating her heart was buried in Leghorn.[36] The Gisbornes' dog Oscar followed Shelley's carriage down the rough road and howled "piteously" for several days outside the empty Villa Valsovano.[37]

Proceeding slowly because of Mary's advanced pregnancy, the family traveled fourteen miles to Pisa where they succeeded in meeting Lady Mount Cashell, missed the year before. As Mrs. Mason, she lived unmarried with George William Tighe and their two young daughters, Laurette and Nerina. Spending the night in Pisa, the Shelleys called again on Mrs. Mason and her family the next morning at their home, Casa Silva.

If Mary was concerned that Mrs. Mason's continuing correspondence with Mrs. Godwin contained scandalous and untrue
stories of the Shelleys that might cloud their reception, she was
pleasantly surprised. Mary soon asked Maria Gisborne to send
a parcel to Mrs. Mason with books, two cantos of *Childe Harold,*
and "the very best green tea."[38] However, it was with Claire, not
Mary, that Mrs. Mason developed a special relationship. Claire
wrote to Maria Gisborne from Florence about meeting Mrs. Mason, "a tall handsome woman" who "kissed" Claire "twice" in one
hour. Claire teased Maria, who, also "tall and handsome," had not
kissed "me *once.*" Maria should look at herself in a mirror "and
think what I suffered."[39] Shelley would find in the outspoken, radical, intelligent, and literary Mrs. Mason the last of his inspira-
tional mother surrogates. She usually signed her letters to the
Shelleys, "Margaretta."

9

Florentine Voices:
Unacknowledged Legislator
and Sophia Stacey

WHEN THE SHELLEY FAMILY SETTLED OCTOBER 2 INTO MADAME DU Plantis's Palazzo Marini boardinghouse, 4395 Via Valfonda, Florence became their fourth city of residence in 1819. Mary expected life to be "solitary & dull" but they soon enjoyed the opera and a "beautiful" ballet. Claire found an excellent singing teacher and, to improve her piano playing, borrowed the landlady's chiroplast, a device for improving keyboard finger position.[1] Charles Clairmont, after a stormy flirtation with Madame du Plantis's daughter, left the household for Vienna in early November.

Mary, twenty-two in August, had written Leigh Hunt before leaving Leghorn of her continuing depression from the deaths of Clara and William.[2] Godwin did not help when, again playing on her guilt, he wrote of expecting a jury ruling on his house rent lawsuit, saying, "Your time, as well as mine, is in October."[3] In early November, shortly before giving birth, Mary wrote Maria Gisborne of receiving "the worst possible news." The decision had gone against Godwin, who would have to produce £1500. Mary said if Shelley had to go to England about this, the journey would be "next door to death for him." She expected "nothing but misery."[4] Godwin vainly asked Shelley for £500. A year later, Godwin was still in his Skinner Street house trying to get £500 from Shelley, who had arranged for Horace Smith to advance Godwin £100.[5] Shelley, with a surfeit of English creditors, wrote Leigh Hunt in mid-October that his doctors "absolutely forbid my travelling to England in the winter" but he might make a spring visit that Hunt should not mention "publickly."[6] Mary's response to her father's continuing plight was to goad Shelley. Revising her incestuous

160

story *Mathilda*, she intended its earnings to go to her father.[7] Both Mary and Shelley had doctor bills, his for medicating the periodic pain in his side. Mary, without Dr. Bell, complained about the high cost and low quality of her obstetrical care and wished they had stayed in Pisa for the winter.[8] Bell had become ill in Rome where he wrote Shelley an affectionate farewell letter before dying several months later.[9]

A letter from Maria Gisborne saying her husband's trip to England was aborted when he became ill in France also brought more financial worry; work on Henry Reveley's steamboat "will be retarded for want of cash." Maria called the Shelleys the project's "patron and patroness," her signal to send the money they apparently had agreed to supply before leaving Leghorn.[10] Shelley answered he was "in torture" until money came from London. Admitting lacking "the discipline necessary for my imagination," Shelley thought John Gisborne would be surprised to learn of his "resolution" to finance Henry's boat. Hinting at the "imprudence" of his financial help, Shelley would "bear the blame & loss (if such a thing were possible) of a reverse." Reaching for "optimism," he thought it "best" Gisborne would return and "best that I should have overpersuaded you & Henry."[11] He sent Henry £50 but a further £200 from London was held up because Shelley's bank account was short of funds. Shelley then borrowed £100 from Horace Smith, who began his vigilant role as Shelley's London financial manager. By the end of 1819, Shelley had provided approximately £275 for the steamboat venture.[12]

Another favor for Maria Gisborne was trying to repay money she owed to an elusive Signora Tonelli. Each time Shelley called on her, he left a carefully handwritten card with his name and address.[13] More fruitfully, he visited the reading room of Delesert's English lending library to peruse political and literary periodicals from home.

Florence was stimulating for Shelley. In less than three months he achieved an astonishing array of creativity, composing poetry and prose in eight different forms: political satire (*Peter Bell the Third*); political essays ("The Carlile Letter"; *A Philosophical View of Reform*); political songs ("Sonnet: England in 1819"); short love lyrics ("Indian Serenade"); lyric drama (act IV of *Prometheus Unbound*); translation (Spinoza's *Tractatus Theologico-Politicus*); artistic commentary (*Notes on Sculptures*); and his most famous personal lyric (*Ode to the West Wind*).

Shelley gloried in the Uffizi Gallery. He and Mary visited there October 11 to glimpse the *Medici Venus,* which Mary found unimpressive. Shelley, returning alone for an entire afternoon,[14] told Maria Gisborne he planned to study the gallery "piecemeal" to fulfill one of his "chief [aims] in Italy . . . observing in statuary and painting . . . the rules according to which . . . ideal beauty . . . is realized in external forms." He told Hogg he "dedicated every sunny day to the study of the gallery," writing notes as he viewed each sculpture.[15]

Venus Anadyomene emerging on a shell from her bath fascinated Shelley with her "all soft and mild enjoyment." In his fullest description of the female body, he found "Her face expresses a breathless yet passive and innocent voluptuousness without affectation . . . at once desire and enjoyment. . . . Her lips . . .are wrought by inextinguishable desire. . . . Her eyes seem heavy and swimming with pleasure. . . . The neck is full and swollen as with the respiration of delight . . . the lines of the curved back flow into and around the thighs, and the wrinkled muscles of the belly. . . . Her pointed and pear-like bosom ever virgin—the virgin Mary might have this beauty, but alas!"[16]

Shelley's longest note was about the grief expressed in the *Niobe* statue, the mother "sheltering" from "inevitable peril" what he imagined was her last "surviving" child. He found "voluptuous" the effect of seeing through the folds of drapery on *Venus Genetrix.* Equally enraptured by unclad male statues, *A Ganymede* had "delicate hands . . . [and] light and delicate feet" while *Apollo* had "softness" and "a womanish vivacity . . . a boyish inexperience exceedingly delightful." One figure's covered penis elicited his "(Curse these fig leaves; why is a round tin thing more decent than a cylindrical marble one?)" Finding *Leda*'s face "very ugly," he wrote, "I should be a long time before I should make love to her." *The Laocoön,* which "nothing . . . [from] antiquity can surpass," evoked a long commentary on the father–son relationship. Only one work of art—a small painting of Medusa's severed head—so fascinated Shelley that it elicited a poem with the line, "Its horror and its beauty are divine."[17]

Crucial to Shelley's next compositions was his anger after reading for the first time in mid-October the personal slanders against him in the vicious long review of *Laon and Cythna* in the April 1819 *Quarterly Review.*[18] Lord Dillon, in Florence at the time, told Medwin he saw Shelley in Delesert's reading "the last *Quarterly.*"

Bursting "into convulsive laughter," Shelley hastily ran down the stairs.[19] More likely, Shelley was reading *Gentleman's Magazine*, eager for any news of his father's health. That periodical had reviews of the two *Peter Bells*,[20] germane to his own work.

Shelley probably first read the savage review of *Laon and Cythna* in a *Quarterly* clipping he received from Ollier in mid-October along with the first of Hunt's three spirited counterattacks in the late September 1819 *Examiner.* Ollier also wrote that Shelley's works were not selling well. Shelley was angered and unsettled by the slashing personal attack in the *Quarterly*'s long, unsigned review: Shelley's "bold convictions," those of "a young and inexperienced man, imperfectly educated . . . shamefully dissolute in his conduct," could carry no weight with those who "live under a paternal government and a pure faith, who look up with love and gratitude to a beneficent monarch, and reverence a zealous and upright priesthood." Shelley would "have us renounce our belief in our religions" and make "Love . . . the sole of the law which shall govern the moral world."[21]

Shelley never learned the reviewer was his fellow Eton and Oxford student, John Taylor Coleridge, two years older than Shelley but in the Fifth Form with him at Eton. Coleridge repeated the schoolyard gossip of Shelley and his background, including his "speculations and his disappointments [began] in early childhood." Shelley was "unteachable in boyhood, unamiable in youth, querulous and unmanly in manhood,—singularly unhappy in all three." Coleridge advised him to turn to the Bible, "which has more poetry in it than Lucretius, more interest than Godwin . . . But it is a sealed book to a proud spirit."

The review's ending—garnered from Shelley's "Ozymandias" published in Hunt's February 1818 *Examiner*—read, "Like the Egyptian of old, the wheels of his chariot are broken, the path of 'mighty waters' closes in upon him behind . . . finally, he sinks 'like lead' to the bottom, and is forgotten. . . . if we . . . tell what we now know about him, it would be indeed a disgusting picture."

Infuriated by this personal slander, Shelley began drafting a letter—apparently never sent—to the *Quarterly*'s editor, William Gifford. Quoting the review's conclusion, he demanded the reviewer or the editor provide proof as to what he "now knows" about him "to the disadvantage of my personal character" that "affords an unanswerable comment" or be labeled a "slanderer."[22] In a later draft about the "slanderous" review, he wrote: "I was too much amused by being compared to the Pharoah not to readily forgive editor printer publisher stitcher or any one, except the despicable writer."[23]

The *Laon and Cythna* review from the Tory stronghold of literary power appeared when Shelley anticipated both *The Cenci* and *Prometheus Unbound* coming before the public. The *Quarterly*'s attack dampened the reception of these major works and probably left an imprint on Shelley's poetic confidence.[24]

After reading the *Quarterly* assault, Shelley wrote Ollier, thinly covering his anger with urbane humor about the *Quarterly*'s "droll remarks" and Hunt's "kind defence" in the *Examiner.* Declaring Southey the reviewer, Shelley defended himself against his charge of imitating Wordsworth and was "amused" at the reviewer's description of "their Omnipotent God . . . pulling me under the sea by the hair of my head, like Pharoah . . . pretending not to be drowned myself when I *am* drowned; and, last, *being* drowned." Later, Shelley told Ollier he was determined to refute the *Quarterly*'s assertion that "my chariot-wheels are broken."[25]

Shelley knew the *Quarterly* had far more influence than Hunt's *Examiner.* In Venice, he and Byron incorrectly believed, as Byron said, "The Son of a Bitch" Southey was the *Quarterly* reviewer who savaged Hunt's *Foliage* and slurred Shelley by innuendo.[26] Because Southey, John Taylor Coleridge's friend, was known as the *Quarterly*'s point man, Shelley assumed his old Keswick neighbor wrote the review of *Laon and Cythna.* In 1817, Southey attacked the reform pamphlet by "The Hermit of Marlow" and wrote Wordsworth that Hunt, visiting Shelley at Marlow, was "in a fair way of becoming as infamous in his domestic conduct."[27] Shelley— later erroneously believing his college-mate the Reverend Henry Hart Milman was the reviewer—wrote Ollier, "Priests & Eunuchs have their privilege."[28]

After his mid-October letter to Ollier, Shelley began composing lines that became *Ode to the West Wind.* Seemingly, he chose to respond to the *Quarterly* attack not with the letter to Gifford but with a poem that crystallized his message with powerful succinctness.

Shelley wrote of the Cascine Forest, bordering the Arno near Palazzo Marini: "I like the Cascini very much where I often walk alone watching the leaves & the rising & falling of the Arno."[29] Several weeks earlier, aware of his prematurely graying hair, he wrote in his notebook:

'Twas the 20th of October
And the woods had all grown sober
As a man does when his hair
Looks as theirs did, grey & spare
When the dead leaves [disappear?]
As to mock the stupid fleg—
Like ghosts . . .

Shelley also wrote,

Within the surface of the fleeting river
The wrinkled image of the mountain lay
Immovably unquiet . . .[30]

In his *Ode,* Shelley replaced these lines with the image of the waters of "Baiae's bay." He retrieved the powerful "wrinkled . . . unquiet" water-mirror image a few months later in *Ode to Liberty,* then in "Evening: Ponte al Mare," and finally in "To Jane. The Recollection."

Shelley, in Dante's Florence, chose that poet's *terza rima* for his *Ode,* writing out twenty-three lines that ended:

But as my hopes were fire, so my decay
   Shall be as ashes covering them. Oh, Earth
Oh friends, if when my   has ebbed away
   One spark be unextinguished of that hearth[31]

Evolving these lines into the final two stanzas, Shelley created a new sonnet form that gave his *Ode* its beautiful symmetry. After drafting in pencil the *Ode*'s initial three stanzas, he wrote "Octr 25" in another notebook and copied these stanzas out in ink, revising as he wrote. A line in Greek near the drafts suggests Shelley was satisfied his *Ode* answered the *Quarterly* reviewer: "By my virtuous power I, a mortal, vanquish thee, a mighty god."

Because the *Ode*'s last two stanzas were completed after October 25, the entire poem probably occupied at least a week's effort if he began it on the twentieth. Months later, before sending the *Ode* to Ollier for publication with *Prometheus Unbound,* he recalled having "conceived and chiefly written" the poem "in a wood that skirts the Arno near Florence, and on a day when that tempestuous wind . . . was collecting the vapours which pour down the autumnal rains [that] began . . . at sunset with a violent tempest of hail and rain, attended by that magnificent thunder and lightning peculiar to the Cisalpine regions."

Ode to the West Wind marked a dramatic growth in Shelley's poetic expression combined with acute observations of natural phenomena, including types of clouds and the interactive effects of wind and ocean currents.[32] The *Ode*'s form builds with the repeated invocation, "O, hear!," as if directed to the attacking *Quarterly* reviewer.

Shelley's choice of the richly symbolic wind perhaps owed something to his continuing translation of Spinoza. Identifying *breath* as one meaning of the Hebrew word for *pneuma* or *spirit*, Spinoza noted, it "literally means a wind."[33] After Ollier's printing of the *Ode*'s first line, "O, WILD West Wind, thou breath of Autumn's being," the stanza ended with the command, "Wild Spirit, which art moving everywhere; / Destroyer and preserver; hear, O, hear!" This "Wild Spirit" next takes the human shape Shelley projected into clouds, a "fierce Maenad" with "bright uplifted hair," "locks of the approaching storm."

Shelley appropriates the threatening "congregated might" of this power's "voice" in order to "trumpet" his words to an "unawakened Earth" in the final two stanzas. Symbolizing this merger is the submersion scene Shelley saw in Naples, where the wind's power reaches "far below" to the foliage of underwater plants. Rewriting his draft's graying hair image, the frightening power now makes the "sapless foliage . . . grow grey with fear / And tremble and despoil themselves."

Shelley, composing while he and Mary anxiously expected the birth of their child, concluded the *Ode* asking that the West Wind "Drive my dead thoughts . . . to quicken a new birth!" Shelley's wish, "Scatter, as from an unextinguished hearth / Ashes and sparks, my words among mankind!" is followed by the skeptical final question, "If Winter comes, can Spring be far behind?" Facing self-doubts from the chilling effects of critics' attacks, Shelley's characteristic response was creative accomplishment.

Anger—and rivalry—directed toward Wordsworth ignited Shelley's next accomplishment, the satire *Peter Bell the Third*. He had read in the *Examiner* of the appearance of Wordsworth's long-gestating poem, *Peter Bell*, first composed in 1798. The April 25 *Examiner* had Keats's anonymous review of John Hamilton Reynolds's parody, *Peter Bell: A Lyrical Ballad,* and Hunt reviewed Wordsworth's poem a week later. The conservative Wordsworth was now fair game for critics. His *Peter Bell* involved a donkey's ennobling influence on a sinner and another 1819 parodist labeled it *The Dead Asses: A Lyrical Ballad.*[34]

Shelley possibly began *Peter Bell the Third* in Leghorn but wrote most of it in Florence the last week in October. The disdain in Shelley's 1816 sonnet "To Wordsworth" was reinforced when Peacock wrote in July 1818 of Wordsworth's active support of the Tories in the Westmorland district election. This conservatism, and its dulling effects on Wordsworth's poetry, became satirical themes of *Peter Bell the Third.*

Mary, awaiting her baby, copied *Peter* as Shelley composed.[35] In a postscript to Shelley's November 2 letter to Hunt enclosing "*my* Peter," Mary complained that the infant clothes she requested had not arrived.[36] The baby clothes arrived too late and *Peter Bell the Third* waited twenty years to be published despite Shelley's appeal to Hunt that Ollier publish it immediately and anonymously. Alluding to his Carlile letter and *A Philosophical View of Reform,* he would soon have "more serious things . . . [for] public attention." Although Shelley later called *Peter* a "joke" and "a trifle unworthy of me seriously to acknowledge," he was still trying to get Ollier to publish it the next May.[37]

Mary believed that Shelley put "much of himself" in *Peter Bell the Third* but did not mention his treatment of Wordsworth.[38] Mimicking Wordsworth's life, Shelley criticized him (Peter) for lacking playfulness and for believing "happiness is wrong," implying Wordsworth bordered on having a sexual perversion—"a certain hungry wish"—having earlier stated Peter was a "moral eunuch":

> He touched the hem of Nature's shift,
> Felt faint, and never dared uplift
> The closest, all-concealing tunic.
>
> (315–17)

Wordsworth, not just "A solemn and unsexual man," had homosexual inclinations, "like a male Molly." An "Impious Libertine," he "commits i[nces]t with his sister / In ruined Abbies," part of a stanza crossed through in Mary's fair copy and never published with the poem.[39] He left intact the next stanza's lines (478–79), "Is not incest enough, / And must there be adultery too?"

After excoriating corrupt government, a bought Parliament, royal Hanoverian despotism, regressive taxation, and prostitution stemming from chaste sexual repression, Shelley satirized lawyers, judges, bailiffs, Chancellors, and Bishops, "whose trade is, over ladies / To lean, and flirt, and stare, and simper."

Shelley concluded with a critique of Coleridge, a "man . . . fair as a maid, / And Peter noted what he said." Although he "was a mighty poet—and/ A subtle-souled Psychologist," his "mind . . . was a mist." Shelley's pseudonym for his poem was "Miching Mallecho, Esq.," from *Hamlet*.

Upon completing *Peter Bell the Third*, Shelley spent three days composing his long letter—*For the Examiner*—protesting the October trial and conviction of Richard Carlile for blasphemous libel. Shelley began by stating Carlile's trial "has filled me with an indignation that will not & ought not to be suppressed."[40] He sent *For the Examiner* to Hunt on November 6, but Hunt had published five letters in the *Examiner* sympathetic to Carlile and Shelley's waited over one hundred years to be printed in its entirety.[41]

Shelley's letter is a radical defense of freedom of the press and a spirited attack on England's pernicious blasphemy laws. Aligning himself with Carlile, he declares he too is a blasphemer willing to go to jail—his only written pronouncement to that effect—albeit from the safety of Italy: "for what was Mr. Carlisle prosecuted? For impugning the Divinity of Jesus Christ? I impugn it. For denying that the whole mass of antient Hebrew literature is of divine authority? I deny it . . . I am prepared both to do my duty & to abide by whatever consequences may be attached to its fulfillment."

Shelley, attacking both religious and social class discrimination, argued that not only was the deist Carlile not judged by deists, but his low economic status did not provide the immunity from blasphemy granted higher-status deists who doubted the existence of God, including Jeremy Bentham and Sir William Drummond. Religion is "the mask & garment," the ideological front that entrenched political interests used to squelch reform. Without reform, including the people's right to "receive a just price for their labours," England was headed for "the alternative of despotism or revolution." Shelley concluded by appealing to Hunt for solidarity despite their political differences: "The tremendous question is now agitating, whether a military judicial despotism is to be established by our present rulers, or some form of government less unfavourable to the real and permanent interests of all . . . our party will be that of liberty & of the oppre[ss]ed."

Shelley—championing immediate annual parliaments, complete abolition of the monarchy, and eventual universal suffrage—was piqued over Hunt's failure to publish his Carlile letter and rebuked him some months later.[42] Carlile may not have known who wrote the *Declaration of Rights* when he printed it, but he printed four pirated editions of *Queen Mab* in addition to publishing poems and articles praising Shelley.[43]

The Carlile letter finished, Shelley soon embarked on his longest prose work and most ambitious political treatise, *A Philosophical View of Reform*. He wrote to the Gisbornes of having "deserted the odorous gardens of literature to journey across the great sandy desert of Politics; not, you may imagine, without the hope of finding some enchanted paradise."[44] His reading—Plato's *Republic* and Clarendon's four-volume *The History of the Rebellion and Civil Wars in England*—suggests the imaginative political sweep of *A Philosophical View of Reform*. Clarendon also gave Shelley background for his still-nascent drama, *Charles the First*. Act IV of *Prometheus Unbound* possibly was contemplated, but he wrote to Hunt in mid-November, "The Prometheus I wish to be printed and to come out immediately."[45] When John Gisborne returned in mid-October with the undelivered *Prometheus Unbound* manuscript, Shelley immediately asked the Gisbornes to send it with the printed copies of *The Cenci* by ship to Ollier. It was mid-December before the ship sailed. Shelley was still writing *A Philosophical View of Reform* on December 23, the day he wrote the Gisbornes that he had finished act IV.[46]

Mary's child was born November 12 after a brief labor. At twenty-two, she had her fourth baby and second son. She had been childless for "5 hateful months"[47] and her spirits lifted slightly. Shelley told Hunt that Mary's being "a little consoled" was "a great relief & a great comfort to me amongst all my misfortunes past present & to come." Perhaps creating one misfortune, Shelley next wrote John Gisborne warning him to sell his government bonds, advice forwarded by Peacock.[48] The Shelleys would regret this warning, which soon propelled the Gisbornes to England.

The day Shelley's heir was born, Henry Reveley cast the steamboat's engine cylinder, the largest in Italy. Shelley wrote him, "Your boat will be to the Ocean of Water what the earth is to the Ocean of Aether—a prosperous & swift voyager."[49] A more romantic version, "Thou art fair, & few are fairer / Of the Nymphs of earth or ocean," soon flowed from Shelley's pen.

Miss Sophia Stacey, recently arrived in Florence, called at Madame du Plantis's boardinghouse two days before Mary delivered. Sophia—a year older than Shelley and the ward of his uncle, Robert Parker—learned that Shelley, his wife, "and her friend Miss Clermont" were living there. The next day, November 11, Sophia and her older female traveling companion, Miss Corbet Parry-Jones, moved into the Palazzo Marini. Orphaned as a child, the personable, dark-haired Sophia was well educated for an upper-middle class young woman. Her most striking physical feature was her "strong, almost lycanthropic" eyes.[50] She was a talented harpist with an attractive singing voice, qualities—along with her orphan status—that soon established her as Shelley's new *inamorata*.[51] The five or more lyrics and fragments Shelley wrote for the well-named Sophia are among his most erotic. He kept them from Mary, who gave them misleading dates when she published some after his death.

Before Shelley met her, Sophia had rejected several "brilliant offers" from suitors during three years in "society" in Brighton and Bath. In 1823, she would marry Lieutenant James Patrick Catty, Royal Engineers, six years her junior. Sophia and her husband had five children and in their travels acquired a home in Florence before he died in 1839. A subsequent marriage seemed unsuccessful and, inheriting her family's extensive property in 1855, she was known as Mrs. Catty until her death in 1874.

Sophia's interest in Shelley was sparked by the many disapproving stories she heard from his aunt, Hellen Parker, Bysshe Shelley's oldest daughter. After receiving a copy of *St. Irvyne* from his young nephew, Robert Parker spoke with Shelley after his Oxford expulsion. Sophia's travel diary, and a brief memoir of Shelley she wrote some years later, provide information about her relationship with Shelley.[52] Shelley quickly appeared in her diary when, on November 13, she recorded in faulty Italian what happened "after dinner," presumably a prearranged rendezvous: "I saw the signal: the light of the lamp." Together, talking of music and verses, Shelley "spoke of his sisters," of his "adventures in youth," and asked her "to give his regards to Mr. Parker."[53] Sophia left no record that Shelley mentioned his parents, whom she knew.

She observed that young William's portrait had "the image of Lady Shelley—lovely eyes."[54]

Recalling their daily contact, Sophia noted "we soon became very close friends," adding decorously, "He was at that time married to his second wife."[55] Within days of her arrival Shelley began writing love poetry to her. Living under the same roof for one and a half months, they had ample opportunity to share their talents and interests. While Mary was preoccupied with her newborn son, Shelley and Sophia saw Florence together. Soon he was feeling better, but as Sophia's departure approached, she expressed concern over Shelley's "suffering much from pain in his side." A week later Sophia wrote in her diary that while the two were engaging in one of their many talks, "he was seized with spasms: he is in very delicate state of health."

As he had with Cornelia Turner, Shelley read Italian with Sophia, including an aria from a Mozart opera. She noted he discoursed on "the Established Church and Radicalism . . . Love, Liberty, Death." Sophia's sweet singing voice and harp playing aroused Shelley's erotic lyricism; some of his love songs she inspired probably were composed to be sung. Mary, perhaps with a jealous edge, wrote Maria Gisborne that Sophia—"*entousiasmée* to see" Shelley—"is lively and unaffected . . . sings well for an english delettanti & if she would learn the scales would sing exceedingly well for she has a sweet voice." Mary complained that Sophia and Miss Jones "assert a claim to our acquaintance on the score of being acquainted with S.'s family. . . . you never see any one except those whom you shut out when you can."[56] Shelley did not shut out Sophia; his love lyrics to her imply some physical intimacy. Claire reported years later: "Miss Stacey was 29. Shelley's study was on the ground floor . . . He made love to Sophia."[57]

Sophia was delighted when Shelley showed her his new son Percy with the comment, "it could do no mischief now" but some day he could be the "conqueror of the provinces." The next day, Shelley introduced her to Mary, whom Sophia described as "a sweetly pretty woman . . . very delicate and interesting." Mary apparently did not object when Sophia suggested "Florence" for little Percy's middle name. Many years later Sophia sent Percy Florence a previously unknown love lyric his father had composed for her in Florence.

Sophia's diary entries, some in halting Italian, were brief and at times cryptic. Learning that Shelley had a carriage but kept no horses, she thought him "humane." Sophia, socially active, observed that the Shelleys "see no company and live quite to themselves." Inviting them to one of her tea parties, she had one other guest, "Mr. Grieves, who had been at college with Shelley." After some "political discussion" Sophia sang and "Mr. Shelley praised me much."[58] Accompanied by Mr. Tomkins, an artist living downstairs, Sophia and Shelley spent four hours in the Uffizi and later walked in the Cascine woods. Finding Shelley a "mysterious, yet interesting character," Sophia upon entering his study noted "Numbers of Greek books were lying about the room." It impressed her that he was "always reading" and at night he wrote at his "little table with pen and ink." She noted Mary also had a writing desk.

When Sophia sang and played the harp for him, or he listened to her vocal practicing, Shelley's enjoyment turned to rapture. She recalled he especially liked her singing Mozart's "Non temer o madre amata" and de Thierry's ballad, "Why declare how much I love thee."[59] Upon hearing her sing the evening of November 16, Shelley promised to write her some verses, which he handed to her the next night after she sang once more. It possibly was the three-stanza poem, "I arise from dreams of thee," one of his most passionate love lyrics, subsequently titled "Indian Serenade" and "The Indian Girl's Song." The third stanza moves from dreams to hope for renewed closeness:

> O lift me from the grass!
> I die, I faint, I fail!
> Let thy love in kisses rain
> On my lips and eyelids pale.
> My cheek is cold and white, alas!
> My heart beats loud and fast,
> Oh! press it close to thine again,
> Where it will break at last.
>
>   (17–24)

In his draft, Shelley had written, "From dreams of thee beloved, I have risen wild & joyous." He also deleted the lines, "O Pillow cold and wet with tears! / Thou breathest sleep no more."[60] One scholar believed Shelley's lines "undisguised poetic eroticism . . . delirium of orgasm."[61]

Some critics have assumed the narrator is a maiden responding to a sexual encounter and that Shelley wrote the poem several years later as a song for an Indian drama. Shelley contributed to this obfuscation by resurrecting the lyric several years later for Jane Williams, recalling it in his notebook for *Hellas*, and by using it in a poem competition with Byron.[62] The poem's appropriate title, its first line, "I arise from dreams of thee," was used by Sophia's son.[63]

Another love lyric for Sophia, "Thou art fair, and few are fairer" ("To Sophia"), surfaced in 1868. She had copied the lines in her diary with the date, December 1819. Nearly five decades later, Sophia copied the lines again, sending them with a letter to the man she helped name. Having inherited his father's passion for sailing, a delighted Sir Percy Florence Shelley, now forty-eight, appropriately replied to Sophia on the stationery of his yacht "Enchantress," asking permission to have the poem published. "Lines written for Miss Sophia Stacey" appeared in William Michael Rossetti's 1870 edition of Shelley's poems. Sophia Catty wrote on the back of one of its illustrations: "Birth of Sir Percy Shelley at Florence x Via Val Fonda—in 1819—I was there x there. SC—named the child."[64]

Sophia recalled that the copy of the lyric, "Thou art fair, and few are fairer," she received from Shelley was headed with the single word "Sophia." and "placed in my hands after hearing me frequently play the harp."[65] Sophia's unusual eyes evoked some of Shelley's most passionate lines:

> Thy deep eyes, a double Planet,
> Gaze the wisest into madness
> With soft clear fire,—the winds that fan it
> Are those thoughts of tender gladness
> Which, like zephyrs on the billow,
> Make thy gentle soul their pillow.
>
> (7–12)

Shelley, his "fainting soul" having heard "thy harp's wild measure," concluded, "As one who feels an unseen spirit / Is my heart when thine is near it."[66]

Shelley did not give Sophia the other love lyrics he secretly was writing. However, on December 28, the day before she left, he placed in her hand a copy of Leigh Hunt's 1819 *Literary Pocket-Book* in which he had written out three verses for her, "Good-Night," "Love's Philosophy" ("An Anacreontic"), and "Time Long Past." In "Good-Night"—also written in Italian—the wish that their two hearts remain close together expresses the same theme in both "I arise from dreams of thee" and "Thou art fair, and few are fairer." Shelley ended his three-stanza poem:

> The hearts that on each other beat
>   From evening close to morning light,
> Have nights as good as they are sweet
>   But never *say* good-night.[67]

Shelley sent Leigh Hunt on November 16 "Love's Philosophy" and, perhaps to deceive Mary's eyes, only mentioned enclosing a political poem.[68] Hunt wrote back immediately about the "delicious love-song" and hinted at its non-marital inspiration by calling it a "boldness of benevolence." Having read it for the "ninth or tenth time," Hunt said he would publish it "incontinently" in *The Indicator*, which he did.[69] That Hunt published Shelley's surreptitious love songs at this time but not his political poems probably fostered Shelley's nineteenth-century reputation as a lyricist rather than a radical political poet.[70] Shelley carefully toned down for Sophia some of the explicit eroticism in "Love's Philosophy" that was in the version he sent Hunt. Soon after the line, "Nothing in the world is single" came the lines "In one another's being mingle / Why not I with thine?" For Sophia, "being" became "spirit." Similarly, in "What are all these kissings worth / If thou kiss me not?" Shelley gave Sophia "sweet work" for "kissings."[71]

The "sweet work" Shelley had in mind appeared more explicitly in a fragment he excluded:

> When we sink to intermingle
>   And the violet tells no tale
>   To the odour scented gale
> For they too have enough to do
> Of such work as I and you[72]

Act IV of *Prometheus Unbound*, as "a rebirth of sexuality,"[73] can be read as a disguised love poem to Sophia, with cosmic couplings of the Choruses followed by the coupling of the Earth and Moon.[74] Shelley's sexual and scientific metaphors in act IV build upon his knowledge of contemporary science, including the nebular theories of Herschel and Laplace, the chemical and electrical advances of Sir Humphry Davy, and the poet-scientist Erasmus Darwin's evolutionary ideas that anticipated those of his grandson.[75] Alfred North Whitehead cited Shelley's powerful ability in act IV to visualize the earth's conical "pyramid of night" in relation to the sun.[76] Shelley, perhaps countering Mary's view in *Frankenstein,* insists that love and science will co-exist in a future Promethean social order.

Composed while Mary was heavily pregnant, Ione's vision—an image of the "Mother of the Months" with her infant enwombed in their crescent-shaped moon-boat chariot—is Shelley's most extended passage in the language of whiteness. More startling is her sister Panthea's vision, an imagining of subatomic orbits enwombing the infant Earth:

> A sphere, which is as many thousand spheres,
> Solid as chrystal, yet through all its mass
> Flow, as through empty space, music and light:
> Ten thousand orbs involving and involved,
>
> With mighty whirl the multitudinous orb
> Grinds the bright brook into an azure mist
> Of elemental subtlety, like light;
>
>   Within the Orb itself,
> Pillowed upon its alabaster arms,
> Like to a child o'erwearied with sweet toil,
> On its own folded wings and wavy hair,
> The Spirit of the Earth is laid asleep,
> And you can see its little lips are moving,
> Amid the changing light of their own smiles,
> Like one who talks of what he loves in dream.

> (IV.238–41, 253–55, 261–68)

The astral love dance of the Earth and Moon is the revealed expression of the unseen lovemaking between Prometheus and Asia in the cave. In a fusion of identities, Mother Earth, a latent Hermaphrodite, is now "Brother." Drawing upon Herschel's notion of an icy lunar surface,[77] Shelley's Moon sings of Earth's erotic warmth "Which penetrates my frozen frame." Earth's response captures the message of act IV:

> Man, one harmonious soul of many a soul,
> Whose nature is its own divine control,
> Where all things flow to all, as rivers to the sea;
> Familiar acts are beautiful through love;

> (IV.400–403)

Concluding act IV, Demogorgon prescribes endurance, forbearance, and forgiveness, firmly rejecting repentance:

> To suffer woes which Hope thinks infinite;
> To forgive wrongs darker than death or night;
>   To defy Power, which seems omnipotent;
> To love, and bear; to hope, till Hope creates
> From its own wreck the thing it contemplates;
>   Neither to change, nor falter, nor repent:
> This, like thy glory, Titan, is to be
>   Good, great, and joyous, beautiful and free;
> This is alone Life, Joy, Empire, and Victory.
>
> (570–78)

Earlier, The Moon—"an insatiate bride"—sang of a "violet's gentle eye," perhaps an echo of Sophia's eyes. Two months after she left Florence, Shelley sent her his lines, later called "On a Faded Violet." Shelley added them without Mary's awareness to her letter to Sophia written the day after he had returned from several days in Leghorn where he consulted the Gisbornes and possibly del Rosso about Elena and blackmail. He wrote out three stanzas, omitting a fourth that seemed to refer to him and deserted Elena, she a "poor blossom" and both having "fortunes . . . alike," possibly the loss of the mysterious lady: "For from the time we [left] her bosom / We both began to wither[.]" After writing out the stanzas to Sophia, Shelley wrote, "if you tell no one *whose* they are, you are welcome to them." The lines include, "The colour from the flower is gone / Which like thy sweet eyes smiled on me."[78]

One of Shelley's lyrics to Sophia Stacey, "I fear thy kisses gentle maiden," was so frank that Mary omitted one stanza when she published it.[79] Mary deleted Shelley's allusion to the "heavy & tight" chain of marriage, a sentiment expressed in a long verse fragment to Sophia that later appeared in *Epipsychidion.*[80]

Shelley began this long Sophia-fragment asserting to "my dear friend" his intention to dedicate his next book of poetry to her. His publication plans included a volume of three autobiographical poems whose scenes would "be laid at Rome, Florence, and Naples . . . all drawn from dreadful or beautiful realities."[81] Abandoning this project, he later alluded to *Epipsychidion*'s origin in Sophian Florence in the poem's "Advertisement."[82]

After the Sophia-fragment's dedication statement, Shelley continued, "What you are, is a thing I must veil." With the "riddle," whether she is "mistress or friend," Shelley introduced his famous passage, later included in *Epipsychidion*, about free love, beginning, "I never was attached to that great sect." Professing to Sophia in the fragment, "I love you!", Shelley playfully wrote, some "Hint that, though not my wife, you are a woman," and still others "swear you're a Hermaphrodite."[83] It is as if harp-playing Sophia had become a fantasy siren lover whose songs helped dissolve his sadness.

Shelley's melancholy was evident in the third lyric he wrote out for Sophia in Hunt's *Literary Pocket-Book*, "Time Long Past." Sophia's "tone . . . is now forever fled, / . . . A love so sweet it could not last" and, regretting her approaching departure, he wrote, "Each day a shadow onward cast/ Which made us wish it yet might last." In the final stanza, his "regret, almost remorse" about their separation evokes little William's death: " 'Tis like a child's belovèd corse/ A father watches."

Sophia, a month after leaving Florence, observed that the bust of Lucio Cesare in the Naples Museum was "like Mr. Shelley." Saying she could "never forget his personal appearance," she later wrote: "His face was singularly engaging, with strongly marked intellectuality. His eyes were however the most striking portion of his face, blue and large, and of a tenderness of expression unsurpassed. In his manner there was an almost childish simplicity combined with much refinement."[84]

After Sophia left, Shelley sat twice for a portrait—now lost—by his neighbor, Mr. Tomkins. Shelley, ill, wore a fur-collared cloak with his usual open neck in the bitter cold early January. Tomkins suggested in vain that Shelley take the sacrament at the English Embassy to overcome Shelley's complaint of cold treatment from the English residents.[85]

English coldness would have been greater had they known his attacks in *A Philosophical View of Reform*, the "political work" he was writing December 23 after finishing act IV.[86] The following May he was asking Hunt's help in promoting the *View*, "boldly but temperately written."[87] Bentham's *Plan of Parliamentary Reform* was selling well and Shelley wanted his message broadcast as well. His entreaty for Hunt's help was in vain; one hundred years elapsed before Shelley's *View* was printed.[88]

In his *View*, Shelley advocated making "all religions, all forms of opinion respecting the origin and government of the universe, equal in the eye of the law." The "standing army" should be dis-

banded as a soldier—"a slave" and "more degraded than a murderer"—was taught "to despise human life and human suffering."
The military was a "profession beyond abhorrence and below contempt."

Shelley's main thrust was economic. Empathy for the poor was
matched by his anger toward their exploitation by the aristocracy
and the "despotism of the oligarchy of party . . . the [pow]er of the
rich . . . [the] king is merely the mask of this power . . . a kind of
stalking-horse. . . . Monarchy is only the string which ties the rob-
ber's bundle."

Arguing that political reform necessitated economic and social
equality, Shelley glanced back toward Godwin's *Political Justice*
but was anticipating the class struggle arguments of Marx and Engels: "When the majority in any nation arrive at a conviction that
it is their duty and their interest to divest the minority of a power
employed to their disadvantage . . . a struggle must ensue." Mary
wrote years later that Shelley believed "a clash between the two
classes of society was inevitable, and he eagerly ranged himself on
the people's side."[89]

Shelley assailed the Church of England's priesthood and Malthus,
"a priest of course, for his doctrines are those of a eunuch and of a
tyrant." Malthus wanted to take from the poor "the one thing which
made it impossible to degrade them below the beasts . . . the soothing, elevating, and harmonious gentleness of the sexual intercourse and the humanizing charities of domestic life which are its
appendages." Malthus "has the hardened insolence to propose as
a remedy that the poor . . . abstain from sexual intercourse, while
the rich are to be permitted to add as many mouths to consume the
products of the labor of the poor as they please." Shelley's class
manifesto was "That the majority [of] people of England are destitute and miserable, ill-clothed, ill-fed, ill-educated . . . they are
impatient to procure a reform of the cause of their abject and
wretched state."

Class differences were exacerbated by paper money and more
importantly by the exorbitant national debt "chiefly contracted in
two liberticide wars, undertaken by the privileged classes of the
country" against France and America. Shelley advocated abol-
ishing the national debt with the excess wealth of the monied
classes, not knowing David Ricardo was making the same recommendation.[90]

Shelley admired the ideas of Godwin's friend Robert Owen, but did not share Owen's socialist utopianism.[91] Shelley's view of history, presented in some detail in the *View*, reflected his Godwinian belief in perfectibility, gradual improvement in the face of great resistance, with inevitable setbacks. Shelley argued that in the broad sweep of history from the Roman Empire until the present social institutions had subverted the capacity for love and liberty. Jesus was a "great Reformer" whose "system" for "liberty and equality . . . was perverted to support oppression." Shelley's psychological position was that precepts originally expressive of freedom become internalized as "mere names," distorted into fixed "symbols" of domination.

Shelley, arguing from Bacon's "idols of the mind," made the psychological tyrannizing effect of internal rigidity the heart of his skeptical view about change.[92] At the dawn of depth psychology, Shelley urged the continuing analysis of "Lord Bacon, Spinoza, Hobbes, Bayle, Montaigne" who first "anatomized the inmost nature of social man." They initiated a "new epoch" that began "deeper inquiries into the forms of human nature" that are incompatible with "popular systems of faith . . . upon which the superstructure of political and religious tyranny, are built."

In ringing, pre-Marxist language, Shelley felt "Modern European society is . . . [an] engine . . . perpetually wearing away & breaking into pieces the wheels of which it is composed."[93] He endorsed the utilitarian view of "the greatest good for the greatest number" which, combined with "liberty and equality," has produced "The system of government in the United States of America . . . the first practical illustration of the new philosophy."

Wrestling with the possibility of insurrection, civil war, and their potentially bloody aftermath, he wrote: "The strongest argument, perhaps, for the necessity of reform is the inoperative and unconscious abjectness to which the purposes of a considerable mass of the people are reduced. . . . The savage brutality of the populace is proportioned to the arbitrary character of their government." As for war, it is "a kind of superstition [that] corrupts the imagination of men . . . the hellish exultation, and unnatural drunkenness of the destruction of the conquerors, the burning of the harvests, and the obliteration of the traces of cultivation."

Shelley appealed for nonviolent action and leadership from "poets, philosophers, and artists," mentioning Godwin and Hazlitt.

Crossing out "Lord Byron," he added Bentham and Hunt.[94] In the *View,* Shelley first wrote of the power of "unacknowledged" poets: "They are the priests of an unapprehended inspiration, the mirrors of gigantic shadows which futurity casts upon the present. . . . Poets and philosophers are the unacknowledged legislators of the world." Nevertheless, Shelley anticipated that if England reached a "point of moral and political degradation . . . it will be necessary to appeal to an exertion of physical strength. If the madness of parties admits no other mode of determining the question at issue."

Although unfinished, *A Philosophical View of Reform* has been recognized as "the most advanced work of political theory of the age," "one of the most advanced and sophisticated documents of political philosophy in the nineteenth century."[95]

Still writing as 1819 ended, Shelley began translating Plato's *Ion* and composed "Ode to Heaven."[96] The ode, published with *Prometheus Unbound,* deflated humanity's "presumption," reducing Heaven to a "globe of dew." Earth and its universe are mere "Drops" in the "unimagined . . . measureless" universes beyond.

Shelley's morale was boosted when he read the laudatory review of *Alastor* in the November *Blackwood's Edinburgh Magazine.* The reviewer also defended Shelley, "a great poet," against the reviewer of *Laon and Cythna* in the *Quarterly,* "a dunce rating a man of genius." Shelley wrote Ollier he was glad "to see the *Quarterly* cut up" and Mary called the review an "antidote" to the *Quarterly's* "bane."[97]

Once again, Shelley complained to the Gisbornes that a letter from Godwin kept Mary's "spirits" from being "good." He plaintively asked, "What shall I, what can I, what ought I to do? You cannot picture to yourself my perplexity." Mary had written Maria Gisborne in mid-December regretting their decision to come to Florence, citing the lack of acquaintances "worth your friendship," presumably including Sophia with her "claim" of kinship. A move to Pisa or the baths in nearby Casciana might help the "rhumatic" pain in Shelley's side. Mary, planning her next novel, *Valperga,* was peeved that Maria Gisborne and Mrs. Mason had no suggestions for someone to guide her research.[98]

Mrs. Mason did locate an Italian-speaking Swiss-German nurse for infant Percy to replace Milly Shields, who returned to Marlow. The day Shelley gave Sophia the *Pocket-Book* with his three poems to her, Mary wrote Maria Gisborne, "he seems a changed man his numerous weaknesses & ailments have left him & settled all in his side."[99]

Sophia also noted his side pain in her diary. After Shelley wrote her a letter of introduction to Signora Dionigi in Rome, Sophia wrote, "Mr. Shelley walks with me to see our carriage to Rome, and the step being high he lifted me out of the carriage." The two then walked to the post office. Shelley last saw Sophia early the morning of December 29, accompanying her and Miss Jones "off on the road to Rome."[100] He had told Signora Dionigi, and Sophia noted in her diary, that he planned "shortly" to go to Rome and then to Venice to see Byron. Thinking Byron would like Sophia's songs, Shelley had tried to arrange for the two to meet but Byron was with Teresa Guiccioli in Ravenna. If Shelley planned to see Sophia in Rome, he never went, as plans for William's grave marker were delayed.[101] On the last day of 1819, Mary wrote in her journal, "I now begin a new year—may it be a happier one than the last unhappy one."

10

Poetic Mothers: Pisa and Leghorn

Sᴏᴘʜɪᴀ ɢᴏɴᴇ, ꜱʜᴇʟʟᴇʏ ᴡʀᴏᴛᴇ ɪɴ ᴛʜᴇ ᴘʀɪᴠᴀᴄʏ ᴏꜰ ʜɪꜱ ɴᴏᴛᴇʙᴏᴏᴋ ᴏꜰ his talks with Claire, each being the "second conscience" of the other. Claire commented in her journal that the number two was "the symbol of division . . . Let this rule be applied to marriage and we shall find the cause of its unhappy querulous state."[1] Mary, seeking companionship, asked Mrs. Mason to send ten-year-old Laurette to visit. Mrs. Mason demurred, urging Shelley to stop taking his two current medications and come to Pisa to see Vaccà, who was "little inclined to giving drugs."[2] Shelley resumed translating Spinoza aloud while Mary transcribed. Claire, hearing of Byron's *cavalier servante* role with Teresa Guiccioli, wrote sarcastically, "The Hero is gone to Ravenna." Mary more precisely noted Byron was "reforming—i.e. making love and becoming a methodist."[3]

In mid-January Shelley, answering a letter from Tom Medwin in Geneva, encouraged him to come live "with me" as they were "fixed" for the year in Tuscany. Giving Leghorn as his future address, Shelley had not "much spirit for writing Poetry" but Florence's "keen air" allowed one to "imagine vividly even in the midst of despondence. . . . my nerves have been racked upon the last ten days."[4]

Mary thought Shelley was better but had "extreme nervous irritability" from the cold. The only "cure" for her "low spirits" was writing, and she told Amelia Curran they were considering consulting Vaccà in Pisa.[5] In a medical sojourn, the Shelleys visited the Gabinetto Fisica, a museum containing wax anatomical models and met the Reverend William Clark, M.D. He wanted copies for Cambridge University and, on Shelley's security, was loaned £30 for the project from Madame du Plantis.[6]

A disturbing event on January 23 solidified plans to move to Pisa. Elise Foggi, living in Florence, called. Unsettled by her reappearance, Shelley immediately wrote to John Gisborne they "suddenly" had decided to go to Pisa and he would visit them soon in Leghorn.[7]

One ritual before leaving was having Percy Florence, in Claire's words, "half baptized" by an English clergyman.[8] Shelley sold his carriage and, in their haste to depart, packed Madame du Plantis's silver-plate spoons, returning them to the irate landlady four months later.[9] Her anger increased upon discovering they also had taken her daughter's piano chiroplast, Shelley intending that Henry Reveley make a copy for Claire. After Madame du Plantis accused Claire of stealing it, Mary hoped never to see her "ugly face" again.[10]

Departing by boat on January 26 in a cold wind, at Empoli they took a carriage to Pisa and lodged at the Tre Donzelle.[11] The next day, they called at Casa Silva on Via Mala Gonella, south of the Arno, where Mrs. Mason gave them some of her Irish political pamphlets from the late 1790s.[12]

Born Margaret Jane King in 1772, Mrs. Mason was the oldest daughter of Viscount Kingsborough, County Cork. She was fourteen when Mary Wollstonecraft became her governess-tutor for one year. Margaret credited the "noble" Mary Wollstonecraft's "affectionate mildness" with curbing her own quick temper, preventing her from turning into a "ferocious animal."[13] A countess at age nineteen, she soon regretted her marriage to the conservative second Earl of Mount Cashell. In the late 1790s, he was a Tory in the Irish House of Lords, while Countess Mount Cashell, a United Irishwoman, entertained leading liberals, including Grattan, Curran, and the visiting Godwin.

With her husband and five children in Paris in 1801, Lady Mount Cashell saw such notable friends of Wollstonecraft's as Thomas Paine, Thomas Holcroft, Amelia Opie, and Helen Maria Williams. She met Talleyrand, Lafayette, and the Bonapartes.[14] Becoming the lover of Irish-born George William Tighe in Rome in 1804, she remained in Europe with him when her husband took the children home. Socially rejected in London for her de facto marriage to Tighe, Lady Mount Cashell adopted the name "Mrs. Mason" from Wollstonecraft's *Original Stories from Real Life*.[15] Tighe and Margaret last visited the Godwins in 1814, days after Shelley, Mary, and Claire eloped.[16]

Shelley, writing Hunt about his attraction to Mrs. Mason, now forty-seven, said it was his "fate" to find another "lady of 45, very unprejudiced and philosophical . . . and a disposition rather to like me, in every town I inhabit . . . But certainly this lady is."[17] (Forty-five was also the age of Lady Charlotte Campbell Bury at this time.) Claire found Mrs. Mason an emotional mainstay, describing her as "very tall, of a lofty presence. . . . Her countenance beamed mildly, with the expression of a refined, cultivated, and highly cheerful mind. . . . I never saw the smallest symptom of the melancholy and discontent which was so striking both in Byron and Shelley."[18]

The retiring George Tighe's nickname, "Tatty," derived from his interest in growing improved potatoes. Claire admired him as "a most accurate and penetrating judge of human nature." Shelley found him "very agreeable," not as inferior to Mrs. Mason as John Gisborne was to his wife.[19] The Masons' second daughter, Nerina, was five.

Pisa provided Shelley a milder climate, pure drinking water, Vaccà's medical care, nearby therapeutic baths, and the Gisbornes in Leghorn. Cleft by the Arno and a few kilometers from the Mediterranean, Pisa allowed Shelley to indulge his passion for boats. Another attraction was the absence of Florence's gossiping English society, rejected by the Shelleys. However, a recent Pisan resident, the prickly classical writer Walter Savage Landor, spurned Shelley's overture because of the stories of his marriage to Harriet he probably heard from his friend Southey. Landor—whose poem *Gebir* Shelley had recited aloud too frequently for Hogg at Oxford—told Mary after Shelley's death he regretted not having extended himself in Pisa.[20]

Pisa's influence and population having dwindled, its reputation now rested on its fine architecture and renowned university where Galileo promulgated his laws of motion. Shelley wrote the Gisbornes that he and Mary were "going to study Mathematics"[21] and borrowed Henry's copy of the *Encyclopedia Britannica*. Claire described Shelley walking "about reading a great quarto Encyclopedia with another volume under his arm."[22]

On January 29, the Shelleys moved into rooms of the Casa Frassi on the Lungarno, unaware for two weeks of the death that day of George III. The Prince Regent, now George IV, was mentioned by Mary in replying to Sophia Stacey's letter from Naples. Mary suggested they would not again see Sophia because she would want to go to England to see the "good-for-nothing" Regent crowned. Mary asked Sophia to "forgive my radicalism" and Shelley added a note and enclosed his poem "On a Faded Violet." Shelley's words were perhaps the last sent to Sophia. Claire recorded three more letters from Sophia to the Shelleys by mid-August but no replies exist.[23]

Three years later, as Mrs. Catty, Sophia was given a wedding reception in Brighton—"a most brilliant entertainment"—by George IV's morganatic wife, Mrs. Fitzherbert.[24] Shelley probably never knew that Lieutenant Tom Medwin in June 1819 had been received by the Regent in a levee at Carlton House.

Sir Timothy Shelley, hearing of the birth of the new potential heir to his title and estates, wrote Whitton about Shelley's unpaid debts: "It is not likely He will soon visit England with so many unwelcome Guests to ask how he does by a Gentle Tap."[25] One "guest," the Bath decorating firm still trying to collect £1100, contacted Timothy who refused to "interfere in this unpleasant business."[26]

The firm wrote Shelley implying he had bought their furniture intending to sell it to get to the Continent and threatened to declare him a legal outlaw unless he paid £500 toward his debt. Shelley protested their "ruinous & disgraceful plan," saying there was "nothing dishonourable in my conduct" as he left England precipitously to "re-establish my health."[27] Meanwhile, Madocks, Shelley's Marlow agent, was holding his books hostage until he was paid what Shelley owed him. On top of this, Shelley wrote Hunt to stall off the debt on the Marlow piano.[28] Later, in a futile move to cover the *post obit* bond they arranged in case Shelley died before his father, the Bath firm took out an insurance policy on Shelley's life with a clause for non-payment if death was by drowning. Six years later the firm went bankrupt never having collected a shilling of Shelley's debt.[29]

Elise's Florence visit had set in motion financial worries concerning Elena Adelaide Shelley. Two days after moving into Casa Frassi Shelley went to Leghorn, probably communicating that his financial problems necessitated curtailing his investment in Henry's steamboat. In a matter of weeks, Shelley retrenched on the project and Henry prepared to go to England with the Gisbornes.

After Shelley returned from Leghorn, Mary skipped her journal entries for almost a week. Shelley and Claire again were sharing activities without her. When Dr. Vaccà visited the family for the first time in early February, Claire's diagnosis of swollen lymph glands elicited her comment, "Vaccà . . . says I am scrofulous and I say he is ridiculous."[30] Vaccà soon convinced Shelley his symptoms were not life-threatening, diagnosing his "disease as entirely nervous and nephritic." Shelley should "leave his complaint to Nature," Vaccà insisting he stop taking all drugs and medication prescribed by his previous physicians.[31] Once again, Shelley had found a renowned physician whose political and humanitarian beliefs mirrored his own. Mary considered Vaccà "very pleasant . . . a great republican & no Xtian."[32] After Shelley's death, Vaccà said "the English . . . never tired of speaking ill of Shelley & of Ld. Byron, but that no man was ever so much loved by his friends as S."[33]

Mary's emotional state was suggested in Claire's early February journal entry, "A Greek author says, 'A bad wife is like Winter in a house.'"[34] Mary was anxious to talk to Maria Gisborne about going to England.[35] She was correcting *Mathilda*, whose heroine's farewell to poet Woodville was, "the turf will soon be green on my grave; and the violets will bloom on it."[36]

Letters from his lawyer, Longdill, and from Horace Smith left Shelley "unwell."[37] Smith added to his financial anxieties by probably confirming Longdill's news that Dr. Hume, the guardian of Ianthe and Charles, reported Shelley was in arrears for a quarter's child support. Shelley wrote Hume asking him to contact Smith for the money and inquired for the first time since leaving England as to "the health & intellectual improvement of my children." The financial mix-up, involving Shelley's failure to communicate with his London bankers, was not settled for another year.[38]

Money for another child—Elena Adelaide—soon concerned Shelley. The Gisbornes' brief visit at the end of February—ostensibly to bring the Shelleys' new maid, Caterina—instigated Shelley's going to Leghorn several days later.[39] Returning to Pisa, he wrote the Gisbornes he had sent the "requisite" letters concerning financial and legal arrangements for Elena Adelaide. He directed his Florence banker to close his account and send the balance to John Gisborne. Shelley probably sent another letter to Elena's caretakers in Naples. Arranging to provide the Gisbornes a set amount of money for Elena, he would "make up the deficiency" between that amount and his Florence bank balance. In this money-laundering plan, the Gisbornes passed Shelley's money to a third party for delivery to Naples. He sent the Gisbornes "an outside calculation of the expenses at Naples calculated in ducats—I think it is as well to put into the hands of Del Rosso or whoever engages to do the business 150 ducats.—or more, as you see occasion.—but on this you will favour me so fa[r as] t[o] allow your judgment to regulate mine." He expressed a "thousand thanks" for their kindness and interest.[40]

Frederico del Rosso—later a lecturer at the University of Pisa—was an eminent Livornese attorney.[41] That Shelley acquired his services indicated some payment change for Elena, now beginning her second year with the Naples caretakers. Shelley's allocation of 150 ducats—about £30—suggests some possible extortion involving Elena. Mary, writing Marianne Hunt, perhaps alluded to Elena's expenses as "claims . . . external or perhaps rather internal for they belong to ourselves."[42]

Linked to Shelley's concern about payments for Elena was his suspicion that his mail was being intercepted in the Pisa post office. Returning from Leghorn, he asked the Gisbornes to address their letters to him as "Medwin." By March 19, increasingly suspicious, he asked the Gisbornes, if they wrote "again on the subject of Del Rosso" to address him "simply 'Mr. Jones.'"[43] In his letter to his Florence banker, he enclosed a second letter to be forwarded to him *Poste Restante*, a possible trick to see if someone would ask for his letter at the Pisa post office.[44]

On March 11, Shelley wrote the Gisbornes his most frank letter concerning his precarious marriage. In a stark appeal, Shelley discussed the depth of Mary's depression, her animosity toward him, and the extent of their alienation from one another. Shelley's letter, preserved by John Gisborne but suppressed by Mary or her daughter-in-law, was not published until 1980.[45]

Expressing his fear that Mary would take her own life, Shelley said his efforts to help only worsened their situation: "Mary has resigned herself, especially since the death of her child, to a train of thoughts, which if not cut off, cannot but conduct to some fatal end." Her "inward change" was expressed in her "Ill temper and irritation at the familiar events of life." Shelley's own irritability "awakens" his annoyance with her and that "all my attempts to restrain exasperate." Repeating her suicidal potential, Shelley added, "Mary considers me as a portion of herself, and feels no more remorse in torturing me than in torturing her own mind— Could she suddenly know a person in every way my equal, and hold close and perpetual communion with him, as a distinct being from herself; as a friend instead of a husband, she would obtain empire over herself that she might not make him miserable—In seeking to make another happy, she would find her own happiness." He entreated Maria Gisborne to come, as Mary has "a greater affection" for her "than for any one else" and her "presence would be a perpetual friendly check upon all evil."

Shelley, companionless in his agonizing isolation from Mary, began composing *The Sensitive Plant*. In early April, Mary wrote John Gisborne, "After some days of weakness Shelley had a very bad nervous attack yesterday he is better today but not well."[46] That same day, another critical letter from Godwin arrived.

Mary, upset about Maria's leaving Italy, told her to come to Pisa and "argue the point." The Shelleys had moved to more rooms on an upper floor of Casa Frassi and Maria could have a "comfortable bed." Mary told her, "You must expect me to shed tears when you go."[47] When Maria left for England in early May, Mary read four of Wollstonecraft's works and Godwin's *Memoirs* of her mother. Shelley, companionless, in April urged Hunt, Medwin, Hogg, and Peacock to visit him in Italy.

Shelley, writing *The Sensitive Plant* in his own room atop Casa Frassi, described to Hunt "the wise and amiable" Mrs. Mason.[48] Shelley told Medwin that he read Greek with Mrs. Mason and that she was his inspiration for *The Sensitive Plant*. Medwin thought her garden "unpoetical," but Shelley suggested it was the poem's setting.[49]

The Sensitive Plant, *mimosa pudica* or modest mimosa, also called "touch-me-not" and "Shame Lady," folds discreetly when touched. Shelley identified with the plant's nervous sensibility,[50] and its sexual hermaphroditism fascinated botanists. Shelley later called himself the "mimosa" when writing Claire.[51]

Gleaning Greek mythology for flowers with particular erotic meaning,[52] Shelley perhaps knew that the mimosa, the only annual among his flowering perennials, was susceptible to early death. The poem, ending in death-like winter, begins in a sexually awakened spring garden. Infused with the "Spirit of Love," the Sensitive Plant "panted with bliss . . . Like a doe in the noontide with love's sweet want." Aroused and "companionless," the plant's frustration introduces the substitute satisfaction of a maternal "undefiled Paradise" whose "flowers (as an infant's awakening eyes / Smile on its mother)."

The maternal "Power in this sweet place," the Lady who tends the garden, also having "no companion," is an idealized mother: "If the flowers had been her own infants she / Could never have nursed them more tenderly." With the passing of summer, this maternal bliss ends as "she died!"

This loss, symbolized by the devastating effect of autumn and winter upon the Sensitive Plant, seemingly suggests the loss of the mysterious lady of Naples: over "the waves of Baiae . . . / She floats up through the smoke of Vesuvius." In increasingly "lurid" stanzas, the decaying flowers—having "stifled the air till the dead wind stank"—are replaced by "loathliest weeds" with "names the verse feels loath" to mention. Shelley probably censored obscene names of plants he knew with "Pale, fleshy" shape.[53] Mary, reprinting the poem, deleted an entire stanza depicting the decaying plants as a human corpse left to rot on a gibbet.

Upon spring's return, the Sensitive Plant was a "leafless wreck." Had the poem ended here with its pessimistic, near-death devastation, its placement in the *Prometheus Unbound* volume after the title poem's sense of hopeful renewal would have seemed strange. Read as either personal or political allegory, *The Sensitive Plant* ends with hopeful skepticism in a Conclusion that leaves unsettled both the fate of the deserted, ravaged Sensitive Plant and the emotional legacy of the deceased Lady of the Garden. "I cannot say" if the Sensitive Plant or the Spirit of Love that sat "within its boughs" "felt this change" of rebirth. However, "It is a modest creed" that "death itself must be / . . . a mockery" and it is we who "are changed;" the "garden sweet, that lady fair" "In truth have never pass'd away." Shelley concluded his poem,

> For love, and beauty, and delight
> There is no death nor change: their might
> Exceeds our organs—which endure
> No light—being themselves obscure.

Shelley, having read Mrs. Mason's annotated copy of *Political Justice,* continued writing *A Philosophical View of Reform.*[54]

Mrs. Mason, reviling Byron, was encouraging Claire to be more assertive about seeing Allegra. Claire, not having seen Allegra in a year and a half, wrote Byron in mid-March begging him to send the child to Pisa.[55] Not hearing from Byron by mid-April, Shelley and Claire tentatively planned to go to Ravenna for Allegra. However, Shelley had "some business" in Leghorn, undoubtedly to see del Rosso about Elena. When the Gisbornes visited the Shelleys on April 20–21, Shelley returned with them to Leghorn.[56]

Claire next wrote Byron she and Shelley would leave Pisa early May to "fetch" Allegra for a healthful summer in Bagni di Lucca away from the "unwholesomeness of the air" of Venice and Ravenna. Because long travel would be "detrimental" to Shelley's health, he would accompany Claire only to Bologna. In this unrealistic scenario, if Byron did not send Allegra to their hotel in Bologna, Claire would "proceed to Ravenna," being "careful not to molest you."[57]

Just before Claire wrote this letter, Byron had written to Hoppner explaining why Allegra "shall not quit me again." He "totally" disapproved of the Shelleys' treatment of children, adding, "Have they ever *reared* one?" Sending Allegra to the Shelleys was "to perish of Starvation, and green fruit—or be taught to believe there was no Deity." In a year or two he intended to send her to England or "put her in a Convent for education." He reiterated that Claire could have the child with her if she lived in the "vicinity."[58]

Mrs. Hoppner immediately conveyed Byron's rejection in a letter to Claire, including his attacks on Shelleyan child-rearing. Mary thought "The Hoppners have behaved shamefully."[59] A volley of letters between Claire and Byron ensued in May and after receiving a "Brutal letter from Albè," Claire took her severe headaches to Mrs. Mason's to spend days putting the library in order.[60]

Before the Gisbornes and Henry sailed on May 2, Mary and Shelley went to Leghorn to say goodbye. Mary, insisting Maria keep a diary of their journey, gave the Gisbornes the manuscript of *Mathilda* to give to Godwin. After Maria's departure, Shelley gave Mary the ten-day task of transcribing seven of the nine short poems to be published with *Prometheus Unbound*. Shelley had accepted John Gisborne's offer to proofread *Prometheus Unbound* while in London, after Ollier refused to send the proofs to Italy. When Ollier gave the proofing job to Peacock, Shelley was very displeased with the result.

Canceling the Ravenna trip, Shelley, in late May, left for Casciana to join George Tighe in taking the baths. Returning through Leghorn, he shipped two alabaster vases to Horace Smith and possibly saw del Rosso again. When he wrote the Gisbornes that Henry's steamboat was "asleep under the walls," they probably felt the boat's sleeping resulted from Shelley promising more than he would deliver, an accusation they were hearing in London from Godwin. Shelley, unrealistically expecting "to have piece of mind" soon, enclosed his final "additions" to *Prometheus Unbound*.[61]

Returning with a bad head cold, Shelley answered a letter from Byron, their first exchange since October 1818. Responding tactfully, Shelley wished Byron "had not expressed yourself so harshly in your letter about Clare" who "was obliged to read it." Shelley assured Byron he would teach a child neither belief nor disbelief and "a regard to chastity is quite necessary, as things are, for a young female."[62] When Claire spent a day away in early June, Mary wrote, "A Better day than most days . . . [even] though Shelley is not well."[63] Mary was now using symbols in her journal, a sunburst for Claire and a crescent moon, possibly signifying Shelley's blackmail payments to Paolo.[64] Shelley journeyed again to Casciana on the tenth to consult George Tighe, who had some law training. Claire recorded, "He who keeps his grief within his own breast, is a cannibal of his heart."[65]

The day after Shelley returned to Pisa, Mary wrote "Paolo" with her crescent moon in her journal. Claire's entry was "Bother & Confusion with packing up." Shelley apparently had suffered another panic attack June 12 in the Pisa post office, where he found letters from Sophia Stacey, John Gisborne, and probably a blackmail letter from Paolo Foggi.[66] Shelley returned to Casa Frassi with the story of being threatened in the post office by his old Tanyrallt nemesis, Leeson. Mary's crescent moon, possibly a lunacy symbol, may indicate Shelley's emotional state from Paolo's blackmail. Neither Mary nor Claire mentioned Shelley's attack in their journals. Repeating his pattern of fleeing after believing he was attacked, Shelley announced they had to leave Pisa immediately; they stayed overnight with Mrs. Mason. Shelley, after spending the next day in Leghorn, allowed the family to return to Casa Frassi. On June 15, they moved to the safety of the Gisbornes' Casa Ricci in Leghorn, near the lawyer, del Rosso.

Claire and Medwin left accounts of Shelley's Pisa post office experience. In the more reliable versions of Claire, related to Edward Silsbee fifty-six years later, Shelley returned from his usual solo trip to the post office saying, "we must be off—Leeson has met me there—threatened to murder me to accuse me of foul crimes & have me imprisoned." George Tighe, returning from Casciana June 14, confronted Shelley, saying it was "unmanly to flee . . . from Such accusations—no Englishman must." Shelley should "meet him & apply to law abt. him." According to Claire, Shelley relented, they returned to Casa Frassi, and Shelley "never again spoke of his being pursued by Leeson who was his fancied assassin."[67] Back at Casa Frassi, Claire wrote of Shelley's fright, "The king of England with all his merry men / Marched up a hill & then marched down again."[68] Mary, using book references in her journal as codes for personal issues, mentioned two of her father's novels right after Shelley's incident; *Fleetwood,* with its Wales locale and near-mad hero, and *Caleb Williams,* a story of guilt and paranoid pursuit.[69]

Paolo's blackmail threats probably triggered Shelley's latest delusional episode involving Leeson. Silsbee noted that Claire commented on Shelley's "persistent hallucination about Leeson." She thought this "fear of Leeson's accusing him of crime has a strange bearing as to his feelings about women & the relations one should have with them."[70] Shelley's possible sexual involvement with Claire about this time cannot be ruled out, despite the "ban" on entering her bedroom she reported a jealous Mary imposed upon Shelley. According to Silsbee, Claire said Shelley considered bedrooms "chambers of horrors."[71]

In Medwin's account, related by Shelley at least five months after it occurred,[72] there was no mention of Leeson. Rather, Shelley was approached in the post office by "a stranger" who was "an Englishman" and "an officer in the Portuguese service." Hearing Shelley's name when he asked for his mail, the "tall, powerful" stranger said, "What, are you that d——d atheist Shelley?" and "struck him such a blow that it felled him to the ground, and stunned him." When Shelley came to, the ruffian had disappeared. "Raving with insult," he immediately sought out Tighe, who learned the stranger had left the Tre Donzelle for Genoa. Not knowing his route, thought of pursuit was abandoned. Medwin's version indicates Shelley had changed his story to accord with the Keswick and Tanyrallt attacks by being physically assaulted and receiving a blow. He possibly lost consciousness, either after opening a threatening letter from Paolo Foggi or after meeting an Englishman in Pisa whom Shelley believed was Paolo's accomplice. Peacock surmised that this incident, like the one at Tanyrallt, was another of his friend's "semi-delusions," a view Trelawny expressed to Claire in 1870.[73]

Without mentioning Shelley's delusional attack, Mary wrote Maria Gisborne from Casa Ricci that "a variety of circumstances have occurred not of the most pleasant nature" that made it necessary "to consult an attorney and we thought of Del Rosso & came here." They believed "Our old friend Paolo" was part of a larger conspiracy against them and "there were other circumstances" that Mary would tell Maria in person. Not knowing if they were "done with" Paolo, "a most superlative rascal," they had "to guess

as to his accomplices." On their "thorny" path of life, Mary's "anxiety" about Godwin was "not the least of my troubles." She wondered if the Gisbornes were "pleased or vexed" that they had
"taken possession" of Casa Ricci, which they planned to occupy for
"1 or 2 months . . . That is if you will not be angry."[74] The Gisbornes
were hearing angry accounts of Shelley from Godwin.

Shelley, now wearing a ring inscribed in Italian, "The good time
will come,"[75] learned that *The Cenci* was selling and urged Ollier
to prepare a second edition. Hearing that the reviews "blaspheme
me at a great rate," he wondered "why I write verses for nobody
reads them."[76]

Shelley used Henry's "raftered" attic room in Casa Ricci as his
writing redoubt[77] and began an epistolary duel with Southey in late
June. Still convinced Southey wrote the slanderous, anonymous
review of *The Revolt of Islam,* Shelley told him he hoped Southey
was not the "unprincipled hireling" who, "with the cowardice, no
less the malignity, of an assassin," could "insult the domestic
calamities of a writer of the adverse party." Southey, citing the
"menace" in Shelley's letter, denied writing the review and implied
that Harriet's suicide resulted from Shelley's rejection of Christianity.[78] Shelley disavowed "any menace" toward Southey and
hoped to meet him in London as "ten minutes' conversation is
worth ten folios of writing." Disclaiming responsibility for Harriet's death, Shelley said, "I shall never make the public my familiar confidant." Southey then replied that Shelley had "corrupted"
and "debauched" Harriet's mind, leading her into a life of "shame"
after their separation. Because Shelley's life was an "Atheist's
Tragedy . . . scarcely less painful, than the story of the Cenci,"
Southey recommended he read the Scriptures.[79] Southey later
wrote a friend that his letters gave Shelley "such a lecture" as his
"execrable history" deserved.[80]

Still suspicious about Southey, Shelley drafted an unfinished
poem, "A Satire upon Satire," with canceled lines recommending
Southey be subjected to the whip with "strokes . . . Till it be broken
on his flinty (soul) heart."[81] Shelley later wrote Hunt that he "meant
to be very severe" in the poem, which "was full of *small knives.*"[82]

Shelley's ongoing conflict with Godwin was punningly characterized by Claire as "Old Sky-Ball & young Sky-Ball."[83] Godwin—
writing to Mary and attacking Shelley for not sending a "shilling"
of the £500 he expected—enclosed a copy of an earlier letter which
Shelley probably kept from her. If Shelley would "not send me"

money, Godwin's "next request is, that he will let me alone" and stop "deluding me."[84] Mary, after consulting a reluctant Shelley, wrote the Gisbornes asking them to loan Godwin £400. Shelley enclosed a promissory note payable to John Gisborne pledging the loan's repayment in £50 quarterly payments with interest. Shelley told Gisborne not to give the money to Godwin unless he was certain it was for the rent settlement. Mary ended her letter, "Shelley is far from well, being nervous to an extraordinary degree."[85]

That same day, June 30, Shelley began another letter to the Gisbornes, which Mary never saw. Stating that Godwin's incessant appeal was only one "cause [that] combines with a thousand greater and lesser accessories to disquiet me," if the Gisbornes rejected making the loan for Godwin—"my bitterest enemy"—neither he nor Mary "shall love you the less." No money was to be paid directly "into Godwin's hands," and the Gisbornes should see all the legal signatures. Shelley, "full of bitterness" making this request, had received alarming news of Elena Adelaide's health. Once again, he poured out his anguish over his strained marital situation and elusive poetic fame: "What remains to me? Domestic peace and fame? You will laugh when you hear me talk of the latter. . . . Domestic peace I might have . . . but have not, for Mary suffers dreadfully from the state of Godwin's circumstances." Shelley, "very nervous, but better in general health," said they "have had a most infernal business with Paolo." Writing "from Henry's study," Shelley was sending "some verses I spawned the first day I came, which will show you how I struggle with despondency."

Shelley then effectively undid Mary's appeal for the loan by insisting the Gisbornes "refuse" to lend Godwin the money unless they could "enforce" Godwin's using it for its intended purpose. He reminded them of his overextended financial obligations and of "Godwin's implacable exactions . . . his boundless and plausible sophistry." Any responses to Shelley that were "unfit for Mary's agitated mind" should be sent "under cover of Mrs. Mason." After copying the verse letter he enclosed, Shelley—wanting more information of the "real state" of Godwin's lawsuit—closed, "You know vultures have considerable appetites."[86]

Shelley's enclosed poem, *Letter to Maria Gisborne,* has an underlying depressive theme deceptively veiled by a casually charming style.[87] In Henry's attic room, "a soft cell," Shelley could "Yield to the impulse of an infancy / Outlasting manhood" by constructing one of his boyhood paper boats "made to float" in Henry's "pretty . . .

walnut bowl" filled with liquid mercury. Among recalled "absent images" is the "wisest lady," Maria Gisborne, who, listening as Shelley recited his "visionary rhyme," was to him "As is a nurse—when inarticulately / A child would talk as its grown parents do."

This parental reference evoked Godwin, "greater none than he / though fallen," the first in a list of Londoners the Gisbornes will see. Also eclipsed is Coleridge, "who sits obscure . . . A hooded eagle among blinking owls." Coleridge told Maria Gisborne in late June of hearing from Southey that Shelley "possessed much genius." Coleridge thought Shelley "a wicked character . . . but allowed of the possibility of misrepresentation."[88] In Shelley's poem, Hunt was "one of those happy souls . . . the salt of the earth" while Hogg "locks" and "barricades" his great "virtues," "a pearl within an oyster shell." Peacock had "Turned into a Flamingo, that shy bird." His unexpected marriage in March 1820 to Jane Gryffydh evoked Shelley's lines, "When a man marries, dies, or turns Hindoo, / His best friends hear no more of him." Horace Smith's "Wit and sense" rounded out Shelley's list of friends. Unmentioned was Keats, whom the Gisbornes would see twice.

Shelley closed his verse letter imploring Maria Gisborne, "Next winter you must pass with me" to read together "books, Spanish, Italian, Greek." And, "as to nerves," Maria was the best treatment: "when you are with me there, / And they shall never more sip laudanum."

Mary recalled an evening walk with Shelley, perhaps June 22, when they heard the skylark's "carolling."[89] Shelley's *To a Sky-Lark* recalls the bird's "shrill delight," "unbodied joy" and "profuse strains of unpremeditated art." Feeling rejected as a poet, he envied what "Thy skill to poet were, thou scorner of the ground!" In perhaps an envious comparison with Byron, Shelley rephrased Maddalo's words ("They learn in suffering what they teach in song") with "Our sweetest songs are those that tell of saddest thought." Shelley had written Byron several weeks earlier after reading *Don Juan*, "Where did you learn all these secrets? I should like to go to school there."[90] *To a Sky-Lark* closes:

> Teach me half the gladness
>   That thy brain must know,
> Such harmonious madness
>   From my lips would flow,
> The world would listen then, as I am listening now.

The exuberant spontaneity of the poem's cascading similes conceals Shelley's carefully wrought draft revisions. "Hail to thee, blithe Spirit! / Bird thou never wert," was initially drafted—under his drawing of a tree—as, "What art thou blithe spirit / For bird thou hardly art."[91]

Shortly after completing these lines, Shelley wrote to the Gisbornes: "My poor Neapolitan, I hear, has a severe fever of dentition. I suppose she will die, and leave another memory to those which already torture me. I am awaiting the next post with anxiety, but without much hope." He added, "We have had a most infernal business with Paolo, whom, however, we have succeeded in crushing. . . . I struggle with despondency." He added a hopeful postscript July 2: "I have later news of my Neapolitan. I have taken every possible precaution for her, and hope they will succeed. She is to come as soon as she recovers."[92] Several days later, after receiving the news that Elena Adelaide died on June 10, he wrote the Gisbornes:

> My Neapolitan charge is dead. It seems as if the destruction that is consuming me were as an atmosphere which wrapt & infected everything connected with me. The rascal Paolo has been taking advantage of my situation at Naples in December 1818 to attempt to extort money by threat[en]ing to charge me with the most horrible crimes. He is connected with some English here, who hate me with a fervour that almost does credit to their phlegmatic brains, & listen & vent the most prodigious falsehoods. An ounce of civet good apothecary to sweeten this dunghill of a world.[93]

Mary, not sharing Shelley's despair, probably enclosed his letter with her lighthearted one to Maria Gisborne, saying, "Our Babe is well & merry."[94] Soon Mary wrote Maria that "Necessity" brought them to Leghorn because Paolo "came here" and "laid an accusation." Their lawyer del Rosso then had him ordered "to quit Leghorn in four hours." They felt the "idea of going to Del Rosso was most fortunate, as otherwise we certainly should have been frightened again, if not unnecessarily teazed."[95] The teasing was not over.

To a Sky-Lark and Ode to Liberty were mailed in time to become the final two poems in the Prometheus Unbound volume. Ode to Liberty had been gestating since March when the Shelleys read in the Examiner of the revolution in Spain against King Ferdinand, whose monarchy had been restored in 1814 with the Inquisition.

Shelley had written to Hunt in April of migrating to Spain, for its warmth and because of the recent "glorious events . . . You know my passion for a republic, or anything which approaches it."[96]

The *Ode*, mostly composed in early July,[97] begins as a call for restored Liberty and ends, "As waves which lately paved his watery way / Hiss round a drowner's head in their tempestuous play." This sadly prophetic vision includes a "wild swan" in flight, doubly killed by a storm's lightning-bolt and by drowning. Ironically, the lightning "bolt" through the swan-poet's brain is also an arrow—Ovid's image of Liberty as the goddess Diana—making Shelley's Liberty an arrow-armed "huntress . . . terror / Of the world's wolves!"

This fiercely destructive Liberty reflects Shelley's long-standing ambivalence about violence in the fight for freedom. In the *Ode*, the free should "stamp the impious name / Of **** [King] into the dust" and "Lift the victory-flashing sword" against him. Liberty should not hesitate "To set thine armed heel on this reluctant worm." Shelley, a veteran victim of English blasphemy and sedition laws, warned Peacock that asterisks might have to substitute in the *Ode* for "King" and "Priest."[98]

Amid the continuing conflict between Mary and Claire, Shelley read, translated, and escaped alone to Pisa. Claire wrote in her journal in early July, "Heigh-ho the Clare & the Ma / Find something to fight about every day."[99] Mrs. Mason, trying to separate Claire from Shelley and Mary, had written her friend Helen Maria Williams in Paris about a position there for Claire. Shelley evidently was to take Claire to Paris but Mrs. Mason's mid-July letter said "our Parisian plan has failed." Claire got another rebuff in an unbending letter about Allegra from Byron's secretary-steward.[100]

Mrs. Mason, well-versed in domestic sexual intrigue, recognized Shelley's continuing need for Claire stunted her being independent and fueled Mary's depressive anger toward Claire and Shelley. In his note to Maria Gisborne, Shelley—avoiding his role in the marital conflict—wished Mary "were as wise now as she will be at 45, or as misfortune has made me" because she "would then live on very good terms with Clare." Shelley asked Maria not to mention to Mary what he discussed in his letters and enclosed an unidentified poem which, "Of course," he had not shown to Mary. In London, the Gisbornes were hearing from Godwin that all three of his daughters "were all equally in love with" Shelley and that Fanny's suicide was due to Shelley's preference for Mary.[101]

In late June, Shelley began reading aloud the comic satirical poem *Il Ricciardetto* and soon adopted its *ottava rima* verse form to freely translate the "infinitely comical" Homeric *Hymn to Mercury*.[102] Perfecting a style of *ottava rima* in *Hymn to Mercury* differing from that of Byron and Keats, Shelley wrote his longest translation, astonishingly finishing the forty-seven stanzas on July 14.[103]

Shelley's infant-trickster hero, Mercury-Hermes, a precocious "schemer subtle," appropriates the family wealth by stealing from his older brother by another mother. Hermes, playing a lyre, sings a parody of Shelley's skylark, an "unpremeditated song" of "blithe noise." In a rare indulgence of anal humor, Shelley's flatulent Hermes "sent out of his belly that which was / A fearful herald of the want behind."

Earlier, Shelley had composed four lyrics for Mary's short mythological dramas, *Midas* and *Proserpine*, completed in early May.[104] For *Midas*, he wrote "Song of Apollo" and "Song of Pan," contrasting the magisterial sun-god's affirmation—"I am the eye with which the Universe / Beholds itself, and knows it is divine,"—with the sexuality of the earth-god's "sweet pipings" near where "Liquid Peneus was flowing— / And all dark Tempe lay." For Mary's other drama, Shelley composed "Song of Proserpine" and "Arethusa," the latter one of his most compelling love lyrics in which the sexual pursuit of nymph Arethusa by river god Alpheus ends in their watery merger of love-making.

In mid-July, Claire returned from a visit at Casa Silva bringing Mrs. Mason, her daughter Laurette, and Miss Mathilda Field, an English schoolmistress.[105] Shelley and Mary having decided to leave Leghorn, he returned to Pisa with this Mason entourage to search for a home outside the city. During his five-day absence, Claire watched another cylinder being cast for the steamboat.[106]

Upon finishing *Hymn to Mercury*, Shelley began reading Catherine Macaulay's *The History of England from the Accession of James I*, part of Mary's encouragement that he follow the success of *The Cenci* with another drama whose revolutionary theme Godwin suggested two years earlier.[107] Shelley, answering Medwin's letter praising *The Cenci*, decried the "squeamishness" that kept it off the stage and mentioned his intention to write another play, "in the spirit of human nature, without prejudice or passion, entitled 'Charles the First'."[108]

Shelley's decision to write *Charles the First*—which he did not start for another year—perhaps was spurred by word at this time

of the political revolution in Naples against Metternich's puppet
government. Claire thought it "glorious"[109] and Shelley approved
the constitutionalists' declaration that they would execute the
royal family if Austria declared war. Hunt printed a fiery passage
from *Lines written among the Euganean Hills* in his *Examiner,*
taking care not to mention Shelley's name.

Another political event arousing the Shelleys was the royal scandal over George IV's attempt to divorce his long-exiled wife, Queen
Caroline. She returned to England in early June amid popular support to claim her crown just as her husband's legal evidence of her
adultery was being presented in the "green bag" to the examining
lords. Shelley—reluctantly siding with Caroline, "this vulgar cook-
maid they call a Queen"—believed it was "really time for the English to wean themselves from this nonsense." His despised
Castlereagh, Eldon, and Sidmouth all had hands in the matter. Referring to Pasiphae's intercourse with a Bull, Shelley suggested "a
Bill will be passed in Parliament to declare that no Minotaur shall
be considered as legal heir to the Crown of *these* realms."[110] Adopting Mary's suggestion, he later depicted Caroline in *Swellfoot the
Tyrant* as "Joan Bull."

In late July, Shelley heard from John Gisborne about Keats's serious condition. When the Gisbornes first met him in June at the
Hunts', Keats responded empathetically to Maria's comment
about a singer's expert breathing by noting it was like "when a
diver descends into the hidden depths of the sea you feel an apprehension lest he may never rise again." Later that same
evening, Keats ruptured another blood vessel at home and moved
into the crowded Hunt house to be cared for. When the Gisbornes
next saw him July 12, they were shocked by his changed appearance as he sat without saying a word. Maria wrote he looked "emaciated" and "under the sentence of death from Dr. Lamb,"[111] the
William Lambe Shelley cited approvingly in *Queen Mab.* Lambe insisted Keats go to Italy, and possibly the Gisbornes and Hunt discussed asking Shelley to invite Keats to stay with him.[112] Shelley
responded quickly to John Gisborne's news of Keats and on July
27 wrote his best-known letter, extending an invitation to Keats.
Writing and mailing the letter in Leghorn, Shelley gave Pisa as his
address, expecting to be living there.

Shelley's gracious invitation to Keats came a week after he extended a similar one to Medwin and to "your friend," Edward
Williams. Qualifying his "sincere welcome," he told Medwin the liv-

ing conditions "may be found deficient."[113] In his letter to Keats, Shelley said if Keats "could [find] Pisa or its neighbourhood agreeable to you, Mrs. Shelley unites with myself in urging the request, that you would take up your residence with us." Referring to Keats's latest setback, Shelley advised him "to pass the winter a[fte]r so [treme]ndous an accident in Italy." Shelley suggested he come by sea to Leghorn, "within a few miles of us."[114]

Keats received Shelley's letter August 12, the day he left Hunt's home distraught, after learning a servant had opened a letter from his beloved Fanny Brawne. Keats wrote to his sister, "Yesterday I received an invitation from Mr Shelley, a Gentleman residing at Pisa, to spend the winter with him: if I go I must be away in a Month or even less." Keats also wrote appreciatively about Shelley's invitation to his friend Charles Armitage Brown.[115] Four days after receiving Shelley's letter, Keats wrote thanking him for his invitation.[116] He gave this letter, and a copy of his just published *Lamia* volume of poems, to the Gisbornes to deliver to Shelley. Keats had conditionally accepted Shelley's invitation, stating that only his prior death could stand in the way: "If I do not take advantage of your invitation it will be prevented by a circumstance I have very much at heart to prophesy." In response to Shelley's invitation, Keats immediately wrote to his publisher John Taylor asking him to inquire about a passage to Leghorn. Taylor viewed Shelley unfavorably, having turned down *Laon and Cythna.* Arranging and financing Keats's trip to Italy, Taylor found passage on a ship to Naples.[117]

Before receiving Keats's letter and poems in October, Shelley heard from Hunt that "Keats, who is better, is sensible of your kindness" and had been "advised to go to Rome, but will call on you in the spring." Three weeks after receiving Keats's letter, Shelley wrote Marianne Hunt in late October: "Where is Keats now? I am anxiously expecting him in Italy where I shall take care to bestow every possible attention on him ... I intend to be the physician both to his body & soul."[118]

The exchange in the two poets' letters, aside from Keats's illness, centered on frank criticisms of the other's poetry. Shelley, not having liked *Endymion* upon first reading it, mentioned he had just read it again "with a new sense of the treasures of the poetry it contains, though treasures poured forth with indistinct profusion." Believing this was why so few copies sold, he added, "I feel persuaded that you are capable of the greatest things, so you but will. . . . In poetry *I* have sought to avoid system & mannerism; I wish those who excel me in genius, would pursue the same plan." Shelley, an exacting self-critic, raised his estimate of his younger rival's genius in October when he read Keats's "Hyperion, A Fragment" in the *Lamia* volume the Gisbornes brought.[119]

Keats acknowledged in his letter to Shelley that his "mind was like a pack of scattered cards" when he wrote *Endymion* but now "I am pick'd up and sorted to a pip." Returning Shelley's critical volley about "indistinct profusion," Keats commented on *The Cenci:* "You I am sure will forgive me for sincerely remarking that you might curb your magnanimity and be more of an artist, and 'load every rift' of your subject with ore." Returning another criticism, Keats recalled Shelley's advice to him on a walk on Hampstead Heath "not to publish my first-blights." Keats expected *Prometheus Unbound* any day from Ollier and wished Shelley had not rushed his lyrical drama into print. Thanking Shelley again for the "kindness" of his invitation, Keats closed his letter, "In the hope of soon seeing you."

On July 30, Shelley rented for three months their next home in Bagni di Pisa—San Giuliano Terme—four miles north of Pisa on the road to Lucca. Writing to Mary from Pisa of the "spacious" apartment's rooms for writing, he said Mrs. Mason was unhappy because Tatty, believing England was on the verge of revolution, planned to go there to secure his financial matters. Shelley did not believe England was on the "eve of exploding" and hoped for "a Reform." Having "no thought of leaving Italy," he would "save money" for several years when perhaps "it will be time for me to assert my rights, & preserve my annu[i]ty." Alluding to his father possibly dying, he added, "Meanwhile another event may decide us."[120]

On August 5, after stopping briefly to see Mrs. Mason, the Shelleys, with Claire, arrived at their new abode, Casa Prini, in San Giuliano. Neither Mary nor Claire mentioned Shelley's twenty-eighth birthday the day before in their journals.

11

Baths of San Giuliano

Mary, PERHAPS INSPIRED BY HAVING HER OWN WRITING ROOM, SOON composed a children's story, *Maurice*, for Mrs. Mason's daughter Laurette. She sent it to Godwin, whose refusal to publish it was remedied after the manuscript was discovered in 1997.[1] The story's setting, a waterside cottage, perhaps was suggested by the canal behind Casa Prini connecting the Serchio and Arno Rivers. Claire began taking the thermal baths with friends from Pisa, including Mrs. Mason, Madame Tantini, and Mrs. Mason's former servant, "Betsy the Nun."[2]

Mary believed the baths soothed Shelley's "nervous irritability,"[3] perhaps aggravated by Godwin's accusing letter demanding money. Addressed to Mary, Shelley kept it from her and wrote a long, blistering reply that Godwin called "scurrilous." The Gisbornes, soured by Godwin's recounting of his financial fight with Shelley, departed for Italy in early September.

Shelley, refusing Godwin money, advised him "not to depend on me for any further pecuniary assistance at the present moment." The "considerable fortune" of "£4 or £5000" he had given to Godwin "might as well have been thrown into the sea." Shelley said he had more deserving creditors than Godwin who, with his "extraordinary accomplishments," could get the £400 himself. Shelley told Godwin that Mary had agreed he could intercept Godwin's letters to determine if they might "disturb her mind." Further, Godwin should cease his financial correspondence with Mary because of the old charges that Godwin was selling his two daughters into prostitution with Shelley. Mentioning his own "most complicated embarrassment," Shelley was concerned that "my very limited resources might involve me in personal peril." Alluding to Paolo's blackmail efforts, he told Godwin, "I fear that you & I are not on such terms as to justify me in exposing to you that actual state of my delicate & emergent situation which the most sacred considerations imperiously require me to conceal from Mary." Shelley refused to elaborate on this "subject now present to my mind" and accused Godwin of "disturbing" their marital harmony by "revenging [Shelley's] witholding of money."[4] Shelley's "sacred considerations" suggests he was still hiding from Mary details about Elena Adelaide,[5] including his relationship with the mysterious lady and his possible fathering of Elena Adelaide. A few weeks after writing Godwin, he again saw del Rosso.

Shelley was again experiencing his periodic "nephritic pains," which Vaccà considered not life-threatening.[6] The arrival of Southey's letter about Shelley's "menace" did not help his peace of mind and Mary wrote Amelia Curran that numerous "spies" were stealing their letters but their attempts at "desperate mischief lately" succeeded "no further than to blacken us among the English." Should Amelia hear this "scandal against us . . . it is all a lie."[7]

To escape these anxieties, Shelley now made his deferred trek up Monte San Pellegrino. The entire household went to Lucca where, the following morning, August 12, Shelley began his solo trip. Mary and Claire visited in Lucca the tomb of Castruccio, the title of the novel Mary was writing, later called *Valperga*.[8] They returned home through Ripafratta and Pugnano along the Serchio, the same river Shelley was following north to Castlenuovo before beginning his ascent. Monte San Pellegrino in Alpe, a pilgrimage spot for Catholics, has a rocky shrine to the Virgin Mary, all parodied in the "enwombèd rocks" of the cave of Shelley's pagan Witch goddess he would soon write about. Shelley probably spent the night atop the mountain, returning to San Giuliano the next day, August 13. Mary later wrote he made his two-day trip "on foot" but he could only have covered this distance by conveyance or horseback, as his notes indicate.[9] Still, it was a strenuous trip and Mary wrote that the "excursion delighted him" but he had "exerted himself too much, and the effect was considerable lassitude and weakness on his return."[10] Feeling lassitude or not, Shelley began the most rapid pace of poetic composition of his life. Starting August 14, in three days he composed the eighty-four *ottava rima* stanzas of *The Witch of Atlas*.

Shelley's "visionary rhyme" has allusions to Spenser's *Faerie Queene*, "Virgil's Gnat," and Forteguerri's *Ricciardetto*, all among his current reading.[11] The beautiful "lady witch" combines urbanity and playfulness, humor and skepticism, light-heartedness and darkness, as well as a teasing sexuality. Her cool detachment, bordering on stern indifference, callousness, and "lack of understanding sympathy,"[12] is best summed up by Shelley's word, "aloof."

Mary, perhaps sensing that the Witch's aloofness and lack of sympathy referred to her, maintained a negative view of the poem. The six opening stanzas, dedicated "To Mary," broadcast the Shelleys' continuing marital quarrel. Shelley subtitled these dedicatory stanzas, "On her objecting to the following poem, upon the score of its containing no human interest." Veiling his hostility with humor, Shelley created a poetic rebuke to Mary. Not surprisingly, she omitted these stanzas when she first published the *Witch:*

> How, my dear Mary, are you critic-bitten
>   (For vipers kill, though dead) by some review,
> That you condemn these verses I have written
>   Because they tell no story, false or true?
> What, though no mice are caught by a young kitten,
>   May it not leap and play as grown cats do,
> Till its claws come? Prithee, for this one time,
> Content thee with a visionary rhyme.
>
>   (1–8)

After comparing Wordsworth's "nineteen years" to clothe "Peter Bell" in "windowed raggedness" to his "three days / in dressing" his wizard lady in "Light the vest of flowing metre," Shelley challenged Mary to "unveil my Witch," an undressing that like "love, when it becomes idolatry," carried no "sin."

Among her three critical responses to the *Witch* after Shelley's death, Mary in 1839 considered it "peculiarly characteristic of his tastes." Seemingly unable to appreciate the poem's almost bitter commentary on the human passions, including sexual love, she derogated the *Witch* as "wildly fanciful . . . discarding human interest and passion." Her efforts to change his "abstract and dreamy" style for one that suited "the popular taste" were in "vain." Saying that "Shelley shrunk instinctively from portraying human passions," Mary evaded the Witch's erotic roles as titillator, voyeuse, exhibitionist, prankster, and gossip.[13] For Mary, Shelley was inspired by "yellow moonshine."

Parodying the Christ-child myth, Shelley's *Witch* features a carnal conception between two parents producing a female deity. Born a full-grown woman, the Witch's nudity was only "garmented in light" but no Wise Men came to "behold" her. Rather, she attracted the "sly serpent," "rude kings," lusty satyrs, and "quaint

Priapus," the phallic fertility god. Reacting to her visitors' admiring glances, she weaves around her naked beauty a "subtle veil," a mere "shadow," to cover the "splendour of her love."

Inside the Witch's visionary cave—"The deep recesses of her odorous dwelling"—are "scrolls of strange device, / The works of some Saturnian Archimage" telling of the "happy" Golden Age before Christianity's original sin, the "native vice" of sexual guilt. The Witch "cannot die as you must" and—like Mary doing research on fourteenth-century Lucca for her novel—"All day the wizard lady sate aloof / Spelling out scrolls of dread antiquity." Shelley's description of the Witch's hearth (stanza 27) contains his loveliest lines about fire: "Each flame of it is as a precious stone / Dissolved in ever moving light."

The Witch produces an infant from a sexual act she finds offensive:

> Then by strange art she kneaded fire and snow
>   Together, tempering the repugnant mass
> With liquid love
>
> (321–23)

Shelley later suggested his Witch may eventually lose her repugnance toward sexuality and know "what love was." However, remaining "chaster," she is a "sexless bee," a promiscuous honeygatherer "Tasting all blossoms and confined to none." The child she creates in her own image, a hermaphroditic "creature," is a "sexless thing" with "no defect / Of either sex, yet all of the grace of both."

The Witch's "feeble" chariot—one of Shelley's flimsy poetic boats—was reconditioned as "the lightest boat" afloat. Fitting her "Hermaphroditus" with "two rapid wings," the Witch commanded, "Sit here!" Captain and navigator, the Witch "played her many pranks" steering to her favorite place, the warm Nile River whose "Mareotid lakes" are "Strewn with faint blooms like bridal chamber floors, / Where naked boys bridling tame Water snakes."

The Witch, like the Egyptian goddess Isis, is able to bring the dead back to life. With voyeuristic delight, she watched sleeping mortals, including "two lovers linked innocently" and those "old and young" in "troubled forms of sleep" with religious nightmares about "custom's lawless law," marriage. The Witch was insensitive to their fears and suffering, "the strife / Which stirs the liquid surface of man's life." Reversing religious dogma, Shelley declared it was the callous Witch who could learn from mortals and "make that Spirit mingle with her own."

This mingling could bring about Shelley's social aspirations: priests would "pull / The old cant down," the king would replace himself with an ape, soldiers would beat their swords into ploughshares, and "timid lovers"—no longer "coy"—take "sweet joy" with such "fulfillment." Rather than the "many thousand schemes which lovers find / The Witch found one" to bring "happiness in marriage warm and kind." As if alluding to Mary's conflicts over Claire, Shelley wishes "Friends who . . . / Were torn apart" the Witch "did unite again." However, the last stanza conveys skepticism that the Witch's "pranks" provided any "panacea" for mortals' malaise.

If Shelley were wishing for marital "happiness" in the *Witch*'s penultimate stanza, his wish went unanswered. The August emotional climate in the Shelley household was decidedly unsettled. Mary, upset by Claire, again left her journal blank for a week. Claire, after escaping again to Casa Silva for Mrs. Mason's advice, planned to spend September in Leghorn at Casa Ricci before the Gisbornes returned.

The nonviolent revolution in Naples helped prompt Shelley in mid-August to begin composing one his most carefully crafted poems, "Ode to Naples."[14] His note to the "Ode" mentioned other "recollections" of Naples[15] that influenced the poem's elegiac tone, including Pompeii—"the city disinterred"—and possibly Elena's death weeks earlier. Shelley entreats all the cities of "eternal Italy" to join Naples in overthrowing foreign oppression so that conflicting political passions might become "harmonizing ardours" of liberty and be humanity's "high hope and unextinct desire."

Wanting to get his political "Ode" quickly into the English press and realizing that the Neapolitan revolution would be short-lived, Shelley bypassed the dilatory Hunt and sent "Ode to Naples" to an opposition paper he increasingly turned to, the Whig London *Morning Chronicle*. The poem appeared September 26 with his initials and the *Military Register and Weekly Gazette* reprinted it in early October, a martial recognition that would have surprised and bemused Shelley.[16]

His next political poem, written immediately after, left no doubt of Shelley's burning anger. *Oedipus Tyrannus; or, Swellfoot the Tyrant*—Shelley's most savagely satiric political writing—was quickly published and just as quickly suppressed and burned in London. *Swellfoot* was a frontal assault on the monarchy of the sexually profligate George IV and the terrible social conditions imposed upon the poor. Queen Caroline's farcical sexual escapades made Shelley's contempt for her only slightly less than that for her reviled husband.

Some scholars dismiss *Swellfoot the Tyrant*, Shelley's most blatantly sexual poem, as a lapse into "bawdy." Beginning with its overtly phallic title, (Oedipus means swellfoot, that is, erect penis), the two-act verse burlesque's sexual jokes and imagery include the royal couple's sex-role reversal: George is a "man-milliner," Caroline the "Bull-Queen." *Swellfoot* displays Shelley's grasp of the sexual idiom of his day, however much he was influenced by such sexually comic classical sources as Hesiod, and Aristophanes' *The Frogs* and *Lysistrata*.[17] The starved pigs—the English masses in *Swellfoot*—reflect Shelley's contempt for Edmund Burke's 1790 epithet, the "swinish multitude," which appeared in *Swellfoot's Dramatis Personnae*. Mary recalled the impetus for Shelley's Chorus of Pigs was a grunting group of hogs outside their windows who "riotously accompanied" Shelley's high-pitched voice as he recited the recently completed "Ode to Naples" to the visiting Mrs. Mason.[18] Shelley's *Swellfoot* abounds with his Field Place hog-knowledge, including spaying of sows, "cut close and deep." Ben Jonson's phrase, "whoring in the pig stalls,"[19] embellished Shelley's attack on Malthus's idea of sterilization of the poor, represented by "Moses" the sow-gelder.[20]

The revolutionary intent of *Swellfoot the Tyrant* and *The Mask of Anarchy* reflects the ideas in *A Philosophical View of Reform*. Despite his ambivalence about a revolution of the lower classes, Shelley was not interested in cosmetic political change. After the stillborn fate of *The Mask*, Shelley sent *Swellfoot* to Horace Smith in the early autumn. It was published anonymously by mid-December 1820. Early in *Swellfoot*, Shelley correctly anticipated the label of sedition pasted on it immediately after its publication. In the opening scene, within a grisly Temple of Famine "built of thighbones and death's-heads, and tiled with scalps" ("scalps of women" in his draft),[21] the obscenely paunched Royal Swellfoot confronts the starving Chorus of Swine. Shelley attacks Southey as the Chorus chants, "I have heard your Laureate sing, / That pity was a royal thing." Hearing the Pigs' words, Swellfoot declares, "This is sedition, and rank blasphemy!"

Swellfoot's final image is the Bull-Queen, cross-dressed like a fox-and-hound huntress who leaps "nimbly" on the back of Ion

Minotaur (John Bull) in response to his invitation, "mount me." Under its surface humor, *Swellfoot* deepens Shelley's increasingly vitriolic view that political change is always subject to subversion by destructive human passions.

Horace Smith wrote that all but seven copies of *Swellfoot* were burned in a "holocaust" at the Inquisition Office by The Society for the Suppression of Vice as soon as "it appeared in the bookseller's window." Smith had refused to give the Society the author's name for prosecution for "seditious and disloyal libel."[22] Smith's action saved the publisher, J. Johnston, from prosecution, but the Society was more successful when they sent William Clark to jail for publishing *Queen Mab* in 1821.[23]

Before taking Claire to Leghorn on August 31, Shelley again wrote Ollier complaining of his "timidity" for not publishing a second edition of *The Cenci* and indicating he had contemplated a trip to London that summer to square some of his debts. Using a long title not known until recently, Shelley asked Ollier if he would be interested in publishing an octavo volume entitled "A Philosophical View of the Question of Reform in the Government of Great Britain."[24] About this time, Shelley received Byron's curt three-sentence reply to Shelley's late-May four-page letter. Irritated by Claire's letters, Byron wanted to hear only from Shelley.[25] Shelley wrote to Mary from Leghorn of a delay in seeing del Rosso—about Paolo's blackmail—and spent several days with Claire before returning home. As usual, he felt "somewhat better" when away from Mary. Soon he wrote to Amelia Curran that should the Tory government fall, he might visit England.[26]

Claire, bathing daily during her month in Leghorn, read novels that mirrored her confusion over Shelley, Mary, and Byron. Charles Brockden Brown's *Ormond*—whose heroine, Constantia, had elicited Shelley's love poems to Claire—involved two women's rivalry for the same man. Claire began Richardson's *Clarissa,* whose tragic heroine's name was similar to hers. After her journal entry, "To pretend to convince a man who knows in his heart he is doing wrong!" she acidly wrote, "Another jiggeting rascal called Biron."[27]

Evidence of the fury of Mediterranean storms was Claire's mid-September entry that the "extremely high wind" produced "waves with sharp edges, dashing among the rocks." Several nights later she dreamed Allegra was coming from Ravenna, not aware that her daughter was frequently ill and living in a villa some distance from her father. Only Teresa Guiccioli visited the child. Shelley arrived September 27 to take Claire back to San Giuliano for a few days before she went to stay several weeks with Mrs. Mason. At Casa Ricci he left Mary's letter to Maria Gisborne, expected imminently from England.

Mary had not received one letter from Maria Gisborne. Finally, in early October, she heard from John Gisborne in Genoa that they hoped to sail for Leghorn the next day and were "anxious to see you." He enclosed Maria Gisborne's long August 23 letter. Mary wrote another invitation for the Gisbornes to visit but they neither visited nor corresponded after arriving in Leghorn. Only on October 10 did the Shelleys learn from Claire of the return of the Gisbornes, who apparently passed through San Giuliano without stopping. Angry and puzzled, Shelley wrote the Gisbornes, "We do not quite understand your silence," reminding them of "your promise when you left Italy" of a first visit. Five days later, getting no response, Mary made a fruitless peace mission to Leghorn. Home the next day, she wrote to Maria that Shelley was "in a state of considerable agitation" after Mary told him of Maria's vague, unspecified "accusations," which Maria had put in a "foolish" letter she never sent to Mary but did not recant. The letter probably included charges about Shelley and Claire by Mrs. Godwin, whom Mary called "that filthy woman." Mary's letter—delivered personally by Shelley—contained an ultimatum: the Gisbornes had to initiate any reconciliation, "join them, or us—the gulph is deep, the plank is going to be removed."[28] Mary did not see Maria Gisborne again until the next April.

A major cause of the rupture was Godwin's letter awaiting the Gisbornes in Leghorn. Apparently, the Gisbornes' last meeting with Godwin left them angry toward him and Shelley, Godwin implying that Shelley's "losses" on the steamboat precluded any aid to Godwin.[29] John Gisborne terminated the steamboat project and sent Henry on October 19 to negotiate with Shelley.

Shelley—in a "long and very explicit conversation" with Henry, whom he soon called a "whipped and trembling dog"—told Henry he "absolutely refused" to have anything more to do with the steamboat unless John Gisborne took no further part in the project. If Gisborne refused, Shelley would take what money he could get from the sale of the parts and tell his friends about "the vile treatment which I had received from him and his family." To obtain four hundred crowns to complete the steamboat, Shelley proposed the engine be mortgaged and resolved "to advance no more money to get it finished" as "The Gisbornes are people totally without faith. . . . the most filthy and odious animals with which I ever came in contact." If they came to visit Mary he would not stay in the house and had "already planned a retreat to Mrs. Mason's."[30]

This outburst against the Gisbornes in his letter to Claire contrasted with Shelley's note to John Gisborne that same day. Not mentioning the steamboat, he apologized for delaying sending Galignani's newspapers and asked John Gisborne's help in his plan to learn Arabic.

Shelley was unhappy when Mrs. Mason found Claire a living arrangement in Florence. Still financially dependent upon Shelley, Claire agreed to a one-month trial visit as a paying guest in the home of Dr. Bojti, his wife, and three children. In her anomalous role, she was neither governess nor a member of the family. However, Bojti, an unusually gifted man, could introduce Claire to sophisticated Florentine society and facilitate her future as a governess. A medical colleague of Vaccà's, Professor Bojti was a distinguished specialist in obstetrics who later attended Byron's Countess Guiccioli. The longtime friend of his patron, the Grand Duke Ferdinand III, Bojti lived directly across from the Pitti Palace.[31]

Shelley and Claire traveled to Florence on October 20, spending the night at an *albergo* before an intermediary, Dr. Tantini, took them to the Bojtis'. Upon returning to Pisa, Shelley learned from Mrs. Mason that Tom Medwin was at the Tre Donzelle. Not having seen Shelley for seven years, Medwin found him "emaciated, and somewhat bent; owing to near-sightedness" as he had "to lean over his books, with his eyes almost touching them." Shelley's "profuse" hair was "partially interspersed with grey . . . but his appearance was youthful." He had "a freshness and purity in his complexion that he never lost."[32]

Traveling to San Giuliano, Medwin mentioned he expected his Genevan friends, Edward and Jane Williams, would soon join them. Medwin's arrival, Claire's departure, and the estrangement from the Gisbornes began a gradual shift in the Shelleys' relationships. Reaching out to a circle of new acquaintances, for the first time in Italy they became more a part of the community in which they lived.

When incessant rain caused the Serchio to overflow, water from the canal and the flooded town square began filling Casa Prini's ground floor the evening of October 25. Shelley and Medwin, at an upstairs window, watched the torch-bearing, half-immersed peasant families driving their cattle through the water toward the dark mountains looming beyond the town. The next morning, with six feet of water on the ground floor, they crawled through an upstairs window to a boat.[33] Shelley found new lodgings in Pisa and on the twenty-ninth they moved into an ample apartment in the Palazzo Galletti on the Lungarno. Next door was the larger marble palazzo inscribed "Alla Giornata" (to the day), an inscription that Shelley told Medwin had "some deep and mystical meaning." Medwin, discussing this "mystery" of the meaning of "Alla Giornata" in his biography of Shelley, mentioned it became the title of a novel but did not mention its author, Lady Charlotte Campbell Bury. Medwin knew that Lady Bury and some of her daughters were in Pisa at this time.[34]

Claire and Shelley corresponded frequently. Her letters are lost but she kept several of his despite his asking her to destroy them. Her absence was "too painful," he missed her "sweet consolation," and were it not "for Mrs. Mason, I should say, come back immediately and give up a plan so inconsistent with your feelings." He found "seclusion" in his new fourth-floor study above Mary's mezzanine room but the "pain" of his recurrent "spasms" produced a "nervous irritability" that "is a great and serious evil to me." Against Vaccà's advice, he hinted of using laudanum again.[35] Medwin noted Shelley was using "Scott's vitriolic baths." Vaccà, perhaps not certain of his diagnosis, reportedly said after Shelley's death he did not believe his patient had nephritis. Vaccà knew Shelley's history of being "messed" by medications, including arsenic, nitric acid, laurel leaves, diuretics, powerful resins, opium, and mercury.[36]

Shelley and Medwin visited Pisa's sights, including the Camposanto frescoes and the Foundling Hospital. Mingling with a raucous carnival crowd along the Lungarno, Shelley was despondent. One pastime he enjoyed, Medwin said, was playing on the floor by the hour with Percy Florence.

Mary found Medwin a bore, not much of an improvement on Claire. Shelley also would find Medwin boring, but initially the two men hatched a variety of schemes. Shelley wrote Claire not to tell Mary of their plan to sail next spring to "Greece, Syria, and Egypt" on a ship owned by Medwin's wealthy friend who also admired Shelley's poetry. This "wealthy" friend perhaps was Edward

Trelawny, hoping to inherit money from his recently deceased father.[37] Earlier, Shelley had tentatively sought Byron's financial backing for this escapist voyage.[38]

Planning to study Arabic with Medwin for this trip, Shelley asked Claire to locate a grammar, dictionary, and other Arabic books in Florence. Writing to Peacock that he and his "schoolfellow" Medwin were studying Arabic, Shelley did not refer to Medwin as his cousin, usually calling him his "friend." Shelley found Keats's *Hyperion* "an astonishing piece of writing," providing "a conception of Keats which I confess I had not before." Shelley, currently "infirm of purpose" in his writing, had "great designs and feeble hopes of ever accomplishing them." Reading primarily Greek and Spanish, he told Peacock, "Plato and Calderon have been my gods." Medwin, aware of Shelley's "dejection and despondency," read aloud to him and Mary from his Indian journal.[39] Shelley successfully urged Ollier to publish Medwin's long poem, *Sketches in Hindoostan*, not "the highest style of poetry." Ironically, with this letter, Shelley sent Ollier "all my saddest verses," which were rejected with *Julian and Maddalo*. Commenting on his *Prometheus Unbound* volume he had received from John Gisborne, Shelley told Ollier it was "most beautifully printed" but full of "errors of the press."[40]

Mary, irked by Medwin and finding the Gisbornes' rejection "inexplicable," got inflamed eyes and suspended pouring through what Shelley called the "fifty old books" for *Valperga*. She again recorded reading *Corinne*, the story of two sisters involved with the same man.[41] Possibly, the book's title was a journal code anticipating Claire's return.

Claire wrote "caricatures" of Byron and Shelley in her journal, angrily parodying Byron and "his dirty mistresses." Shelley was "looking very sweet & smiling. a little ~~child playing~~ Jesus Christ ... grasping a small knife & looking mild. . . . I will quietly murder that little child." She added, "Shelley's three aversions. God Almighty, Lord Chancellor & didactic Poetry."[42]

Against his wishes, Claire preserved Shelley's long mid-November confidential letter containing his insistence that she return "instantly" and not extend her contract with the Bojtis. Although Mrs. Mason was "opposed strongly" to Claire's return, Shelley rationalized she would come around to his view. Claire was complaining her glands were acting up and he insisted, "How I long to see you again, and take what care I can of you."[43] That day

Mary's journal entries ceased for an entire week until her sunburst symbol noted Claire's return on November 21, the day Medwin became ill.[44]

Vaccà was summoned and Medwin recalled Shelley "tended me like a brother" with "assiduous . . . affectionate care" for six weeks, applying leeches and giving him medicine. During this time, Medwin read many of Shelley's works, including recent drafts in his manuscript notebook. Medwin's enthusiasm for his poems surprised Shelley. Echoing what he recently wrote to Peacock, Shelley told Medwin, "I am disgusted with writing, and were it not for an irresistible impulse, that predominates my better reason, should discontinue so doing." Conversing about Chatterton, Medwin recalled that Shelley, after saying "four of his friends had committed suicide," lapsed into one of his melancholy moods that was "most distressing to witness." Medwin observed, "I have reason to think . . . he had contemplated such a termination of his ills."[45]

Mary was annoyed whenever Medwin interrupted their evening reading to discuss literature. Shelley listed for him the few books needed for a good library, including the Greek plays, Plato, Bacon, Shakespeare, the older English dramatists, Milton, Goethe, Schiller, Dante, Petrarch, Boccaccio, Machiavelli, Calderón, and the Bible. Medwin said Shelley considered *Paradise Lost* superior to any other poem and the dungeon scene in Webster's *The Duchess of Malfi* equal to anything in Shakespeare. Shelley praised a novel of contemporary Greece, Thomas Hope's *Anastasius*, telling Medwin he avoided reading inferior prose or poetry "for fear of unconsciously spoiling his style." They read together Schiller's *The Maid of Orleans*, Shelley admiring its treatment of Christianity as a mythology.

Claire recalled Shelley had "the voice of a child—high tenor from the back of the head,"[46] but Medwin believed that Shelley's voice, unmatched when reading poetry, "was a cracked soprano, but in the variety of its tones, and the intensity of feeling which he displayed in the finest passages, produced an effect almost electric." As he had earlier for Byron, Shelley translated aloud Aeschylus's *Prometheus*, Medwin commenting it was as fluent as if written in French or Italian. After Medwin and Shelley read Calderón's *La cisma D'Inglaterra* [*The Schism in England*], Medwin attempted a translation which Shelley corrected, taking special care with lines about the taper and the moth, "His sunflower wings their own funereal pyre." The two read Dante, Shelley hinting he might translate the entire *Divina Commedia,* insisting it be in *terza rima* to do justice to the author. Medwin reported Shelley considered substituting his talent for translation for his lack of success with original composition.[47]

Now, in addition to Claire, another dark-haired young woman entered the Shelleys' lives, thanks to the November 24 visit of the eccentric Professor Francesco Pacchiani. Tall, dark-countenanced with black eyes and known as "il diavolo Pacchiani," the forty-nine-year-old erstwhile priest soon would be dismissed from the University of Pisa where he was professor of logic, metaphysics, and physical chemistry since 1801. He had not fulfilled the early promise such scientists as Volta, Cuvier, and Humboldt had placed in him. But for this failed academic and unsavory priest, *Epipsychidion* probably would not have been written. Perhaps Henry Reveley mentioned Shelley to his former teacher, Pacchiani. A crafty denizen of the Pisa–Florence–Lucca circuit and attracted to moneyed Englishmen and their ladies, Pacchiani supplemented his meager university salary with nefarious teaching and real estate kickback schemes.

Pacchiani initially charmed Shelley and Mary with his literary pretensions, knowledge of Uffizi art, and brilliant repartee. Mary wrote to Leigh Hunt that their friends incorrectly called Pacchiani "mad" and "eccentric," he was "the only Italian that has a heart and a soul . . . the highest mind, a profound genius, and an eloquence that transports." Medwin said Shelley compared Pacchiani's eloquence with Coleridge's. Shelley wrote to John Gisborne, "Henry will tell you how much I am in love with Pacchiani."[48] Soon Mary called him the "Black Genius," Claire found him "indecent," and he offended Shelley "by telling a dirty story."[49]

An ordained canon, Pacchiani contemptuously referred to his priest's cap as "Tartuffemetro," "measure of hypocrisy."[50] He was the confessor to the family of the powerful Governor of Pisa, Marchese Niccolò Viviani, whose two daughters, Teresa and the younger Ferdinanda, he tutored. Teresa, nineteen, was sixteen when she was sent to live in Pisa's Convent of Santa Anna, actually a conservatory school with ties to the Tuscan State. Too old to be a student, Teresa lived in a sort of open confinement as a special resident awaiting an arranged marriage. Two young attorneys, Biondi and Danielli, were interested in her. Teresa, estranged from her young mother and controlled by her old authoritarian father, soon triggered Shelley's rescue fantasies.

After Pacchiani enthused about Teresa, Medwin recalled that the priest took him and Shelley to see her. Entering the conservatoria on Via Carducci through a "gloomy portal" in the high stone wall, Medwin recalled he and Shelley were struck by Teresa's "profuse black hair, tied in the most simple knot." Her "features possessed a rare faultlessness, and almost Grecian contour, the nose and forehead making a straight line," her eyes having a "sleepy voluptuousness."[51] More likely, Claire was the first person in the Shelley household to meet her.[52] On November 29, Claire noted that she and Mary attended a memorial service at the nearby Church of San Nicola and that Pacchiani and the "Campbells" were there. Claire "Then went with Pacchiani to the Convent of St. Anna. The beautiful Teresa Viviani."[53] On her third visit, December 1, Claire probably introduced Teresa to Mary, having received a letter from Teresa the day before. On the third, Claire, Mary, and Shelley called on Teresa.[54]

The Shelleys soon called her Emilia, perhaps after the Boccaccio heroine who had two suitors.[55] Visiting frequently, Shelley, Mary, and Claire also corresponded with Emilia. Agreeing with Shelley's request that they call each other brother and sister, Emilia asked him to "embrace my very dear and beautiful sister Mary." Shelley brought her books and a little writing desk, Mary sent her a slender chain, and both gave her a pair of birds. Claire recalled that Shelley "by bribery . . . used to pass his evenings" at the convent.[56]

In late November, John Taaffe, an Irishman, paid the first of many visits to the Shelleys. A Pisan resident who had published an unrecognized poem, Taaffe's literary ambitions and modest talent earned him Mary's dismissive characterization, "the poet laureate of Pisa."[57] Like Shelley, Taaffe contracted in 1811 an ill-defined, ill-fated marriage in Edinburgh. His second marriage resulted in two children born in Pisa before their mother died in 1819. Late in life, Taaffe—always a staunch Catholic—wrote warmly of Shelley and his "rich and musical language." Shelley "knew English better than any person I ever met" and his conversation was "singularly mellifluous and full of heat." Taaffe recalled Shelley telling him that "he composed best when he was ill." Like others, Taaffe remembered Shelley's "custom of lying on the carpet like a dog . . . there was something wizened in his freckled face . . . something of the faded flower."[58]

Pacchiani brought to the Shelleys' the *improsivvatore*, Tommaso Sgricci, whose artistry—performing *poesia espontanea*—

immediately impressed Shelley. Sgricci, near his greatest fame, performed public *accademie,* passages in blank verse and *terza rima* followed by a complete tragedy. Each dramatic improvisation, constructed from several Greek dramatists, was recited like a spontaneous imaginative outpouring. Impressed with Sgricci's rendering of the death of Hector in a January performance, Shelley wrote a glowing review in Italian.[59]

Although Shelley complimented Sgricci as the "Dante among the ghosts" of Pisa, at a public performance Taaffe had to prevent a university professor from verbally chasing Sgricci from the theater.[60] Byron, seeing Sgricci in Milan, called him a "celebrated Sodomite . . . not known to have b——d anybody here as yet." Mary defended Sgricci against such slurs.[61]

The day Pacchiani introduced Claire to Princess Argyropoulo of the Greek expatriate society in Pisa,[62] he brought to the Shelleys' home the Princess's cousin, Prince Alexander Mavrocordato, future leader in the Greek revolution and the new republic's first president. Mary noted Mavrocordato's appearance with the upbeat "delightful weather."[63] Turning the tables on Shelley and Claire, she enjoyed Mavrocordato's attentions for the next six months.

One year older than Shelley, Mavrocordato was short with "bushy jet black hair and prodigious whiskers . . . thick eye-brows and huge mustache [that] gave a wild, romantic, expression to his features." Despite "large Asiatic eyes, full of fire and wit," he had difficulty looking people in the face.[64] Mavrocordato, exchanging language lessons with Mary, quickly picked up English as Mary's Greek improved. Shelley, a somewhat jealous classicist, disparaged Mavrocordato's Greek pronunciation and emendations when they read *Agamemnon* together. Admiring Mavrocordato as "one Greek of the highest qualities," Shelley matched wits with him over chess; Medwin observed neither had great skill.[65]

Shelley visited Emilia frequently but despite the mild winter, Mary noted he "suffers a great deal of pain in every way." A "cold" in his eyes kept him from reading and writing for two weeks in December.[66] Contributing to his malaise was Claire's decision to return to Florence.

Aroused by the Gisbornes' news of Keats's deteriorated health, Shelley drafted, but apparently never sent, a letter to William Gifford, editor of *The Quarterly Review.* Still smarting from the *Quarterly*'s anonymous review of *Laon and Cythna,* Shelley referred to the *Quarterly*'s savaging of *Endymion,* insisting the poem "with

all its faults is a remarkable production for a man of Keats's age."
"Hyperion" was "surely the highest style of poetry" and its author
was "coming to pay me a visit in Italy."[67] Shelley was unaware that
by the end of November Keats was in Rome, just down the Spanish Steps from Amelia Curran. He had less than three months left
of his "posthumous existence."

When Shelley's spasms continued into December, Medwin, becoming his health practitioner, told him of seeing animal magnet-
ism practiced in India. Medwin's having benefited from it in
Geneva elicited Shelley's "earnest request" to undergo the experience when he had his next attack. Medwin's report that Shelley
had not "previously heard of Mesmerism" seems unlikely.[68]

On the evening of December 15, Medwin placed his hand on
Shelley's forehead, producing a "deep slumber" that "instantly"
stopped his spasms. Shelley's eyes remained open during his
trance and, as Medwin led him from one end of the room to a sofa,
he responded to questions with the same pitch as Medwin's voice.
Once out of the trance, Shelley had the usual amnesia for what had
occurred. However, according to Claire, Shelley "begs them not to
ask him more questions because he shall say what he ought not."
After hypnotizing Shelley a second time, Medwin reported Shelley
"improvised" for the first time "faultless" verses in Italian. Medwin noted that Mary later magnetised Shelley but soon ceased
when, in a return of his old sleepwalking habit, he went to a window that fortunately was barred.[69]

Medwin's hypnotism provided Shelley temporary relief at best.
Mary said he was "very unwell" December 22, the day before
Claire's departure for a six-month stay in Florence. Arriving at the
Bojtis, Claire became ill and soon noted "My gland is opened." Writing letters to Shelley not for Mary's eyes, she chastised him for being insensitive to her feelings and he lectured her that her gland
problem came from "dejection of spirits" that could be remedied by
"society and amusement." Although Vaccà had reassured him to the
contrary, he was sure he would "be cut for the stone" and he reproached her that "it would have been better for you to have remained at Pisa." He casually mentioned "sometimes" seeing Emilia
who "continues to enchant me infinitely; and I soothe myself with
the idea that I make the discomfort of her captivity lighter to her by
demonstration of the interest which she has awakened in me."[70]

At the time of writing this early January letter to Claire, Shelley
probably had begun composing *Epipsychidion*. He developed

boils and a swollen face[71] and on January 11 he begged off going with Mary to Lucca to see Sgricci perform. During her two-day absence, he visited Emilia and worked on *Epipsychidion*.[72] He wrote Claire again of seeing Emilia and responded to her insinuation that he was in love with Emilia by declaring *his* kind of "*love*" for Emilia was not the same as what Claire called love.[73] That day, Shelley first met Jane Williams.

12

"Emily . . . my heart's sister"

J ane and Edward Williams had been urged by Medwin to come to Pisa "to chase Shelley's melancholy." Leaving Geneva in October with their infant son "Meddy," they were accompanied by a recent acquaintance, the Cornishman Edward John Trelawny, who also agreed to follow Medwin to Italy in search of Shelley. Trelawny had a copy of *Queen Mab* and after reading Medwin's copy of *The Cenci* he was eager to meet this poet who shared his political and social beliefs. First, however, he left the Williamses in Chalon-sur-Saône to proceed to England, his father having died. The Williams family, in late December, traveled to Marseille and fortuitously found a ship for Leghorn, where they arrived January 13. It was another year before Trelawny got to Pisa.

Medwin helped the Williamses find accommodations in Pisa, but only Jane, seven months pregnant, dined with the Shelleys at their first meeting, January 16. Shelley immediately wrote Claire that Jane was "an extremely pretty & gentle woman—apparently not *very* clever. I like her very much. I have seen her only an hour but I will tell you more another time. Mary will write you sheets of gossip."[1]

The gossip perhaps included the fact that Jane still was legally married to Captain John Edward Johnson of the East India Company Maritime Service. The Shelleys possibly learned that Jane Cleveland—born January 21, 1798—was sixteen when she married the ten-years-older sea captain in St. Pancras Church August 1814, just weeks after Shelley and Mary completed their romancing there and eloped to the Continent. Jane suffered "irreparable injuries" from her husband, later considered a gambler and a cheat. Claire would report that Jane and Edward met in India and returned to England together. In another version, while Jane's husband was away in 1817 on a year-long voyage, she may have written Edward Williams, proposing they elope. She had recently met

219

him in England, perhaps for the first time, after he returned from army service in India, where she had lived sometime before 1814.[2]

Mary enjoyed the Williamses' company, though Shelley was preoccupied with Emilia and composing *Epipsychidion.* Shelley helped Medwin translate Dante but Mary derided Medwin's effort "as a rotten apple is like a fine nonpareil."[3] The Williamses' plan to stay in Pisa only a month before going to Florence was canceled and Jane joined Mary, Claire, and Emilia as the fourth young woman in Shelley's Pisan orbit. Of the four, only Mary was unmentioned in Shelley's clandestine mid-January letter to Claire in which he denied being neglectful and wished that she would "love me better than you do." Confirming Claire's suspicions about his feelings for Emilia, he admitted finding "pleasure" in "an excessive susceptibility to nature . . . the smell of a flower affects me with violent emotions."[4]

Emilia was the "flower." Drafting a letter in Italian to her, Shelley considered her "lovelier to behold than the white lily on its green stem."[5] Perhaps after Emilia sent flowers to Palazzo Galletti, Shelley drafted the poem—printed by Mary as "To E*** V***"— beginning, "Madonna, wherefore hast thou sent to me / Sweet basil and mignonette?" Shelley asked, "Alas, and they are wet! / Is it with thy kisses or tears?"

Ten years later, Claire was greatly impressed when told by Emilia that "after Shelley's love for her . . . she never could be happy . . . with anyone else . . . after what had passed between Shelley and her." According to Edward Silsbee, these remarks—and *Epipsychidion*—made Claire think "Shelley was a lover of hers." Claire said Emilia called Shelley "adorable sposo" but Claire "could not tell whether S. was in <u>love</u> with her." Claire was "struck" that when Emilia married, Shelley "never felt it" or "seemed to mind it." Claire, looking back in her late seventies, believed Shelley's relationship with Emilia had been part of his "ruling passion . . . to shock the world." Apparently referring to Shelley's profession of love for Emily in *Epipsychidion,* Silsbee noted Claire told him: "They all saw it Medwin, Lady M. Cashel & all Mrs. S—— too wondered at him & how he could do it. Mrs. S was disturbed by it."[6] Disturbing too were lines Shelley drafted of a night reverie about Emilia's "trembling lips" creating "joys" that "Yet quiver thro' my burning face."[7]

Shelley also expressed his intense infatuation in his Italian letters, which she answered—to him and to Mary—in Italian. His romance with Emilia became a more lavish version of that with Sophia Stacey a year earlier. Emilia had composed sonnets and from her effusive essay, "Il Vero Amore," Shelley quoted lines on the "loving soul" as an epigraph to *Epipsychidion*.[8]

Mary loaned her Bible—*Corinne*—to Emilia, who recognized her own "sad . . . lot is the same."[9] Mary's sympathy for Emilia now became a tolerant skepticism. Shelley's letters and poetry to Emilia suggest they shared physical intimacies; his description of sexual intercourse with her in *Epipsychidion* is the most vivid erotic encounter in his poetry. Writing to John Gisborne, Shelley alluded to other sexual activities at the convent he found abhorrent, "most singular facts" that "belong to a part of human nature from which I shrink, I will be silent on them."[10]

Emilia, writing in Italian to Shelley, said that Claire would be "*jealous*" if she read her letter to him and asked if Mary "loves me less than the others do?" She concluded another letter, "I love you with all my heart, dear Brother!" and hoped "Mary won't be *jealous*."[11] Emilia, effectively combining naïveté, a manipulative bent, and a brazen frankness, wrote Mary, "I know that your husband said well when he said that your apparent coldness is only *the ash which covers an affectionate heart*."[12] Emilia later wrote Mary that "the only trait lacking in your perfections" was warmth, adding, "Accept my most tender kisses, which, being distant, will not be too warm for you, and will not have the effect of the *Sun* upon your *ice*, or limpid *drop from a frozen fountain*."[13] About this time, Shelley was using the sun-ice metaphor as he wrote about both women in *Epipsychidion*.

Mary got revenge when she satirized Emilia as Clorinda Saviani in her story, "The Bride of Modern Italy." A seventeen-year-old English painter—Shelley—makes "frequent" and "unwatched" visits to the conniving Clorinda. Mary, calling them "the lovers," wrote that the painter is only saved from "the folly he had been about to commit" by Clorinda's arranged marriage. In Mary's story was Claire's journal entry, "Emilia says that she prays always to a Saint, and every time she changes her lover, she changes her Saint, adopting the one of her lover."[14] The painter "had no tutelar saint" but he and Clorinda with "one kiss sealed their infidelity."[15]

Small-town Pisa's gossip about Shelley's convent visits no doubt grew when Emilia visited Palazzo Galletti January 19.[16] She reassured him in December about his concern that if he successfully liberated her they might be divided: "My soul, my heart, can never be parted from my brother . . . Emilia will seek you everywhere. . . . I always pray to God to grant that I may live with you always." Mary began reading Dante's *Vita Nuova* with Shelley in late January. If she knew he was writing the poem about Emilia as a Beatrice, she never mentioned it in her journal or letters. Shelley translated parts of *Epipsychidion* into Italian for Emilia before sending the fair copy in his hand to Ollier February 16. That day, Mary had visited Emilia and then was "alone"[17] while Shelley spent the evening at Casa Silva, probably completing his fair copy and writing Ollier. Already disavowing *Epipsychidion,* he told Ollier to publish it immediately and anonymously so it "should not be considered as my own; indeed in a certain sense, it is a production of a portion of me already dead; and in this sense the advertisement is no fiction." Intended "for the esoteric few," his "secret" as its author was "to avoid the malignity of those who turn sweet food into poison." He wanted only one hundred copies printed even though the number "who are capable of judging and feeling rightly with respect to a composition of so abstruse a nature, certainly do not arrive at that number." Further, "it would give me no pleasure that the vulgar should read it."

He had written the fair copy, "so as to give very little trouble, I hope, to the printer." Stung by Peacock's errors in proofreading *Prometheus Unbound,* and desiring anonymity, he asked Ollier to correct the proofs. With *Epipsychidion,* Shelley enclosed "Ode to Naples" and "a sonnet," probably "To the Republic of Benevento,"[18] whose lines suggest his inner struggle: "Man who man would be, / Must rule the empire of himself."

Shelley, ambivalent about anonymity, signed his introductory advertisement to *Epipsychidion,* "S." Ollier printed at least two hundred copies of *Epipsychidion* but Mary omitted it from her 1824 edition of Shelley's poems, placing it in her 1839 edition. It was Shelley's only major poem upon which she failed to comment except by her silence.

In late 1821 or early 1822, Shelley wrote Ollier to withdraw *Epipsychidion* from the market. In June 1822, he would write to John Gisborne:

The 'Epipsychidion' I cannot look at; the person whom it celebrates was a cloud instead of a Juno; and poor Ixion starts from the centaur that was the offspring of his own embrace. If you are anxious, however, to hear what I am and have been, it will tell you something thereof. It is an idealized history of my life and feelings. I think one is always in love with something or other; the error, and I confess it is not easy for spirits cased in flesh and blood to avoid it, consists in seeking in a mortal image the likeness of what is perhaps eternal.[19]

It was Shelley's most starkly autobiographical poem and Mary could not hide the repeated references to "Emily" or the quasi-anonymity Shelley bestowed on its full title, *Epipsychidion: Verses Addressed to the Noble and Unfortunate Lady, Emilia V——, Now Imprisoned in the Convent of ——*. Mary could not have been pleased with the preface or "Advertisement" that Shelley drafted four times. Harking back to Sophia Stacey's departure, he began, "The Writer of the following Lines died at Florence," omitting one draft's, "in January 1820." Most of what have been considered "Fragments Connected with *Epipsychidion*" probably was written a year earlier. Shelley apparently imported "almost word for word"[20] into *Epipsychidion* lines written in the same notebook in Florence, including the lines beginning, "I never was attached to that great sect" and ending with his discourse on "True love." Among other lines drafted earlier and incorporated into *Epipsychidion* were those Mary was to entitle, "Fiordispina."

Epipsychidion, more than a love poem to Emilia, is Shelley's self-analysis, "an inquiry into his *psychidion,*"[21] stemming from his failed relationships with women, including his two marriages. Shelley's coined Greek word, "epipsychidion" ("On the little soul"), indicates the poem's focus on the feminine aspect of his psyche.[22] Anticipating Jung's archetype of the *anima,* Shelley never named this internalized feminine, referring to it as "this soul out of my soul" and "a soul within the soul," a phrase in his earlier essay, *On Love.* Emilia was Shelley's latest "antitype," the person upon whom he projected his unconscious idealized "miniature," a process in *Epipsychidion* that relates to psychoanalytic concepts.[23]

Shelley's second draft of his preface to *Epipsychidion* contains a geographically accurate premonition of his death and a plot suggesting his curious idea for effecting Emilia's escape from the convent: "[The following Poem was found in the P.F. of a young Englishman, who died on his passage from Leghorn to the Levant] He was accompanied by a lady . . . supposed to be his wife, & an effeminate looking youth, to whom he shewed . . . so [singular] excessive an attachment as to give rise to the suspicion, that she was a woman—At his death this suspicion was confirmed."[24]

This *ménage à trois* voyage with maritally dubious Mary, and Emilia as a cross-dresser, seems related to Shelley's androgynous scheme that Claire persuade Mrs. Mason to dress as a man, marry Emilia, and receive her dowry. Free of the convent, Emilia would join the Shelley family. Mrs. Mason evidently had dressed as a man when studying medicine in Jena.[25] In another escape plot, Claire was to get a widower Pisan lawyer to marry Emilia. When Mrs. Mason foiled this plan, Shelley apparently burst out in anger toward her.[26]

The poem's beginning exemplifies Shelley's fondness for multiple allusions:

> Sweet Spirit! Sister of that orphan one,
> Whose empire is the name thou weepest on,
> In my heart's temple I suspend to thee
> These votive wreaths of withered memory.
>
> Poor captive Bird!
>
> (1–5)

The "orphan" can be Shelley, Mary,[27] or the orphaned Sophia Stacey. "Sister" Emilia also echoes Shelley's sister Elizabeth, "captive" at Field Place and a "withered memory." Poetically releasing Emilia from her "narrow cage" for her ascent beyond the heavens as "my adored Nightingale!," Shelley professes, "Emily, / I love thee," "Would we two had been twins of the same mother! / . . .I am not thine: I am part of *thee*."

Recognizing his romantic cul-de-sac, "Mine own infirmity!", he interspersed images of death with some of his most erotic images:

> She met me, Stranger, upon life's rough way,
> And lured me towards sweet Death;
>
> And from her lips, as from a hyacinth full
> Of honey-dew, a liquid murmur drops,
> Killing the sense with passion;
>
> (72–73, 83–85)

His wish, that "though dissimilar," they might endure "Such difference without discord," leads to Shelley's famous lines rejecting the institution of marriage:

> I never was attached to that great sect,
> Whose doctrine is, that each one should select

Out of the crowd a mistress or a friend,
And all the rest, though fair and wise, commend
To cold oblivion, though it is in the code
Of modern morals, and the beaten road
Which those poor slaves with weary footsteps tread,
Who travel to their home among the dead
By the broad highway of the world, and so
With one chained friend, perhaps a jealous foe,
The dreariest and longest journey go.

(149–59)

Mary, certainly "jealous," probably resented Shelley's implication of being his "foe." Continuing with lines written in Florence, Shelley rationalized his own needs: "True Love in this differs from gold and clay, / That to divide is not to take away." He added new lines:

Narrow
The heart that loves, the brain that contemplates,
The life that wears, the spirit that creates
One object, and one form, and builds thereby
A sepulchre for its eternity.

(169–73)

In his Advertisement, Shelley said—in Italian—it "would be a great shame" if a reader could not "know how to denude his words" to see his true meaning. Scholars, accepting his challenge, have deciphered the identities of his women.[28]

Following a strict chronology, Shelley began his history "In the clear prime of my youth's dawn" with "a Being whom my spirit oft / Met on its visioned wanderings, far aloft," seemingly his sister, Elizabeth, the "loadstar of my one desire," who "Past . . . / Into the dreary cone of our life's shade." Associating his loss of Elizabeth with his depressive episode—"my despair"—that brought him home from Eton, a seemingly hallucinatory "voice" told him, "The phantom is beside thee whom thou seekest" as he cast about for his lost "soul out of my soul."

In *Epipsychidion*, Shelley carefully recorded, sometimes for the first time, the depth of his emotional disturbance at each crisis in his life. Elizabeth's withdrawal from him was "this Chaos . . . / Of which she was the veiled Divinity." After losing Elizabeth, he hastily joined in schoolboy "stumbling" pursuit of sexual experience with other Etonians, all "untaught foresters," seeking "If I could find one form resembling hers, / In which she might have masked herself from me." Recounting his apparent sexual episode at Eton, perhaps with a prostitute—"One whose voice was venomed melody" and whose "touch was as electric poison"—the result, "hair grown grey," had the same "blanched . . . locks" in his 1820 tale of this encounter, *Una Favola.*

Subsequent relationships failed, as "In many mortal forms I rashly sought / The shadow of that idol of my thought." These "many" disappointing women extended from 1808 to 1814, when he met Mary:

> And some were fair—but beauty dies away:
> Others were wise—but honeyed words betray:
> And One was true—oh! why not true to me?
>
> (269–71)

Shelley's sense of betrayal by "wise" women included Elizabeth Hitchener, his first soul sister. The "One . . . not true to me" seems a composite of Harriet Grove and Harriet Shelley.

Addressing Mary's sexual coldness, Shelley, with brutal frankness, wrote perhaps the most hurtful lines Mary would read in *Epipsychidion:*

> The cold chaste Moon, the Queen of Heaven's bright
> isles,
> Who makes all beautiful on which she smiles.
> That wandering shrine of soft yet icy flame
> Which is ever transformed, yet still the same,
> And warms not but illumines.
>
> And there I lay, within a chaste cold bed:
> Alas, I then was nor alive nor dead:—
> For at her silver voice came Death and Life.
>
> (281–85, 299–301)

There follows one of *Epipsychidion's* most allusive passages, ostensibly about Harriet's drowning:

> What storms then shook the ocean of my sleep,
> Blotting that Moon, whose pale and waning lips
> Then shrank as in the sickness of eclipse;—
> And how my soul was as a lampless sea,
> And who was then its Tempest; when She,

The Planet of that hour, was quenched, what frost
Crept o'er those waters, 'till from coast to coast
The moving billows of my being fell
Into a death of ice, immovable;—
And then—what earthquakes made it gape and split,
The white Moon smiling all the while on it,
These words conceal:—If not, each word would be
The key of staunchless tears. Weep not for me!

(308–20)

Mary, "that Moon," is eclipsed by the first storm—Fanny Imlay's suicide—followed by Harriet's suicide, the "Planet" who was "quenched." The "Tempest" behind this storm likely was Eliza Westbrook, whom Shelley held responsible for Harriet's suicide as well as for the loss of his children.[29] This passage has overtones of the subsequent stormy events in Naples involving the mysterious lady and Elena Adelaide, melancholy losses evoking "staunchless tears" that Shelley's "words conceal." The "Tempest" alludes to Shakespeare's play about Naples (and Milan), a titled and motherless daughter, the stormy sea, and the enchanted isle to which Shelley will elope with Emilia.

Abruptly, Emilia appears as "The Vision I had sought through grief and shame." In Shelley's pantheon of astronomical loves, Emilia is the Sun. Her sexuality, both "soft" and "penetrating," arouses his "dreaming clay" that—"lifted"—ends the "long night" of Mary-Moon's sexual coldness: "I knew it was the Vision veiled from me / So many years—that it was Emily." Mary and Emily are "Twin Spheres of light who rule this passive Earth, / This world of love, this *me*."

Shelley next summons Claire to rejoin his Pisan sisterhood:

Thou too, O Comet beautiful and fierce,
Who drew the heart of this frail Universe
Towards thine own; till, wreckt in that convulsion,
Alternating attraction and repulsion,
Thine went astray and that was rent in twain;
Oh, float into our azure heaven again!

(368–73)

Shelley's relationship with Claire—"Alternating attraction and repulsion"—involved the "convulsion" of 1815 when their probable sexual relationship led to her expulsion to Lynmouth. Repulsed, in

1816 she went "astray" in Byron's bed with results that left her "rent in twain."

Recognizing his failed sisterhood of love, Shelley ended *Epipsychidion* with an apocalyptic sexual fantasy with Emilia, his "lady of solitude":

> Emily,
> A ship is floating in the harbour now,
> A wind is blowing o'er the mountain's brow;
> There is a path on the sea's azure floor,
> No keel has ever ploughed that path before;
>
> (407–11)

However virginal Emilia was, their sexual union on "an isle under Ionian skies" occurred near an ivy-twined ruined tower "pleasure-house." Exceeding the eroticism of the incestuous union of Laon and Cythna, Shelley created Romantic poetry's lushest imagery of sexual intercourse, a blissful annihilation of boundaries between self and other:

> Our breath shall intermix, our bosoms bound,
> And our veins beat together; and our lips
> With other eloquence than words, eclipse
> The soul that burns between them, and the wells
> Which boil under our being's inmost cells,
>
> We shall become the same, we shall be one
> Spirit within two frames, oh! wherefore two?
> One passion in twin-hearts, which grows and grew,
> 'Till like two meteors of expanding flame,
> Those spheres instinct with it become the same,
> Touch, mingle, are transfigured; ever still
> Burning, yet ever inconsumable:
> In one another's substance finding food
>
> (565–69, 573–80)

This climactic sexual fantasy with Emilia brings a painful awareness that his marital "chains of lead" carry greater authority than his "winged words." Neither the agonized cathartic poetic history of defeated love in *Epipsychidion* nor his fantasies about Emilia have changed his life. Returning to his real relationships, he concluded with the wish that his verse will affect "the hearts" of "Marina" (Mary), "Vanna" (Jane), and "Primus" (Edward Williams):

And bid them love each other and be blest:
And leave the troop which errs, and which reproves,
And come and be my guest,—for I am Love's.

(602–4)

Shelley, attending to love's realities, on the day he sent *Epipsychidion* to Ollier also sent to Claire a check for her next two months with the Bojtis. He hoped soon to tell Claire "of Del Rosso," whom he had just paid.[30] Silsbee's account from Claire was that Paolo threatened Shelley "for bad conduct" and Shelley "draws money . . . more than once."[31]

Shelley soon wrote Claire that "Keats is very ill in Naples" and he had "written to him to ask him to come to Pisa, without however inviting him to our own house" as "We are not rich enough . . . Poor Fellow!"[32] In Naples in early November 1820, Keats received what Severn called "a most generous letter" from Shelley, who did not learn Keats was in Rome until late March. Keats never saw Shelley's February 1821 letter. He died in Rome several days after it was written.

Shelley, soon to begin *A Defence of Poetry,* wrote Ollier of "high and new designs in verse . . . labours of years, perhaps." Not having begun *Charles the First,* he ordered more books, including one on geology and histories of Spain and England.[33] Medwin, before leaving February 27 for Florence and Rome, copied a number of Shelley's prose works which he published shortly after Shelley's death.[34]

Medwin's absence—and Mavrocordato's daily visits—lightened Mary's mood and Shelley asked Ollier to send her desk for her resumed writing.[35] Jane was in her final month of pregnancy, and she and Williams often dined with the Shelleys. During his brief stint at Eton, Williams apparently had not known Shelley, who was there at the same time.

In early March, the Shelleys moved to another Lungarno residence, Casa Aulla. Mary attended the birth of Jane Williams's daughter, Jane Rosalind, called Dina. Her middle name, from *Rosalind and Helen,* reflected Mary's role as her godmother.[36] Claire was "miserable" in Florence from disheartening news about Allegra that Shelley and Mary passed on from Byron.[37] Confirming what she had heard of Byron's intentions, Claire learned that Allegra was sent on March 1 to the convent school of San Giovanni Battista in Bagnacavallo, a small town in the marshy plains twelve

miles west of Ravenna. Byron, in Ravenna with an illegal cache of
Carbonari arms he had paid for, used the deteriorating military
and political scene as one reason for sending Allegra away.[38]

Allegra, only four, was three years younger than the age for ad-
mission at the school run by Capuchin nuns, known for poverty and
strictness. Byron, sending Allegra to Bagnacavallo with Ghigi, his
Ravenna banker, never saw nor inspected the convent.[39] Claire accused Byron of breaking his promise in Geneva that their expected
child "should never be away from one of its parents." Inquiring
about convent schools, Claire found they were "nothing less than
most miserable." Allegra was "being condemned" by Byron to "a
life of ignorance & degradation," a "condemnation" Claire said was
confirmed by Byron having paid "double" to assure Allegra
"proper treatment." Claire, unaware of Mrs. Hoppner's animosity
toward her, would "submit" to that "worthy" woman's "sound judgment" concerning Allegra's education. Claire proposed Allegra be
sent "at my own expense" to "the very best english boarding
school" that Byron's "own friends" should chose.[40] Byron sent her
letter to the Hoppners with an acid comment about what the Hoppners had told him they heard from Elise, that Claire left her newborn baby in Naples.

Shelley, kowtowing to Byron, wrote to him that he and Mary "entirely agree" with Byron's decision about Allegra and that Claire's
"unreasonable" opposition is "the result of a misguided maternal
affection, which is to be pitied, while we condemn." Byron, gratified that Shelley and Mary "do not disapprove," replied that Allegra's placement was "merely temporary."[41] He wrote Hoppner
that only "amiable Claire" disapproved and he had no intention of
giving "a *natural* Child an English education." Byron's £5000
"dowry" for Allegra was "a pittance" for a respectable English
marriage but was fine in Italy's marriage market. Besides, he was
determined "She should be a R[oma]n *Catholic* . . . the best religion" because it was Christianity's oldest branch.[42]

Unmentioned in Byron's reasons for sending Allegra away was
his relationship with Countess Teresa Guiccioli. Byron considered
Allegra and Teresa—seventeen years apart—his "two little
girls"[43] and Claire later reported that Teresa's jealousy of Allegra
led to the child's being "put in a poor convent."[44]

Adding to Claire's irritation were two "ridiculous" anonymous
love letters she accused Shelley of writing. In his bantering rejoinder, he did not flatly deny writing them, saying that "certain intox-

icating moments" helped relieve his depression. A weather change brings only a mood "change," not a "relief of ills."[45]

Shelley, writing *A Defence of Poetry*, had abandoned previous versions, including a dialogue between his persona, Lionel, and Keats.[46] In late January, Shelley had written Ollier taking exception to Peacock's "article," *The Four Ages of Poetry*, in Ollier's *Literary Miscellany*. It "excited" Shelley's "polemical faculties so violently" that he would send Ollier his answer to this "very clever . . . very false" essay for the *Miscellany*.[47] In February he jokingly wrote Peacock that *The Four Ages* "excited me to a sacred rage . . . I had the greatest desire to break a lance with you" but was "too lazy" to respond. Peacock had "unhorsed poetry," but Shelley— "the knight of the shield of shadow and the lance of gossamer"— had "a whole quiver of arguments." His arrows came partly from Plato's *Ion*, which he suggested Peacock re-read.[48] Shelley kept Ollier informed of his progress on the essay, which grew ever longer. Mary spent a week in mid-March copying *A Defence*. Shelley, refusing payment for it, sent it to Ollier on the twentieth with permission to omit text but not to alter it. Telling Ollier it was the first section of a three-part essay, Shelley was unaware the *Miscellany* had expired after the first issue. *A Defence* became another of his major works destined for posthumous publication.

Shelley argued against Peacock's views that poetry had no utility in the modern age of science and technology. Peacock—at thirty-three a failed poet when he joined the East India Company in late 1818—was now financially independent from Shelley. In *The Four Ages of Poetry*, Peacock was developing his version of the utilitarian ideology of his East India Company colleague, James Mill.[49]

After the "golden age" of Homer, Peacock thought poetry had declined to its present "brass age" exemplified by "egotistical rhapsodies" of "a morbid dreamer like Wordsworth." Peacock also tarred Byron, Southey, Scott, and Coleridge, but avoided mentioning Shelley, Keats, or Hunt in his essay. Serious intellectuals pursued science or philosophy while the poet is "raking up the ashes of dead savages to find gewgaws and rattles for the grown babies of the age." Shelley's reactions to these ideas was his most bravura prose performance.

The beauty and power of Shelley's language in *A Defence of Poetry* illustrate his thesis that "The distinction between poets and prose writers is a vulgar error." The beautiful language and thought of Plato and Lord Bacon made them "essentially" poets:

"All the authors of revolution in opinion are not only necessarily poets as they are inventors . . . their periods are harmonious and rhythmical and contain in themselves the elements of verse; being the echo of the eternal music."[50]

Shelley turned Peacock's arguments around by defending poetry with utilitarian arguments.[51] Having just ordered the latest scientific work in geology and the complete works of Milton, Shelley saw no essential distinction between poetry and science. He refused to devalue the utility of either the rational mind or the imagination: "whatever strengthens and purifies the affections, enlarges the imagination, and adds spirit to sense, is useful."

Poets with this "power" often in "their nature, have little apparent correspondence with that spirit of good of which they are the ministers." Sounding "the depths of human nature . . . they are themselves perhaps the most sincerely astonished at its manifestations, for it is less their spirit than the spirit of the age."

Making a significant correction, Shelley concluded, "Poets are the [priests] hierophants of an unapprehended inspiration, the mirrors of the gigantic shadows which futurity casts upon the present . . . Poets are the unacknowledged legislators of the world." More than a personal affirmation of Shelley's sorely tested poetic identity, *A Defence* is a reasoned affirmation of his belief in the role of poetry—and all the arts—in promoting the more moral, politically humane society he envisioned in *A Philosophical View of Reform.*

After completing *A Defence,* Shelley wrote Peacock he had "written little this winter" because of his "severe ophthalmia" but admitted making an "acquaintance, in an obscure convent . . . the only Italian for whom I have ever felt any interest." In remote Pisa, the "revolutionary volcanoes . . . give more light than heat: the lava has not yet reached Tuscany."[52]

As the revolution in Italy died, Mavrocordato kept the Shelleys confidentially informed of the impending Greek uprising against the Turks led by his cousin, Prince Alexander Ypsilanti. When Mavrocordato brought word April 1 the Greek revolution had started,[53] Mary wrote Claire, "Greece will most certainly be free." She was saddened when Mavrocordato had to join the Greek army and Shelley wrote to Medwin in Rome that the Greek revolution put an end to their planned voyage to Greece.[54] Mary, helped by Shelley, translated Ypsilanti's proclamation of revolution and sent a copy to the *Examiner.* Shelley sent his translation to the *Morning Chronicle.* In her editorial letter, Mary reiterated Mavrocordato's view that the revolt was an overtly religious crusade, "The war of the Cross against the Crescent, for which our fathers bled." Shelley omitted religious references in his letter. Only their letters were printed as each paper already had published the proclamation.[55]

Probably at Mary's instigation, Shelley asked Peacock to procure a gem with the head of Alexander, and two letter seals ringed with the Greek words, "I am a prophet of glorious struggles." This line—from Sophocles' *Oedipus at Colonus,* which Mary and Alexander Mavrocordato had just read together—became Shelley's epigraph for *Hellas,* which he dedicated to Mavrocordato. The gem and one letter seal probably were intended as gifts from Mary to Mavrocordato. She could use the other seal when corresponding "with my Greek."[56]

Mavrocordato, who did not sail for Greece until late June, continued his frequent visits and walks with Mary. In one of his warm letters to her in fluent French, he despaired over the Greek political scene. Hoping that evening for her consolation, he asked her not to tell Shelley of his feelings.[57]

April 11 brought shocking news from Horace Smith that "overturns us."[58] Smith's letter probably was the Shelleys' first word of Keats's death in February: "Keats . . . died at Rome under lamentable circumstances, and whom all lovers of poetry may regret as a young genius destined to do great things." More urgently disturbing, Smith, calling at Shelley's bank for his quarterly allowance, was told by the puzzled bankers "they had received notice *not to advance anything more on your account, as the payments to them would in future be discontinued.*" Smith told Shelley to draw on his stock exchange account and promised to pursue "the apparent mystery . . . knowing you are not over regular in matters of business, you may, perhaps, have made new arrangements for your money, and by some inadvertency omitted to apprise me."

Smith quickly learned that Shelley's allowance was being withheld because of a Chancery suit against Shelley for a year's nonpayment of his quarterly £30 child-support payments to Dr. Thomas Hume for Ianthe and Charles. Shelley felt optimistic upon receiving Smith's next letter April 13 and blithely reassured Claire it was a "false alarm." He only owed "£30 to Hume" and blamed "that rascal Longdill" for issuing "an order against my whole income."[59] However, Shelley was in arrears £120 to Hume. Smith soon wrote of being "engaged in warlike operations" determined "to ferret out the mystery of this Chancery suit" brought on with "alacrity" by Timothy's lawyer Whitton in "a cowardly cabal against an absent man." Smith was uncovering Byzantine miscues and legal intrigue leading up to the Chancery suit. He was still "very angry" with Shelley for his "total want of regularity," for ordering his bank not to pay Dr. Hume, and for telling Smith that he had given "positive orders to pay" Hume when all agreed that Shelley "had done no such thing."[60] Shelley had neglected to ask his bankers to countermand his previous stop payment order. By February 1821 he was a year in arrears for his children's income even though almost the full amount was in Hume's banker's hands waiting an order to be paid. The suit Whitton brought against Shelley was joined in by Hume, Longdill, and the Westbrooks.

In this legal intrigue, Smith correctly surmised that neither the arrears nor the suit against Shelley holding up his income was known to Shelley's father. Smith wrote a long letter to the surprised Sir Timothy, introducing himself with "pride" as Shelley's "particular friend" who remitted his quarterly income to Italy. After explaining Shelley's careful assignment of part of his quarterly income for Dr. Hume, he informed Timothy of the "legal proceedings." Carefully omitting Whitton's name, Smith protested that Shelley's income ceased "without a syllable of explanation." Smith concluded, "you, Sir, I am sure, would never have become a party, but from some great misapprehension of the real circumstances of the case."[61]

Chagrined, Timothy immediately replied this was his "first intimation" of either the arrears problem or the lawsuit. He would show Smith's letter to Whitton in order determine why "my name" was part of the suit.[62] Once again, Whitton was having it both ways with Timothy in his enduring role as Shelley's de facto father. Exercising authority over Shelley without Timothy's awareness—something Timothy had encouraged since his son's expulsion—Whitton continued to pocket fees from Shelley family legal proceedings. Whitton's invasiveness into Shelley family matters apparently did not stop there. Smith told Shelley in his April 17 letter of hearing a conversation in a coach about the pending marriage of "Whitton's daughter . . . to a Captain Shelley, who was stated to be a natural son of Sir Timothy's."[63]

Enclosing Timothy's reply, Smith wrote Shelley that the lawyers had *cooked up* the lawsuit. Whitton had taken "a most scandalous liberty" in making Sir Timothy "a party without his privity" and stopping "your money on his own authority." Smith would let Whitton "get out of this dilemma as well as he can." He did not know Whitton "but I seem to dislike him by instinct." Smith expressed the hope of seeing Shelley in Italy by the summer or autumn.[64]

In mid-June, Smith wrote Shelley "the whole affair" was settled more agreeably than he expected. Shelley did not have to pay the court costs and the Chancellor decreed £30 be regularly reserved for Dr. Hume. There is no record that Hume answered Shelley's 1820 query about Ianthe and Charles, who were eight and seven in 1821. However, Shelley heard about *Queen Mab* and its Ianthe, Smith informing him the Society for the Suppression of Vice was prosecuting William Clark for pirating publication of *Queen Mab*. The press covered the "hue and cry" and Smith was "often stopped in the streets, and asked whether you are really guilty of all the enormities laid to your charge. Of course I assert their utter false-hood, but the good Christians never stick at confirming one an-other's lies against a common enemy, as they consider you." He hoped Shelley had withheld his "sanction from the publication."[65]

On June 22, Shelley wrote both Hunt and Ollier that he had asked his solicitor "to apply to Chancery for an injunction to restrain the sale" of *Queen Mab*. Deliberately belittling his poem and taking two years off his age, he said he wrote it when eighteen "in a suffi-ciently intemperate spirit" for "my personal friends" and it doubt-less was "perfectly worthless in point of literary composition . . . crude and immature." He was still "a devoted enemy to religious, political, and domestic oppression." He still protested "this system of inculcating the truth of Christianity and the excellence of Monarchy . . . by such equivocal arguments as confiscation, and im-prisonment, and invective, and slander, and the insolent violation of the most sacred ties of nature and society."[66] This was Shelley's final written attack on Lord Chancellor Eldon for removing his children from him.

13

"A Love in desolation masked"

Shelley, preferring sailing for his health, had rejected Vaccà's prescription of horseback riding. He wrote Claire that a sailboat cost less and he had enough trouble "taming his own will" without worrying about that of a horse. He had asked Henry Reveley to buy an inexpensive flat-bottomed, ten-foot boat, "a very nice little shell."[1] Shelley hardly mentioned his recent life-threatening sailing accident in his "shell" when he and Williams decided to sail the craft from Leghorn to Pisa on the canal. Maria Gisborne, knowing Shelley could not swim and was unfamiliar with the canal, insisted Henry, a strong swimmer, go with them.[2]

Halfway through their voyage Williams stood up and, grabbing the mast to steady himself, capsized the boat. Finding no bottom in the deep canal, Henry told Williams, who "could swim a little," to swim ashore. Henry caught hold of Shelley and "told him to be calm and quiet" in order to take him ashore. Shelley answered, "All right never more comfortable in my life do what you will with me." When Henry laid him on the ground, Shelley "fell flat down on his face in a faint." After Henry recovered the boat, the three found food and shelter in a moonlit farm house. Henry reported "Shelley was in ecstacies of delight after his ducking; Williams and I did not care for it." Williams wrote Trelawny shortly after, "A few nights ago I nearly put an end to the Poet and myself . . . the wind blew very hard, and fair, we . . . started with a huge sail, and at 10 o'clock P.M. capsized her."[3]

Soon Henry, in Leghorn, read Shelley's letter saying, "Our ducking last night has added fire instead of quenching the nautical ardour which produced it." Shelley thought it "a good omen in any enterprise that it begins in evil." Enclosing Williams's directions for modifications, he urged quick repairs as "the approaching season invites expedition."[4] When Henry delivered the repaired skiff, Shelley proposed they sail back to Leghorn. Henry reported that

236

despite the boat's "diminutive size and frail nature," the two made the May 4 voyage "with ease and comfort."

In his letter to Henry, Shelley said he looked forward to the visit of the Gisbornes, "our false friends." Arriving for their four-day conciliation visit, the Gisbornes announced they planned to return to England. Irritated by their visit, Shelley wrote Claire he was "gentle, but cold" to them. They did not mention the steamboat; "in fact my money seems as irretrievable as Henry's character, & it is fortunate that I value it as little." Shelley was "incapable of composition."[5] The recent news of Keats's death stirred his expectation of not outliving his father. Shelley told Claire, "The incumbent of my reversion still flourishes . . . the sensations with which it has pleased the Devil to endow the frame of his successor, are not the strongest pledges of longevity."[6]

These feelings of personal vulnerability helped prompt his composition of *Adonais,* probably begun in April shortly after hearing of Keats's death. In early June, he wrote Claire he was "never well" but had "a great desire & interest to live, & I would submit to any inconveniences to attain that object." His only "relief" was "from the composition of poetry, which necessitates contemplations that lift me above the stormy mist of sensations which are my habitual place of abode. . . . I have lately been composing a poem on Keats."[7]

Mavrocordato's increased attentiveness to Mary in April and May led Shelley to write Claire, "I reproach my own savage disposition that so agreable accomplished and aimiable [a] person is not more agreable to me." After a ship arrived for Mavrocordato in early June, Shelley acknowledged the Prince's relationship with Mary helped their marital relationship: "He is a great loss to Mary, and *therefore* to me—but not otherwise."[8]

Claire compared her lonely life in Florence to her stay in Lynmouth, believing "every hour" of the last five years "has brought its misfortune, each worse than the other." Considering joining her brother in Vienna, she diligently studied German. Obsessed with Byron, she found his poetry had "the body of Man: there is so much of leg & so much of thigh" to the neglect of "the soul." She dreamed that Tatty had returned Allegra to her from Bagnacavallo and that she told Shelley Allegra "shall never go back again." In early June, she dreamed a letter came saying "Allegra was ill and not likely to live."[9] Shelley wrote to Claire of his continuing bipolar mood swings, "irritability & depression; or moments of almost supernatural elevation of spirits." As for suicidal thoughts, "in spite of the strong motives which should impel me to desire to exist under another form," he thought his overall health was better.[10]

Moving his family to San Giuliano in early May, Shelley told Claire of seeing Emilia twice a week but he was "very ill, body & soul, but principally the latter." Boating only "overfatigued me & made me worse." The baths gave some benefit but the best help was "solitude, & not seeing polite human faces, & hearing voices."[11] Their house faced the mountains and the Williamses had rented a marchesa's villa in nearby Pugnano in late April. Pugnano's proximity to San Giuliano allowed easy contact between the two families, either by walking or by the canal.

Shelley expected Emilia's pending marriage would take a "great & painful weight . . . off my mind. . . . Poor thing! she suffers dreadfully in her prison."[12] Emilia told Shelley to expect a visit from her new suitor and to discourage her current suitor, Francesco Danielli.[13] Shelley joked to Claire he was "worthy of taking my degree of M.A. in the art of Love." He next mentioned Emilia's replacement: "I like & I have got reconciled to Jane." Early in June they saw "a good deal of the Williams's—who are very good people, & I like her much better than I did."[14]

Talented in drawing, Edward Williams had literary ambitions. He began writing a play, *The Promise,* for which Shelley included a bridal hymn, probably written earlier for Emilia Viviani.[15] Williams, who would paint the best likeness of Shelley, wrote to Trelawny that the "extraordinarily young" Shelley was "a man of most astonishing genius." Shelley had a "wonderful command of language" and spoke with "ease" on "abstruse subjects . . . his ordinary conversation is akin to poetry." If Shelley only "wrote as he talked, he would be popular enough. Lord Byron and others think him by far the most imaginative poet of the day." Williams thought Byron wrote to Shelley like "a pupil . . . asking his opinion, and demanding his advice on certain points."[16] Williams believed Shelley suggested "the idea" of *Manfred* to Byron as well as "metaphysical notions" in the third Canto of *Childe Harold,* an assessment now considered "essentially correct."[17]

The fifty-mile boating trip Shelley and Williams took the last day of May to Lake Bientina, a (now-drained) swamp-lake east of Pisa, probably was the basis of Shelley's poem, "The Boat on the Serchio." Part of the lake's appeal was the habitable floating islands formed from decayed vegetation.[18] Their guide was Shelley's servant, "Dominic, the boat-man" of the poem. "Lionel" and "Melchior"—Shelley and Williams—are exiles living in Italy who "stowed tenderly" in straw their "bottles of warm tea." This evoked Shelley's poetic memory "at Eton" where with other "wanton schoolboys" he enjoyed forbidden "freedom" on twilight picnics "couched on stolen hay."

Shelley found companionship with Williams and Jane but felt neglected by his friends in England. Claire was away, Emilia was increasingly demanding, and Mary's emotional distance struck home after Mavrocordato left. Shelley's identification with Keats's lonely death in Rome became more vivid when he learned of Keats's burial in the Protestant Cemetery near his beloved little William. After Shelley's death, Mary wrote, "Adonais is not Keats's it is his own elegy." Hunt said Shelley told him "it was more an elegy on himself than the subject of it."[19] Both poets had been subjected to "savage" critical attacks and Shelley turned the critics' attacks upon Keats into a belief they caused his death, an erroneous idea expressed in *Adonais*.[20]

Shelley was proud of his artistry in *Adonais;* his highest poetic aspirations were evoked by Keats's death. Dowden accurately believed *Adonais* is "the costliest monument in verse ever erected to the memory of an English singer."[21] After completing *Adonais,* Shelley wrote the Gisbornes it was "a highly wrought piece of art, perhaps better in point of composition than anything I have written." Saying the same to Claire, he added it was "worthy both of him & of me." He wrote Ollier it "is perhaps the least imperfect of my compositions."[22]

Shelley's conflicted and competitive feelings about Byron influenced *Adonais,* which rebutted Byron's derogatory views about Keats's poetry.[23] Shelley argued with Byron about Keats in five letters they exchanged before, during, and after the composition of *Adonais*. Shelley lavishly praised Byron, now "at the age at which those eternal poets . . . have ever begun their supreme poems." Concluding *Adonais,* Shelley desired to join Adonais/Keats in his "spirit's bark" to "where the Eternal are," including Byron. Shelley, praising Keats, conveyed the news of his death to Byron in a distorted, personalized version based partly on Hunt's letter about Keats's burst blood vessel and on Shelley's intense feelings of being abused by the reviewers. This version provided both the imagery for the death of Adonais/Keats and for Shelley's bitter anger in *Adonais* towards his own mauling by the *Quarterly*. Shelley wrote Byron, "Young Keats, whose 'Hyperion' showed so great promise, died lately at Rome from the consequence of breaking a blood-vessel, in paroxysms of despair at the contemptuous attack on his book in the *Quarterly Review*."[24] Shelley knew too well Byron's close association with the conservative *Quarterly*'s publisher, John Murray.[25]

Byron's disparaging comments about Keats suggest the magnitude of Shelley's task in trying to change Byron's view of Keats. Byron called Keats "a tadpole of the Lakes" after he slighted Byron's favorite poet, Pope.[26] Byron's comments to Murray about the *Lamia* volume included "Johnny Keats's p-ss a bed poetry"; "No more Keats . . . flay him alive . . . the drivelling idiotism of the Mankin"; "the Onanism of Poetry . . . this miserable Self-polluter of the human Mind"; "writing a sort of mental masturbation—he is always f-gg-g his Imagination . . . a Bedlam vision produced by raw pork and opium"; "that dirty little blackguard Keates."[27] In letters to Murray, Byron twice referred to Keats as "Mr. John Ketch," a hanged murderer. Such invective came from the poet who silently used phrases from Keats's *Endymion* when composing the first canto of *Don Juan*.[28] Shelley, exacting revenge in *Adonais*, praised Byron as "The Pythian of the age" but made him "The Pilgrim of Eternity," the first mourner at Keats's bier.

Responding to Keats's death, Byron wrote Murray that when he was attacked by a critic, "Instead of bursting a blood-vessel—I drank three bottles of Claret—and began an answer."[29] Byron's letter to Shelley the same day perhaps was the final stimulus provoking his composition of *Adonais* for the following six weeks. Byron wondered if Keats's death were "*actually true* . . . I did not think criticism had been so killing." Byron did not share Shelley's "estimate" of Keats, who had "such inordinate self-love he would probably have not been very happy." Further, the *Endymion* review was not as "severe as many reviews." His next remark, "man should calculate his powers of resistance before he goes into the arena," crept into *Adonais*. Byron then criticized *The Cenci*, inviting Shelley to take "revenge" on his own latest drama, *Marino Faliero*.[30] Shelley kept his view of *Marino* from Byron but told Hunt, "if 'Marino Faliero' is a drama, the 'Cenci' is not."[31]

Byron, rejecting Shelley's wish that he write "a great Poem," hoped that Shelley would come "alone" to Ravenna during the summer. In reply, Shelley invited Byron to "spend this summer with us," noting Claire would not be "at Pisa." If Byron declined,

Shelley would "certainly try" to visit him but "many circumstances will conspire to make it short, and inconvenient to me."[32]

Shelley next rebuked Byron for comparing Byron's reaction to adverse criticism to that of Keats: "*Your* instance hardly applies." Byron's "argument" did not justify "contemptuous and wounding expressions against a man just because he has written bad verses; or, as Keats did, some good verses in bad taste." Expressing a metaphor that appeared twice in *Adonais*, Shelley defended Keats: "Some plants, which require delicacy in rearing, might bring forth beautiful flowers if ever they should arrive at maturity." As for himself, Shelley was "perhaps, morbidly indifferent to this sort of praise or blame; and this, perhaps, deprives me of an incitement to do what now I shall never do, i.e., write anything worth calling a poem." Urging Byron to read *Hyperion*, Shelley stressed the "energy and beauty" of Keats's "powers." Byron was impressed after reading *Hyperion*, writing Murray to "omit all that is said about him [Keats] in any M.S.S. of mine—or publication."[33]

Despite having told Byron of his indifference to criticism, Shelley expressed unabated anger toward Southey, the chief critic he attacked in *Adonais*. He addressed Southey in the Preface with Hamlet's words, "Nor shall it be your excuse, that, murderer as you are, you have spoken daggers, but used none." Shelley thanked Taaffe for advising canceling in his Preface a "whole passage relating to my private wrongs." However, he rejected Taaffe's advice to delete the poem's lines comparing his own bloodied brow to "Cain's or Christ's." Shelley identified with both as exiles persecuted by the orthodoxy.[34] Shelley's identification with the fratricidal Cain suggests both his envious ambivalence about Keats and his survivor guilt in relation to his younger poetic brother. Other poets who died young that were mentioned in *Adonais* included Chatterton, Sidney, and Lucan, all "inheritors of unfulfilled renown."

Two critics quickly crucified Shelley for his juxtaposition of Cain and Christ, one suspecting that even quoting the line in his review might "be criminal." He branded "wretched" Shelley for this "profanation . . . any man who . . . denies the being of God, is essentially mad." *Adonais* was "*contemptible* . . . the refuse of a schoolboy's commonplace book."[35] Shelley learned from John Gisborne in early 1822 of the *Quarterly's* review attacking *Prometheus Unbound* for its "unintelligibility" and of the "extraordinarily abusive review" of *Adonais* in the *Literary Gazette*. Shelley saw few, if any, of these reviews, but wrote John Gisborne, "It is absurd in any review to criticize Adonais, & still more to pretend the verses are bad. . . . I know what to think of Adonais." As for *Prometheus Unbound,* it "was never intended for more than 5 or 6 persons."[36]

Shelley, speaking of *Adonais,* quoted to the Gisbornes and to Claire his earlier satiric lines on Southey: "I have dipped my pen in consuming fire to chastise his [Keats's] destroyers; otherwise the tone of the poem is solemn & exalted."[37] Shelley, returning Southey's advice that he embrace Christianity, paraphrased the New Testament in his Preface, "Against what woman taken in adultery, dares the foremost of these literary prostitutes to cast his opprobrious stone?"

The Preface also mentioned the dying Keats was cared for by Joseph Severn, "a young artist of the greatest promise." Shelley had more recent news of Keats's death that John Gisborne obtained from the Reverend Robert Finch. Shelley wrote Gisborne that he would have been unable to compose *Adonais* if he had seen this "heart rending account."[38] Medwin arrived in Rome in March but had not responded to Shelley's early April request for word of Keats.[39]

Shelley, often in Pisa the first half of June completing his elegy, arranged for its printing and visited Emilia. Revising and adding until the last, he probably completed *Adonais* shortly before the first copy came off the press on July 12.[40] He told Ollier that, to avoid the "errors" of *Prometheus Unbound, Adonais* was being printed in Pisa. The printer, Niccolò Capurro, had reprinted Byron's *Lament of Tasso* in 1818. Shelley, proud of the poem and its printing, lavished more care on its production than on any other of his works. For a frontispiece, he sent Ollier Williams's sepia drawing of the poem's final stanza, instructing it be engraved like those in "Lord Byron's works." The engraving never appeared, nor did a larger "octavo edition" Shelley contemplated. Ollier sold few of the Pisan quarto copies Shelley sent in mid-July. Shelley's previous comment, "It is little adapted for popularity," had proven correct.[41]

Mary first read *Adonais* when the initial copy arrived from the press in July. The bitter parody of the biblical marriage vow, "No more let Life divide what Death can join together," gave added meaning to Shelley's immediately previous famous stanza 52:

> The One remains, the many change and pass;
> Heaven's light forever shines, Earth's shadows fly;

> Life, like a dome of many-coloured glass,
> Stains the white radiance of Eternity,
> Until Death tramples it to fragments.—Die,
> If thou wouldst be with that which thou dost seek!

Shelley coined the name "Adonais" from the Greek "Adonai" of Theocritus and the Athenian women's rites of Adonia that celebrated the death of Adonis, gored in the groin by a boar.[42] Shelley's "mighty Mother" Urania in *Adonais* was an important change of the Adonis myth, transforming the lovers Adonis and Venus to the mother–son story of Adonais and Urania. Emphasizing maternal abandonment, Urania is asked twice in the second stanza, "Where wert thou mighty Mother . . . / When Adonais died?" Later, Urania tried to kiss breath into Adonais's dead lips with a "vain caress." Shelley's double meaning of "vain" is not lost.

Ambivalence also colored Shelley's self-portrait in *Adonais,* his "frail" and "companionless" Actaeon self-image combining with that of Bacchus-Dionysus.[43] In Dionysian rites, maenad-like women tear apart Dionysus's animal companion, a live panther. Shelley, a "pardlike Spirit" ("pantherlike" in a draft),[44] was "A Love in desolation masked."

Urging, "go to Rome," Shelley revisits the "all too young" grave of his son, next to that of Keats, where he too would "From the world's bitter wind / Seek shelter in the shadow of the tomb." Shelley concluded with his final poetic voyage:

> I am borne darkly, fearfully, afar:
> Whilst burning through the inmost veil of Heaven,
> The soul of Adonais, like a star,
> Beacons from the abode where the Eternal are.

While *Adonais* was being printed, Claire, after a failed one-day reconciliation with Mary, returned June 23 to Leghorn accompanied by Shelley. When he rejoined Mary on June 25, Shelley again suffered "from his side & nervous irritation."[45] He ignored Vaccà's advice to stop self-medicating and later wrote Claire of taking a "double dose of opium" to help him sleep.[46]

As the Gisbornes prepared to leave Leghorn, Shelley exchanged a copy of *Adonais* for their maps of Italy. Responding to the Gisbornes' praise of his elegy, Shelley was "fully repaid for the painful emotions from which some of the verses of my poem sprung. . . . The poet & the man are two different natures: though they exist together they may be unconscious of each other, & incapable of deciding upon each other's powers & effects by any reflex act." As to the "decision" about his poetic "posterity," "the court is a very severe one, & I fear that the verdict will be guilty death."[47] Although concerned about the critical reception of *Adonais,* he made light to Taaffe of the "ridiculous violence of the prejudices which are conceived against me. . . . I laugh at this comic pantomime which the good people in London exhibit, with my shadow for their Harlequin."[48]

Shelley was especially self-deprecating about *Adonais* when he sent Byron a copy. Perhaps he had been "carried away too far by enthusiasm of the moment" and had "erred" by "considering Keats rather as he surpassed me in particular, than as he was inferior to others." He wondered why he kept "writing verses . . . I execute so awkwardly." Not having heard from Byron after inviting him to Pisa, or realizing that Teresa Guiccioli soon would reluctantly leave Byron to join her family in politically safe Florence, Shelley said he would visit Ravenna "for a week or so in the autumn" and again approved Byron's decision to place Allegra in the convent. Shelley's words would have infuriated Claire: "I feel more and more strongly the wisdom of your firmness. . . . I applaud it the more because I know how weak I should have been in your case. . . . Allegra's happiness depends upon your perseverance."[49] Claire, probably upset upon receiving the report on Allegra containing her handwriting, went to Pisa for a week to be with the Masons where she told Shelley that word reached Leghorn of Napoleon's death in May.[50]

Shelley accompanied the Gisbornes to Florence on their late-July departure for England. Mary wanted to spend the coming winter in Rome but Shelley stayed longer in Florence searching for a house. His enthusiasm for Florence came from Claire's expected return to the Bojtis' household and from the Williamses' idea of moving there. Shelley visited the Uffizi Gallery for the last time,[51] as events soon changed any plans for leaving Pisa.

While Shelley was away, Williams painted a miniature of Mary, her intended surprise birthday present for Shelley. On returning from Florence August 2, Shelley received a letter from Byron offering to cover his expenses to visit and asking for a quick reply.[52] Shelley left the next day. In his letter, Byron mentioned the likelihood of moving to Switzerland with Teresa Guiccioli and her politically exiled family. Byron did not tell Shelley that he was central to his plan of having the Gambas remain in Italy. Before Shelley arrived, Byron wrote to Teresa's brother, Pietro Gamba, that he could not leave as he momentarily expected "a relation of Allegra's ... to decide about the child's future." After Shelley arrived, Byron wrote Pietro that his visiting "friend" would write Teresa "some forcible reasons why it would be better to stay in Italy."[53]

Shelley apparently was not entirely forthcoming with Mary and Claire concerning his trip. On August 3, he went to the Masons, where Mary later joined him, bade him goodbye, and wrote "S. departs" in her journal, without mentioning his next stop. Shelley backtracked to Leghorn, spending his twenty-ninth birthday with Claire before proceeding to Ravenna. This detour perhaps arose when he found at the Mason's Claire's secret August 1 letter. Scarcely a week before, Shelley and Claire had spent much of the day together in Pisa. It is unclear if Mary was aware he was returning to Leghorn. On his birthday morning, Shelley and Claire rose at five to row in the harbor. Later, they sailed "out into the sea" and dined before Shelley left.[54] Mary spent Shelley's birthday with the Williamses, Edward finishing her portrait. Claire's lighthearted description of sailing with Shelley contrasted with Mary's journal entry on Shelley's final birthday: "S birthday—7 years are now gone—What changes What a life—we now appear tranquil—yet who know[s] what wind—I will not prognosticate evil—We have had enough of it—When I came to Italy—I said all is well if it were permanent—it was more passing than an Italian twilight—I now say the same—May it be a polar day—Yet that too has an end."[55]

Shelley, keeping his visit with Byron from Claire, told her he was going to Florence to continue house hunting. Claire expected to see him August 9, but he wrote her from Florence saying, without explanation, that it was impossible. His brief letter to Mary from Florence, hand carried to her by a third party, possibly kept her from knowing he got to Florence later than she expected. The next day he wrote Mary from Bologna with a vague excuse as to why he had not arrived there earlier. Once again, separation from Mary relieved his physical symptoms despite being "pitched" down a slope when his carriage overturned. He advised Mary "to invite Claire to spend a few days with you," but Claire was not to know he was visiting Byron. He ended asking Mary to give "his love to the Williams's," to kiss "my pretty" Percy, and "accept an affectionate one from me in return for the cold [?]."[56] The cancellation, probably Mary's, implied her cool Pisan farewell, possibly because she knew or suspected his plans to see Claire. Mary did not resume her journal until the end of August.

After Shelley was greeted in Ravenna the evening of August 6 by a delighted Byron, the two talked until five in the morning. Waiting for Byron to awaken, Shelley wrote to Mary but saved the shocking news until last. First, he told her that Byron's "permanent sort of liaison with Contessa Guiccioli" had improved his health. They talked "a great deal of poetry" and "as usual differed . . . I think more than ever." Byron reported that Allegra, "grown very beautiful" with a "violent and imperious" temper, would accompany him to Switzerland if he went.

Turning to the real news, Shelley wrote, "Lord Byron has also told me a circumstance that shocks me exceedingly." Byron had shown him Hoppner's letter of the previous September reporting Elise's story that Shelley was the father of a child born to Claire in Naples and had placed it in a foundling home there. Shelley, not mentioning Foggi's blackmail, was "at a loss to account" for such "a degree of desperate & wicked malice."

Hoppner had written that his changed opinion of Shelley was due to a "fearful secret" that "I trust, for his unfortunate wife's sake, if not out of regard to Mrs. Hoppner and me," Byron would not let "the Shelleys know that we are acquainted with it." Hoppner stated "that at the time the Shelleys were here Clara was with child by Shelley: you may remember to have heard that she was constantly unwell, and under the care of a Physician, and I am charitable enough to believe that the quantity of medicine she then took was not for the mere purpose of restoring her health." Claire's pregnancy was the reason she stayed "alone" at Este. In Naples, "one night Shelley was called up to see Clara who was very ill." Mary "thought" this "very strange," not being "aware of the nature of the connexion between them." Hoppner reported that Mary "had sufficient proof of Shelley's indifference, and of Clara's hatred for her." A "half-hour" after the child's birth they bribed a midwife "to carry it to the Pieta," having bought "the physician's silence with a considerable sum." Mary was treated by "these beasts . . . in the most brutal manner," Claire attempting to get Shelley "to abandon" Mary. Elise said that Mary "knows nothing of their adventure in Naples" and "Clara does not scruple to tell Mrs. Shelley she wishes her dead, and to say to Shelley in her presence that she wonders how he can live with such a creature." Hoppner agreed with Byron that Claire "is a damned bitch" but disagreed "that man can be, as you say, 'crazy against morality', and have honour."[57]

In his letter to Mary, Shelley said Elise was "actuated either by some inconceivable malice for our dismissing her—or bribed by my enemies—or making common cause with her infamous husband." Not explicitly denying Elise's charge "that Clare was my mistress," Shelley said, "that is all very well & so far there is nothing new: all the world has heard so much & people may believe or not believe as they think good." He accused Hoppner of accusing him of giving Claire medicine for an abortion, something Hoppner only implied. Shelley, after misreporting that Hoppner said he "beat" Mary, was most indignant of his charge that he was the kind of person who would abandon his own child in a foundling hospital.

There followed three unreadable lines, perhaps Shelley's most significant, heavily obliterated by someone. He then told Mary to write the Hoppners "refuting the charge in case you believe & Know & can prove that it is false: stating the grounds & the proofs of your belief.—I will not dictate what you should say, nor I hope inspire you with warmth to rebut a charge which you only can effectually rebut." She should send her letter to him and he would forward it to the Hoppners. The next illegible line is heavily scored through and the letter's ending is missing.[58]

Shelley's indignation about the Hoppner scandal in this first Ravenna letter to Mary had dissipated when he wrote her a day later. He was sure it had given her "pain" but "it was necessary to look the affair in the face" and she "alone" could answer the "calumny." He thought these accusations were "the source of the violent denunciations of the Literary Gazette," a reviewer branding Shelley as one whom "after debauching, had abandoned any woman." Shelley's statement to Mary, that the Hoppner accusations should be suppressed if "only for the sake of our dear Percy," seemed an afterthought. Most of this letter contained details of Ravenna's ancient churches and his disgust with the "rude & tasteless" Christian art.[59]

Shelley had given Mary the onerous task of exoneration by making a public statement about their troubled marriage. She knew the Pisan gossip of Shelley's relationship with Emilia. Hoppner's letter contained a number of charges but Shelley twice asked Mary to rebut "the charge," as if to give her scope. Greatly shaken when she read Shelley's letter on the tenth, Mary immediately wrote her letter of rebuttal to Isabella Hoppner, enclosing it with a letter to Shelley and Elise's last letter to her.[60]

Writing Mrs. Hoppner about the "falsehoods" spread by Elise, "this miserable girl," Mary mentioned the discovery in Naples of Elise's pregnancy, the danger of her miscarriage, her marriage to Paolo, his "scheme of extorting money from Shelley by false accusations," and giving Paolo's letters to "a celebrated lawyer . . . to silence him." Mary mentioned Elise's recent letter "with great professions of love," asking Mary to send her money. Mary next dealt with Elise's charges that Shelley and Claire had been lovers, and that Claire had a child by him. These were the most disturbing charges for her to rebut and she made numerous slips and revisions:

> She says Claire was Shelley's ~~miss~~ mistress . . . I am perfectly convinced, in my own mind that Shelley never had an improper connexion with Claire—At the time specified in ~~Claires~~ Elise's letter, the winter after we quited ~~Nap~~ Este, I suppose while she was with us, and that was at Naples, we lived in lodgings where I had momentary entrance into every room and such a thing could not have passed unknown to me. . . . I now do remember that Claire did keep her bed there for two days— but I attended on her—I saw the physician—her illness was one that she had been accustomed to for years—and the same remedies were employed as I had before ministered to her in England. Claire had no child—the rest must be false. . . . ~~I th~~ That my beloved Shelley should stand thus slandered in your minds—~~He~~ He, the gentlest & most humane of creatures
>
> It is all a lie—Claire ~~if anything~~ is timid; she always shewed respect even for me—poor dear girl! she has ~~many~~ some faults—you know them as well as I—but her heart is good—and if ever we quarelled, which was seldom, it was I, and not she, that was harsh, and our instantaneous reconciliations were sincere & affectionate.
>
> Need I say that the union between my husband and ~~hims~~ myself has ever been undisturbed—Love caused our first imprudence, love which improved by esteem, a perfect trust one in the other, a confidence and affection, which visited as we have been by severe calamities (have we not lossed two children?) has encreased daily and knows no bounds.
>
> I will add that Claire has been separated from us for about a year— She lives with a respectable German family at Florence—The reasons of this were obvious—her connexion with us made her manifest as the Miss Clairmont, the Mother of Allegra
>
> Shelley is incapable of cruelty as the softest woman—To those who know him his humanity is almost a proverb.—He has been unfortunate

as a father. the laws of his country & death has cut him off from his dearest hopes—~~But~~ His enemies have done him incredible mischief

Mary's postscript said she was sending this letter to Shelley in Ravenna so "he may see it" as well as Byron who, she mistakenly wrote, "gave no credit to the tale."[61]

Mary's statement, "Claire had no baby," undoubtedly true, evaded the issue of her possible pregnancy and miscarriage. Neither Mary nor Shelley acknowledged in their letters that a baby, Elena Adelaide Shelley, was born in Naples. Shelley had downplayed to Mary the accusation that Claire was his mistress, but this was the prime charge Mary took pains to rebut, as well as the associated charge that he had abused Mary. In her covering letter to Shelley, Mary, sensitive to the charges about him and Claire, warned him not to be "imprudent" and "Consider well if Florence be a fit residence for us." Mary wrote, "our bark is indeed tempest tost but love me as you ever have done." He should not think Mary "imprudent in mentioning Claire's illness at Naples—It is well to meet facts—they are as cunning as wicked." Mary implored Shelley "for a thousand reasons" to make a copy of her letter to Mrs. Hoppner. He did not, telling Mary that had he "recopied your letter" to Mrs. Hoppner it would "necessarily destroy its authenticity." He gave it to Byron who intended "to send it with his own comments to the Hoppners."

Shelley seemingly had a sense of completion in the entire matter after reading her letter. Having initially told Mary of possibly "prosecuting Elise before the Tuscan tribunals," he then wrote, "I speedily regained the indifference which the opinion . . . amply merits. . . . So much for nothing."

The unresolved controversy about whether Byron ever sent Mary's letter to Mrs. Hoppner, or if he even referred to it in writing to the Hoppners, has divided Shelley and Byron scholars. Mary's letter to Mrs. Hoppner was intended primarily for Shelley and Byron. Shelley's ambiguous "in case you believe" to Mary was her opening to declare to him that, despite their marooned marriage, she intended they would stay together. To Byron, whose esteem she valued, she was asserting her loyalty to Shelley. Her slip and ambiguous phrasing that she was convinced Shelley "never had an improper connexion with Claire—At the time specified in ~~Claire's~~ Elise's letter . . . at Naples" can be read as subverting her conscious intention to make the blanket assertion that Shelley never had a sexual relationship with Claire. Emphasizing her ability to oversee their conduct in their Naples lodgings, she avoided mentioning the two and a half weeks Shelley and Claire were together before Mary joined them at Este. Trying to convince Mrs. Hoppner of her sound marriage, Mary exaggerated the length of time Claire had not been living with them and revealed her real feelings about her marriage when she made the slip, "the union between my husband and hims myself has ever been undisturbed." Mary's "Claire had no child" was neither a denial that someone else had a child nor a denial that Claire was pregnant, although her assertion that Claire was suffering from her chronic menstrual problems was meant to convey that she had not miscarried.

In his October 1820 reply to Hoppner, Byron tempered his acceptance of Hoppner's story with a skeptical proviso about Elise. He did not "doubt" her story about "Shiloh," but Elise was like "a sort of *Queen's* evidence," first eager to return to them and then turning on them with abuse. He had "little doubt" of the facts and assured Hoppner he would "keep your counsel." Compounding his rush to judgment against Shelley, Byron enclosed a letter from "Shiloh." Calling Shelley "Shiloh" was Byron's way of ridiculing his messianic fervor.[62] When Byron sent Claire's letters to Hoppner in April 1821, he still did not doubt "the main points" about her "having planted a child in the N[aples] Foundling" but questioned Elise's total accuracy.[63]

Byron's breaking his promise of secrecy to Hoppner involved the complex relationship between the two poets. Shelley, responding to Byron's hospitality, stayed longer in Ravenna than he had planned. But, as he wrote to Mary, he had no illusions about the limits of their unequal friendship:

Lord Byron and I are excellent friends, & were I reduced to poverty, or were a writer who had no claims to a higher station than I posess—or did I posess a higher than I deserve, we should appear in all things as such, & I would freely ask him any favour. Such is not the case—The demon of mistrust & of pride lurks between two persons in our situation poisoning the freedom of their intercourse . . . I think the fault is not on my side; nor is it likely, I being the weaker. . . . What is passing in the heart of another rarely escapes the observation of one who is a strict anatomist of his own—[64]

If Shelley were poor, had no talent as a poet, or were overrated as a poet, he would pose no threat to the easily threatened Byron.

In this same letter, having heard Byron read Canto V of *Don Juan*, Shelley praised him as "not above but far above all the poets of the day; every word has the stamp of immortality." Shelley added, "I despair of rivalling Byron, as well I may; and there is no other with whom it is worth contending." These rivalrous feelings for Byron were in *Adonais*, which Byron did not mention during Shelley's visit. He did praise *Prometheus Unbound* and censured *The Cenci*.[65]

Byron's showing Shelley Hoppner's almost year-old accusatory letter came from very mixed motives. Perhaps consciously he wanted Shelley to exonerate himself from this scandalous gossip, but revealing the letter was an unconscious passive-aggressive act. The letter's attack on both Claire and Shelley expressed Byron's anger toward them, linked as they were in his feelings from his first encounter with her. Her aggressive pursuit of Byron after feeling spurned by Shelley gave Byron the status of a substitute, second-best sexual rival. Byron's sexual involvement with Claire was the one instance when Shelley had greater power over Byron, feeding his underlying sense of powerlessness that always threatened him. Claire, the woman who most threatened Byron's sense of power, became the woman toward whom he was most cruel, surpassing his feelings toward his wife, "that infernal fiend, whose destruction I shall yet see."[66] Claire threatened Byron not only by her sexual aggressiveness but by not allowing him to evade direct paternal responsibility for his child. For once in his life, Byron was not an absentee father to a child of his. His occasional comment that Shelley was Allegra's father expressed his wish that this were so. Byron's anger toward Claire, the "damned bitch" who was the "atheistical mother" of Allegra, carried over indirectly to Mary. It was as if Byron said to Shelley, "this will hurt your wife, but get her to rebut this story of you and Claire."

Shelley had told Mary, after giving her letter to Byron, "Lord Byron is not a man to keep a secret good or bad—but in openly confessing that he has not done so he must observe a certain delicacy—& therefore he wished to send the letter himself—& indeed this adds weight to your representations."[67] Byron's "delicacy" was such that he probably did not send Mary's letter to the Hoppners. After Byron's death, Mary's letter was found with the seal(s) broken among his papers, inconclusive evidence as to whether it was sent.[68] Aside from not wanting the Hoppners to know he violated their confidence, Byron had other reasons for not sending the letter. Irritated that the puritanical Hoppners disapproved of his liaison with Teresa, he perhaps thought twice about disabusing them of their censure of Shelley. Byron avoided antagonizing Hoppner, who did his bidding in a variety of personal tasks. In September 1821, Hoppner asked Byron if he received a letter (now lost) he had recently sent with "some details of the [Shiloes (partially erased)] which I should be sorry to travel about the world, or to fall into any other hands but yours." Whatever Hoppner heard, he and his wife remained antagonistic to Claire and the Shelleys.[69]

Claire probably was pregnant by Shelley when they arrived at the Hoppners in Venice, August 1818. Hoppner plausibly stated in his September 1820 letter to Byron that this was the reason Claire was unwell at Este, was seeing a physician for medication in Padua, and remained in Este with the children when the Shelleys stayed in Venice for two weeks in October. Elise's charge that Claire had a baby in Naples probably merged Claire's miscarriage or abortion in late December with the birth of Elena Adelaide. Claire's missing journal from June 1818 to March 1819 seems not accidental. Mary's "Claire had no baby" is consistent with Claire having lost a fetus that was probably a little over four months old. Mary's December 27 entry, her only journal mention of Claire in Naples, referred to Claire's recurrent menstrual problem, but none of Claire's journal entries suggested any interruption with her usual activities at these times, including being "in bed." The blackmail charges Paolo Foggi fomented in June 1820 probably included charges of Claire's having a baby by Shelley. In two subsequent letters, Shelley mentioned to a concerned Claire that he had not yet seen the lawyer del Rosso, but when he had he would "write of it."

Shelley accommodated Byron and wrote persuasively in French to Teresa Guiccioli dissuading her from going to Geneva. His "fee" for this letter, he told Mary, was Byron's agreement to live in Tuscany. Inquiring if Mary had "heard anything of my poor Emilia," he admitted Emilia wrote him "the day of my departure" about her briefly postponed marriage. Shelley had told Byron about Emilia, asking him not to divulge what he said lest Mary be "much annoyed."[70]

Byron provided Shelley his carriage and black-bearded servant Tita as personal valet. Shelley wrote Peacock that Byron's exotic living arrangements included a freely roaming menagerie of "ten horses, eight enormous dogs, three monkeys, five cats, an eagle, a crow, and a falcon." He had "just met on the grand staircase five peacocks, two guinea hens, and an Egyptian crane." After their all-night talks, Shelley forced himself to stay in bed until noon but Byron always slept until two. After their evening gallops "through the pine forests" they dined and sat up "gossiping till six in the morning."[71]

Byron, convinced that Shelley's letter to Teresa would have the desired effect, told him the day after it was sent he would move to Pisa. Shelley immediately wrote Mary inquiring if "any of the large palaces are to be let" and to keep this news "a profound secret from Clare." However, since Claire and the Williamses still beckoned Shelley to Florence, he wanted Mary's "full opinion" about wintering there before returning to Pisa "to enjoy the society of the noble lord."[72]

Quickly forgetting Florence, Shelley asked Mary, "What think you of remaining at Pisa?" They could form "a society of our own class. . . . Our roots were never struck so deeply as at Pisa & the transplanted tree flourishes not." He believed the Williamses probably would stay and Hunt might join them, not to mention "Lord Byron and his Italian friends." Although Byron's "great regard for us" came at a price, it "is better worth it, than those on whom we bestow it from mere custom." He had in mind Mrs. Mason, whose "perverseness is very annoying to me especially as Mr. Tighe is seriously my friend." Although his "greatest content" would be to "utterly desert all human society" and go to a "solitary island . . . build a boat . . . read no reviews & talk with no authors . . . it does not appear" they will be "alone."

As for Allegra, Shelley could not suggest any alternative to Bagnacavallo. He described his trip the previous day to see her, a twelve-mile journey Byron never made. Slighter and paler from "improper food," she still had "deep blue eyes." Her initial shyness yielded to his caresses but her delight in the gold chain he gave her indicated "her dominant foible seems the love of distinction & vanity." Before Shelley left, she made him run with her "all over the convent like a mad thing" as she rang the bell that called the sleeping nuns to assembly. Shelley was dismayed that her "intellect is not much cultivated here," her talk being full of "Paradise & angels . . . a prodigious list of saints . . . and the Bambino. . . . the idea of bringing up so sweet a creature in the midst of such trash till sixteen!"[73]

Leaving Ravenna about August 17, Shelley agreed to deliver Byron's letters to Teresa in Florence. She was "very much" pleased by Shelley whose "health seems to be very poor . . . how is it possible to be so thin, so worn out?"[74] Claire, at San Giuliano when Shelley returned, heard for the first time the unexpected news of Byron's pending arrival. Shelley quickly negotiated a one-year lease for the Palazzo Lanfranchi on the Lungarno for Byron. Writing to Medwin in Geneva, Shelley asked if he had taken his translation of Plato's *Symposium* "by mistake" and stated that "Whilst you were with me . . . I was harrassed by some severe disquietudes, the causes of which are now I hope almost at an end."[75] As Emilia's September marriage to Luigi Biondi approached, she wrote to Shelley that her parents forbade him further visits. Wishing to maintain the "faithful friendship" of Shelley, Mary, and Claire, she offered to return his writing desk and his copy of *La Nouvelle Héloïse*. She ended, "don't get angry."[76]

Because Byron was upset that the Lanfranchi had too few stables for his eight horses, Shelley dutifully found extra stalls and agreed to purchase extra furniture to fill the large palazzo. Immersed in the logistics of moving Byron's immense household, Shelley arranged for eight wagons to be sent from Pisa to Ravenna after Byron complained of the expense at his end.[77] Reluctant to leave Ravenna, Byron wrote Teresa he expected "very serious evils" in Pisa for her father, her brother, and "especially" for her.[78] Moving to Pisa with her father and brother at the end of August, Teresa soon met Mary but not Claire, who was in Leghorn. The Gambas, with temporary passports and under political surveillance, rented lodgings on the Lungarno. After Byron's arrival, Teresa continued to live with her family to avoid any Pisan scandal. When she wrote to Byron of Shelley's offer to teach her English, Byron vetoed the idea because of the "horrible things" being said about both him and Shelley.[79]

Shelley assured Byron that Teresa Guiccioli's qualities made him "secure against any of my female friends here" but Shelley would "trust you" with Mrs. Williams. Still uncertain of Byron's real views on the Hoppners' accusations, he was sure Byron had "seen enough" to convince him that their charges were "void of foundation."[80]

Besides Byron, the key person in Shelley's emerging Pisan community was Leigh Hunt, about whom the two poets had conversed in Ravenna. Hunt had written to Shelley in late August his desire to come to Italy had seemed a "beautiful impossibility; but your friendship has put it in my power." Hunt, at a low point, was suf-

fering "in money matters." The *Examiner* was failing, his brother
John was in prison, and illness struck most of his brood of six children.[81] Shelley had presented Hunt a plan for a periodical with Byron and told Hunt he only wanted to be the "link between you and
him." Shelley said the profits from such a venture with Byron
"must . . . be very great," but added "a secret" he withheld from Byron, "nothing would induce me to share in the profits . . . I desire to
be, nothing." Shelley believed he could again impose on Horace
Smith for aid to bring Hunt to Italy and tried to reassure Hunt
about Byron, who "has many generous and exalted qualities, but
the canker of aristocracy wants to be cut out." In late September,
Hunt wrote, "We are coming." Hunt realistically declined Shelley's
offer of Horace Smith's aid but unrealistically wrote they would
leave for Italy in a month. Shelley included in his letter his "Italian
impromptu," the three-stanza "Buona Notte," a farewell to Emilia
Viviani that echoed his "Good-Night" stanzas for Sophia Stacey.[82]

Emilia, hearing Byron was coming, asked Shelley for money for
a female "friend"—obviously herself—and suggested Byron and
Shelley together could "make up the amount indicated." She would
"be content with less" if that were too risky.[83] In Ravenna, Byron
possibly agreed to loan Shelley 224 Tuscan crowns for Emilia, an
amount Shelley repaid in late January 1822.[84]

After Emilia's marriage, Shelley wrote to Hogg that the "very interesting Italian lady" he knew last winter is "now married; which
to quote our friend Peacock, is you know the same as being
dead."[85] The death of his love for Emilia entered into several beautiful lyrics drafted in 1821, a collective elegy. "To ———," was left unfinished in the same notebook as *Epipsychidion* and his Italian letters to Emilia:

> Music, when soft voices die,
> Vibrates in the memory—
> Odours, when sweet violets sicken,
> Live within the sense they quicken.

Other poems in the notebook include "A Lament," "Remembrance," *Ginevra,* and "The Fugitives." In "Remembrance," after
Emilia's "summer's flight," "joy is fled, / I am left lone, alone." He
had sent a near-duplicate to Sophia Stacey. Shelley would present
a copy to Jane Williams with a note about "this melancholy old
song . . . Do not say it is mine to any one, even if you think so."[86]

Shelley later wrote to John Gisborne: "The Epipsychidion is a mystery—As to real flesh & blood, you know that I do not deal in those articles,—you might as well go to a ginshop for a leg of mutton, as expect anything human or earthly from me. I desire Ollier not to circulate this piece except to the Σύνετοι [cognoscenti], and even they it seems are inclined to approximate me to the circle of a servant girl & her sweetheart."[87]

Fig. 10. Percy Bysshe Shelley, watercolor by Edward Williams, 1821 or 1822, courtesy of The Pierpont Morgan Library, New York. 1949.3.

Fig. 11. Mary Wollstonecraft Shelley by Richard Rothwell, 1841, courtesy of the National Portrait Gallery, London.

Fig. 12. Jane Williams by George Clint, ?1820s–1830s, Shelley Relics 4, courtesy of the Bodleian Library.

Fig. 13. Edward Ellerker Williams, pastel self-portrait, courtesy of the Carl F. Pforzheimer Collection of Shelley and His Circle, The New York Public Library, Astor, Lenox and Tilden Foundations.

Fig. 14. Lady Mount Cashell (Mrs. Mason), miniature, courtesy of The Carl F. Pforzheimer Collection of Shelley and His Circle, The New York Public Library, Astor, Lenox and Tilden Foundations.

Fig. 15. Villa Magni with the *Don Juan*, 1822, from a watercolor by Captain Daniel Roberts, R.N., courtesy of The Provost & Fellows of Eton College.

Fig. 16. Edward John Trelawny, lithograph by Seymour Kirkup, courtesy of the National Portrait Gallery, London.

Fig. 17. Shelley's grave, Protestant Cemetery, Rome. Photograph by author.

PERCY BYSSHE SHELLEY

COR · CORDIUM

NATUS IV AUG. MDCCXCII

OBIIT VIII JUL. MDCCCXXII

Nothing of him that doth fade.
But doth suffer a sea-change
Into something rich and strange

Fig. 18. Sir Percy Florence Shelley, color drawing/painting, courtesy of The Huntington Library.

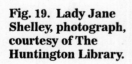

Fig. 19. Lady Jane Shelley, photograph, courtesy of The Huntington Library.

14

The Last Pisan Winter

ON EMILIA'S WEDDING DAY IN EARLY SEPTEMBER, SHELLEY, MARY, and Claire left on a four-day excursion to La Spezia. Shelley, considering spending the following summer on the Gulf of Spezia, took the two tentatively reconciled women sailing.[1] Back in San Giuliano, Horace Smith's letter from Paris brought news that his wife's illness caused him to cancel his "long-cherished plans" to join Shelley in Italy. Smith had praised *Adonais* as second only to *The Cenci* among Shelley's works because it was devoid of "the metaphysical abstraction" that could "puzzle the uninitiated." Shelley was pleased, fearing *Adonais* was too "metaphysical." He probably was composing *Hellas* and told Smith "All public attention is now centered on the wonderful revolution in Greece." He "dare not . . . hope that slaves can become freemen so cheaply" but if the Greeks had Mavrocordato's "highest qualities," all would "go well."[2]

Shelley, stalled in composing *Charles the First,* told Ollier it was "conceived but not born."[3] Mary was copying her novel *Valperga,* determined its royalties would go to her father. One heroine in *Valperga,* "Euthanasia," Claire believed was "Shelley in female attire" and after Shelley's death, Mary felt Euthanasia's drowning was a "catastrophe strangely prophetic."[4] Claire was back in Leghorn in early October when she heard from Shelley that Byron was not bringing Allegra to Pisa. Shelley stayed four days in Leghorn with Claire before returning with her to Pugnano, where she would spend the rest of October with the Williamses.

Shelley, writing Ollier that his "dramatic poem called 'Hellas' will soon be ready," ordered James Mill's *History of British India.*[5] Despite his enthusiasm about Greece's revolution for freedom, Shelley was considering immigrating to colonial India. In late October he told Hogg he was thinking of going to India "if I could get a respectable appointment," or "any where, where I might be compelled to active exertion" and "enter into an entirely new sphere of action."[6] Previously, Shelley inquired of Peacock about employment through the East India Company in some political capacity "at the court of a native prince." Peacock thought this was "altogether impossible," given the Company's bureaucratic structure, but nothing "would be more beneficial" for Shelley than to follow "some scheme of flesh and blood." Peacock would try to locate an alternative opportunity for Shelley.[7] In early 1822, Shelley would write to Peacock that receiving "no encouragement about India" he still wished "I had something better to do than furnish this jingling food for the hunger of oblivion, called *verse*."[8]

Shelley's discontent was related to the anticipated arrival of that brighter poetic star, Byron. His self-doubts were not decreased when Peacock wrote that only *Don Juan* "in recent literature" was "good for anything." Although *Adonais* was "very beautiful," Shelley should think "of your audience . . . The number who understand you, and sympathise with you, is very small." If Shelley would "adapt" his composition to such understanding and sympathies, he "would attain the highest degree of poetical fame."[9]

To garner popular sympathy, Shelley wanted *Hellas* printed quickly, capitalizing on the English enthusiasm for the Greek cause. He sent *Hellas* to Ollier on November 11, urging its "*immediate* publication," a necessary precondition for "What little interest this Poem may ever excite." Two months later, its publication delayed, Shelley was again angry with Ollier.[10]

Shelley probably made several false starts on a poem about the Greek Revolution before writing *Adonais*.[11] His conversations in Ravenna with Byron and "good rumours" there brought him back to his Greek war poem.[12] Byron later told Lady Blessington that Shelley, had he not died, was to accompany him to Greece.[13] The length and complex structure of *Hellas* indicate it was composed from late August into November. Shelley's three-stanza lyric in the *Hellas* notebook ("Mutability"), beginning "The flower that smiles today / Tomorrow dies," suggests his political message merged with a personal sense of transience.

Abandoning a long fragment—a "Prologue to *Hellas*"—involving Christ, Satan, and Mahomet, Shelley turned to Aeschylus's *Persians* for his poem's structure.[14] Williams, perhaps suggesting the poem's title, took five days to write out the fair copy and correctly feared the poem was "so far above the level of common apprehension (as indeed most of his writings are) that I am doubtful of its popularity."[15] Shelley's disdain to write down to his readers collided with his desire to promote his political agenda against the non-interventionist policy of his hated Castlereagh. *Hellas* rightfully has been considered the pre-eminent artistic work of the Panhellenic movement. Neither Shelley nor Byron outlived the revolution, but both recognized its importance as the major revolutionary struggle in Europe at that time. The revolutions in Spain and Italy had evoked odes from Shelley, but *Hellas* was subtitled *A Lyrical Drama*, the same artistic status as *Prometheus Unbound*. The title *Hellas* underscored Shelley's desire to promote the ideals of classical Greek democracy, however short of these ideals a bloody victory over the Turks might fall.

Despite apologizing in his Preface for relying upon his "newspaper erudition" in composing *Hellas*, Shelley followed the events closely, including the atrocities both sides committed. Casting aside pure pacifism in a revolution for liberty, Shelley supported military action in *Hellas* even as he wished it contained. He twice praised the United States and wrote in his Preface, "We are all Greeks—our laws, our literature, our religion, our arts have their root in Greece." Similar words appeared in the *Examiner*, which reported the campaign in detail and raised a subscription for the Greek cause.

Behind its rallying cry, Williams sensed the more somber message in *Hellas*. Shelley's Notes warned against assuming poets could disentangle "the Gordion knot of the origin of evil" and that for a poet "to anticipate however darkly a period of regeneration and happiness is a hazardous exercise." Aeschylus's *Persians* was a historical drama of Greek victory told from the vantage point not of the victors but of the vanquished Persian leaders. Adopting this viewpoint in *Hellas*, Shelley tempered the pessimism and doubt of the Turkish Sultan Mahmud with a chorus of his enslaved Greek women who sing some of Shelley's finest lyrics of cyclical renewal:

> Worlds on worlds are rolling ever
> From creation to decay,
> Like the bubbles on a river,
> Sparkling, bursting, borne away.

(197–200)

The future resided in the humane thought inherited from Greece, not in warfare or "Temples and towers" that "must decay":

> But Greece and her foundations are
> Built below the tide of war,
> Based on the chrystalline sea
> Of thought and its eternity;
> Her citizens, imperial spirits,
>   Rule the present from the past,
> On all this world of men inherits
>   Their seal is set.
>
> (696–703)

The final great song of the Chorus begins by asserting Shelley's belief in renewal:

> The world's great age begins anew,
>   The golden years return,
> The earth doth like a snake renew
>   Her winter's weeds outworn:
> Heaven smiles, and faiths and empires gleam
> Like wrecks of a dissolving dream.
>
> (1060–65)

Taking a long view of history, Shelley ended *Hellas* on a darker tone and commented: "The final chorus is indistinct and obscure." Lacking prophecy, he finds "authority and my excuse" in "Isaiah and Virgil, whose ardent spirits . . . saw the possible and perhaps approaching state of society in which 'the lion shall lie down with the lamb'." After intoning, "A brighter Hellas rears its mountains / From waves serener far," and "Another Athens shall arise," the Chorus strikes a questioning tone of angry resignation:

> O cease! must hate and death return?
>   Cease! must men kill and die?
> Cease! drain not to its dregs the urn
>   Of bitter prophecy.
> The world is weary of the past,
> O might it die or rest at last!
>
> (1096–1101)

Hellas marked the final appearance of Shelley's old persona, Ahasuerus, the Wandering Jew. Through a hypnotic-like influence, Ahasuerus induces a confrontation in Mahmud with his Phantom forbear, Mahomet. Mahmud, denied the insight Prometheus gained of his curse on his father, was allowed only the sad awareness that his predecessor Mahomet's earlier conquest of the last vestiges of the Roman Empire foretold his own defeat at the hands of the Greeks.

Shelley's giving Ollier permission "to suppress" any passages in the Notes to *Hellas* that "should alarm you"[16] resulted in a deleted paragraph in the Preface that began, "Should the English people ever become free" and referred to "those ringleaders of privileged gangs of murderers and swindlers, called Sovereigns." Ollier also deleted "this holy alliance [of] all the despots of the earth," an allusion to Metternich and Castlereagh. Ollier soon wrote of Shelley and his "Holy Pisan Alliance."[17]

Printed at the end of *Hellas* was Shelley's remarkable poem, "Written on Hearing the News of the Death of Napoleon." It actually is about the "Earth" as "Mother" who, after the tyrant's death, is asked, "What, Mother, do you laugh now he is dead?" Her lengthy reply starts with a feisty rejoinder, as if she comments on Shelley's revealing of family secrets in his poetry:

> "Who has known me of old," replied Earth,
> "Or who has my story told?
> It is thou who art overbold."
>
> (17–19)

Awaiting Byron to join his tenuous Pisan alliance, Shelley wrote to its third member, advising Hunt to bring his family by sea.[18] Receiving from Byron Cantos 3–5 of *Don Juan*, Shelley responded: "It is a poem totally of its own species . . . it [has] at once the stamp of originality and a defiance of imitation. Nothing has ever been written like it in English." Shelley was "content" that *Don Juan* approximated the epic he had encouraged Byron to write.[19]

Shelley complained to Byron of his "ill health . . . my habitual disorder . : . a tertian fever" and wrote to Hogg of being "weak & with much nervous irritability . . . [my] spirits . . . by no means good." He added in Italian, "I feel sensibly the weariness and sorrow of past life." The idea of doing something new in India "I dare say is a mere dream," and he would probably "finish as I have begun," a poet.[20]

Confirming his intent to stay fixed, he wrote John Gisborne that same October day of their furnished house in Pisa, a "headquarters" where, with "all my books," he would "intrench myself—like a spider in a web." Shelley asked Gisborne to help Peacock send his books from Marlow and mentioned "just finishing" *Hellas*. He defended Godwin's *Answer to Malthus* against the "lies" of a recent review, calling his father-in-law's work "victorious & decisive." Shelley played humorously with his ambivalence about Godwin, adding, "compared with these miserable sciolists he is a vulture (you know vultures have considerable appetites) to a worm." Earlier, he told Claire that Godwin's latest work was "dry" and "clever," a "decent interspersion of cant and sophistry."[21]

On October 25, the Shelleys moved into the first and last home in Italy in which they intended to live for an extended period, occupying rooms on the top floor of the Tre Palazzi di Chiesa. This four-story structure on Pisa's Lungarno Galileo Galilei was diagonally across the Arno from Byron's Palazzo Lanfranchi.[22] Writing to Peacock from their "lofty palace" with views toward the Mediterranean, Shelley assured him their new furniture "cost fewer shillings than that at Marlow did pounds sterling." Peacock was still negotiating the Albion House expenses and Shelley enclosed a signed "certificate," a *post obit* bond to cover his debt to the Bath outfitters. He also had filled out a medical questionnaire for an insurance policy his creditors took out on his life that excluded payment if death occurred by drowning at sea.[23] Among the extensive new furnishings Shelley omitted mentioning to Peacock was a sofa bed for his study that afforded sleeping accommodations separate from Mary's.[24]

Byron's bed, arriving at Palazzo Lanfranchi before milord, had as its most impressive feature, according to Williams, a coat of arms "emblazoned, with the well adapted motto of 'Crede Byron'!" The Williamses, moving to Pisa, stayed with the Shelleys for three weeks in November until they occupied an apartment a floor below. Shelley told Williams "he always 'writes best in the air,'—under a tree— in a garden or on the bank of a river; there is an undivided spirit reigns abroad, a mutual harmony among the works of Nature."[25]

Claire, staying with Mrs. Mason, asked Williams to escort her to the Tre Palazzi as "Shelley won't do to fetch me because he looks singular in the streets."[26] Perhaps he still wore the long gown Claire said caused him to be called "signora" on the streets of Rome. On her way to Florence November 1, Claire caught a glimpse of Byron heading toward Pisa when his "travelling train" passed her carriage. Having last seen him in Geneva, she never saw him again.

Years later, Claire told Mary that Shelley had maligned Claire to Byron in an apparent effort to defuse Byron's anger and to influence him about Allegra. Not mentioning Shelley by name, Claire said she had "a friend whom I loved entirely and who certainly loved me much; yet immense were the lies he told of me." She loved "him still as if he had never spoken ill of me . . . he told me himself in his calm voice and with the gentlest looks that it was absolutely necessary he should traduce me and that he expected I should submit without a murmur to it." She had acquiesced "with the greatest cheerfulness" believing that such "frankness and honour would redeem any calumny . . . besides one feels ennobled in being the victim of necessity."[27]

Byron, coldly, had not said goodbye to Allegra before leaving Ravenna. However, he did have an emotionally charged experience traveling to Pisa upon encountering his younger friend from Harrow—whose name was the homophone of Claire—Lord Clare. Meeting briefly near Bologna, Byron was "agitated" as they touched and could not recall "an hour of my existence" that compared to their five minutes together on the road.[28] After Shelley's death, Byron told Mary of his inability to feel someone was a friend: "As to friendship, it is a propensity in which my genius is very limited. I do not know the male human being, except Lord Clare . . . for whom I feel any thing that deserves the name . . . I did not even feel it for Shelley, however much I admired and esteemed him."[29]

Medwin, the man who would try to befriend both poets, joined the Pisan community in November after hearing from Shelley that Byron was coming.[30] He found Shelley "an altered man" after eight months. His health was "sensibly improved" and he had "shaken off much of that melancholy and depression, to which he had been subject during the last year."[31] However, Shelley soon had "leeches on his side" and Medwin was "confined with rheumatism."[32]

Byron's all-male congregations in Palazzo Lanfranchi left the excluded women to ride horseback together. Byron visited Teresa at the Gambas' several hours each evening.[33] Mary's comment, Pisa "has become a little nest of singing birds," was literally true.[34] All the men were published writers except Williams, who was writing a play called *The Promise*. Teresa would follow Mary as an author. Jane, who sang, soon starred in Shelley's lyrics.

What Williams called the "Pisan circle" revolved around Byron. He preferred staying within the Lanfranchi, partly to avoid the English, whose invitations he declined, and partly not to display his halting gait caused by his foot deformity. As chief cavalier, Byron rode about on a thickset Dutch horse and provided mounts for others. Pistol shooting was a regular pastime. Emilia's father, Governor Viviani, forbade shooting within the small walled garden behind the Lanfranchi but approved Byron's use of a garden-vineyard two miles east in Cisanello.[35] Byron's favorite target for his "pistol party" was a half-crown coin lodged in a forked stick at fourteen paces. He was the first to hit the coin, despite his trembling hand. Shelley's pistol hand "was all firmness" and soon he and Williams were regularly hitting the coin. Being frugal, Shelley often made his own bull's-eye targets. Byron told Medwin that Shelley was "a much better shot than I am, but he is thinking of metaphysics rather than of firing."[36]

Williams now helped Shelley with his long-term project, translating Spinoza's *Tractatus Theologico-Politicus*. Shelley dictated as Williams wrote and the translation—now lost—was completed in less than a week. Byron had given his permission to add his name to Shelley's translation which, with a prefatory biography of Spinoza, was to have been printed in Pisa.[37]

Shelley was visiting Leghorn with the Williamses in late November when a well-dressed Italian offered to be his companion-guide, saying he could introduce him to "first families" and "pleasures now unknown to you." After seriously asking, "For how much," and being told 10,000 crowns a year, Shelley thanked him, saying, "my means are proportionate to my wishes which are both extremely moderate." The man replied, "Sir, I know the contrary," as Shelley drove off with the Williamses.[38]

Corresponding frequently with Claire, Shelley wanted a "confidential letter" from her "detailing" her "intimacies" and "future plans." She should not think "I ever love you less although that love has been & still must be a source of disquietude to me." Referring to Byron's group, Shelley considered himself "the Exotic who unfortunately belonging to the order of mimosa . . . cannot endure the company of many persons & the society of one is either great pleasure or great pain." This allusion to Byron led to admitting he "had no spirits for serious composition." Lacking "confidence . . . to write [in] solitude or put forth thoughts without sympathy is unprofitable vanity." He requested, "Tell me ~~dearest~~ what you mean to do." The cancellation apparently was Claire's.[39]

Claire's letters to Shelley—not for Mary's eyes—were always addressed to Mrs. Mason. After his late December solo trip to Leghorn,[40] he wrote cryptically to Claire that the foul weather prevented his gaining some "intelligence" for her from "an expected person" and Claire's "desires on this subject are the object of my anxious thought."[41] Claire's anxieties, including her increasing concern about motherless Allegra, were expressed in anxiety dreams of a child falling into a well, another of a beheaded Jane Williams, and one in which Jane's little boy died.[42]

Byron, unconcerned about Allegra, was exchanging locks of hair with his legitimate daughter Ada in England. Having earlier promised Teresa he would stop writing *Don Juan* after the fifth canto, he wrote Murray that she, like "all women," had the "illusion" of exalting "the sentiment of the passions," an illusion *Don Juan* "strips off."[43] In addition to the fifth canto, Byron's prolific creativity before arriving in Pisa included *Sardanapalus, The Two Foscari, Cain,* and *The Vision of Judgment,* a satiric attack on Southey's *A Vision of Judgment.*

Shelley read *Cain* soon after Byron arrived in Pisa and told Williams it was "second to nothing of the kind." Mary believed it was Byron's "finest production."[44] Shelley, writing glowingly of *Cain* twice to John Gisborne, called Byron "this spirit of an angel in the mortal paradise of a decaying body." *Cain* was "apocalyptic . . . a revelation . . . [no] finer poetry . . . has appeared in England since the publication of Paradise Regained." Shelley complained he could only write "by fits." Increasingly feeling in Byron's shadow, Shelley said *Charles the First* "succeeds very well" but he could not "seize the conception of the subject as a whole yet, & seldom touch the *canvas.*"[45]

The Hunts' erroneous mid-November message that they were sailing immediately for Italy led the Shelleys to buy furniture for their friends. Byron, with what Mary called "unpretending generosity,"[46] provided £50 for the furniture and made available Lanfranchi's ground floor for the eight-member Hunt family. Late-December storms plagued the Mediterranean and by year's end, when the Hunts had not arrived, Shelley could not sleep for fear of their safety. His anxiety would have been greater had he known that the small brig they first sailed on was a floating bomb, surreptitiously carrying fifty barrels of gunpowder for the Greeks. However, the Hunts were back in England because unfavorable winds twice forced their ship back to port. Worse, Marianne Hunt had become alarmingly ill, throwing up blood. It was mid-May before the Hunts embarked on another ship.[47]

Mary and Jane began attending Sunday church services in the Tre Palazzi apartment of the Reverend George Frederick Nott, who apparently invited the two women. At one of the services Mary attended, Nott delivered a sermon against atheism as he looked and preached directly at Mary. Reacting to his "impertinent" behavior, she wrote Nott asking if he "intended any personal allusion." Nott denied he was attacking Shelley and sent another note, via Medwin, denying Vaccà's report making the round of English Pisan gossip. It seems Nott had called Shelley a *scellerato* (wicked one) at Mrs. Beauclerk's, a visiting Englishwoman. Satisfied with Nott's explanation, Mary defensively wrote about her church-going to Maria Gisborne, who had written of Hogg's being "shocked" at Mary's church attendance.[48]

Medwin called the Reverend Nott a "licensed libeller" and "Slipknot" because he had evaded marital engagements. Medwin, keeping records of his daily conversations with Byron for future publication, copied Byron's nine-stanza satire that included, "Thou shalt, Nott! bear false witness against thy neighbour." Mrs. Mason, not to be outdone by Byron, composed her own satirical verse. Reflecting Shelley's bemused attitude toward the whole episode, she entitled her satire, "Twelve cogent reasons for supposing P B Sh-ll-y to be the D-v-l Inc-rn-t-."[49]

Shelley's indignation over religion did become aroused by the rumor a man was to be burned alive soon in Lucca for "sacrilege." Racing to tell Byron, he found Medwin there with the same rumor. Presumably, a priest had denounced the "Wretch," whose crime was taking "consecrated wafers from the altar" and throwing them "contemptuously about the church." The priest had told Medwin "burning is too light a death."[50]

According to Medwin, Shelley proposed they "arm ourselves . . . and immediately ride to Lucca" to take the prisoner to the safety of the Tuscan frontier. Shelley's zeal infused Byron, who would join the wild plan if their representations to the authorities failed. Learning that the execution would not take place the next day, Byron asked a skeptical Taaffe to try to get the sentence changed. Meanwhile, Byron and Shelley each wrote letters on the same piece of paper to Lord Guildford in Leghorn to intervene. Taaffe soon returned with the news that the culprit, a Florentine priest who stole a Communion cup, had escaped to the safety of Florence.

In a note to Byron about their letters to Lord Guildford, Shelley wrote that the "burning of my fellow serpent has been abandoned." Byron sent Shelley's note to Thomas Moore saying that Shelley's use of "fellow Serpent" was Byron's "buffoonery" derived from

Goethe's Mephistopheles. Shelley, like the serpent, walks "on the tip of his tail."[51] Byron's characterization probably came from Shelley himself, who had written of the serpent having "hopped along on its tail" in his 1820–1821 satirical essay *On the Devil, and Devils*.[52] After Shelley learned from Byron that Moore—detecting *Queen Mab*'s atheism in *Cain*—warned Byron from being involved with "the snake," he asked Horace Smith to personally convey to Moore a gentlemanly message of denial.[53] Shelley was being modest; he undoubtedly noted numerous paraphrases of *Queen Mab* in *Cain*, something Medwin also suggested. Byron, perhaps to forestall any idea of borrowing from *Queen Mab*—which he may have re-read in 1821—wrote to Murray upon finishing *Cain* that he "highly" admired the poetry of *Queen Mab* but Shelley knew "his opinions and mine differ materially upon the metaphysical portion of that work."[54]

Williams heard in early January that his play *The Promise* was rejected by Covent Garden and immediately began writing a tragedy with Shelley's muted encouragement.[55] Shelley and Williams often sailed on the Arno during the last half of December, despite weather that posed an obvious danger in their fragile skiff. After sailing in a "Violent wind" on Christmas Day, Shelley ordered a new sail. The swollen Arno, overflowing its banks, threatened to take away bridges. The September trip to La Spezia had whetted Shelley's appetite for sailing in the sea, and Mary wrote Maria Gisborne they "may probably" spend the next summer there.[56] Toward the end of December Williams wrote to Trelawny in Genoa that he and Shelley "must" have a boat and would be pleased if Trelawny's friend, Captain Daniel Roberts, would build it. Williams added that Byron desired to "join our party" for the summer in La Spezia.[57]

As 1821 ended, Mary was suffering. She wrote to Maria Gisborne of fancying herself in a "hermitage," staying up late at night in "solitude." Her "social intercourse" was "so contracted" that it shut out "most" of her continuing painful headaches.[58] Only a single entry appears in her journal between December 20 and January 13. Shelley, exchanging letters secretly with Claire, told her Mary's severe "rheumatism in her head" had "entirely" deprived her of sleep "for some successive nights." She was treating herself with "blisters and laudanum" and was "somewhat better." Shelley confessed he too "suffered considerably from pain and depression of spirits."[59] Amid this domestic pain, Shelley was increasingly attracted to Jane, telling John Gisborne she was more "amiable and beautiful . . . [a] spirit of embodied peace in our circle of tempests."[60]

In his letter to Claire, Shelley mentioned attending after "much solicitation" one of Mrs. Beauclerk's evening socials. Mrs. Beauclerk had done "me the favour to caress me exceedingly" but if she did not call on Mary he would not attend any more of her soirees. Williams, to lure Trelawny to Pisa, informed him that Mrs. Beauclerk, "with her litter of seven daughters," was "the gayest lady, and the only one who gives dances, for the young squaws are arriving at that age when, as Lord Byron says, they must waltz for their livelihood."[61] When Trelawny soon arrived, he took a fancy to one of the daughters.

Mrs. Beauclerk's sons were in Geneva with their father, Charles Beauclerk. Four years after marrying Emily ("Mimi") Beauclerk in 1799, he built St. Leonard's Lodge near Field Place. Mrs. Beauclerk was the long-term mistress of Lord Dudley, who possibly fathered some of her thirteen children.[62] Medwin, a social climber questing after a wealthy wife, regularly attended Mrs. Beauclerk's evening open houses. He reported that Byron had a falling out with her after Medwin had arranged—at the request of both—a meeting between the two "by accident." According to Medwin, Mrs. Beauclerk wished she could have seen more of Shelley. Teresa Guiccioli later recalled Medwin's detailed and "disgusting" boast about his success with Mrs. Beauclerk, which Byron called "imaginary fire." Medwin's relationship with Mrs. Beauclerk grew stormy and he soon would leave Pisa.[63]

Mary and Jane dined alone Christmas Day, when Byron held one of his all-male dinners. Shelley and Williams, after a long sail, joined Medwin and Taaffe at Lanfranchi for Byron's feast.[64] Shelley ate little and drank less at Byron's regular weekly banquets, actually two successive lavish dinners each with many courses elaborately laid out with decanters of wine. Shelley wrote to Horace Smith that his "nerves are generally shaken to pieces" watching the others, drinking until three in the morning "vats of claret." Byron, worried about his weight, ate sparingly the rest of the week.[65]

The Christmas dinner was notable for a wager Byron proposed and Shelley accepted. The first to come "to their estate" would pay the other £1000,[66] a wager pitting the death of Byron's rich mother-in-law, Lady Noel, against that of undying Sir Timothy. Lady Noel died a month later but Byron, hearing of her death in mid-February, neither honored his bet by paying Shelley nor said he intended to. Although Williams believed Byron "came into" Lady Noel's annual income of £10,000,[67] it was somewhat less but enough to double his annual income.[68] Medwin's claim—that Williams, disgusted at Byron, "never afterwards" entered his "doors"—is inaccurate.[69] However, both Williams and Shelley were annoyed, and repercussions from the unpaid bet continued after Shelley's death.

The day Mary recorded the news of Lady Noel's death, Shelley wrote an awkward letter to Byron, enclosing Hunt's letter requesting that Shelley ask Byron for a £250 loan and promising to repay Byron. Shelley said "poor Hunt's promise to pay in a given time" was not "worth very much." Having previously sent Hunt £150, Shelley was holding another £50 for him even though his own resources were at a "low ebb." Appreciating all Byron had done for the Hunts, Shelley told him he "should be happy to be responsible" if Byron loaned the money to Hunt.[70] If Shelley were fishing for some recompense from Byron over their wager, he was disappointed. However, Byron did provide £250 for Hunt with Shelley's agreement to repay the amount when his father died. Writing to Hunt of Byron's "*tolerable willingness*" for this arrangement, Shelley added, "Many circumstances have occurred between myself & Lord. B. which make the intercourse painful to me, & this last discussion about money particularly so." He repeated that he would take "no more share" in the proposed Byron–Hunt literary journal "than is absolutely necessary to your interests." In a postscript, Shelley said Lady Noel was dead and "Lord B is rich, a still richer man."[71]

Lady Noel's will stipulated that Byron take the Noel arms and name. He began signing his letters "Noel Byron" or "N. B.," pleased that his initials were now those of Napoleon Bonaparte.[72] Shelley knew Byron admired Napoleon and collected Napoleonic items, including a pin and a snuffbox, each with the emperor's likeness, and an engraved portrait. Byron's huge carriage was a replica of Napoleon's and his extensive coin collection had many valuable napoleons, some of gold.[73] About this time, Byron wrote he would not pay for the expense of a bust of anyone, excepting Napoleon and a few others, and criticized the "hankering for public fame" of those who had their bust sculpted. Early in January, Williams found Byron sitting for his bust by the famous sculptor, Lorenzo Bartolini.[74] Shelley added to Byron's memorabilia by presenting him with a collection of Napoleon commemorative medals in an undated leather case inscribed "P. B. Shelley to Lord Byron."[75]

The medals possibly were Shelley's gift for Byron's thirty-fourth birthday, January 22. Shelley was writing "Sonnet to Byron," perhaps intending it to accompany the Napoleon medals. Shelley's self-abasing sonnet of praise clearly conveys his envy and resentment toward Byron. Shelley presents himself as "The worm beneath the sod" who "May lift itself in worship to the God."[76] Shelley prefaced his draft of the sonnet with, "I'm afraid these verses will not please you but." In a poetic fragment seemingly written at this time, "The False Laurel and the True," Byron, as Milton, wore the true poetic laurel.[77] Shelley, increasingly disaffected with Byron, apparently thought better of giving Byron the sonnet for his birthday.[78]

The New Year heightened Shelley's competitive malaise as Byron completed his drama, *Werner.* Mary, again Byron's copyist, read aloud the first two acts as Shelley worked on the first act of *Charles the First.* Finding his drama "a devil of a nut to crack," Shelley, while spending most of January 5 playing billiards with Williams at Lanfranchi, talked "seriously" of "taking in hand a steam yacht to work between Leghorn and Genoa."[79]

Shelley told Ollier that *Charles the First* would be ready "by the Spring" and offered him the right of refusal. Shelley said his drama "promises to be good, as Tragedies go . . . not coloured by the party spirit of the author."[80] Subduing his political passion among characters with whom he could not clearly identify, Shelley was caught in a cul-de-sac of historical writing. *Charles the First* and Mary's *Valperga* share some common themes, but Shelley did not discuss his play with Mary as he had *The Cenci.*[81]

Concerned with money and poetic fame, Shelley asked Gisborne to negotiate selling the copyright of *Charles the First* to Ollier, hoping to get "150 or 200 pounds." He wrote Hunt that if he completed his drama "according to my present idea [it] will hold a higher rank [than] the Cenci as a work of art." Shelley then shared with Hunt his current suspicious turn: "My firm persuasion is that the mass of mankind as things are arranged at present, are cruel deceitful & selfish, & always on the watch to surprize those few who are not—& therefore I have taken suspicion to me as a cloak, & scorn as an impenetrable shield . . . [my] faculties are shaken to atoms & torpid. I can write nothing."[82] Shelley stopped work on *Charles the*

First about January 26, the day after his letter to Hunt. In early March, writing Hunt about *Charles the First,* he said he had "written nothing for this last two months; a slight circumstance gave a new train to my ideas & shattered the fragile edifice when half built."[83]

January 26 seemed pivotal. Writing that day to John Gisborne, Shelley mentioned difficulty in conceiving *Charles the First* "as a whole," adding, "My convent friend . . . is married" and he was "in a sort of morbid quietness." Jane, not Emilia, seemingly was part of the "slight circumstance" that brought down the drama. On January 26, the Williamses received his first poem about Jane, "The Serpent Is Shut Out of Paradise."

In drafting five scenes of his drama, Shelley perhaps empathized with Charles I, whom he presented as caught in a bind of securing money and power.[84] Of two minds about Charles I, Shelley followed *King Lear,* giving the monarch's fool, Archy, the most insightful and pithy lines. The Archbishop of Canterbury, Laud, was to be a major villain, as was Cromwell. Medwin, recalling talks with Shelley about the drama, believed "Shelley could not reconcile his mind to the beheading of Charles," looking "upon him as the slave of circumstances, as the purest in morals, the most exemplary of husbands and fathers." Shelley "reprobated" the "arch-hypocrite, Cromwell" and "hated the Puritans,—not their tenets so much as their intolerance."[85]

Hearing nothing from Ollier about the reception of *Adonais,* Shelley testily inquired if Ollier had either published his elegy or republished it with his corrections. After personally offering Ollier the copyright to *Charles the First,* he said that if Ollier didn't begin to pay more attention to his letters "you will scarcely think it extraordinary that this should be the last time I intend to trouble you."[86]

Trelawny's arrival from Genoa January 14 energized the Pisan circle. In his iconic version of his first encounter with Shelley, written thirty-six years later, Trelawny saw a "pair of glittering eyes" outside the room. Jane Williams "laughingly said, 'Come in, Shelley, it's only our friend Tre just arrived.'" "Swiftly gliding in, blushing like a girl . . . a tall thin stripling" with "flushed, feminine, and artless face," Shelley took Trelawny's hands in his own. Trelawny, "silent from astonishment," wondered, "was it possible this mild-looking, beardless boy, could be the veritable monster at war with all the world?" Shelley was dressed "like a boy, in a black jacket and trowsers, which he seemed to have outgrown." When Jane asked him "what book he had in his hand? His face brightened, and he answered briskly. 'Calderon's Magico Prodigioso, I am translating some passages in it.'" When asked to read it, Shelley "masterly ... analyzed the genius of the author." Trelawny was struck by "his lucid interpretation of the story, and the ease with which he translated into our language the most subtle and imaginative passages of the Spanish poet." When Trelawny looked up and asked where Shelley had gone, Jane replied, "Who? Shelley? Oh, he comes and goes like a spirit, no one knows when or where."

Shelley, after returning with Mary, left the room again as she asked Trelawny of "the news of London and Paris." Trelawny, adding three years to Mary's age, believed "she was rather under the English standard of woman's height, very fair and light-haired, witty, social, and animated in the society of friends, though mournful in solitude." Her "power of expressing her thoughts in varied and appropriate words" contrasted "with the scanty vocabulary used by ladies in society."[87]

Mary, intrigued by Trelawny, wrote volubly in her journal several days later: "Trelawny is extravagant ... partly natural, & partly perhaps put on ... his abrupt, but not unpolished manners ... are nevertheless in unison with his Moorish face ... his dark hair his herculean form." Pleased by his "extreme good nature," she was assured by his smile that "his heart is good." His "strange ... horrific" stories of himself added to his "rare merit of interesting my imagination."[88] She described Trelawny to Maria Gisborne as a "half Arab Englishman ... six feet high.... His company is delightful for he excites me to think and if any evil shade the intercourse that time will unveil—the sun will rise or night darken all."[89]

Trelawny, probably the most physically imposing man Mary had met, lavishly embroidered his tales of his seafaring years. Nine years later, he wove these tales into his partly accurate and partly fictitious story of his early life, *Adventures of a Younger Son*. The second son of an abusive, tyrannical father and a disinterested mother, both from old Cornish families, rebellious young Edward John Trelawny shared some of Shelley's formative influences. His father, a member of parliament, inherited property and sent Edward away to school when he was eight. Expelled two years later for leading a violent student revolt, Edward entered the Royal Navy in 1805 at age twelve, barely missing action at Trafalgar. His grueling experiences as a midshipman in a series of twelve ships in Mauritius, India, and the East Indies became the basis of his fictional persona as a corsair-privateer in *Younger Son*. This fantasy self-image was nurtured by his avid identification with the heroes of Byron's romances, including *The Corsair*.

After being wounded, Trelawny was discharged in 1812 without attaining his self-anointed rank of lieutenant. He married in 1813, had two children, and reacted to his wife's unfaithfulness by obtaining a divorce. During the extended divorce proceedings and trial, his wife's infidelities received the usual lurid display in the London press.[90] Headlined as "Lieutenant Trelawny," he was considered one of the handsomest men in London. After his father's death, his annual income of £300 was considerably more than the army half-pay Williams and Medwin received.

Trelawny, just months younger than Shelley, became Mary's best answer to her husband's interest in Jane by becoming her daily visitor and evening consort. Years later, after talking with Trelawny, William Rossetti wrote, "Shelley never walked out with his wife in Trelawny's time."[91] Mary, dissatisfied with Shelley's antisocial bent, wrote Maria Gisborne she "had thought of being presented" at "the Court here, balls &c," but "Shelley would not take the necessary steps, and so we go on in our obscure way." She had "hope" that Shelley's *Charles the First*, "now on the anvil, will raise his reputation." Byron's poetry was "an overflowing river . . . sometimes it is a cataract."[92]

In late January Shelley asked Horace Smith, in Versailles, to buy a "good pedal harp" for which he was prepared to pay "from 70 to 80 guineas," plus "5 or 6 napoleons' worth of harp music." Giving detailed shipping instructions, Shelley did not say for whom it was intended. He wanted this "present" right away; "if I were to delay, the grace of my compliment would be lost."[93] Smith declined to indulge Shelley's wish. Two weeks earlier, when Shelley wrote to John Gisborne that Jane was more beautiful than ever, he merged her image with that of Margaret in the edition of *Faust* containing Retzsch's illustrations. Margaret's "wonderful" picture "makes all the pulses of my head beat—those of my heart have been quiet long ago."[94]

In subsequent letters to John Gisborne, Shelley "was never satiated" looking at the *Faust* etchings. Jane's presence was like a line from *Faust*, "Remain, thou, thou art so beautiful." He now understood better the "Hartz Mountain scene" from the etching which depicted Mephistopheles and Faust surrounded by the nude young witches in the orgy of the Walpurgis Night. This was one of two sections of *Faust* Shelley had by now translated, although he believed only Coleridge could do justice to the original.[95]

Shelley's reveries about Jane were first expressed poetically in his late-January seven stanza "The Serpent Is Shut Out from Paradise." Sending it downstairs with a brief letter to "Signor Williams," he discreetly avoided a personal confrontation with the poem's object and her husband. Shelley's note to Williams indicates "The Serpent" was a love poem to Jane. Paraphrasing his drafted prefaces to *Epipsychidion,* he again is "my friend" who "found" the verses in the same "portfolio" where "those I sent you the other day were found." These verses were "too dismal for me to keep" but "If any of the stanzas should please you, you may read them to Jane, but to no one else,—and yet on second thought I had rather you would not [about six words scratched out]."[96]

Shelley titled the stanzas, "To ——." Despite William Rossetti's misleading 1870 title—"To Edward Williams"—the poem was directed to Jane, not Edward. Mary waited until 1839 to publish "The Serpent" as "Stanzas," after it appeared in Ascham's 1834 pirated edition of Shelley's poems. Williams, indicating Jane read the poem, wrote, "S sent us some beautiful but too melancholy lines." The next day, Shelley, Jane, and Williams sailed on the Arno.[97]

"The Serpent" apparently was written after Mary asked Shelley to limit his visits to the Williamses' apartment. By the first of March, the quarantine apparently ineffective, Mary requested a private "Embassy" with Edward who discreetly recorded, "Called on Mary by appointment."[98] Mary's newly prescribed limits begin the first stanza:

> The serpent is shut out from Paradise—
> The wounded deer must seek the herb no more
> In which its heart's cure lies—
> The widowed dove must cease to haunt a bower
> Like that from which its mate with feigned sighs
> Fled in the April hour.

Shelley, hinting that his domestic emotional crisis contributed to his ceasing work on *Charles the First,* was echoing the final lines of scene V he had recently written for that drama:

> A widow bird sate mourning her love
> Upon a wintry bough;
> The frozen wind crept on above,
> The freezing stream below.

In "The Serpent," Shelley, the "widowed dove" who must "cease to haunt" Jane's bower, implies that Mary's affection was "feigned." As if merging his feelings toward Mary with those toward literary critics, he wrote:

> Of hatred I am proud,—with scorn content;
>> Indifference, which once hurt me, now is grown
>> Itself indifferent.
> But not to speak of love, Pity alone
> Can break a spirit already more than bent.
>
> (9–13)

Dropping any pretense that the poem is not for Jane alone, "Dear friends" is followed by "dear *friend*" in the third stanza. He appeals to her not to withdraw from him and even "if now I see you seldomer," she should

>> know that I only fly
>> Your looks, because they stir
>> Griefs that should sleep
>>
>> (18–20)

Shelley, returning "to my cold home," and, "forced" to wear the "idle mask" of poet, seeks "Peace . . . but in you I found it not."

Realizing Jane cannot reciprocate his feelings, Shelley wonders if "She loves me, loves me, not," resigned to the recognition that his love for her is "a Vision long since fled." Thoughts of death intrude in the penultimate stanza: "Doubtless there is a place of peace / Where *my* weak heart and all its throbs shall cease."

As for his relationship with Mary, Shelley concluded his poem saying he had "asked her, yesterday, if she believed / That I had resolution." His answer to himself was negative because he "relieved / His heart with words" rather than "what his judgment bade / Would do, and leave the scorner unrelieved." Mary as "scorner" echoes his repeated use of "scorn" in passages in *Julian and Maddalo* referring to his relationship with her.

Shelley sent these stanzas to Jane the day after requesting her harp from Horace Smith, having written in *Charles the First,* that "Lady Jane" should "place my lute, together with the music / Mari received last week from Italy."

Reacting to his literary and romantic frustrations, Shelley turned to another passion, sailing.

15
Drawn to the Sea

THE EVOLUTION OF SHELLEY'S NEW BOAT BEGAN THE DAY AFTER
Trelawny arrived. Williams noted that Trelawny brought to Tre
Palazzi "the model of an American schooner on which it is settled
with S[helley] & myself to build a boat 30 feet long."[1] Williams's
words indicate the three planned joint ownership of the boat.
Trelawny, having briefly served on a captured American schooner,[2]
wrote that same day to his friend in Genoa, the retired Royal
Naval Commander, Captain Daniel Roberts, "to commence on it
directly."

Trelawny and the Williamses joined the Shelleys for a celebra-
tory dinner. Mary dubbed the three men "The Corsair Crew" and
later recalled that night was "one of gaiety and thoughtlessness—
Jane's and my miserable destiny was decided. We then said laugh-
ing each to the other, 'Our husbands decide without asking our consent, or having our concurrence: for, to tell you the truth, I hate this
boat, though I say nothing.'" Agreeing, Jane said to speak out was
"to spoil their pleasure."[3]

When the Corsair Crew dined with Byron on January 16, the talk
of their new boat infected Byron, who wanted a boat modeled on
theirs for competition in sailing. Byron's boat was to be larger and,
unlike the other, would be decked. Trelawny wrote to Roberts that
Byron's boat—to be named "The Countess Gamba Guiccioli"—
was to have a "water closet" and be "sumtuously fitted up: with all
kinds of conveniences for provisions, wine, Books, tables, sofas,
hooks for pistols, rifles, beautifully painted, but not gaudily!"[4] After
Teresa Guiccioli protested, Byron renamed his boat the *Bolivar*.[5]
It was probably about thirty to thirty-five feet in length, not the
large, elegant square-rigger often pictured.[6] Trelawny, calling the
Bolivar a "small schooner," soon informed Byron his vessel could
not have a water closet. However, its expensive fittings made it a
high-cost plaything.

The frugal Crew soon had second thoughts about their proposed craft's cost. Trelawny, after inspecting a boat for sale in Leghorn,[7] consulted Shelley and wrote new "*definitive*" instructions to Roberts. Work was to continue on Byron's boat, with a cabin "as *high* and *roomy* as possible, no *expence* to be spared to make her a complete Beauty!" Its four guns should be "as *large* as you think *safe*—to make a devil of a noise!" Trelawny added that they had decided to postpone "our Boat" and Roberts should build instead a smaller craft, "about 17 or 18 feet," as a tender for Byron's larger boat. If Roberts thought this tender for Byron's boat was not enough, he should also build Byron "a little dinghy." Trelawny urged Roberts to make Byron's planned auxiliary boat "a thorough Varment at pulling and sailing!"[8] At this juncture, Byron had as many as three boats under construction or consideration, Shelley none.[9]

Shelley, desiring separation from Byron, decided to be sole owner of his own craft. He became nettled with Trelawny, who probably collaborated with Byron in naming Shelley's boat the *Don Juan*. Shelley later wrote John Gisborne that it "was originally intended to belong equally to Williams, Trelawny, and myself, but the wish to escape from the third person induced me to become sole proprietor." Its cost, £80, "reduced me to some difficulty in point of money."[10] Trelawny's apparent proposal that Byron join their summer colony led to Mary's fear that Byron's presence would threaten the colony's "unity."[11]

The design and exact size of the *Don Juan* are somewhat obscure. Trelawny did not mention bringing to Pisa a model for the future boat. He later erroneously claimed the final plan of Shelley's boat was based on a model Williams had brought from England, a plan Trelawny said that Williams insisted upon against Roberts's advice. Trelawny said he, Williams, and Shelley drew plans of their projected boat in the sand as they considered islands to visit on a map of the Mediterranean.[12] Careful analysis of the *Don Juan*,[13] correcting previous misconceptions, indicates it probably was between twenty-four and twenty-eight-feet long, had a beam of eight feet, and was round bottomed. According to Trelawny and Roberts, to bring the *Don Juan* down into the water, heavy ballast of pig iron was added, weighing at least two thousand pounds and reducing the freeboard of the open boat. The ballast was dangerously heavy, especially with the added weight of cargo and the eighty-six-pound tender. The boat's twin masts could carry seven sails, including the topsails. Although it might not be considered over-rigged, in a storm the topsails could be difficult to take down, adding to the danger of swamping.

Trelawny, spending time with Shelley, recalled driving him to Leghorn in Trelawny's gig. After visiting a Greek felucca, they boarded an "American clipper" where Trelawny claimed he "seduced Shelley into drinking a wine-glass of weak grog, the first and last he ever drank." Shelley pleased the ship's mate by toasting George Washington. Riding home, Shelley was "in high glee" and "full of fun."[14]

Trelawny's effort to teach Shelley to swim failed. Shelley, observing Trelawny's "aquatic acrobatics" in a deep pool in the Arno, wondered why he could not swim, as "it seems so very easy." After Trelawny explained how to float, Shelley doffed his clothes, jumped in and "lay stretched out on the bottom like a conger eel, not making the least effort or struggle to save himself." Fished out by Trelawny, Shelley asked that Mary not be told of the episode, adding, "It's a great temptation; in another minute, I might have been in another planet."[15] Trelawny described Shelley's body as that of "a young Indian, strong-limbed and vigorous . . . he beat us all in walking."[16] Byron's foot deformity preoccupied Trelawny, whose first anecdote about Byron was that "His halting gait was apparent, but he moved with quickness. . . . His lameness certainly helped to make him sceptical, cynical, and savage."[17] The day Byron first met Trelawny he told Teresa he was "the personification of my Corsair . . . He sleeps with the poem under his pillow."[18]

On a lovely early February morning, Shelley invited Jane to join him and Mary on a walk through Pisa's Cascine pine forest. Williams stayed home, awaiting their mid-afternoon return.[19] Their walk to the sea under graceful umbrella pines induced two of Shelley's finest love lyrics, "To Jane. The Invitation" and "To Jane. The Recollection." Mary, the unmentioned chaperone, published them in 1824 as one poem, "Pine Forest of the Cascine, near Pisa," from Shelley's rough draft. Only later did she learn that Shelley, in exquisite handwriting, had given fair copies of each poem to Jane. His note with "Recollection" was, "To Jane: not to be opened unless you are alone, or with Williams." Shelley's manuscript notations at the end of "Recollection" suggest that he omitted a final stanza he considered not "appropriate to send to the wife of a friend."[20]

Jane is addressed in the first line of the "Invitation," "Dearest, best and brightest, come away." Her warm presence, implicitly contrasting with Mary's coldness, heralds a spring that could thaw winter's "frozen streams." The implied criticism of Mary continues, as Shelley and Jane are

> Where the soul need not repress
> Its music lest it should not find
> An echo in another's mind.
>
> (24–26)

With musical Jane, "the touch of Nature's art / Harmonizes heart to heart." Closing his invitation, he urged Jane, "Radiant Sister of the day, / Awake, arise and come away."

The anticipation in the "Invitation" gives way to memories of the day in the "Recollection," with its deeper, elegiac, and more complex mood. Back home alone with "Sorrow," "Despair," and "Care," Shelley composes an "epitaph" to the "loveliest" day that "is dead." Alluding to Mary, "A frown is on the Heaven's brow." Invoking imagery from the previous week's "The Serpent Is Shut Out from Paradise," they paused in the sunlight of "Paradise" among pines whose trunks suggestively twisted "as rude as serpents interlaced." The remainder of the poem evokes a "magic circle" of "calm" with Jane, "one fair form that filled with love / The lifeless atmosphere."

"Recollection" is a poem of mirroring, trees and sky reflected in pools of water "More perfect" than the reality being mirrored. The lyric becomes a poetic version of his essay *On Love*, where Shelley wrote, an "ideal prototype" is like "a mirror whose surface reflects only the forms of purity and brightness . . . a circle around its proper paradise."[21] "Recollection" ends with the idealized, mirrored image lasting only

> Until an envious wind crept by,
>   Like an unwelcome thought
> Which from the mind's too faithful eye
>   Blots one dear image out.—
> Though thou art ever fair and kind
>   And forest ever green,
> Less oft is peace in S[helley]'s mind
>   Than calm in water seen.
>
> (81–88)

Mary—the "envious wind" and "unwelcome thought" blotting out Jane's "dear image"—would be part of the lack of "calm" in "Shelley's mind" in the stressful months ahead.

Several days after this walk, Shelley and Williams went to La
Spezia seeking houses for the summer colony. After vainly exploring "every hovel" in La Spezia, they crossed to Lerici where an old
fisherman showed them two houses that pleased them. The next
day they learned that only the beach house was available, at one
hundred crowns a year. Shelley probably was relieved that no
house was suitable for Byron's establishment. Returning to Pisa,
their "Spezia plan" was still unsettled.[22] Every evening they were
gone, Mary was Trelawny's companion at the opera and Mrs. Beauclerk's ball. She wrote glowingly of feeling "tenderness" to those
who had awakened in her such "harmony & thrilling music."[23]

Byron began talking "vehemently" of performing *Othello* in the
main hall of the Lanfranchi with "all Pisa" as the audience. *Othello*
was a favorite of Trelawny's since his days of hobnobbing with London actors. Inevitably, his swarthy countenance and physical presence landed him the title role. Byron took the choice role of the conniving Iago while Shelley, finding contact with Byron "painful,"[24]
was noticeably absent from the cast. Mary was cast as Desdemona, Williams as Cassio, Jane as Emilia, and Medwin as Roderigo.
Trelawny and Mary agreed that Iago had "no better representa-
tive" than Byron[25] but after only a few rehearsals the play was
called off. Medwin believed Teresa "put her Veto" on the play, perhaps from jealousy about Desdemona, now possibly either Mrs.
Beauclerk or one of her daughters.[26]

Shakespeare resurfaced when Trelawny burst into the Shelleys'
apartment excited about the boat being built, saying "we must all
embark—all live aboard—'We will all suffer a sea change.'" Shelley, delighted with Trelawny's quoting Ariel from *The Tempest*,
said he would use it for the motto of his boat.[27]

The two poets held differing views of Shakespeare, whom Byron
liked to derogate. Samuel Rogers, visiting Byron in April, recalled
a Lanfranchi dinner attended by Trelawny and Shelley. Byron's
criticism of the Bard provoked Shelley's "meek yet resolute" defense, despite Byron's "rude" interruption, "Oh, that's very well *for
an atheist.*"[28] Perhaps this dinner discussion produced a dialogue
published anonymously in 1830, "Byron and Shelley on the Character of Hamlet." Its content suggests Shelley's ideas; the writing
may have been Mary's. Responding to Byron's attacks, Shelley
praised Shakespeare's genius, the drama's unity, and "the deep
meaning signified" in the dialogue between Hamlet and his
mother. Shelley considered the play's "moral" was Hamlet's ob-

servation that we learn "There's a divinity that shapes our ends / Rough-hew them how we will." The dialogue ends: "Shelley, as he finished, looked up, and found Lord Byron fast asleep."[29]

Byron respected Shelley's literary acumen and asked his views of his *The Deformed Transformed*. Shelley said he liked it least of anything Byron had written, it being "a bad imitation of 'Faust;' and besides, there are two entire lines of Southey's in it." Responding to Byron's query, Shelley repeated the lines, identifying them from *The Curse of Kehama*. Byron instantly threw the sheet into the fire.[30]

Byron also became enraged when Medwin showed him Southey's recent attack upon him in *The Courier*. Southey, having read Byron's attack on him, denied spreading scandal about Byron and the Shelleys in Switzerland. He accused Byron of concealing the basis of his criticisms of the "Satanic School," which included the unnamed Shelley. Byron responded by asking his friend Douglas Kinnaird to challenge the Poet Laureate to a duel in France. Byron had upheld his honor by challenging Southey, who—Byron knew—would not budge from Keswick.[31]

Byron, in turn, was provoking Shelley's private thoughts of a duel. When he told Byron *The Deformed Transformed* was a bad imitation of *Faust*, Shelley recognized that his talks with Byron about the Doppelgänger motif in Goethe and Calderón had given Byron the idea to use it in his drama. Further, Shelley recognized that his translation for Byron from a Calderón drama about a "second self" had been integrated into *The Deformed Transformed*. Shelley had other irritations aside from Byron's appropriation of his ideas. He was at an impasse composing *Charles the First*, had heard nothing of the critics' response to *Adonais*, had heard from Hunt of being attacked by Hazlitt, and did not know if Ollier had published *Hellas*. Meanwhile, Medwin said Byron "threatened to make himself as voluminous & prolific an author as Shakespeare."[32]

Shelley indicated to Claire ideas of silencing Byron by challenging him to a duel: "It is of vital importance both to me and to yourself, to Allegra even, that I should put a period to my intimacy with L[ord] B[yron], and that without *éclat*." He "strongly" suspected Byron of "the basest insinuations and the only mode in which I could effectually silence him I am reluctant (even if I had proof) to employ during my father's life." Only Claire's "immediate feelings" kept Shelley from "suddenly and irrevocably" leaving "this country which he inhabits, nor ever enter it but as an enemy to determine our differences *without words*."[33]

Byron's "basest insinuations" that provoked this letter were his innuendos about Claire and Shelley parenting a child. Many years later Claire reported a questionable incident presumably related by Mrs. Mason's former servant, Betsy Parker. She supposedly witnessed an angry Shelley telling Mrs. Mason "he could with pleasure have knocked Lord Byron down" after seeing Byron's "gleam of malicious satisfaction" when told of Claire's "declining health."[34]

Claire was upset that Byron "confessed he had not made the smallest inquiry" about her complaints concerning Allegra's convent. She said she learned about the terrible convent conditions from Mr. Tighe who, she claimed, made a trip to Allegra's convent without the Shelleys' knowledge.[35] Claire also had "low Spirits" in mid-January after experiencing "Disagreeable questioning" at the home of her wealthy friend in Florence, Madame Boutourlin. The previous May, Claire had met at the Boutourlins' members of Lady Charlotte Bury's entourage, Countess Charleville and her daughter, Louisa Tisdale.[36]

The evening of February 7, 1822, Claire met Elise Foggi at Casa Boutourlin. Three days later Elise called on Claire, who wrote a line in her journal she later tried hard to obliterate: "E's report of Naples and me." Claire was familiar with some version of these charges from Paolo's blackmail efforts.[37] The next day, Elise called again and Claire wrote, "Spend a very unhappy day."[38] Claire and Elise would meet twenty times over the next two months.

Claire, probably communicating about Elise's visits, wrote to Shelley and to Mrs. Mason and received quick replies from each. Claire, after staying home all day February 16 with "terrible anxiety," received a letter from Shelley conveying pessimism about Byron's yielding on Allegra. Claire, "wretched" and "miserable," drafted her last fruitless appeal to Byron, imploring him to let her visit Allegra at Bagnacavallo. Having an "inexplicable internal feeling" of never seeing Allegra again, she said her visit was urgent, as "I shortly leave Italy, for a new country." Her brother Charles had just written from Vienna, probably concerning a position there as governess. It would be, she told Byron, "a disagreeable and precarious course of life" and it was better she "were dead" so as "to escape all the sufferings which your harshness causes me." After writing, "I conjure you do not make the world dark to me, as if my Allegra were dead," she ended plaintively, "I wish you every happiness."[39] The next day, still "miserable," Claire wrote letters to her brother, Shelley, Mrs. Mason, and Mary, informing each of her decision to leave Italy.[40]

Alarmed by Claire's letter, Mary consulted Shelley and dispatched their servant Domenico Bini to fetch Claire with Mary's brief note to come "directly" and Shelley "will return with you to Florence."[41] After four days in Pisa, Claire was dissuaded from leaving Italy. She did not see Byron but shared Trelawny's company on three occasions.

When Claire left, Mary, uncharacteristically, wrote at length in her journal of her own dejected feelings. Her "invaluable" feelings had "bought" only "Contempt discontent & disappointment." She wanted to love "in my fellow creatures . . . that which is" and not "fix" her "affections on a fair form endued with imaginary attributes." She possibly had read Shelley's recent poem to Jane ("The Recollection") with its phrase, "fair form." Soon after this entry, Mary convened her private "Embassy" with Edward Williams.[42]

Preoccupied with his new tragedy, Williams showed the first act to Shelley, who "found some faults but generally approved." Trelawny told Williams that Byron—who suggested it be titled *The Secret*—viewed the drama favorably and offered to write a prologue and epilogue to help ensure its success.[43] Shelley stayed home the evening of February 17, while Mary and Trelawny went with the Williamses to the *veglione,* a masked ball lasting until three in the morning. When Jane became ill the next day, Williams noted, "S[helley] turns Physician." She was well enough that evening to appear in "an Hindoostani dress" she had brought from India. Mary donned a Turkish costume and Williams sketched Jane in her dress.[44] Shelley, responding to her singing Hindustani airs, gave Jane a copy of "I Arise from dreams of thee." This poem, probably evoked by Sophia Stacey's singing, next saw duty in a verse contest between Byron and Shelley instigated by the English tenor, John Sinclair, performing that winter in the Pisan opera and at Mrs. Beauclerk's socials. Sinclair was fond of Shelley's verses and considered adapting them to music. Byron's effort was "Stanzas to a Hindoo Air," and Shelley's resurrected Stacey-poem has come to be known as "The Indian Girl's Song."[45]

Another Indian theme, based on a story Trelawny told, crept into an unfinished drama Shelley began for his circle's entertainment. It has overtones of *The Tempest* and Shelley possibly intended it to replace Byron's production of *Othello*. The theme—of lost love on an island peopled by an Enchantress, a Spirit, an Indian youth, a lady, and a pirate—seemingly owes as much to Shelley's personal situation as to Trelawny's tale of himself as a pirate. The youth passionately desires the pirate's lady who, responding to him only with "sisterly affection," causes his "hell of waking sorrow."[46]

Loss of love also pervades Shelley's haunting "When the lamp is shattered." Possibly intended for the unfinished Indian drama,[47] it is Shelley's most personal lament of emotional bereavement among his last lyrics, expressing an inability to respond or seek restored love. Among images of death, the second stanza ends as his "mute" spirit hears only "the mournful surges / That ring the dead seaman's knell." In the next stanza, "When hearts have once mingled / Love first leaves the well-built nest," the loss is endured by the "weak one," implicitly Shelley. The lines end as the "nest"

> Will rot, and thine eagle home
> Leave thee naked to laughter,
> When leaves fall and cold winds come.
>
> (30–32)

After his March 1 "Embassy" with Mary, Williams joined Shelley on the Arno in the little skiff. About ten days later Medwin departed for Rome and Naples. Trelawny had become Medwin's competitor, both with the ladies and in collecting anecdotes about Shelley and Byron. Trelawny recalled that Shelley, unable to resist giving Medwin money before he left, dumped a pile of coins on his library's hearth rug. Using a fire shovel, he apportioned half for household expenses and a quarter for Mary. Shelley told Mary his quarter was for moneyless "poor Tom Medwin." Mary later assured Trelawny she controlled the money, allowing Shelley an occasional *scudo* as "he can't be trusted with money, and he won't have it."[48] When Mrs. Beauclerk departed after Medwin, Claire called them Pisa's "two great conductors of gossip."[49]

Shelley's writing of shipwrecks continued in his translation of scenes from Calderón's *El mágico prodigioso*. A Shelley-like solitary scholar, Cyprian, whose searching "intellect / Can find no God," becomes "enamoured" of Justina. After she "disdains him," he retired "to a solitary seashore" to meet his Doppelgänger, the Daemon-Lucifer, a "friendless guest" who emerged from the "watery eclipse" of a ship wrecked in a "tempest." The Daemon, misleading Cyprian, vows to forge Cyprian's "destruction."

Mary, now scorning Emilia Viviani, wrote to Maria Gisborne that Emilia's request for money concluded "our friendship." Mary was reminded of a nursery rhyme about a "pretty maid" on "Cranbourne lane"—the Covent Garden district of prostitutes—who, after being given "cakes" and "wine," asked "for some brandy." Mary believed the story of this "little naughty girl" was the "whole story of Shelley['s] Italian platonics."[50] Unaware of Shelley's poems for Jane, Mary was aware of a new, unsettling reality. By mid-March, after three years, she was again pregnant, qualifying Trelawny's report that Shelley, in Pisa, slept on his own sofa for two years.[51]

In Florence, Claire fretted over two commissions from Mary and Shelley concerning Elise Foggi, who visited her almost daily. Feeling "miserable," Claire entered in her journal, "Give the Naples commission to her Husband," words she later tried to cross out.[52] This commission to Paolo Foggi possibly concerned demands related to Shelley's Neapolitan child. Claire's other commission was to enlist Elise in trying to squelch the scandal. The peculiar tactic was for Elise to deny to Mrs. Hoppner that she, Elise, had told her what in fact she had about Claire's and Shelley's putative Neapolitan child. Soon, Elise was asked to write Mary a denial letter as well. Confused, Claire wrote Mary asking what Elise was "to say to you" and Mrs. Hoppner. Claire received her instructions and Elise dutifully wrote in French messages of denial to Mary and to Mrs. Hoppner.[53] This unresolved drama's final act came in 1843 when Mary wrote Claire from Florence that the Hoppners were there and "I cut them completely."[54]

Claire, increasingly fearful for Allegra, in mid-March concocted two wild plots to extricate her from the convent. Without telling the Shelleys, she and Mrs. Mason devised the idea of Claire converting to Catholicism and entering the Bagnacavallo convent as a pensioner boarder. She told Edward Silsbee of this plan five decades later, saying it required that Shelley "advance the money" for Claire's board at Bagnacavallo.[55]

Claire's other scheme, conveyed to Mary, was for Shelley to write a forged letter apparently containing Byron's request that the child be released. Once freed, Claire and Allegra would live in some unspecified locale, again financed by Shelley. Mary wrote that she and Shelley consulted "seriously" about this unrealistic plan which could only result in a "duel" between Byron and Shelley. Mary agreed Allegra should be separated from Byron, who was "as remorseless as he is unprincipled." She reminded Claire that

Shelley's urging Byron to remove Allegra from the convent caused the "exasperated" Byron to vow if Claire annoyed him again he would place Allegra in a secret convent and Claire would have nothing to do with her. Mary reassured Claire that Allegra's health was in no great danger as Bagnacavallo's "salutary" air was "the best" in Italy.

Counseling Claire to wait for a more auspicious time, Mary reminded her, "Spring is our unlucky season" and listed each spring's "ill luck" since 1815, including that of "Emilia" in 1821. She and Shelley were still "in great uncertainty as to our summer residence" but "We have thought of Naples."[56] Shelley's postscript assured Claire their house would be "far from Lord Byron's" in his effort to end "his detested intimacy." Byron, after a recent heated conversation, was jealous "of my regard for your interests" and "inaccessible to my suggestions."

Several days later, Shelley wrote Claire that her "plan about Allegra" would end in "inevitable destruction," adding—words Claire later tried to obliterate—"I *would not* in any case make myself the party to a forged letter." Shelley said he could not refuse Byron's challenge to a duel. Claire's "fraudulent" plan was "madness" and "shocked" him. Shelley had "no money" for this "impossible" idea but would "try to" finance Claire's trip to Vienna should she go.

Shelley was "convinced" Claire could "never obtain Allegra," who was in Byron's "power." Claire partially obliterated his reminder of "when you rejected my earnest advice & treated me with that contempt which I have never merited from you, & how at Milan, & how vain is now your regret!" He ended mysteriously about soon writing her "on another subject" about "which, however, all is as you already know."[57] A week later, Shelley instructed Claire to address him at the Post Office "not Hodgson . . . but Joe James."[58] Claire also tried to obliterate these words.

Claire had another aggravating involvement with her two poets. After Shelley aroused Byron's interest in Goethe's *Memoirs*, Byron offered to pay him for a translation of Goethe's life. Shelley got Claire to do the translation but misunderstood her wish to have her name on the translation, telling Byron the translator was in Paris. Claire's unfinished translation was praised by Shelley, but she received no recompense.[59]

In late March, Claire received Shelley's news of his life-threatening experience, "yesterday's affray." He reported being "struck from my horse, & had not Capt. Hay warded off the sabre with his stick must inevitably have been killed." Captain John Hay, Byron's friend, received "a severe sabre wound across the face."[60] The morning of the incident, the Williamses accepted Mary's invitation for dinner. Shelley and Trelawny joined Byron, Hay, and Pietro Gamba for the customary afternoon horseback ride to the *podere* for pistol shooting. Williams stayed home to work on his tragedy.

Riding home in the late afternoon, the men were met by Mary and Teresa, in their carriage, and Taaffe, who rode alongside Byron, Shelley, and Trelawny. Approaching the city gate, a uniformed horseman who overtook them from the rear apparently brushed Taaffe, whose startled horse reared, bumping into Byron's horse. Mary reported Taaffe cried out about "this man's insolence" and Byron's vow to "bring him to an account" began the chase. Taaffe, calming his frightened horse, did not rush to join the rest.[61]

The offending dragoon, Sergeant-Major Stefani Masi of the Tuscan Royal Light Horse, was first overtaken by Shelley. Trelawny joined him in blocking the dragoon. Shelley, the Italian speaker, politely asked the dragoon to explain his conduct. According to Shelley, Masi replied with curses and insults. By this time, Byron and the other men arrived.

Pietro Gamba then enraged Masi by striking him with his riding whip and calling him "Ignorante." Trelawny, struck on the legs with the flat of Masi's saber, yelled to Shelley, asking if he had any pistols. His pistols empty, Shelley attempted to come between Trelawny and Masi, who slashed at Shelley with his saber. Shelley was saved by Hay's parrying the blow and by the close quarters of the skirmish. However, Shelley was hit on the head by Masi's saber's hilt and knocked off his horse, falling senseless on the ground for some moments. Masi, after cutting Hay across the nose, pummeled Byron's courier.

His head hurting badly, Shelley came to and vomited. Mounting his horse, he was riding toward town when Masi began a confrontation with Trelawny. Shelley's arrival caused the dragoon to ride off toward Byron's palace. Shelley, Trelawny, and the still-bleeding Hay proceeded toward Lanfranchi, where Byron was armed with a sword-stick. Across the river, the unwitting Williamses waited to dine in the Shelleys' apartment. As the dragoon rode past Lanfranchi, someone struck him in the side with a lance and the seriously wounded Masi fell in a faint to the ground before being carried to the hospital.

Mary, calming the hysterical Teresa, asked that the Williamses be informed. Taaffe, arriving last, hurried off to report the fray to Governor Viviani. The entire group went from Lanfranchi to the Shelleys' apartment. Shelley was still feeling sick from his blow and Byron, "foaming with rage," held fainting Teresa on his arm. Mary looked "philosophically upon this interesting scene."

The next morning Taaffe had news that Masi's wound was a "mere scratch" but Mary returned from the hospital saying he was not expected to live. Amid rampant rumors of an English insurrection, Shelley heard from Mrs. Beauclerk that he was in danger. Trelawny armed himself with Williams's pistols.

Williams thought Taaffe was "highly blameable" and Jane's tag, "False Taaffe," was quickly adopted. Shelley wrote Claire: "My part in the affair, if not cautious or prudent, was justifiable; nor can I take to myself any imputation of rashness or want of temper. My words and my actions were calm and peaceable although firm." He thought the fault, if any, started with Taaffe. Shelley, on "the swiftest horse," said once he began pursuing Masi he "could not have allowed the man to escape."[62] Vaccà, attending the recovering Masi, criticized the English involved in the affair. The dilatory authorities began taking testimony from the participants, including Mary.[63]

Byron's innocent servant Tita and a servant of the Gambas were held in the wounding of Masi after the actual assailant, Byron's coachman, was released. Byron, fearful that distorted stories of the affair might appear in the London press, wrote friends in Britain, including Sir Walter Scott. Hiring a lawyer in Florence, Byron threatened to bring the matter before Parliament and had Mary send copies of the depositions to Hunt for the *Examiner* and to Medwin in Rome. Mary told Hunt the affair was "a matter of perfect indifference" and that Shelley, "in infinitely better health," had "got over this winter delightfully."

This did not square with Shelley's actual feelings. He wrote Claire of his war with his "rebel faculties"[64] and informed Hunt both his health and Mary's "obliged" them to seek "sea air." Shelley confided to Hunt he was the only one to whom "I have breathed a syllable of my feelings" of becoming "misanthropical and suspicious," like others he had "formerly condemned." Hoping Hunt's presence could "cure" him, he mentioned the hurt Byron inflicted: "how deep the wounds have been, you partly know and partly can conjecture. Certain it is, that Lord Byron has made me bitterly feel the inferiority which the world has presumed to place between us and which subsists nowhere in reality but in our own talents, which are not our own but Nature's—or in our rank, which is not our own but Fortune's."[65]

The Masi affair was a catalyst in dispersing the Pisan circle. Williams and Jane inquired without luck about houses in Leghorn. Hay found for Byron's summer residence the Villa Dupuy on a hillside in Montenero, several kilometers south of Leghorn.[66] The salmon-colored sprawling house had room for Byron, Teresa, and the Gambas, but would prove almost unbearable in the unusually hot summer of 1822. With Teresa's permission, Byron resumed *Don Juan*.[67] Williams, without living arrangements, constantly wrote of being "unsettled" in his journal. Despite this, he and Shelley negotiated for a boat to take their families and furniture to La Spezia. On April 5, the two sailed the Arno and heard from Roberts that Shelley's new boat would be finished in ten days.[68]

Shelley urged Claire to join "our party in the country," where they "shall be quite alone" and distant from Byron's villa.[69] That same day, he wrote Hunt about moving near the sea, specifying "near Spezia" to John Gisborne and Horace Smith. Receiving *Hellas*, Shelley found it was "prettily printed" but quickly sent Ollier a list of errata and admitted the poem was "in general more correct than my other books."[70]

Shelley told John Gisborne that "changes" made it "necessary" to make a new will. Gisborne had witnessed Shelley's changed will three years earlier when Mary was pregnant with Percy and perhaps understood another child was expected.[71] Shelley wanted to add a £2,000 legacy for Hunt[72] and perhaps intended to drop his £6,000 provision for Allegra.

In this long letter to Gisborne, Shelley, laying out in detail his financial situation, estimated his inherited estate "At my fathers death" was "from 5 to 7000 a year." Placing his debts at £22,500, he thought a good lawyer could reduce the amount to "£14 or £15[000]," a reduction made easier if he did not return to England. His firm decision, "I *will not* come" to England when his father died, was based on more than money: "with regard to my own feelings, I should lose everything" if he returned to England. His family at Field Place had never extended any consolation at the deaths of his children in Italy. Unable to send John Gisborne the "5 to 10 pounds" he owed him, Shelley said returning meant confronting the Godwins, who "are forever plotting & devising pretexts for money; none of which however they get: *1st* because I *can't,* & *2nd* because I *wont.*"

On the day Claire arrived in Pisa, April 15, word came that the houses Shelley had wanted near La Spezia were refused to them. Byron suspected it was because the Piedmontese government had heard of Shelley's involvement in the Masi imbroglio. Given this setback, Shelley and Williams soon searched unsuccessfully for houses in Montenero and Antignano.[73] Williams's relationship with Shelley had just weathered another setback, Shelley's presentation to Jane of a guitar and its accompanying poem, "With a guitar. To Jane." Shelley copied the poem on fine, thin paper in his most beautiful hand.

Williams, carefully avoiding mentioning the gift in his journal, sent a note upstairs to "My dear S——" veiling his jealous anger in a lighthearted invitation to a duel: "Jane begs me to say that she can only answer your kindness in person. As for my movements I am going to shoot this Evening—that is, I feel that I must parade you at 10 paces if you go on thus—If you will call yourself or send your second we will point out the ground."[74]

After Horace Smith refused to lend Shelley money for Jane's musical instrument, Shelley answered, "I have contrived to get my musical coals at Newcastle itself."[75] The guitar, in a black wooden case, was made in Pisa by Ferdinando Bottari, another resonance from *The Tempest,* whose Ferdinand would be Williams in "With a guitar. To Jane."[76]

Trelawny's recollection years later was of finding Shelley composing the poem one spring day in the Cascine pine forest under a fallen tree by a mirror-like pond. Searching for the poet with Mary, who stopped to rest, Trelawny met an old man who knew the secluded haunt of "L'Inglese malinconico." A rapt Shelley was writing in "a frightful scrawl," the words so smeared and written over one another that Trelawny could only decipher the opening lines, "Ariel, to Miranda take / This slave of music." Told Mary was anxiously awaiting him, Shelley sighed in reply, "Poor Mary! her's is a sad fate . . . she can't bear solitude, nor I society—the quick coupled with the dead."[77]

The poem's Ariel, Shelley, and Miranda, Jane, are in contrast to "the silent Moon," Mary, who "is not sadder in her cell / Than deserted Ariel." Mary, "interlunar," is invisible and in a "swoon," an allusion to her pregnancy with its eclipse on sexual relations. Shelley is both "deserted Ariel" and the slave guitar waiting to be strummed by Miranda-Jane, the "only" one who can make his "de-lighted spirit glow." Seemingly commenting on Mary restricting his contact with Jane, "the poor sprite" Shelley "is / Imprisoned for some fault of his."

Mary's prenatal state yields Shelley's own birthing fantasy of be-ing the guitar "wrought" from a tree that is "dreaming . . . all of love." Ariel, the "spirit that inhabits" the guitar, "will not tell / To those who cannot question well" all "it knows . . . / These secrets of an elder day." The guitar "keeps its highest holiest tone / For our beloved Jane alone."

A disturbing letter about Allegra arrived April 17 from Byron's Ravenna banker, Ghigi. After a recurrence of "little slow fevers," the doctor, believing she was consumptive, bled her three times. Soon Ghigi wrote that Allegra "has been very ill, of a dangerous ill-ness" but with all the doctors and nuns, "If there is any fault, it is of too much care." The Abbess also wrote about Allegra's "little in-flammation" and of the care being lavished upon her. These letters arrived April 19, two days after the child's condition became so crit-ical she was confirmed by the Bishop of Faenza.[78]

On April 22, word reached Byron's secretary that Allegra had died two days earlier "after a convulsive catarrhal attack." The nuns believed their five-year-old gifted charge died because she was "too intelligent to live." Byron, hearing the news from Teresa, "remained immovable" for an hour, not shedding a tear, "his coun-tenance manifested . . . so profound, so sublime a sorrow."[79] Byron planned that Allegra's embalmed body be sent to Harrow Church, where he too wished to be buried. When her body arrived in Leghorn in early May, Byron refused to see the two men who ac-companied the casket or pay them for their services. Byron angrily refused to pay the exorbitant embalming fee, not to mention the modest bill sent by the nuns at the convent.[80]

Teresa brought what Mary called "Evil news" on April 23 and By-ron wrote Shelley, "The blow was stunning and unexpected; for I thought the danger over." Dealing with his guilt, Byron did "not know that I have any thing to reproach in my conduct . . . it is a mo-ment when we are apt to think that, if this or that had been done, such an event might have been prevented."[81] Mary wrote Maria Gisborne of Byron's "remorse, for he felt he had acted against every body's councils and wishes, and death had stamped with truth the many and often urged prophecies of Claire." Allegra "died of a typhus fever" that was "raging in the Romagna" and about which they were uninformed.[82]

The morning of April 23 Claire had departed with Williams and Jane to find houses in La Spezia, all three unaware of Allegra's death. Finding no suitable houses, they returned two days later. Shelley apparently had told Byron that he would delay telling Claire about Allegra and he now planned to put distance between Claire and Byron by moving both Tre Palazzi households immediately to La Spezia. Claire resisted, wanting to return to Florence, but Shelley, with difficulty, persuaded her to go to La Spezia.

The initial contingent would be Mary, Percy, Claire, and Trelawny. Shelley hoped that Villa Magni, the house on the beach near Lerici he had liked in February, was still available from its owner in Sarzana. Mary, still "unwell" from her pregnancy, was to contract for it and try to find a house for the Williamses, who also needed some persuasion by Shelley to move.

When Claire's group departed April 26, Williams noted she was "quite unconscious of the burden on her friends' minds." The next morning, Shelley and the Williamses loaded their household belongings on two boats moored in front of Tre Palazzi before departing by road for Lerici. The next day, the Lerici harbormaster reported no houses were available and the duty on their furniture would be at least £300. Reacting to this "devil of a mess," Williams resolved to send his family's goods back to Pisa without unloading them. Shelley wrote to Mary, who was with Trelawny in La Spezia, anxiously inquiring how she had "sustained the trials of the journey" and urging her to go to Sarzana to close on Villa Magni.[83] That day, April 28, Trelawny left for Genoa to fetch the *Bolivar*. Shelley and Williams, with the harbormaster's help, avoided, at least temporarily, the customs charge on their goods. Williams was only "somewhat calmed" on hearing from Mary in Sarzana that she had secured Villa Magni but there was "no hope" for a house for the Williams family. Jane agreed with Williams to send their goods back to Pisa and the two went to La Spezia intent on finding lodgings for their family.

The "impertinence" of the innkeeper to ask "32 francs a day" caused the Williamses to return to Lerici, where Mary had arrived from Sarzana. The two boats of household goods were towed across the little bay from Lerici to San Terenzo, a small, rustic village on whose southern shore the Villa Magni hugged the beach.

The boats soon were unloaded on the beach and both families' goods were stowed in Villa Magni. The dispirited Williamses, unsure where they would live, spent that night at the inn in Lerici. They returned the next morning, May 1, to Villa Magni where the Shelleys "contrived to give us rooms—without them Heaven knows what we should have done."[84]

Villa Magni had cramped living quarters for the five adults and three children. Above the dirt ground floor, used for storage, were three small bedrooms around a larger dining room. The top floor provided quarters for each family's servants, who soon quarreled. The sea lapped at the entrance of Shelley's "white house with arches."[85] Spanning the front of the house was a raised terrace, accessed from the living quarters. The families passed the first night "talking over our folly and our troubles." Soon, Claire wanted to return to Florence and Mary, discontent with the new house, wrote in her journal May 4, "The Rest of May a blank."[86]

Williams's journal fills the void. On May 2, he and Shelley sailed in the little skiff despite stormy weather, fished without luck among the rocks, and vainly pursued wild ducks. More seriously, Claire's insistence on returning to Florence had to be confronted. The Williamses and Shelleys were conferring in Jane's room when Claire entered and guessed "the purpose of our meeting." Shelley "broke the unhappy news" about Allegra to Claire, who, "after her first burst of grief, and despair . . . reconciled herself to her fate, sooner than we expected."[87]

When Shelley wrote Byron of being "compelled" to tell Claire of Allegra's death, he declined describing "her grief" as Byron had "already suffered too much." Because Claire wished to see the coffin, Shelley said he would accompany her to Leghorn but, "on many accounts," not to Pisa, where Byron remained until May 20. Shelley expressed relief that despite what he had "dreaded" Claire "retains her senses." He conveyed Claire's request that Byron send a portrait of Allegra and a lock of her hair.[88]

Byron, sending these mementos to Shelley, also returned Claire's attacking letter he had just received. Mrs. Mason called this now-lost letter "furious," Claire apparently saying the Shelleys joined her in condemning Byron's placing Allegra in a convent.[89] Shelley wrote to Byron that he "had no idea that her letter was written in that temper" and regardless of what he and Mary thought of Byron's ideas concerning Allegra's education, they would not have "allowed such a letter to be sent to you had we suspected it's contents." He had dissuaded Claire from going to Leghorn to visit Allegra's coffin and she had no objection to Allegra's burial in England.[90]

Although Allegra's death relieved Shelley from his awkward role as mediator between the child's parents, he was still linked with Byron. At Byron's request, Shelley took in his servant Tita, released from prison and banished from Tuscany.[91] Shelley's more troubling tie to Byron was the pending arrival of Hunt and his family. Before Byron moved to Montenero, Shelley notified him that Hunt would embark May 13, adding optimistically, "We may therefore expect him every day at Leghorn."

Shelley expressed qualms about Byron's legal representation against Masi and encouraged him to "intercede for the poor devil."[92] Despite Byron's urging, Shelley reiterated he had "not the least desire to proceed against the poor devil" but was "willing to act as you think best."[93] Byron rejected Shelley's meliorating, saying he would "be very much surprized" if Shelley did not prosecute.[94] There is no record that Shelley ever wrote to Byron again.

In early May, Shelley had written Byron, "we are dismal . . . the accommodations are as wretched as the scenery is divine." However, the Williamses were "a great relief and consolation." Six days later, he wrote Byron of his "shattered health & spirits" and of being "so exhausted." Confused, he began this letter with "Spezia," crossed out for "Lerici," and misdated the year as 1821.[95] Three days earlier, May 6, Shelley had experienced the first of two acute hallucinatory episodes at Villa Magni.

Williams left the only account of this first experience. He and Shelley were having an evening talk while walking on the terrace that overlooked the beach. Watching the moonlight upon the water, Shelley shared some "rather melancholy" feelings with Williams, who shared his own similar feelings.

> Shelley . . . complained of being unusually nervous, and stopping short he grasped me violently by the arm and stared steadfastly on the white surf that broke upon the beach under our feet. Observing him sensibly affected I demanded of him if he was in pain—but he only answered, saying, "There it is again!—there!"—He recovered after some time, and declared that he saw, as plainly as then he saw me a naked child rise from the sea, clap its hands as if in joy and smiling at him. This was a trance that it required some reasoning and philosophy entirely to awaken him from, so forcibly had the vision operated on his mind.[96]

This hallucinated child probably was Allegra, although he had lost William, Clara, and Elena Adelaide. Years later, Mary wrote, ambiguously, that Shelley's vision was of "the child of a friend who had lately died."[97]

This first terrace episode occurred when Shelley and Williams were anticipating the arrival of Shelley's boat from Genoa. The powerful sea swells fascinated Williams, who misunderstood their origin and was kept awake by their breaking on the beach "like heavy artillery."[98] He and Shelley, trying to launch the small flat-bottomed boat by pushing it through the heavy seas, were swamped attempting to land. The next day, Shelley had his vision of the child. The morning of May 7, heavy surf prevented their going out but Williams, believing the seas had calmed in the afternoon, tried to put to sea with Jane. Two waves successively struck the boat, which almost swamped before Williams could land a "half drowned" Jane onto the rocks. A late afternoon heavy thunder and lightning storm was further evidence of the Mediterranean's potential for treachery.

They heard from Trelawny on May 8 that the *Don Juan* would arrive the next day and "Every eye strained in hope of seeing the boat come in." Their anxiety mounted when the boat had not arrived by May 10 and the heavy sea swells returned. Bad weather had forced the *Don Juan* to return to Genoa several days before. Finally, on the afternoon of May 12, Williams spotted from the terrace a sail rounding the point of Portovenere. It was Shelley's boat, manned by a "Mr. Heslop and two English seamen," one of whom, eighteen-year-old Charles Vivian, Shelley hired as crew.[99]

The *Don Juan*'s maiden voyage from Genoa had been stormy and a gale was still blowing from the southwest when Heslop moored the new craft at Lerici. Shelley and Williams quickly arrived to try her out before dark even though Shelley found the weather "very squally." Discovering there were too few reefs to shorten the sail in the strong wind, they soon returned to avoid capsizing. Williams, overconfident, was elated at how "she fetches whatever she looks at . . . we have now a perfect plaything for the summer." That night and the next day the heavy gale continued with torrential rains. Williams thought the heavy surf crashing upon Villa Magni made them feel in their beds "as if we were on board ship." That afternoon Shelley and Williams walked again to see their boat, but delayed taking it out until the next morning when the weather had calmed. Hoisting the topsails and flying jib, they sailed "on a wind" in an hour and a half to La Spezia and back. Heslop left for Genoa carrying a letter from Shelley inviting Roberts to stay with them at Villa Magni, "although I cannot boast very capital accommodation." The *Don Juan*, "a most beautiful boat," so far surpassed their expectations that they thought Roberts had sent Byron's *Bolivar* "by mistake." The next morning, the two men took Mary and Jane for a sail to Portovenere. Williams felt the boat "sailed like a witch."[100]

It was painfully clear to Shelley that his new boat was indeed the *Don Juan*. He did not mention to Roberts his resentment that painted on his boat's mainsail was the name of Byron's epic. According to Mary, after Shelley decided to be sole owner of the boat, he gave it the name *Ariel*, but Byron "chose to take fire at this" and wrote Roberts that the earlier chosen name be painted on the sail. *Don Juan* stuck as the boat's name, but Mary said that unless the words on the sail were eradicated they would "make a coal-barge of our boat."[101] Not mentioning the name on the sail, Shelley wrote to Byron that his new boat "serves me at once for a study & a carriage." Writing Trelawny, Shelley caustically commented, "we must suppose the name to have [been] given her during the equivocation of sex which her godfather suffered in the Harem." Shelley was referring to the transvestite scene in *Don Juan*'s fifth canto, if not to Byron's bisexual proclivities. Trelawny later scratched out Shelley's complaint that "my noble friend, carrying the joke rather too far" had "Don Juan . . . written on the mainsail." Shelley wondered if Byron intended "to write Bolivar on his own mainsail." Shelley, exaggerating Williams's sailing prowess and deferring to him as the boat's commander, told Trelawny, "Williams declares her to be perfect, & I participate in his enthusiasm inasmuch as would be decent for a landsman." They had not yet raced against larger boats but "she passes the small ones as a comet might pass the dullest planets of the Heavens." Anxious about its final cost, Shelley joked to Trelawny that Roberts's estimate of £50 would grow to £500.[102]

Shelley, without mentioning his boat, wrote to Horace Smith despairingly about Byron's inhibiting influence on his creativity: "I do not write—I have lived too long near Lord Byron & the sun has extinguished the glowworm." Another aggravation was Godwin, whose disturbing letters Mary was still not reading. Losing the lawsuit and having to leave the house on Skinner Street, Godwin wrote Mary, "forget that you have a Father." Playing his guilt card,

Godwin said he had lived long enough and should stop writing to Mary. Shelley's anger heightened when Godwin wrote of arranging another *post obit* loan with Shelley's moneylender, Willats. In his game of emotional blackmail with Shelley, Godwin did not mention that he refused to sell the copyright of Mary's *Valperga* because he thought he would not get enough for it. Godwin ended with a histrionic flourish: "I fear—I fear—I am a drowning man, catching at a straw."

Shelley played his straw, asking Horace Smith for a £400 loan for Godwin. Going through the motions for Mary's sake, Shelley accurately anticipated Smith's refusal. Godwin, rescued financially by his friends, soon returned to the book business with his wife on the Strand.[103]

Mrs. Mason's May letters to Shelley attributed Mary's loss of "good health and spirits" not to her pregnancy but to the presence of the other women in Shelley's household: "I dread Clare's being in the same house for a month or two, and wish the Williams' were a half mile from you."[104] Her implied criticism of Shelley might have been even more pointed had she known of the love lyrics Shelley continued composing for his Miranda.

16

A "watery eclipse"

THE TRIP THAT SHELLEY AND JANE TOOK TO CARRARA MAY 17 PROB-
ably was the only entire day they enjoyed each other's company
away from their spouses. Williams, after scrubbing the *Don Juan*,
was unsuccessful in having their Lerici harbormaster friend
Magliana erase the mainsail's letters which "Lord B[yron] in his
contemptible vanity" had Roberts "inscribe." Williams and Shelley
sailed the next day to Isola Palmaria, off Portovenere. Hearing
murmurs on approaching a small unfamiliar island, they dubbed it
"Syren's island" before discovering the sound came from their
boat's taut lanyard. The inexperienced seamen then almost struck
the rocks after being caught in the islet's strong current.[1]

Shelley's hopes for retrieving his books that Peacock sent were
dashed when the Customs Inspector refused to release them. Having passed from Tuscany into the Piedmont, the books legally had
to be sent to Genoa for inspection. Shelley's vehement appeal
"proved ineffective and with the curses of all parties away went the
books for Genoa."[2]

Williams, with Shelley's approval, now kept busy building a
small, light boat of reeds and tarred canvas to serve as a dinghy for
the *Don Juan*. Williams said his overbuilt eighty-six-pound dinghy
stowed "easily" but its dimensions, eight by four feet, meant space
was limited when aboard. If towed astern, it could affect the steering of the twenty-four to twenty-eight-foot *Don Juan*.[3]

Williams's continual fussing with the *Don Juan* led Jane to
comment, "ah Ned you are decorating your coffin."[4] Jane's other
concerns were Shelley's increasing emotional attachment and her
dissatisfaction with their cramped quarters. Mary, experiencing
problems with her pregnancy, wanted to leave the uncomfortable
house. Of the three women, only Claire escaped from the tense
household. Calm and resigned in the weeks after Allegra's death,
she left Villa Magni May 21 for a brief trip to Florence.

Shelley, ignoring Mrs. Mason's views that Claire should be distant, wrote to Claire in Florence that she "would be happier here this summer than anywhere else." After offering to meet her in Viareggio to bring her back to Villa Magni, he said, "Mary continues to suffer terribly from languor and hysterical affections; and things in every respect remain as they were when you left us." He was writing "a little . . . and enjoy for the first time these ten years something like health.—I find however that I must neither think or feel, or the pain returns to its old nest."[5] This was the first indication that sometime in late May he had begun composing *The Triumph of Life*. Having turned the cook's "room into a study . . . the occupation of a few mornings in composition has somewhat shaken my nerves."[6]

Shelley's "shaken" nerves perhaps came from his difficulty in beginning *The Triumph*; at least four drafts of a start exist, including one on a May 26 letter from Mrs. Mason to Mary.[7] Shelley told Claire in late May that Williams "seems happy and content" but Jane "pines after her own house and saucepans. . . . It is a pity that any one so pretty and amicable could be so selfish."[8] He still insisted Claire "would be happier here . . . near me." Byron would not bother her as "a great gulph" had arisen between him and Shelley that "must daily become wider." Shelley ended his letter, "Mary, though ill, is good."[9]

Mary was not "good." The day before, Shelley wrote a rare letter to Mrs. Godwin saying he had not shown her letter or Godwin's to Mary because of her "present state of health & spirits." This "caution" was necessary as Mary was "about three months advanced in pregnancy,—and the irritability & languor which accompany this state is always distressing, & sometimes alarming." Mary "feels too intensely her fathers distress, which she would sacrifize all she posesses to remedy."[10]

Once again, with Mary pregnant, Shelley seclusively returned to a major writing project, *The Triumph of Life*. Simultaneously, he was composing secret love lyrics about Jane, intended neither for Mary's eyes nor for publication.

Stormy weather and high seas in late May curtailed sailing and Williams, in a rare self-revelation, felt "as unsettled as the weather." The next day, despite continuing strong wind, Williams and Shelley sailed with Magliana for Massa, where they managed a treacherous landing through surf and strong currents. The return home, "with a strong westerly wind straight in our teeth," took seven hours. Shelley wrote Claire they "returned late at night against a high sea and heavy wind in which the boat behaved excellently." When a Sarzana sailmaker finally cut "*Don Juan*" from the sail, Shelley was pleased that "The superscription of my poor boat's infamy is erased."[11]

On June 6, Shelley, Williams, and Charles Vivian sailed for Viareggio to pick up Claire. Three hours out a "baffling" wind left them becalmed four miles off shore until six in the evening when thunderclouds threatened them with a squall. After rowing ashore, they were stopped by a soldier; Shelley and Williams brandished pistols and, with Vivian's help, subdued the guard. Trudging inland three miles, they slept at Massa. After being becalmed in the morning's hot, oppressive air, they were finally propelled home by a wind to await Claire's arrival that evening.[12]

In early June, Mary wrote to Maria Gisborne that "Shelley's boat is a beautiful creature . . . only 24 by 8 feet, she is a perfect little ship, and looks twice her size." Shelley's "incessant boating" had improved his health and Mary was better after being "very unwell for some time past." Initially, they had trouble finding food. The locals lived in poverty "beyond anything," were "coarse," and spoke "a detestable dialect." However, the seashore was better than any other north of Naples, with excellent air and no "English society." Alluding to her unborn child, Mary said "fate decrees" they spend next winter in Pisa.[13]

On June 8, Mary's "Unwell" in her journal hinted at the pending dire event. She once again read Madame de Staël, the writer she always turned to when under duress with childbearing. Rather than *Corinne*, she read de Staël's essay on her guilt-laden relationship with her father. Williams discretely noted that Mary was "alarmingly unwell" but "strangely better" that night.[14] However, weeks later she wrote to Maria Gisborne of being in "great ill health" all week until Sunday, June 16, when, at least two weeks into her second trimester, she suffered a near-fatal miscarriage at eight in the morning. Hemorrhaging and "nearly lifeless" for seven hours, she "kept from fainting by brandy, vinegar eau de Cologne." Shelley's earlier medical reading proved decisive. After ice arrived, overruling Claire and Jane, his "unsparing application" of the ice "restored" Mary.[15]

Shelley wrote details of his life-saving efforts to John Gisborne two days after Mary's "severe miscarriage." Her condition "for some hours was alarming" and, with no "medical assistance,"

Shelley "took the most decisive resolutions, by dint of making her sit in ice, I succeeded in checking the hemorrhage and the fainting fits." When the physician arrived, "all danger was over, and he had nothing to do but to applaud me for my boldness." Mary was "now doing well, and the sea-baths will restore her."[16]

Three days before Mary's miscarriage, the *Bolivar*, captained by Trelawny with Roberts aboard, sailed into Lerici firing six shots from two brass cannon. These guns, inscribed with Byron's seal, added to official concern about Byron's political intent and the authorities soon restricted the use of the *Bolivar*. Williams and Shelley had rushed out in the *Don Juan* to greet her big sister, but Byron's boat's speed gave "no chance" to catch her. Williams thought the *Don Juan* kept "as good a wind," but admitted the *Bolivar* was "the most beautiful craft I ever saw." Byron was outraged that the boat cost over £1000, ten times more than Roberts had indicated. Lacking Shelley's passion for sailing, Byron seldom went aboard his "little thing of about 22 tons."[17]

Trelawny claimed to have sailed in the *Don Juan* with Shelley and Williams to observe their seamanship. Shelley, receiving steering instructions from Williams, held a book in one hand while incorrectly moving the tiller with the other. When a gleeful Shelley lost his hat overboard, Williams took the helm. Trelawny thought Williams needed practice but was a better sailor than he expected. Writing decades later, Trelawny said he admonished the two that they would have to swim for it if they displayed such seamanship in a squall. Shelley reportedly replied, "Not I: I should have gone down with the rest of the pigs [ballast] in the bottom of the boat."[18]

Williams's dinghy delighted Shelley, who paddled it out to sea and let the wind drive him ashore. Trelawny recalled that one evening, just before her miscarriage, Mary yelled out from the verandah, "Percy will be drowned; the boat is upset." Shrieking with glee as waves knocked him down in the shallow water, Shelley struggled to save the little boat until Trelawny waded out to rescue him.

In another incident that Trelawny related, and Jane told William Michael Rossetti in her old age, Shelley rowed a frightened Jane and her two children perilously far offshore in the flimsy dinghy. To Shelley's "Now let us together solve the great mystery," Jane replied that she and the children wanted dinner first. Attempting to escape, she capsized the boat in shallow water. After her rescue by Williams and Trelawny, Shelley emerged from the water with the boat on his back like a turtle. Trelawny was the only real swimmer in the group. Neither Shelley nor Roberts could swim, and Trelawny thought Williams did not swim "well." Another Trelawny tale, probably apocryphal, had a nude Shelley appearing dripping wet in Villa Magni's salon room before several visiting ladies. He tried to pass unnoticed, screened by the Italian maid before the shocked visitors. Drawing himself up "in full view," he stated it was his usual bathing hour and his skiff had capsized with his clothes. Reappearing from his room, he left to fetch his clothes before they washed out to sea.[19]

Leigh Hunt and his family finally arrived in Genoa on June 15, a day in which threatening swells off Villa Magni required the *Bolivar* be towed for safety to Lerici. The next day, a strong gale blowing, Mary endured her miscarriage. She would write Maria Gisborne she "hated our house & the country around it," finding the native folk "wild & hateful." She was "not well in mind or body," her "nerves were wound up to the utmost irritation and the sense of misfortune hung over my spirits." Shelley, who "reproached" her for her attitude, "never was in better health or spirits . . . the place was quite after his own heart." Her walks in the woods only made her "weep & shudder" and her "only moments of peace were on board that unhappy boat, when lying down with my head on my knees I shut my eyes & felt the wind & our swift motion alone." Attributing some of her malaise to her pregnancy, she admitted all that had gone on before "now weighed on me." In her drawing of their living quarters, Shelley's bedroom was next to that of "Mrs. [Williams]." On the opposite side of the dining hall was the bedroom Mary shared with little Percy.[20]

When Trelawny sailed without Roberts on June 18 for Leghorn to deliver the *Bolivar,* he was escorted out of the bay by Shelley and Williams in the *Don Juan.* Returning ashore, Shelley immediately wrote a crucial letter to Trelawny arranging payment for the *Don Juan* and mentioning that Roberts and Williams were busily refitting the *Don Juan.* Shelley then made a very personal request. He reminded Trelawny of their recent conversation and would consider it a "great kindness" if Trelawny could "procure me a small quantity" of "Prussic Acid, or essential oil of bitter almonds" which "requires the greatest caution in preparation & ought to be highly concentrated." Shelley "would give any price for this medicine" because of his "desire of avoiding needless suffering." He had "no intention of suicide at present" but it would "comfort" him to own this "golden key to the chamber of perpetual rest." After writing "Let this rest," several words were smeared out, probably by Trelawny, who published this letter twice omitting this partially obliterated sentence, which perhaps ended, "between us."[21]

Despite thoughts of suicide, Shelley seemed set for a summer of healthful sailing at Villa Magni. A week earlier, he wrote Taaffe of being "delighted with this place," offering him "the rude hospitality of these rocks." Before writing Trelawny about the prussic acid, Shelley wrote to his London bankers to forward his June quarterly income to his Leghorn banker.[22]

The day he wrote his "golden key" letter to Trelawny, Shelley, in a long letter to John Gisborne, expressed a deeply felt lack of sympathy from Mary, recovering from her miscarriage: "I only feel the want of those who can feel, and understand me. . . . Mary does not . . . I like Jane more and more. . . . She has a taste for music, and an elegance of form and motions that compensate in some degree for the lack of literary refinement." Jane and his boat were momentary pleasures without a future: "Williams is captain, and we drive along this delightful bay in the evening wind, under the summer moon, until earth appears another world. Jane brings her guitar, and if the past and the future could be obliterated, the present would content me so well that I could say with Faust to the passing moment, 'Remain, thou, thou art so beautiful.'" Shelley was quoting words that Faust said would make him wish to die.[23]

Further revealing his inner crisis, he discussed why he discontinued writing *Charles the First:* "I feel too little certainty of the future, and too little satisfaction with regard to the past, to undertake any subject seriously and deeply. I stand, as it were, upon a precipice, which I have ascended with great, and cannot descend without greater, peril, and I am content if the heaven above me is calm for the passing moment." Seeking support in his impasse with Mary, Shelley wished the Gisbornes would "return to Italy for my sake."

Shelley, increasingly dubious about the Hunt–Byron journal, saw "little of Byron" and would not "permit Hunt" to be a link between Byron and himself. He added, "I detest all society—almost all, at least—and Lord Byron is the nucleus of all that is hateful and tiresome in it." He added, bitterly, that *Cain,* the "perfection" of Byron's "coarse music," had "touched a chord to which a million hearts responded." Protesting "supreme indifference" to popular opinion, he wanted Gisborne to pass on what was said about himself in a recent critical memoir "besides my being an Atheist."[24] He did not tell Gisborne, or perhaps anyone else, that he was composing the brooding, introspective *The Triumph of Life*.

Shelley had told Hunt that Jane was "a delightful person," the "exact antitype of the lady in the Sensitive plant—though this must have been a pure anticipated cognition as it was written a year before I knew her."[25] Jane stimulated his most delightful love lyrics, including "Lines written in the Bay of Lerici" and "To Jane" ("The keen stars are twinkling"), both interspersed in his draft of *The Triumph of Life*. "To Jane" renders her sensuous singing as she played the guitar during a moonlit sail under the stars. More circumspect than "To Constantia," written in response to Claire's Marlow piano playing and singing, the "tinkling" of the playing of "Dear Jane" is given "soul" by "your voice most tender." With muted eroticism, the final stanza ends with the "Delight" of a fantasy

> Of some world far from ours,
> Where music and moonlight and feeling
> Are one.

Shelley sent Jane a note saying his ariette "might be profane— but it was vain to struggle with the ruling spirit, who compelled me to speak of things sacred to yours & Wilhemeister's indulgence— I commit them to your secrecy & your mercy & will try & do better another time." The poem's publication history indicates Jane kept Shelley's trust.[26] A poem probably written to Jane, "One Word Is Too Often Profaned," expresses his preference for "pity from thee more dear / Than that from another." Although "I can give not what men call love," his was "The devotion of something afar, / From the sphere of our sorrow."

"The Magnetic Lady To Her Patient" overtly celebrates Jane's therapeutic hypnotizing of Shelley but implicitly reveals their private talk of love. Awakening him from the spell, she asks, "What would . . . / . . . cure your head and side?" Shelley replies,

> "What would cure that would kill me, Jane,
> And as I must on earth abide
> Awhile yet, tempt me not to break
> My chain."[27]

The temptation of breaking his marital "chain," if not that of his life, was real as June progressed. Jane's solace through hypnosis veiled his erotic enticement and her seductiveness. Perhaps the trance-inducing warmth of Jane's hand on his brow was the extent of their physical contact. Like a ventriloquist, Shelley's "Magnetic Lady" speaks his seductive words, including her harsh analogy that his relationship to Mary is one of "weeds" compared to the relationship "full of flowers" between Jane and Edward. Inducing a deeper trance, Jane asks him to "forget me, for I can never / Be thine," saying for the third time she does not belong to him. Jane gives voice to his desire that he regain his "second youth again" so that, in his least veiled allusion to sexual embrace in the poem, "By mine thy being is to its deep possessed."

Mary recognized that Shelley's "Italian platonics" were not over, but a conspiracy of denial and avoidance about his emotional state, including his feelings for Jane, settled over the household.

The smoldering resentment of Roberts toward the younger Byron, including not being made captain of the *Bolivar,* influenced his zeal in directing the refitting of the *Don Juan.* During its construction he added two tons of iron ballast for stabilizing the boat in a breeze, telling Trelawny that Shelley could recoup this extra expense by selling the iron when he finished using the boat.[28] More expense was incurred at Lerici when Roberts consulted with Williams and Shelley about adding "a false stem and stern" to the *Don Juan.* Shelley wrote to Trelawny that the two "seem determined that she shall enter Leghorn in style—I am no great judge of these matters."[29]

The day Shelley was preoccupied with Mary's miscarriage, Roberts, with Williams's enthusiastic help, took down the *Don Juan*'s main and mizzen masts and began adding "tressel trees" to support the addition of new, taller topmasts. The added canvas carried by these topmasts increased the boat's speed and its susceptibility to heel over and swamp, if not capsize, especially with its complement of seven sails.[30] With the inexperienced crew when Roberts was not aboard, and the round-bottomed boat's open deck that easily shipped water, the *Don Juan* seemingly was an accident waiting to happen in the hazardous Mediterranean. Williams enthused over the "beautiful appearance" of the two refitted masts, noting the work took place during days of "strong gales and tremendous swell." Several days after being hauled out of the water on June 19, the *Don Juan* got a new bowsprit and false stern. Now two feet longer, Williams thought "she looks like a vessel of 50 tons." Probably seeking more speed, the topsails were altered again on July 1, the day the *Don Juan* left Lerici for the last time. Perhaps the most accurate depiction of the boat, including its extremely high masts, was the watercolor Roberts painted in 1822 showing a crew of three (possibly the last rendition of Shelley before his death) and a dog on board just offshore Villa Magni. In the woodcut made from this painting that Trelawny published in his 1858 *Recollections,* one crew member, the dog, and the top floor of Villa Magni are missing.[31]

Shelley's next psychic storm appeared in Williams's journal on June 23: "During the night S[helley] sees spirits and alarms the whole house."[32] Sometime after this episode, Shelley told Mary that "he had had many visions lately." Mary wrote Maria Gisborne that Shelley said he "had often seen these figures when ill." Mary thought the "strangest thing" was Jane's seeing Shelley twice in a "vision" just before Mary's miscarriage. In her mood of denial, Mary wrote, "we thought [no] more of these things."

Mary reported Jane's "vision" occurred during the day, probably June 14, when Williams and Roberts went inland to fish.[33] Jane, standing with Trelawny looking out a window onto the terrace, thought she saw Shelley twice "pass by the window . . . without coat or jacket," both times going in the same direction across the terrace without having returned. Since he would have had to pass the window returning, Jane "was struck at seeing him pass twice" going the same way. When he disappeared, Jane cried out, "'Good God can Shelley have leapt from the wall? Where can he be gone?'" She "trembled exceedingly" as Trelawny assured her Shelley had not been on the terrace. Mary, confirming Shelley was "far off," thought this episode was inexplicable: "Jane though a woman of sensibility, has not much imagination & is not in the slightest degree nervous."[34]

Jane's "vision" of Shelley occurred about the time he had one of himself "which met him as he walked on the terrace & said to him—'How long do you mean to be content.'" Mary thought these were "no terrific words" and "certainly were not prophetic" of Shelley's fate only weeks later.[35] Shelley told Mary of this terrace vision immediately after his terrifying nightmare that Williams said disturbed the entire house on June 23, a little more than a week after Jane's "vision" of Shelley.

Mary's account of Shelley's nightmare indicates he had two sets of frightening visions which, combined with sleepwalking, resembled a night terror. She believed her illness had "caused a return" of Shelley's "nervous sensations & visions as bad as his worst times." Mary, still unable to walk and confined to her bed, was awakened in the middle of the night by Shelley's screaming. When he "come rushing into my room" she thought he was asleep and "tried to waken him by calling on him." His continued screaming so panicked Mary that she "jumped out of bed & ran across the hall" to Jane's room. Williams went to Shelley, who told Mary he had not been asleep but had been frightened by a vision. However, because he denied having screamed, Mary knew he "certainly [had] a dream & no waking vision." He had been "frightened" by dreaming that Jane and Williams came to him "in the most horrible condition, their bodies lacerated—their bones starting through their skin, the faces pale yet stained with blood, they could hardly walk, but Edward was the weakest & Jane was supporting him." Williams said, "Get up, Shelley, the sea is flooding the house & it is all coming down." Shelley thought he "went to his window that looked on the terrace & the sea & thought he saw the sea rushing in." His vision suddenly changing, Shelley "saw the figure of himself strangling me," causing him to "rush into my room, yet fearful of frightening me he dared not approach the bed." Mary's "jumping out" of bed "awoke him, or as he phrased it caused his vision to vanish."[36]

Shelley's attempt to strangle Mary in his nightmare probably caused his screams of fright. His hallucinatory "visions" do not indicate Shelley was psychotic.[37] His complex personality structure negates any simple diagnostic formulation. He appeared to be reacting to the cumulative emotional stresses. Mary's near-fatal miscarriage perhaps triggered Shelley's guilt over an unconscious wish for her death, guilt possibly fed by his erotic feelings for Jane.

Shelley's last lyric probably was "Lines written in the Bay of Lerici." His frustrated desire for Jane, suggested in a number of canceled lines in his draft, included "But now I desired, I dare not."[38] The lines, "She left me, and I staid alone / Thinking over every tone," are hauntingly repeated, "She left me at the silent time."

Mary—"Bright wanderer, fair coquette of Heaven," "given / To change and be adored for ever"—has a rival, Jane, "One fair as [thou], but far more true." Most deeply, Shelley felt abandoned, a "guardian angel gone" replaced by a "demon . . . / In my faint heart" that left him "disturbed and weak." He concluded contemplating a fate like that of the rock-bound fish of San Terenzo, as "the fisher with his lamp / And spear" now "struck the fish who came / To worship the delusive flame." Probably unfinished, the poem's final line may be either "Destroying life alone not peace." or "Seeking Life alone not peace."[39]

The day after Shelley's frightening nightmare, a letter arrived from Hunt. Barely a week had passed since Mary's miscarriage, but Shelley impulsively made ready to embark for Genoa, a voyage much longer than any he had attempted in the *Don Juan.* He and Williams rigged the boat, hoping to reach Genoa the next day before dark. Williams noted the weather was calm but there was a "Heavy sea running." Shelley wrote to Roberts asking him to go along, but did not send it, using the sheet for composing more of *The Triumph of Life.* Shelley canceled the trip when, as he wrote Hunt, "poor Mary suffered a relapse, which though in the issue not serious was sufficient to warn me of the necessity of remaining with her for the present." She was "now much better, although still confined to the sofa." It was fortunate the trip was canceled. The next day, when they would have been at sea, Williams noted, "Strong gale and threatening weather." He and Roberts spent the day making a new main topmast for the *Don Juan.*[40] Mary, increasingly eager to leave Villa Magni, wrote to Hunt in late June, "let me entreat you let no persuasions induce you to come. . . . I wish I cd break my chains & leave this dungeon."[41]

Shelley spent the last week of June composing more of *The Triumph of Life* while Williams and Roberts tinkered with the *Don Juan.* Despite the local peasants' prayers, the hot and sultry weather produced little rain until a morning thunderstorm June 29. Shelley sailed his re-rigged boat for the first time on that day and got an added boost when his books arrived from Genoa. The censors, not too diligent, returned *Queen Mab,* which Williams thought "an astonishing work."[42]

Williams never saw the more subtle and elegant poetry of *The Triumph of Life* which Shelley was composing on forty sheets of paper, including the backs of letters. The ten years between *Queen Mab* and *The Triumph* produced dramatic differences between the two poems. Each featured a guide and pupil, both female in the earlier poem, both male in the latter. The ethereal, all-wise maternal "Fairy Queen" was replaced by Rousseau. Unlike Mab, Rousseau is a flawed exemplar lacking a clear future vision to offer his younger companion, Shelley's narrator in *The Triumph of Life.* Shelley's feminine spirit of Ianthe, eager to embrace Mab's bright, hopeful future "of visioned bliss," is replaced in *The Triumph* with a "ghastly dance" of humanity wildly fornicating in a dusty, public highway led by a blind charioteer within whose car huddles dark, death-like Life. Shelley seemingly intended his own view in *The Triumph* to be a stance toward life that resisted the narrow, disillusioned visions of both Rousseau and the poet-narrator.[43] His need to accomplish this poetic mission in the face of his depressive impasse speaks for the resilient power of the remarkable creative force in his personality.

The Triumph can be seen as Shelley's final dialogue with himself. The near-extinguished Rousseau represents that part of himself contemplating life's end, while his younger poet-narrator questioner is that part of Shelley still searching for an inner calm, reflected in the moving tranquility of the first forty lines. Shelley's long-term identification with Rousseau[44] evolved from his 1811 disparagement of the *Confessions* into his later enthrallment with *Julie*, the work "of a mighty Genius," the greatest since Milton. Now, Shelley replaced the flawed Rousseau with the flawed Byron as the greatest poet since Milton.[45] *Julie* stemmed from Rousseau's unconsummated passion for the last love of his life. Among the love lyrics intermingled in his drafts of *The Triumph*, Shelley wrote either, "Alas I kiss you Julie," or "Alas I kiss you Jane."

The narrator's opening early-dawn "waking dream" is replaced by the "maniac dance" of the passing multitude of humanity, in whose midst is a "cold glare," the headlight of a "rushing" "ill . . . guided" chariot with two dark figures. Missing in the entire parade of humanity were Socrates and Jesus, "the sacred few who could not tame / Their spirits to the conquerors." With maenad-like eroticism, the "ribald crowd" around the chariot engaged in a "fierce and obscene . . . wild dance" as they "Mix with each other . . . To savage music." "Maidens and youths" were "tortured by their agonizing pleasure / Convulsed . . . [in] unholy leisure."

In the first of a series of hallucinatory-like visual transformations, the "old root" of a chestnut tree becomes the decayed head of Rousseau, perhaps a victim of terminal venereal disease.[46] Acknowledging he should have "forborne" being in this sexual parade, Rousseau advises his young companion to resist joining "the dance." Rousseau calls himself "one of that deluded crew" who do not "know themselves" and thus "Could not repress the mutiny within."

Asked by the youth-narrator, "Whence camest thou and whither goest thou?", Rousseau describes his gestation "Under a mountain" in "a cavern, high and deep" from which he emerged into a "light diviner than the common sun." This light, the feminine "shape all light," will become the dark, deathly figure of Life crouching in the chariot. She is the rainbow goddess Iris, making "silver music" and holding "a crystal glass" of "Nepenthe," the drug that erases all sorrows. Gazing at her dancing feet as she sings her "sweet tune," Rousseau experiences his thoughts "blot" out. His "mind was strewn beneath / Her feet like embers" and "she, thought by thought, / Trampled its fires into the dust of death."

Replying to Rousseau's request to "Shew whence I came, and where I am, and why," the "shape all light," like a dangerous enchantress, commands him to drink from the cup of Nepenthe.[47] Touching his "faint lips" to the cup, "suddenly my brain became as sand," signaling the transformation of the "shape all light" into a "new Vision," the dark shape the poet-narrator had seen crouching in the chariot blindly leading the dusty "stream" of humanity "like bubbles on an eddying flood." The Lucretian deathly visions of Rousseau's world include "Phantoms" who, like "a flock of vampire-bats," blot out the sun. Others, more ominously, "fling / Shadows of shadows."

Shelley's final assault on patriarchal political and religious institutions is a series of searing tragi-comic images of ruling "apes" with "ermined capes" or wearing "the tiar / Of pontiffs." Rousseau, "the cripple," growing "weary of the ghastly dance" and fallen "by the wayside," is asked by his perplexed young companion, "Then, what is Life?" His answer, the final words of *The Triumph*, "Happy those for whom the fold / Of," remained forever incomplete.

If *The Triumph of Life* is "Shelley's death mask,"[48] it bears his most ironically enigmatic expression. Was it essentially finished, or did he envision a longer poem? Would any ending he intended have been decisively more life-affirming, as might be implied by the final allusion to the folding star, or would he have ended more darkly? Had he continued his poem, perhaps he would have disdained any definitive closure.[49]

The *Triumph* is like a dark dream vision within a dark dream vision, a structure not unrelated to the hallucinations and nightmares Shelley was experiencing at this time. The repetitions in the fragment suggest continuing threatening fantasies. Despite what some have argued, *The Triumph* was neither a suicide note nor a proto-Sartrean philosophical manifesto espousing existential nothingness, the futility of human existence, or the deconstruction of meaning.

Writing about English politics to Horace Smith at the end June, about the time he broke off *The Triumph,* Shelley stated, "I once thought to study these affairs & write or act in them" but was "glad that my good genius said refrain. I see little public virtue, & I foresee that the contest will be one of blood & gold." Earlier in the letter, Shelley expressed perhaps the guiding motif of *The Triumph of Life.* Decrying "the inefficacy of the existing religions no less than political systems for restraining & guiding mankind," he added, "Let us see the truth whatever that may be.—The destiny of man can scarcely be so degraded that he was born only to die."[50]

Always seeking to accommodate his idealism with his lifelong skepticism, Shelley, on the eve of his thirtieth birthday, had deepened into a greater acceptance of life's contrary forces, reflected in the poem's initial lines:

> Swift as a spirit hastening to his task
> Of glory and of good, the Sun sprang forth
> Rejoicing in his splendour, and the mask
>
> Of darkness fell from the awakened Earth.
>
> (1–4)

In addition to the classical and more recent literary forebears that influenced Shelley's imagery, the most immediate goad was Byron's continuing "cold glare" that was eclipsing Shelley's poetic sun.[51] Trelawny, writing to Shelley on June 22, said Byron had finished two more cantos of *Don Juan* and then added a postscript: "Your letter [of June 18] shall be attended to respecting the two poisons of gold and prussic acid, for they are near of kin."[52]

Shelley told Horace Smith in his late June letter that as soon as he heard from Hunt he would "weigh anchor in my little schooner & give him chase to Leghorn, where I must occupy myself in some arrangements for him with Lord Byron." He added, "Between ourselves I greatly fear this alliance will not succeed, for I, who could never have been regarded as more than the link of the two thunderbolts, cannot now consent to be even that." He then thought of a more apt metaphor: "how long the alliance between the wren &

the eagle may continue I will not prophesy." He ended with perhaps his last words from Lerici: "I still inhabit this divine bay, reading Spanish dramas & sailing & listening to the most enchanting music. We have some friends on a visit to us, & my only regret is that the summer must ever pass, or that Mary has not the same predilection for this place that I have, which would induce me never to shift my quarters."[53]

Shelley was responding to Horace Smith's early June letter turning down Shelley's request of a £400 loan for Godwin. Thanking Smith for his "refusal," Shelley said he had no intention of helping Godwin by dipping into his "patrimony . . . already too much diminished." Ten years after writing to Godwin that he was "the Son of a man of fortune," Shelley closed his financial book on Mary's father.

Unknown to Shelley, the Hunts had left Genoa on June 28 and experienced at sea a terrible thunder and lightning storm. On June 30, the *Don Juan*'s new topsails were "unbent" for more alterations and Shelley apparently heard from Hunt that he was leaving Genoa.[54] Leghorn beckoned. The next morning, Monday, July 1, Williams rose at four "to get the topsails altered" and by noon a "fine breeze from the westward tempted us to weigh for Leghorn."[55] Williams carefully left his gold watch with Jane. At two in the afternoon, he, Shelley, and Charles Vivian sailed over to Lerici to take on board Roberts, who apparently intended to return with the three from Leghorn. By two-thirty, they cleared the little bay for the run to Leghorn. Shelley, unaware of its message, carried Mary's brief letter to Hunt warning him not to come to their San Terenzo "dungeon." Remaining at Villa Magni were Mary, Jane, Claire, and the three children.

Mary wrote later that she was physically well enough "to crawl from my bedroom to the terrace" but, in "bad spirits," she "could not endure" Shelley's going, fearing more for Percy's well-being than Shelley's. Crying "bitterly," she called Shelley back several times, telling him "if I did not see him soon I would go to Pisa with the child."[56]

It is uncertain what closeness Shelley and Jane had shared by the time he left Villa Magni. Medwin stated he did not know "a purer being," Mrs. Williams being beyond "a breath of scandal." Trelawny reportedly was "certain there was no intrigue between Shelley and Mrs. Williams" whom he likened to the "Virgin Mary."[57] In early April, Shelley had written to Hunt, "Alas, how I am fallen from the boasted purity in which you knew me once exulting!" Sensitive to Shelley's sexual innuendoes, Hunt wrote to another, "Does he mean . . . veal cutlets, or that he has fallen in love with someone who does not deserve it?"[58] Jane's attraction to Shelley perhaps has been underplayed. Her biographer considered her less passive romantically than often depicted and that her love for Edward did not rule out her possible "deep and growing affection and attraction for Shelley." Unhappily married, she became Williams's lover and instigated their elopement.[59] Even if Shelley wrote "Julie," not "Jane," after "Alas I kiss you" in his draft, some physical intimacy possibly passed between them.[60]

When the *Don Juan* left for Leghorn, it had not been sailed seriously since its new rigging and hull changes. With the experienced Roberts on board, Williams recorded sailing the "45 to 50" miles to Leghorn in only seven and one half hours, dropping anchor astern of Byron's *Bolivar* at nine that evening. Unable to get quarantine clearance to go ashore because the health office was closed, the *Bolivar*'s cushions provided bedding for the night on the *Don Juan*.[61] The next morning, July 2, they heard that the *Bolivar* was about to sail for Genoa and that Byron was departing imminently because the authorities ordered the Gambas to leave Tuscany by July 4. On shore, they met the Gambas leaving the police office. Locating Byron at his merchant-agent's, Dunn's, Shelley learned Byron's uncertain next destination might be the United States, Genoa, or Lucca. Shelley next had an emotional meeting with Hunt at his hotel.

Shelley was ecstatic to see Hunt and the two friends tearfully embraced. Thornton Hunt, now twelve, later recalled that Shelley, rushing into his father's arms, exclaimed in his "shrill" voice of being "so inexpressibly delighted!—you cannot think how inexpressibly happy it makes me!" Thornton noticed Shelley's chest was larger and his "voice was stronger, his manner more confident."[62] Leigh Hunt observed he was "embrowned" by the sun and "the youthful smoothness of his face was gone; the temples seemed beaten in; the forehead had wrinkles in it; and his glossy brown locks were now dullened and mixed with grey." His garb included "a large-brimmed leghorn hat . . . a jane jacket and waistcoat, and nankeen trousers, all fitting loosely to the body." Without a neckcloth, his upturned collar fell to one side giving his whole "appearance not decidedly the reverse of negligé."[63]

Hunt and Byron, first meeting at Villa Dupuy, hardly knew each other, milord "grown so fat," Hunt "grown so thin."[64] Byron's household was in turmoil, Teresa's brother Pietro having been stabbed trying to break up fighting servants. Byron dismissed the assailant, but Shelley later gave him some money, believing no one else would help "such an ill-looking fellow."[65]

Hunt recalled taking Shelley aboard Hunt's ship where Shelley, spreading a large piece of paper, "made a dot on it with his pen," saying, "That is the experience of mankind." Asked if the white "is our inexperience," Shelley replied that with all the paper in the world, only "the dot is history."[66]

On July 3, Shelley helped the Hunts settle into the Lanfranchi where Marianne Hunt, "in a desperate state of health," was examined by Vaccà. He gave her a year to live, considering her case "hopeless" and "inevitably" fatal.[67] She bore four more children and died thirty-five years later.

Byron first met the ill Marianne Hunt at Lanfranchi and, hardly noticing her, did not speak. His conduct "cut H[unt] to the soul."[68] Williams had remained in Leghorn, impatient to return to Jane and his children. July 4, he noted, was a "fine" day. Religious processions prayed for rain "but the Gods are either angry or Nature is too powerful." It was his final journal entry.[69]

Shelley returned to Leghorn July 7 after caging the eagle and the wren in several days' negotiations. Byron wanted to dissociate himself from the journal but Shelley convinced him to stay involved and to provide more money for Hunt. Byron promptly offered Hunt the copyright of *The Vision of Judgment* for the journal, which Byron initially intended be named *Hesperides* before it became *The Liberal.*[70]

By July 4, Shelley had received two very unsettling letters from Mary. In Pisa, he unburdened upon Hunt the "cloud" hanging over his relationship with Mary. Hunt had observed Shelley's "pain" on reading a letter from Mary,[71] probably his third letter from her since leaving Villa Magni.

Williams, hearing daily from Shelley, wrote to Jane on July 6 that Shelley received a "most gloomy" letter from Mary the previous day, adding, "this mood of hers aggravates my uneasiness to see you."[72] Mary would write Maria Gisborne that she was increasingly depressed after Shelley's departure and had "entreated him to return." While Jane and Claire "took their evening walk," Mary would "patrole [*sic*] the terrace, oppressed with wretchedness."[73]

Mary had written asking Shelley not to buy the *Bolivar* and to inquire about a house in Pugnano. Shelley answered he had ruled out buying the *Bolivar* and dismissed Pugnano: "I have no time to spare from Hunt's affairs; I am detained unwillingly here." He told Mary that Williams might come in the *Don Juan* before he returned, "but that would be decided tomorrow." He wondered "whether you are not more reconciled to staying at Lerici at least during the summer." His last words to Mary were of finding his *Symposium* translation, misplaced a year earlier.[74]

Shelley then wrote Jane the final letter of his life, a brief, melancholy prose love lyric. Saying she would "probably see Williams" before he could "disentangle" himself from Pisa, he intended to go to Leghorn that evening and urge Williams "to sail with the first fair wind without expecting me. I have thus the pleasure of contributing to your happiness when deprived of every other—and of leaving you no other subject of regret, but the absence of one scarcely worth regretting." He wrote, "I figure to myself the countenance which has been the source of such consolation to me, shadowed by a veil of sorrow," concluding, "How soon those hours past, & how slowly they return to pass so soon again, & perhaps for ever, in which we lived together so intimately so happily!—Adieu, my dearest friend—I only write these lines for the pleasure of tracing what will meet your eyes."[75]

Jane's July 6 reply, sent to Pisa and postmarked July 8, probably was not seen by Shelley before he and Williams set sail from Leghorn July 8. Despite his preoccupation with Byron and the Hunts, Shelley had written to Jane two days before Williams who, with ample time, finally wrote her for the first time.

Jane told Shelley, "Your few melancholy lines have indeed cast your own visionary veil over a countenance that was animated with the hope of seeing you return with far different tidings." Having heard he was returning accompanied by the *Bolivar*, she went to the terrace at five in the morning and imagined seeing the *Bolivar*. She wondered, "what can this mean?" saying, "Hope, and uncertainty, have made such a chaos in my mind, that I don't know what to think." Her "Neddino" had not written "a single word: surely I shall see him tonight! Perhaps too you are with him." Mary, getting on "well," was talking "of going to Pisa." Jane wanted Shelley to "gather consolation" from her "prophecy" that "whatever may be the present difficulties and disappointments," they were "small" compared to those had Byron remained. Ending with "Buona notte," she added, "Why do you talk of never enjoying moments like the past, are you going to join your friend Plato or do you expect I shall do so soon?"[76] Jane was eager to assure a despairing Shelley of her continuing presence for him.

Williams, in his tardy letter to Jane of July 6, wished he could fly to her on the hard "gale" blowing on the Leghorn quay toward Lerici. He was "tired to death of waiting" and if Shelley were still "detained" the next day, he would "depart in a Felucca," leaving the *Don Juan* behind. He said Shelley "desires that I should return to you, but I know secretly wishes me not to leave him in the lurch." Williams said, tellingly, "He, too, by his manner, is as anxious to see *you* almost as I could be." He ended this Saturday letter saying that unless the weather was bad he should be home no later than Tuesday evening.

As Mary said, Shelley's "skrewing LB's mind to the sticking place about the journal" made better headway than Williams expected.[77] On Sunday, July 7, Shelley felt he had done what he could to secure Byron's continued involvement with *The Liberal.* That day, Byron loaned £50 to Shelley and soon arranged that more manuscripts be sent to *The Liberal.* Hunt, still optimistic, wrote to his sister-in-law of Byron's "great ardour" for the new journal and that Shelley had "some excellent" manuscripts ready for it.[78]

Sunday afternoon Shelley took Hunt on a tour of Pisa. Hunt recalled they walked "arm-in-arm . . . he was looking better than I had ever seen him" and they "anticipated a thousand pleasures." Shelley spoke fondly of Horace Smith and laughed when Hunt told some of Hogg's jokes. After seeing the Leaning Tower and the Baptistery, they sat in the Duomo listening to the organ, both agreeing, "What a divine religion might be found out, if charity were really made the principle of it, instead of faith."[79] At twilight they entered the galleried cloisters of the holy burial grounds, the Camposanto. Hunt described the large fresco, "The Triumph of Death," a Petrarchan damnation scene that possibly influenced *The Triumph of Life.*

Before leaving Pisa, Shelley called on Mrs. Mason, who had never seen him "in better health and spirits." Her last glance of him was of his happy face, but she had two sad dreams the next night, one of a penniless Shelley looking "very pale & fearfully melancholy," refusing her offer of food. In her other dream, little

Percy had died.[80] Hunt detected that Shelley was less hopeful than formerly. Saying goodbye to Marianne Hunt on July 7, Shelley said, "If I die tomorrow I have lived to be older than my father, I am ninety years of age."[81] Timothy would die when ninety.

Before Shelley took the post chaise back to Leghorn Sunday night, Hunt gave him Keats's *Lamia* volume, telling him "to keep it till he gave it to me with his own hands." Shelley promised Hunt he would not sail in bad weather and planned to sign his will the next morning in Leghorn before sailing for Lerici.[82] It was his last voyage. After Mary's journal entry, the two words "Monday 8th," came two hundred twenty-six blank pages.

Sifting fact from fiction as to what occurred on that fateful Monday, July 8, and on the agonizing days afterward, has been rare.[83] That morning, while Shelley and Williams prepared for returning to Lerici, a passing thunderstorm probably did little to break Leghorn's hot, sultry summer air. Trelawny's 1858 recollection was that after accompanying Shelley to his banker's, presumably to cash Byron's £50 note, the two went to a store. Trelawny's 1875 version had Shelley leaving his banker's with "a canvas bag full of Tuscan crown pieces."[84] The 245 Tuscan crowns Williams obtained earlier from his banker were recovered from his locked trunk.[85] Also stowed on the *Don Juan* were supplies for Villa Magni and a hamper of wine, a gift for the friendly Lerici harbormaster. This cargo, plus the cumbersome dinghy, probably made for little room aboard the *Don Juan*. If Shelley signed a new will, about which he had written John Gisborne in April, it has never surfaced.

The report that Williams's banker, De Young, accompanied Shelley to the pier and unsuccessfully tried to argue him out of departing is uncorroborated.[86] Two other unsubstantiated reports said that others disagreed with Shelley about sailing that day. The weather at the time of departure had cleared, according to the earliest accounts of both Roberts and Trelawny. The departure time, variably reported, most likely was between twelve-thirty and one o'clock. Mary told Maria Gisborne that Roberts, on July 12, told her that "about noon" after an "early" thunderstorm "the weather was fine & the wind right for Lerici—They were impatient to be gone." Roberts apparently had qualms about the weather, as Mary quoted him as saying to Shelley, "Stay until tomorrow to see if the weather is settled; & S. might have staid but Edward was in so great an anxiety to reach home—saying they would get there in seven hours with the wind—that they sailed!" Mary said Shelley was "in one of those extravagant fits of good spirits in which you have sometimes seen him." He had recently told Mary that only when he was in high spirits could he prophesy something dire happening.[87]

Trelawny's plan to accompany the *Don Juan* some distance in the *Bolivar* was aborted because he lacked papers to pass quarantine officials. In one early account, Trelawny wrote, "we weighed our anchors at a little after twelve—with a light and favourable breeze from the S.E." Anchoring after being detained, Trelawny said "the breeze gradually freshened and in 3 hours their Boat was out of sight—at half past three the sun became overcast and small dark clouds rising from the sea ascended and moved rapidly along against the wind—which indicated a change to the N.W. and the horizon in that quarter became dense and alarming."[88] In another early account, Trelawny said he watched as the *Don Juan* "made all sail out of the harbour for Spezia" until the boat became "a speck on the horizon—which was becoming thick & dark with heavy clouds moving rapidly." Retiring to his cabin, a half hour later "a man on deck told me a heavy squall had come on."[89] Roberts was unmentioned in Trelawny's early accounts. Decades later, in his *Recollections,* Trelawny changed numerous details in his account.

Roberts told Mary he went to the end of the *molo* to watch the *Don Juan* sail at one o'clock making seven knots. Still on the *molo* "about three," seeing an approaching storm "from the Gulph," he climbed a tower and claimed to see through a glass the *Don Juan* "about ten miles out at sea, off Via Reggio, they were taking their topsails." However, "the haze of the storm" hid the boat and after the storm cleared "I looked again fancying that I should see them on their return to us—but there was no boat on the sea." If the distance were ten miles, given the probable hazy conditions, it is unlikely Roberts could have seen them.

Roberts, writing to Byron on July 20, reported that a sailor had told him, "at four o'clock Monday evening he bore up in a heavy squall of wind to run back to Leghorn and passed close to the Don Juan . . . taking in her Gaff Topsails and a Sailor boy was at the Mast head." A few minutes later the boat "disappeared and [ ] foundered." The wind "blew too hard for him to haul his wind to assist or save the ~~Men~~ Crew, in about 17 fathoms of water and thinks he could point out the spot within a mile or two." Roberts told Byron the main boom and part of a sail were found but right after the squall cleared "nothing whatever" was seen floating. Roberts thought his informant gave "a good description of the boat" and his statement could be "depended upon."[90]

Earlier, during his July 12 talk with Mary, Roberts said "several spars" belonging to the *Don Juan* were found on the fishing boat. Mary wondered, "perhaps they let them perish to obtain these" but she said nothing about the *Don Juan* being rammed, something she would have reported had Roberts mentioned it. Indeed, Roberts, after inspecting the raised *Don Juan*, wrote Mary September 14 that "she was not upset, but I think must have filled by a heavy sea."[91] The theory that the *Don Juan* was rammed and sunk by one of the larger feluccas—whether accidentally, as a piracy attempt, or for political reasons—was not in the first accounts of either Trelawny or Roberts. Both later changed their initial stories that the vessel swamped in the heavy seas. Recounting these events in 1858, Trelawny substituted himself for Roberts and the spars became an "English-made oar" discovered by his Genoese mate immediately after the tragedy.[92] Trelawny's 1858 (*Recollections*) and 1878 (*Records*) accounts have been given too much credence.

Strangely, Trelawny's accounts break off soon after the storm, whose "fury" lasted no "more than twenty minutes." Seeing no sign of his friends' boat, he went ashore. Another storm moved through the entire area that night, apparently the one Hunt witnessed in Pisa, thinking Shelley was safely in Lerici. Trelawny reported returning to the *Bolivar* on the morning of July 9, but was vague about his activities and whereabouts from July 10 to July 13. Waiting vainly for a letter from Villa Magni, it was three days before Trelawny went to see Byron in Pisa.[93]

What Roberts told Mary in Leghorn four days after the tragedy differs in several important respects from what he related in 1828 to some English acquaintances.[94] In this later account, Roberts reportedly said he was the last person to see Shelley alive and had "set out" with Shelley in the *Don Juan* "from Leghorn & after going some distance returned in a boat which had followed." Roberts presumably said, "Trelawny was to have been of the party but had had words with Shelly [*sic*] the morning they sailed." This account's veracity may be no greater than Trelawny's later accounts, but Roberts had reasons for returning with Shelley to Lerici, including being offended by Byron's greeting when the two first met in Leghorn the day Shelley arrived. Williams wrote to Jane on July 6 that "the way he [Byron] received our friend Roberts at Dunn's door, shall be described when we meet—it must be acted." Byron was put out by what he considered was Roberts's exorbitant bill for the *Bolivar.* Roberts later accused Trelawny of being "bigoted" in Byron's favor.[95]

Trelawny never mentioned a disagreement with Shelley that final morning. If Roberts started out in the *Don Juan,* a disagreement over the threatening weather may have prompted his return to Leghorn. Roberts, like Shelley, could not swim. Mary's account states that Roberts had urged Shelley to remain another day in Leghorn for the weather to clear. Roberts, perhaps guilty about not accompanying the inexperienced crew of the *Don Juan,* would not have wanted Mary to know he turned back or of any disagreement Shelley might have had with Trelawny or himself.

The actions of Shelley, Williams, and Vivian during the fatal storm will never be known. The early accounts of Roberts and Trelawny, supplemented by officials' reports after the tragedy, indicate the *Don Juan* was probably about two to three hours out from Leghorn when, seeing the approaching storm, the crew had only enough time to furl the dangerous topsails before being swamped. The open boat, with low freeboard and heavy ballast, did not need extremely rough seas to ship water and sink immediately. Roberts, seeing the *Don Juan* after it was raised, reported that the complete "29 Piggs of iron ballast" were still aboard her.[96]

It is unclear how far offshore the *Don Juan* sank and in what depth of water. Trelawny gave widely varying estimates about what had happened somewhere off the shore of Viareggio. One of his early accounts had them "about four or five miles at sea, in 15 or 16 fathom water, with a light breeze under a crowd of sail" when the "violent squall" struck the "unprepared" crew. He claimed the *Don Juan* "filled to leeward, and having two tons of iron ballast, and not decked, went down on the instant."[97]

Taaffe's 1826 narrative, "clearly a fabrication,"[98] has provided speculation for those who have proposed Shelley was engaging in an act of suicide and murder by restraining Williams (or Vivian) from lowering the sails.[99] This unacceptable hypothesis requires believing Shelley would sacrifice others' lives. Despite his depression and mental anguish at Villa Magni, there is no reason to believe other than that he and his companions drowned as hapless victims of a sudden squall, an inexperienced crew in a boat susceptible to sudden filling in such a storm.

This does not mean Shelley had not contemplated ending his life, something he entertained in earlier life crises and about which he had asked Trelawny for help only weeks earlier. Unraveling layers of self-destructive trends in Shelley's complex personality allows for no simple, categorical statement. Shelley repeatedly found himself in life-threatening boating situations before Lerici. Death by drowning was a recurrent theme in his poems. The conscious form of death he was contemplating, poisoning, would have robbed his life story of its dramatic ending.

17

Life Terminable and Interminable

Mary and Jane were not alarmed when the *Don Juan* failed to arrive by Tuesday. Monday having been stormy, they presumed the men would not leave Leghorn in such weather. It rained all of Tuesday and when a felucca arrived Wednesday from Leghorn with word the *Don Juan* had sailed Monday, the women did not believe it. Failing to see "the tall sails of the little boat" by midnight, they "began to fear not the truth, but some illness" had detained the men. Jane decided on Thursday to go to Leghorn the next day, ignoring Mary's plea to await word in Friday's mail. Jane did wait, as Friday's "heavy sea & bad wind" prohibited boats from leaving Lerici.[1]

Friday brought Hunt's July 9 letter to Shelley which Mary read trembling before dropping the paper. Hunt wanted to know how Shelley and Williams got home because "you must have been out in the bad weather, and we are anxious."[2] Jane uttered, "Then it is all over!" but Mary replied, "No . . . but this suspense is dreadful." Weak from her miscarriage, Mary proposed they immediately take the "swift" post to Leghorn "to learn our fate." Leaving the children with Claire and the nurse Caterina, the two women crossed the bay to Lerici, where no one had heard of an accident.[3]

Believing Byron was still in Leghorn, they stopped in Pisa at midnight to ask "the fearful question" of Hunt, whom Mary had not seen in four years. Hunt was in bed so Mary "staggered" up the marble staircase to Byron's apartments to be met by smiling Teresa Guiccioli. Mary, barely able to speak, asked about any word of Shelley. Her agony rose when Teresa said they only knew he sailed Monday and "bad weather" came later that afternoon. Teresa and Byron told Mary later she looked like a "ghost," her face white as "marble." Byron had sensed the worst since July 9 or 10, when Trelawny arrived from Leghorn expecting a letter from Villa Magni. Finding none, after relating his fears to Hunt, he went to Byron, whose "lips quivered" and "voice faltered" as he questioned Trelawny about Shelley's departure.[4]

Mary and Jane, clutching a semblance of hope, arrived in Leghorn after two in the morning. Up early after sleeping fitfully in their clothes, they found Roberts whose face "seemed to tell us that the worst was true." He recounted Shelley's activities in Pisa, the final preparations, the departure of the *Don Juan,* and its disappearance after the storm cleared. Mary's hopes rose after hearing reports that they might have been blown over to Corsica and a courier was sent up the coast to check at each tower for any information. Deciding to return quickly to Lerici, the two women stopped in Pisa long enough to deliver a letter to Byron from Roberts. Byron permitted Roberts to use the *Bolivar* to search for the *Don Juan* but Roberts's letter erased "the slender hope" Byron still had about Shelley.[5]

Joined by Trelawny, Mary and Jane stopped at Viareggio. There, Mary wrote, "our calamity first began to break on us." The *Don Juan*'s dinghy and a water cask had been found "five miles off."[6] The cask unsettled Mary most as she knew they may have jettisoned the little boat. That night, approaching Lerici, Mary struggled not to show her feelings to Jane. Rowing across the bay to Villa Magni, their "desolate" mood, accompanied by "the roaring sea" and the "scirocco wind," formed a macabre contrast to the bright lights of San Terenzo's *festa* celebration. Claire had heard nothing of the *Don Juan* or its occupants during the day and a half Mary and Jane were on their exhausting trip.

Amid the "detestable chant" of the locals dancing "like wild savages . . . on the sands close to our door," they kept their vigil at Villa Magni. After three days, Trelawny departed for Leghorn the evening of July 18, possibly having heard the rumors of a body washed ashore. A letter from Hunt, probably written July 18, said that he, Byron, and Roberts had "just returned . . . from making an inquiry at the mouth of the Serchio about a body lately buried." Hunt thought it was neither Shelley nor Williams.[7] It was Williams's body, which washed ashore July 17 about sixteen miles north of Leghorn and south of Viareggio, near the mouth of the Serchio and the Tower of Migliarino, just over the border of the Duchy of Lucca in Tuscan territory. When Byron, Hunt, and Roberts got to the mouth of the Serchio on July 18, Williams's body had already been buried in the sand with lime by the health officers who would not permit it to be disinterred. His body was only identified definitively a month later before cremation.

The day after Trelawny left, Mary became ill and Roberts's July 15 letter to Trelawny arrived. Trelawny had asked Mary to open it if it came after his departure but Claire intercepted it, not letting either Mary or Jane see it. Claire immediately wrote Hunt that Roberts, believing "there was no hope," was going to Viareggio to check on a rumor that bodies were found "3 miles" from that town. Claire doubted the report as they had received a letter written July 15 from the Captain of the Port of Viareggio stating "nothing had been found." She told Hunt she was not "capable of giving" Mary and Jane "consolation," her own "spirit" being "weakened . . . from constant suffering." Asking Hunt's "consul," Claire ended, "Death would be the greatest kindness to us all."[8]

The seas were rough on July 18 when Shelley's badly mutilated body washed ashore at Viareggio sometime late in the day, thirty hours after Williams's body came ashore. Byron, Hunt, and Roberts had just left the area. Trelawny, arriving shortly after Shelley's body was discovered, identified it before it too was covered with lime and buried in the sand. Shelley's body came ashore about a mile north of Viareggio's small harbor, about five and a half miles north of Williams's body. That same day, Vivian's barefoot body washed ashore further north. Like Shelley's body, the flesh not covered by clothing, including the face and extremities, had disappeared. Still visible were Vivian's striped sailor's trousers and cotton jacket. The authorities possibly cremated Vivian's body, burying his remains in the sand.[9] Vivian's body came ashore at Massa about ten and a half miles north of Shelley's, near the area where the cask from the *Don Juan* was found. Of the three bodies, Shelley's was found closest to where the dinghy from the *Don Juan* came ashore, at Motrone.[10]

When Trelawny had not returned to Villa Magni by late afternoon of July 19, Mary reassured Jane there possibly was hope as he would have come back sooner had "any thing been found." When Trelawny returned at seven that evening, Caterina shrieked as he entered the doorway and walked upstairs unannounced to the waiting women: "I neither spoke, nor did they question me. Mrs. Shelley's large grey eyes were fixed on my face. I turned away. Unable to bear this horrid silence, with a convulsive effort she exclaimed—'Is there no hope?' I did not answer but left the room, and sent the servant with the children to them."[11]

What Trelawny had seen at Viareggio was too devastating to re-late to Mary. His early grim written accounts of the horrible con-dition of Shelley's body after ten days in the water were censored in his later narratives. He identified Shelley's body from the "dress and stature," recognizing Shelley's nankeen trousers, boots, white silk socks, and double-breasted jacket. In a jacket pocket was Keats's *Lamia* volume that Hunt had given to him; only the cover remained.[12]

Mary told Maria Gisborne that Trelawny was generous "to a dis-tressing degree." She most appreciated his considerate behavior that Friday "night of agony" after his return to Villa Magni with the fatal news. Avoiding giving her "cruelly useless" consolation, "he launched forth into . . . overflowing & eloquent praise of my divine Shelley."[13]

The next day, July 20, Trelawny accompanied the families back to Pisa. Byron had suggested they might stay at the Lanfranchi, but they preferred their apartments in the Tre Palazzi. Trelawny, for the next three weeks, took responsibility for the final disposi-tion of the bodies of Shelley and Williams. Matters were compli-cated because both the Lucchese and Tuscan governments had to be dealt with; Shelley's body came ashore in the former territory, Williams's in the latter. Edward Dawkins, the British chargé d'af-faires in Florence, negotiated with the authorities in the two gov-ernments to approve disinterment of the bodies. Jane wanted to ship Williams's body to England, but Trelawny suggested burial ei-ther in Leghorn or with Shelley at Rome. Trelawny had a leaden coffin and a walnut coffin made for Shelley's body, but before Williams's coffins were made the local officials insisted both bod-ies be cremated to meet health regulations. Mary paid a dis-counted amount for the unused coffins. For the ashes, Trelawny or-dered two walnut cases be made, each a foot and a half long, covered with black velvet. Attached on top was a brass plate with Hunt's Latin inscription, "simply stating their loss by shipwreck, age, country &c." Trelawny ordered construction of "a kind of caul-dron" for burning the bodies, "a machine of iron five feet long, two broad . . . supported by legs of two feet high."[14]

Mary had visited Shelley's burial spot, where sticks in the sand marked the grave. The day she expected both bodies to be cre-mated, August 15, she wrote Maria Gisborne that Byron, Hunt, and Trelawny "are gone to the desolate sea coast to perform the last offices to their earthly remains." She planned to have Shelley's ashes buried in the Protestant Cemetery of Rome next to little William's grave. Jane would take Williams's ashes to England.[15]

Trelawny correctly anticipated the cremations would be gruesome, stressful events for him, Byron, and Hunt. Despite this, all three commented on the eerie beauty of the funeral pyres' flames. In his early narratives, Trelawny, preferring to leave the bodies buried on the seashore, attacked "the humbling & degrading manner in which the severity of Quarantine Laws & bigotry of religion (Catholicism) had consigned . . . their mangled corses—which had been dragged on shore by hooks and tumbled into shallow holes— barely covered with loose sand." Departing for the cremations, Trelawny gathered the two boxes for the ashes, the burning machine, and procured "incense, honey, wine, salt, and sugar to burn with the body."[16] Byron contributed a bottle of wine from Florence and two pounds of incense, bought at *del Serpente* pharmacy.[17]

Trelawny sailed August 13 on the *Bolivar* from Leghorn for Viareggio, accompanied by his friend, Captain Shenley. Roberts, disliking Shenley, was absent. Arriving in Viareggio the next day, Trelawny discharged the Livornese sailors who, for six days, dragged unsuccessfully for the *Don Juan*. On the morning of August 15, Trelawny, Shenley, and a health officer arrived at Williams's marked grave, close to the surf. Joined by Byron and Hunt, the blistering heat made walking on the sand almost unbearable. Four dragoons from the nearby Tower of Migliarino helped Trelawny probe for the body. Identification of Williams was uncertain until they found a boot that matched one brought for the occasion. Trelawny said Byron claimed he could identify Williams by his teeth and immediately pronounced the fleshless skull was that of Williams.

Standing in "mournful silence" around the "emense" fire, they threw "incense honey wine & sugar" on the flames, adding to their "fierceness." In the intense heat, Byron, followed by Trelawny and Shenley, stripped and plunged into the sea for a swim. Trelawny recalled Byron becoming violently ill after swimming out for a mile or two. Returning after an hour, the body was still unconsumed until a shed next to the pyre caught fire. It being late afternoon, they agreed to meet the next day to cremate Shelley's body.

This solemn, grisly ordeal[18] began the morning of August 16. Trelawny, Shenley, the health officer, and several seamen from the *Bolivar* proceeded by boat about a mile or two up the coast from Viareggio toward Massa before arriving at the white sticks demarcating Shelley's grave. While they were locating the body, Byron's carriage arrived. The accompanying dragoons and foot soldiers proved necessary to keep at a distance the local people, including "a great number of well dressed women," whose "inordinate curiosity" was provoked, as on the previous day, by such a rare event. The delay in locating the body, and the emotional press of the previous day's events, led Byron to leave the scene. Hunt remained in the carriage, "now looking on, now drawing back with feelings that were not to be witnessed."[19] Byron swam out to the *Bolivar*, a three-mile round trip, returning several hours later, after the burning of Shelley's body had concluded. Byron's swim seemed an act of self-mortification and identification with his fellow poet. The midday sun gave him a "broiling," badly burning his back, arms, and shoulders. In "pain" with a "feverish attack," he suffered his "whole skin's coming off . . . one large continuous blister." Perhaps thinking of Shelley, Byron said his new skin was now "glossy as a snake in its new suit."[20]

Byron, taking his swim, and Hunt, huddled in the carriage, did not see the disinterment of Shelley's buried body after a spade "struck the skull violently." Describing graphically the badly "mutilated decomposed & destroyed" remains, Trelawny wrote in a passage later crossed out that the task was so sickening the soldiers had to gain composure "by drinking brandy." In one early account, Trelawny noted Byron "wished much to have the skull if possible" but, being "unusually thin and strikingly small," it broke into pieces. Years later, in his effort to elevate Shelley and denigrate Byron, Trelawny freely embellished both cremations.[21]

Shelley's body took longer to consume than Williams's. Its "unusually small" heart, resisting burning, had a "bright blue flame around it" from the "oily fluid," probably blood that "flowed freely from it." Editing Trelawny's version, Hunt made Shelley's heart "unusually large."[22] Physicians have speculated that its resistance to burning may have been due to calcification, possibly from an earlier tubercular infection.[23]

Shelley's heart soon caused discord between Mary and Hunt. Trelawny apparently gave it to Hunt, who had "begged" for it. Hunt wrote a rather bizarre letter to Mary the day after the cremation, refusing her request that she have the heart. Discounting Byron's support for Mary's claim, Hunt told her his "love for my friend" Shelley negates "the claims of any other love, man's or woman's." Besides, Byron had "no right to bestow the heart."[24]

Mary, avoiding Hunt for nine days, arranged, with Trelawny's help, for delivery of Shelley's ashes to Rome.[25] Hunt kept the heart "preserved in spirits of wine," according to an indifferent Byron, who remarked that Hunt would keep it in a glass case and write sonnets about it.[26] Jane prevailed upon Hunt to return the heart to Mary, telling him Shelley's gentle spirit would be dismayed by such bitterness between them.[27]

Anticipating the future, the three women were anxious about their desperate financial situations. Jane planned to take her two children to England. Claire, before leaving for Vienna, apparently noted in her journal a brief intimacy in Pisa with Trelawny, "Friday the 6th. of September." Exactly three years later, she wrote that the "sweets" might not have vanished had Trelawny been different.[28] Trelawny, in Genoa with his mistress, the wife of a Captain Wright, implored Claire in vain to stay with him and not go to Vienna. Rushing from Genoa, Trelawny failed to intercept Claire before she left Pisa on September 15.[29] Mary viewed Claire's involvement with Trelawny as a "hasty & ill formed junction."[30] After Claire left, Trelawny, in a series of love letters, exclaimed, "You! You! Torture me Clara, your cold cruel heartless letter has driven me mad." He had loved her even "before I saw you," but she "loathed" him and "heaped on me contumelies and neglect" until they separated. Claire scratched out some passages as Trelawny pressed his case for months.[31]

Shelley's ashes, without his heart, were delivered in Rome to John Freeborn, a Via Condotti wine merchant and agent to the English Rome Consul.[32] In late November Freeborn led the Reverend Dr. Richard Burgess down into his wine cellar. Pointing to the walnut box, Freeman asked Burgess to bury it, explaining to the puzzled clergyman that it contained "Mr. Shelley's ashes Sir." Burgess, knowing Shelley was a great English poet and having heard "sensational rumors" in Rome about his death and cremation, including the possibility of suicide, decided to help end the stories by interring the remains in the "usual way."[33] In early January, Mary wrote to the wandering Trelawny that Hunt had heard that Joseph Severn was still in Rome and "about to fulfill the last scene of misery for me."[34]

Ordinarily, Protestants were buried at night in Rome, but the English received exceptions for early morning burials. Because Papal authorities forbade further burials in the old Protestant burial ground, where little William Shelley was buried, Mary obtained permission for her son's body's exhumation for burial with Shelley's ashes.[35] Seeking the grave, a shocked Severn, finding an adult buried under little William's gravestone, abandoned further search.[36]

In the early morning hours of January 21, 1823, Severn, Freeborn, Burgess, and another English clergyman, Reverend W. Cook, accompanied Shelley's box of ashes, placed in a regular coffin, through the streets of Rome to the "new" section of the cemetery. Probably nine people gathered for the service at eleven, including Severn, the artists Seymour Kirkup and Richard Westmacott, a Mr. Scoles, Freeborn, the two clergymen, General Sir George Cockburn, and Sir Charles Styles.[37] The courageous Reverend Burgess, recalling the event decades later, did not mention being abused for conducting Shelley's burial service. Severn, despite being warned by his family to avoid "that atheist, republican, and free-liver," later esteemed Shelley's praise of him in the Preface to *Adonais*, considering Shelley "the only real religious poet of the age."[38]

Shelley's ashes had yet to find a final resting place. Trelawny, arriving in Rome March 1823, with Severn's help located Shelley's grave "mingled in a heap with five or six common vagabonds." Trelawny found "the only interesting spot" for the new gravesite, a solitary place just below the ruins of a tall tower that forms part of the old Roman wall running down to the nearby pyramid of Cestius, "protected . . . from every possible molestation." Trelawny had masons prepare two adjacent gravesites, his own next to Shelley's.

Trelawny, eschewing Severn's design, had inscribed on Shelley's gravestone an abbreviation of Hunt's Latin epitaph, Cor Cordium ("Heart of Hearts"), with the dates of Shelley's birth and death. Trelawny wrote a pleased Mary that he had added Ariel's three lines from *The Tempest* that had so delighted Shelley:

> Nothing of him that doth fade,
> But doth suffer a sea-change
> Into something rich and strange.

Trelawny planted eight cypress trees and "as many laurels" around the two tombs.[39]

Shelley's ashes found their final resting place long before the stories were put to rest that the *Don Juan* had been rammed and sunk. On September 20, 1822, after the *Don Juan* had been found and raised, Mary wrote Maria Gisborne that the boat "did not up-

set, but filled & went down," repeating Roberts's words in his September 14 letter. Neither Mary nor Roberts entertained a ramming
theory at this time. Trelawny, who had not seen the *Don Juan* after it was raised, apparently was the first to circulate the idea. In
October, Mary wrote to Jane Williams (in London) that "Trelawny
tells me that in his, Roberts & every other sailor's opinion she was
run down; of course by that Fishing boat—which confessed to
have seen them." Mary talked to Roberts about this the following
May after Roberts had refitted the *Don Juan* and taken care to
provide the safety of a deck. Roberts deceptively told Mary he had
sailed her in "various experiments, hazardous ones" to determine
what caused "the catastrophe" and that it was "plain to every eye"
that "she was run down from behind . . . a great hole knocked in the
stern timbers."[40]

By 1839, Mary wrote only of the boat's "defect" and "that it was
never seaworthy," apparently changing her mind about the ramming theory.[41] Writing probably in the spring of 1823, Trelawny
stated, "one of the many large Fishing Craft" struck the *Don Juan*
"on the weather quarter filled her to Leaward when she
foundered." However, he ended with an afterthought, "Shelley's
boat might have foundered & the damage of her hull done in getting her up—not by having been run down."[42] Roberts spent
months with Trelawny before first mentioning the ramming theory
to Mary in 1823. He reportedly said in 1828 that the boat was "stove
in," adding he "believes" the boat was run down, avoiding an un-
equivocal assertion.[43] Trelawny twice printed in the 1870s a letter
from his daughter, Laetitia Call, containing a story of a sailor
who "died a little while ago" after a deathbed confession to a priest
that he was in the crew that ran down the boat, thinking Byron and
his money were on board. This story, soon challenged in the
Atheneum, has been proved erroneous.[44]

The *Don Juan* was found "fifteen" miles off shore by two Viareggio fishing boats.[45] The multiple damage to the gunwale possibly
was incurred raising the vessel—laden with heavy ballast and
mud—with the crude equipment of the day in what was probably
deep water. Roberts, about to "put the hull in condition," would
have mentioned the "great hole" he later mentioned to Mary had
one existed.[46] Trelawny, guilty of changing facts in his *Recollections,* changed Roberts's letter to Mary to a short letter to
Trelawny. A letter from Roberts to Trelawny was edited to remove
statements about the stove-in gunwale that ran counter to the

ramming theory. Trelawny's invented postscript claimed that on "close examination of Shelley's boat" many broken timbers on the starboard quarter made him "think for certain" that feluccas ran down the *Don Juan* in the squall.[47] As Cameron asserted, the running-down theory rests on "no firm evidence."[48] Trelawny and Roberts undoubtedly promulgated the ramming theory to avoid guilt about their roles in the unsafe design of the *Don Juan,* including its rigging. Trelawny wrote to Claire in September 1822, "I designed the treacherous bark which proved his Coffin." He repeated his words a few months later.[49]

Among supposed eyewitnesses interviewed in 1890 was eighty-seven-year-old Antonio Canova, a presumed crew member of the salvage vessel that caught the *Don Juan* in its net, "five" miles off Viareggio and the Tower of Migliarino. After beaching and bailing her, items found included a trunk with clothes, cheques, other papers, a hundred francs in silver, sixteen sandbags for ballast, iron spades, and several hampers of bottled beer.[50] These sailors' late reports gain credence as they agree with contemporary reports that the boat's main sails were up and that it sank quickly.[51]

Hunt wrote to his sister-in-law about Shelley's death, asking her to notify Hogg and enclosing a notice that appeared August 4 in the *Examiner,* the first public account in England of Shelley's death.[52] The posthumous castigation of Shelley began the next day when the conservative *Courier* announced, "Shelley, the writer of some infidel poetry, has been drowned; *now* he knows whether there is a God or no." The *Courier* carefully pointed out William Clark's simultaneous prosecution for "republication" of *Queen Mab*.[53] *The Country Literary Chronicle* account said Shelley was "a man of extraordinary but perverted talents." The Tory *John Bull,* quoting Shelley's "blasphemy" in *Queen Mab,* considered God arranged the drowning as a warning and attacked the Whig *Morning Chronicle* for calling the "Atheist" Shelley "divine-minded." Defending Shelley was the long obituary in *The Paris Monthly Review* of August 1822, written by Horace Smith. The "catastrophe" of Shelley's death "had snatched from English literature a votary of warmest enthusiasm blended with the most pre-eminent genius. . . . Perhaps there never existed a greater enthusiast for the happiness of mankind than Mr. Shelley . . . [who] has never had fair play. . . . his works were scarcely known, except by those objectionable passages which his opponents sedulously intruded upon the public." *Gentleman's Magazine* attacked Shelley as "a fitter subject for a penitentiary dying speech, than a laudatory elegy; for the muse of the rope, rather than that of the cypress."[54]

This press abuse, and the fact that several of the notices identified Shelley as the son of "Sir Timothy Shelley, Bart.," added to Timothy's hostile attitude toward Mary in the years ahead, including his prohibitions against her publication of his son's biography.[55] Notified by Whitton of Shelley's death, Timothy briefly mentioned the tragedy in his reply, saying, "God's will be done!" Peacock wrote to Timothy of Shelley's death, mentioning that his uninsured life left "his widow and her infant son . . . without any provision." That same day, Timothy received a letter from the executor of the estate of Elizabeth Hitchener, who died early in 1822, asking for £100 that Shelley owed her. Timothy, not deigning to write Peacock, sent both letters to Whitton saying that the lack of "proper mourning clothes" prohibited his coming to London. Besides, "etiquette" dictated "not to appear in Public . . . until we have been to Church." Because of "the peculiar circumstances the general acceptation of the world may be at rest in regard to the Family." Although losing "an eldest son . . . is truly melancholy . . . it has pleas'd the Great Author of our Being so to dispose of him I must make up my mind with resignation." Wrapping himself in religious piety, Timothy never acknowledged his son's greatness as a poet. Timothy's letters never mentioned Lady Shelley's response to her son's death.[56]

Godwin's cold response to Shelley's death equaled Timothy's. After hearing the "the afflicting intelligence," he wrote Mary chastising those in Italy for not notifying him, "perhaps" excusing Mary but blaming Claire and Lady Mount Cashell, whose silence was "peculiarly cruel." Finances were paramount for Godwin, who was "impatient to hear" of Shelley's monetary provisions for Mary. If she made him her "lawyer," his negotiations with Shelley's solicitor, Longdill, would have "more effect." He urged Mary to come home soon as "We have no battle to fight . . . that is over now."[57] Mary assured Godwin her friends "worship" Shelley and she was not "so desolate as you might think."[58]

Medwin, arriving in Pisa from Geneva after Shelley's cremation, first implied he was present but later admitted arriving "some hours . . . too late."[59] Returning briefly to England, Medwin was "quite disgusted by the want of feeling" of Timothy and the entire Shelley family, for whom he had "a thorough contempt."[60]

Byron, deeply moved by Shelley's death, had written Thomas Moore early in 1822, "As to poor Shelley, who is another bugbear to you and the world, he is, to my knowledge, the *least* selfish and mildest of men—a man who has made more sacrifices of his fortune and feelings for others than any other I ever heard of." In August, Byron wrote to John Murray that he and others were "brutally mistaken" concerning Shelley, who was "without exception —the *best* and least selfish man I ever knew." A few days later he wrote Thomas Moore, "There is thus another man gone, about whom the world was ill-naturedly, and ignorantly and brutally mistaken. It will, perhaps, do him justice *now*, when he can be no better for it."[61]

Although Byron was itching for new horizons, "fluctuating" between South America and Greece,[62] he and the remaining Pisan colony moved to Genoa in September. Mary, Jane, and the children departed first, to be followed by Byron and the Hunts. The ruckus over Shelley's heart had cast a veil over Mary's dealings with Hunt, but Trelawny convinced her she should not live alone. She explained to Godwin why her friends had persuaded her she should stay in Italy for a year. Because Shelley's quarterly allowance ceased when he died and his will could not be acted upon until his father's death, Mary would live on the money she had. Byron, believing Sir Timothy would give her an allowance, paid Mary to transcribe his work, including his new cantos of *Don Juan*. She planned to earn money editing Shelley's manuscripts for publication and from her writing. Jane soon left for England, and Mary leased a large unfurnished house, just outside Genoa in Albaro, that she would share with the Hunts. A mile up the hill was Byron's casa.[63]

Hobhouse, visiting Byron in Pisa in mid-September, tried to persuade him to drop *The Liberal*. Byron demurred, partially out of loyalty to Shelley's memory. Byron failed to persuade Hunt to return to England or stay in Pisa, Hunt being fearful that his tenuous financial lifeline, *The Liberal*, would snap if he and Byron were so distant.[64] Byron generously told Hunt to ask his secretary Lega for whatever money he needed, only to have Marianne Hunt complain that Shelley knew better "how to do a favour."[65] Byron, consoled that his casa was a mile from the Hunt children, "dirtier and more mischievous than Yahoos,"[66] bought the Shelleys' and Williamses' Pisan furniture to help Mary and Jane. In late September, separate overland caravans carried the Hunts and Byron's larger entourage from Pisa to Lerici. Meeting Trelawny with the *Bolivar*, Byron was sick in bed four days following a swimming match with Trelawny to his boat.[67]

Mary waited several weeks for the Hunts and Byron to arrive, alone in her grief with Percy Florence, not yet three. Concerned about who would pay the allowance for little Percy's half-siblings, Charles and Ianthe, Mary was unaware that in early 1822 Timothy Shelley had approved the children's new custodians selected by the Westbrooks. Although Charles was now the successor to Timothy's baronetcy, his grandfather balked at paying more than one quarterly allowance for him and his sister. The matter was resolved in 1823 when Chancery made Timothy Charles's guardian. Ianthe became the guardian of Mr. Westbrook and Eliza Westbrook, now Mrs. Farthing Beauchamp.[68]

Mary had prepared Jane's future with Hogg in a letter Jane hand delivered to him in London. She told Hogg that Jane was "the friend" Shelley "saw daily for nearly two years, to whom he was affectionately attached." Mary asked Hogg "to do all in your power" for Jane, including "what little you can to amuse her."[69] He quickly complied. Hogg and Jane discreetly became lovers and plotted, in his words, "to add a few more chapters to our secret history & surprizing adventures." Both lamented Mary's probable return to England, Hogg expecting "Her conversation will be painful, just as her letters are, because, to those who saw behind the scenes, the subject of it is a mere fable." Jane undoubtedly was telling Hogg, and perhaps others, of Shelley's disastrous marriage to Mary and of his feelings for Jane. Hogg told Jane, "our loss is real" but that Mary's, "however painful, is in fact imaginary for to suppose that matters co^d have continued as they were, wo^d have been the vanity of vanities, & any other terminations wo^d have been for her, except as to money-matters, infinitely worse."[70] Jane had told Hogg she believed that Shelley was not going to continue to live with Mary.

Jane and Hogg hid their mutual attraction from Mary. He told Jane that his copy of Shelley's juvenile poems reminded him of her.[71] In February 1823, Jane wrote Mary that Hogg seemed "strongly interested in me." Jane had not told Hogg that she was unmarried to Edward Williams and that her husband lived in London. That spring, Jane had her own lodgings to receive Hogg. Mary wrote to Jane of her hope that she and Jane would live together in Florence.

Jane and Hogg began living together as Mr. and Mrs. Hogg in 1827, had two children, and remained unmarried to the time of his death in 1862. Their relationship was the most Shelleyan episode of the poet's afterlife. Shelley's death allowed Hogg, finally, to consummate a relationship with one of Shelley's loves.

Claire revered Shelley for the remainder of her long life even as she criticized his views on love. She had judged correctly the mercurial Trelawny, who would have three marriages followed by a common-law wife and a live-in relationship with an adolescent female he called his "niece."[72] Trelawny twice wrote to Claire that Shelley was "a thorough mormon" who anticipated "the sect." Trelawny "would gladly have joined him and founded a settlement . . . the poet should have had fifty wives—five would have done for me."[73]

With financial help from Trelawny and Mary, Claire went to Vienna. In late 1822, Mrs. Mason, without Claire's knowledge, wrote Byron asking him to provide for Claire. Despite telling Mary he would do so, Byron did not help Claire. Mary, from what she earned working on *The Liberal*, sent fifteen napoleons to Claire. To assuage his conscience, Byron offered to channel funds to Claire through Mary, who rejected his devious plan.[74]

In early October, Mary began her new journal, titling it, "The Journal of Sorrow—Begun 1822 But for my Child it could not End too soon."[75] Soon she received her cherished desk left in Marlow. It was delivered to Byron who, before passing it along to Mary, read the letters it contained written by Mary to Shelley from Marlow when he was in London. Her agony increased when she found in the desk locks of hair, those of Shelley and of little Clara, the child Mary thought most resembled her father.[76] Mary quickly devoted herself to the challenging task of editing and publishing Shelley's poetry and prose.[77] By November, she decided to write Shelley's life, a project she began but soon ceased when Timothy Shelley forbade it. Although she returned to her memoir of Shelley years later, only in her notes to his poems, and in her stories and novels, was she able to recreate something of her husband's biography.[78]

Mary wrote to Jane from Albaro that Trelawny was "the only one in Italy" with "a sincere affection for me." She told Claire that "Hunt does not like me; it is both our faults & I do not blame him."[79] Byron wrote his disapproving English friends that *The Liberal* was Hunt's journal even though Byron's writing kept it afloat. Mary mediated between Hunt and Byron even as her own relationship with each was strained. *The Liberal* would have four issues, the first appearing October 15, seven thousand copies being printed.

Mary, determined to earn money from her writing, composed two articles that appeared in *The Liberal*. She asked Peacock to send the manuscript of *A Defence of Poetry* for *The Liberal* and hoped *The Witch of Atlas* would also appear. Neither did.

Byron, at Mary's request, contacted Whitton to determine what provision Timothy Shelley intended to make for Mary and her son.[80] Whitton, after discussion with Timothy, denied support to Mary. Byron then wrote tactfully to Sir Timothy stating that he "had the honour of being" Shelley's "friend" and asked that Timothy's "destitute . . . daughter-in-law and her child" be given a "simple provision." Timothy sent Byron's letter to Whitton, intimating he might allow Mary £160 a year. However, Whitton conferred with Timothy and drafted a letter for Timothy to send Byron attacking Mary, rejecting any allowance for her, and offering "suitable protection and care" of Percy "if he shall be placed with a person I shall approve." Timothy told Byron his other responsibilities "limited" the amount he could give Percy. Listing his accusations against Mary, Timothy told Byron, "Mrs. Shelley was, I have been told, the intimate friend of my son in the lifetime of his first wife and to the time of her death, and in no small degree as I suspect estranged my son's mind from his family and all his first duties in life." He disagreed with Byron "that Mrs. Shelley is innocent. . . . I must therefore decline all interference in matters in which Mrs. Shelley is interested."[81]

Mary's response, shocked anger, was not at the accusations about her behavior with Shelley but at the idea of relinquishing her only child, especially to someone approved by the detested Timothy. She received another shock when Byron told her she should accept Timothy's offer and relinquish her child. Mary now began to question Byron's moral and practical judgment, maintaining an outward "docility" toward him. Obsessed over whether to return to England, she wrote to everyone she knew for advice. Jane and Hogg wanted her to stay in Italy. Byron, counseling Mary to return to England, confided to her in early April 1823 he would go to Greece in July. Mary noted that this would alleviate him of his tired relationship with Teresa Guiccioli, a liaison, she observed, that had cost him nothing monetarily. Mary wrote to Jane that she would return to England after attending the birth of Marianne Hunt's seventh child in June. If Byron left for Greece in July, she knew Trelawny would go with him. Thinking "the Liberal looks dismal," she could not "live under Hunt's roof," angered that Hunt wanted to have his "selfish" sister-in-law join them. Marianne vetoed having Bessy Kent come.[82]

Mary's relationship to Hunt, Shelley, and herself decisively changed in early June when she confronted Hunt about his dislike for her. Hunt told Mary what Shelley had told him just before he died about his dissatisfaction with Mary who, bursting into tears, spoke of her great remorse. Having fought with her over Shelley's heart, Hunt realized she had "worshipped" Shelley all these past months and upbraided himself for being "cold" and "almost cruel" toward her. Calling Mary "a torrent of fire under a Heckla snow," he believed her "impulses of fire may be turned to good & great purpose." Hunt mentioned that Trelawny had told him that Shelley, even when "most uneasy" about Mary, believed "she had excuses of suffering little known to any body but himself." Hunt, having discussed Shelley's marital situation with Jane after his death, now blamed Jane for misleading him about the Shelleys' relationship. Hunt, never fond of Jane, said she "has not quite intellect enough to see very far into a case where great thoughts, passions &c. are concerned." Mary had told him that "though others had seen the worst part of her tempers towards S., they had not seen the amends, & request of pardon, which she always made him in private."[83]

Mary's guilt after Shelley's death now became more intense. Addressing "My Shelley" in her journal after her talk with Hunt, she asked him if at the time of his death, "did you think of the faults, the coldness & weaknesses of your unhappy Mary" and of her "tears" during their "parting embrace, of the love that deeply dwelt in her heart—of her sufferings—her Anguish -?" She continued, "I cannot grieve for you, beloved Shelley," stating her grief was for his friends, the world, his child, and for herself. She "ever felt" that she was "unworthy of you . . . most bitterly and deeply now."[84] Soon she wrote a long introspective poem, "The Choice," a poetic "tale of unrequited love." It addressed the anger, guilt, inhibition, and depression that blocked her loving feelings and led to "cold neglect." Her analysis was that "My heart was all thine own—but yet a shell / Closed in its core, which seemed impenetrable." She asked his forgiveness that the "gaping" tear in their relationship had not been repaired when he died.[85] Hunt's emotional blinders and his adoration of Shelley rendered him unable to help Mary see the role that Shelley's faults had played in their difficult marriage.[86]

At Hunt's request, Bessie had shown Jane his letter in which he blamed his coldness toward Mary on what Jane had told him of

Mary's behavior toward Shelley. In April 1824, Jane wrote to Hunt protesting his "unjust" placing of blame on her, reminding him they had both witnessed "on a certain occasion (which I need not mention)" a "sad circumstance" concerning Mary's behavior. Further, while she had spoken of "Mary's conduct," Hunt knew Mary well enough to discern "whether a persons temper be bad or good" and Jane remembered Hunt telling her "that our Shelley mentioned several circumstances on that subject that distressed you during the short week you were together." Jane reminded him of Shelley's "pain" when he received a letter from Mary in Leghorn and asked Hunt not to discuss "these things" with Mary.[87] Before leaving Italy, Mary wrote Jane that she was still the "the only one I greatly love" in England.[88] Four years later she felt totally betrayed by Jane.

Mary's problems in leaving Italy the summer of 1823 put a final sour note on the complicated Shelley–Byron relationship. The day after Marianne Hunt had her baby in early June, Mary told Byron she was ready to leave. After promising to pay for Mary's travel, Byron became annoyed with her wavering about departing. Mary was irked by Byron's "air of unwillingness & sense of obligation" and Hunt told Byron "there was no obligation" because Byron owed Mary the £1000 from his bet with Shelley.[89] Byron, communicating with Mary through Hunt, wrote him that Mary refused Byron's assistance because "of what she is pleased to call 'estrangement.'" Byron, still offering to finance her journey "*handsomely and conveniently*," to spare her "any fancied humiliation," proposed he give the money to Hunt who would pass it to Mary with the explanation that Hunt had raised the money. Byron expressed "utter astonishment" at what Hunt told him that day, perhaps something Shelley had told Hunt. Byron stated he was resigning as an executor of Shelley's estate and declined the £2000 Shelley left him in his will.[90] Mary wrote Jane that Byron's "notes and letters [were] full of contempt against me & my lost Shelley" and that Jane would "laugh" because Byron had told Hunt that Shelley had lowered "himself down to the level of democrats."[91]

Refusing Byron, Mary asked Trelawny for money, and with her own £30 and some from Mrs. Mason, she could return to England. Hunt accepted Byron's offer to finance moving his family to Florence and asked "to be exonerated" from his £250 debt to Byron. He also asked Byron to take care of his brother John's bill for £130. Byron apparently acceded to all these requests. Mary wrote to Teresa

Guiccioli wishing Byron success in Greece but did not see him before he and Trelawny departed on the *Hercules* July 16.

In Greece, Byron allied himself with Mavrocordato in Missolonghi while Trelawny joined the eastern rival Greek faction of Odysseus Androutsos. When Trelawny heard that Byron had died on April 19, 1824, he rushed to Missolonghi. Upon leaving, he angered Mavrocordato by taking half of his artillery back to Odysseus's cave redoubt at Mount Parnassus. Trelawny wrote Claire that they had both lost their "evil genius," Byron.[92] One of Trelawny's English cave-mates, bribed by Mavrocordato, in June 1825 shot and nearly killed Trelawny. His recovery took weeks but he spared the life of the would-be assassin. Claire happily read in September that "he was well and still in his cavern."[93]

Briefly in England in 1828, Trelawny found Claire was a domesticated spinster and ended a letter to her, "Adieu old Aunt."[94] Displeased with Mary for providing material to Thomas Moore for his biography of Byron, Trelawny left for Florence without saying goodbye. Her refusal shortly after to provide material to Trelawny for a memoir of Shelley so angered him that he threatened to mention in his book her collaboration with Moore, for which John Murray sent her £100.[95] Claire refused to join Trelawny in Florence to educate his young daughter Zella but when she changed her mind in 1830, Trelawny said he had other plans.[96]

Trelawny, giving up on his biography of Shelley, published with Mary's generous assistance in 1831 his own half-concocted life, *Adventures of a Younger Son*. He hinted in his letters to Mary that he was "united" with her by "fate" but she responded firmly that she would not marry him "nor any body else—Mary Shelley shall be written on my tomb." A month later she reiterated, "My name will <u>never</u> be Trelawny . . . Mary Shelley will <u>never</u> be yours."[97] Later, Mary said Trelawny was "Endued with genius . . . but destroyed by <u>being</u> <u>nothing</u>. . . . I never feel comfortable with him."[98] Trelawny achieved fame in 1858 with his *Recollections of the Last Days of Shelley and Byron*, in which Mary received fair treatment. However, when revised in 1878, with the assistance of William Michael Rossetti, as *Records of Shelley, Byron, and the Author*, Mary was treated with scorn in the appendix. Four years earlier, Trelawny had been immortalized in John Millais's large painting, *The North West Passage;* the rebel corsair had unknowingly endorsed British imperialism. Doggedly atheistic, vegetarian, and teetotaler to the end, Trelawny, the last of Shelley's male friends, died at the age of eighty-eight on August 13, 1881. After nearly sixty years, he joined Shelley in the Protestant Cemetery.

While en route to England from Italy, Mary wrote to Jane, "you I trust love me," admitting that in her relationship with Shelley she had not "been all I sh^d have been."[99] Arriving in London in late August 1823, Mary wrote Hunt, "I found myself famous!" A stage production of *Frankenstein* was "to be repeated for the 23rd night" and Godwin republished *Frankenstein* by the time she arrived.[100] Mary, with Peacock's assistance, extracted from Timothy an annual income for Percy Florence of £100 and an equal amount for herself. Timothy, ever tight, demanded both incomes be paid with interest against the estate Mary would inherit when Timothy died.[101]

Aside from little Percy, Jane was now the most important person in Mary's life. Her first eruption with Jane occurred the end of January 1825 when, probably realizing Hogg and Jane were lovers, she twice called herself a "fool" in her journal. Jane, still not living with Hogg, reestablished a close relationship with Mary, who wrote to Hunt of "my Janey's . . . power . . . over me . . . my sole delight." She later wrote Trelawny that at that time "I was so ready to give myself away—& being afraid of men, I was apt to get tousy-mousy for women." Mary found her close friendship with Caroline Norton "fascinating" and "Had I been a man I should certainly have fallen in love with her. . . . she might have wound me round her finger."[102]

Hogg and a pregnant Jane moved into their Maida Vale home in April 1827 as Mr. and Mrs. Jefferson Hogg. Mary learned in July that Jane had betrayed her by talking about her behind her back to a number of friends, probably about her difficult marriage with Shelley and his attraction to Jane. She wrote in her journal that her "friend has proved false & treacherous. . . . for four years I was devoted to her—& earned only ingratitude."[103] Contact was renewed months later, but Mary never forgot Jane's betrayal.

Mary also became immersed in the convoluted sexual relationship between Isabel Robinson and Mary Diana Dods, a transvestite with Tory sympathies. When "Doddy" and a pregnant Isabel became a "married" couple and went to France, Mary assisted their departure with the help of her friend, the American playwright John Howard Payne.[104] Payne became her "Amabilissimo Cavaliere" but, after he professed his love, Mary indicated that his close friend Washington Irving was her real interest. Payne tried unsuccessfully to arouse Irving's interest in Mary by showing him letters she wrote to Payne. Undeterred, Mary several years later enlisted Thomas Moore's help in promoting a non-productive meeting with reluctant Irving.[105] Two other writers unsuccessfully pursued Mary, Arthur Brooke (John Chalk Claris) and Prosper Mérimée. One of the "delicately healthed Poets" to whom she was attracted was Bryan Waller Procter (Barry Cornwall). She was hurt upon reading in the paper of his marriage.[106]

A more mysterious romantic relationship began in 1832 with Major Aubrey Beauclerk, the brother of her dear friend Georgina Beauclerk Paul, a young girl when Mary first knew her in Pisa. Aubrey, a much younger and distinctly minor reincarnation of Shelley in terms of his radical political and social views, became an M.P. in 1832. Mary's recollection of "ineffable bliss" with Aubrey may indicate they were lovers and his marriage in 1834 probably contributed to her depression at that time. After Beauclerk became a widower in 1838, Mary's journal entries suggest her hopes of uniting with him. The next year she received a jolt upon learning Beauclerk was to marry Mary's young protégée, Rosa Robinson.[107] Years later, Claire told Edward Silsbee that Mary had accepted Aubrey's marriage proposal but when his family objected, she "drew back . . . chagrined."[108]

Mary's final infatuation was Ferdinand Gatteschi, a handsome thirty-year-old Carbonari Italian expatriate living in Paris. Encouraging him with money obtained from Claire, Mary gave him her portrait and exchanged letters with him. Disbelieving Claire's warning not to trust him, Mary was blackmailed in 1845 by Gatteschi, who threatened to expose her letters to him unless she gave him money. If not love letters, they probably contained much about her personal life with Shelley. Mary mentioned repeatedly that the letters could "destroy" her. The Paris police retrieved the letters, which Mary burned.[109]

After Jane and Hogg's first daughter died, they had another daughter in 1836. Jane had survived a blackmail attempt by her husband, whose death in 1840 ended their twenty-six-year marriage. Perhaps deferring to Shelley's ideas, Hogg chose not to marry Jane. Increasingly remote, Hogg was often away on his circuit and fortyish Jane became romantically interested in two younger men. One, her nephew Henry Cleveland, lived in Jane's house until she died. The other was the Hunts' son Henry Sylvan Hunt. Mary wrote to Claire that the kisses Jane bestowed upon Henry Hunt aroused the jealousy of Jane's nephew and that Jane "certainly has betrayed a degree of interest & passion which her children think strange." She assumed Jane's behavior had not "passed all limits."[110] When Jane's daughter Dina became pregnant by young Hunt, Claire encouraged their eventual marriage.[111] After Hogg died in August 1862, his brother John's obituary-memoir made no mention of Jane, who died twenty-two years later in November 1884 at age eighty-six. The last living member of Shelley's circle, Jane had been largely ignored by Shelleyans who missed what she might have contributed to his biography.

Claire, too, had a long life. She went to Moscow in 1823 as governess in a prosperous family. The family's tutor—a passionate, intellectual German poet and composer, Hermann Gambs, the same age as Shelley and Trelawny—could not get Claire to fully return his affection. Claire told Jane she felt for Gambs the way Jane felt about Shelley. Jane advised her to fall in love, but Claire responded by alluding to her affair with Byron, a brief "happy passion" of "ten minutes" that "discomposed the rest of my life."[112]

Claire, back in London in 1828, wrote a story, "The Pole," which can be read as a veiled version of Shelley's Neapolitan child and the Campbell sisters. Claire asked Mary to complete the last scene and publish it under the pseudonym "Mont. Obscur."[113] Claire's life as governess took her to Dresden, Nice, Florence, Naples, and then to Pisa in late 1831 to live with Mrs. Mason where, she wrote Mary, "I am as her child." After ten years of hiding her background and being silent about her beliefs, she now "had no need to disguise my sentiments." Among these, she told Mary, was her continuing love of Shelley despite the "immense . . . lies he told" about her.[114]

After Lady Mount Cashell died in 1835, Claire wrote to Mary of her grief and her continued "extreme contempt and obstinate aversion" to the dead Byron, who had "so wantonly willfully destroyed my Allegra." Claire told Mary she disbelieved her after Mary wrote she too had no affection for Byron. Claire added she knew Byron "hated Shelley" and "despised his poetry and his principles." She regretted that although she had "incessantly entreated" Shelley to break with Byron, he could not do so because of his "ill-advised gentleness" and his belief "he might lead Lord Byron to good works and good ways."[115]

Claire returned to England in late 1835, only months before eighty-year-old Godwin died in April 1836, the same month that Maria Gisborne died. Henry Reveley, married in 1824, made a name for himself as architect and engineer in a new colony in Western Australia, to be called Perth. Shortly after Godwin's death,

Mary wrote to Trelawny her most explicit account of her lifelong vexed relationship with Claire, saying they "were never friends . . . never loved each other." Mary's "idea of Heaven was a world without Claire," who could still make her "more uncomfortable than any human being—a faculty she, unconsciously perhaps, never fails to exert whenever I see her."[116]

Claire, after her mother died in 1841, arranged to receive an annuity against her future inheritance. Aided by a gift of £100 from Mary, she moved to Paris. Having come into the full £12,000 legacy Shelley left her when Sir Timothy died in 1844, Claire returned in 1846 to England before moving in 1859 to Florence, her home the last twenty years of her life.[117]

From 1872 until 1876, Edward Silsbee periodically intruded his way into her home, which included Claire's niece Pauline, who fell in love with Silsbee. He recorded his conversations with Claire about Shelley and his circle before leaving Claire for the last time February 1879, weeks before her death. He had obtained Shelley's (Harvard) Manuscript Book, but not his letters, enough to provide Henry James the idea for his novella, *The Aspern Papers*. Claire, having embraced her mother's Catholicism in 1849, wrote Trelawny in 1870 defending Mary against his charges that she was a religious hypocrite. Claire believed "Life is only the prologue to an Eternal Drama. . . . My life has been most desolate; no one cared for me no one helped me." She considered writing a book to "illustrate from the lives of Shelley and Byron the dangers and evils resulting from erroneous opinions on the relations of the sexes."[118] Claire died at age eighty on March 19, 1879. Her names, inscribed on her tombstone in a cemetery outside Florence, included the "Constantia" from Shelley's poems: "In Memory of Clara Mary Constantia Jane Clairmont . . . She passed her life in sufferings, expiating not only her faults but also her virtues."[119]

Byron's death gave Medwin his chance to make literary capital. In less than two months he assembled from memory and his "copious" notes his *Conversations of Lord Byron*.[120] He wrote to a disdainful Mary that Shelley was "a very prominent feature" of the book and "There are some topics I have cautiously avoided, and of course you are one."[121] Ten days after *Conversations* appeared in October 1824, Medwin parlayed his £500 from the book and his new fame into a marriage to a widowed countess with a fortune of about £10,000. After four years of marriage, they were living and entertaining in a palazzo in Florence when, having squandered all her money, he deserted her and their two young daughters. Trelawny, in Florence, helped the distraught and completely duped wife cope with the huge debt Medwin had left her.[122] Years later, Medwin, angry at Mary for objecting to his writing the first biography of Shelley, wrote a letter to Jane hinting he had incriminating information about Shelley in Naples and with Emilia Viviani.[123] Mary, believing Medwin tried to extort money from her not to publish the biography, may never have read his *Life of Percy Bysshe Shelley*. Despite her fears, and his factual inaccuracies, Medwin treated her and Emilia with sensitive taste and did not mention Elena Adelaide Shelley.

Mary's closeness to Shelley, and her familiarity with his writing habits and illegible handwriting, helped in the task of transforming his often chaotic notebooks and drafts into a poetic corpus. Her efforts have been called "Herculean," placing her "somewhere between Shelley's collaborator and his co-author."[124] She told Hunt, "I hate to mutilate,"[125] but this was the fate of Shelley's writing. Only in the late twentieth century has his poetry and prose received more definitive scholarly editing. Mary's 1824 *Posthumous Poetry* was designed to create a non-controversial, ethereal Shelley for the poetic middle-class mainstream by downplaying his radical ideas and emphasizing his lyrical gifts. Presenting a pure, spiritual, and lyrical Shelley, she essentially disembodied his radical and subversive views on politics, sex, and religion. This strategy also accommodated her fear of losing her allowance from Shelley's father.

When more than three hundred of the five hundred copies of Mary's 1824 edition of Shelley's poetry were sold in the first two months, an irate Sir Timothy, again negotiating with Mary about finances, ordered the unsold copies called back. Her name, omitted on the title page, did appear on the glowing introductory memoir of Shelley's last years. Mary wrote of Timothy's reaction, he "writhes under the fame of his incomparable son as if it were the most grievous injury done to him."[126] She had to promise not to bring his name before the public again during Timothy's lifetime. Further, Whitton convinced Timothy that Shelley's prose manuscripts should be placed in Peacock's care, erasing Mary's plans for a prose edition.[127] Since Timothy was seventy, Mary was not too disturbed; however, he lived another twenty years.

Seemingly unnoticed by the Shelley group, twenty-four-year-old Eliza Ianthe Shelley, in 1837, married Edward Jeffries Esdaile. Of their seven children, only one passed on the genes of Shelley and Harriet.[128]

Shelley's son Charles Bysshe died at age eleven of tuberculosis at Field Place, September 11, 1826. Five years later, the same disease in the same house was fatal to Shelley's thirty-seven-year-old unmarried sister Elizabeth. Timothy had grown fond of his grandson Charles, sending him to Syon House Academy. Charles's parents' names were on the burial notice signed by Shelley's first tutor, Vicar "Taffy" Edwards, but Charles was listed on his burial plaque in Warnham Church only as the grandson of Sir Timothy Shelley and Lady Elizabeth Shelley.

Mary, noting that six-year-old Percy was "now Shelley's only Son,"[129] hoped that his being heir to the baronetcy might alleviate her financial situation. An annoyed Timothy had temporarily suspended Mary's allowance when she published her 1826 novel, *The Last Man*, because the title page read, "by the author of *Frankenstein*." Finally, with Peacock's help, her annual allowance became £250 with the understanding it would increase to £300 for Percy's education expenses. Timothy still refused to see Mary but upon meeting young Percy wrote to Whitton of being "unman'd" by emotion and gratified the boy was "very clean in his person." Shelley's younger brother John married in 1827 and soon caused financial "trouble" for his father who wrote indulgently to Whitton something he would never have written about John's older brother, "We were all young once." Denying he ever had "unchristian-like Feelings" for Mary, Timothy ruled out Eton for young Percy. Mary sent him to Harrow and Cambridge.[130]

Timothy's 1824 embargo on Mary's publication of Shelley's works and life gave the pirate publishers free hand to cash in on Shelley's now-profitable reputation. Even John Murray tried to get copyright to his poems. Although publication of *Queen Mab* brought immediate trials of blasphemy, pirated editions appeared as well as twenty-six editions of his other poetry between 1821 and 1841. The proliferation of new liberal and radical newspapers spread his views among the working-class political movements. Robert Owen, in his utopian-socialist writing, quoted Shelley freely, helping to promulgate him as a political poet. From the late 1820s and extending in the 1850s, Shelley's political thought, in both his poetry and prose, was quoted and revered by the working-class Chartist Movement. Eleanor Marx recalled that her father and Engels both spoke about the Chartists' "Shelley-worship," confirmed by analysis of Chartist publications of the time. Commonly printed were extracts from *Queen Mab, The Revolt of Islam,* and *The Mask of Anarchy,* as well as such shorter political poems as "Song to the Men of England" and "Sonnet: To the Republic of Benevento."[131]

Amidst this publication flurry, Mary got Timothy to agree to the publication in 1839 of her four-volume edition of Shelley's *Poetical Works* with her name, "Mrs. Shelley," as editor, on the title page. After Whitton's death in 1832, his replacement, John Gregson, proved more an ally for Mary, increasing her allowance to £400 when Percy went to Harrow in 1832 and evoking Timothy's remark to Gregson, "Her Diamond Eyes had cut your Glass Heart."[132] Mindful of her husband's handicap, Mary insisted Percy learn to swim before going to Harrow, where she soon wrote Gregson that Percy's Master "was pleased with his progress & his docility."[133] Passive intellectually and socially, Percy lived with his mother after graduating from Cambridge's Trinity College.

Becoming Sir Percy when his grandfather died, April 24, 1844, Shelley's son acquired the first of ten yachts he owned. Percy wanted to live in the decayed hulk of Castle Goring but sold it and briefly studied law. Shelley's mother had stripped Field Place to the walls when she moved out after Timothy's death. Percy rented it out until 1848 when he moved in with Mary and his new wife, Jane Gibson St. John. She was one of nine natural children of a northern banker and was widowed at the same age as Mary, twenty-four. Before his marriage, Percy dropped out of the race for a Parliament seat in Horsham. Running as an independent radical, he decided the marriage his mother had orchestrated was a more certain alternative.

Mary found Field Place "a swamp." A visit from Claire aroused the old animosity between the two stepsisters. In the ensuing row, Mary exclaimed she did not want to be left alone with Claire, "the bane of my existence." Percy, once Claire's delight but now estranged from her, moved with his mother and Lady Jane to London where Mary's headaches were diagnosed as a brain tumor. Stoically facing death, she refused Trelawny's offer of his burial plot next to Shelley's grave because of the cost and bother, preferring St. Pancras where her mother and father were buried and where she and Shelley had become lovers. Paralyzed and unconscious for a week, she died February 1, 1851, at age fifty-three. Percy was devastated and Lady Jane, taking charge as the Shelley family manager, changed Mary's burial site to St. Peter's Church, Bournemouth, where she and Percy would live in Boscombe Manor. Lady Jane had the remains of Godwin and Mary Wollstonecraft disinterred, but not those of the second Mrs. Godwin, and buried them with Mary. Shelley's elusive heart (if, indeed, it was not his liver) seemingly was placed either in the common grave or in nearby Christchurch Priory,[134] where Lady Jane beatified Shelley with Henry Weekes's Pietà-like statue of Mary holding the dead Christ-Shelley. Later, in 1891, she commissioned Onslow Ford's statue of a frontal-nude drowned Shelley for his grave in Rome. After it was rejected by Trelawny's daughter, University College installed it near Shelley's rooms.

Sir Percy and his wife, childless, brought her niece, Bessie Florence Gibson, into their home and later legally adopted her.[135] After Mary's death, Lady Jane and Sir Percy commissioned Hogg to write the biography of Shelley. The publication in 1858 of the first two of Hogg's four projected volumes infuriated Percy and Lady Shelley. Reacting to Hogg's deliberate lies, distortions, and self-aggrandizement, they stopped publication. Peacock, Harriet's defender, soon rebutted Hogg's bias against her in *Fraser's Magazine* and in his *Memoirs of Shelley*. Sir Percy, appealing to Leigh Hunt to save "Shelley's beloved memory" from Hogg, elicited Hunt's characterization of Hogg's biography as "This foolish book of an imbecile pretender."

Hunt, who returned with his family to England in 1825 and endured Hazlitt's written attacks on Shelley, eschewed writing his friend's biography. Before his death in 1858, Hunt had written lovingly of Shelley in his 1828 *Lord Byron and Some of His Contemporaries* and in his 1850 *Autobiography*. To counter Hogg's biography, Lady Shelley enlisted the help of Edmund Ollier in publishing a brief adulatory biography as *Shelley Memorials* in 1859. Later, in 1882, her multi-volume *Shelley and Mary* contained letters, excerpts from Mary's journal, and Lady Shelley's handwritten notes blaming Harriet for Shelley's elopement with Mary.

With the death of Sir Percy in 1889 and his wife in 1892, Shelley's only direct descendants are from Ianthe Shelley Esdaile's son Edward. Ianthe died just before her sixty-third birthday in 1876 and is buried under a copper beech tree in the Cothelstone Churchyard, Somerset. Her headstone, unlike that of her brother Charles, recognizes her father. She was the "Daughter of the Poet Shelley."

Notes

1. THE DARK AUTUMN OF SUICIDES

1. To LB, 8 September 1816, *L*, 1:504.
2. To LB, 20 November, 29 September 1816, *L*, 1:512–14, 506–8; to John Murray, 2 October, 30 October 1816, *L*, 1:508–9, 511.
3. CC to LB, 12 September 1816, *CC*, 1:70–71.
4. Ingpen, 469–70.
5. Ingpen, 470; *SC*, 4:825–28.
6. *SC*, 5:27–31.
7. CC to LB, 29 September 1816, *CC*, 1:76–78.
8. FG to MWG, 26 September 1816, *CC*, 1:74–75.
9. *JMS*, 1:138; FG to MWG, 3 October 1816, *CC*, 1:80–82.
10. StC, 410, 552 n. 13.
11. Sunstein, 430 n. 32; *CC*, 1:85 n. 1, 86–89 n. 2; B. R. Pollin, "Fanny Godwin's Suicide Re-examined," *Etudes Anglaises* 18 (July–September 1965): 258–68.
12. Sunstein, 126–27.
13. Box 7, file 2, Silsbee.
14. FG to WG, 8 October 1816, *CC*, 1:85; *JMS*, 1:139.
15. Box 7, file 2, 3, Silsbee.
16. CC to EJT, 30 May 1875, *CC*, 2:629.
17. *JMS*, 1:138–40.
18. *CC*, 1:86; Dowden, 2:57.
19. FG was familiar with Swansea, having visited relatives in May 1814 in adjacent Pentredwr, a trip the Godwins presumably promoted because of her attraction to PBS.
20. CC reported, "When Shelley got to Swansea she was dead & buried." Box 7, file 2, Silsbee. Locke, 274, provides no reference for his statement that PBS saw FG's body.
21. WG to MWG, 13 October 1816, *SM*, 148.
22. Charles Clairmont to MWS, 9 August 1817, *CC*, 1:108.
23. CC to LB, 27 October 1816, *CC*, 1:89.
24. *JMS*, 1:142.
25. *JMS*, 1:141–44; *SC*, 4:767.
26. Box 7, file 2, Silsbee; Peacock, 33.
27. *SG*, 72–73; MS. Shelley adds. c. 4, f. 68 (folder 7), Bodleian.

28. G. M. Matthews, "Whose Little Footsteps? Three Shelley Pieces Re-Addressed," in Donald H. Reiman, Michael C. Jaye, and Betty T. Bennett, eds., *The Evidence of the Imagination* (New York: New York University Press, 1978), 236–63.

29. *SG*, 73.

30. *GWLJ*, 39.

31. Pollin, "Suicide Re-examined," 258–68; *CC*, 1:87–89.

32. To PBS, 17 December 1816, *LMWS*, 1:24.

33. *JMS*, 1:141–45.

34. To LB, 20 November 1816, *L*, 1:512–14.

35. Thompson, 620–21.

36. Dawson, chap. 5; *GY*, 115–19.

37. To R. W. Hayward, 5 November 1816, *SC*, 5:766.

38. To WG, 24 November 1816, *L*, 1:514–15.

39. *JMS*, 1:148; Peck, 2:437; Dowden, 2:61.

40. To PBS, 5 December 1816, *LMWS*, 1:22–24.

41. To LH, 8 December 1816, *L*, 1:516–19.

42. *JMS*, 1:150; *SC*, 5:403.

43. Arthur H. Beavan, *James and Horace Smith* (London, 1899), 136–38.

44. *AM*, 186.

45. Thomas Hookham to PBS, 13 December 1816, *SC*, 4:776–77.

46. To MWG, 16 December 1816, *L*, 1:519–21. For this letter's authenticity, see Newman I. White, Frederick L. Jones, Kenneth N. Cameron, *An Examination of the Shelley Legend* (Philadelphia: University of Pennsylvania Press, 1951), 67–71.

47. Dowden, 2:64.

48. HS to John Frank Newton, 5 June 1816, *L*, 1:476–77.

49. *SC*, 4:776 n. 26.

50. *SC*, 4:777.

51. *AM*, 197. For HS's last days, see *SC*, 4:769–802; *GY*, 42–43, 578 n. 147.

52. WG to William Baxter, 12 May 1817, *SC*, 4:787.

53. *SG*, 75.

54. To MWG, 11 January 1817, *L*, 1:528; *SG*, 75.

55. Dowden, 1:424.

56. *GY*, 41–42. WG's "authority" for his information probably was Eliza Westbrook, who had confided late details about HS to Mrs. Godwin.

57. To Southey, 17 August 1820, *L*, 2:231.

58. Charles Clairmont to Francis Place, 12 January 1816, *CC*, 1:18.

59. CC to EJT, 30 August-21 September 1875, *CC*, 2:631.

60. White, 1:676; *GY*, 578 n. 147.

61. *GY*, 42–43; *SC*, 4:790–91; White, 1:674–76.

62. CC to EJT, 30 August-21 September 1875, *CC*, 2:631–62. Maxwell's regiment was sent to India in March 1816. If Maxwell did not leave until late March, he could have fathered HS's child. See *SC*, 4:791 n. 58; *CC*, 2:633 n. 8.

63. *Records*, 186.

64. Ingpen, 648–50; *SC*, 4:777–81. For the 1859 report that HS avoided "the revolting burial" of suicide, see *SC*, 4:779.

65. *SC*, 4:783 n. 4.

66. Ingpen, 481–82, first reported HS's burial record in the register of the parish of Paddington. PBS may not have known where she was buried. Her exact burial place

is uncertain, but St. George's cemetery on Bayswater Road near Hyde Park is probable. See SC, 4:797–98; *GY,* 43–45, 578 n. 151.

67. *GY,* 44.

68. Ingpen, 649; *SC,* 4:778; *GY,* 45.

69. HS to Eliza Westbrook, ? 7 December 1816, *SC,* 4:802–10.

70. *SC,* 4:795; *Records,* 186.

71. *GY,* 46.

72. *ALH,* 1:28.

73. Peacock, 88–89.

74. To LB, 17 January 1817, *L,* 1:529–30.

75. PBS and MWS to LH and Marianne Hunt, 30 June 1817, *L,* 1:543–44.

76. Peacock, 68.

77. To LB, 17 January 1817, *L,* 1:529–30. A family story suggests Eliza's ill treatment of Ianthe in later years. See *SC,* 5:86 n. 10.

78. To Eliza Westbrook, 18 December 1816, *L,* 1:522–23.

79. Medwin, 468, App. III.

80. *JMS,* 2:560.

81. White, 2:516; *L,* 1:555.

82. Dowden, 2:76.

83. To PBS, 17 December 1816, *LMWS,* 1:25.

84. Peacock, 88; *SC,* 3:96; CC to EJT, ? April 1871, *CC,* 2:617, 618–19 n. 4.

85. StC, 44, 553.

86. Ingpen, App. X.

87. CC to EJT, ? April 1871, *CC,* 2:617. See also R. Glynn Grylls, *Claire Clairmont* (London: John Murray, 1939), 262. StC, 415, gave some credence to this report, but not Sunstein, 431 n.43. Edward Silsbee recorded CC's 1870 comments: "Mary sat one end of Room her parents opposing when Shelley objected he cd not marry against his principles &c &c She advanced put her hand on his shoulder Said . . . if you won't marry me I'll do as Harriet did. The parents left them . . . S. turned very pale. Miss C. says after these 2 deaths/suicides . . . s was never the same." Box 7, file 2, Silsbee.

88. David Booth to Isabel Booth, 9 January 1818, *SC,* 5:391–92; text, London *Star,* 22 March 1894.

89. To CC, 30 December 1816, *SC,* 5:31–33.

90. Mary Jane Godwin to Archibald Constable, 3 February 1817, *SC,* 5:33–34.

91. WG to Hull Godwin, 21 February 1817, C. K. Paul, *William Godwin: His Friends and Contemporaries* (London, 1876), 1:246.

92. *JMS,* 1:152.

93. Sunstein, 128–32.

94. Dowden, 2:77.

95. Medwin, 463–68.

96. White, 2:513–15; Medwin, 468–70; *Shelley's Lost Letters to Harriet,* ed. Leslie Hotson (London: Faber and Faber, 1930).

97. To MWS, 11 January 1817, *L,* 1:527. See also, *SG,* 75; *SC,* 5:85.

98. Medwin, 470.

99. William Whitton to TS, 17 January 1817, Ingpen, 491–92. *A Letter* was not introduced into the trial. See White, 2:515.

100. White, 2:App.IV, 515–17.

101. To LB, 17 January 1817, *SC,* 5:82–83.

102. W. B. Willcox and W. L. Arnstein, *The Age of Aristocracy: 1688 to 1830* (Lexington: University of Kentucky Press, 1983), 277.

103. Dowden, 2:83–84.

104. *JMS*, 1:155–56.

105. Dowden, 2:84; *JMS*,1 :157 n. 4.

106. To CC, 30 January 1817, *SC*, 5:87.

107. Dowden, 2:86–88. See also, StC, 419.

108. Dowden, 2:90.

109. Peacock, 66–67.

110. MWS to Marianne Hunt, 6 August 1817, *LMWS*, 1:40.

111. *SC*, 6:647–52.

2. ALBION HOUSE

1. MWS to LB, 13 January 1817, *LMWS*, 1:26–27; PBS to LB, 17 January 1817, *SC*, 5:82.

2. Peck, 1:520; *SC*, 5:516 n. 6; Dowden, 1:110.

3. Peacock, 64–65.

4. David Booth to Isabel Booth, 9 January 1818, London *Star*, 22 March 1894; *SC*, 5:392.

5. *SC*, 8:827–46.

6. To Hogg, 1 July 1820, *L*, 2:209.

7. Blunden, 170.

8. *ALH*, 2:29; Peacock, 64.

9. *AM*, 187.

10. *ALH*, 2:32–35; Dowden, 2:107.

11. *ALH*, 1:220–21.

12. To PBS, 16 August 1820, *LJK*, 2:323.

13. Dowden, 2:132 n.

14. *ALH*, 2:36.

15. To Benjamin Bailey, 8 October 1817, *LJK*, 1:170.

16. *Autobiography of Benjamin Haydon*, ed. Edmund Blunden (Oxford: Clarendon, 1927), 220–21. See also, *SC*,7:95–96.

17. William Sharp, *Life and Letters of Joseph Severn* (London, 1892), 116–17.

18. To the Shelleys, 11 July 1821, *The Correspondence of Leigh Hunt*, ed. Thornton Hunt (London, 1862) 1:166. See also, *JMS*, 1:163; Dawson, 187.

19. To LH, 27 September 1819, *L*, 2:123.

20. To PBS, 17 December 1816, *LMWS*, 1:25. For Coulson, see *SC*, 5:314–18.

21. *SC*, 5:104–17.

22. To LB, 23 April 1817, *L*, 1:539. See also, Sunstein, 130.

23. Thompson, 631–49; Scrivener, 108–12.

24. To Charles Ollier, 22 February 1817, *L*, 1:534. See also, *SC*, 5:124–29; Murray, 1:415.

25. R. G. Thorne, *The History of Parliament: The House of Commons 1790–1812*, vol. 5 (London: Secher and Warburg, 1986).

26. *GY*, 121–27; Dawson, 170–75; Scrivener, 112–19; *SC*, 9:241–45.

27. Dawson, 170–71, 187–89.

28. Murray, 1:246–71, 459–60.

29. Murray, 1:175–76.

30. To Ollier, ? February 1817, *L*, 1:532–34. See also, Murray, 1:316–17; Scrivener, 115–16.

31. *GY*, 123, 592 n. 27, 28; Scrivener, 109, 118.

32. *JMS*, 1:166.

33. *ALH*, 2:30; Hunt, 192; *SC*, 5:482.

34. *JMS*, 1:166–69; Robinson, 1:lxxxiv–lxxxv.

35. *JMS*, 1:167 n. 2.

36. *ALH*, 2:30–31.

37. Peacock, 70; *ALH*, 2:28–29.

38. Dowden, 2:121–22.

39. *ALH*, 2:30.

40. *JMS*, 1:169; Robinson, 1:lxxxv–lxxxviii.

41. Robinson, 1:lxvi–lxxi.

42. To Lackington, Allen & Company, 23 October 1817, *L*, 1:565.

43. To PBS, 24 September 1817, *LMWS*, 1:42.

44. *JMS*, 2:App.I.

45. PBS to Joseph Kirkman, 24 April 1817, *SC*, 6:522.

46. Dowden, 2:115.

47. Peacock, 45–46; *JMS*, 1:170, 194 n. 4.

48. To Lackington, Allen & Company, 22 August 1817, *L*, 1:553. See also, Robinson, 1:lxxxvii–lxxxviii; *SC*, 5:27–31, 395–98.

49. *PW*, 544–55; *SG*, 79.

50. To LB, 9 July 1817, *L*, 1:546–47.

51. *SC*, 5:142–51.

52. *SC*, 5:405–6 n. 16. Keats began *Endymion* April 1817, completing the draft in November.

53. *JMS*, 1:176–77.

54. To Hogg, 6 July 1817, *L*, 1:545–46; *JMS*, 1:177.

55. To PBS, 24 September 1817, *LMWS*, 1:41.

56. Obituary of Miss Selina Furnivall, age 100, London *Times*, 29 April 1926.

57. Ibid.

58. Peacock, 65–66.

59. *AM*, 188–89.

60. To PBS, 24 September 1817, *LMWS*, 1:42.

61. To Marianne Hunt, 6 August 1817, *LMWS*, 1:39.

62. Robinson, 1:lxxxviii–lxxxvix.

63. MS. Shelley adds. c. 4, fols. 184–85 [184r], Bodleian; *BSM*, 13. Printed in *SG*, 83.

64. *BSM*, 13:189–203.

65. *SC*, 5:145–46 n. 13; to PBS, 28 September 1817, *LMWS*, 1:45.

66. To LB, 24 September 1817, *L*, 1:556.

67. *SC*, 5:293.

68. To PBS, 26 September 1817, *LMWS*, 1:43.

69. Dowden, 2:120, 123–24; *SG*, 93.

70. To MWS, 6 October 1817, *L*, 1:560.

71. To PBS, 28 September 1817, *LMWS*, 1:47.

72. To Brookes & Company, 29 September 1817, *L*, 1:560.

73. To PBS, ? 2 October 1817, *LMWS,* 1:50.

74. To PBS, 5 October 1817, *LMWS,* 1:52.

75. To PBS, 30 September 1817, *LMWS,*1:49.

76. To PBS, 18 October 1817, *LMWS,* 1:57.

77. To MWS, 8 October 1817, *L,* 1:561–63.

78. To PBS, 18 October 1817, *LMWS,* 1:56–57.

79. Ingpen, 522–26; White, 1:541.

80. To MWS, 6, 8 October 1817, *L,* 1:560–62.

81. Sunstein, 146.

82. To George and Tom Keats, 21, ? 27 December 1817, *LJK,* 1:194.

83. Thompson, 668.

84. *JMS,* 1:183–84; Murray, 1:447–51; *SC,* 5:125 n. 7.

85. *SC,* 5:301.

86. London *Star,* 1 March 1894; *SC,* 5:339–40.

87. London *Star,* 15, 22 March 1894; *SC,* 5:388–92.

88. *PW,* 188.

89. Judith Chernaik, *TLS,* 6 February 1969; Chernaik, 195–97; *SPP,* 107–8.

90. *JCC,* 79; to Ollier, 22 January 1818, *L,* 1:594. See also, *CW,* 3:328; *SC,* 2:910–12.

91. Chernaik, 195, 197 n. 44.

92. *GY,* 296–97.

93. Box 7, file 2, Silsbee; *JCC,* 143 n. 41; *CW,* 10:252 n. 2.

94. To LB, 24 September 1817, *L,* 1:556–58.

95. To [A Publisher], 13 October 1817, *L,* 1:563–64. See also, Charles E. Robinson, "Percy Bysshe Shelley, Charles Ollier, and William Blackwood," in Everest, 190–91.

96. To Ollier, 3 December 1817, *L,* 1:571.

97. To WG, 1 December 1817, *L,* 1:569–70.

98. To WG, 7 December 1817, *L,* 1:572–74.

99. To WG, 11 December 1817, *L,*1:576–78.

100. *SC,* 5:161.

101. *SC,* 5:163–64; *SC,* 9:247–50; Thompson, 721–22.

102. To Ollier, 11 December 1817, *L,* 1:579.

103. To Ollier, 13 December 1817, *L,* 1:581–82.

104. Peacock, 65, 88–89; *JMS,* 1:187.

105. *CW,* 1:422–27.

106. To Thomas Moore, 16 December 1817, *L,* 1:582–83. See also *SC,* 5:350–53.

107. *UH,* 125–26; *RR,* 136; Robert Morrison, "De Quincey, Champion of Shelley," *KSJ* 41 (1992): 36–41.

108. *UH,* 133.

109. *SC,* 6:931 n. 15.

110. *PW,* 35–37.

111. Stuart M. Sperry, "The Sexual Theme in Shelley's *The Revolt of Islam,*" *Journal of English and Germanic Philology* 82 (January 1983): 32–49; Sperry, chap. 3; Reiman, 34–43; John Donovan, "Incest in *Laon and Cythna:* Nature, Custom, Desire," *KSR* 2 (1987): 49–90; Peter Finch, "Shelley's *Laon and Cythna:* The Bride Stripped Bare . . . Almost," *KSR* 3 (1988): 23–46; Brown, Ch. 10; Teddi Lynn Chichester, "Shelley's Imaginative Transsexualism in *Laon and Cythna,*" *KSJ* 45 (1996): 77–101; J. Andrew Hubbell, "*Laon and Cythna:* A Vision of Regency Romanticism," *KSJ* 51 (2002): 174–97.

112. To [A Publisher], 13 October 1817, *L,*1:563–64.

113. Sperry, 50.
114. *JMS*, 1:75; Peck, 1:430; Sperry, 45, 210 n. 10.
115. Sperry, 48.
116. Richard Cronin, *Shelley's Poetic Thoughts* (New York: St. Martin's Press, 1981), 98.
117. Sperry, 60.

3. "Paradise of exiles, Italy"

1. To LB, 17 December 1817, *L*, 1:583–84; *SC*, 5:363–64.
2. To Douglas Kinnaird, 13 January 1818, *BLJ*, 6:7.
3. Horace Smith, "A Greybeard's Gossip about his Literary Acquaintance," *New Monthly Magazine and Humorist*, 79 (1847): 289–90.
4. *SPP*, 109. Earlier erroneous accounts of the sonnet's origin in Holmes, 410, and in H. M. Richmond, "Ozymandias and the Travelers," *KSJ* 11 (1962): 65–71, were refuted. See Tony Venables, "The Lost Traveller," *KSR* 15 (2001): 15–21. See also E. M. Waith, "Ozymandias: Shelley, Horace Smith, and Denon," *KSJ* 44 (1995): 22–28; M. K. Bequette, "Shelley and Smith: Two Sonnets on Ozymandias," *KSJ* 26 (1977): 29–31.
5. To [Sir Walter Scott], 2 January 1818, *L*, 1:590.
6. Medwin, 193.
7. *PW*, 157.
8. *JMS*, 1:189
9. WG to MWS, 5 January 1818, *L*, 1:592.
10. *JCC*, 79; CC to LB, 12 January 1818, *CC*, 1:109–11.
11. *JCC*, 81; Ingpen, 517.
12. *SC*, 5:478–92.
13. WG to PBS, 31 January 1818, *L*, 1:597–98.
14. *SC*, 5:482.
15. To George and Tom Keats, ? 14 February 1818, *LJK*, 1:227–28. See also, *PW*, 552.
16. *JCC*, 83. Keats, declining Smith's invitation, requested, "Remember me to Shelley." See John Keats to Horace Smith, 19 February 1818, *LJK*, 1:234.
17. LH to MWS, 25–27 July, 1819, *SC*, 6:846.
18. *JMS*, 1:193; *JCC*, 83.
19. *JMS*, 1:194.
20. *SC*, 5:507–8; Sunstein, 148.
21. *JMS*, 1:196; *L*, 2:65 n. 1.
22. White, 1:559–60.
23. Ingpen, 529; *JMS*, 1:196.
24. *JMS*, 1:197; *SC*, 5:511–12; *SC*, 6:579.
25. Murray, 1:285–88, 492.
26. Peacock, 70.
27. TLP to Hogg, 20 March 1818, *SC*, 6:518–22.
28. *SC*, 5:497.
29. PBS to Brookes & Company, 12 March 1818, *SC*, 5:514–16.
30. To LH, 13 March 1818, *L*, 2:1.
31. *JMS*, 1:197–98; MWS to the Hunts, 22 March 1818, *LMWS*, 1:62–63.
32. *SC*, 6:527 n. 8; Brown, 9; *JMS*, 1:198 n. 3.
33. *SC*, 6:528 n. 10; *JMS*, 1:198 n. 4.

34. To LH and Marianne Hunt, 22 March 1818, *L*, 2:2–3.

35. *JCC*, 88; *JMS*, 1:200.

36. *JMS*, 1:200.

37. *CC*, 1:114; *CC*, 2:603; MWS to PBS, 29 May 1817, *LMWS*, 1:36. See also Emily W. Sunstein, "Louise Duvillard of Geneva, the Shelley's Nursemaid," *KSJ* 29 (1980): 27–30; Sunstein, 429 n. 7. Elise (b. 1795) was listed in the Geneva census at the Duvillard-Romieux address until the end of 1815. If Aimée was Elise's child, her age was about five months when Elise joined the Shelley household in Geneva in 1816. For an assertion that Elise was a mother at this time, see Mrs. Julian Marshall, *The Life and Letters of Mary Wollstonecraft Shelley*, 2 vols. (London, 1889), 1:234. MWS's statement in her 6 April 1818 letter to the Hunts that "Aimee is very beautiful with . . . a more beautiful mouth than her Mothers expressive of greatest sensibility" seems more likely a comparison with Elise's mouth than with that of Elise's mother, whom the Hunts had never met.

38. *JCC*, 88–89.

39. To TLP, 6 April 1818, *L*, 2:4; *JMS*, 1:202.

40. To the Hunts, 6 April 1818, *LMWS*, 1:64.

41. To TLP, 20 April 1818, *L*, 2:7–8.

42. To TLP, 6 April 1818, *L*, 2:4; MWS to the Hunts, 6 April 1818, *LMWS*, 1:64.

43. To TLP, 20 April 1818, *L*, 2:8.

44. *JMS*, 1:92, 98.

45. To LB, 24 September 1817, *L*, 1:556–57.

46. To TLP, 20 April 1818, *L*, 2:6.

47. *JCC*, 91.

48. To LB, 13 April 1818, *L*, 2:5.

49. To LB, 22 April 1818, *CC*, 1:113–14.

50. To James Wedderburn Webster, 8 September 1818, to Hobhouse, 3 March 1818, *BLJ*, 6:66, 19. LB signed a codicil to his will on November 1818 bequeathing £5000 to "Allegra Biron" upon becoming twenty-one or married, conditioned upon her not marrying "a Native of Great Britain." See *SC*, 6:748.

51. *JMS*, 1:207; *SC*, 5:452.

52. To TLP, 20 April 1818, *L*, 2:9.

53. To LB, 22 April 1818, *SC*, 6:564–66.

54. To Hobhouse, 24 April 1818, *BLJ*, 6:37.

55. To Augusta Leigh, 21 September 1818, *BLJ*, 6:69.

56. To LB, 28 April 1818, *L*, 2:12–13.

57. To CC, 24 March 1822, *L*, 2:400.

58. To LB 24 March 1821; to EJT, 1870, *CC*, 1:163–64; *CC*, 2:603–4.

59. *JMS*, 2:585. MWS perhaps was sensitive about the Godwins' attacks on PBS imparted in 1814 to Lady Mount Cashell in London after MWS and PBS eloped. See *SC*, 8:912–13.

60. *JMS*, 1:209.

61. WG to Maria Gisborne, 10 March 1818, *SC*, 5:512.

62. *JCC*, 468–70; *GWJL*, 3–6; *SC*, 10:1116–23.

63. *PW*, 635.

64. PBS to Hogg, 30 April 1818, *SC*, 6:584.

65. *JMS*, 1:211. For the fate of MWS's transcription of "Relazione della morte della Famiglia Cenci, seguita in Roma il de 11 Maggio, 1599," completed 25 May 1818, see *SC*, 5:464; *SC*, 6:896–98.

66. To TLP, 24 August 1819, *L*, 2:114. "Slawkenburgian" is from Sterne's *Tristram Shandy*.

67. To the Hunts, 13 May 1818, *LMWS*, 1:66–68.

68. WG to PBS, 8 June 1818, *SM*, 281–83.

69. To LB, 17 May 1818, *CC*, 1:116–17.

70. MWS to Maria Gisborne, 5 June 1818, *LMWS*, 1:71; *JMS*, 1:212; *SC*, 6:599.

71. To TLP, 5 June 1818, *L*, 2:18.

72. To Maria Gisborne, 26 July 1818, *LMWS*, 1:76.

73. Biographers since Dowden (Dowden, 2:210 n) have speculated that G. B. Chiappa was either the owner or manager of Casa Bertini. However, Domenico Bertini's descendant, Francesco Bertini, probably still owned the house. See *SC*, 6:657 n. 2. There is no indication the Shelleys changed residences in Bagni di Lucca. PBS's 23 August 1818 letter to MWS (*L*, 2:38) is addressed to her at "Casa Bertini," which has often been confused (as in Holmes, 336, 424) with adjacent Villa del Chiappa.

74. To Maria Gisborne, 15 June 1818, *LMWS*, 1:72–73. Casa Bertini is divided into two living quarters, each with their own entrance. The garden MWS described is that of Villa del Chiappa. Signore Chiappa probably offered the use of his garden to the new arrivals.

75. To Maria Gisborne, 15 June 1818, *LMWS*, 1:72–73.

76. *JMS*, 1:216.

77. Medwin, 198; Dowden, 2:215; Peck, 2:86.

78. To Ollier, 28 June 1818, *L*, 2:19.

79. To Ollier, 16 August 1818, *L*, 2:31–32. This undated letter had the same London postmark, "1 September 1818" as PBS's 16 August letter to TLP.

80. *SC*, 6:666–68. Presumably WG was not the third party as PBS sent him £50 in July. See also, PBS to Brookes, Son & Dixon, 31 July 1818, *SC*, 6:653.

81. On June 28 and August 16 (*JMS*, 1:216, 223) PBS wrote "Zuchino" in MWS's journal, possibly misspelling zecchino, a small coin (sequin) of the time. Such entries possibly were records of payments to "A. B." or of household payments.

82. *JMS*, 1:222; MWS to Maria Gisborne, 17 August 1818, *LMWS*, 1:77.

83. *JMS*, 1:219.

84. To TLP, 26 July 1818, *L*, 2:25.

85. To TLP, 26 July 1818, *L*, 2:25–26.

86. Ibid.; *SC*, 6:659 n. 5.

87. *SC*, 6:618–33.

88. G. M. Matthews, "A New Text of Shelley's Scene for *Tasso*," *KSMB* 11 (1960): 39–47; *SC*, 6:591.

89. To TLP, 26 July 1818, *L*, 2:20.

90. *CW*, 7:227.

91. *JMS*, 1:217–22.

92. To WG; to TLP, 26 July 1818, *L*, 2:22, 20.

93. Benjamin Farrington, "The Text of Shelley's Translation of the Symposium of Plato," *Modern Language Review* 14 (1919): 325–26. Quoted in *GY*, 303.

94. *On Love* was possibly a "prefatory essay" that evolved into the *Discourse*. See *SC*, 6:633–39.

95. Crompton, 20.

96. To TLP, 16 August 1818, *L*, 2:29.

97. Crompton, 19–21, App.

98. *Prose*, 222.

99. Crompton, 288–91; Kenneth J. Dover, *Greek Homosexuality* (Cambridge: Harvard University Press, 1978; updated 1989).

100. *Prose*, 221; James A. Notopolous, *The Platonism of Shelley* (Durham, N.C.: Duke University Press, 1949), 409–10, 531–32.

101. *Prose*, 223.

102. To Ollier, 16 August 1818, *L*, 2:31.

103. To WG, 26 July 1818, *L*, 2:22.

104. To Maria Gisborne, 26 July 1818, *LMWS*, 1:75.

105. To TLP, 16 August 1818, *SC*, 6:656–57.

106. *JMS*, 1:223.

107. Iris Origo, *Allegra* (London: Hogarth Press, 1935), 39.

108. To Augusta Leigh, 3 August 1818, to John Murray, 3 August 1818, *BLJ*, 6:62.

109. To MWS, 19 August 1818, *L*, 2:32; *JMS*, 1:223.

110. To Maria Gisborne, 17 August 1818, *LMWS*, 1:77–78.

111. To TLP, 6 April 1819, *L*, 2:94.

112. To MWS, 19 August 1818, *L*, 2:32–34. See also *SC*, 6:679 n. 11.

4. EUGANEAN ISLES OF MISERY

1. To MWS, 23–24 August 1818, *L*, 2:34–38. For MWS's censored version of this letter, see *SC*, 6:672–75.

2. To TLP, 8 October 1818, *L*, 2:42.

3. To MWS, 23 August 1818, *L*, 2:36.

4. To TLP, 8 October 1818, *L*, 2:42.

5. *Byron*, 2:759.

6. To MWS, 23–24 August 1818, *L*, 2:36–37.

7. *JMS*, 1:225

8. To LB, 13 September 1818, *L*, 2:38.

9. *JMS*, 1:225.

10. *JMS*, 1:226; to Maria Gisborne, c. 13 September 1818, *LMWS*, 1:78–79.

11. To Maria Gisborne, c. 13 September, *LMWS*, 1:78–79.

12. *JMS*, 1:226.

13. *BSM*, 9:lxvi; to MWS, 22 September 1818, *L*, 2:39–40.

14. *PW*, 203–4.

15. To LB, 13 September 1818, *L*, 2:38–39.

16. To MWS, 22 September 1818, *L*, 2:40.

17. To Augusta Leigh, 21 September 1818, *BLJ*, 6:69.

18. To EJT, 26 July 1831, *LMWS*, 2:143–44. CC told LB (October 1816) he was "afraid of me." See *CC*, 1:83–84.

19. To MWS, [22 September 1818], *L*, 2:39–40.

20. To CC, 25 September 1818, *L*, 2:40–41.

21. CC always recorded regular 27–28 day intervals of her periods in her journal.

22. *SC*, 6:694.

23. WG to MWS, 27 October 1818, Dowden, 2:232.

24. To CC, 25 September 1818, *L*, 2:41.

25. To LB, 3 October 1818, *LMWS*, 1:80. See also *JMS*, 1:228; Sunstein, 160; *Byron*, 2:744 n.

26. MS 408, Pierpont Morgan Library, reprinted in StC, 465, and (in part) Dawson, 49. See also CG, 241 n. 33; *SC*, 6:956.

27. To TLP, 8 October 1818, *L*, 2:43.

28. *PW*, 167; PBS's Advertisement to *Rosalind and Helen*.

29. To Maria Gisborne, 2 November 1818, *LMWS*, 1:80–81.

30. Ibid.

31. To LB, 17 October 1818, *L*, 2:44.

32. To TLP, 8 October 1818, *SC*, 6:662; *L*, 2:44.

33. To TLP, 17–18 December 1818, *L*, 2:58.

34. Crompton, 243–44.

35. To Hogg, 21 December 1818, *L*, 2:69.

36. To TLP, 17–18 December 1818, *L*, 2:58.

37. *SC*, 6:857–65.

38. *YS*, 256, 613 n. 13; *Byron*, 2:720.

39. White, 2:46; *YS*, 261.

40. To TLP, 8 October 1818, *L*, 2:42.

41. *Don Juan*, Dedication, stanzas 3 and 11; "dry bob" meant coition without emission.

42. *Shelley and Byron*, 63.

43. Chernaik, 239; *Shelley and Byron*, 111, 264 n. 38; *SPP*, 137 n. 1.

44. To TLP, 6–7 November 1818, *L*, 2:45–48; *JMS*, 1:235; to Maria Gisborne, c. 3 December 1818, *LMWS*, 1:83.

45. To TLP, 7 November 1818, *L*, 2:47.

46. G. M. Matthews, "A New Text of Shelley's Scene for Tasso," *KSMB* 11 (1960): 39–47.

47. To TLP, 25 February 1819, *L*, 2:80–81.

48. To LH, c. 20 August 1820, *L*, 1:112.

49. JMS, 1:236.

50. *JMS*, 1:222 n. 1, 235–36 n. 6.

51. To TLP, 20 November 1818, *L*, 2:54–57; *JMS*, 1:236.

52. To TLP, 20 November 1818, *LMWS*, 1:82; *L*, 2:57.

53. To TLP, 17–18 December 1818, *L*, 2:58–60.

54. *Shelley and Byron*, 76–80.

55. *Shelley Papers*, 129.

56. *EL*, 1:x.

57. Medwin, 207.

58. *Shelley Papers*, 50.

59. To TLP, 17–18 December 1818, *L*, 1:60.

60. To Maria Gisborne, c. 3 December 1818, *LMWS*, 1:83.

61. To TLP, 17–18 December 1818, *L*, 1:60; MWS to Maria Gisborne, *LMWS*, 1:83.

5. PARADISE OF DEVILS

1. To TLP, ?18–19 December 1818, *L*, 2:60.

2. To Sophia Stacey, 7 March 1820, *LMWS*, 1:130. For complete letter, see *KSJ* 56 (1997):53–56.

3. *JMS*, 1:245.

4. *Shelley Papers*, 51.

5. Madame de Staël, *Corinne, or Italy,* trans. and ed. A. H. Goldberger (New Brunswick: Rutgers University Press, 1987), Introd.; J. C. Herrold, *Mistress of an Age: A Life of Madame de Staël* (New York: Bobbs-Merrill, 1958), chap. 15.

6. *JMS,* 1:242.

7. To TLP, ?18–19 December 1818, *L*,2:61.

8. To Hogg, 21 December 1818, *L,* 2:69.

9. To TLP, ?18–19 December 1818, *L,* 2:57–64.

10. *JMS,* 1:244.

11. To LH, ? 20 December 1818, *L,* 2:68.

12. To Hogg, 21 December 1818, *L,* 2:69.

13. *SG,* 105; *L,* 2:74 n 10.

14. To TLP, 23–24 January 1819, *L,* 2:70–76.

15. *L,* 2:71 n 5.

16. *JMS,* 1:245; Robinson, 1:xcvii.

17. CG, 112–15.

18. To TLP, 23–24 January 1819, *L,* 2:76; MWS to Maria Gisborne, 22 January 1819, *LMWS,* 1:85.

19. To TLP, 25 February 1819, *L,* 2:82.

20. CG, 113, 115; Roskilly practiced medicine in Naples until his death in 1864.

21. *EL,* 2:194.

22. Charles MacFarlane, *Reminiscences of a Literary Life,* ed. J. F. Tattersall (London: Murray, 1917), 6.

23. To TLP, 23–24 January 1819, *L,* 2:76; to Maria Gisborne, 22 January 1819, *LMWS,* 1:84–85.

24. To Isabella Hoppner, 10 August 1821, *LMWS,* 1:206. No record of the Naples marriage has been found. See Roe, 172.

25. Marcel Kessel, "The Mark of X in Claire Clairmont's Journals," *PMLA* 66 (December 1951):1180–83. Resuming her journal 7 March 1819, CC recorded her next period on 22 March (*JCC,* 102). Assuming her rather regular twenty-eight–day cycle, the onset of her period the previous December could have been the twenty-seventh.

26. White, 2:App.VII. Further independent investigations produced "only inconclusive negative evidence" about the child and its parentage. See *CC,* 2:App.B.

27. "Padurin" perhaps was a phonetic rendering of Godwin which PBS did not correct and which appeared accurately on the birth registration but as "Gebuin" on the death certificate. Both White, 2:71, and Holmes, 46, inaccurately state the birth registration gives 7 P.M. as the time of birth; it was the time PBS appeared to register the child on 27 February 1819.

28. PBS gave his occupation on the birth certificate as "Proprietario," proprietor; on the death certificate it was "Possidente," landowner.

29. My 1997 visit to Vico Canale confirms Roe, 176, that it is a "rather poor" neighborhood. No. 45, opening onto the crowded, narrow, and dark street, is in a building occupying the entire block. Roe found in the 1950s a family named Liguori had left the neighborhood for Sicily about 1920.

30. *CC,* 2:650.

31. CG, 54–68.

32. Holmes, 483.

33. To WG, 25 July 1818, *L,* 2:21; to Maria Gisborne, 17 August 1818, *LMWS,* 1:77–78. MWS perhaps had earlier mentioned a possible trip to Naples to the Gisbornes.

34. Medwin, 210, 116.

35. Roe, 174–75. MWS (*LMWS*,1:86) wrote to Maria Gisborne, 22 January 1819, of a Carbonari conspiracy in Spain. Edward Silsbee noted in 1875–1876 that CC "has often said she thinks Shelley joined the Carbonari" and that she "has a great desire to know whether he was a Carbonari thinks he might have been & that his great [?aversion] to Byron was caused by this perhaps." See Box 7, file 3, Silsbee.

36. To the Gisbornes ? 7 July 1820, *L*, 2:211; *GY*, 73.

37. Elise Foggi to MWS, 26 July 1821, *LMWS*, 1:208.

38. *LAS*, 85–86.

39. Dowden, 2:4–5, 252; box 7, file 3, Silsbee; box 8, file 4, Silsbee; *CC*, 2:651. CC told Edward Silsbee in 1875 and 1876 about "the lady at Naples" and CC's "promise" not to divulge her name. Marion K. Stocking, letter to author, 6 January 1993, believed Dowden's reference to W. M. Rossetti as the source of this information concerning CC's knowledge of the lady came from a reported conversation or from manuscripts now lost that were among the Forman papers.

40. *GY*, 72.

41. *JCC*, 110.

42. Medwin, 204–8; *Shelley Papers*, 50–51; *Conversations*, 254.

43. Nora Crook, email to the author, 5 July 2003. I am indebted to Crook's astute observations.

44. *GY*, 583 n. 32. Emily Sunstein, telephone conversation with the author, November 25, 1992, expressed the same belief.

45. Roe, 171; *GY*, 583 n. 34. For Stocking's excellent summary of Elena Adelaide Shelley and the possible Campbell involvement, see *CC*, 2:App.B. Cameron, *GY*, 583, noted that Lady Charlotte's daughter Adelaide Constance was presumably a child at that time and that a possible source for the name Adelaide was Amelia Adelaide of Saxe-Meineingen who in July 1818 married the Duke of Clarence and later was Queen Adelaide.

46. Pam Perkins, "Lady Charlotte Susan Maria Campbell Bury, 1775–1861," in *Scottish Women Writers of the Romantic Period*, eds. Stephen Behrendt and Nancy Kushigan (Alexandria, VA: Alexander Street Press, 2002) [web].

47. Harriet Charlotte Beaujolois Campbell, *A Journey to Florence in 1817*, ed. Sir Gavin de Beer (London: G. Bless, 1951). I am indebted to Marion K. Stocking for alerting me to the late Sir Gavin's helpful archives on Lady Charlotte, Rare Manuscripts Department of University College Library, London. See also, *Three Generations of Fascinating Women*, Lady Constance Russell of Swallowfield (London, 1904); *Memoirs of a Highland Lady: The Autobiography of Elizabeth Grant* (London, 1898); [Lady Charlotte Bury], *Diary of a Lady in Waiting* (London: John Lane, 1908) Introd.; *DNB*, 8:22–23.

48. Lady Charlotte sailed on the royal yacht in 1815 from Villefranche to Genoa to join the Princess of Wales. The yacht's commander, Captain Pechell, later purchased Castle Goring from PBS's son. Lady Charlotte's surviving daughter Bianca by her second marriage married David Lyon of Goring Park, Sussex.

49. Perkins, "Lady Charlotte Bury."

50. Harriet Campbell, *Journey to Florence*, preface; entry February 1818.

51. *Memoir and Correspondence of Susan Ferrier*, ed. J. A. Doyne (London, 1898).

52. Harriet wrote in her journal, 15 February 1818, "After three weeks with us Eliza went to Naples"; on 12 April 1818, "Eleanora is gone to Naples. I could write much, but I am unable. Perhaps at some future period I may again endeavour to relate all

that has happened. The last weeks have been a trial for me." On 4 May 1818 Harriet, age fifteen, wrote: "A curious vacuum has taken place in my journal. I fear it is one which will never be filled up. Yet why should I regret it: All I could have written would have been painful: and as such why should I wish to prolong sad remembrance . . . time had effaced the feeling of disgust natural to all belonging to it, I should not probably have liked to pursue some account. . . . I have received a stroke which I could hardly have expected to have effected me so much." Although this may refer to Lady Charlotte's marriage to Bury, the earlier references to Eliza and Eleanora going to Naples may be relevant. Traveling to Camaldoli, near Florence, with her mother, her younger sister Adelaide, and a man named Rawson, Harriet wrote on 16 July 1818, "Mr. Bury met us . . . [he] nervous at meeting Rawson. Harriet had quarrel with Mamma about a letter to Eleanora which was written perhaps too freely. She had promised to tell the whole story to Bury and I was afraid that we should immediately be at swords draw. But all went smoothly." In August 1818, Harriet was with her mother and Bury looking for a house in Siena before they went to Rome the end of November 1818. That Lady Charlotte gave her daughters born in Italy the Italian name Bianca indicates Elena Adelaide need not reflect Italian parentage.

53. Birthdates for the three youngest Campbell daughters are inconsistent: Adelaide, probably born 1808, married Lord Arthur Lennox in 1835, had five children and died 1888; Emma, probably born 1806, married William Russell in 1828 and died 1886; Julia, perhaps born before 1806, married Peter Brooke in 1836 and died 1858.

54. Medwin, 280; *JCC,* 189; Dowden, 2:370.

55. *JCC,* 229. CC lived in Florence when Harriet Campbell married there, February 1821. CC, active in Florentine society, mentioned on 3 March 1821 (*JCC,* 213), "News of one of Lady Oxford's daughters" in Geneva. Lady Oxford, once a lover of LB, was a close friend of Lady Charlotte Bury.

56. Box 7, file 3, Silsbee (22 July 1875); box 8, file 4, Silsbee (April 1876). See also, *CC,* 2:651.

57. CC wrote MWS in 1845 that a woman acquaintance "got into a scrape" and had to get married. See *CC,* 2:446.

58. Stocking considered March 12 to May 7, 1818, as the probable conception dates; Reiman considered the dates to be March 15 to June 1, with a high probability it was between April 1 and April 15. See *CC,* 2:645; *SC,* 6:578.

59. *JCC,* 91; *SC,* 5:452; *JMS,* 1:207.

60. To TLP, 20 April 1818, *L,* 2:6.

61. To the Gisbornes, 6 April 1819, *L,* 2:90.

62. The first act to legalize adoption in England was in 1819; not until 1926 was complete legal status available. See White, 2:79, 571 n. 107.

63. Lovell, 315–16.

64. To Maria Gisborne, 22 January 1819, *LMWS,* 1:85–86.

65. Medwin, 207–8.

66. *PW,* 570–71.

67. White, 2:78, 570–71 n. 106. William Michael Rossetti, *Athenaeum,* July 15, 1882 (No. 2855): 79, reported his conversation with EJT: "Shelley, he says, attempted suicide in Naples."

68. To Ollier, 10 November 1820, *L,* 2:246.

69. White, 2:51. Fraistat notes, "a more accurate list awaits further work in dating." See *BSM,* 9:xciii.

70. White, 2:51.

71. *BSM*, 9:lviii.

72. Chernaik, 82 n. 15.

73. *JMS*, 1:248; to TLP, 25 February 1819, *L*, 2:77.

74. MacFarlane, *Reminiscences*, chap. 1; Peck, 2:113–14; White, 2:64–65, 566–67. Neither MWS nor PBS mentioned meeting MacFarlane. As White indicated, Mac-Farlane's account should be accepted as genuine, but distortion in some details undoubtedly occurred after thirty-seven years.

75. To Maria Gisborne, 26 February 1819, *LMWS*, 1:87.

76. To Ollier, 27 February 1819, *L*, 2:83.

77. *JMS*, 1:249.

78. The novel's attack occurred at an inn in Terracina, where the Shelleys stayed after leaving Capua.

6. ROMAN TRAGEDY AND CREATIVITY

1. *JMS*, 1:250–51; to TLP, 23 March 1819, *L*, 2:83–84.

2. *JCC*, 99.

3. To TLP, 23 March 1819, *L*, 2:87.

4. To TLP, 6 April 1819, *L*, 2:93; *JCC*, 104.

5. To Maria Gisborne, 26 April 1819, *LMWS*, 1:95.

6. To Hobhouse, 31 March 1817, *BLJ*, 5:199.

7. *JCC*, 100.

8. To Marianne Hunt, 12 March 1819, *LMWS*, 1:88–90; *JMS*, 1:253.

9. To TLP, 6 April 1819, *L*, 2:94; *SPP*, 202–3.

10. To the Gisbornes, 6 April 1819, *L*, 2:90.

11. To LH, 6 April 1819, *LMWS*, 1:90.

12. To Maria Gisborne, 9 April 1819, *LMWS*, 1:93.

13. To Maria Gisborne, 26, 27 April 1819, *LMWS*, 1:94, 96.

14. *JCC*, 104.

15. *DNB*.

16. *JMS*, 1:278–80.

17. To LB, 18 May 1819, *CC*, 1:127–28. See also, *CG*, 112, 115.

18. Chap. 16; *CG*, 108; Gelpi, 131 n. 5.

19. *JCC*, 101, 104.

20. To LH, 6 April, to Marianne Hunt, 12 March 1819, *LMWS*, 1:90–92, 89.

21. To Maria Gisborne, 9 April 1819, *LMWS*, 1:93–94.

22. To John Murray, 15 May 1819, *BLJ*, 6:126; Robinson, 1:xcviii.

23. G. M. Matthews, "'Julian and Maddalo':the Draft and the Meaning," *Studia Neophilologica* XXXV (1963): 57–84; *SC*, 6:858–65.

24. *PW*, 335; Barbara Groseclose, "A Portrait Not by Guido Reni of a Girl Who is not Beatrice Cenci," in *Studies in Eighteenth-Century Culture*, ed. H. C. Payne, vol. 2 (Madison: University of Wisconsin, 1982), 107–32. MWS stated they also saw a Beatrice portrait at the Palazzo Doria.

25. *JMS*, 1:263; *SPP*, 144–45.

26. To LB, ? 15 May 1819, *CC*, 1:127.

27. Dowden, 2:328–29.

28. To LB, ? 15 May 1819, *CC*, 1:126–28.

29. To Hobhouse, 6 April 1819, *BLJ*, 6:108; *Byron*, 2:773–74; *SC*, 7:384–85.

30. *JCC*, 108.

31. To Maria Gisborne, 26 April 1819, *LMWS*, 1:94.

32. Box 8, file 3, Silsbee.

33. PBS first met Amelia Curran in 1812, the year Aaron Burr described her as having the "genius and eloquence of her father." Henry Crabb Robinson found her "very plain" but "free and sometimes graceful in her freedom." See *JCC*, 108 n. 34; *SC*, 6:498–500.

34. *JCC*, 110.

35. Ibid., 111. For the fate of Amelia Curran's portraits of MWS and PBS, see *JMS*, 1:264 n. 3; *JMS*, 2:496 n. 2.

36. *SC*, 5:500. PBS's 5 August 1819 letter to Amelia Curran, (*L*, 2:107), suggests he had not paid her for the portraits.

37. To Maria Gisborne, 11 May 1819, *LMWS*, 1:97.

38. To Maria Gisborne, 30 May 1819, *LMWS*, 1:97–98.

39. Mary Shelley, "The Sisters of Albano" (1829), in *Mary Shelley: Collected Tales and Stories*, ed. Charles E. Robinson (Baltimore: Johns Hopkins University Press, 1976), 57.

40. To Maria Gisborne, 30 May 1819, *LMWS*, 1:98. See also, *CC*, 1:128.

41. *JMS*, 1:262; *JCC*, 110.

42. Previous biographers conflated the Rome and Pisa post office events, two separate occurrences.

43. *JMS*, 1:264; to Maria Gisborne, 30 May 1819, *LMWS*, 1:98.

44. *JCC*, 113; *JMS*, 1:279.

45. *SC*, 6:838.

46. CC and MWS to Maria Gisborne, 3, 5 June 1819, *LMWS*, 1:99.

47. *JCC*, 113; to Marianne Hunt, 28 August 1819, *LMWS*, 1:103.

48. To TLP, ? 20–21 June 1819, *L*, 2:99.

49. To Hogg, 25 July 1819, *L*, 2:104.

50. To Amelia Curran, 5 August 1819, *L*, 2:107.

51. To TLP, 8 June 1819, *L*, 2:97.

52. *JCC*, 113–14.

53. To LB, 26 May 1820, *L*, 2:198.

54. To Ollier, 14 May 1820, *L*, 2:196.

55. To Ollier, 6 September 1819, *L*, 2:116. Possibly with act IV in mind, PBS wrote TLP in late September not to give *Prometheus Unbound* to Ollier "until I write to that effect." See *L*, 2:120.

56. To TLP, 6 April 1819, *L*, 2:94.

57. Curran, 114.

58. J. B. Twitchell, "Shelley's Metapsychological System in Act IV of *Prometheus Unbound*," *KSJ* 24 (1975):29–48.

59. To Ollier, 6 September, 15 October, 15 December 1819, 6 March 1820, *L*, 2:116, 127, 164, 174.

60. *Records*, 54, 122.

61. LH to PBS, 1 March 1821, in *Leigh Hunt: Selected Writings*, ed. D. J. Dibley (Manchester: Carcanet, 1990), 168.

62. *UH*, 133–50.

63. *Shelley and Byron*, 30–31.

64. *The Selected Poetry and Prose of Percy Bysshe Shelley*, ed. Carlos Baker (New York: Modern Library, 1951), vi.

65. Sperry, 69.

66. Reiman, 68.

67. Sperry, 85.

68. Gelpi, 178–81.

69. Sperry, 115–16.

7. LEGHORN'S "SAD REALITY"

1. To TLP, ?20–21 June 1819, *L*, 2:98–99.

2. To TLP, 6 July 1819, *L*, 2:99–100.

3. To Hogg, 25 July 1819, *L*, 2:105.

4. *PW*, 336.

5. *BSM*, 9:xlvii–xlix.

6. *PW*, 336.

7. Nora Crook, "The Enigma of 'A Vision of the Sea,' or 'Who Sees the Water-spouts?',", in *Evaluating Shelley*, ed. Timothy Clark and J. E. Hogle (Edinburgh: Edinburgh University Press, 1996), 152–63. See also *MYR*, 4:xxx, lvii, 191.

8. *PW*, 337.

9. WG to MWS, 30 March 1820. In C. K. Paul, *William Godwin: His Friends and Contemporaries*, vol. 2 (London, 1876), 272.

10. To Marianne Hunt, 28 August 1819; to LH, 24 September 1819, *LMWS*, 1:104, 108.

11. To Hogg, 25 July, to TLP, 24 August, to TLP, 21 September 1819, *L*, 2:105, 115, 120.

12. To Augusta Leigh, c. 10–23 September 1819, *BLJ*, 6:223; *JCC*, 114.

13. To TLP, c. 25 July 1819, *L*, 2:101–3. See also, *SC*, 6:897 n. 1; *SG*, 114.

14. Neither the translation nor the presumed print of Beatrice was printed with the play. See *Shelley's Cenci*, 40–46; *SC*, 6:896–900.

15. *L*, 2:102 n. 6.

16. To Amelia Curran, 18 September 1819, *LMWS*, 1:106.

17. To Ollier, 15 October 1819, *L*, 2:127.

18. To LH, c. 17–19 August 1819, *L*, 2:111–13. For the Dedication's dating, see *SC*, 6:865–74.

19. *JMS*, 1:294–95. See also, *SC*, 6:896–900.

20. *SC*, 6:900 n. 14, n. 16.

21. *Shelley's Cenci*, 5–6; *SC*, 6:897.

22. Peacock, 73; *GY*, 396, 636–37 n. 15; *Shelley's Cenci*, 39–40; *PW*, 337.

23. To Maria Gisborne, 13–14 October 1819; to Ollier, 15 December 1819, *L*, 2:126, 163.

24. To LH, 5 April 1820, *L*, 2:181.

25. To Ollier, 15 December 1819, *L*, 2:163.

26. *UH*, chap. 7.

27. To PBS, 26 April 1821, *BLJ*, 8:103.

28. *Records*, 60; *Henry Crabb Robinson on Books and Their Writers*, ed. E.J. Morley, 3 vols. (London: Dent, 1938), 1:409; to PBS, 16 August 1820, *LJK*, 2:322–23.

29. *Shelley's Cenci*, 192.

30. Ibid., 237–46; *GY*, 396–97, 637 n. 17; Michael Worton, "Speech and Silence in *The Cenci*," in *Essays on Shelley*, ed. Miriam Allott (Liverpool: Liverpool University Press, 1982), 121–22.

31. To Maria Gisborne, 16 November 1819, *L*, 2:154. *Los cabellos de Absalón (The Hair of Absalom)* was one of three Calderón plays dealing with incest that attracted PBS, the others being *La devoción de la cruz (Devotion to the Cross)* and *La vida es sueño (Life is a dream)*. See Edwin Honig, *Calderón and the Seizures of Honor* (Cambridge: Harvard University Press, 1972), chap. 8.

32. *SN*, 2:87.

33. Corrado Ricci, *Beatrice Cenci*, 2 vols. (New York: Boni and Liveright, 1925), chap. 28.

34. *CW*, 2:159–166. See also *BSM*, 10; T. G. Steffan, "Seven Accounts of the Cenci and Shelley's Drama," *Studies in English Literature* 9 (1969):601–18; *SC*, 6:897–98; *SG*, 112.

35. George Yost, *Pieracci and Shelley, an Italian ur-Cenci* (Potomac, Maryland: Scripta Humanistica, 1986). Yost states PBS's Camillo probably was from Pieracci, a character not in other sources available to PBS. Both PBS and Pieracci omitted similar sexual facts (sodomy) about Count Cenci. Yost believes "beyond reasonable doubt" that PBS drew secondarily upon Pieracci's play, published in Florence, pointing out that PBS's play is far more dramatic than that of Pieracci. In his draft Preface to *The Cenci*, Shelley wrote that the story "is a tragedy which has been already acted & which has received . . . approbation & success." See *MYR*, 4; *SN*, 2:90.

36. Sperry, 134–35, 140; Ronald Tetreault, *The Poetry of Life: Shelley and Literary Form* (Toronto: University of Toronto Press, 1987), 136; Worton, "Speech and Silence," 120.

37. Sperry, 139.

38. *MYR*, 4.

39. Sperry, 132–34; Worton, "Speech and Silence," 117.

40. Honig, *Seizures of Honor*, 5–6. Calderón's influence on *The Cenci* deserves extended treatment. See Timothy Webb, *The Violet and the Crucible: Shelley and Translation* (Oxford: Clarendon Press, 1976), 221–22.

41. Paul Smith, "Restless Casuistry: Shelley's Composition of *The Cenci*," *KSJ* 13 (1964):77–85.

42. Reiman, 70.

43. *Recollections*, 76.

44. R. H. Fogle, *The Imagery of Keats and Shelley* (Chapel Hill: University of North Carolina Press, 1949), 180–81. See also Curran, 128; Rieger, 112.

45. To Medwin, 20 July 1820, *L*, 2:219.

46. MS. Shelley adds. e. 13, f. 86, Bodleian. Reproduced in Sunstein, opp. 210. See also, Sunstein, vii; *SG*, 112; *BSM*, 10:272.

47. Medwin, 221; to TLP, 24 August 1819, *L*, 2:115.

48. To Marianne Hunt, 29 June, to Amelia Curran, 27 June 1819, *LMWS*, 1:101, 100.

49. *JMS*, 1:293.

50. WG to MWS, 9 September 1819, *SM*, 410A-10B.

51. *JMS*, 1:294; *BSM*, 4:xxxii; *SG*, 116.

52. *GWJL*, 44.

53. To LH, 15 August 1819, *L*, 2:109.

54. Edmund Blunden, *Leigh Hunt* (London: Cobden-Sanderson, 1930), 137.

55. To LH, 27 September 1819, *L*, 2:122.

56. *SC*, 6:859–65; *SPP*, 119; Nora Crook, "Pecksie and the Elf: Did the Shelleys Couple Romantically?", *Romanticism on the Net* 18 (May 2000).

57. To LH, 15 August 1819, *SC*, 6:850–53. See also, *SC*, 6:859.

58. To Ollier, 15 December 1819, *L*, 2:164.

59. To CC, ? 2 January 1821, *L*, 2:254.

60. *YS*, 261–62; White, 2:46; *SC*, 6:860–65; G. M. Matthews, "A New Text for Shelley's Scene for *Tasso*," *KSMB* 11 (1960):45.

61. Mary Wollstonecraft Shelley, *Mathilda*, ed. Elizabeth Nitchie, *Studies in Philology*, Extra Series #3, No. 3, October 1959 (Chapel Hill: The University of North Carolina Press), 77–78; *BSM*, 4:251.

62. *GY*, 264–65.

63. Mary Shelley, *Mathilda*, 64, 73.

64. PBS usually did not mention time periods casually. The "two years" could be an oblique reference to the "mysterious lady" who seemingly reappeared in his life in two-year intervals starting in 1814.

65. To Ollier, 23 December 1819, *SC*, 6:1099–1103.

66. To Ollier, 14 May 1820, *L*, 2:196–97. For PBS's fair copy manuscript of *Athanase: A Fragment*, and its history and dating, see *SC*, 7:132–60. See also, Donald H. Reiman, "Shelley as Athanase," *SC*, 7:110–32; *CG*, 166–70; "Athanase," ed. Kelvin Everest, *KSR* 7 (1992):62–84.

67. *SC*, 7:118.

68. Reiman considered *Julian and Maddalo* and *Athanase* represent PBS developing a "new" self. See *SC*, 7:114; 126–27.

69. *SC*, 6:1086–87; *SC*, 7:150; Webb, *The Violet*, 79.

70. *PW*, 158–59; Irving Massey, *Posthumous Poems of Shelley* (Montreal: McGill University Press, 1969), 131–57.

71. MS. Shelley adds. e. 12, Bodleian; *SG*, 118; Chernaik, 247.

72. Sunstein, 171.

73. Mary Shelley, *Mathilda*, 65; *SG*, 116.

8. "A VOICE FROM OVER THE SEA"

1. To TLP, 9 September 1819; to Ollier, 6 September 1819, *L*, 2:118–19, 117.

2. To TLP, 21 September 1819, *L*, 2:120. Richard Cronin, "Asleep in Italy: Byron and Shelley in 1819," *KSR* 10 (1996): 151–80.

3. To TLP, 24 August 1819, *L*, 2:115.

4. Thompson, 685–87.

5. To TLP, 23–24 January 1819, *L*, 2:70.

6. Thompson, 683; Scrivener, 197–98.

7. Thompson, 700.

8. Samuel Bamford, *Passages in the Life of a Radical*, ed. Henry Dunckley (London, 1893),2:155–57. Quoted in *GY*, 344–45; Thompson, 686–87.

9. *SN*, 2:173. From Wordsworth's *Ode: 1815*, "Carnage is thy [God's] daughter."

10. *GY* 343–50, 623–25.

11. To LH, [16] November 1819, *L*, 2:152.

12. Holmes, 532.

13. *CW,* 3:225–33.

14. LH to PBS, 20 September 1819, *SM,* 413.

15. Paul Foot, *Red Shelley* (London: Sidgwick & Jackson, 1980), 219; to LH, 23 December 1819, *L,* 2:166–67.

16. *JMS,* 1:297; White, 2:294; Curran, 186–92; Fogle, 134–38.

17. Bryan Shelley, *Shelley and Scripture: The Interpreting Angel* (Oxford: Oxford University Press, Clarendon Press, 1994), 89–90.

18. Scrivener, 288.

19. Ibid., 199; Stephen C. Behrendt, *Shelley and His Audiences* (Lincoln: University of Nebraska Press, 1989), 198–99.

20. *GY,* 350, 626 n. 15.

21. Scrivener, 238; *PW,* 575–76.

22. Scrivener, 207.

23. To LH, 1 May 1820, *L,* 2:191.

24. Scrivener, 227; Neil Fraistat, *The Poem and the Book: Interpreting Collections of Romantic Poetry* (Chapel Hill: University of North Carolina Press, 1985), 29, 198 n. 13.

25. Scrivener, 227.

26. William McTaggart, *England in 1819: Church, State and Poverty* (London: Keats-Shelley Memorial Association, 1970).

27. *CW,* 3:154.

28. To LH, 23 December 1819, *L,* 2:167.

29. To Maria Gisborne, 24 November 1819, *LMWS,* 1:114.

30. To TLP, 21 September 1819, *L,* 2:119–20; *JMS,* 1:296.

31. To Amelia Curran, 18 September 1819, *LMWS,* 1:106.

32. *JMS,* 1:297; *SC,* 8:920, 922.

33. To LH, 27 September 1819, *L,* 2:122.

34. To CC, 12 August 1845, *LMWS,* 3:200.

35. Sunstein, 175; *JCC,* 469.

36. Sunstein, 175.

37. Maria Gisborne to MWS, 11 October 1819, *GWJL,* 53.

38. To Maria Gisborne, 5 October 1819, *LMWS,* 1:110.

39. To Maria Gisborne, 13 November 1819, *CC,* 1:133.

9. FLORENTINE VOICES

1. To Maria Gisborne, 5 October 1819, *LMWS,* 1:109–10; *JMS,* 1:298.

2. To LH, 24 September 1819, *LMWS,* 1:108.

3. WG to MWS, 15 October 1819, *SM,* 420a–21b.

4. To Maria Gisborne, 9 November 1819, *LMWS,* 1:112.

5. To WG, 7 August 1820, *L,* 2:225.

6. To LH, 13, 16 November 1819, *L,* 1:151; *SC,* 6:1080–82.

7. *JMS,* 1:296–98; Sunstein, 175; *BSM,* 4:xxxii.

8. To Maria Gisborne, ? 13 December 1819, *LMWS,* 1:119.

9. *SM,* 463–64.

10. Maria Gisborne to MWS, 11 October 1819, *GWJL,* 54.

11. To Maria Gisborne, 13–14 October 1819, *L,* 2:124–25.

12. To the Gisbornes, 23 December 1819, *L*, 2:165; *SC*, 9:287 n. 7.

13. One card is in the Huntington (Jerome Kern) copy of *Prometheus Unbound.*

14. To Marianne Hunt, 24–25 November 1819, *LMWS*, 1:114; *JMS*, 1:298–99.

15. To Maria Gisborne, 13–14 October 1819, to Hogg, 20 April 1820, *L*, 2:126, 186; F. S. Colwell, "Shelley on Sculpture: The Uffizi Notes," *KSJ* 28 (1979): 59–77; E. B. Murray, "Shelley's Notes on Sculptures: The Provenance and Authority of the Text," *KSJ* 32 (1983): 150–71.

16. *Prose*, 348.

17. For text and commentaries about PBS's "On the Medusa of Leonardo da Vinci, in the Florentine Gallery," see *RC*. The painting, not by Leonardo, is attributed to the seventeenth-century Flemish School.

18. *SC*, 6:931–32; *BSM,* 1; *GY*, 351, 626–27 n. 21.

19. Medwin, 225–26.

20. *BSM*, 1:7; *SC*, 6:934 n. 26.

21. *The Quarterly Review*, 21 (April 1819): 460–71.

22. To The Editor of *The Quarterly Review*, ? October 1819, *L*, 2:130.

23. To William Gifford, ? November 1820, *SM*, 561–63.

24. *SC*, 6:931–32.

25. To Ollier, 15 December, 15 October 1819, *L*, 2:163, 126–28.

26. To John Cam Hobhouse, 11 November 1818, to John Murray, 24 November 1818, *BLJ*, 6:76, 83.

27. *NLRS*, 2:156.

28. To Ollier, 11 June 1821, *L*, 2:298–99.

29. To the Gisbornes, 6 November 1819, *L*, 2:150.

30. *SN*, 1:170, 162.

31. Ibid., 1:171–72.

32. Desmond King-Hele, *Shelley: His Thought and Work*, 3d ed. (Rutherford: Fairleigh Dickinson University Press, 1984), 213–18.

33. *SC*, 8:732.

34. Stephen Gill, *William Wordsworth: A Life* (Oxford: Oxford University Press, Clarendon Press, 1989), 476 n. 72.

35. *JMS*, 1:300; *BSM,* 1:5–6.

36. To Marianne Hunt, 2 November 1819, *LMWS*, 1:111.

37. To Ollier, 14 May 1820, 30 April 1820, 15 December 1819, *L*, 2:196, 189, 164; to LH, 2 November 1819, *L*, 2:134–35.

38. *PW*, 363.

39. *BSM*, 1:108–13.

40. *L*, 2:136–48.

41. Hoagwood, 163, 229 n. 28; *GY*, 119–21.

42. To LH, 5 April 1820, *L*, 2:181.

43. *GY*, 120; *UH*, 95–98.

44. To the Gisbornes, 6 November 1819, *L*, 2:150.

45. To LH, 16 November 1819, *SC*, 6:1080–82.

46. To the Gisbornes, 23 December 1819, *L*, 2:165.

47. To Marianne Hunt, 24 November 1819, *LMWS*, 1:114.

48. To LH, 13 November 1819, to John Gisborne, 16 November, 1819, to TLP, [?2] May 1820, *L*, 2:150, 156–57, 192–93.

49. To Henry Reveley, 17 November 1819, *L*, 2:157–58.

50. Rodney M. Bennett, letter to author, 3 September 1994.

51. Sophia was the fifth of six children of Flint Stacey, a partner in a brewery firm and mayor of Maidstone. Her great-great-grandson, Rodney M. Bennett, kindly provided information about her, including his note, *KSJ* 35 (1986):16, her portrait by Bouton, her obituary, *Maidstone & Kentish Journal,* 4 January 1875, and her date of birth, May 25, 1791. Her portrait was also painted in 1819 by Grimaldi, court painter to the Prince Regent.

52. Sophia's now lost travel diary and her memoir are extracted in Angeli, 95–105. The diary was described in the *Atheneum* in 1908 by Sophia's son Corbet S. Catty, whose son informed N. I. White in 1936 he did not know what became of the diary. Angeli informed White she had extracted and printed "practically all" of the PBS material in the diary. See White, 2:586 n. 47, 172–75. Angeli, 100, presumed Sophia wrote the brief memoir "some years, perhaps many years, later."

53. Angeli, 97. Sophia's Italian translated by Angeli.

54. Ibid., 98.

55. Ibid., 101.

56. To Maria Gisborne, ? 2, 13 December 1819, *LMWS,* 1:118, 119–20.

57. Box 7, file 3, Silsbee.

58. Angeli, 98. For Grieves, see *SC,* 10:871.

59. Angeli, 102.

60. Chernaik, 249–50.

61. Brown, 62–65.

62. *BSM,* 16:l–liii; *MYR,* 3:443.

63. Corbet Stacey Catty, "Shelley's 'I arise from dreams of thee' and Miss Sophia Stacey," *Atheneum,* No. 4199 (April 18, 1908): 478.

64. Inscription in HM copy, William Michael Rossetti, *The Poetical Works of Percy Bysshe Shelley,* 2 vols. (London: 1870), 1:116.

65. Angeli, 102; *SG,* 127.

66. Rossetti, *Poetical Works.*

67. Leigh Hunt, *The Literary Pocket-Book,* 1822.

68. To LH, [16] November 1819, *L,* 2:151–53; *SC,* 6:1085.

69. LH to PBS, 2 December 1819, *SC,* 6:1089–91.

70. *SC,* 6:1094.

71. *The Indicator,* December 22, 1819.

72. *SN,* 2:11–12. Forman (*SN,* 2:13) considered "Love's Philosophy" might be "licentious."

73. Sperry, 117.

74. MWS stated (*PW,* 271) that PBS conceived act IV "in Florence." See also Fraistat, *BSM,* 9:lxx; *SC,* 6:1074; Tatsuo Tokoo, "The Composition of *Epipsychidion:* Some Manuscript Evidence," *KSJ* 42 (1993):101.

75. Carl Grabo, *A Newton Among Poets* (Chapel Hill: University of North Carolina Press, 1930), 30–79, chaps. 8–11; King-Hele, *Shelley,* 162–64, chaps. 8–9; *GY,* 15.

76. Alfred North Whitehead, *Science and the Modern World* (New York: Macmillan, 1925), chap. 5.

77. Grabo, *A Newton,* 93–94, 161–65; *GY,* 555.

78. *SC,* 10:867–86; *BSM,* 9:xcviii; Betty T. Bennett, "Newly Uncovered Letters and Poems by Mary Wollstonecraft Shelley," *KSJ* 46 (1997):53–56.

79. Chernaik, 278–79; *CW,* 4:44–45; White, 2:174.

80. *PW*, 426–29, lines 1–141; Tokoo, "Composition of *Epipsychidion*," 98–99; *BSM*, 9.
81. To Ollier, 15 December 1819, *L*, 2:164.
82. *PW*, 425.
83. Hermaphroditic female statues with a penis were common throughout Italy; PBS possibly saw one in Naples or Rome, if not in Florence. See *JMS*, 1:245; *L*, 2:81.
84. Angeli, 101.
85. Dowden, 2:312 n; *JCC*, 115–16; Angeli, 105.
86. To the Gisbornes, 23 December 1819, *L*, 2:165.
87. To LH, 26 May 1820, *L*, 2:201.
88. *SC*, 6:955–58; *Prose*, 230–61.
89. *PW*, 588.
90. *GY*, 137–40, 594–96; *SC*, 6:1003–4.
91. *GY*, 118–19, 145–47.
92. Hoagwood, 172–74.
93. *SC*, 6:973–74.
94. Ibid., 6:1060.
95. *GY*, 149; Hoagwood, 209; Foot, *Red Shelley*, 11.
96. *BSM*, 9:xxxii–xlii.
97. To Maria Gisborne, ? 13 December 1819, *LMWS*, 1:120; to Ollier, 15 December 1819, *L*, 2:163. For the *Blackwood's* review, see *RR*, Part C, I, 118–24. See also *SC*, 6:931 n. 16.
98. To Maria Gisborne, ? 13, 28 December 1819, *LMWS*, 1:119–21, 122.
99. To Maria Gisborne, 28 December 1819, *LMWS*, 1:122.
100. Angeli, 99.
101. To Amelia Curran, 18 November 1819, *L*, 2:158–59. For William's final headstone, see *SC*, 10:838–40.

10. POETIC MOTHERS

1. *JCC*, 116–17; *BSM*, 18:f.103a.
2. Mrs. Mason to MWS and PBS, *SM*, 449–53.
3. To Maria Gisborne, 12 January 1820, *LMWS*, 1:124; *JCC*, 116.
4. To Thomas Medwin, 17 January 1820, *L*, 2:169–70.
5. To Amelia Curran, 19 January 1820, to Maria Gisborne, 12, 18 January 1820, *LMWS*, 1:127, 124, 125.
6. *SC*, 8:915–18, 920–21.
7. To John Gisborne, 24–25 January 1820, *L*, 2:171.
8. *JCC*, 118; *JMS*, 1:307.
9. To Horace Hall, 24 March, 26 May 1820, *SC*, 8:918, 1059.
10. Marion Kingston, "Notes on Three Shelley Letters," *KSMB* 6 (1955): 13–15; *L*, 2:172–73 n. 1; Mary Shelley to Sophia Stacey, 7 March 1820, *KSJ* 56 (1997): 53–56; *JCC*, 122–23 n. 85.
11. *JMS*, 1:307.
12. *JCC*, 119 n. 74; *JMS*, 1:307 n. 5.
13. E. C. McAleer, *The Sensitive Plant: A Life of Lady Mount Cashell* (Chapel Hill: University of North Carolina Press, 1958), 38–43, 53.
14. Mary Shelley, *Maurice*, ed. Claire Tomalin (London: Viking, 1998), Introd.

15. McAleer, *Sensitive Plant*, 47; *SC*, 1:59.
16. Mrs. Mason possibly met PBS in 1812. See McAleer, 124–25.
17. To LH, 5 April 1820, *L*, 2:180.
18. Dowden, 2:317.
19. To Hogg, 20 April 1820, *L*, 2:186; *JCC*, 139 n. 30; Dowden, 2:317–18.
20. *BSM*, 9:xcviii; *JCC*, 146 n. 53; White, 2:588 n. 3.
21. To the Gisbornes, 9 February 1820, *L*, 2:172.
22. *JCC*, 146; *JMS*, 1:318–19.
23. To Sophia Stacey, 5–7 March 1820, *LMWS*, 1:130–31; *KSJ* 56 (1997): 53–56.
24. *Maidstone & Kentish Journal*, 4 January 1875.
25. TS to William Whitton, 18 January 1820, *SC*, 8:772–73.
26. TS to Edmund English, 21 April 1821, *SC*, 8:1001.
27. To English, English, & Becks, 10 March 1820, *SC*, 8:878–80.
28. To TLP, c. 10 March 1820, to LH, 5 April 1820, *L*, 2:176–77, 179–80.
29. *SC*, 8:827–47.
30. *JCC*, 122.
31. *PW*, 635; to Maria Gisborne, 13 December 1820, *LMWS*, 1:168.
32. To Marianne Hunt, 24 March 1820, *LMWS*, 1:136.
33. *JCC*, 466.
34. Ibid., 123.
35. To Maria Gisborne, c. 19 February 1820, *LMWS*, 1:128.
36. Mary Shelley, *Mathilda*, 80.
37. *JMS*, 1:307, 309; *JCC*, 129.
38. To Dr. Thomas Hume, 17 February 1820, *SC*, 9:283–89; *JMS*, 1:309 n. 2, 360–61 n. 4.
39. *JMS*, 1:311.
40. To the Gisbornes, 8 March 1820, *L*, 2:175–76.
41. White, 2:589–90 n. 11.
42. To Marianne Hunt, 24 March 1820, *LMWS*, 1:136.
43. To the Gisbornes, 19 March 1820, *L*, 2:179.
44. To Horace Hall, 19 March 1820, *SC*, 8:891, 896.
45. To the Gisbornes, 11 March 1820, David M. Stocking and Marion K. Stocking, "New Shelley Letters in a John Gisborne Notebook," *KSMB* 31 (1980): 2–4.
46. To John Gisborne, 4 April 1820, *LMWS*, 1:142.
47. To Maria Gisborne, ? 13 April 1820, 22 March 1820, *LMWS*, 1:142, 134–35.
48. To LH, 5 April 1820, *L*, 2:180.
49. Medwin, 265.
50. Stuart Curran, *Poetic Form and British Romanticism* (New York: Oxford University Press, 1986), 122–23; CG, 203–7.
51. To CC, 11 December 1821, *L*, 2:368.
52. *SPP*, 287 n. 6; Richard S. Caldwell, "'The Sensitive Plant' as Original Fantasy," *Studies in Romanticism* 16 (1976): 221–52. See 232–37.
53. CG, 205; *SPP*, 293 n. 5.
54. *SC*, 8:897–915.
55. To LB, 16 March 1820, *CC*, 1:140–41.
56. *JMS*, 1:315.
57. CC to LB, 23 April 1820, *CC*, 1:142–43.
58. To Richard Hoppner, 22 April 1820, *BLJ*, 7:80.

59. To Maria Gisborne, 8 May 1820, *LMWS*, 1:145.

60. *JCC*, 145–49.

61. To the Gisbornes, 26 May 1820, *L*, 2:201–3.

62. To LB, 26 May 1820, *L*, 2:197–99.

63. *JMS*, 1:320; *JCC*, 150.

64. *JMS*, 1:320, 321 n. 3; *SC*, 8:1081 n. 2; *JMS*, 2:App.I.

65. *JCC*, 150.

66. *JMS*, 1:321; *JCC*, 150.

67. Box 7, files 2, 3, Silsbee. Silsbee's three accounts about this "Leeson" event differ in minor details.

68. *JCC*, 151.

69. *JMS*, 1:322–23.

70. Box 7, file 3, Silsbee.

71. Ibid.

72. *The Atheneum*, 1832; *Shelley Papers*, 58–59; Medwin, 239–41.

73. Peacock, 75–76, incorrectly placed the episode in Florence. EJT wrote to CC, 5 January 1870: "his vivid imagination might occasionally delude as it does others—for instance his account of the parson [sic] assaulting him at the post office—I doubted—but it may have been—in all ordinary circumstances of life he was truthful." See *LEJT*, 224.

74. To Maria Gisborne, 18 June 1820, *LMWS*, 1:146–49.

75. To TLP, c.10 March 1820, *L*, 2:177.

76. To TLP, 12 July 1820, *L*, 2:213.

77. Box 7, file 3, Silsbee.

78. To Southey, 26 June 1820, Southey to PBS, [July 1820], *L*, 2:203–5. See also, *Shelley's Satire*, 84–86.

79. To Southey, 17 August 1820, Southey to PBS, [? September 1820], *L*, 2:230–33.

80. Southey to Joseph Cottle, 25 June 1823, *NLRS*, 2:249.

81. *SN*, 1:145; *Shelley's Satire*, 77–83; *PW*, 625–26.

82. To LH, 25 January 1822, *L*, 2:382–83.

83. *JCC*, 147.

84. WG to MWS, 25 April, 13 June 1820, *SC*, 8:1069–72.

85. To Maria Gisborne, 30 June 1820, *LWMS*, 1:151; PBS to John Gisborne, 30 June 1820, *LWMS*, 1:152.

86. To the Gisbornes, 30 June–2 July 1820, *L*, 2:206–8.

87. "July 1" on *Letter to Maria Gisborne* is the date it was copied (*JMS*, 1:325), not the composition date. Confirming PBS's statement that *Letter to Maria Gisborne* was composed soon after arriving in Leghorn, before *To a Sky-Lark*, is John Gisborne's journal notation of the receipt of PBS's 30 June–2 July letter with "letter in verse" enclosed. See *LMWS*, 1:151–52 n. 1.

88. *GWJL*, 36–37.

89. *PW*, 635; *JMS*, 1:323; White, 2:594 n. 54.

90. To LB, 26 May 1820, *L*, 2:198.

91. *SG*, 139.

92. To the Gisbornes, 30 June–2 July 1820, *L*, 2:206–8.

93. To the Gisbornes, ? 7 July 1820, *L*, 2:211.

94. To Maria Gisborne, 7 July 1820, *LMWS*, 1:153.

95. To Maria Gisborne, 19 July 1820, *LMWS*, 1:155.

96. To LH, 5 April 1820, *L*, 2:180.

97. *GY*, 365, 630–31 n. 5.

98. To TLP, 12 July 1820, *L*, 2:213–14.

99. *JCC*, 153; *JMS*, 1:324.

100. *JCC*, 155 n. 87, 467–68; To Maria Gisborne, 19 July 1820, *LMWS*, 1:157, *L*, 2:214–18.

101. *GWJL*, 39.

102. *JMS*, 1:324–27; to TLP, 12 July 1820, *L*, 2:213.

103. *JMS*, 1:326.

104. Ibid., 1:316 n. 3; *LMWS*, 1:419 n. 1; *SPP*, 367 n. 1.

105. *JCC*, 156–57. Miss Field stayed with the Masons one year; CC later considered starting a school with her.

106. *JCC*, 157–58.

107. *JMS*, 1:324–26.

108. To Medwin, 20 July 1820, *L*, 2:218–20.

109. *JCC*, 156.

110. To the Gisbornes, 30 June, 19 July 1820, to TLP, 12 July 1820, *L*, 2:207, 218, 213.

111. *GWJL*, 36, 37, 40, 44–45.

112. *SC*, 5:412.

113. To Medwin, 20 July 1820, *L*, 2:219.

114. To John Keats, 27 July 1820, *L*, 2:220–21.

115. To Fanny Keats, 13 August 1820, to Charles Brown, 14 August 1820, *LJK*, 2:314, 321. PBS's letter to Keats arrived in London August 10, addressed to Hunt's *Examiner* office. Keats received it two days later at Hunt's Mortimer Place home. See *GWJL*, 44–45; *LJK*, 2:313 n. 1, n. 2.

116. To PBS, 16 August 1820, *LJK*, 2:322–23.

117. To John Taylor, 14 August 1820, *LJK*, 2:318. See also, *SC*, 6:530–39.

118. To Marianne Hunt, 29 October 1820, *L*, 2:239–40; LH to PBS, 23 August 1820, *SM*, 532.

119. To TLP, 8 November 1820, *SC*, 5:416. See also *SC*, 5:401–18.

120. To MWS, 30 July 1820, *L*, 2:222–23.

11. BATHS OF SAN GIULIANO

1. *SM*, 698C-98D; *JMS*, 1:328.

2. *JCC*, 168, 130 n. 2, 466–67.

3. *PW*, 388.

4. To Godwin, 7 August 1820, *L*, 224–29, 229 n. 8. See also *GWJL*, 48.

5. Sunstein, 182.

6. To WG, n.d., *L*, 2:229.

7. To Amelia Curran, 17 August 1820, *LMWS*, 1:158–59.

8. *JCC*, 169; *JMS*, 1:328–29.

9. Ms. Notebook adds. e. 9., 33, Bodleian.

10. *PW*, 388.

11. Richard Cronin, *Shelley's Poetic Thoughts* (New York: St. Martin's Press, 1981), 55–63; Hogle, 211–16.

12. *SPP*, 365.

13. Sperry, 144–46.

14. *JMS*, 1:329–30; *PW*, 480–81.

15. Chernaik, 109.

16. Charles E. Robinson, "Shelley to the Editor of the Morning Chronicle: A Second New Letter of 5 April 1821," *KSMB* 32 (1981): 54–58.

17. *Shelley's Satire*, 191–92 n. 33, n. 40.

18. *JMS*, 1:329–30; *PW*, 410; *JCC*, 172.

19. *Shelley's Satire*, 131, 189 n. 18.

20. *GY*, 327, 629 n. 39.

21. *BSM*, 6:50.

22. Arthur H. Beavan, *James and Horace Smith* (London, 1899), quoted in *GY*, 357; see also *GY*, 628–29 n. 38, Medwin, 254. For *Swellfoot* as the "Critics' Stepchild," *see SC*, 10:772–825.

23. White, 2:304–5.

24. To Charles Ollier, 27 August 1820, in Christopher Goulding, "An Unpublished Shelley Letter," *Review of English Studies*, n.s., 52, (2001):233–37. I am indebted to Charles E. Robinson for alerting me to this letter.

25. To PBS, 25 August 1820, *BLJ*, 7:162.

26. To MWS, 1 September 1820, *L*, 2:234–35; to Amelia Curran, 17 September 1820, *SC*, 10:831–32.

27. *JCC*, 172–73.

28. To Maria Gisborne, 17 October 1820, *LMWS*, 1:160–61.

29. WG to Maria Gisborne, 15 September 1820, *SM*, 536–37.

30. To CC, 15 November, 29 October 1820, *L*, 2: 247–50, 241–44.

31. *JCC*, 470.

32. Medwin, 233–34.

33. *JMS*, 1:338; Medwin, 234; *PW*, 635–36.

34. Medwin, 234–35, 280. In 1826, Lady Charlotte Bury published anonymously *Alla Giornata, or To the D*ay. See *DNB*, 8:22–23.

35. To CC, 29 October 1820, *L*, 2:241–44.

36. CG, 115–16, 245 n. 52; Dowden, 2:356 n; *Records*, 189.

37. *Trelawny*, 40–41.

38. To LB, 17 September 1820, to CC, 29 October 1820, *L*, 2:237, 242.

39. *JMS*, 1:339; Medwin, 267; to TLP, 8 November 1820, *L*, 2:244–45.

40. To Ollier, 10 November 1820, *L*, 2:246.

41. *JMS*, 1:340.

42. *JCC*, 183–84.

43. To CC, 15 November 1820, *L*, 2:247–50.

44. *JMS*, 1:340.

45. Medwin, 235–37.

46. Box 8, file 4, Silsbee.

47. Medwin, 242–49; to Maria Gisborne, 16 November 1819, *L*, 2:154–55.

48. To John Gisborne, late November 1820, *L*, 2:250; MWS to LH, 3 December 1820, *LMWS*, 1:165.

49. To Maria Gisborne, [? 15 December 1820], *LMWS*, 1:169; *JCC*, 194.

50. *JCC*, 189.

51. Medwin, 277–79.

52. Edward Silsbee noted CC told him "She (C)[CC] introduced her [Teresa Vi-

viani] to Mrs S[helley]" and "She to Shelley," suggesting either CC or MWS introduced PBS to Teresa. See Box 7, file 3, Silsbee.

53. *JCC,* 189.

54. Ibid., 190–91; *JMS,* 1:341.

55. *SPP,* 390; *JCC,* 188–90.

56. Box 7, file 3, Silsbee.

57. To Maria Gisborne, 7 March, 6 April 1822, *LMWS,* 1:223, 227; *JCC,* 189.

58. Cline, 23–24, chap. 2; *JMS,* 2:App.II.

59. P. M. S. Dawson, "Shelley and the *Improvvisatore* Sgricci: An Unpublished Review," *KSMB* 32 (1981): 19–29.

60. To LH, 29 December 1820, *LMWS,* 1:171–72.

61. To Hobhouse, 3 March 1820, *BLJ,* 7:51–52; MWS to CC, 24 January 1821, *LMWS,* 1:182.

62. *JCC,* 190.

63. *JMS,* 1:341.

64. *JCC,* App. C, 473–76.

65. Medwin, 263–64.

66. To LH, to Maria Gisborne, 29 December 1820, *LMWS,* 1:169, 173.

67. To William Gifford, Editor of *The Quarterly Review,* [? November 1820], *L,* 2:251–53.

68. Medwin, 269–70; *JCC,* 196 n. 85; *PW,* 822.

69. *PW,* 667; Medwin, 270.

70. To CC, [? 2 January 1821], *L,* 2:254.

71. MWS to CC, 14–15 January 1821, *LMWS,* 1:175.

72. *JMS,* 1:349.

73. To CC, 16 January 1821, *L,* 2:256–57.

12. "EMILY . . . MY HEART'S SISTER"

1. To CC, [16 January] 1821, *L,* 2:256–57.

2. Box 7, file 3, Silsbee; Rees, chap. 3.

3. To CC, 14–15 January 1821, *LMWS,* 1:177–78.

4. To CC, 16 January 1821, *L,* 2:256–57.

5. *L,* 2:App.I, 449. See also, White, 2:App.II; Rogers, App. V, 238–41.

6. Box 7, files 2, 3, Silsbee.

7. White, 2:254.

8. Medwin, 281–84; Enrica Viviani Della Robbia, *Vita di una Donna,* (Florence, 1936).

9. White, 2:468.

10. To John Gisborne, 26 January 1822, *L,* 2:388.

11. Emilia Viviani to PBS, 12 December 1820, *SM,* 555–56; Emilia Viviani to PBS, ? December 1820, Robbia, *Vita,* 87–88; White, 2:472–74, 480.

12. Emilia Viviani to MWS, 24 December 1820, *SM,* 557–58; White, 2:476.

13. Emilia Viviani to MWS, 14 January 1821, *SM,* 637; Robbia, *Vita,* 89; White, 2:253, 605 n. 12. PBS's daughter-in-law omitted the italicized words when printing this letter in *SM.*

14. *JCC,* 243.

15. *Mary Shelley: Collected Tales and Stories,* ed. Charles E. Robinson (Baltimore: Johns Hopkins University Press, 1976), 28.

16. *JMS,* 1:350.

17. Ibid., 1:353.

18. To Ollier, 16 February 1821, *L,* 2:262–63; *SG,* 153.

19. To John Gisborne, 18 June 1822, *L,* 2:434.

20. Tatsuo Tokoo, "The Composition of *Epipsychidion:* Some Manuscript Evidence," *KSJ* 42 (1993): 97–103.

21. Wasserman, 428.

22. Hogle, 280, 387 n. 26; Wasserman, 418–20; *SPP,* 392. Silsbee noted CC pronounced "Epip-sychidion thinks Shelley did so." See Box 8, file 4, Silsbee.

23. Sperry, chap. 9.

24. *PW,* 425.

25. Box 7, files 2, 3, Silsbee.

26. Ibid.

27. *SPP,* 393 n. 5.

28. Kenneth N. Cameron, "The Planet-Tempest Passage in *Epipsychidion,*" *PMLA* 63 (1948): 950–72; *GY,* 280–88; Sperry, 170–76.

29. *GY,* 284.

30. To CC, 16 February 1821, *L,* 2:264.

31. Box 7, file 2, Silsbee.

32. To CC, 18 February 1821, to John Keats, [c. 18 February 1821], *L,* 2:265–68.

33. To Ollier, 16, 22 February 1821, *L,* 2:262–63, 268–70.

34. Murray, 1:xxvii.

35. To Ollier, 4 March 1821, *L,* 2:271.

36. *JMS,* 1:357; *GWJL,* 103, 121.

37. *JCC,* 216.

38. *Byron,* 2:901–2.

39. Iris Origo, *Allegra* (London: Hogarth Press, 1935), chap. 4; *Byron,* 2:903–5.

40. To LB, 24 March 1821, *CC,* 1:163–65.

41. To PBS, 26 April 1821, *BLLJ,* 501–2; to LB, 17 April 1821, *L,* 2:283–84.

42. To Richard Hoppner, 3 April, 11 May 1821, *BLJ,* 8:97–98, 112–13.

43. To Teresa Guiccioli, 7 August 1820, *BLJ,* 7:152.

44. Box 7, file 3, Silsbee.

45. To CC, 2 April 1821, *L,* 2:279–80; *JCC,* 212, 216.

46. To Editor of *The Literary Miscellany,* February–March 1821, *L,* 2:272–77; *BSM,* 6:1–8; Rogers, 16–17, 256–58; *SG,* 154–55.

47. To Ollier, 20 January 1821, *L,* 2:258.

48. To TLP, 15 February 1821, *L,* 2:261.

49. Butler, 186–88. For *The Four Ages of Poetry,* see *Shelley's Critical Prose,* ed. Bruce R. McElderry, Jr. (Lincoln: University of Nebraska Press, 1967), 158–72.

50. *SPP,* 510–35; MS. Shelley e. 6, Bodleian.

51. Butler, 292; Hoagwood, 203–4.

52. To TLP, 21 March 1821, *L,* 2:275–76.

53. *JMS,* 1:359.

54. To CC, 2 April 1821, *LMWS,* 1:186–87; to Medwin, 4 April 1821, *L,* 2:280.

55. Charles E. Robinson, "The Shelleys to Leigh Hunt: A New Letter of 5 April 1821," *KSMB* 31 (1980): 52–56; "Shelley to the Editor of the *Morning Chronicle:* A Second New Letter of 5 April 1821," *KSMB* 32 (1981): 55–58. See also *LMWS,* 3:399–400.

56. To Maria Gisborne, c. 21 March 1821, *LMWS*, 1:185; to TLP, 21 March 1821, *L*, 2:276–77.

57. Mavrocordato to MWS, ?3 February, 3 April 1821, *SM*, 581, 600–602.

58. *JMS*, 1:360; Horace Smith to PBS, 28 March 1821, *SM*, 599–600. See also, *Shelley Memorials*, 181.

59. To CC, [? 13 April 1821], *L*, 2:281.

60. Ms. Abinger Dep. c. 516, Bodleian, quoted in *JMS*, 1:361 n. 4. Lady Shelley deleted this section of the letter in *SM*.

61. Horace Smith to TS, 13 April 1821, *SM*, 613–15.

62. TS to Horace Smith, 17 April 1821, *SM*, 615.

63. Horace Smith to PBS, 17 April 1821, *SM*, 612.

64. Horace Smith to PBS, 19 April 1821, *SM*, 616.

65. Horace Smith to PBS, 15 June 1821, *SM*, 639–40.

66. To LH, 22 June 1817, to Ollier, 22 June 1817, *L*, 2:304, 305.

13. "A LOVE IN DESOLATION MASKED"

1. To CC, 29 April 1821, *L*, 2:288.

2. *SC*, 10:1147–49; *GWJL*, 70–71.

3. *Records,* 63.

4. To Henry Reveley, 17, 19 April 1821, *L*, 2:285–86, 286–87. See also *SG*, 157.

5. To CC, 29 April 1821, *L*, 2:288.

6. To CC, ? 14 May 1821, *L*, 2:292.

7. To CC, 8 June 1821, *L*, 2:296.

8. To CC, 8 June, ? 14 May 1821, *L*, 2:296, 292.

9. *JCC*, 235.

10. To CC, 29 April, 8 June 1821, *L*, 2:288, 296.

11. To CC, ? 14 May 1821, *L*, 2:292.

12. To CC, 29 April 1821, *L*, 2:288.

13. Herbert Huscher, "A New Viviani Letter," *KSMB* 14 (1963): 30–33.

14. To CC, 8 June, ? 14 May 1821, *L*, 2:296, 292.

15. *SG*, 162; *JMS*, 1:367 n. 2.

16. EW to EJT, ? 19 April 1821, *Recollections*, 12–14.

17. *Shelley and Byron*, 18, 43.

18. Nora Crook, "The Boat on the Serchio," *KSR* 7 (1992): 85–97.

19. *Percy Bysshe Shelley: Poems and Prose*, ed. Timothy Webb (London: Everyman, 1995), 435; to Maria Gisborne, 15 August 1822, *LMWS*, 1:249.

20. *GY*, 426.

21. Dowden, 2:411.

22. To Ollier, 11 June 1821, to the Gisbornes, 5 June 1821, to CC, 8 June 1821, *L*, 2:299, 294, 296.

23. *Shelley and Byron*, 162–68.

24. To LB, 16 April 1821, *L*, 2:283–84.

25. *SC*, 5:419; *Shelley and Byron*, 61.

26. *Byron*, 2:846; *Shelley and Byron*, 161–62.

27. To John Murray, 12 October, 4, 9, 18 November 1820, *BLJ*, 7:200–2, 217, 225, 229.

28. *Shelley and Byron*, 162, 271 n. 52; John Barnard, "Byron's Use of *Endymion* in *Don Juan*, Canto I," *KSR* 3 (1988): 62–69.

29. To John Murray, 26 April 1821, *BLJ,* 8:102.

30. To PBS, 26 April 1821, *BLLJ,* 501–2.

31. To LH, 26 August 1821, *L,* 2:345.

32. To LB, 4 May 1821, *L,* 2:289–91.

33. To John Murray, 30 July 1821, *BLJ,* 8:162. See also *Shelley and Byron,* 168–70.

34. To John Taaffe, 4 July 1821, *L,* 2:306–7; Timothy Webb, *Shelley: A Voice Not Understood* (Manchester: Manchester University Press, 1977), 166–69.

35. *UH,* 288–89.

36. To John Gisborne, 10 April 1822, 26 January 1822, *L,* 2:406, 388.

37. To CC, to John Gisborne, 16 June 1821, *L,* 2:302, 300; *GY,* 430.

38. To John Gisborne, 16 June 1821, *L,* 2:299–300. See also *L,* 2:299–300 n. 1; *GWJL,* 71–72.

39. To Medwin, 4 April 1821, *L,* 2:280.

40. *GY,* 427, 643–44 n. 20.

41. To Ollier, 11 June, [late] July 1821, *L,* 2:298–99, 310–11. See also Peck, 2:222–23; *SC,* 5:421–22.

42. *GY,* 432; Hogle, 302, 390–91 n. 57.

43. *GY,* 436; *CG,* 173–80; Carlos Baker, *Shelley's Major Poetry* (Princeton: Princeton University Press, 1948), 245.

44. Anthony D. Knerr, *Shelley's Adonais: A Critical Edition* (New York: Columbia University Press, 1984), 85–86, 256–57 n. 16.

45. To Maria Gisborne, 30 June, 1821, *LMWS,* 1:203; *JMS,* 1:371; *JCC,* 237–38.

46. To CC, 5 August 1821, *L,* 2:314.

47. To the Gisbornes, 19 July 1821, *L,* 2:310.

48. To John Taaffe, 4 July 1821, *L,* 2:307.

49. To LB, 16 July 1821, *L,* 2:308–10.

50. *JCC,* 242–43.

51. To MWS, 31 July 1821, *L,* 2:313.

52. To PBS, 30–?31 July 1821, *BLJ,* 8:163.

53. To Count Pietro Gamba, 5, 9 August 1821, *BLJ,* 8:171, 175.

54. *JCC,* 244; *JMS,* 1:376.

55. *JMS,* 1:377.

56. To MWS, 6 August 1821, to CC, 5 August 1821, *L,* 2:315–16, 313–14.

57. Richard Hoppner to LB, 16 September 1820, *L,* 2:318. Printed in full in *Lord Byron's Correspondence,* ed. John Murray (London: John Murray, 1922) 2:179–83.

58. To MWS, 7 August 1821, *L,* 2:316–19.

59. To MWS, 8 August 1821, *L,* 2:320–22, 320 n. 2.

60. To PBS, 10 August 1821, *LMWS,* 1:204; Elise Foggi to MWS, 26 July 1821, *LMWS,* 1:208–9.

61. To Isabella Hoppner, 10 August 1821, *LMWS,* 1:205–8.

62. To Richard Hoppner, 1 October 1820, *BLJ,* 7:191. "Shiloh" refers to the delusional millenarian Joanna Southcote.

63. To Richard Hoppner, ? 3, 3 April 1821, *BLJ,* 8:97–98.

64. To MWS, 10 August 1821, *L,* 2:324.

65. To LH, 26 August 1821, *L,* 2:345.

66. *Byron,* 2:697.

67. To MWS, 16 August 1821, *L,* 2:336–38.

68. Dowden, 2:429; Grylls, 149–50; Moore, 255–57; 493–94; *Byron,* 2:925–26 n. 2.

69. *Byron,* 2:925–26 n. 2.

70. To MWS, 10 August 1821, to The Countess Guiccioli, 10 August 1821, to LB, 14 September 1821, *L*, 2:322–25, 325–29, 347.

71. To TLP, ?10 August 1810, *L*, 2:330.

72. To MWS, 11 August 1821, *L*, 2:331–32.

73. To MWS, 15–16 August 1821, *L*, 2:333–39.

74. *LA*, 277–78.

75. To Medwin, 22 August 1821, *L*, 2:341.

76. Emilia Viviani to PBS, n.d., *SM*, 576–77.

77. To PBS, 26 August 1821, to Teresa Guiccioli, 26 August 1821, *BLJ*, 8:189–90; PBS to LB, late August 1821, 14 September 1821, *L*, 2:343, 346.

78. To Teresa Guiccioli, 24 August 1821, *BLJ*, 8:188.

79. To Teresa Guiccioli, 9 September 1821, *BLJ*, 8:204–5.

80. To LB, 14 September 1821, *L*, 2:346–47.

81. LH to PBS, 28 August 1821, *SM*, 696–99.

82. To LH, 26 August 1821, LH to PBS and MWS, 21 September 1821, *L*, 2:343–46.

83. Emilia Viviani to PBS, 3 September 1821, White, 2:484–85.

84. Moore, 251.

85. To Hogg, 22 October 1821, *L*, 2:360.

86. To JW, [? 1822], *L*, 2:386–87.

87. To John Gisborne, 22 October 1821, *L*, 2:363.

14. THE LAST PISAN WINTER

1. *JMS*, 1:379; *JCC*, 247.

2. Horace Smith to PBS, 30 August, 3 October 1821, *L*, 2:348, 350–51; PBS to Horace Smith, 14 September 1821, *L*, 2:348–50.

3. To Ollier, 25 September 1821, *L*, 2:352–55.

4. To Maria Gisborne, 6 May 1823, *LMWS*, 1:336; CC to MWS, 15 March 1836, *CC*, 2:341.

5. To Ollier, 11 October 1821, *L*, 2:356–57.

6. To Hogg, 22 October 1821, *L*, 2:361.

7. TLP to PBS, 11 October 1821, *SM*, 699–700, *L*, 2:361 n. 5.

8. To TLP, ? 11 January 1822, *L*, 2:374.

9. TLP to PBS, 28 February 1822, *L*, 2:374–75.

10. To Ollier, 11 January 1822, *L*, 2:372.

11. *BSM*, 16:xxix–xlvii.

12. To MWS, 10 August 1821, *L*, 2:324.

13. Ernest J. Lovell, ed., *His Very Self and Voice: Collected Conversations of Lord Byron* (New York: Macmillan, 1954), 447.

14. *GY*, 375–80, 633 n. 33; Reiman, 120; Wasserman, 395.

15. *GWJL*, 106–11.

16. To Ollier, 11 November 1821, *L*, 2:365.

17. Charles E. Robinson, "Percy Bysshe Shelley, Charles Ollier, and William Blackwood," in Everest, 203.

18. To LH, 6 October 1821, *L*, 2:355–56.

19. To LB, 21 October 1821, *L*, 2:357–58.

20. To Hogg, 22 October 1821, *L*, 2:359–62.

21. To CC, 16 June 1821, to John Gisborne, 22 October 1821, *L*, 2:303, 362–64.

22. A marker on Tre Palazzi di Chiesa recognizes PBS's residency but the section containing his apartments was destroyed in 1943 by Allied bombing.

23. To TLP, ? 11 January 1822, *L*, 2:373–74. See also *SC*, 8:827–42.

24. Sunstein, 203, 438 n. 1.

25. *GWJL*, 105–6.

26. To MWS, 31 October 1821, *CC*, 1:167.

27. To MWS, 9 March 1834, *CC*, 1:309. Sunstein, 204, believed CC was speaking about PBS; Stocking, *CC*, 1:311 n. 9, is unable "to identify this friend."

28. "Detached Thoughts," Pisa, 5 November 1821, *BLJ*, 9:49.

29. To MWS, [? 16 November] 1822, *BLLJ*, 574.

30. *GWJL*, 112.

31. Medwin, 327.

32. *GWJL*, 114.

33. *Conversations*, 62; Cline, 53.

34. To Maria Gisborne, 30 November 1821, *LMWS*, 1:209.

35. Angeli, 264; Cline, 54.

36. Medwin, 328–29; *GWJL*, 116–17.

37. *SC*, 8:737–43; *GWJL*, 111–12.

38. *GWJL*, 114–15.

39. To CC, 11 December 1821, *L*, 2:367–68.

40. Unrecorded by MWS.

41. To CC, 31 December 1821, *L*, 2:370–71.

42. *JCC*, 260, 265.

43. To John Murray, 6 July 1821, *BLJ*, 8:147–48.

44. To Maria Gisborne, 21 December 1821, *LMWS*, 1:212; *GWJL*, 109.

45. To John Gisborne, 26 January, 12 January 1822, *L*, 2:388, 376.

46. To Maria Gisborne, ? 20 December 1821, *LMWS*, 1:212. See also Moore, App. 11; *JMS*,1:385.

47. John Hunt to PBS, 16 November 1821, *SM*, 706–8.

48. To Maria Gisborne, [?] January, 7 March 1822, *LMWS*, 1:214, 223; *JMS*,1:386; *GWJL*, 117; Medwin, 360–64.

49. Paula R. Feldman, "Shelley, Mrs. Mason and the Devil Incarnate: An Unpublished Poem," *The Library Chronicle of the University of Texas at Austin* 12 (1979): 21–29; Medwin, 362–64.

50. Medwin, 364–67; Cline, 60–65, 231 n. 1.

51. To Thomas Moore, ? 13 December 1821, *BLJ*, 9:81; PBS to LB, 13 December 1821, *L*, 2:368–69.

52. *Prose*, 266, 274; *RC*.

53. To Horace Smith, 11 April 1822, *L*, 2:412; *Records*, 80; *Shelley and Byron*, 196.

54. *Shelley and Byron*, 197–99, 276 n. 54; Medwin, 334.

55. *GWJL*, 124–26.

56. To Maria Gisborne, 21 December 1821, *LMWS*, 1:212–13; *GWJL*, 118–19.

57. Edward Williams to EJT, [26] December 1821, *Recollections*, 12–14.

58. To Maria Gisborne, 21 December 1821, *LMWS*, 1:213.

59. To CC, 31 December 1821, *L*, 1:370.

60. To John Gisborne, 12 January 1822, *L*, 2:376.

61. Edward Williams to EJT, 26 December 1821, *GWJL*, 160.

62. DK (1995), 30; Susan C. Djabri, "The Beauclerks of St. Leonard's Lodge," Horsham, n.p., 1995; Sunstein, 316, 449 n. 13.

63. MWS to EJT, 15 December 1829, *LMWS*, 2:94; Medwin, 367–69; *JMS*,1:398; Lovell, 103–6.

64. *GWJL*, 119.

65. Moore, 267–73; PBS to Horace Smith, 25 January 1822, *L*, 2:379.

66. *GWJL*, 119; Medwin, 375.

67. *GWJL*, 130.

68. *Byron*, 3:971.

69. Medwin, 375.

70. To LB, 15 February 1822, *L*, 2:389; *JMS*, 1:398.

71. To LH, 17 February 1822, *L*, 2:389–90.

72. *Byron*, 3:971.

73. *Byron*, 2:603; Moore, 253–54.

74. *GWJL*, 122; "Detached Thoughts," *BLJ*, 9:21.

75. Byron Collection, Harrow. The medals, made about 1820 by Andrieu, depict famous events in Napoleon's life.

76. PBS's fair copy, dated January 22, titled "Lines to—." See also *MYR*, 8:246–51; Andrew Nicholson, "Review of *BSM* XII (ed. Nora Crook)," *KSR* 7 (1993): 166–67.

77. *Shelley and Byron*, 208–9.

78. Medwin, 285, wrote, "Byron never saw" the sonnet. PBS made two fair copies, one perhaps intended for LB.

79. *GWJL*, 123; PBS to TLP, [? 11 January 1822], *L*, 2:373.

80. To Ollier, 11 January 1822, *L*, 2:371–72.

81. *BSM*, 12:xxx.

82. To LH, 25 January, to John Gisborne, 12 January 1822, *L*, 2:380, 375.

83. To LH, 2 March 1822, *L*, 2:394.

84. *Shelley and Byron*, 212; Reiman, 126–27.

85. Medwin, 342–43.

86. To Ollier, 11 January 1821, *L*, 2:372.

87. *Recollections*, 22–23.

88. *JMS*, 1:390–91.

89. To Maria Gisborne, 9 February 1822, *LMWS*, 1:218.

90. *Trelawny*, 28.

91. *The Diary of W. M. Rossetti*, ed. Odette Bornand (Oxford: Oxford University Press, Clarendon Press, 1977), 170; *BSM*, 12:lxi.

92. To Maria Gisborne, ? 18 January 1822, *LMWS*, 1:214–16.

93. To Horace Smith, 25 January 1822, *L*, 2:378–79.

94. To John Gisborne, 12 January 1822, *L*, 2:376.

95. To John Gisborne, 10 April, 18 June 1822, *L*, 2:407, 435–36.

96. To Edward Williams, 26 January 1822, *L*, 2:384. The heavily obliterated final words probably were not censored by PBS.

97. *GWJL*, 127.

98. Ibid., 132; *JMS*, 1:400.

15. DRAWN TO THE SEA

1. *GWJL*, 125.

2. Anne Hill, "Trelawny's Family Background and Naval Career," *KSJ* 5 (1956): 11–32; *Trelawny*, 65–67.

3. *JMS,* 1:390 n. 1, 392.

4. EJT to Captain Roberts, 7 February 1822, Cline, 74–75.

5. *LA,* 298; *Trelawny,* 215 n. 18.

6. Joseph A. Dane, "On the Instability of Vessels and Narratives: A Nautical Perspective on the Sinking of the *Don Juan," KSJ* 47 (1998), 71–73. In Williams's pen-and-ink sketch of the two boats (*JMS,* 1:211; *SG,* 182), that on the left is almost certainly not the *Bolivar.* That on the right resembles Roberts's version of the *Don Juan* and Villa Magni.

7. *GWJL,* 128.

8. EJT to Captain Roberts, 5 February 1822, *LEJT,* 1–2. See also *GWJL,* 128 n. 87.

9. Dane, "Nautical Perspective," 75–76.

10. To John Gisborne, 18 June 1822, *L,* 2:435.

11. To Maria Gisborne, 9 February 1822, *LMWS,* 1:217–18.

12. *Recollections,* 97–100.

13. Dane, "Nautical Perspective," 75–79.

14. *Recollections,* chap. 9.

15. Ibid., chap. 7.

16. *Records,* Preface.

17. *Recollections,* chaps. 4, 21. For LB's clubfoot, see *Byron,* 3:1238 n. line 19.

18. *LA,* 298.

19. *GWJL,* 128; *JMS,* 1:393.

20. *SPP,* 470–71 n. 1; Chernaik, 162, 266. For texts of both poems, see *SPP,* 470–74.

21. *Prose,* 170.

22. *GWJL,* 130–31.

23. *JMS,* 1:394–97; *GWJL,* 128–30.

24. To LH, 17 February 1822, *L,* 2:390.

25. *LMWS,* 1:470 n. 7.

26. *Conversations,* 190–91.

27. *JMS,* 1:397; MWS to Maria Gisborne, 3 May 1823, *LMWS,* 1:334.

28. *Byron,* 3:991.

29. *New Monthly Magazine and Literary Journal* n.s. 29, pt. ii (1830): 327–66. Reprinted in McElderberry, *Shelley's Critical Prose,* App. A. See also *Shelley and Byron,* 148–49, 270 n. 30.

30. Medwin, 334–35; *Conversations,* 153–54. See also *Shelley and Byron,* 213–17, 278.

31. *JMS,* 1:394; *Byron,* 3:967–69; *GWJL,* 135.

32. *Shelley and Byron,* 213–16, 278 nn. 23–29.

33. To CC, [n.d.], *L,* 2:391–92.

34. Dowden, 2:487; *JCC,* 128 n. 96, 466–67.

35. Dowden, 2:483, 486.

36. *JCC,* 229. Harriet Campbell married the Countess's son in Florence, February 1821.

37. MWS had not responded to Elise's mid-1821 letter asking for money and Elise possibly was hinting further blackmail when she met CC.

38. *JCC,* 274–75.

39. To LB, 18 February 1822, *CC,* 1:169–70.

40. *JCC,* 274–76.

41. To CC, 20 February 1822, *LMWS,* 1:220.

42. *JMS,* 1:399–400.

43. *GWJL*, 132–34.
44. Ibid., 131.
45. Medwin, 317–18; *LA*, 298–99.
46. "Fragments of an Unfinished Drama." See *CW*, 4:129–137, 414; *Trelawny*, 64.
47. *SC*, 7:48; Chernaik, 156–58, 254–56.
48. *Records*, 123–24.
49. To MWS, 9 April 1822, *CC*, 1:172.
50. To Maria Gisborne, 7 March 1822, *LMWS*, 1:223.
51. H. J. Massingham, *The Friend of Shelley: A Memoir of Edward John Trelawny* (London: Cobden-Sanderson, 1930), 215.
52. *JCC*, 278 n. 2.
53. To MWS, 9 April 1822, *CC*, 1:172; *SM*, 786–87; *GY*, 70, 582 n. 18.
54. To CC, 20 February 1843, *LMWS*, 3:58.
55. Box 8, file 4, Silsbee; *CC*, 1:173 n. 1.
56. To CC, 20 March 1822, *LMWS*, 1:225–26.
57. To CC, 24 March 1822, *L*, 2:399–401.
58. To CC, 31 March 1822, *L*, 2:402–3.
59. *Conversations*, 261; *JCC*, 278 n. 99, 283.
60. To CC, 25 March 1822, *L*, 2:401.
61. Cline, chaps. 6, 7; *GWJL*, 136–37; MWS to Maria Gisborne, 6 April 1822, *LMWS*, 1:227–28.
62. To CC, 31 March 1822, *L*, 2:403.
63. *JMS*, 1:406; Cline, 241–42 n. 101.
64. To CC, 31 March 1822, *L*, 2:403; MWS to LH, 13 April 1822, *LMWS*, 1:234.
65. To LH, 10 April 1822, *L*, 2:405.
66. To John Hay, 6 April 1822, *BJL*, 9:135.
67. *Byron*, 3:988; *GWJL*, 143.
68. *GWJL*, 141.
69. To CC, 10 April 1822, *L*, 2:403–4.
70. To Ollier, 11 April, to John Gisborne, 10 April 1822, *L*, 2:410–11, 406.
71. John Gisborne to Hogg, 12 August 1822, *GWJL*, 88. PBS's presumed 1819 will, never located, was unmentioned in his letters.
72. To LH, 30 October 1826, *LWMS*, 1:535.
73. *GWJL*, 143.
74. MS. Shelley adds. c. 12, fol. 24, Bodleian; *SG*, 178.
75. To Horace Smith, 11 April 1822, *L*, 2:412.
76. The guitar is dated 1815 or 1816. See *SG*, 176. PBS apparently owned another similar guitar in a black case (Pforzheimer Collection, New York Public Library) made in 1817 in Naples.
77. *Recollections*, chap. 8; *Records*, 310 n. 20.
78. *LA*, 310–11; Moore, 318–21; *Byron*, 3:991–92.
79. *BLLJ*, 567–68.
80. *LA*, 311; Moore, 321–24.
81. To PBS, 23 April 1822, *BJL*, 9:147–48; *JMS*, 1:404.
82. To Maria Gisborne, 2 June 1822, *LMWS*, 1:235.
83. To MWS, 28 April 1822, *L*, 2:413–14.
84. *GWJL*, 146.
85. To LH, 19 June 1822, *L*, 2:438; *GWJL*, 146.

86. *JMS*, 1:410.
87. To Maria Gisborne, 2 June 1822, *LMWS*, 1:236; *GWJL*, 146.
88. To LB, 3 May 1822, *L*, 2:415–16.
89. Mrs. Mason to MWS, 14 January 1823, *JCC*, 294–95.
90. To LB, 9 May 1822, *L*, 2:416–17.
91. Cline, 139–47.
92. To LB, [? 12 May] 1822, *L*, 2:417–18.
93. To LB, 16 May 1822, *L*, 2;420.
94. To PBS, 20 May 1820, *BLJ*, 9:160–61.
95. To LB, 3, 9 May 1822, *L*, 2:415–16, 416–17.
96. *GWJL*, 147.
97. *EL*, 2:347.
98. *GWJL*, 147. For Williams's nautical naïveté and arrogance about his prowess, see Dane, "Nautical Perspective," 85–86.
99. *GWJL*, 148.
100. Ibid., 148–49; PBS to Captain Roberts, 14 May 1822, *L*, 2:419.
101. To Maria Gisborne, 2 June 1822, *LMWS*, 1:236.
102. To EJT, 16 May, to LB, 16 May 1822, *L*, 2:421–22, 420–21 n. 5.
103. To Horace Smith, c. 21 May 1822, *L*, 2:423–25; WG to MWS, 19 April, 3 May 1822, *L*, 2:423–24 n. 2; Horace Smith to PBS, 5 June 1822, *L*, 2:425–26 n. 3. See also, StC, 465–66; *SM*, 811–14.
104. Mrs. Mason to PBS, 12 May, ? May 1822, *SM*, 800–2.

16. A "WATERY ECLIPSE"

1. *GWJL*, 149.
2. Ibid., 150.
3. Ibid., 150–51, 154; Dane, "Nautical Perspective," *KSJ* 47 (1998), 80.
4. Box 7, file 3, Silsbee.
5. To CC, 28 May 1822, *L*, 2:427.
6. To CC, 30 May 1822, *L*, 2:430.
7. Betty T. Bennett and Alice G. Fredman, "A Note on the Dating of Shelley's "The Triumph of Life," " *KSJ* 31 (1982): 13–15. See also Donald H. Reiman, *Shelley's "The Triumph of Life": A Critical Study* (Urbana: University of Illinois Press, 1965); *BSM*, 1:116–17.
8. To CC, 28 May 1822, *L*, 2:427.
9. To CC, 30 May 1822, *L*, 2:429–30.
10. To Mary Jane Godwin, 29 May 1822, *L*, 2:428–29.
11. To CC, 28, 30 May 1822, *L*, 2:427, 430; *GWJL*, 151–52.
12. *GWJL*, 153; *JMS*, 1:411.
13. To Maria Gisborne, 2 June 1822, *LMWS*, 1:234–37.
14. *GWJL*, 153–54.
15. To Maria Gisborne, 15 August 1822, *LMWS*, 1:244.
16. To John Gisborne, 18 June 1822, *L*, 2:434.
17. To Edward J. Dawkins, 26 June 1822, *BLJ*, 9:178.
18. *Records*, chap. 10.
19. Ibid.

20. To Maria Gisborne, 15 August 1822, *LMWS*, 1:244–45.

21. To EJT, 18 June 1822, *L*,2: 432–33.

22. To John Taaffe, 11 June 1822, to Brookes & Company, 15 June 1822, *L*, 2:431, 432.

23. Rieger, 233; *Shelley and Byron*, 221.

24. To John Gisborne, 18 June 1822, *L*, 2:434–37. See *UH*, 389.

25. To LH, 19 [? 20] June 1822, *L*, 2:437–39.

26. *SPP*, 479 n. 1; Chernaik, 260.

27. Chernaik, 259.

28. Roberts to EJT, 28 March 1822. See B. C. Barker-Benfield, "The Honeymoon of Joseph and Henrietta Chichester, with Daniel Roberts' Memories of Byron and Shelley," *Bodleian Library Record* 12 (April 1986): 126, 137 n. 39.

29. To EJT, 18 June 1822, *L*, 2:432. See also, Diana Pugh, "Captain Roberts and the Sinking of the *Don Juan*," *KSMB* 26 (1975): 18–22; Dane, "Nautical Perspective," 79.

30. Dane, "Nautical Perspective," 79, lists the seven sails as a main, mizzen, two (untested) topsails, and "perhaps three foresails."

31. Roberts's 1822 painting, acquired by Eton College in 1997, was first published in *KSR* 16 (2002). See also *GWJL*, 154–56. For the woodcut in *Recollections*, see *GWJL*, 14–15.

32. *GWJL*, 155.

33. Ibid., 154.

34. To Maria Gisborne, 15 August 1822, *LMWS*, 1:245–46.

35. Ibid.

36. Ibid.

37. Cameron (*GY*, 90–95) considered these episodes indicated PBS was not "psychotic" but hesitated to label him "neurotic." White, 2:372, believed the episodes "owe a great deal" to Shelley's "manic-depressive psychology." Holmes, 727, thought Shelley's visions "his Zoroastrian double."

38. *BSM*, 1:f. 35 v.

39. *SPP*, 481 n. 3; Chernaik, 276 n. 58.

40. *GWJL*, 155; to LH, 24 June 1822, *L*, 2:401.

41. To LH, c. 30 June 1822, *LMWS*, 1:238.

42. *GWJL*, 156.

43. Hugh Roberts, *Shelley and the Chaos of History: A New Politics of Poetry* (University Park: The Pennsylvania State University Press, 1997), 397–407.

44. *GY*, 460–62, 468, 649 n. 31.

45. *Shelley and Byron*, 227–28. For *Julie* and *The Triumph*, see Donald H. Reiman, "Shelley's "*The Triumph of Life*": The Biographical Problem," *PMLA* 78 No.5 (December 1963): 536–50; Roberts, *Shelley and Chaos*, 203–6.

46. CG, 215–17.

47. *Shelley and Byron*, 225–26.

48. William A. Ulmer, *Shelleyan Eros* (Princeton: Princeton University Press, 1990), 182.

49. Hogle, 398 n. 124.

50. To Horace Smith, 29 June 1822, *L*, 2:442.

51. *Shelley and Byron*, 228–36.

52. EJT to PBS, 22 June 1822, *SM*, 823–24.

53. To Horace Smith, 29 June 1922, *L*, 2:442–43.

54. *ALH*, 2:102; *Byron*, 3:1006 n. line 5.

55. *GWJL,* 156.

56. To Maria Gisborne, 15 August 1822, *LMWS,* 1:246.

57. *Rossetti Papers,* quoted from Reiman, "The Biographical Problem," 544; Medwin, 318–19.

58. *The Correspondence of Leigh Hunt,* ed. Thornton Hunt (London, 1862), 1:182; PBS to LH, 10 April 1822, *L,* 2:405.

59. Rees, chap. 2, 93.

60. G. M. Matthews, "On Shelley's '*The Triumph of Life*'," *Studia Neophilologica* 34 (1962): 129–32. For the reading "Julie," see Reiman, "The Biographical Problem," 536–50.

61. *GWJL,* 156.

62. *AM,* 189–91.

63. *ALH,* 2:132–33; White, 2:528.

64. *ALH,* 2:125.

65. Ibid., 2:126; Cline, 172–75.

66. Blunden, 299–300.

67. To MWS, 4 July 1822, *L,* 2:444; *ALH,* 2:126.

68. Edward Williams to JW, 6 July 1822, *Recollections,* 109–12.

69. *GWJL,* 156.

70. To MWS, 4 July 1822, *L,* 2:444. See also *Byron,* 3:1026; W. H. Marshall, *Byron, Shelley, Hunt, and "The Liberal"* (Philadelphia: University of Pennsylvania Press, 1960).

71. JW to LH, 28 April 1824, *GWJL,* 166.

72. Edward Williams to JW, 6 July 1822, *GWJL,* 162–63.

73. To Maria Gisborne, 15 August 1822, *LMWS,* 1:246.

74. To MWS, 4 July 1822, *L,* 2:443–44.

75. To JW, 4 July 1822, *L,* 2:445.

76. JW to PBS, 6 July 1822, *Records* (1878), 124–25; *GWJL,* 160–61.

77. To Maria Gisborne, 15 August 1822, *LMWS,* 1:248.

78. Lovell, *His Very Self and Voice,* 304.

79. *ALH,* 2:133.

80. To Maria Gisborne, 15 August 1822, *LMWS,* 1:244–50.

81. To Maria Gisborne, c. 27 August 1822, *LMWS,* 1:255.

82. *ALH,* 2:129–30.

83. *GY,* 98–111. For EJT's numerous accounts, see Leslie A. Marchand, "Trelawny on the Death of Shelley," *KSMB* 4 (1952): 9–34. Internal contradictions and apparent fabrications in the oft-cited later reports by EJT and Roberts place their probable self-serving testimony in serious question.

84. *Records,* chap. 11. Letter to the *Times,* December 1875; *Recollections,* chap. 11.

85. *Trelawny,* 226–27; *GWJL,* 156.

86. White, 2:632 n. 43.

87. To Maria Gisborne, 15 August 1822, *LMWS,* 1:248.

88. Marchand, "Trelawny on the Death," 29–30, Narrative 2, dated by EJT "Sep.br 1822" but probably written in Rome April 1823. Original, Keats-Shelley Memorial House, Rome.

89. Narrative 5, Marchand, "Trelawny on the Death," Add. 39168 S., BL.

90. Roberts to LB, 20 July 1822, MS. Shelley adds d. 4, fols. 17–18, Bodleian; see also *JMS,*1:414, Barker-Benfield, "Daniel Roberts' Memories," 130.

91. Capt. Daniel Roberts to MWS, 14 September 1822, Add. 52361, BL.

92. *Recollections,* chap. 11.

93. Marchand, "Trelawny on the Death," 15.

94. Barker-Benfield, "Daniel Roberts' Memories," 122.

95. *Recollections,* chap. 14.

96. Captain Daniel Roberts to MWS, 14 September 1822, Add. 52361, BL. Also found were "7 torn sails."

97. Narrative 5, Marchand, "Trelawny on the Death," Add. 39168 S., BL.

98. Dane, "Nautical Perspective," 82. See *The Journal of Clarissa Trant,* ed. C. G. Luard (London: John Lane, 1925), 198–99; Peck, 2:287; *GY,* 100, 388 n. 124.

99. Rieger, 221–36.

17. LIFE TERMINABLE AND INTERMINABLE

1. To Maria Gisborne, 15 August 1822, *LMWS,* 1:246–48.

2. LH to PBS, 9 July 1822, *SM,* 838.

3. To Maria Gisborne, 15 August 1822, *LMWS,* 1:246–48.

4. *Records,* chap. 11.

5. To Captain Roberts, 14 July 1822, *BLJ,* 9:184.

6. Records, App.

7. LH to EJT, "8 o'clock, p.m. 17th July," *The Correspondence of Leigh Hunt,* 1:184.

8. To LH, 19 July 1822, *CC,* 1:176.

9. Guido Biagi, *The Last Days of Percy Bysshe Shelley* (London, 1898), 83.

10. *Records,* App.

11. *Recollections,* chap. 11.

12. Biagi, *Last Days,* 77–80, 83; *Records,* chap. 11, App.

13. To Maria Gisborne, c. 27 August 1822, *LMWS,* 1:253–54.

14. Biagi, *Last Days,* 84–105; MWS to Edward Dawkins, 21 August 1822, *LMWS,* 1:251. See also Peck, 2:App.K.

15. To Maria Gisborne, 15 August 1822, to Edward Dawkins, 21 August 1822, *LMWS,* 1:249, 251.

16. Leslie A. Marchand, "Trelawny on the Death of Shelley," *KSMB* 4 (1952): 9–34. Narratives 1 and 3.

17. Moore, 345.

18. *LEJT,* 10–14; Add. 39168, BL.

19. *ALH,* 2:130.

20. To Thomas Moore, 27 August 1822, *BLLJ,* 564–65.

21. *Recollections,* chap. 12; *Trelawny,* 217 n. 3.

22. "16th August 1822," Add. 39168, BL.

23. A. M. Z. Norman, "Shelley's Heart," *The Journal of the History of Medicine* (1955): 114; *LMWS,* 1:256; Gelpi, 131. Frederick L. Hildebrand, M.D., a pulmonary specialist, in a letter to the author, 11 November 1996, noted that heart calcification is extremely rare and would have caused a protracted illness with heart failure, inconsistent with Shelley's physical health at the time of his death. If Shelley did have tuberculosis, Hildebrand considered he "certainly could have had tuberculosis pericarditis" in which ultimately calcium is laid down as part of the healing process.

24. LH to MWS, 17 August 1822, *Letters of Mary W. Shelley,* ed. F. L. Jones (Norman: University of Oklahoma Press, 1944), 1:187.

25. To Maria Gisborne, c. 27 August 1822, *LMWS*, 1:253–54.

26. To Thomas Moore, 27 August 1822, *BLLJ*, 565. See also *Byron*, 3:1025.

27. *GWJL*, 88–89.

28. *JCC*, 284, 356.

29. *LEJT*, 15–19; *LMWS*, 1:282; *CC*, 1:177–78.

30. To JW, 12 January 1823, *LMWS*, 1:306.

31. EJT to CC, 4 December [1822], 10 December 1822, 20 April 1823, MS Ashley 5119, BL. See also *LEJT*, 28–32; *JCC*, 284 n. 19.

32. To John Parke, 7 September 1822, *LMWS*, 1:256–57.

33. Angeli, 317–19.

34. To EJT, 7 January 1823, *LMWS*, 1:302. See also Dowden, 2:536 n.

35. H. Nelson Gay, "The Protestant Burial-Ground in Rome," *Bulletin & Review Keats-Shelley Memorial Rome* 2 (1913), 54.

36. *Life and Letters of Joseph Severn*, ed. William Sharp (London, 1892), 122–23; Hay, "Protestant Burial-Ground," 52–54; White, 2:383, 634 nn. 58–59.

37. Hay, "Protestant Burial-Ground," 54.

38. Grylls, 79.

39. EJT to MWS, 2 April, 27 April 1823, *SM*, 930–31, 933–36.

40. To Maria Gisborne, 20 September 1822, to JW, 15 October 1822, to Maria Gisborne, 3 May 1823, *LMWS*, 1:262, 282, 334–35.

41. *PW*, 676–78, 679–80 n. 1.

42. Marchand, "Trelawny on the Death," 29–31, narrative 2.

43. B. C. Barker-Benfield, "The Honeymoon of Joseph and Henrietta Chichester, with Daniel Roberts' Memories of Byron and Shelley," *Bodleian Library Record* 12 (April 1986), 122.

44. *GY*, 102–3, 105–6; *Records*, chap. 11; *Atheneum* 25 December 1875.

45. Biagi, *Last Days*, 142–47.

46. *GY*, 98–111, 587–90; Diana Pugh, "Captain Roberts and the Sinking of the *Don Juan*," *KSMB* 26 (1975): 18–22; *Trelawny*, 183–86; Barker Benfield, "Daniel Roberts' Memories," 139 n. 75.

47. *Recollections*, chap. 10.

48. *GY*, 103–6.

49. To CC, 22 September 1822, 22 November 1822, *LEJT*, 20, 25.

50. Biagi, *Last Days*, 163–64. Canova, "not present" at PBS's cremation, reported "it took place near the Du'fosse", a reference to Fossa dell Abate and Focette, two adjacent locales just north of Viareggio near Motrone, where PBS's body was found. Canova remembered seeing "smoke rising there."

51. *GY*, 106.

52. *UH*, 321; LH to Elizabeth Kent, 20 July 1822, *A Shelley Library*, ed. Thomas James Wise (London: Private Circulation, 1924), 105–6.

53. Norman, 15–16.

54. *UH*, chap. 13.

55. Ingpen, 559.

56. TS to Whitton, 6, 8 August 1822, TLP to TS, 6 August 1822, H. Holste to TS, 6 August 1822, Ingpen 549–53.

57. WG to MWS, 9, 6 August 1822, *SM*, 843–44, 840A–40B.

58. WG to Mrs. John Taylor, 16 August 1822, *LMWS*, 3:401; StC, 467–68.

59. *Conversations*, 306, 319; Medwin, 394–95.

60. Medwin to JW, 25 February 1823, Abinger Collection, Bodleian; Lovell, 138.

61. To Thomas Moore, 8 August 1822, *BLLJ*, 563–64; to John Murray, 3 August 1822, *BLJ*, 9:189–90; to Thomas Moore, 4 March 1822, *BLLJ*, 552.

62. To Thomas Moore, 27 August 1822, *BLLJ*, 565.

63. To Maria Gisborne, 17, 20 September 1822, *LMWS*, 1:260–62.

64. Moore, 352–53.

65. *Byron*, 3:1030–33; *BLJ*, 9:209–10.

66. To MWS, 4 October 1822, *BLJ*, 10:11. See also Moore, 350–51.

67. *Byron*, 3:1033–36; *Records*, chap. 14; *JMS*, 2:432.

68. Ingpen, 511–12; MWS to Maria Gisborne, 20 September 1822, *LMWS*, 1:261.

69. To Hogg, 9 September 1822, *LMWS*, 1:257–58.

70. Hogg to JW, 17 April 1823, *JMS*, 2:502–3 n. 2.

71. Rees, 111–12.

72. *Trelawny*, 169, 191.

73. To CC, 27 November 1869, 5 January 1870, *LEJT*, 221–24.

74. To JW, 12 January, 19 February 1823, *LMWS*, 1:306, 312.

75. *JMS*, 2:facing 429.

76. To JW, 15 October 1822, *LMWS*, 1:283; *JMS*, 2:435.

77. *LMWS*, 1:267–68 n. 3.

78. *JMS*, 2:444–45 n. 4.

79. To CC, 19 December 1822, to JW, 15 October 1822, *LMWS*, 1:300, 280.

80. To John Hanson, 23 October 1822, *BLJ*, 10:16.

81. TS to LB, 6 February 1823, Ingpen, 566–67; LB to TS, 7 January 1823, Ingpen, 563–65.

82. To JW, 10 April 1823, *LMWS*, 1:328–31.

83. LH to ? Elizabeth Kent, c. August 1823, #3:35, Keats–Shelley Memorial House, Rome. See also Sunstein, 238–39. My inspection of LH's letter indicates it may not have been written to Bessy Kent.

84. *JMS*, 2:466–67.

85. "The Choice," ed. H. Buxton Forman, (London, 1876); *JMS*, 2:490–94.

86. Sunstein, 238.

87. JW to LH, 28 April 1824, *GWJL*, 165–67. See also Rees, 139.

88. To JW, 31 May 1823, *LMWS*, 1:341.

89. To JW, c. 2 July 1823, *LMWS*, 1:344.

90. To LH, 28 June 1823, *BLJ*, 10:205–6.

91. To JW, c. 2 July 1823, *LMWS*, 1:344.

92. To CC, September 1824, *LEJT*, 87–89.

93. *JCC*, 358–59.

94. *LEJT*, 116; *JCC*, 417.

95. To EJT, 1 April, 27 July 1829, *LMWS*, 2:72, 82; EJT to MWS, 3 July 1829, *LEJT*, 126–27; Sunstein, 287, 297–98; *Trelawny*, 134.

96. *JCC*, 418; *CC*, 1:282 n. 2.

97. To EJT, 26 June, 14 June 1831, *LMWS*, 2:143, 139. See also, *LEJT*, 162, 166.

98. *JMS*, 2:526–27.

99. To JW, 13 August 1823, *LMWS*, 1:366–67.

100. To LH, 9 September 1823, *LMWS*, 1:378.

101. Ingpen, 574–75.

102. To EJT, 12 October 1835, *LMWS*, 2:256; to LH, 12 August 1826, *LMWS*, 1:527–28.

103. *JMS*, 2:488–89.

104. Sunstein, 280–85.

105. *LMWS*, 1:493–94 nn. 1–2, 495 n. 4; Sunstein, 266–68; *JMS*, 2:468 n. 1, 472 n. 4; Norman, 64–65.

106. *JMS*, 2:481–82 n. 2, 488–89.

107. Ibid., 2:563–64; *CC*, 2:356–57 n. 6.

108. Box 7, file 3, Silsbee. See also *CC*, 2:356–57 n. 6; Sunstein, 315–16, 321–22, 449 n. 13; *LMWS*, 2:xxii–xxiii, 184 n. 1; *LMWS*, 3:374 n. 1; *JMS*, 2:600–601.

109. *CC*, 2:385 n. 2, 470 n. 1; *LMWS*, 3:xxvii–xxviii; Sunstein, 370–72.

110. To CC, 16 August 1842, *LMWS*, 3:36.

111. Rees, 156–62; Scott, 239–42; *CC*, 2:367 n. 2; *LMWS*, 3:33 n. 2.

112. To JW, 20 June 1825, December 1826, *CC*, 1:230, 240–41. See also *JCC*, 298–303; *CC*, 1:219 n. 7.

113. *Mary Shelley: Collected Tales and Stories*, ed. Charles E. Robinson (Baltimore: Johns Hopkins University Press, 1976), 347–72, 399–400.

114. To MWS, 26 October 1832, 9 March 1834, *CC*, 1:290–91, 309.

115. To MWS, 2 June, 16 September 1835, *CC*, 2:319, 327–28.

116. To EJT, 14 May 1836, *LMWS*, 2:271.

117. *CC*, 2:426–27 n. 2.

118. To EJT, 26 December 1870, *CC*, 2:614. See also *CC*, 2:App.C; Marion Kingston Stocking, "Miss Tina and Miss Plin: The Papers Behind *The Aspern Papers*," in *The Evidence of Imagination*, eds. Donald H. Reiman et al. (New York: New York University Press, 1978), 372–84. Marion Stocking is the only living Shelley scholar to have personally known a descendent of CC who had personally known CC.

119. *CC*, 2:664.

120. Lovell, 160–70.

121. Medwin to MWS, 10 July 1824, 13 [August] 1824, Abinger Collection. See also, Lovell, 161, 168.

122. Lovell, chap. 7; DK (1995), 41–43.

123. Ibid., 315–16.

124. Neil Fraistat, "'I Hate to Mutilate': Mary Shelley and the Transmission of Shelley's Textual Corpus," lecture, CUNY Graduate Center, November 1990. See also *SPP*, 645–53.

125. To LH, 6 October 1839, *LMWS*, 2:326.

126. To LH, 22 August 1824, *LMWS*, 1:444.

127. Ingpen, 576–85.

128. Only three of Ianthe's seven children lived to adulthood: Eliza Margaret Esdaile (1841–1930) was unmarried; William Esdaile (1846–1915) married but had no children; Charles Edward Jeffries Esdaile (1845–1922) had six sons and five daughters, one of whom was Ianthe Margaret Esdaile (1875–1937). Her brother Percy Charles Esdaile (1882–1926) had a daughter, Elizabeth Dorothy Warmington (b. 1917) of Cothelstone, my kind informant about the family history.

129. *JMS*, 2:498.

130. Ingpen, 580–98. John Shelley's son Edward (1827–1890) became the 4th Baronet in 1889 when Sir Percy Florence died; Edward's brother Charles (1838–1902) became 5th Baronet, succeeded by his son John. John's brother Percy Bysshe Shelley (b. 1872) became the 7th Baronet and was succeeded in 1953 by his brother.

131. Bouthaina Shaaban, "Shelley in the Chartist Press," *KSMB* 34 (1983):41–60. See also, White, 2:chap.30.

132. TS to John Gregson, 20 November 1832, MS. Shelley adds. d. 14, f. 57r., Bodleian. Quoted in Sunstein, 315.

133. To John Gregson, 8 October 1832, *LMWS*, 2:174.

134. Norman, 263–66.

135. Bessie Florence (d. 1934) married in 1871 Leopold James York Campbell, grandson of the 1st Baron Abinger. Her male descendents continued the Abinger line of barons. The 8th Baron Abinger (d. 2002) has been succeeded by his son, the 9th Baron Abinger. See *LMWS*, 3:374 n. 5.

Selected Bibliography

The sources listed include some writings not cited in the endnotes. A few other works that were influential, including Melville's *Moby-Dick*, rest too deep to be cited.

CHRONOLOGY OF PUBLICATION OF SHELLEY'S WORKS

Those published during his lifetime list author(s)'s name (if any) as printed.

Zastrozzi, a Romance. By P. B. S. London: G. Wilkie and J. Robinson, 1810.

Original Poetry; by Victor and Cazire. Worthing: Printed by C. and W. Phillips and Sold by J. J. Stockdale, 41, Pall Mall, and All Other Booksellers, 1810.

Posthumous Fragments of Margaret Nicholson; Being Poems Found Amongst the Papers of that Noted Female Who Attempted the Life of the King in 1786. Edited by John Fitzvictor. Oxford: J. Munday, 1810.

St. Irvyne; or The Rosicrucian: A Romance. By A Gentleman of the University of Oxford. London: J. J. Stockdale, 1811. Remainders reissued by Stockdale with 1822 date.

The Necessity of Atheism. Worthing: Printed by C. & W. Phillips, [1811].

An Address, to the Irish People. By Percy Bysshe Shelley. Dublin: n.p., 1812.

Proposals for an Association of those Philanthropists, Who Convinced of the Inadequacy of the Moral and Political State of Ireland to Produce Benefits which Are Nevertheless Attainable Are Willing to Unite to Accomplish its Regeneration. Percy Bysshe Shelley. Dublin: Printed by I. Eton, 1812.

Declaration of Rights. [Broadside; Dublin: n.p., 1812].

The Devil's Walk, a Ballad. [Broadside: printing circumstances unknown, 1812].

A Letter to Lord Ellenborough, Occasioned by the Sentence which he passed on Mr. D. I. Eaton, as Publisher of the Third Part of Paine's Age of Reason. [Barnstaple: Printed by Syle, 1812].

Queen Mab; a Philosophical Poem: with Notes. By Percy Bysshe Shelley. London: Printed by P. B. Shelley, 23, Chapel Street, Grosvenor Square. 1813.

A Vindication of Natural Diet. Being One in a Series of Notes to Queen Mab, a Philosophical Poem. London: J. Callow, 1813.

A Refutation of Deism: in a Dialogue. London: Printed by Schulze and Dean, 1814.

Alastor; or, The Spirit of Solitude: and Other Poems. By Percy Bysshe Shelley. London: Baldwin, Cradock, and Joy; and Carpenter and Son, 1816.

A Proposal for Putting Reform to the Vote Throughout the Kingdom. By The Hermit of Marlow. London: C. and J. Ollier, 1817.

"We Pity the Plumage, but Forget the Dying Bird." An Address to the People on the Death of the Princess Charlotte. By The Hermit of Marlow. [1817]. [No copy extant of this edition.]

History of a Six Weeks' Tour through a Part of France, Switzerland, Germany, and Holland: with Letters Descriptive of a Sail Round the Lake of Geneva, and of the Glaciers of Chamouni. [Shelley and Mary Shelley]. London: T. Hookham, Jun. and C. and J. Ollier, 1817.

Laon and Cythna; or, The Revolution of the Golden City: A Vision of the Nineteenth Century. By Percy B. Shelley. London: Sherwood, Neely, & Jones; and C. and J. Ollier, 1818. Suppressed and reissued with emendations as *The Revolt of Islam; a Poem, in Twelve Cantos.* By Percy Bysshe Shelley. London: C. and J. Ollier, 1818.

Rosalind and Helen, A Modern Eclogue; with Other Poems. By Percy Bysshe Shelley. London: C. and J. Ollier, 1819.

The Cenci: A Tragedy in Five Acts. By Percy B. Shelley. Italy: C. and J. Ollier, 1819. 2nd ed. London: C and J Ollier, 1821.

Prometheus Unbound: A Lyrical Drama in Four Acts with Other Poems. By Percy Bysshe Shelley. London: C and J Ollier, 1820.

Œdipus Tyrannus; or, Swellfoot the Tyrant. A Tragedy. In Two Acts. Translated from the Original Doric. London: Published for the Author, by J. Johnston, 1820.

Epipsychidion: Verses Addressed to the Noble and Unfortunate Lady Emilia V—— Now Imprisoned in the Convent of —— London: C and J Ollier, 1821.

Adonais: An Elegy on the Death of John Keats, Author of Endymion, Hyperion etc. By Percy B. Shelley. Pisa: With the Types of Didot, 1821.

Hellas: A Lyrical Drama. By Percy B. Shelley. London: Charles and James Ollier, 1822.

Posthumous Poems of Percy Bysshe Shelley. [Edited by Mary Shelley]. London: John and Henry L. Hunt, 1824.

The Masque of Anarchy. A Poem. By Percy Bysshe Shelley. Now first published, with a Preface by Leigh Hunt. London: Edward Moxon, 1832.

The Shelley Papers. Memoir of Percy Bysshe Shelley by T. Medwin, Esq. and Original Poems and Papers of Percy Bysshe Shelley. Now First Collected. London: Whittaker, Treacher & Co., 1833. Published serially in *The Atheneum*, 1832–33, as "Memoir of Shelley" (Nos. 247–52) and "Shelley Papers" (Nos. 253–286). For chronology of Medwin's published works, see Lovell, *Captain Medwin*, 333–37.

Medwin, Thomas. *The Angler in Wales, or Days and Nights of Sportsmen.* 2 vols. London: Richard Bentley, 1834. Biographical allusions to Shelley and Byron. First publication of Shelley's "Buona Notte" and part of his translation from Dante's *Purgatorio*.

The Poetical Works of Percy Bysshe Shelley. Edited by Mrs. Shelley. 4 vols. London: Edward Moxon, 1839.

Essays, Letters from Abroad, Translations and Fragments, By Percy Bysshe Shelley. Edited by Mrs. Shelley. 2 vols. London: Edward Moxon, 1840.

Shelley Memorials: From Authentic Sources. To which is added An Essay On Christianity by Percy Bysshe Shelley. Now First Printed. Edited by Lady [Jane] Shelley. London: Smith, Elder & Co., 1859.

Relics of Shelley. Edited by Richard Garnett. London: Edward Moxon, 1862.

Rossetti, William Michael. "Shelley in 1812–13: An Unpublished Poem and Other Particulars." *Fortnightly Review* 49 (January 1871): 67–85. Shelley under surveillance at Lynmouth; "Devil's Walk, a Ballad."

The Wandering Jew. A Poem by Percy Bysshe Shelley. Edited by Bertram Dobell. London: Printed for The Shelley Society, by Reeves and Turner, 1887.

A Philosophical View of Reform, Now Printed for the First Time. Edited by T. W. Rolleston. London: Oxford University Press, 1920.

Verse and Prose from the Manuscripts of Percy Bysshe Shelley. Edited by Sir John C. E. Shelley-Rolls and Roger Ingpen. London: Privately printed, 1934.

Notopolous, James A. *The Platonism of Shelley: A Study of Platonism and the Poetic Mind.* Durham, N.C.: Duke University Press, 1949. Texts of Shelley's translations of Plato.

The Esdaile Notebook: A Volume of Early Poems by Percy Bysshe Shelley. Edited with Notes by Kenneth Neill Cameron. New York: Knopf, 1964; corrected ed. London: Faber and Faber, 1964.

CHRONOLOGY OF EDITIONS OF SHELLEY'S WORKS, LATE NINETEENTH TO TWENTY-FIRST CENTURY

Rossetti, William Michael, ed. *The Poetical Works of Percy Bysshe Shelley.* Introduction, "Memoir of Shelley." 2 vols. London: Moxon, 1870; rev., 3 vols., 1878.

Forman, H. Buxton, ed. *The Poetical Works of Percy Bysshe Shelley.* 4 vols. London: Reeves and Turner, 1876; *The Works of Percy Bysshe Shelley in Verse and Prose.* 8 vols. 1880.; *Poetical Works*, 2 vols., 1882; 5 vols. ["Aldine Edition"], George Bell, 1892.

Woodberry, George E. *The Complete Poetical Works of Percy Bysshe Shelley.* 4 vols. (Centenary Edition). Cambridge, Mass.: Riverside Press, 1892. Cambridge Edition, 1 vol., 1901.

Hutchinson, Thomas, ed. *The Complete Poetical Works of Shelley.* London: Oxford University Press, 1905. Reset in 1943 as *Shelley: Poetical Works.* Oxford Standard Authors. New ed., corrected by G. M. Matthews, 1970. Most complete one volume edition; with translations.

Koszul, A. H., ed. *Shelley's Prose in the Bodleian Manuscripts, Edited with Corrections, Additions, Notes and Unpublished Fragments.* London: Frowde, 1910.

Locock, C. D., ed. *The Poems of Percy Bysshe Shelley.* 2 vols. London: Methuen, 1911.

Ingpen, Roger, and Walter E. Peck, eds. *The Complete Works of Percy Bysshe Shelley.* (Julian Edition). 10 vols. London: Ernest Benn, 1926–1930. Reprint, New York: Gordian Press, 1965. Poetry, prose, and letters.

Clark, David Lee, ed. *Shelley's Prose: or The Trumpet of a Prophecy.* Albuquerque: University of New Mexico Press, 1954. The prose awaits a scholarly, complete edition.

McElderry, Bruce R. Jr., ed. *Shelley's Critical Prose.* Lincoln: University of Nebraska Press, 1967.

Behrendt, Stephen C., ed. *Percy Bysshe Shelley: Zastrozzi and St Irvyne.* Oxford: Oxford University Press, 1986. Both works in one volume.

Matthews, Geoffrey, and Kelvin Everest, eds. *The Poems of Shelley.* vols. 1, 2. London: Longman, 1989, 2000. Scholarly with insightful notes.

Murray, E. B., ed. *The Prose Works of Percy Bysshe Shelley.* vol. 1. Oxford: Clarendon Press, Oxford University Press, 1993. Authoritative, 1811–1818; excludes *Zastrozzi* and *St. Irvyne.*

Reiman, Donald H., and Neil Fraistat, eds. *The Complete Poetry of Percy Bysshe Shelley.* vol. 1. Baltimore: Johns Hopkins University Press, 1999. Vol. 2 of this multi-volume definitive edition expected 2004.

———, eds. *Shelley's Poetry and Prose: Authoritative Texts and Criticism.* 2nd ed. New York: Norton, 2002. The most useful, scholarly selection of works, with notes and critical articles.

PUBLISHED MANUSCRIPT SOURCES, CATALOGUES, CONTEMPORARY REVIEWS, AND REDACTIONS

Barker-Benfield, B. C., ed. *Shelley's Guitar: A Bicentenary Exhibition of Manuscripts, First Editions and Relics of Percy Bysshe Shelley.* Oxford:

Bodleian Library, 1992. Exact scholarship with facsimiles and illustrations of many unusual items.

Cameron, Kenneth Neill, Donald H. Reiman, and Doucet Devin Fischer, eds. *Shelley and His Circle, 1773–1822.* 10 vols. Cambridge: Harvard University Press, 1961–2002. Through 1820. Manuscripts, with commentaries and essays, in the Carl F. Pforzheimer Collection of Shelley and His Circle, The New York Public Library.

Ellis, F. S. *A Lexical Concordance to the Poetical Works of Percy Bysshe Shelley.* London, 1892. Reprint, New York: Burt Franklin, 1968.

Forman, Harry Buxton. *The Shelley Library: An Essay in Bibliography.* London: Reeves and Turner, 1886.

———, ed. *Note Books of Percy Bysshe Shelley: From the Originals in the Library of W. K. Bixby.* 3 vols. Boston: Bibliophile Society, 1911. Three draft notebooks, now in the Huntington Library; available in *Manuscripts of the Younger Romantics,* vols. 4, 6, and 7.

Knerr, Anthony D. *Shelley's* Adonais: *A Critical Edition.* New York: Columbia University Press, 1984.

Matthews, G. M. "On Shelley's 'The Triumph of Life.'" *Studia Neophilologica* 34 (1962): 104–34.

———. "A New Text of Shelley's Scene for *Tasso.*" *Keats–Shelley Memorial Bulletin* 11 (1960): 39–47.

Reiman, Donald H. *Shelley's "The Triumph of Life": A Critical Study, Based on a Text Newly Edited from the Bodleian Manuscript.* Urbana: University of Illinois Press, 1965.

———, ed. *The Romantics Reviewed: Contemporary Reviews of British Romantic Writers. Part C: Shelley, Keats, and London Radical Writers.* 2 vols. New York: Garland, 1972.

———, ed. *The Romantic Context: Poetry.* 128 vols. New York: Garland, 1976–79. Includes biographical account and works of Elizabeth Hitchener.

———, general ed. *The Manuscripts of the Younger Romantics: A Facsimile Edition, with Scholarly Introductions, Bibliographical Descriptions, and Annotations. Percy B. and Mary W. Shelley.* 9 vols. New York: Garland, 1985–96.

———, general ed. *The Bodleian Shelley Manuscripts: A Facsimile Edition, with Full Transcriptions and Scholarly Apparatus.* 23 vols. New York: Garland, 1986–2001. A great advance for Shelley scholarship.

Robinson, Charles E., ed. *The Frankenstein Notebooks: A Facsimile Edition.* vol. 9, two parts, *The Manuscripts of the Younger Romantics.* New York: Garland, 1996. Includes scholarly analysis of Shelley's contributions to *Frankenstein.*

White, Newman Ivey. *The Unextinguished Hearth: Shelley and His Contemporary Critics.* Durham, N.C.: Duke University Press, 1938. Reviews of Shelley's works through 1824.

Wise, Thomas James. *A Shelley Library: A Catalogue of Printed Books, Manuscripts and Autograph Letters by Percy Bysshe Shelley, Harriet Shelley and Mary Wollstonecraft Shelley.* London: Privately printed, 1924. Many useful descriptions and facsimiles.

Woodberry, G. E., ed. *The Shelley Notebook in the Harvard College Library.* Cambridge: John Barnard Associates, 1929. Available in *Manuscripts of the Younger Romantics: Percy Bysshe Shelley,* vol. 5.

Zillman, Lawrence John, ed. *Shelley's* Prometheus Unbound: *A Variorum Edition.* Seattle: University of Washington Press, 1959.

CHRONOLOGY OF BIOGRAPHIES OF SHELLEY AND REMINISCENCES

Medwin, Thomas. *Journal of the Conversations of Lord Byron: Noted during a Residence with His Lordship at Pisa, in the Years 1821 and 1822.* London, 1824. Subsequently printed as *Conversations of Lord Byron with Thomas Medwin, Esq.* 2 vols. London: Henry Colburn and Richard Bentley, 1832; *Medwin's Conversations of Lord Byron.* Edited by Ernest J. Lovell, Jr. Princeton: Princeton University Press, 1966.

Stockdale, John James, ed. *Stockdale's Budget.* London, 1826–27. First nine of sixteen numbers contain articles about Shelley.

Hunt, James Henry Leigh. *Lord Byron and Some of His Contemporaries; with Recollections of the Author's Life, and of His Visit to Italy.* London: Henry Colborn, 1828.

Barker-Benfield, B. C. "The Honeymoon of Joseph and Henrietta Chichester, with Daniel Roberts' Memories of Byron and Shelley." *Bodleian Library Record* 12 No. 2 (April 1986), 119–41. Roberts's 1828 reports about Shelley.

Hogg, Thomas Jefferson. "Reminiscences of Shelley at Oxford." *The New Monthly Magazine,* 1832. Reprinted and edited by R. A. Streatfeild. *Shelley at Oxford.* London: Methuen, 1904.

Montgomery, Robert. *Oxford, a Poem.* 3d ed. London, 1833. John Slatter's references to Shelley in notes.

[Merle, Joseph Gibbons]. "A Newspaper Editor's Reminiscences." *Fraser's Magazine* 23 (June 1841):699–710.

Medwin, Thomas. *The Life of Percy Bysshe Shelley.* 2 vols. London: Thomas Cautley Newby, 1847. First biography of Shelley.

Hunt, James Henry Leigh. *The Autobiography of Leigh Hunt: With Reminiscences of Friends and Contemporaries.* 2 vols. New York: Harpers, 1850.

MacFarlane, Charles. *Reminiscences of a Literary Life.* Introduction by John F. Tattersall. London: Murray, 1917. Recalls Shelley in Naples; written in 1856.

Hogg, Thomas Jefferson. *The Life of Percy Bysshe Shelley.* 2 vols. London: Moxon, 1858. The life up to 1814; two subsequent volumes suppressed. Reprinted and edited by Humbert Wolfe. *The Life of Percy Bysshe Shelley by Thomas Jefferson Hogg, The Recollections of Shelley & Byron by Edward John Trelawny, Memoirs of Shelley by Thomas Love Peacock.* 2 vols. London: Dent, 1933.

Peacock, Thomas Love. "Memoirs of Percy Bysshe Shelley." *Fraser's Magazine,* June 1858; "Memoirs of Shelley." Fraser's Magazine, January 1860; "Percy Bysshe Shelley. Supplementary Notice." Fraser's Magazine, March 1862. Reprinted and edited by Howard Mills. *Thomas Love Peacock: Memoirs of Shelley and other Essays and Reviews.* New York: New York University Press, 1970.

Trelawny, Edward John. *Recollections of the Last Days of Shelley and Byron.* London: Edward Moxon, 1858.

Reveley, Henry W. "Notes and observations to the 'Shelley Memorials'." *Shelley and His Circle.* Vol. 10: 1134–52. Written after October 1859.

Bentley, Nicholas, ed. *Selections from The Reminiscences of Captain Gronow.* London: Folio Society, 1977. Fellow Etonian's interesting but faulty recollections. First published variously as *Recollections and Anecdotes.* 4 vols. London: Smith, Elder, 1861–66.

[Hunt, Thornton L.] "Shelley. By One Who Knew Him." *Atlantic Monthly,* February 1863, 184–204. Reprinted in Blunden, *Shelley and Keats.*

Rennie, Sir John. *Autobiography.* London, 1875. Shelley at Syon House; written 1867.

Trelawny, Edward John. *Records of Shelley, Byron, and the Author.* London: Basil Montague Pickering, 1878. Reprint, edited by David Wright. Harmondsworth, Middlesex: Penguin Books, 1982.

Houston, Mrs. Matilda C. *A Woman's Memories of World-Known Men.* 2 vols. London: F. V. White, 1883. Visited Shelley's parents after his death.

Dowden, Edward. *The Life of Percy Bysshe Shelley.* 2 vols. London: Kegan Paul, Trench & Co., 1886. Still a valuable work.

Letters to and from Charles Kirkpatrick Sharpe. Edited by Alexander Allardyce. 2 vols. Edinburgh and London, 1888. Shelley at Oxford.

Webb, Alfred. "Harriet Shelley and Catherine Nugent." *The Nation* 48 No. 1249 (1889): 464–86. Recollections by one whose father was Nugent's close friend in Dublin.

Rolleston, Maud. *Talks with Lady Shelley.* London: G. G. Harrop, 1925. Her visits with Lady Shelley began in 1894.

Smith, Elizabeth Grant. *Memoirs of a Highland Lady.* Edited by Lady Strachey. London, 1899.

Koszul, A. H. *La jeunesse de Shelley.* Paris: Bloud & cie, 1910.

[Medwin, Thomas.] *The Life of Percy Bysshe Shelley by Thomas Medwin: A New Edition printed from a copy copiously amended and extended by the Author and left unpublished at his death*. Edited by H. Buxton Forman. London: Humphrey Milford / Oxford University Press, 1913.

Ingpen, Roger. *Shelley in England: New Facts and Letters from the Shelley-Whitton Papers*. London: Kegan Paul, Trench, Trubner, 1917.

Maurois, André. *Ariel: The Life of Shelley*. Translated by Ella D'Arcy. New York: D. Appleton, 1925. First published in France, 1923. Popularized with invented conversations.

Brett-Smith, H. F. B., and C. E. Jones, eds. *The Works of Thomas Love Peacock* (Halliford Edition). 10 vols. London: Constable, 1924–34.

Blunden, Edmund, ed. *Shelley and Keats: As they struck their Contemporaries*. London: Beaumont, 1925.

Peck, Walter Edwin. *Shelley: His Life and Work*. 2 vols. Boston: Houghton Mifflin, 1927. Appendices with Shelley's financial accounts.

Blunden, Edmund. *Shelley: A Life Story*. London: Collins, 1946.

White, Newman Ivey. *Shelley*. 2 vols. New York: Knopf, 1940. Reprint, New York: Octagon Books, 1972. Enduring pillar of Shelley scholarship.

Cameron, Kenneth Neill. *The Young Shelley: Genesis of a Radical*. New York: Macmillan, 1950. Valuable political approach with detailed notes.

Marchand, Leslie A. "Trelawny on the Death of Shelley." *Keats–Shelley Memorial Bulletin* 4 (1952): 9–34. Trelawny's numerous accounts.

Fuller, Jean Overton. *Shelley: A Biography*. London: Jonathan Cape, 1968.

Cameron, Kenneth Neill. *Shelley: The Golden Years*. Cambridge: Harvard University Press, 1974. Emphasizes analyses of later poetry and prose.

Holmes, Richard. *Shelley: The Pursuit*. London: Weidenfeld & Nicholson, 1974; New York: Dutton, 1975.

Reiman, Donald H. *Percy Bysshe Shelley*. Updated ed. Boston: Twayne, 1990. Concise, scholarly account.

BIOGRAPHIES OF SHELLEY'S ASSOCIATES AND SPECIALIZED BIOGRAPHICAL OR BIBLIOGRAPHICAL STUDIES

Angeli, Helen Rossetti. *Shelley and His Friends in Italy*. London: Methuen, 1911.

Barker-Benfield, B. C. "Shelley's Bodleian Visits." *Bodleian Library Record* 12 No. 5 (October 1987), 381–99.

Bate, Walter Jackson. *John Keats*. Cambridge: Harvard University Press, 1963.

Beavan, Arthur H. *James and Horace Smith, Joint Authors of 'Rejected Addresses': a Family Narrative*. London: Hurst and Blackett, 1899.

Beazley, Elizabeth. *Madocks and the Wonder of Wales: The Life of W. A. Madocks, M. P., 1773–1828, Improver, 'Chaotic' . . . Regional Planner . . .*

with some Account of his Agent, John Williams. London: Faber and Faber, 1967.

Benzi, William. *Dr. F. J. Furnivall: Victorian Scholar Adventurer.* Norman, Okla.: Pilgrim Books, 1983. Recollections of Shelley's physician's son, who founded the Shelley Society.

Biagi, Guido. *The Last Days of Shelley: New Details from Unpublished Documents.* London: T. Fisher Unwin, 1898.

Bieri, James. "Shelley's Older Brother." *Keats–Shelley Journal* 39 (1990): 29–33.

Blainey, Ann. *Immortal Boy: A Portrait of Leigh Hunt.* London: Croom, Helm, 1985.

Blunden, Edmund. *Leigh Hunt: A Biography.* London: Cobden-Sanderson, 1930.

Boas, Louise. *Harriet Shelley: Five Long Years.* London: Oxford University Press, 1961.

Brailsford, H. N. *Shelley, Godwin, and Their Circle.* London: Williams and Norgate, 1913.

Cameron, Kenneth Neill, ed. *Romantic Rebels: Essays on Shelley and His Circle.* Cambridge: Harvard University Press, 1973. Collected from *Shelley and His Circle,* vols. 1–4.

Chancellor, E. Beresford. *The Regency Rakes.* Vol. 6. *The Lives of the Rakes.* London: Philip Alan, 1925. Personal details about the eleventh Duke of Norfolk.

Cline, C. L. *Byron, Shelley, and their Pisan Circle.* Cambridge: Harvard University Press, 1952.

Croft, Margaret L. "A Strange Adventure of Shelley's and Its Belated Explanation." *Century Magazine* 48 (October 1905): 905–9. Contains Miss Holland's copy of Shelley's drawing of the Tanyrallt devil.

Crook, Nora and Guiton, Derek. *Shelley's Venomed Melody.* Cambridge: Cambridge University Press, 1986. Bravura study of Shelley's medical history.

Djabri, Susan Cabell, and Jeremy Knight. *Horsham's Forgotten Son: Thomas Medwin Friend of Shelley and Byron.* Horsham: Horsham Museum, 1995. New Information.

Dowling, H. M. "The Attack at Tanyrallt." *Keats–Shelley Memorial Bulletin* 23 (1972): 40–43.

Felton, Felix. *Thomas Love Peacock.* London: George Allen & Unwin, 1973.

Gay, H. Nelson. "The Protestant Burial-Ground in Rome: A Historical Sketch." *Bulletin and Review of the Keats–Shelley Memorial Rome* 2 (1913): 33–58.

Gittings, Robert, and Jo Manton. *Claire Clairmont and the Shelleys 1798–1879.* Oxford: Oxford University Press, 1992. Marion Stocking's works are authoritative.

Godwin, William. *Memoirs of the Author of a Vindication of the Rights of Woman.* London: J. Johnson; and G. G. and J. Robinson, 1798. Godwin's biography of Mary Wollstonecraft, written shortly after her death. Its frankness quickly led to a second (altered) edition.

Grylls, R. Glynn. *Mary Shelley: A Biography.* London: Oxford University Press, 1938.

———. *Claire Clairmont: Mother of Byron's Allegra.* London: John Murray, 1939.

Hand, Sally. "Timothy Shelley, Merchant of Newark: The Search for Shelley's Ancestor." *Keats–Shelley Journal* 29 (1980): 31–42.

Häusermann, H. W. *The Genevan Background.* London: Routledge & Kegan Paul, 1952. Details and context of Shelley's 1816 Swiss home.

Hawkins, Desmond. *Shelley's First Love: The Love Story of Percy Bysshe Shelley and Harriet Grove.* London: Kyle Cathie, 1992. Written by an authority on the Grove family.

———. "The Groves of Cwm Elan." *The Radnorshire Society Transactions* (1985): 45–49.

———. *The Life and Times of Captain John Pilfold.* Horsham: Horsham Museum Society, 1998.

Hill, Anne. "Trelawny's Family Background and Naval Career." *Keats–Shelley Journal* 5 (1956): 11–32.

Locke, Don. *A Fantasy of Reason: The Life and Thought of William Godwin.* London: Routledge & Kegan Paul, 1980.

Looker, Samuel J. *Shelley Trelawny and Henley.* Worthing, Sussex: Aldridge Bros., 1950. Details of Shelley's Worthing imprint on *The Necessity of Atheism* and *Victor and Cazire,* both reproduced in facsimile.

Lovell, Ernest J. Jr., ed. *His Very Voice: Collected Conversations of Lord Byron.* New York: Macmillan, 1954.

———. *Captain Medwin: Friend of Byron and Shelley.* Austin: University of Texas Press, 1962.

Mac-Carthy, Dennis Florence. *Shelley's Early Life: From Original Sources. With Curious Incidents, Letters, and Writings, Now First Published or Collected.* London: John Camden Hotten, 1872. Among the book's gems, frontispiece engraving of John Lawless.

MacDonald, D. L. *Poor Polidori: A Critical Biography of the Author of The Vampyre.* Toronto: University of Toronto Press, 1991.

Marchand, Leslie A. "A Note on the Burning of Shelley's Body." *Keats–Shelley Memorial Bulletin* 6 (1955): 1–3.

———. *Byron: A Biography.* 3 vols. New York: Knopf, 1957.

Marshall, Peter H. *William Godwin.* New Haven: Yale University Press, 1984.

Massingham, H. J. *The Friend of Shelley: A Memoir of Edward John Trelawny.* London: Cobden-Sanderson, 1930.

McAleer, Edward C. *The Sensitive Plant: A Life of Lady Mount Cashell.* Chapel Hill: University of North Carolina Press, 1958.

Mellor, Anne K. *Mary Shelley: Her Life, Her Fiction, Her Monsters.* New York: Methuen, 1988.

Moore, Thomas. *Life, Letters, and Journals of Lord Byron: Complete In One Volume with Notes.* London: John Murray, 1839. Original edition, 2 vols., 1829–1830. With Mary Shelley's assistance.

Nitchie, Elizabeth. *Mary Shelley: Author of "Frankenstein."* New Brunswick: Rutgers University Press, 1953.

———, ed. *"Mathilda:* by Mary Wollstonecraft Shelley." *Studies in Philology* Extra Series No. 3 (October 1959): 1–104.

Norman, Sylva. *Flight of the Skylark: The Development of Shelley's Reputation.* London: Max Reinhardt, 1954.

Origo, Iris. *Allegra.* London: Hogarth Press, 1935.

———. *The Last Attachment: The story of Byron and Teresa Guicciloi as told in their unpublished letters and other family papers.* London: Jonathan Cape, 1949.

Paul, C. Kegan. *William Godwin: His Friends and Contemporaries.* 2 vols. London: Henry S. King, 1876.

Rees, Joan. *Shelley's Jane Williams.* London: William Kimber, 1985.

Scott, Winifred. *Jefferson Hogg.* London: Jonathan Cape, 1951.

Seymour, Miranda. *Mary Shelley.* London: John Murray, 2000.

St Clair, William. *Trelawny: The Incurable Romancer.* New York: Vanguard Press, 1977.

———. *The Godwins and the Shelleys: The Biography of a Family.* London: Faber and Faber, 1989.

Sunstein, Emily W. *Mary Shelley: Romance and Reality.* Boston: Little Brown, 1989.

Tomalin, Claire. *The Life and Death of Mary Wollstonecraft.* New York: Harcourt, Brace, Jovanovich, 1974.

Trelawny, Edward John. *Adventures of a Younger Son.* London, 1831. Semifactual autobiography.

Ward, Eileen. *John Keats: The Making of a Poet.* New York: Viking Press, 1963. Helpful psychological insights.

LETTERS, JOURNALS, DIARIES, AND RECOLLECTIONS

Albery, William, ed. *Reminiscences of Horsham: being Recollections of Henry Burstow.* Folcroft, Pa.: Folcroft Library, 1975. Horsham and Shelley's parents after the poet's death.

Bennett, Betty T., ed. *The Letters of Mary Wollstonecraft Shelley.* 3 vols. Baltimore: Johns Hopkins University Press, 1980–88.

Bury, Lady Charlotte. *Diary Illustrative of the Reign of George the Fourth.* London, 1838.

Campbell, Harriet Charlotte Beaujolois. *A Journey to Florence in 1817.* Edited by Sir Gavin de Beer. London: G. Bless, 1951.

Curry, Kenneth, ed. *New Letters of Robert Southey.* 2 vols. New York: Columbia University Press, 1965.

De Ricci, Seymour. *A Bibliography of Shelley's Letters, Published and Unpublished.* Bois-Colombes, France: Privately printed, 1927. Incomplete but useful.

Djabri, Susan Cabell and Knight, Jeremy, eds. *The Letters of Bysshe and Timothy Shelley and other documents.* Horsham: Horsham Museum Society, 1999. Old Bysshe and son.

Feldman, Paula R. and Scott-Kilvert, Diana, eds. *The Journals of Mary Shelley: 1814–1844.* 2 vols. Oxford: Clarendon Press, Oxford University Press, 1987.

Forman, H. Buxton, ed. *The Letters of Edward John Trelawny.* London: Milford, 1910.

Garnett, Richard S., ed. *Letters about Shelley Interchanged by Three Friends—Edward Dowden, Richard Garnett and Wm. Michael Rossetti.* London: Hodder & Stoughton, 1917.

Gates, Eleanor M., ed. *Leigh Hunt: A Life in Letters.* Essex, Conn.: Fall River, 1998.

Hawkins, Desmond, ed. *The Grove Diaries: The Rise and Fall of an English Family 1809–1925.* Stanbridge, U.K.: Dovecote Press, 1995. Includes Harriet's diary, 1809–10, and that of her sister Charlotte, 1811–58. Harriet Grove's diary was privately printed in London, 1932, by Roger Ingpen and subsequently printed in *Shelley and His Circle* 2: 507–40.

Hotson, Leslie, ed. *Shelley's Lost Letters to Harriet.* London: Faber and Faber, 1930.

[Hunt, Thornton L., ed.]. *The Correspondence of Leigh Hunt.* 2 vols. London: Elder, 1862.

Ingpen, Roger, ed. *The Letters of Percy Bysshe Shelley.* 2 vols. London: Pitman, 1909; rev. ed., 1915.

Jones, Frederick L., ed. *Letters of Mary W. Shelley.* 2 vols. Norman: University of Oklahoma Press, 1944.

———, ed. *Mary Shelley's Journal.* Norman: University of Oklahoma Press, 1947.

———, ed. *Maria Gisborne & Edward E. Williams: Shelley's Friends Their Journals and Letters.* Norman: University of Oklahoma Press, 1951.

———, ed. *The Letters of Percy Bysshe Shelley.* 2 vols. Oxford: Clarendon Press, Oxford University Press, 1964.

"The Last of the Calverts." *Cornhill Magazine* 14 (May 1890): 494–520. Shelley's Keswick friends.

A List of the Officers of the Army and Royal Marines, Retired and Half-Pay. London: War Office, 1801–59.

Marchand, Leslie A., ed. *Byron's Letters and Journals.* 12 vols. Cambridge: Belknap Press, Harvard University Press, 1972–82.

———, ed. *What Comes Uppermost: Byron's Letters and Journals.* Supplementary Volume. Newark: University of Delaware Press, 1994.

Marshall, Mrs. Julian [Florence A.]. *The Life and Letters of Mary Wollstonecraft Shelley.* 2 vols. London: Richard Bentley & Son, 1889.

Moore, Doris Langley. *The Late Lord Byron.* London: John Murray, 1961.

———. *Lord Byron: Accounts Rendered.* London: John Murray, 1974.

Norman, Sylva, ed. *After Shelley: The Letters of Thomas Jefferson Hogg to Jane Williams.* London: Oxford University Press, 1934.

Robinson, Charles E. "The Shelleys to Leigh Hunt: A New Letter of 5 April 1821." *Keats–Shelley Memorial Bulletin* 31 (1980): 52–56.

———. "Shelley to the Editor of the *Morning Chronicle:* A Second New Letter of 5 April 1821." *Keats-Shelley Memorial Bulletin* 32 (1981): 55–58.

Rogers, Neville. "An Unpublished Shelley Letter." *Keats-Shelley Memorial Bulletin,* 24 (1974): 20–24.

Rollins, Hyder E., ed. *The Letters of John Keats.* 2 vols. Cambridge: Harvard University Press, 1958.

Rossetti, William Michael, ed. *The Diary of Dr. John William Polidori, 1816, Relating to Byron, Shelley, etc.* London: Elkin Matthews, 1911.

Scott, W. S., ed. *New Shelley Letters.* New Haven: Yale University Press, 1949.

Schwarzback, F. S. "'Harriet 1812': Harriet Shelley's Commonplace Book." *Huntington Library Quarterly* 56 (1993): 41–66.

[Shelley, Lady Jane, ed.] *Shelley and Mary.* 3 or 4 vols. n.p.: Privately printed, 1882. Brief foreward by Sir Percy Florence Shelley; numerous handwritten commentaries and excised passages by Lady Shelley.

Stocking, David M., and Marion Kingston Stocking. "New Shelley Letters in a John Gisborne Notebook." *Keats–Shelley Memorial Bulletin* 31 (1980): 1–9.

Stocking, Marion Kingston, ed. *The Journals of Claire Clairmont.* Cambridge: Harvard University Press, 1968.

———, ed. *The Clairmont Correspondence: Letters of Claire Clairmont, Charles Clairmont, and Fanny Imlay Godwin.* 2 vols. Baltimore: Johns Hopkins University Press, 1995.

Thurman, William Richard Jr. "Letters about Shelley from the Richard Garnett Papers." Ph.D. diss., University of Texas at Austin, 1972.

Yorke, Philip C., ed. *The Diary of John Baker.* London: Hutchinson & Co., 1931. Recollections, 1751–78, about Shelley's grandfather Bysshe.

SOURCES RELEVANT TO SHELLEY, HIS WORKS, AND HIS THOUGHT

Aeschylus. *Prometheus Bound.* Translated by James Scully. Introduction and annotations by C. J. Hetherington. Foreword by William Arrowsmith. New York: Oxford University Press, 1975. Appendix has the fragments of Aeschylus's *Prometheus Unbound.*

Albery, William. *Parliamentary History of the Ancient Borough of Horsham.* London: Longmans, 1927.

Allott, Miriam. "Attitudes to Shelley: the vagaries of a critical reputation." In *Essays on Shelley.* Edited by Miriam Allott.Totowa, N.J.: Barnes & Noble, 1982.

Allsup, James O. *The Magic Circle: A Study of Shelley's Concept of Love.* Port Washington, N.Y.: Kennikat Press, 1976.

Bachelard, Gaston. *The Psychoanalysis of Fire.* Translated by Alan C. M. Ross. Preface by Northrop Frye. Boston: Beacon Press, 1964. Noteworthy chapters on Prometheus and Empedocles.

——. *The Poetics of Space.* Translated by Maria Jolas. Foreward by Etienne Gilson. Boston: Beacon Press, 1969. Provocative chapters on "Shells" and "Intimate Immensity."

Bak, R. C. "Being in Love and Object Loss." *International Journal of Psycho-analysis* 54 (1973): 1–8.

Baker, Carlos. *Shelley's Major Poetry: The Fabric of a Vision.* Princeton: Princeton University Press, 1948.

Barnard, Ellsworth. *Shelley's Religion.* Minneapolis: University of Minnesota Press, 1937.

Bean, John C. "The Poet Borne Darkly: The Dream-Voyage Allegory in Shelley's *Alastor.*" *Keats–Shelley Journal* 13 (1974): 60–76.

Behrendt, Stephen C. *Shelley and His Audiences.* Lincoln: University of Nebraska Press, 1989.

Bennett, Betty T., and Stuart Curran, eds. *Shelley: Poet and Legislator of the World.* Baltimore: Johns Hopkins University Press, 1996.

Blank, G. Kim, ed. *The New Shelley: Later Twentieth-Century Views.* London: Macmillan, 1991.

Bloom, Harold. *Shelley's Mythmaking.* New Haven: Yale University Press, 1959; Ithaca: Cornell University Press, Cornell Paperbacks, 1969.

——. "Shelley and His Precursors." Chap. 4 in *Poetry and Repression: Revisionism from Blake to Stevens.* New Haven: Yale University Press, 1976.

————. *Wallace Stevens: The Poems of Our Climate*. Ithaca: Cornell University Press, 1977. *The Auroras of Autumn* and Shelley's vision.

Bloom, Harold, Paul de Man, Jacques Derrida, Geoffrey Hartmann, and J. Hillis Miller. *Deconstruction and Criticism*. New York: Seabury Press, 1979. *The Triumph of Life* through the decontructionist lens.

Blos, Peter. *Son and Father: Before and Beyond the Oedipus Complex*. New York: Free Press, 1985. With Margaret Mahler (below), crucial to Shelley's life.

Bonca, Teddi Chichester. *Shelley's Mirrors of Love: Narcissism, Sacrifice, and Sorority*. Albany: State University of New York Press, 1999.

Bornstein, George. *Yeats and Shelley*. Chicago: University of Chicago Press, 1970.

Brisman, Leslie. *Romantic Origins*. Ithaca: Cornell University Press, 1978.

Brown, Nathaniel. *Sexuality and Feminism in Shelley*. Cambridge: Harvard University Press, 1979. Essential study that opened new views.

Butler, Marilyn. *Peacock Displayed: A Satirist in his Context*. London: Routledge & Kegan Paul, 1979. Shelley in relation to Peacock.

Caldwell, Richard S. "'The Sensitive Plant' as Original Fantasy." *Studies in Romanticism* 16 (1976): 221–52.

Cameron, Kenneth Neill. "The Social Philosophy of Shelley." *Sewanee Review* 50 (Autumn, 1942): 457–66. Reprinted in Reiman, Donald H. and Sharon Powers, eds. *Shelley's Prose and Poetry*. New York: Norton, 1977.

————. "The Planet-Tempest Passage in *Epipsychidion*." *PMLA* 63 (1948): 950–72. Reprinted in Reiman and Powers, *Shelley's Prose and Poetry*.

Carpenter, Edward, and George Barnefield. *The Psychology of the Poet Shelley*. London: George Allen & Unwin, 1925. Early foray into Shelley's psyche, entirely written by Carpenter, an enthusiastic admirer.

Chandos, John. *Boys Together: English Public Schools 1800–1864*. New Haven: Yale University Press, 1984.

Chernaik, Judith. *The Lyrics of Shelley*. Cleveland, Ohio: Case Western Reserve Press, 1972. Sensitive and scholarly.

Chernaik, Judith, and Timothy Burnett. "The Byron and Shelley Notebooks in the Scrope Davies Find." *Review of English Studies* 29 (February 1978): 36–49.

Chernaik, Judith. *Mab's Daughters*. London: Macmillan, 1991. Published as *Love's Children: A Novel*. New York: Knopf, 1992. Imaginative recreation of Shelley's relationships with Mary Godwin, Fanny Godwin, Claire Clairmont, and Harriet Westbrook, 1816–1817.

Clark, Timothy. *Embodying Revolution: The Figure of the Poet in Shelley*. Oxford: Oxford University Press, Clarendon Press, 1989.

Chichester, Teddi Lynn. "Shelley's Imaginative Transsexualism in *Laon and Cythna*." *Keats-Shelley Journal* 45 (1996): 77–101.

Clark, Timothy, and Jerrold E. Hogle, eds. *Evaluating Shelley*. Edinburgh: Edinburgh University Press, 1996.

Cooper, Andrew M. "Repetition and Realization in Locke, Hume, and Shelley"; " 'Things Not as They Were': The Phenomenology of *Alastor*." Chaps. 1 and 8 in *Doubt and Identity in Romantic Poetry*. New Haven: Yale University Press, 1988.

Croce, Benedetto. *History of the Kingdom of Naples*. Edited by H. Stuart Hughes. Translated by Frances Frenaye. Chicago: University of Chicago Press, 1970.

Crompton, Louis. *Byron and Greek Love: Homophobia in Nineteenth-Century England*. Berkeley and Los Angeles: University of California Press, 1985.

Cronin, Richard. *Shelley's Poetic Thoughts*. New York: St. Martin's Press, 1981.

———. Review of *Red Shelley*, by Paul Foot; *The Unacknowledged Legislator: Shelley and Politics*, by P. M. S. Dawson; *Radical Shelley: The Philosophical Anarchism and Utopian Thought of Percy Bysshe Shelley*, by Michael Henry Scrivener. *Keats–Shelley Memorial Bulletin* 35 (1984): 76–83. Keen analysis and appreciation of Foot vis-à-vis the other two.

———. "Asleep in Italy: Byron and Shelley in 1819." *Keats–Shelley Review* 10 (1996): 151–80.

Crook, Nora. "Shelley and the Solar Microscope." *Keats–Shelley Review* 1 (1986): 49–60.

———. "Shelley's Earliest Poem?" *MLA Notes* (December 1987): 486–90.

———. "The Enigma of 'A Vision of the Sea,' or 'Who Sees the Waterspouts?'" In Clark and Hogle, *Evaluating Shelley*.

———. "The Boat on the Serchio." *Keats–Shelley Review* 7 (1992): 85–97.

———. "Pecksie and the Elf: Did the Shelleys Couple Romantically?" *Romanticism on the Net* 18 (May 2000). www.ron.umontreal.ca.

Curran, Stuart. *Shelley's Cenci: Scorpions Ringed with Fire*. Princeton: Princeton University Press, 1970.

———. *Shelley's Annus Mirabilis: The Maturing of an Epic Vision*. San Marino: Huntington Library, 1975.

———. *Poetic Form and British Romanticism*. New York: Oxford University Press, 1986.

Dane, Joseph A. "On the Instability of Vessels and Narratives: A Nautical Perspective on the Sinking of the *Don Juan*." *Keats–Shelley Journal* 47 (1998): 63–86.

Davis, Phillips G. "The Attack on Shelley at Tanyrallt: a Suggestion." *Keats–Shelley Memorial Bulletin* 23 (1972): 40–43.

Dawson, P. M. S. "Shelley and the Irish Catholics." *Keats–Shelley Memorial Bulletin* 34 (1978): 18–31.

————. *The Unacknowledged Legislator: Shelley and Politics*. Oxford: Clarendon Press, 1980.

Deane, Seamus. *The French Revolution and Enlightenment in England 1789–1832*. Cambridge: Harvard University Press, 1988.

De Beer, Gavin. "An 'Atheist' in the Alps." *Keats–Shelley Memorial Bulletin* 9 (1958): 1–15.

Donovan, John. "Incest in *Laon and Cythna*: Nature, Custom, Desire." *Keats–Shelley Review* 2 (1987): 49–90.

Dover, K. J. *Greek Homosexuality*. Updated ed. Cambridge: Harvard University Press, 1989.

Duffy, Edward. *Rousseau in England: The Context for Shelley's Critique of the Enlightenment*. Berkeley and Los Angeles: University of California Press, 1979.

Engell, James. *The Creative Imagination: Enlightenment to Romanticism*. Cambridge: Harvard University Press, 1981.

Esolen, Anthony M., ed. and trans. *Lucretius: On the Nature of Things; De rerum natura*. Baltimore: Johns Hopkins University Press, 1995. Book Five, 736–37: "... close on the heels / Of the West Wind mother Flora strews their way."

Everest, Kelvin, ed. *Shelley Revalued: Essays from the Gregynog Conference*. Totowa, N.J.: Barnes & Noble, 1983.

————, ed. "Athanase." *Keats–Shelley Review* 7 (1992):62–84.

Ferber, Michael. *The Poetry of Shelley*. London: Penguin Books, 1993. Excellent essay on *Alastor*, reprinted in Reiman and Fraistat, *Shelley's Poetry and Prose*.

Finch, Peter. "Shelley's *Laon and Cythna*: The Bride Stripped Bare. . .Almost." *Keats–Shelley Review* 3 (1988): 23–46.

————. "Monstrous Inheritance: The Sexual Politics of Genre in Shelley's *St. Irvyne*." *Keats–Shelley Journal* 48 (1999): 39–68.

Foot, Paul. *Red Shelley*. London: Sidgwick & Jackson, 1980.

Fraistat, Neil. "Poetic Quests and Questioning in Shelley's *Alastor* Collection." *Keats–Shelley Journal* 33 (1984): 261–81.

————. *The Poem and the Book: Interpreting Collections of Romantic Poetry*. Chapel Hill: University of North Carolina Press, 1985. Interrelations of the poems in the *Prometheus Unbound* volume.

————. "'I Hate to Mutilate': Mary Shelley and the Transmission of Shelley's Textual Corpus." Paper presented at annual meeting of the MLA, Washington, D.C., 1994.

Francis, Joe. "Doubting the Mountain: An Approach to *Mont Blanc*." *Keats–Shelley Review* 16 (2002): 14–21.

Freeman, John. "Shelley's Letters to his Father." *Keats–Shelley Memorial Bulletin* 34 (1983): 1–15.

————. "Shelley's Early Letters." In Everest, *Shelley Revalued.*

Freud, Sigmund. "On Narcissism: An Introduction." In *The Standard Edition of the Complete Psychological Works of Sigmund Freud.* Translated and edited by James Strachey. vol. 14, 73–102. London: Hogarth Press, 1957.

————. "Mourning and Melancholia." *Standard Edition,* vol. 14, 243–58. Shelley's epipsychidion in Freud: ". . . the attachment of the libido to a particular . . . loved person . . . was shattered . . . [and] served to establish an identification of the ego with the abandoned object. Thus the shadow of the object fell upon the ego . . . the narcissistic identification with the object then becomes a substitute for the erotic-cathexis."

————. "On Transience." *Standard Edition,* vol. 14, 305–7. Perhaps Freud's most poetic work, written after World War I by invitation of the Berlin Goethe Society.

————. "The Ego and the Id." ["Das Ich und Das Es."] *Standard Edition,* vol. 19, 12–66.

————. "A Devil-Neurosis in the Seventeenth Century." [my translation, "Eine Teufelsneurose im Siebzehnten Jahrhundert."] *Standard Edition,* vol. 19, 72–105. "When a boy draws grotesque faces and caricatures, we may no doubt be able to show that he is jeering at his father in them; and when a person . . . is afraid of robbers and burglars at night, it is not hard to recognize these as split-off portions of the father."

Gallant, Christine. *Shelley's Ambivalence.* New York: St. Martin's Press, 1989. Jung's archetypes sensitively integrated with psychoanalytic ideas.

Gathorne-Hardy, Jonathan. *The Old School Tie: The Phenomenon of the English Public School.* New York: Viking Press, 1977.

Gelpi, Barbara Charlesworth. *Shelley's Goddess: Maternity, Language, Subjectivity.* New York: Oxford University Press, 1992. Fine psychoanalytic study focusing on *Prometheus Unbound.*

————. "The Nursery Cave: Shelley and the Maternal." In Blank, *The New Shelley.*

Goslee, Nancy Moore. "Shelley at Play: A Study of Sketch and Text in his *Prometheus* Notebooks." *Huntington Library Quarterly* 48 (1985): 210–55. Importance of Shelley's neglected drawings in his creative process.

Grabo, Carl. *A Newton Among Poets: Shelley's Use of Science in Prometheus Unbound.* New York: Cooper Square Publishers, 1930.

————. *The Magic Plant: The Growth of Shelley's Thought.* Chapel Hill: University of North Carolina Press, 1936.

Hampshire, Stuart. *Spinoza: An Introduction to his Philosophical Thought.* Harmondsworth, Middlesex: Penguin Books, 1987. Shelley, Lucretius, and Freud find a place in this analysis.

Hoagwood, Terence Allen. *Skepticism and Ideology: Shelley's Political Prose and Its Philosophical Context from Bacon to Marx.* Iowa City: University of Iowa Press, 1988. Illuminating scholarship.

Hodgson, John A. *Coleridge, Shelley, and Transcendental Inquiry: Rhetoric, Argument, Metapsychology.* Lincoln: University of Nebraska Press, 1989. Shelley, unlike Coleridge, takes Hell seriously.

Hoeveler, Diane Long. *Romantic Androgyny: The Women Within.* University Park: The Pennsylvania State University Press, 1990. Questions some views in Brown, *Sexuality and Feminism in Shelley.*

Hogg, James, ed. *Shelley 1792–1992: Romantic Reassessment 112. Salzburg Studies in English Literature.* Lewiston, N.Y.: Edwin Mellen Press, 1993. Shelley scholars from many lands.

Hogle, Jerrold E. *Shelley's Process: Radical Transference and the Development of His Major Works.* New York: Oxford University Press, 1988.

Honey, J. R. de S. *Tom Brown's Universe: The Development of the Victorian Public School.* London: Millington, 1977.

Hubbell, J. Andrew. "*Laon and Cythna:* A Vision of Regency Romanticism." *Keats–Shelley Journal* 51 (2002): 174–97.

Hudson, T. P. *A History of Horsham.* Chichester: West Sussex Council, 1988.

Hughes, A. M. D. *The Nascent Mind of Shelley.* Oxford: Oxford University Press, Clarendon Press, 1947.

Jones, Ken Prichard. "The Influence of Field Place and Its Surroundings upon Percy Bysshe Shelley." *Keats–Shelley Review* 8 (1993–94): 132–50.

Jones, Steven E. *Shelley's Satire: Violence, Exhortation, and Authority.* DeKalb: Northern Illinois University Press, 1994.

Keach, William. *Shelley's Style.* New York: Methuen, 1984.

King-Hele, Desmond. *Shelley: His Thought and Work.* 3d ed. Rutherford, N.J.: Fairleigh Dickinson University Press, 1984. An appreciation by a mathematician-scientist.

Lacan, Jacques. "The mirror stage as formative of the function of the I." In *Écrits: A Selection.* Translated by Alan Sheridan. New York: Norton, 1977.

Leighton, Angela. *Shelley and the Sublime: An Interpretation of the Major Poems.* Cambridge: Cambridge University Press, 1984.

Lichtenstein, Heinz. "The Role of Narcissism in the Emergence of a Primary Identity." *International Journal of Psycho-analysis* 45 (1964): 50–54.

———. *The Dilemma of Human Identity.* New York: Jason Aronson, 1977.

Lyte, Sir Henry C. Maxwell. *A History of Eton College.* 4th ed. London, 1911.

Mahler, Margaret S. *On Human Symbiosis and the Vicissitudes of Individuation.* New York: International Universities Press, 1968.

Mahler, Margaret S., Fred Pine, and Anita Bergman. *The Psychological Birth of the Human Infant.* New York: Basic Books, 1975.

Marshall, W. H. *Byron, Shelley, Hunt, and "The Liberal".* Philadelphia: University of Pennsylvania Press, 1960.

Matthews, G. M. "A Volcano's Voice in Shelley." *ELH*, 24 (1957):191–228. Reprinted in Reiman and Fraistat, eds. *Shelley's Poetry and Prose.*

———. "Shelley and Jane Williams." *The Review of English Studies* 45 (1961): 40–48.

———. "'Julian and Maddalo': the Draft and the Meaning." *Studia Neophilologica* 35 (1963): 57–84.

———. "Whose Little Footsteps? Three Shelley Pieces Re-Addressed." In Reiman, et al., eds. *The Evidence of the Imagination.*

McCalman, Iain. *Radical Underworld: Prophets, Revolutionaries, and Pornographers in London, 1795–1840.* Cambridge: Cambridge University Press, 1988; reprint, Oxford: Clarendon, 1993.

McDougall, Joyce. *Theaters of the Body: A Psychoanalytic Approach to Psychosomatic Illness.* New York: Norton, 1989.

McNiece, Gerald. *Shelley and the Revolutionary Idea.* Cambridge: Harvard University Press, 1969.

McTaggart, William. *England in 1819: Church, State and Poverty.* London: Keats–Shelley Memorial Association, 1970.

Morley, Edith J., ed. *Henry Crabb Robinson on Books and Their Writers.* 3 vols. London: Dent, 1938.

Morrison, Robert. "De Quincey, Champion of Shelley." *Keats–Shelley Journal* 41 (1992): 36–41.

Murray, E. B. "Shelley's Notes on Sculptures: The Provenance and Authority of the Text." *Keats–Shelley Journal* 32 (1983): 150–71.

———. "The Dating and Composition of Shelley's *The Assassins*." *Keats–Shelley Journal* 34 (1985): 14–17.

Nitchie, Elizabeth. "Shelley at Eton: Mary Shelley vs. Jefferson Hogg." *Keats–Shelley Memorial Bulletin* 11 (1960): 48–54.

O'Malley, Glenn. *Shelley and Synaesthesia.* Evanston: Northwestern University Press, 1964.

O'Neill, Michael. *Percy Bysshe Shelley: A Literary Life.* London: Macmillan, 1989.

———. *The Human Mind's Imaginings: Conflict and Achievement in Shelley's Poetry.* Oxford: Oxford University Press, Clarendon Press, 1989.

Orange, Ursula. "Elise, Nursemaid to the Shelleys." *Keats–Shelley Memorial Bulletin* 6 (1955): 24–34.

Patlock, Robert. *The Life and Adventures of Peter Wilkins.* London: J. M. Dent, 1928; reprint, Westport, Conn.: Hyperion Press, 1974. This 1751 *voyage imaginaire* greatly impressed the youthful Shelley.

Pollin, B. R. "Fanny Godwin's Suicide Re-examined." *Etudes Anglaises* 18 (July–September 1965): 258–68.

Pugh, Diana. "Captain Roberts and the Sinking of the Don Juan." *Keats–Shelley Memorial Bulletin* 26 (1975): 18–22.

Pulos, C. E. *The Deep Truth: A Study of Shelley's Scepticism.* Lincoln: University of Nebraska Press, 1962.

Rajan, Tilottama. "Visionary and Questioner: Idealism and Skepticism in Shelley's Poetry." Chap. 2 in *Dark Interpreter: The Discourse of Romanticism.* Ithaca: Cornell University Press, 1980.

Reiman, Donald H. "Shelley's 'The Triumph of Life': The Biographical Problem." *PMLA* 78 (December 1963):536–50. Also in Reiman, Donald H. *Romantic Texts and Contexts.* Columbia: University of Missouri Press, 1987. Takes issue with Matthews's "Shelley and Jane Williams" vis-à-vis *The Triumph of Life.*

———. "Roman Scenes in *Prometheus Unbound* III.iv." *Philological Quarterly* 46 (January 1967): 69–78. Also in Reiman, *Romantic Texts and Contexts.*

———. "*Shelley as Agrarian Reactionary.*" *Keats–Shelley Memorial Bulletin* 30 (1979): 5–15. Also in Reiman, *Romantic Texts and Contexts.*

———. "Shelley as Athanase." *Shelley and His Circle* vol. 7 (1986): 110–32.

———. *Intervals of Inspiration: The Skeptical Tradition and the Psychology of Romanticism.* Greenwood, Fla.: Penkevill, 1988.

———. *The Study of Modern Manuscripts: Public, Confidential, and Private.* Baltimore: Johns Hopkins University Press, 1993. Useful observations about Shelley.

Reiman, Donald H., Michael C. Jaye, and Betty T. Bennett, eds. *The Evidence of the Imagination.* New York: New York University Press, 1978.

Ricci, Corrado. *Beatrice Cenci.* Translated by Morris Bishop and Henry Longan Stuart. 2 vols. New York: Boni and Liveright, 1925.

Rieger, James. *The Mutiny Within: The Heresies of Percy Bysshe Shelley.* New York: George Braziller, 1967.

Roberts, Hugh. *Shelley and the Chaos of History: A New Politics of Poetry.* University Park: The Pennsylvania State University Press, 1997. Advances Shelley studies by considering contemporary scientific thought and Lucretius.

Robinson, Charles E. *Shelley and Byron: The Snake and the Eagle Wreathed in Fight.* Baltimore: Johns Hopkins University Press, 1976. Each poet's influence on the other, emotionally and creatively.

———, ed. *Mary Shelley: Collected Tales and Stories.* Baltimore: Johns Hopkins University Press, 1978.

———. "Percy Bysshe Shelley, Charles Ollier, and William Blackwood: the contexts of early nineteenth-century printing." In Everest, *Shelley Revalued,* 183–213.

Roe, Ivan. *Shelley: The Last Phase*. London: Hutchinson, 1953.

Rogers, Neville. *Shelley at Work*. 2d ed. Oxford: Clarendon Press, 1967.

Santayana, George. "Shelley: or The Poetic Value of Revolutionary Principles." In *Winds of Doctrine*. London: J. M. Dent and Sons, 1913. Reprinted in Norman Henfrey, ed., *Selected Writings of George Santayana*. vol. 1. Cambridge: Cambridge University Press, 1968. Santayana defends Shelley against Matthew Arnold.

Schapiro, Barbara A. *The Romantic Mother: Narcissistic Patterns in Romantic Poetry*. Baltimore: Johns Hopkins University Press, 1983.

Scrivener, Michael Henry. *Radical Shelley: The Philosophical Anarchism and Utopian Thought of Percy Bysshe Shelley*. Princeton: Princeton University Press, 1982.

Shaaban, Bouthaina. "Shelley in the Chartist Press." *Keats–Shelley Memorial Bulletin* 34 (1983): 41–60.

Shelley, Bryan. *Shelley and Scripture: The Interpreting Angel*. Oxford: Oxford University Press, Clarendon Press, 1994.

Slater, Philip E. *The Glory of Hera: Greek Mythology and the Greek Family*. Boston: Beacon Press, 1968.

Smith, Robert Metcalf. *The Shelley Legend*. New York: Scribner's, 1945. For rebuttal, see White, Newman Ivey, Frederick L. Jones, and Kenneth N. Cameron. *An Examination of The Shelley Legend*. Philadelphia: University of Pennsylvania Press, 1951.

Sperry, Stuart M. "The Sexual Themes in Shelley's *The Revolt of Islam*." *Journal of English and Germanic Philology* 82 (January 1983): 32–49.

———. *Shelley's Major Verse: The Narrative and Dramatic Poetry*. Cambridge: Harvard University Press, 1988. Astute criticism informed by psychoanalytic understanding.

St. George, Priscilla P. "Cwm Elan and Nantgwillt: Two Vanished Sites." *Keats–Shelley Journal* 17 (1968): 7–9.

Steffan, T. G. "Seven Accounts of the Cenci and Shelley's Drama." *Studies in English Literature* 9 (1969): 601–18.

Stocking, Marion Kingston. "Miss Tina and Miss Plin: The Papers Behind the *Aspern Papers*." In Reiman et al., eds. *The Evidence of the Imagination*, 372–94.

Stone, Lawrence. *Family, Sex and Marriage in England 1500–1800*. London: Oxford University Press, 1977.

———. *Road to Divorce: England 1530–1987*. New York: Oxford University Press, 1990.

Sunstein, Emily W. "Louise Duvillard of Geneva, the Shelleys' Nursemaid." *Keats–Shelley Journal* 29 (1980): 27–30. The elusive Elise Foggi.

Tetreault, Ronald. *The Poetry of Life: Shelley and Literary Form*. Toronto: University of Toronto Press, 1987.

Thomas, C. B., and K. R. Duszynski. "Words of the Rorschach, Disease, and Death." *Psychosomatic Medicine* 47 (No. 2, March/April 1985): 201–11.

Thompson, E. P. *The Making of the English Working Class.* New York: Vintage, 1966.

Thompson, F. M. L. *English Landed Society in the Nineteenth Century.* London: Routledge and Kegan Paul, 1963.

Thorne, R. G. *The History of Parliament: The House of Commons 1790–1812.* vol. 5. London: Secker and Warburg, 1986.

Tokoo, Tatsuo. "The Composition of *Epipsychidion:* Some Manuscript Evidence." *Keats–Shelley Journal* 42 (1993): 97–103.

Twitchell, James B. "Shelley's Metapsychological System in Act IV of *Prometheus Unbound.*" *Keats–Shelley Journal* 24 (1975): 39–48.

Ulmer, William A. *Shelleyan Eros: The Rhetoric of Romantic Love.* Princeton: Princeton University Press, 1990.

Venables, Tony. "The Lost Traveller." *Keats–Shelley Review* 15 (2001): 15–21. Unraveling myths about "Ozymandias."

Wasserman, Earl R. *The Subtler Language.* Baltimore: Johns Hopkins University Press, 1959.

———. *Shelley: A Critical Reading.* Baltimore: Johns Hopkins University Press, 1971.

Webb, Timothy. *The Violet and the Crucible: Shelley and Translation.* Oxford: Clarendon Press, 1976.

———. *Shelley: A Voice not Understood.* Manchester, U.K.: Manchester University Press, 1977.

———. "'The Avalanche of Ages': Shelley's Defence of Atheism and *Prometheus Unbound.*" *Keats–Shelley Memorial Bulletin* 35 (1984): 1–39.

Weinberg, Alan M. *Shelley's Italian Experience.* London: Macmillan, 1991. Italy's influence on Shelley's poetry.

Weiskel, Thomas. *The Romantic Sublime: Studies in the Structure and Psychology of Transcendence.* Baltimore: Johns Hopkins University Press, 1976. Psychologically informed.

West, David. *The Imagery and Poetry of Lucretius.* Edinburgh: University of Edinburgh Press, 1969. Reprint, Norman: University of Oklahoma Press, 1994. Vivifies why Shelley was influenced by Lucretius.

Whitehead, Alfred North. "The Romantic Reaction." In *Science and the Modern World.* New York: Macmillan, 1925. Reprint, New York: Free Press Paperbacks, 1967. Shelley as the poet of science.

Winnicott, D. W. *Playing and Reality.* New York: Basic Books, 1971. Key chapters are "Transitional Objects and Transitional Phenomena," "Creativity and Its Origins," and "Mirror-role of Mother and Family in Child Development."

Woodings, R. B., ed. *Shelley: Modern Judgments*. London: Macmillan, 1969.

Woodring, Carl. *Politics in English Romantic Poetry*. Cambridge: Harvard University Press, 1970.

Woods, Margaret L. "Shelley at Tanyrallt." *Nineteenth Century* 70 (November 1911): 890–903. Good account of Tremadoc about 1813.

Worton, Michael. "Speech and Silence in *The Cenci*." In Allott, *Essays on Shelley*.

Wu, Ya-Feng. "'The Assassins': Shelley's Appropriation of History." *Keats–Shelley Review* 9 (1995): 51–62.

Yeats, William Butler. "The Philosophy of Shelley's Poetry." In *Essays and Introductions*. New York: Macmillan, Collier Books Edition, 1968. Writing in 1900, Yeats discusses Shelley's "ruling symbols."

Yost, George. *Pieracci and Shelley, an Italian ur-Cenci*. Potomac, Md.: Scripta Humanistica, 1986.

Index

Page numbers in italics refer to illustration pages.

A. B.: secret recipient of PBS correspondence, 68, 72, 73, 363 nn. 79–81

A'Court, Sir William (British envoy, Naples), 103

Actaeon, 128, 243

Adelaide, Queen, 110, 367 n. 45

Aeschylus: *Agamemnon,* 216; *The Persians,* 69, 265, 266; *Prometheus Bound,* 41, 59, 126–27, 213

Afghanistan, 41

Aglietti, Dr. Francesco, 79

Ahasuerus, the Wandering Jew, 127, 267

Albano, 122

Albano, Monte, 88

Albaro, 340

Albion House, 32–33, 37–38, 40, 41, 44, 46, 55, 56, 58, *94,* 105, 269

Alcibiades, 70

Alfieri, Vittorio: *Myrrha,* 79

Allegra. *See* Byron, Allegra

Andrieu, Bertrand, 388 n. 75

androgyny, 71, 89, 224

Androutsos, Odysseus, 346

Angeli, Helen Rossetti, 376 n. 52

Antignano, 297

Antinous, 89

Apennines, 64, 67, 88, 133

Apollo (sculpture), 162

Argyll, Duke of, 108

Argyropoulo, Princess, 216

Ariosto, Lodovico, 87; *Orlando Furioso,* 67

Aristophanes: *The Clouds,* 69; *The Frogs,* 207; *Lysistrata,* 207

Arno River, 68, 164, 165, 183, 184, 202, 269, 274, 281, 285, 291, 296

Arqua Petrarcha, 81

Artaud, Antonin, 137

Arveiron River, 88

Ascham, John, 281

Atheneum, 337, 376 n. 52

Avernus, Lake, 99–100

Bacon, Sir Francis, 55, 127, 179, 213, 231

Bagnacavallo, 229–30, 237, 253, 289, 292–93

Bagni di Lucca, 66–69, 72–74, 77–80, 100, 105, 122, 123, 190, 363 n. 73

Bagni di Pisa. *See* San Giuliano

Baiae, Bay of, 99, 165, 189

Balthus (Balthasar Klossowski de Rola), 137

Bamford, Samuel, 151

Bandinelli, Baccio: *The Laocoön,* 162

Baptistery (Pisa), 323

Barthélemy, Jean-Jacques: *Anarcharsis,* 69

Basilica of the Madonna, 88

Bath (Avon), 11–15, 32

Bath Herald, 11

Baths of Caracalla, 2, 117

Baudelaire, Charles, 114

Baxter, William, 20, 21, 37, 46, 57

Bayle, Pierre, 179

Beauclerk, Maj. Aubrey, 348

Beauclerk, Charles, 275
Beauclerk, Emily ("Mimi"), 273, 287, 290, 291, 295
Bell, Dr. John, 119, 120–23, 133, 158, 161
Bell, Mrs. John, 119, 120
Belzoni, Giovanni, 55
Bennett, Rodney M., 376 n. 51
Bentham, Jeremy, 168, 180; "Paederasty," 71; *Plan of Parliamentary Reform*, 177
Bequette, M. K., 361 n. 4
Berry, Duc de, 109
Bertini, Domenico, 67, 363 n. 73
Bertini, Franceso, 363 n. 73
Bible, 37–38, 213
Bilby, Mr., 66
Bientina, Lake, 238
Bini, Domenico (Dominic), 290
Biondi, Luigi, 214, 254
Birmingham, 150
Bisham Wood, 37
Blackstone, Sir William: *Commentaries*, 70
Blackwood's Edinburgh Magazine, 49, 51, 137, 180
Blake, William, 39
Blessington, Lady, 265
blindness, 147
Boccaccio, Francesco, 104
Boccaccio, Giovanni, 142, 213, 215
Boinville, (Mrs.) Harriet de, 20, 135
Bojti, Dr. Antonio, 210, 212, 217, 244
Bolivar (Byron's boat), 283–84, 299, 303, 308, 309, 312, 320, 322, 325, 327, 330, 333–34, 340, 389 n. 6
Bologna, 64, 75, 78, 87, 190, 245
Bonaparte, Napoleon, 66, 119, 183, 244, 267, 276, 388 n. 75
Booth, David, 46, 58
Booth, Isabel Baxter, 43, 46, 47, 57
Borghese, Prince, 66
Borghese, Princess Pauline, 66–67, 119, 122
Borghese Gardens, 116, 121–22
Boscombe Manor, 354
Bottari, Ferdinando, 297
Bouton, Charles-Marie, *96*, 376 n. 51
Boutourlin, Madame, 289

Brawne, Fanny, 200
Bristol, 13
British Museum, 57
Brooke, Arthur (John Chalk Claris), 348
Brown, Charles Brockden: *Ormond*, 47, 208; *Wieland*, 47
Browne, Charles Armitage, 200
Browning, Robert, 137
Burdett, Sir Francis, 29, 151
Burgess, Rev. Dr. Richard, 335–36
Burke, Edmund, 207
Burr, Aaron, 370 n. 33
Bury, Bianca Augusta Romana, 109, 110, 367 n. 48, 367–68 n. 52
Bury, Lady Charlotte Susan Maria Campbell, 108–10, 121, 184, 211, 289, 367 nn. 45, 47, and 48, 367–68 n. 52, 368 n. 55; *Alla Giornata, or To the Day*, 381 n. 34; *The Divorced*, 108; *Flirtation*, 108; *Self-Indulgence*, 108; *The Three Great Sanctuaries of Tuscany*, 108, 110
Bury, Rev. Edward John, 109, 367–68 n. 52
Byron, Ada, 272
Byron, Allegra (Clara Allegra, "Alba"), 32, 35, 37, 39, 40, 42, 43, 44, 46, 54–58, 62–64, 66, 72–73, 75–76, 78, 79, 80, 83–84, 112, 121, 143, 189–91, 197, 208, 229–30, 237, 244–46, 248, 251, 253, 264, 269, 272, 288–90, 292–93, 296, 298–302, 305, 349, 362 n. 50
Byron, Augusta (Mrs. Leigh, Byron's half sister), 49, 63, 79, 105, 135
Byron, Lady (Annabella Milbanke), 251
Byron, Lord (George Gordon) 25, 35, 39, 44, 57, 59, 90, 101, 105, 108, 117, 126–27, 143, 149, 164, 173, 180, 197, 198, 211, 212, 231, 238, 273–74, 305, 307, 308, 312, 318, 320, 322, 323, 326–27, 329–35; and the Carbonari, 106, 230, 367 n. 35; as center of the Pisan/Genoa circle, 270–76, 283–84, 287, 294, 340–43, 345; and Claire Clairmont and daughter Allegra ("Alba"), 11–12, 15, 16, 32, 40, 43, 47,

55–56, 58, 62–64, 66, 72–73, 75–76, 79, 80, 83–84, 119, 121, 135, 189–91, 208, 228, 229–30, 237, 240, 244, 251, 253–54, 264, 269–70, 272, 288–90, 292–93, 298, 300–301, 306, 342, 349, 362 n. 50, 364 n. 18; and the Countess Guiccioli, 121, 135, 181, 182, 208, 210, 230, 244–46, 252–54, 270, 272, 283, 287, 294–96, 298, 329, 343; cynicism/nihilism of, 84, 85, 89; death in Greece of, 346; and death/cremation of PBS, 334, 339–40, 345; deformity of, 270, 285; homosexuality/bisexuality of, 83, 270, 303; household and spending of, 72, 75, 252–53, 269, 272, 275, 283–84; inheritance of, 275–77; on Keats, 239–41, 321; knowledge of the mysterious lady by, 108; and Mary, 80–81, 120, 158, 249, 270, 272, 277, 280, 284, 292, 340, 342–43, 345–46, 349; in PBS's poetry, 76–77, 82, 84–86, 277, 388 n. 78; physical descriptions of, 76, 285, 321; renewed friendship with PBS in Italy of, 75–77, 79, 83, 85, 181, 190–91, 244–46, 250–54, 265; and riding, 76–77, 83, 85, 253, 254, 270–71, 294; rivalry of PBS with, 61, 85, 195, 239–40, 250–51, 265, 271, 272, 277, 287–88, 295–96, 303, 310, 316, 318–19; sexual profligacy of, 62–63, 72–73, 83, 121; and status, 63, 255, 296. Works: *The Bride of Abydos*, 57; *Cain*, 272, 274, 310; *Childe Harold*, 11, 83, 85, 159, 238; *The Corsair*, 280, 285; *The Deformed Transformed*, 288; *Don Juan*, 81, 85, 195, 240, 251, 265, 268, 272, 296, 303, 340, 365 n. 41; *Lament of Tasso*, 61, 242; *Manfred*, 40, 48, 49, 238; *Marino Faliero*, 240; "Mazeppa," 81; *Memoirs*, 81; "Ode on Venice," 81; *Parisina*, 48; "Prometheus," 127; *Sardanapalus*, 272; "Stanzas to a Hindoo Air," 290; *The Two Foscari*, 272; *The Vision of Judgment*, 272, 321; *Werner*, 277
"Byron and Shelley on the Character of Hamlet," 287–88

Calderón de la Barca, Pedro, 135, 138, 140, 148, 212, 213, 288, 372 nn. 31 and 40; *Los cabellos de Absalón*, 372 n. 31; *La cisma D'Inglaterra*, 213; *La devoción de la cruz*, 372 n. 31; *El màgico prodigioso*, 279, 291; *La vida es sueño*, 372 n. 31
Call, Laetitia, 337
Cambrian (Swansea), 14
Cambridge University, 70, 352, 353
Cameron, Kenneth Neill, 107–8, 338, 356 n. 46, 392 n. 37
Campbell, Adelaide Constance, 110, 367 n. 45, 367–68 n. 52, 368 n. 53
Campbell, Lady Charlotte. *See* Bury, Lady Charlotte Susan Maria Campbell
Campbell, Eleanora, 109–10, 147, 211, 349, 367–68 n. 52. *See also* mysterious lady
Campbell, Eliza, 109–10, 147, 211, 349, 367–68 n. 52. *See also* mysterious lady
Campbell, Emma, 110
Campbell, Harriet Charlotte Beaujolois (later second Countess Charleville), 109–10, 367–68 n. 52, 368 n. 55, 389 n. 36
Campbell, Leopold James York, 398 n. 135
Camposanto, 211, 323
Canova, Antonio, 67, 338, 395 n. 50
Capitol (Rome), 116, 121
Capua, 115–16
Capurro, Niccolò, 242
Carbonari, 106, 230, 348, 367 n. 35
Carlile, Richard, 151–53, 168–69
Carlton House, 185
Caroline, Princess (later Queen), 109, 199, 207, 367 n. 48
Cartwright, Maj. John, 36
Casa Bertini, 66–67, 72, 363 nn. 73 and 74
Casa Boutourlin, 110, 289
Casa del Chiappa, 67
Casa Frassi, 184, 185, 188, 191
Casa I Capuccini, 77, 78, 83, 86
Casa Prini, 201, 202, 210

Casa Ricci, 65, 191–93, 206, 209
Casa Silva, 158, 183, 206, 222
Cascades of Mármora, 88
Casciana, 180, 190, 191
Cascine Forest, 164, 172, 285, 297
Castellamare, 118, 119
Castlereagh, Viscount (Robert Stewart), 29, 85, 150, 153–54, 156, 199, 266, 268
Castle Goring, 353, 367 n. 48
Castruccio, 203
Caterina (nursemaid), 186, 329, 331
Catholic emancipation, 29
Cato Street Conspiracy, 150
Catty, Corbet S., 376 n. 52
Catty, Lt. James Patrick, 170
Catty, Sophia. See Stacey, Sophia
Cenci, Beatrice, 120–21, 135, 138–41, 369 n. 24, 371 n. 14
Cenci family, 65, 120, 135
Cenci, Count Francesco, 121, 135, 138–41, 372 n. 35
Cenci, Giacomo, 140
Cenci Palace, 121
Cervantes: Don Quixote, 16
Cesare, Lucio, 177
Cestius, pyramid of, 89, 124, 336
Charles I, 73, 278
Charleville, first Countess, 110, 289, 389 n. 36
Charlotte, Princess, 45
Charters, Thomas, 15, 58
Chartist Movement, 352–53
Chatterton, Thomas, 213, 241
Chiappa, Signore G. B. del, 67, 363 nn. 73 and 74
Christchurch Priory, 354
Clairmont, Charles, 14, 21, 27, 37, 148, 160, 237, 289
Clairmont, Claire (Clara Mary Jane), 18, 21, 22, 26, 30, 35, 37, 45, 50, 54, 58, 60, 61, 65, 68, 102, 105, 106, 107, 110, 120–22, 143, 158–59, 170, 184, 191–92, 199, 233, 236–39, 242, 275, 291, 297, 319, 321, 329–31, 348, 349, 355 n. 20, 357 n. 87, 367 n. 35, 368 nn. 55 and 57, 380 n. 105, 383 n. 22, 389 n. 37; and Byron, 11–12, 15, 16, 32, 47, 58, 62–64, 66, 74–76, 79, 84, 119, 121, 135, 182, 184, 189–91, 197, 208, 212, 228, 229–30, 237, 240, 251, 253–54, 264, 269, 288–89, 298–301, 306, 342, 346, 349, 364 n. 18; closeness to and financial dependence on PBS of, 12, 25, 27, 35, 37, 39, 42, 44, 73, 78, 80, 83, 99, 103, 110, 145, 182, 185, 188, 192, 197, 208–13, 216–18, 220, 227–29, 230, 239, 245, 247–52, 269–70, 271–72, 292, 304, 306, 331, 342, 349, 387 n. 27; as "Constantia," 47–48, 56, 208, 311, 350; death of, 350; and death of Allegra, 299–301, 305, 349; and death of PBS, 331, 335, 342; departure/separation from Shelley household of, 210–13, 216, 217–18, 229, 237, 243, 244, 248; and Emilia Viviani, 215–18, 220, 221, 224, 381–82 n. 52; governess career of, 210, 289, 349; journal of, 98, 104, 116, 117, 123–25, 185, 186, 191, 197, 201, 208, 212, 221, 252, 289, 292, 364 n. 21, 366 n. 25; later years of, 349–50, 353; lost literary efforts of, 37; and Mrs. Mason, 159, 184, 189–90, 197, 198, 202, 206, 209–12, 224, 244, 269, 271, 289, 290, 292, 304, 306, 342, 349; and music, 39, 47, 57–58, 117, 135, 160, 183, 311; on the mysterious lady, 110–11, 367 n. 39; and Peacock, 48, 56–58, 60, 66; pregnancy(ies?) of, 11, 13, 16, 26–27, 32, 79, 80, 81, 100, 103–4, 230, 246–50, 289; separation from Allegra of, 64, 65, 72–76, 79, 83–84, 121, 135, 189–90, 208, 229–30, 237, 244, 264, 269–70, 272, 288–90, 292–93, 298; short story "The Pole" of, 349; translation of Goethe's Memoirs by, 293; and Trelawny, 335, 338, 342, 346, 350
Clairmont, Pauline, 350
Clare, John Fitzgibbon, second Earl of, 270
Clarendon, Edward, Earl of: The History of the Rebellion and Civil Wars in England, 169
Clark, William, 208, 235, 338
Clark, Rev. William, M.D., 182

Clarke, Charles Cowden, 34
Clement VIII, Pope, 138
Cleveland, Henry, 348
Clint, George, 259
Cobbett, William, 36; "Address to Journeymen and Labourers," 16
Cockburn, Gen. Sir George, 336
Coleridge, John Taylor, 51, 163, 164
Coleridge, Samuel Taylor, 39, 168, 195, 231, 281; *Kubla Khan,* 18
Colosseum, 89, 116
Como, Lake, 61–63, 74, 111
Convent of Santa Anna, 97, 214, 215, 223, 232, 292
Cook, Rev. W., 336
Cothelstone Churchyard (Somerset), 354
Coulson, Walter, 35, 37, 45
Country Literary Chronicle, The, 338
Courier, The, 288, 338
Covent Garden Theatre, 135, 136, 274
Croker, John Wilson, 52
Cromwell, Oliver, 73, 278
Crook, Nora, 108, 367 n. 43
Cumming, Lady Eliza Campbell. *See* Campbell, Eliza
Cumming, Sir William Gordon, 109
Curran, Amelia, 94, 122, 123–24, 136, 141, 142, 157, 182, 203, 208, 217, 370 nn. 33, 35, and 36
Curran, John Philpot, 183, 370 n. 33
Cuvier, Georges, Baron, 214

d'Agnano, Lago, 114
Dane, Joseph A., 391 n. 98
Danielli, Francesco, 214, 238
Dante Alighieri, 146, 164, 213, 216, 220; *The Divine Comedy,* 60, 214; *Vita Nuova,* 222
Darwin, Erasmus, 174
Davies, Mr., 120
Davy, Sir Humphry, 174
Dawe, George, 17
Dawkins, Edward, 332
Dead Asses, The: A Lyrical Ballad, 167
de Beer, Sir Gavin, 367 n. 47

Delesert's lending library (Florence), 161, 162–63
del Rosso, Federico, 106, 176, 186–87, 189, 190–92, 196, 203, 208, 228, 252
De Quincey, Thomas, 51
de Thierry: "Why declare how much I love thee," 172
De Young (banker), 324
Dillon, Lord, 162
Diodorus, 55
Dionigi, Signora Marianna Candida, 116, 120, 181
Dods, Mary Diana, 347
Doges' Palace (Venice), 87
Don Juan (PBS's boat), *261,* 284–85, 287, 302–3, 305–9, 312–13, 315, 318, 319–20, 322–27, 329–31, 333, 336–38, 389 n. 6
Dowden, Edward, 107, 239, 363 n. 73, 367 n. 39
Drummond, Sir William, 121, 168; *Academical Questions,* 121
Drury Lane Theatre, 136–37
Dudley, Lord, 275
Duomo, 64, 323
du Plantis, Madame Marveilleux, 158, 160, 170, 182, 183
Duvillard, Louise. *See* Foggi, Elise

East India Company, 136, 149, 231, 265
Edinburgh, 108
Edinburgh Review, 49
Edwards, Rev. Evan ("Taffy"), 352
Egypt, 211
Eldon, Lord John Scott, 27–30, 35, 150, 154, 199, 212, 235
Elgin Marbles, 57
Elise (nursemaid). *See* Foggi, Elise
Ellenborough, first Baron (Edward Law), 50
Elysian Fields, 99
Encyclopedia Britannica, 184
Engels, Friedrich, 178, 352
England: censorship of the theater in, 137; debt of, 178; and the Manchester Massacre, 149–51; repression in, 29, 35–37, 40, 45, 50, 149–52; revolutionary feeling in, 16,

England (*continued*)
35–36, 45, 149–50, 156, 177–78, 201; Tory government of, 29, 35, 137, 149–54, 167, 199, 208; wars of, 178

English, English, and Beck, 32, 185, 269

English Rome Consul, 335

Esdaile, Charles Edward Jeffries, 397 n. 128

Esdaile, Edward (Ianthe's son), 354

Esdaile, Edward Jeffries (Ianthe's husband), 351

Esdaile, Eliza Margaret, 397 n. 128

Esdaile, Ianthe Margaret, 397 n. 128

Esdaile, Percy Charles, 397 n. 128

Esdaile, William, 397 n. 128

Este, 77, 78, 80, 81, 106, 143, 246, 248, 250, 252

Eton, 110, 163, 225–26, 239, 352, 392 n. 31

Euganean Hills, 77, 81

Euripides, 65, 117; *The Cyclops,* 147

Examiner, 16–17, 30, 35–36, 45, 48, 49, 50, 51, 55, 57, 137, 142, 151, 152, 162, 166–68, 196, 199, 232, 255, 266, 295, 338

Falconet, Madame, 102

Ferdinand, King, 114, 196–97

Ferdinand III, Grand Duke, 210

Ferrara, 86–87

Field, Mathilda, 198, 380 n. 105

Field Place, 53, 58, 207, 224, 275, 296, 352, 353

Finch, Rev. Robert, 242

Finden (engraver), *94*

Fitzherbert, Mrs., 185

Florence, 64, 66, 72, 73, 74, 75, 76, 78, 81, 88, 115, 133, 157, 159–62, 165, 167, 171, 176, 180, 182, 184, 186, 210, 211, 216, 225, 244, 245, 248, 249, 253, 290, 292, 299, 300, 305–6, 332, 341, 346, 350, 368 n. 55, 376 n. 74, 389 n. 36

Foggi, Elise, 37, 45, 58, 59–60, 64, 66, 72, 75, 81, 103, 107, 110, 112, 182, 185, 230, 246–50, 252, 289, 292, 362 n. 37, 389 n. 37

Foggi, Paolo, 67, 73, 77, 78, 81, 102–4, 106, 107, 112, 115, 191, 192, 194, 196, 202, 229, 246, 248, 252, 289, 292

Ford, Onslow, 354

Fornarina, La (Margarita Cogni), 80, 121

Forteguerri, Niccolò: *Il Ricciardetto,* 198, 203

Forum, 89, 116

Foundling Hospital (Pisa), 211

Fraser's Magazine, 354

Freeborn, John, 335–36

French Revolution, 37, 52, 129

Furnivall, Dr. George, 41, 44

Gabinetto Fisica, 182

Galignani's Messenger (Paris), 210

Galileo Galilei, 184

Gamba, Pietro, 245, 294, 321

Gambs, Hermann, 349

Gandhi, Mohandas, 156

Garnett, Richard, 107

Gatteschi, Ferdinand, 348

Gavita, Vicenzo, 115

Geneva, 74, 85, 90, 109, 362 n. 37

Genoa, 109, 275, 283, 299, 302–3, 305, 309, 315, 319, 335, 340, 367 n. 48

George III, 184, 274

George, Prince Regent (later George IV), 35, 150, 152, 154, 184–85, 199, 207

Gentleman's Magazine, 163, 338–39

Gifford, William, 11, 163, 216

Gisborne, John, 65–66, 77, 78, 106, 112, 115, 118, 119, 126, 133, 135, 158, 161, 169, 180, 182, 184–91, 194–97, 199–202, 206, 209–10, 212, 214, 221, 225, 237, 239, 241–44, 256, 268, 275, 278, 280, 296, 307, 310–11, 379 n. 87

Gisborne, Maria, 58, 64–67, 73, 77, 78, 80, 102, 106, 112, 115, 118–24, 133, 135, 137, 138, 158–62, 169, 171, 180, 184–90, 192–97, 199–202, 206, 209–10, 212, 236, 237, 239, 242, 243, 244, 273, 274, 279, 280, 292, 298, 307, 309, 313, 321, 324, 332, 336, 349, 367 n. 35

Godwin, Fanny Imlay, 11–16, 24, 27, 197, 227, 355 nn. 19 and 20

Godwin, Mary Jane Clairmont (second wife of William), 12, 17, 26–27, 35, 39, 65, 159, 209, 304, 306, 350, 354, 356 n. 56

Godwin, William, 35, 37, 56, 57, 63–64, 68, 70, 72, 73, 80, 146, 163, 179, 183, 190, 195, 197, 198, 202, 347, 354; death of, 349; and death of PBS, 339; early advice to PBS of, 33; as editor of PBS's statement of beliefs, 30; and Fanny's suicide, 13–14, 16, 197; and financial concerns, 12, 16–17, 26–27, 37, 39, 42, 44, 48–49, 56, 58, 66, 120, 142, 146, 148, 160–61, 190, 193–94, 202–3, 209, 296–97, 303–4, 319, 339, 363 n. 80; on Harriet Shelley, 20, 21, 28, 356 n. 56; literary acquaintances of, 34–35; and Malthus, 81, 269; relationship with the PBS and Mary of, 13–14, 25, 26–27, 37, 39, 44, 57–58, 65, 66, 141–42, 160, 180, 188, 193–94, 202–3, 303–4, 306, 339–40, 362 n. 59; responses to works by PBS of, 49, 126, 134–35, 142; views on marriage of, 26. Works: *Answer to Malthus,* 269; *Caleb Williams,* 192; *Cloudesley,* 88; *Fleetwood,* 192; *Mandeville,* 37, 49; *Memoirs,* 188; *Political Justice,* 127, 178, 189

Goethe, Johann Wolfgang von, 213; *Faust,* 274, 280–81, 288, 310; *Memoirs,* 293

Grattan, Henry, 183

Greece, 211, 216, 232–33, 264–68, 272, 340, 343

Gregson, John, 353

Grieves, Mr., 172

Grottes des Eschelles, 59

Grove, Harriet, 151, 226

Grove, Thomas, Sr., 151

Gryffydh, Jane, 195

Grylls, R. Glynn, 357 n. 87

Guarini, Battista, 87

Guiccioli, Count Alessandro, 121, 135

Guiccioli, Countess Teresa Gamba Ghiselli, 121, 135, 181, 182, 208, 210, 230, 244–46, 252–54, 270, 272, 275, 284, 287, 294–96, 298, 321, 329, 343, 345–46

Guildford, Lord (Frederick North, fifth Earl), 117, 273

Habeas Corpus Suspension Act, 35, 37

Hades, 99

Hamilton, Duchess of, 108

Hampden, 41

Hampden Clubs, 35

Hampstead Heath, 18, 33

Harrow, 270, 352, 353

Harrow Church, 298

Harry (manservant), 37, 43

Hay, Capt. John, 294, 296

Haydon, Benjamin Robert, 34, 92

Hayward (solicitor), 16–17

Hazlitt, William, 34, 35, 179, 288, 354

Herodotus: *Histories,* 69

Herschel, John F. W., 174, 175

Hesiod, 207

Heslop, Mr., 302, 303

Hildebrand, Frederick L., M.D., 394 n. 23

Hitchener, Elizabeth, 226, 339

Hobbes, Thomas, 179

Hobhouse, John Cam, 63, 121, 340

Hogg, John, 349

Hogg, Thomas Jefferson, 35, 37, 41, 56, 57, 64, 83, 99, 101, 119, 120, 124, 162, 184, 188, 195, 255, 264, 268, 273, 323, 338, 341, 343, 348–49, 354

Holcroft, Thomas, 183

Holy Alliance, 154

Holmes, Richard, 361 n. 4, 392 n. 37

Homer, 41, 231; "Hymns," 56; *Hymn to Mercury,* 198

homosexuality, 70–72, 83

Hone, William, 50, 120

Hookham, Thomas, 18, 19, 20

Hope, Thomas: *Anastasius,* 213

Hoppner, Isabella (Mrs. R. B.), 72–73, 75–76, 80, 83–84, 103, 121, 190, 230, 246–52, 254, 292

Hoppner, Richard Belgrave, 72–73, 75–76, 77, 80, 83, 84, 190, 230, 246–47, 250–52, 254, 292

Hoppner scandal, 103, 246–52, 292

Horsham, 29, 35, 353

Humboldt, Alexander von, 214

Hume, Dr. Thomas, 30–31, 186, 233–35
Hume, Mrs. Thomas, 30–31
Hunt, Henry ("Orator"), 149–51
Hunt, Henry Sylvan, 348–49
Hunt, John, 152, 255, 345
Hunt, Leigh, 16–20, 24, 25, 26, 30, 33–40,
    44, 45, 56–58, 64, 66, 92, 101, 118–20,
    136, 146, 158, 159, 166–67, 180, 183,
    185, 188, 193, 195, 197, 199, 200, 214,
    231, 240, 253–55, 268, 272, 276, 277–78,
    295, 296, 301, 311, 340, 347, 351, 354,
    396 n. 83; on the government, 45,
    151–52; imprisonment of, 152; in
    Italy, 309, 310, 315, 318–24, 326,
    329–36, 338, 342–45, 380 n. 115; as
    publisher and literary ally of PBS,
    16–17, 35, 36, 51, 126, 137, 142–43, 152,
    163, 164, 167–69, 174, 199, 235, 239,
    288; relationship with sister-in-law
    of, 49, 164, 338, 344; withdrawal from
    political concerns of, 152, 156, 174,
    177, 206. Works: *Autobiography*, 354;
    Foliage, 37, 57, 164; *Literary Pocket-
    Book*, 173, 177, 180; *Lord Byron and
    Some of His Contemporaries*, 354;
    "On the Nile," 56; *Story of Rimini*,
    49. See also *Examiner; Indicator,
    The; Liberal, The*
Hunt, Marianne, 18, 26, 35, 37, 40, 42,
    44, 57, 58, 59, 64, 66, 117, 120, 187, 199,
    200, 272, 309, 319, 321, 324, 340,
    343–45
Hunt, Thornton, 18, 33, 40, 41–42, 320

Imlay, Fanny. *See* Godwin, Fanny
    Imlay
incest, 46, 48–52, 65, 70, 79, 85, 120–21,
    135–42, 161, 167, 228, 372 n. 31
India, 41, 212, 217, 264–65, 268, 280, 290
India House, 57, 58
Indicator, The, 152, 174
Inquisition (Spain), 196
Inquisition Office, 208
Irish rebellion, 153
Irving, Washington, 347–48
Isola Palmaria, 305
Italy, 27, 40, 43, 44, 45, 46, 48–49, 55–56;
    the English in, 62–63, 67, 91, 103, 107,
118, 122, 177, 184, 196, 203, 214, 270,
    273, 307; and PBS's view of Italians,
    62, 69, 83, 232; revolution in, 199, 206,
    232, 265; trip into, 58–60. *See also
    names of individual cities, houses,
    and sites*

James, Henry: *The Aspern Papers*, 350
Jesus Christ, 34, 36, 50, 87, 128–29, 168,
    179, 204, 241, 265, 316
John Bull, 338
Johnson, Capt. John Edward, 219
Johnston, J., 208
Jones, Frederick L., 356 n. 46
Jonson, Ben, 207
Julian the Apostate, 84
Jung, Carl, 223

Kean, Edmund, 57, 135
Keats, John, 39, 51, 93, 137, 166, 195,
    198, 231, 361 n. 16; critical exchange
    with PBS of, 200–201; death of, 229,
    233, 237, 239–40, 242; distance from
    PBS of, 33–34; illness of, 199–200,
    216; invitation letter from PBS to,
    199–200, 380 n. 115; in Italy, 217;
    meetings of PBS and, 17, 33, 45,
    56–57; PBS's assessments of, 72,
    200, 212, 216–17, 233, 239–41; on
    PBS's literary reputation, 45; social
    background of, 34. Works:
    Endymion, 41, 52, 72, 200, 216–17,
    240, 359 n. 52; *Hyperion*, 201, 212,
    217, 239, 241; *Lamia*, 200–201, 240,
    324, 332; "On the Nile," 56
Kendall, Reverend, 30
Kent, Elizabeth (Bessy), 37, 49, 164,
    338, 344, 396 n. 83
Keswick, 123, 164, 192, 288
Kingsborough, Viscount, 183
Kinnaird, Douglas, 11, 288
Kirkup, Seymour, 262, 336

Lackington, Allen & Company, 40
Lady Castlereagh (ship), 58
Lafayette, Marquis de, 183
Lamb, Charles, 34, 57
Lamb, Mary, 57

Lambe, Dr. William, 199
Landor, Walter Savage, 184; *Gebir,* 184
Laplace, Pierre-Simon, Marquis de, 174
La Scala, 60
La Spezia, 264, 274, 287, 296, 297, 299, 301, 303
Laud, William (archbishop of Canterbury), 278
Lausanne, 109
Lawrence, William, M.D., 43
Leaning Tower of Pisa, 64, 323
Leda (sculpture), 162
Leeson, Robert, 191–92, 379 n. 67
Leghorn, 64, 66, 97, 101, 105, 107, 109, 115, 120, 125, 133–35, 136, 142, 147, 148, 157–58, 161, 167, 182–86, 189–90, 196, 198, 200, 206, 208–9, 236, 243–45, 254, 271, 273, 296, 298, 300–301, 309, 312, 319, 320, 322–25, 327, 329, 330, 333, 345, 379 n. 87
Leochares: *A Ganymede,* 162
Lerici, 287, 299–302, 305, 308, 309, 312–13, 319, 322–24, 326, 328–30, 340
Les Eschelles, 59, 88
Lewis, Matthew Gregory ("Monk"), 108
Liberal, The, 321, 323, 340, 342–43
Lido, 76, 80, 83
Liguori, Antonio, 105
Literary Gazette, 241, 247
Literary Miscellany, 231
Liverpool, Lord (Robert Jenkinson), 29, 35
Livorno. *See* Leghorn
Livy, 102
Lockhart, J. G., 51
Longdill, P. W. (PBS's solicitor), 11–12, 19, 28, 30, 40, 186, 233–34, 339
Lucan, 241
Lucca, 66, 77–79, 123, 203, 218, 273, 320
Lucian: *Dialogues,* 16
Lucretius, 117, 163, 317
Lynmouth, 227, 237

Macaulay, Catherine: *The History of England from the Accession of James I,* 198

MacFarlane, Charles, 102, 114–15, 369 n. 74
Machiavelli, Niccolò, 213
madness, 46, 53, 61, 84–87, 111, 113, 120, 125, 142–47
Madocks, Robert, 32, 185
Madocks, Mrs. Robert, 38
Magliana (harbormaster), 305, 306, 324
Maida Vale, 347
Malthus, Thomas Robert, 127, 157, 207
Manchester Massacre, 149–53, 156, 157
Marchand, Leslie A., 393 n. 83
Marlow, 11, 17, 32, 34, 35, 37, 38, 39, 43, 44, 45, 46, 50, 56, 73, 94, 111, 118, 164, 180, 185, 268, 269, 311, 342
Marshall, Mrs. Julian, 362 n. 37
Marx, Eleanor, 352
Marx, Karl, 178, 352
Masi, Sergeant-Major Stefani, 294–95, 297, 301
Mason, Mrs., 58, 64–65, 158, 180, 182–84, 188–91, 194, 197, 198, 201, 202, 207, 209–12, 220, 224, 244, 245, 253, 260, 269, 271, 273, 289, 290, 292, 300, 304, 306, 323–24, 339, 342, 345, 349, 362 n. 59, 380 n. 105
Masquerier, John James, 94
Massa, 306, 307, 331, 333
Mavrocordato, Prince Alexander, 217, 229, 232–33, 237, 239, 264, 346
Maxwell, Lt. Col. Christopher, 20, 21–22, 356 n. 62
McMillan, Buchanan, 48
Medici Venus (sculpture), 162
Mediterranean Sea, 184, 208, 269, 272, 284, 301–2, 312
Medwin, Thomas, 40–41, 89, 90, 106–10, 112, 123, 133, 141, 162, 182, 185, 188, 191–92, 198, 199, 229, 242, 254, 274, 280, 350–51; and death of PBS, 339; in Italy, 210–15, 217, 219–20, 232, 270, 273, 275, 276, 278, 287, 288, 291, 295, 319, 339, 350–51. Works: *The Angler in Wales,* 108; *Conversations of Lord Byron,* 350; *Lady Singleton,* 108; *Life of Percy Bysshe Shelley,*

Medwin, Thomas (*continued*)
     351; *Sketches in Hindoostan*, 212;
     "Similes," 156
Mérimée, Prosper, 348
Mesmerism/hypnosis, 217, 311–12
Metaurus River, 88
Metternich, Klemens Wenzel von, 153,
     199, 268
Michelangelo, 88
Milan, 58–60, 62, 63, 107, 109, 111, 227,
     231, 293
Milanie, Mlle, 39
*Military Register and Weekly
     Gazette*, 206
Mill, James, 231; *History of British
     India*, 264
Millais, John: *The North West
     Passage*, 346
Milman, Rev. Henry Hart, 164
Milton, John, 108, 213, 232, 277, 316;
     Paradise Lost, 56, 126, 213;
     Paradise Regained, 272
Missolonghi, 346
Montagu, Basil, 29
Montaigne, Michel de, 67, 179
Montanvert, 88
Montenero, 66, 296, 297, 301
Moore, Thomas, 30–31, 51, 273–74,
     339–40, 346, 348
Morning Chronicle (London), 49, 206,
     232, 338
Mount Cashell, Lady Margaret. *See*
     Mason, Mrs.
Mozart, Wolfgang Amadeus, 171; *Don
     Giovanni*, 39, 57; "Non temer o
     madre amata," 172
Munday, John, 47
Murray, John, 11, 39, 40, 51–52, 57, 120,
     240, 241, 274, 340, 346, 352
mysterious lady, 62, 73–74, 88, 90–91,
     99, 100, 106, 107–12, 147, 176, 189, 203,
     227, 367 nn. 39 and 45, 373 n. 64

Naples, 73–74, 79, 81, 86, 88–91, 95,
     98–100, 103–15, 118, 119, 121–22, 132,
     147, 150, 166, 176, 177, 184, 186, 187,
     189, 199, 206, 227, 229, 246, 249, 250,
     293, 351, 366 nn. 20 and 33, 367 n. 39,
     367–68 n. 52

Naples Museum, 177
Neapolitan child. *See* Shelley, Elena
     Adelaide
Nero, 117
Newstead Abbey, 122
Newton, John Frank, 18, 20, 41
Newton, Mrs. John Frank, 18, 20
Niobe (sculpture), 162
Noel, Lady Judith (Milbanke), 275–76
Norfolk, eleventh Duke of (Charles
     Howard), 59
Norton, Caroline, 347
Nott, Rev. George Frederick, 272–73
Novello, Vincent, 39, 57

Ollier, Charles, 35, 36, 48, 49, 50, 51, 58,
     72, 73, 82, 113, 115, 125, 126, 136, 137,
     143, 145, 149, 162, 164–67, 169, 180,
     190, 193, 201, 208, 212, 222, 229, 231,
     235, 239, 242, 256, 264, 265, 268,
     277–78, 288, 296, 370 n. 55
Ollier, Edmund, 354
Ollier, James, 35, 48
O'Neill, Eliza, 135
opera, 39, 57, 58, 60, 100, 125, 133, 160,
     171, 290
Opie, Amelia, 183
ottava rima, 198, 203
Ovid: *Metamorphoses*, 53, 197
Owen, Robert, 179, 352
Oxford, Jane, Lady, 368 n. 55
Oxford University, 29, 70, 108–9, 163,
     170, 184
Oxford University and City Herald,
     47

Pacchiani, Francesco, 214–15
Padua, 74–80, 81, 103, 252
Paestum, 114
Paget, Henry. *See* Uxbridge, Earl of
Paine, Thomas, 183; *The Age of
     Reason*, 152; *The Rights of Man*,
     45–46
painting, 87–88, 117, 120, 211, 162, 323,
     369 n. 24, 375 n. 17
Palatine, 117
Palazzo Colonna, 120
Palazzo Doria, 117, 369 n. 24
Palazzo (Casa) Galletti, 211, 220, 221

Palazzo Lanfranchi, 254, 269, 270–72, 275, 277, 287, 294, 321, 332
Palazzo Marini, 158, 160, 164, 170
Palazzo Mocenigo, 72, 75, 77, 80, 83
Palazzo Verospi, 116
Paley, William, 127
Pantheon, 116
Paris Monthly Review, The, 338
Parker, Betsy, 202, 289
Parker, Hellen, 170
Parker, Robert, 170
Parnassus, Mount, 346
Parry-Jones, Corbet, 170, 171, 181
Paul, Georgina Beauclerk, 348
Payne, John Hayward, 347
Peacock, Thomas Love, 17, 24, 26, 30, 35, 41, 44, 58, 143, 146, 167, 169, 188, 190, 192, 197, 222, 255, 305, 339, 343, 347, 351, 352; and *The Cenci,* 135–38; and Claire, 48, 56–58, 60, 66; employments of, 57, 58, 136, 231, 265; as friend of Harriet Shelley, 20, 354; letters from PBS in Italy to, 60, 61, 64, 66, 69, 71, 73, 75, 76, 81, 83, 84, 87, 88, 89, 91, 100–103, 106, 111, 114, 117–19, 124, 125, 133, 135, 141, 149, 150, 213, 231–32, 252, 265, 269, 370 n. 55; marriage of, 195; on PBS's poetry, 126, 265; as memoirist, 15, 50, 379 n. 73. Works: *The Four Ages of Poetry,* 231–32; *Memoirs of Shelley,* 354; *Nightmare Abbey,* 133; *Rhododaphne,* 37, 41, 58
Persia, 41
"Peterloo." *See* Manchester Massacre
Petrarch, 77, 81, 213; *Trionfo della Morte,* 153
Phidias, 57
Pieracci, Vincenzo: *Beatrice Cenci,* 138, 372 n. 35
Pilfold, Capt. John, 44–45
Pisa, 43, 64, 65, 97, 108, 110, 118, 123, 158, 161, 180, 182–84, 187, 189, 191, 198, 200, 211, 214–16, 219–21, 229, 236, 238, 240, 242, 244, 253, 254, 264, 268–72, 275, 285, 287, 290, 291, 292, 297, 299, 300, 307, 322, 323, 326, 329, 330, 332, 335, 340, 348
Pitti Palace, 210

Pius VII, Pope, 117
Plato, 18, 127, 212, 213, 231, 323; *Ion,* 180, 231; *Symposium,* 69–70, 90, 254, 322; *Phaedrus,* 71; *Republic,* 169
Pliny the Younger, 61
Plutarch, 41, 55, 117
Polidori, Dr. John William, 11
Pompeii, 101, 114, 119
Pope, Alexander, 240
Portovenere, 302, 303, 305
Prato Fiorito, Il, 67–68
Procter, Bryan Waller (Barry Cornwall), 348
Protestant Cemetery (Rome), 89, 124, 239, 262, 333, 335–36, 347
Puritans, 278

Quarterly Review, 37, 51, 57, 162–66, 180, 216, 239–41

Rameses II, 55
Raphael, 86–87; *St. Cecilia,* 87
Ravenna, 121, 181, 182, 208, 230, 240, 244–47, 249, 250, 253, 254, 255, 298
Reform Act of 1832, 150, 152
Reiman, Donald H., 146, 368 n. 58, 373 nn. 66 and 68
"Relation of the Death of the Family of Cenci," 138, 362 n. 65
Reni, Guido, 120; *The Rape of Proserpine,* 87
Republican, 152
Retzsch, Moritz von, 280
Reveley, Henry, 65, 66, 133, 148, 157–59, 161, 169–70, 183, 184, 185, 190, 194, 198, 209, 214, 236, 237, 349
Reveley, Maria James. *See* Gisborne, Maria
Reveley, Willey, 65
Reynolds, John Hamilton: *Peter Bell: A Lyrical Ballad,* 166
Ricardo, David, 178
Richardson, Samuel: *Clarissa,* 208
Richmond, H. M., 361 n. 4
Roberts, Capt. Daniel, 261, 274, 283, 284, 296, 303, 305, 308, 309, 312–13, 315, 319, 320, 324–27, 330, 331, 333, 337, 389 n. 6, 392 n. 31, 393 n. 83
Robertson, Henry, 57

Robinson, Charles E., 38
Robinson, Henry Crabb, 370 n. 33
Robinson, Isabel, 347
Robinson, Rosa, 348
Roe, Ivan, 108, 366 n. 29
Rogers, Samuel, 40, 287
Rome, 65, 81, 88–91, 101, 103, 106, 109, 115, 116–25, 136, 158, 176, 181, 217, 229, 244, 332
Romilly, Sir Samuel, 29
Rose, Polly, 43
Roskilly, Dr. John, 102, 104, 106, 114–15, 119, 366 n. 20
Rossetti, William Michael, 107, 173, 280, 281, 308, 367 n. 39, 368 n. 67
Rossini, Gioacchino, 100, 133; *Il Barbiere di Siviglia,* 58
Rothwell, Richard, *258*
Rousseau, Jean-Jacques, 59, 315–17; *Confessions,* 316; *Julie, ou La Nouvelle Héloïse,* 254, 316
Royal Museum (Naples), 101, 102, 114
Rua, Monte, 81
Ryan, Mr. (Major), 21

San Giovanni Battista (convent school), 229–30
San Giuliano, 123, 201, 203, 209, 210, 254, 264
San Giuseppe a Chiaia, Church of, *95,* 104
San Nicola, Church of, 215
San Pellegrino, Monte, 67–68, 203
San Terenzo, 299, 314, 319, 330
Sarzana, 299
Schiller, Friedrich: *The Maid of Orleans,* 213
Schlegel, Friedrich von: *Lectures on Dramatic Art and Literature,* 59
Scoles, Mr., 336
Scott, Sir Walter, 55, 108, 231, 295
sculpture, 33, 37, 67, 161, 162, 377 n. 83
"Scythrop's tower," 133
Seditious Meetings Act, 37
Serchio River, 66, 202, 210, 330
Serpentine River, 18, 23
Severn, Joseph, *2, 34, 93,* 117, 242, 335–36

Sgricci, Tomaso, 215–16, 218
Shakespeare, William, 34, 72, 135, 137, 213, 288; *Hamlet,* 65, 168, 241, 287–88; *King Lear,* 278; *Othello,* 287, 291; *The Tempest,* 227, 287, 290, 297–98, 336
Sharpe, Charles Kirkpatrick, 108
Shaw, George Bernard, 137
Shelley, Bessie Florence Gibson, 354, 398 n. 135
Shelley, Sir Bysshe, 170
Shelley, Sir Charles (1838–1902; fifth Baronet), 397 n. 130
Shelley, Charles Bysshe (son of PBS and HS), 18, 19, 21, 23, 25, 27, 30–31, 42, 186, 233, 235, 341, 352, 354
Shelley, Clara Everina, 42, 44, 45, 57, 58, 74, 77–81, 106, 132, 160, 302
Shelley, Sir Edward, 397 n. 130
Shelley, Elena Adelaide, 90, *95,* 104–12, 115, 118, 176, 185, 186–87, 189, 194, 196, 203, 206, 227, 249, 252, 292, 302, 349, 351, 366 nn. 26, 27, and 28, 367 n. 45, 367–68 n. 52, 368 n. 58
Shelley, Elizabeth (sister of PBS), 224, 225, 352
Shelley, Lady Elizabeth Pilfold (mother of PBS), 27, 170–71, 339, 352, 353
Shelley, Harriet (née Westbrook, first wife of PBS): inquest for, 20, 22; last message to PBS of, 23–24; marriage to PBS of, 26, 28–30, 50, 184, 193, 226, 343, 354; stories about, 20–23, 28, 193, 356 nn. 56 and 62; suicide of, 18–25, 35, 193, 226, 227, 356 n. 64, 356–57 n. 66, 357 n. 87
Shelley, Ianthe Eliza (later Mrs. Esdaile), 18, 23, 25, 27, 30–31, 42, 186, 233, 235, 341, 351–52, 354, 357 n. 57, 397 n. 128
Shelley, Lady Jane, 187, *263,* 353–54; *Shelley and Mary,* 354; *Shelley Memorials,* 354, 382 n. 13
Shelley, John (PBS's brother), 352, 397 n. 130
Shelley, Sir John (sixth Baronet), 397 n. 130

Shelley, Mary Wollstonecraft Godwin (second wife of PBS), 258; as amanuensis to PBS, 45, 56, 57, 69, 73, 87, 102, 135, 167, 182, 190, 231; biographical work on PBS by, 339, 342, 351, 352; and Byron, 80–81, 120, 182, 249, 270, 272, 277, 280, 284, 292, 340, 342–43, 345–46, 349; commentary on PBS's poetry by, 204, 222, 239, 342; death of, 353–54; and death of PBS, 329–32, 334–36, 341, 342, 344–45; and deaths of Clara and William, 77–81, 83, 106, 124, 134, 141, 160, 187; depression of, 67, 73–75, 77, 80, 82, 86, 102, 112, 120, 124, 133–34, 141–44, 147, 157–58, 160, 169, 180–81, 182, 186, 187, 197, 274, 304, 309, 315, 321–22, 344–45, 348; desire that PBS write more human poetry of, 39, 43, 134; and drawing lessons, 117; early relationship of PBS and, 21; earnings and writing after PBS's death of, 340, 342, 343; as editor/publisher of PBS's writing, 15, 50, 70, 87, 102, 112–13, 133, 138, 146, 156, 167, 176, 189, 204, 220, 222, 223, 245, 281, 285, 340, 342, 351, 353; and Elena's adoption, 104–6, 112, 115, 118, 196; frustration with Claire of, 17, 25, 27, 39, 42, 44, 63, 68, 73, 75, 80, 145, 192, 206, 212–13, 246, 304, 350, 353; and Harriet, 25, 28, 147, 343, 354; and jealousy of Emilia Viviani, 220–21, 223, 225, 252, 292, 293; and jealousy of Jane Williams, 281, 290, 298, 304, 309, 312, 313; journal of, 13, 39, 72, 73, 78, 80, 98, 102, 104, 105, 111, 112, 115, 123–24, 141, 185, 191–92, 201, 206, 213, 222, 245, 246, 252, 279, 290, 300, 324, 342, 347, 354; late friendships and attractions of, 347–48; and the letter to Mrs. Hoppner defending her marriage, 247–51; marriage to PBS of, 16, 18–19, 25–27, 32, 357 n. 87; and Mavrocordato, 217, 229, 232–33, 237, 239; physical descriptions of, 57, 171, 279; pregnancies and miscarriage of, 17, 18, 25, 37, 39, 42, 106, 116–18, 122–23, 133, 157, 161, 166, 167, 175, 292, 297–98, 299, 304–10, 312–15, 329; reading of, 65, 67, 99, 100, 148, 188, 196, 212, 222, 323; relationship with father of, 25–27, 39, 44, 57–58, 65, 141–42, 160–61, 180, 193–94, 202–3, 303–4, 306, 339–40, 362 n. 59; reputation of, 50, 203; response to Fanny's suicide of, 15, 16; and study of languages, 148, 216; and translation of Alfieri's *Myrrha*, 79; and Trelawny, 279–80, 287, 290, 332, 335, 336, 340, 342, 345–47, 350; willfulness/dominance of, 41–42, 44, 144–45, 160, 187; writing lapse of, 120; writing plans on Charles I of, 73, 79; writing room of, 202.
—Works and Editions: "The Bride of Modern Italy," 221; "The Choice," 344; "For Two Political Characters of 1819," 156; *Frankenstein*, 11, 15, 27, 37–38, 42, 55, 74, 81, 102, 120, 175, 347, 352; *History of a Six Weeks' Tour* (with PBS), 37, 41; *The Last Man*, 124, 352; *Lodore*, 115; *Mathilda* (*The Fields of Fancy*), 121, 142, 144, 147–48, 161, 186, 190; *Maurice*, 202; *Midas*, 198; *Poetical Works*, 353; *Posthumous Poetry*, 351; *Proserpine*, 198; *Valperga*, 180, 203, 212, 264, 277, 304

Shelley, Percy Bysshe, 2, 257; anti-monarchical views of, 34, 46, 132, 169, 178, 199, 206–7, 235, 268, 317; aversion to military of, 177–78, 206; and boating, 32, 37, 41–42, 55–56, 99, 148, 158, 161, 169–70, 173, 185, 209, 236–38, 245, 264, 274, 275, 281, 282, 283–85, 291, 296, 300, 302–3, 305–10, 312–13, 315, 319–22, 324–28; and botany, 61, 99, 188–89; childhood and youth of, 53, 72, 86, 163, 170, 225; and class awareness, 36, 45–46, 81, 83, 132, 149, 168, 178–79, 207; contribution to *Frankenstein* of, 38; correspondence of, 20–21, 25, 30, 55, 56, 58–60, 63–64, 68, 72, 73, 75, 76, 83,

Shelley, Percy Bysshe (*continued*)
84, 87, 89, 91, 98, 100–103, 106, 111–12,
114, 117–19, 124–26, 133, 135, 141, 142,
149, 150, 152–53, 156, 157, 158, 160,
182, 183, 185, 187, 193–203, 208,
211–14, 216–17, 219–22, 229–32,
236–42, 246–47, 252, 254, 255, 265, 268,
269, 271, 273, 276–78, 280–81, 296,
300–301, 303, 306, 307, 309–10, 322,
370 nn. 36 and 55, 380 n. 115; custody
battle for children with Harriet of,
18–19, 24–25, 27–30, 33, 40, 154, 227,
235; death and burial of, 223, 264,
313, 324–38, 395 n. 50; death notices
of, 338–39; delusional episodes and
nightmares of, 191–92, 301–2, 313–14,
379 nn. 67 and 73, 392 n. 37;
depression and marital discord with
Mary of, 73–74, 77, 81–82, 84–86, 90,
98, 100–102, 111–15, 125, 132, 133–134,
141–47, 177, 187–88, 194, 196, 197,
204–6, 208, 211–13, 225–26, 231,
237–39, 245–46, 268, 270, 274, 281–82,
286, 291, 301, 309–310, 311–12, 321,
327–28, 341, 344–45, 347, 368 n. 67,
392 n. 37; diet and vegetarianism of,
15, 38, 43, 49, 190, 285; drug use/self-
medication of, 25, 182, 186, 195, 211,
243; as "Elfin Knight," 16–17, 49; and
exile motif, 40, 46, 53, 58, 85, 119, 127,
153, 241; fantasy and play of, 18, 33,
43, 211; and father-son conflict, 127,
131, 140, 167; financial settlement
with father of, 11–12; generosity of,
37, 38, 44, 115, 119, 146; grave of, 262,
335–36; greatest productive periods
of, 81, 117–18, 125, 152–53, 161, 203;
and guilt over Fanny's death, 15, 24,
27, 227, 357 n. 87; and guilt over
Harriet's death, 19, 23, 24–25, 227,
357 n. 87; health problems of, 11, 15,
24, 40, 41, 42, 43, 44, 48–49, 56, 60, 73,
78–79, 98, 100–102, 119, 121, 124, 132,
133, 142, 147, 157–58, 160, 171, 177,
180–81, 182, 185–86, 188, 191, 203, 211,
215–18, 231, 243, 268, 270, 301, 306,
307, 394 n. 23; heart of, 334–35, 340,
344, 354, 394 n. 23; imagery in poems
by, 47–48, 52, 82, 133–34, 140–41,
143–44, 150, 153–55, 165–66, 174–76,
188–89, 196, 197, 205, 207–8, 221,
224–28, 286, 291, 312, 318; interest in
medicine of, 182, 307–8; linguistic
skills of, 148, 171, 173, 195, 210, 212,
216, 220, 225, 279; love lyrics of, 48,
170–77, 198, 208, 220, 221, 223–24, 228,
255–26, 270, 278, 281–82, 290–91,
297–98, 304, 306, 311–12, 314–15, 316;
marriage to Harriet of, 26, 28–30, 50,
184, 193, 226, 343, 354; marriage to
Mary of, 16, 18–19, 25–27, 32, 357 n.
87; maternal surrogates of, 159, 188;
mysteries of, 62, 68, 72–74, 88, 90–91,
99–112, 121, 123, 132, 142–43, 170, 174,
176, 203, 211, 227, 363 n. 81, 373 n. 64;
notebooks of, 117, 124, 139, 141, 147,
162, 165, 173, 182, 213, 223, 255, 265,
351; and observation of natural
phenomena, 59, 61, 69, 88, 99–101,
117, 166; personality of, 18, 46, 177;
physical descriptions of, 18, 43, 89,
102, 114, 164–65, 177, 210, 253–54,
278–79, 285, 320; pseudonymous and
anonymous publication of, 16, 35, 45,
49, 55, 164, 208, 222–23; reading of,
16, 18, 37–38, 41, 53, 55, 56, 59, 60, 61,
65, 67, 69, 72, 90, 99–102, 117, 133, 135,
148, 153, 161, 162–63, 169, 172, 184,
188, 195, 196, 198, 203, 212, 213, 216,
222, 229, 231, 268, 279; and religion,
27–28, 30, 34, 40, 48–52, 55, 87, 107,
126, 129, 168, 171, 177–79, 190–91, 193,
205, 212, 233, 235, 247, 273, 278, 311,
317–18, 323, 336, 339, 351; as
reviewer, 37, 49, 58, 216; reviews of
works by, 12, 37–38, 51, 57, 126, 137,
142, 162–66, 180, 193, 216, 239, 241–42;
rivalry with Byron of, 61, 85, 195,
239–40, 250–51, 265, 271, 272, 287–88,
295–96, 303, 310, 316, 318–19; on the
role of the poet, 179–80, 231–32, 266;
and science/technology, 148, 174–75,
229, 231–32; self-assessments as
poet by, 49, 61, 69, 72, 101–2, 125–26,
136, 140, 152, 153, 167, 169, 193, 195,
212–15, 222, 237, 239, 244, 256, 265,

271, 277, 303; and sexual politics, 26, 30, 50–54, 70–72, 107, 127, 157, 168, 178, 351; sociopolitical thought of, 16, 28–30, 34–36, 45–46, 51–54, 85, 106, 125–27, 131–32, 148–57, 167–69, 171, 177–80, 197, 199, 201, 206–8, 264–68, 317–18, 336, 351, 352–53; success during lifetime of, 137; wills of, 12, 35, 296, 324, 340, 345, 390 n. 71; and women, 15, 192, 223, 226, 228
—Works:
——Poetry and Drama: *Adonais*, 237, 239–44, 251, 264, 265, 278, 288, 336; *Alastor*, 12, 17, 42, 53, 61, 125, 130, 180; "Arethusa," 198; *Athanase: A Fragment*, 134, 145–47, 373 nn. 63 and 68; "Ballad of the Starving Mother" ("A Ballad: Young Parson Richards"), 157; "The Boat on the Serchio," 238–39; "Buona Notte," 255; *The Cenci*, 97, 105, 118, 120, 121, 125, 133–42, 149, 152, 164, 169, 193, 198, 201, 208, 219, 240, 251, 264, 277, 371 n. 14, 372 nn. 35 and 40; *Charles the First*, 153, 169, 198–99, 229, 264, 272, 277–78, 280–82, 288, 310; "The Cloud," 69; "Death," 113; "England in 1819," 152, 157, 161; *Epipsychidion*, 67, 118, 176–77, 214, 217–18, 220–29, 255–56, 281, 383 n. 22; "Evening: Ponte al Mare," 165; "The False Laurel and the True," 277; "Fiordispina," 223; "The Fugitives," 255; *Ginevra*, 255; "Good-Night," 173–74, 255; *Hellas*, 173, 233, 254–68, 288, 296; *Hymn to Intellectual Beauty*, 16; "I arise from dreams of thee" ("Indian Serenade" or "The Indian Girl's Song"), 161, 172–74, 290; "I fear thy kisses gentle maiden," 176; *Julian and Maddalo: A Conversation*, 76–77, 84–87, 113, 118, 120, 122, 125, 134, 142–47, 152–53, 195, 212, 373 n. 68; "A Lament," 255; *Laon and Cythna* (revised as *The Revolt of Islam*), 37, 38, 40–43, 45, 48–54, 70, 85, 101, 118, 125, 126, 162–64, 180, 193, 200, 216, 228, 353;

Letter to Maria Gisborne, 194–95, 379 n. 87; "Lift Not the Painted Veil," 113, 134; "Lines written in the Bay of Lerici," 311, 314–15; *Lines written among the Euganean Hills*, 81–83, 102, 199; "Love's Philosophy" ("An Anacreontic"), 173, 174; "The Magnetic Lady To Her Patient," 311–12; "Marianne's Dream," 40; *The Mask of Anarchy*, 118, 149–57, 207, 353; "Misery.—A Fragment" ("Invocation to Misery"), 113, 133–34; *Mont Blanc*, 41; "Mutability," 265; "Ode to Heaven," 180; *Ode to Liberty*, 165, 196–97; "Ode to Naples," 206, 207, 222; *Ode to the West Wind*, 99, 101, 118, 161, 164–66; "An Ode written October, 1819, before the Spaniards had recovered their Liberty" ("Ode to the Assertors of Liberty"), 156; *Oedipus Tyrannus; or, Swellfoot the Tyrant*, 199, 206–8, 381 n. 22; "On a Faded Violet," 113, 176, 184; "On the Nile," 56; "One Word Is Too Often Profaned," 311; *Original Poetry by Victor and Cazire*, 39; "Ozymandias," 55, 163, 361 n. 4; "The Past," 113; *Peter Bell the Third*, 118, 153, 161, 166–68; *Prometheus Unbound*, 59, 78–79, 81, 83, 85, 86, 99, 101, 117–18, 120, 125–32, 138–40, 156, 157, 161, 164, 165, 169, 174–76, 180, 189, 190, 196, 201, 212, 222, 241, 242, 251, 267, 370 n. 55, 376 n. 74; *Queen Mab*, 28, 42, 45, 48, 121, 125, 169, 199, 208, 219, 235, 274, 315–16, 338, 352–53; "The Question," 113; "Remembrance," 255; *Rosalind and Helen: A Modern Eclogue*, 43, 46, 57, 61, 67, 68, 72, 81, 106, 111, 229; "A Satire upon Satire," 193; *The Sensitive Plant*, 188–89, 311; "The Serpent is Shut Out of Paradise" ("To ——"), 255, 278, 281–82, 286; "Song of Apollo," 198; "Song of Pan," 198; "Song of Proserpine," 198; "Song to the Men of England," 353;

Shelley, Percy Bysshe
—Works:
——Poetry and Drama (*continued*)
"Sonnet to Byron," 277, 388 n. 78;
"Stanzas written in Dejection—
December 1818, Near Naples," 90,
111, 113–14, 115; *St. Irvyne,* 170;
Tasso, 69, 87; "Thou art fair, and few
are fairer" ("To Sophia"), 173, 174;
"Time Long Past," 173, 177; "To
Constantia," 47, 56, 311; "To E***
V***," 220; "To Jane" ("The keen
stars are twinkling"), 311; "To Jane.
The Invitation," 285–86; "To Jane.
The Recollection," 165, 285–86; "To
the Lord Chancellor," 154; "To the
Republic of Benevento," 222, 353;
"To S.[idmouth] and C.[astlereagh],
156; *To a Sky-Lark,* 195–96, 379 n. 87;
"To William Shelley," 40; "To
Wordsworth," 167; *The Triumph of
Life,* 146, 153, 306, 311, 315–18, 323;
"The Two Spirits—An Allegory,"
85–86; *Una Favola,* 226; "What Men
Gain Fairly," 156; "When the lamp is
shattered," 291; *The Witch of Atlas,*
203–6, 343; "With a guitar. To Jane,"
297; "Written on Hearing the News
of the Death of Napoleon," 268
——Prose: *An Address, to the Irish
People,* 29, 36; *Address to the People
on the Death of the Princess
Charlotte,* 45–46, 164; *The Coliseum,*
89, 99, 106; *Declaration of Rights,*
150, 152, 169; *A Defence of Poetry,*
229, 231–32, 343; *A Discourse on the
Manners of the Antient Greeks
Relative to the Subject of Love,*
70–72, 363 n. 94; *For the Examiner*
("The Carlile Letter"), 152–53, 161,
167–69; *History of a Six Weeks' Tour*
(with Mary), 37, 41; *A Letter to Lord
Ellenborough,* 28; *Notes on
Sculptures,* 161; *On Christianity,*
34, 36; *On the Devil, and Devils,*
274; *On Love,* 70, 223, 286, 363 n. 94;
A Philosophical View of Reform,
153, 161, 167, 169, 177–80, 188, 207,

208, 231; *A Proposal for Putting
Reform to the Vote throughout the
Kingdom,* 35–37; *Proposals for an
Association of Philanthropists,* 36
——Translations: *Aristippus*
(Wieland), 65; *The Cyclops*
(Euripides), 147; "Hymns" (Homer),
56; *Hymn to Mercury* (Homer), 198;
Ion (Plato), 180; *El màgico
prodigioso* (Calderón), 279, 291;
Prometheus Bound (Aeschylus), 41,
127, 213; *Symposium* (Plato), 69–70,
90, 254, 322; *Tractatus Theologico-
Politicus* (Spinoza), 45, 161, 166, 182,
271
Shelley, Sir Percy Bysshe (b. 1872;
seventh Baronet), 397 n. 130
Shelley, Sir Percy Florence (surviving
son of PBS and MWG), 169, 171, 173,
180, 183, 196, 211, 245, 247, 263, 296,
299, 308, 309, 324, 340, 343, 347,
352–54, 367 n. 48, 397 n. 130
Shelley, Sir Timothy (father of PBS),
20, 44, 56, 170, 185, 201, 234–35, 275,
296; as Charles's guardian, 341, 352;
death of, 324, 350, 353; and death of
PBS, 339; and the Duke of Norfolk,
59; embargo on Mary's biographical/
editorial work on PBS of, 339, 342,
351–53; financial settlement with
PBS of, 11–12; and hostile attitude
toward Mary and grudging financial
support of Mary and Percy, 339, 342,
343, 347, 351–53; illegitimate son of,
234; in Parliament, 29, 35; and PBS's
custody battle, 27–28
Shelley, William (son of PBS and
MWG), 18, 27, 29–30, 35, 40, 44, 57, 58,
78, 83, 95, 117, 120, 122–25, 132, 134,
141, 142, 160, 171, 177, 181, 239, 302,
333, 335–36
Shelley Society, 137
Shenley, Capt., 333
Sherwood, Neely, and Jones, 48
Shields, Amelia ("Milly"), 37, 45, 57, 58,
63, 64, 78, 180
Sidmouth, first Viscount (Henry
Addington), 29, 150, 154, 156, 199

Sidney, Sir Philip, 241
Silsbee, Edward, 107, 110, 191–92, 220, 229, 292, 348, 350, 357 n. 87, 367 nn. 35 and 39, 379 n. 67, 381–82 n. 52, 383 n. 22
Sinclair, John, 290
Sistine Chapel, 116
Six Acts, 150
slavery, 154
Smith, Benjamin, 20, 22, 23
Smith, Horace, 17–18, 33, 34, 37, 44, 45, 55, 57, 64, 68, *94*, 135, 160, 161, 186, 195, 207–8, 233–35, 255, 264, 274, 275, 280, 282, 296, 297, 303, 304, 318, 319, 323, 338, 361 n. 16; "Sonnet: To the Author of *The Revolt of Islam*," 57
Society for the Suppression of Vice, 208, 235
Socrates, 70, 316
Sophocles: *Oedipus at Colonus,* 233
Southey, Robert, 37, 51, 85, 164, 193, 195, 203, 231, 241, 242, 288; *The Curse of Kehama,* 288; *A Vision of Judgment,* 272
Spa Fields, riot of, 16
Spain, 156, 196–97, 229, 265, 367 n. 35
Spenser, Edmund, 37, 41; *Faerie Queene,* 101–2, 203
Spenserian stanza, 37
Spinoza, Baruch, 179; *Tractatus Theologico-Politicus,* 45, 161, 166, 182, 271
Spoleto, 88
Stacey, Sophia, *96,* 169–77, 180–81, 182, 184–85, 191, 221, 223, 224, 255, 290, 376 nn. 51 and 52
Staël, Madame de, 307; *Corinne, or Italy,* 98–101, 107, 122, 212, 221, 307
St Clair, William, 357 n. 87
St. Croix, Marianne de, 60
Stendhal (Marie-Henri Beyle): *Les Cencis,* 120
Sterne, Laurence: *Tristram Shandy,* 363 n. 66
St. Leonard's Lodge, 275
St. Mildred's, Church of, 26
Stocking, Marion K., 108, 111, 367 nn. 39, 45, and 47, 368 n. 58, 387 n. 27, 397 n. 118

St. Omer, 58
St. Pancras Church, 219, 353
St. Peter's (Rome), 89, 116, 117
St. Peter's Church (Bournemouth), 354
St. Peter's Field (Manchester), 149–51
Styles, Sir Charles, 336
suffrage, 35–36, 150, 169
Sun (London), 20
Sunstein, Emily W., 357 n. 87, 362 n. 37, 367 n. 44, 387 n. 27
Swansea, 13–14, 355 n. 19
Syon House Academy, 352
Syria, 211

Taaffe, John, 215–16, 241, 244, 273, 275, 294–95, 310, 327
Talleyrand-Périgord, Charles-Maurice de, 183
Tantini, Dr., 210
Tantini, Madame, 202
Tanyrallt, 123, 191
Tartary, 41
Tasso, Torquato, 61, 65, 85, 87, 111, 143
Taylor, John, 200
Teatro San Carlo, 100
Terme Bagno alla Villa, 67
Terni, 88, 125
Terracina, 116
terza rima, 146, 165, 214, 216
Thames, 32, 37, 42
Theatre of Cruelty, 137
Theatrical Inquisitor, 137
Theocritus, 243
Tighe, George William ("Tatty"), 158, 183–84, 191, 201, 237, 253, 289
Tighe, Laurette, 158, 182, 198, 202
Tighe, Nerina, 158, 184
Tisdale, James, 110
Tisdale, Louisa, 110, 289
Tita (Giovanni Battista Falconieri), 252, 295, 301
Tomkins, Mr. (neighbor/artist), 172, 177
Tonelli, Signora, 161
Tower of Migliarino, 330, 333, 338
Trelawny, Edward John, 113, 192, 211–12, 219, 236, 238, 262, 274, 275,

Trelawny, Edward John (*continued*) 278–80, 283–85, 287, 290, 291, 292, 294–95, 297, 299, 302–3, 308–10, 312, 313, 318, 319, 324–38, 340, 342, 345, 346–47, 350, 351, 353; *Adventures of a Younger Son*, 279–80, 346, 368 n. 67, 379 n. 73, 393 n. 83; *Recollections of the Last Days of Shelley and Byron*, 313, 325, 337, 346, 392 n. 31; *Records of Shelley, Byron, and the Author*, 326, 346

Trelawny, Zella, 346, 354

Tre Palazzi di Chiesa, 269, 272, 283–85, 299, 332, 387 n. 22

Trevi Fountain, 116

"Triumph of Death, The" (fresco), 323

Tullamore, Lord, 110

Turner, Cornelia, 171

Tylecote, Mr., 32

tyranny, 30, 40, 52, 126, 127, 139, 153, 156, 157, 168, 179, 206–7

Uffizi Gallery, 162, 172, 214, 244

United States of America, 178, 179, 266, 320

University College, Oxford, 29, 109, 354

University of Pisa, 214

Uxbridge, Earl of (Henry Paget, later second Marquis of Anglesey), 109, 110

Vaccà Berlinghieri, Dr. Andrea, 43, 182, 184–86, 203, 210, 213, 217, 236, 243, 273, 295, 321

Vale of Health, 17

Vatican, 89, 116, 120

Velletri, 116

Venables, Tony, 361 n. 4

Venice, 63, 64, 66, 72–73, 77–80, 82, 83, 87, 105, 107, 181, 190, 252

Venus Anadyomene (sculpture), 162

Venus Genetrix (sculpture), 162

Vesuvius, 91, 98, 100, 103, 189

Viareggio, 307, 325, 327, 330–33, 337–38, 395 n. 50

Vienna, 148, 160, 237, 289, 293, 335, 342

Villa Borghese, 116

Villa del Chiappa, 363 nn. 73 and 74

Villa Dupuy, 296, 321

Villa (Casa) Magni, *261*, 299–303, 305, 306, 309, 310, 313, 319, 321, 324, 328–31, 389 n. 6

Villa Pliniana, 61–62, 74

Villa Valsovano, *97*, 133, 158

Virgil, 102, 267; "Virgil's Gnat," 203

Virginia Water, 41

Vivian, Charles, 302, 307, 319, 327, 331

Viviani, Emilia (Teresa), *97*, 110, 112, 214–17, 220–24, 227, 232, 238, 242, 247, 252, 254, 255, 264, 278, 292, 293, 351, 381–82 n. 52; "Il Vero Amore," 221

Viviani, Ferdinanda, 214

Viviani, Marchese Niccolò, 214, 271, 295

Volta, Alessandro, 214

Voltaire, 59

Waith, E. M., 361 n. 4

Warmington, Elizabeth Dorothy, 397 n. 128

Warnham Church, 352

Washington, George, 285

Webb, Timothy, 372 n. 40

Webster, John: *The Duchess of Malfi*, 213

Weekes, Henry, 354

Westbrook, Eliza (Mrs. Farthing Beauchamp), 19, 21–25, 28–30, 42, 136, 227, 234, 341, 356 n. 56, 357 n. 57

Westbrook, Harriet. *See* Shelley, Harriet

Westbrook, John, 18, 22–25, 27, 30, 42, 234, 341

Westmacott, Richard, 336

White, Newman Ivey, 356 n. 46, 369 n. 74, 376 n. 52

Whitehead, Alfred North, 174–75

Whitton, William (Shelley family solicitor), 12, 27, 28, 44, 185, 234–35, 339, 343, 351–53

Wieland, Christoph: *Aristippus*, 65

Willats, William, 56, 304

Williams, Edward Ellerker, 199, 210, 219–20, 228, 229, 236, 238–39, 242, 244, 245, 253, 257, 260, 264, 265–66, 269,

271, 274–78, 280, 281, 283–85, 287, 291, 294–97, 299–315, 319, 320, 322–24, 327, 330–33, 389 n. 6, 391 n. 98; *The Promise,* 238, 270, 274, 290; *The Secret,* 290

Williams, Helen Maria, 183, 197

Williams, James, 50

Williams, Jane, 210, 218–20, 228, 229, 239, 244, 245, 253–55, 259, 264, 269–72, 278–83, 287, 290, 294–314, 316, 319–23, 329–32, 335, 337, 340–45, 349, 351; death of, 349; discussion of the Shelleys' marriage and betrayal of Mary by, 341, 344–45, 347; husband in London of, 219, 341, 348; liaison with Hogg after PBS's death of, 341–42, 347, 348; as love interest and poetic subject of PBS, 173, 238, 270, 275, 278, 280–82, 285–86, 290, 297–98, 306, 310, 311–12, 316, 319–20,

322, 323, 341, 347; Shelleyans' neglect of, 349

Williams, Jane Rosalind ("Dina"), 229, 349

Winckelmann, Johann Joachim, 102

Wollstonecraft, Mary, 14, 15, 16, 52, 65, 141, 183, 188, 354; *Letters from Norway,* 15; *Original Stories from Real Life,* 183

Wordsworth, William, 34, 39, 52, 126, 137, 151, 164, 231; *Peter Bell,* 163, 166–67, 204

Xenophon: *Memorabilia Socratis,* 69

Yeats, William Butler: "The Second Coming," 129

Yeomanry, 151

Yost, George, 372 n. 35

Ypsilanti, Prince Alexander, 232